UNDER SIEGE

UNDER SIEGE

The Independent Labour Party
in Interwar Britain

Ian Bullock

AU PRESS

Copyright © 2017 Ian Bullock

Published by AU Press, Athabasca University
1200, 10011 – 109 Street, Edmonton, AB T5J 3S8

ISBN 978-1-77199-155-1 (pbk.)   ISBN 978-1-77199-156-8 (pdf)
ISBN 978-1-77199-157-5 (epub)   DOI: 10.15215/aupress/9781771991551.01

Cover design by Marvin Harder, marvinharder.com
Interior design by Sergiy Kozakov
Printed and bound in Canada by Marquis Book Printers

Library and Archives Canada Cataloguing in Publication

Bullock, Ian, 1941-, author

    Under siege : the Independent Labour Party in interwar Britain / Ian Bullock.

Includes bibliographical references and index.
Issued in print and electronic formats.

    1. Independent Labour Party (Great Britain)—History—20th century. 2. Political parties—Great Britain--History—20th century. 3. Great Britain—Politics and government—1910-1936. I. Title.

JN1129.I52B85 2017   324.241'097   C2017-902958-4
                                                                                                                                                 C2017-902959-2

Athabasca University Press acknowledges the assistance provided by the Government of Alberta, Alberta Media Fund.

Albertan
Government

This publication is licensed under a Creative Commons licence, Attribution–Noncommercial–No Derivative Works 4.0 International: see www.creativecommons.org. The text may be reproduced for non-commercial purposes, provided that credit is given to the original author.

To obtain permission for uses beyond those outlined in the Creative Commons licence, please contact AU Press, Athabasca University, at aupress@athabascau.ca.

For Sue,
Chloe and Paul (and Tigerlily),
James, Rob, and Andrew

And in memory of my greatly missed friends
Andy Durr, John Gurney, and Fred Herbert

The word Revolution is as ambiguous and deceptive as it is necessary.

—John Middleton Murry, draft of an address
delivered at the ILP's summer school, August 1932

Contents

List of Abbreviations   xi
Acknowledgements   xiii

Introduction   3

PART I Searching for a New Role

1 Democracy, Foreign Policy, and Parliamentary Reform: The Legacy of F. W. Jowett   11
2 An Existential Dilemma: Reactions to the Labour Party's 1918 Constitution   27
3 Ramsay MacDonald and the ILP: A Mutual Ambivalence   41
4 A "Distinctive Program": Variations on the Way Forward   57
5 The 1922 Constitution and the Allen Regime   67

PART II Socialism in Our Time?

6 The Rise of MacDonald and the First Labour Government   85
7 Preparing the Ground for the Living Wage Policy   99
8 The Year of the General Strike—and of *The Living Wage*   113
9 Pursuing the Living Wage Policy   125
10 James Maxton and Increasing Tension with Labour   141

PART III Leaving Labour

11 The Second Labour Government   159
12 The Road Towards Departure   177
13 Disaffiliation Wins the Day   189
14 What Is a Revolutionary Policy?   203
15 Turbulent Waters: A United Front—or a United ILP?   217

PART IV Unity Remains Elusive

16 Lancashire Revolts: Continuing Conflict over the United Front   235

17 The Abyssinian Crisis and the Fate of Democratic Centralism   249

18 Soviet Foreign Policy and the League of Nations: Growing Criticism in the ILP   265

19 The ILP and the USSR: From Doubt to Disillusionment   279

20 Calls for Unity as War Approaches   297

21 The Ex-ILP: A Case for Continuity   315

Conclusion: The Legacy of the ILP's Interwar Years   333

Notes   349
Bibliography   399
Index   409

Abbreviations

BSP	British Socialist Party
CPGB	Communist Party of Great Britain
IBRSU	International Bureau for Revolutionary Socialist Unity
IE	Inner Executive
ILP	Independent Labour Party
ISP	Independent Socialist Party
NAC	National Administrative Council
NEC	National Executive Committee
PLP	Parliamentary Labour Party
POUM	Partido Obrero de Unificación Marxista
RPC	Revolutionary Policy Committee
SDF	Social-Democratic Federation
SL	Socialist League
SLP	Socialist Labour Party
SSIP	Society for Socialist Inquiry and Propaganda
SSP	Scottish Socialist Party
TUC	Trades Union Congress
UDC	Union of Democratic Control

Acknowledgements

I am grateful for a British Academy grant that helped to fund frequent expeditions to the British Library of Political and Economic Science, at the London School of Economics and Political Science, and to the British Library at St. Pancras and its newspaper collection, then at Colindale, as well as research trips to Manchester and Edinburgh. Thanks also to Amelia Wakeford, research development officer at the University of Sussex, for her help in securing the grant, and to Paul Grant, research grant administrator.

Thanks are due to the librarians at the institutions already mentioned, to the People's History Museum, Manchester, and especially to Sue Donnelly, Anna Townslon, Elinor Robinson, and Catherine MacIntyre, archivists at the British Library of Political and Economic Science; to Rona Morrison, at the Centre for Research Collections, University of Edinburgh Library; to Lynette Cawthra, at the Working Class History Museum, Salford; to Kirsty Meehan, of the National Galleries of Scotland; and to Antony Penrose.

I am grateful to my friends Peter France, Siân Reynolds, and Marilyn and Tony Carew for their hospitality during research trips. For initial advice, guidance, and encouragement, I am indebted to Logie Barrow, Tony Carew, Gidon Cohen, Alvin Finkel, Kevin Morgan, Dennis Pilon, and Victor Rabinovitch. In the later stages of the project, I was greatly helped by the dedicated and expert editing of Joyce Hildebrand and, especially, Pamela Holway, at AU Press.

Barry Winter and Sue Bullock both spent long hours reading each chapter in draft and making vital comments. Barry was particularly diligent in discouraging my tendency to write sentences of Proustian length. As ever, Sue played an indispensable part in keeping me sane and (mostly) cheerful throughout what proved to be a lengthy project. I cannot thank her enough.

INDEPENDENT LABOUR PARTY.
(West London Federation.)

GREAT
LABOUR RALLY

UNDER SIEGE

Town Hall, Uxbridge,

FRIDAY, MARCH 2nd, at 8 p.m.

J. KEIR HARDIE, M.P.

Will speak, supported by

C. A. CAVE, C.A., B.Sc. (Int.), J. COCHRANE,
W. HERBERT, R. W. HUDSON, F. ROLFE,
T. ROWLEY, F. YOUENS,
(Labour Candidates for Uxbridge Urban Council,)
Councillor C. R. WESCOTT, and Others.

Chairman: Councillor L. W. SPENCER.

ADMISSION FREE. Reserved Seats, 1s., 6d., 3d.

Introduction

"She had heard someone say something about an Independent Labour Party, and was furious she had not been asked." So wrote Evelyn Waugh of his character Agatha Runcible, one of Britain's so-called Bright Young People, whom he satirized in his novel *Vile Bodies*.[1] Waugh's character was based, quite unmistakably, on Elizabeth Ponsonby—who, while certainly very fond of parties, would probably not have mistaken the reference. The daughter of Arthur Ponsonby, a prominent figure on the British Left who was active in the Independent Labour Party (ILP) after the First World War, Elizabeth was romantically involved in the early 1920s with John Strachey, who was soon to join the Labour Party and the ILP, himself.[2] Waugh, of course, was not known for his warm embrace of left-wing views. Yet his quip serves to remind us that in 1930, the year that *Vile Bodies* appeared, the ILP was a well-known actor on the political stage, having existed, at that point, for nearly forty years.

Founded in 1893, the ILP had initially pursued the "Labour Alliance" strategy of one of its most prominent leaders, Keir Hardie, combining with trade unions to secure parliamentary representation for the working class—an initiative that culminated in 1900, with the formation of the Labour Representation Committee (LRC). From the start, the LRC was often referred to as the "Labour Party," and this became its official title in 1906. At this stage, the Labour Party was a federation of socialist organizations and British trade unions. Among the former, the ILP was the largest, and its members accounted for many, if not most, of the local activists who held public meetings, knocked on doors, and delivered leaflets during elections. The ILP's situation would change in 1918, however, when the Labour Party adopted a new constitution. To Labour's federal structure was added, for the first time, the possibility of joining the party directly, as an individual member, and contributing to the activities of one of the party's newly forming local branches. These changes challenged the traditional role of the ILP within the federation, raising, for the ILP, the urgent question of what part it should, or could, play within the new arrangement.

The founding, in 1920, of the Communist Party of Great Britain (CPGB) likewise altered the landscape of the British Left, and the ILP was, of course, obliged to respond to this new presence. With respect to the interwar period, historians sometimes tend to view the Labour Party and the CPGB as the only two significant forces on the British Left, with the ILP accordingly presented as lacking a clear-cut ideological identity—as struggling to distinguish itself, on the one hand, from an increasingly cautious and conventional Labour Party and, on the other, from the self-proclaimed revolutionary Communists. In his pioneering history of the party, *Left in the Centre*, Robert Dowse argues, for example, that the "lack of identity" of the ILP was "exacerbated" by the emergence of the CPGB. "The I.L.P. had its birth-right filched," he writes; "it was no longer the most significant left-wing Party in Britain."³

But, while the CPGB was certainly a competitor, the creation of that party hardly sounded the death knell of the ILP. At the time, the ILP was indeed an important presence on the British Left, with an impressive range of local branches, especially in Scotland and in the industrial heartland of England. It was an active publisher of party literature, including a national newspaper, the *Labour Leader* (later to become the *New Leader*). It also enjoyed the support of a number of local and regional papers, among them the *Merthyr Pioneer*, the *Leicester Pioneer*, the *Huddersfield Worker*, the Glasgow-based *Forward*, the *Bradford Pioneer*, the *Birmingham Town Crier*, and *Labour's Northern Voice*.⁴ Granted, party membership declined and much of this support was lost after 1932. All the same, as Gidon Cohen points out at the start of his groundbreaking book on the ILP in the 1930s, at the time of its disaffiliation from Labour, the party had five times the membership of the CPGB.⁵ In short, the ILP was far from a moribund organization during the interwar period.

As Dowse's title suggests, a tendency also exists to adopt (whether consciously or not) a Leninist perspective on the ILP and view the party as a "centrist" organization. While no doubt this is exactly how many political activists and observers saw the ILP in the interwar period (and, in some cases, even after 1932), the label almost inevitably suggests a rather indecisive group of people uneasily adrift between the "realistic" politicians of the mainstream Labour Party, to the right, and, to the left, the sharp-witted Marxist-Leninist intellectuals of the British communism. But obscured by this view is the fact that the ILP had ideas of its own, including some that arguably situated the party to the left of the CPGB. Moreover, in the later 1930s, it was the ILP that opposed participation in any "popular front" that included "bourgeois" parties, while the CPGB sought affiliation to the very Labour Party that the ILP had left in 1932 in order to pursue a "revolutionary policy" of its own.

But if the identity of the ILP was in some sense under siege, it was not only from the Communists. The postwar period saw former Liberal Party MPs, such as Charles Trevelyan and Arthur Ponsonby, join the party, bringing with them new perspectives. In particular, these newcomers tended to place considerably greater priority on international affairs than was customary among ILP members. Given the rise of the ILP's Ramsay MacDonald to Labour Party leadership and the prospect that Labour would form the next government, membership in the ILP was also, for a short period, an attractive option for those seeking to gain seats in the House of Commons. For a while, writes Fenner Brockway, secretary of the ILP at the time, "wealthy careerists buzzed around us, anxious to be adopted as candidates, proffering contributions in the hope of securing rewards."[6] In addition, former ILP member Oswald Mosley, who broke with the Labour Party in 1930, continued to have his supporters within the ILP—some of whom even followed him into his British Union of Fascists. At the same time, the 1930s also saw a number of the earliest British Trotskyists join the ILP.

Another major besieger was the Labour Party itself, whose revised constitution of 1918 threatened to make the ILP redundant. Even within the ILP itself, there were those who argued at the time that the ILP should be dissolved or turned into what we might now call a socialist think tank. In addition, many ILP members questioned whether the ILP would be able to press its own radical policies through its group of Labour MPs, and it was this perceived threat that underlay the struggle against the standing orders of the Parliamentary Labour Party—a struggle that contributed significantly to the ILP's decision in 1932 to disaffiliate from Labour.

During the early postwar period, the ILP *might* have given in to the pressure to conform to Labour Party orthodoxy. Equally, it might have been completely absorbed by the Communists. In the early 1920s, in the wake of the founding of the CPGB, a group known as the "Left Wing of the ILP" made a concerted effort to persuade the party to leave the Labour Party and affiliate instead to the Third International, otherwise known as the Communist International, or Comintern. Had this effort been successful, it could only have resulted in the speedy integration of the ILP into the CPGB, as the Comintern would accept only one affiliate from a given country. A merger with the CPGB seemed again to be a possibility in the 1930s, after the ILP left the Labour Party to pursue its "revolutionary policy."

Historians of the ILP generally agree that disaffiliation from the Labour Party in 1932 was a fatal mistake. Dowse has relatively little to say about the period after 1932: he seems to view disaffiliation as such a disaster that what subsequently happened to the ILP is hardly worth discussing. Indeed, within just a few years, erstwhile leading advocates and supporters of disaffiliation within the ILP had already begun to doubt the wisdom of the decision—doubts that culminated in August 1939, when the ILP's National Administrative Council (NAC) voted in favour of seeking reaffiliation.[7] Granted, Cohen takes a more nuanced and generally more positive view of the ILP post-disaffiliation than does Dowse. What needs to be more widely recognized, however, is that, at the time, both alternatives seemed fraught with danger. Some within the ILP feared that if the party chose to remain beneath Labour's umbrella, this would be the beginning of a process that would see the ILP's radicalism tamed or even totally extinguished. In retrospect, this fear seems misplaced, at least insofar as one can judge from the activities of former ILP members who remained in the Labour Party. But to those contemplating the choice that lay before the party, the possibility that continued affiliation would spell the end of the ILP's radicalism seemed very real. As for disaffiliation, the chief concern was that, its ties to Labour severed, the ILP would eventually be absorbed by the Communists—who, during the 1930s, made a very serious attempt to infiltrate the newly independent party.[8] If, in the end, disaffiliation proved to be a mistake, the ILP in fact escaped both of these possible outcomes: neither was it tamed, nor was it absorbed.

The aim of this study is not to tell, once again, the same sad story of the decline of the ILP. Rather, my aim is to examine the distinctive ideas that animated the ILP during the interwar years—ideas that not only help us understand more fully the British politics of the period but also constitute the ILP's lasting contribution to democratic socialist thinking and remain the most significant part of its legacy. Some of those within the wider labour movement of the period distrusted the ILP, seeing it as a band of "intellectuals." The ILP did include among its members a number of influential writers and thinkers, such as John Middleton Murry and, later, George Orwell, whom history has recognized as intellectuals, even if they tended to remain in the party for a relatively short time. But ILP policy was shaped as much by the ideas of those who would not claim such a title, and my focus accordingly falls at least equally on their contributions to the party's ongoing internal debates. As Kevin Morgan put it so succinctly in the context of his exhaustive exploration of the impact of Bolshevism on the British Left, "it is not intellectual history, if that means the history of intellectuals."[9]

During the interwar period, the ILP became a sort of residuary legatee of the pre-Leninist British Left, as it existed prior to the 1917 Russian Revolution, and of nonconformist currents of the early postwar period. The party's policy on radical parliamentary reform, first articulated by MP Fred Jowett before the First World War, continued to be supported by party members long after the war. During the 1920s, the ILP also embraced some of the principles of guild socialism and, in the 1930s, had a serious flirtation with the idea of workers' councils.

Like so much of the pre-1917 Left, the ILP stressed the virtues of internal democracy, though it did adopt what it called "democratic centralism" in the 1930s—with no obvious success. For many years, the ILP also pursued a radical economic policy, predicated on the ideas of J. A. Hobson, among others. This was exemplified by its policy initiative known as both the Living Wage and

Socialism in Our Time. That something of this combination of constitutional and economic radicalism—a strain of distinctive radical democratic socialism—survived into the post-1945 period in the Labour Party and among its supporters can be attributed to the ILP more than to any other single organization, particularly if we include the various offshoots of the ILP, such as the Socialist League and the Scottish Socialist Party.

It would be wrong, of course, to claim that everything the ILP did in the interwar period exemplified some form of democratic socialism or that all members of the party deserved the designation of democratic socialist. And it would be ridiculous to pretend that there were no democratic socialists and strains of democratic socialist thinking in Britain outside the party's ranks. But more than any other organization in Britain over the two decades in question, the ILP did much, however imperfectly, to keep such ideas alive. In 1921, George Clarke, a member of the ILP's Altrincham branch, declared at a Lancashire Division conference "we are the only Party that can consistently stand for democracy."[10] While no doubt coloured by party pride, Clarke's claim was not, in the end, that far off the mark.

In this book, my focus falls on ideas and proposed policies that led to substantial debate within the ILP. Many of the party's positions, although contentious in a broader public context, were accepted with something close to unanimity among ILP members themselves. The opposition to war and warmongering, to capital punishment, and to imperialism are some obvious examples, as is the party's support of internationalism in the wider world and of devolution within the United Kingdom. The ILP was, from its inception, more supportive of women's rights than most other political groupings, including other left-wing organizations, and accordingly less apt to be dominated by men. A number of women were prominent members of the ILP in its early years, during the 1890s, and we will meet others who were active in the party during interwar period. The ILP was also a strong supporter of democracy in the Empire—and especially of the movement in India. That such issues will not receive greater attention in what follows does not, of course, in any way lessen their significance.

All of the debates and events involving the ILP during the interwar years contributed—directly and indirectly—to the policies, culture, and ambience of the labour movement after 1945. Fenner Brockway, who became the ILP secretary in 1923 and was the party's chairman from 1931 to 1934, appears frequently in the pages that follow. During his long and very active life (he died at the age of ninety-nine), Brockway went on to become the most high-profile former ILPer of the postwar period. Among his many activities, he was a founding member of the Campaign for Nuclear Disarmament, War on Want, and the

Introduction

World Disarmament Campaign, as well as chair of the Movement for Colonial Freedom and the British Council for Peace in Vietnam. One thinks also of his attempts, while a Labour MP in the 1950s and early 1960s, to promote legislation outlawing racial discrimination.

The main sources for this study are the ILP archives, housed at the British Library of Political and Economic Science at the London School of Economics; the party's weekly national paper, *Labour Leader* and then the *New Leader*; and, especially for the early 1930s, the Glasgow-based *Forward* and *Labour's Northern Voice*, published by the party's Lancashire Division. The two major studies of the ILP in this period, by Robert Dowse and Gidon Cohen, have, of course, been invaluable and are essential reading for anyone wishing to understand the ILP within its broader context. So, too, is the work of David Howell—notably, his book *MacDonald's Party*—and Matthew Worley's *Labour Inside the Gate*. In addition, Kevin Morgan's magisterial *Bolshevism and the British Left* trilogy offers countless invaluable insights into the Left during the interwar years. For anyone wishing to follow the fortunes of the ILP beyond the interwar years, I recommend Peter Thwaites's dissertation, "The Independent Labour Party, 1938–1950," as well as Barry Winter's *The ILP Past and Present*, which covers the entire history of the organization.

The chapters of this volume are thematic but follow a broadly chronological sequence. One partial exception is the first chapter, which provides a wide sweep of the history of the ILP from its foundation, in 1893, until just before the outbreak of the Second World War, in 1939. The story of these decades is told through an examination of F. W. (Fred) Jowett and his ideas about the radical reform of parliamentary procedure and representative government. Although, as this book will amply illustrate, the ILP's ideological positions shifted considerably during the interwar years, Jowett's views represent a strand of continuity, in the form of an underlying commitment to radical and democratic socialism that survived in the ILP—if only, at times, precariously.

PART I
Searching for a New Role

Democracy, Foreign Policy, and Parliamentary Reform
The Legacy of F. W. Jowett

If one had to nominate a single figure to exemplify the Independent Labour Party's enduring allegiance to democratic socialism, it would surely have to be F. W. (Fred) Jowett (1864–1944). Widely known as "Jowett of Bradford," after the Yorkshire town in which he was born, he would serve on the local council, and later represent as an MP. Bradford was also where the party's founding conference was held. Jowett would remain an influential figure in the ILP for the rest of his life. Every position he took was infused by a fundamental commitment to socialism, democracy, and the spirit of egalitarianism, which together formed the ideological bedrock of the ILP. Although this commitment would be seriously challenged during the interwar period, it was never totally submerged or abandoned.

The Early Years of the ILP

An emphasis on local autonomy and a firm resistance to centralizing tendencies were enduring characteristics of the ILP. This emphasis on the local was conveyed by the use of the term "council" in the name of the party's national coordinating body, the National Administrative Council, a choice no doubt intended to underscore that this was *not* a national "executive." Likewise, "administrative" suggested that the National Administrative Council was concerned with routine organizational matters rather than making or carrying out political decisions. The party grew out of significant local organizations centred in the industrial areas of Lancashire and Yorkshire—most notably, the Manchester Independent Labour Party and the Bradford Labour Union. Jowett had been a leading figure in the latter, and, in 1892, he became the first socialist elected to Bradford's city council. After failing to make an electoral breakthrough in the 1895 general election, the new party devoted itself with renewed vigour to the "Labour Alliance" strategy promoted by its leading figure and former MP, Keir Hardie. This meant uniting ILP socialists with trade unionists—a process that eventually saw the formation of the Labour Representation Committee in 1900.

The Labour Representation Committee achieved a foothold in the House of Commons in 1906, as the Liberals swept to victory in the landslide election of that year, and shortly thereafter changed its name to the "Labour Party." For the rest of the prewar period, there was much criticism from the Left—including within the ILP—of the apparent docility and subservience to the Liberal government of Labour's parliamentary representatives. In the early years of its existence, the Labour Party had no formal leader, but its leading figures were Keir Hardie (who died in 1915), Ramsay MacDonald, and Philip Snowden.

The most distinctive stance of the ILP was its uneasy, though not entirely consistent, opposition to the Great War, while, on the domestic front, its most original—and controversial—position was its commitment to a complete transformation of the British parliamentary system. The instigator and most persistent advocate of this policy, formally adopted in 1914, was Jowett, who was to become one of the more memorable Labour MPs of the twentieth century. Robert Dowse sees Jowett as "representative of the majority" of the early membership of the ILP. He clearly has in mind Jowett's background as a largely self-educated working-class man from a northern industrial city who, having started work as a "half-timer" in a weaving shed at the age of eight, rose to white-collar employment as an "overlooker" and, later, a mill manager.[1] But Jowett was anything but typical in most other respects. J. B. Priestley, another famous son of Bradford, wrote that though Jowett may have sometimes been wrong, he was never "stupidly or ignobly wrong." Always at odds with the Labour establishment, and the wider British one, he was not a charismatic rebel or, as Priestley put it, a "spectacular figure." But in Priestley's view, he was "a great man of a new kind, which the history books have not caught up with yet."[2]

A consistent major theme in Jowett's political life was his determination to make parliamentary democracy work in a way that brought the executive under the control of the elected representatives and made elected members fully accountable to their constituents. For him, this was an essential condition for socialism. His experience as a Bradford city councillor was a key formative influence, especially in the development of his central idea about parliamentary reform—replacing cabinet rule by a committee system similar to the kind then used in local government.

Jowett was elected as Labour MP for Bradford West in 1906; he retained the seat in the elections of 1910 but lost it in the "khaki election" of December 1918—a fate that likewise befell other prominent members of the ILP who opposed the war or at least failed to offer sufficiently unequivocal support for it (notably MacDonald and Snowden). Re-elected in 1922, this time for Bradford East, he served under MacDonald in the minority Labour government of January to November 1924, as First Commissioner of Works. In spite of his determined opposition to what he called "cabinet government," Jowett had accepted MacDonald's invitation to join the government while apparently not expecting to be included in the cabinet. But he was. Like another prominent ILPer, John Wheatley, the new Minister of Health, Jowett refused to wear the customary morning dress and top hat to receive his seal of office at Buckingham Palace. In the same egalitarian spirit, he insisted on including the less elevated members of the ministry staff in his inaugural reception.

Defeated at the October 1924 election, Jowett was once again elected for Bradford East in 1929, losing the seat in the Labour debacle of 1931. In the meantime, he had not been invited to serve in MacDonald's second government. Arthur Marwick, in his book on Clifford Allen, characterizes Jowett as a "traditionalist."[3] In that particular context, this may, arguably, be justified, but plainly, this characterization can hardly be applied to Jowett's approach to parliamentary government.

Jowett's Campaign for Parliamentary Reform

Besides the refusal to wear court attire and the inclusive reception at his ministry, a more substantial way in which, according to his biographer, Jowett defied tradition during his brief period in government was by bringing his departmental estimates forward to early April. Fenner Brockway explains that the normal practice was to save such matters until late July in order to limit the time available for parliamentary discussion before the summer recess. Jowett was motivated not only by the desire to help provide employment but also to ensure adequate time for discussion of his proposals in Parliament. To attempt to avoid or limit such discussion, says Brockway, "did not suit Jowett's democratic principles."[4]

Jowett's democratic principles, while by no means unique, were distinctive, above all in the single-minded doggedness with which he pursued them throughout the early decades of the twentieth century. Unlike some radical socialists of the pre-1914 era, he did not wish to replace representative government with "direct democracy" in the form of the referendum and initiative, though he conceded that there was a case for such procedures replacing the House of Lords, or any second chamber, as an ultimate expression of the sovereignty of the people.[5] Nor, after 1917, was he an enthusiast—as many in the ILP were, especially in the years immediately following the Russian Revolution—of "soviet democracy."[6] Jowett's democratic principles centred on making parliamentary government as genuinely democratic as he could conceive.

Jowett did share with critics of parliamentary government the belief that "the first bulwark of the propertied classes is the House of Commons," and, like them, he asserted that the "old Parliamentary hands know that even if the majority of members of the House of Commons were Socialists, the forces of reaction could prevent rapid progress being made with the help of the ancient machinery now in use."[7] But, unlike those on the Left who believed that the parliamentary system—or "bourgeois" representative systems of all varieties— were beyond repair, Jowett advocated radical reform. Soon after becoming an MP in 1906, he rejected the then current system of British government. "It is not Democracy, it is not even representative government—it is something different from either," he wrote in the *Clarion*, a popular socialist paper.[8]

Jowett's formative political experience occurred during his years on Bradford city council. At that time (and indeed until relatively recently), local government in Britain operated quite differently than did its national equivalent. Local authorities—essentially administrative bodies set up, defined, and regulated by statute—used a system whereby each department, staffed by council employees, was controlled by a committee whose membership reflected as accurately as possible the proportion of each party represented on the full council. Jowett wished to see many changes in the national system, but his central idea was to extend the committee system to the House of Commons as a substitute for cabinet government.

This was not an entirely new idea. Back in 1884, H. M. Hyndman, the leading figure in the then recently formed Social-Democratic Federation (SDF), had called for committees to be elected "to conduct our Foreign Affairs, our Commerce, our Legislature, our Railways and other departments of State."[9] In 1901, H. Russell Smart, a prominent ILP activist, had urged the Labour Representation Committee to contest "the tremendous power vested in that close oligarchy known as the Cabinet."[10]

Jowett began his own critique of cabinet government before his election in 1906. His "I.L.P. Letter" appeared regularly in the *Clarion*, and in March 1905, he described the theory of Cabinet responsibility to the House of Commons as "one of the most mischievous delusions that constant repetition has ever succeeded in foisting upon the public." It should, he urged, be broken down by the Labour Party at the earliest opportunity.[11] Jowett's *Clarion* contributions became regular "Notes on Parliament" following the election in 1906, and a few weeks after becoming an MP, he repeated his attack on cabinet government and argued for its replacement by a system of committees composed of members of all parties. This would, he claimed, bring an end to both "bureaucracy" and "Party Government."[12]

In order to promote his agenda of radical reform of parliamentary procedure, Jowett submitted a motion in 1908 for the setting up of a committee composed exclusively of new MPs who had not become familiar with the "unbusinesslike" practices of the Commons. Its role would be to propose changes in parliamentary procedures.[13] Probably more effective than this motion, however, at least in getting his ideas before a wider audience, was his contribution to the *Clarion*'s "Pass On Pamphlets" series, titled *What Is the Use of Parliament?* Here, he explained in greater detail his proposal to replace the cabinet with a committee system. He had no time for maintaining tradition at all costs, taking the view that "ancient machinery which is obsolete and beyond repair should be thrown out." For Jowett, it was clear that "whoever else . . . can afford to tolerate the present system of conducting the business of the country, the Socialist and Democrat is not of the number."[14]

Like virtually everyone on the Left, Jowett wanted to see an end to the House of Lords, arguing that, with regard to important national issues, it was, even at its very best, functioning only as a clumsy, and in some cases misleading, substitute for the referendum. But Jowett believed that above all a radically reformed House of Commons was what was desparately needed. As long as procedures in the Commons remained unchanged, the position of the House of Lords in the State would be "buttressed and strengthened," Jowett argued.[15] Effective publicity was essential to accountability, but such accountability was impossible "under a system of single Ministerial control, checked only by an annual discussion" and could not possibly cover even "one point in every hundred on which Ministers should be cross-examined, and, if necessary, over-ruled."[16]

According to Jowett, the key change needed for a fundamental reform of the parliamentary system and the establishment of genuine representative government was the replacement of cabinet rule with a committee system. Committees of a sort had been introduced but were "cursed by a system of procedure similar to that of the House of Commons itself."[17] Jowett was particularly dismissive of committees of the whole House, in which "a body of 670 members is supposed to be engaged not only in deciding between the alternative issues presented by each clause of a complicated Bill, but in selecting the fittest words to express the objects of the Bill and its clauses." For the most part, MPs did not even pretend to be following the proceedings.[18]

In 1913, in response to the government's statement of its legislative program for the coming parliamentary session, Lord Robert Cecil, an Independent Conservative MP, moved an "amendment to the address," expressing his regret that no mention had been made of "proposals for the improvement of the procedure of this House." Jowett made a substantial speech in support of this motion, claiming that "the great county councils do their business in a far better way and with far more sense of responsibility than we do." He supported Cecil's proposal to have the committee stage of legislation carried out by an actual committee rather than by the entire House, with members hardly listening to the debate. It was "a scandal," he said, "that encouragement should be given to the rushing in of Members to vote upon points which they have never heard discussed."[19] That same year saw the passage, at the ILP's annual conference, of a motion hostile to single ministerial control of government departments and supporting the creation of select committees of the House of Commons whose members would be drawn from all parties.[20]

Following the inconclusive elections of 1910, the minority Liberal government was dependent in part on Labour Party support in order to remain in power. Were the Liberals to sustain a defeat on an important piece of legislation, a failure that could be construed as evidence of a lack of confidence in the government, the party would have little real choice but to abide by convention and resign, thereby triggering an election. In this situation, Jowett was concerned that Labour MPs would be tempted to compromise, voting in favour of legislation that in some way ran counter to Labour's own agenda rather than risk a potentially fatal Liberal defeat that might pave the way for the return of the Tories. More generally, as part of his strategy to make Parliament more democratic and more effective, Jowett sought to put an end to the convention whereby governments were bound to resign when defeated on a matter of confidence.

Jowett and his Bradford ILP branch had therefore begun, in 1911, to advocate what became known as the "Bradford Resolution"—which, if adopted by Labour, would instruct members of the Labour Party's parliamentary group to vote on each bill according to its merits from Labour's point of view, ignoring any effect on the government's prospects for survival. The hope was that this policy, if consistently pursued, would eventually undermine the existing convention, to the point that it would be abandoned. Especially in view of the present fragility of the Liberal government, however, the proposed policy caused great controversy. It was, in particular, fiercely opposed by Ramsay MacDonald, then the chairman of the Parliamentary Labour Party, who believed that it was vital to keep the Liberals in power at all costs.[21]

Put to a vote at the ILP conferences in 1912 and 1913, the resolution was twice defeated, although with substantial minority support. Not so in 1914, however, when the policy was emphatically approved. This shift in fortunes owed much to the fact that MacDonald was suspected of participating in discussions about an alliance of the Labour Party with the Liberals—a prospect that was anathema to most ILPers. The motion was carried decisively by 233 votes to 78, and Jowett was elected as chairman of the party for the second time, having held the office in 1909–10.[22] There seemed to be at least an outside chance that the Bradford policy would be adopted by the Labour Party, but before that could be tested, war intervened.

The Great War: Democracy and Foreign Policy

Foreign affairs and, above all, the question of military alignments and alliances was an area of particular concern to Jowett—and to many others in both the Labour and Liberal parties. If proper accountability was lacking in government generally, it seemed virtually nonexistent in these crucial areas. In 1908, Jowett complained about Edward VII being "encouraged to meddle in affairs for which he cannot be called to account" in relation to the formation of the Triple Entente with France and Russia.[23] In 1911, in the House of Commons, he asked Foreign Secretary Sir Edward Grey whether, "during his term of office, any undertaking, promise, or understanding had been given to France that, in certain eventualities, British troops would be sent to assist the operations." *Hansard* records the reply of Thomas McKinnon Wood, then Under-Secretary of State for Foreign Affairs: "The answer is in the negative."[24] Several months later, writing in the *Clarion*, Jowett attacked "secret diplomacy and the overpowering influence which experts and permanent officials exercise over successive ministers in turn"—a clear case, in his view, for establishing parliamentary control through a committee system.[25]

Jowett continued his attack on secret diplomacy in a local Bradford paper, the *Bradford Daily Telegraph*: "People may desire peace, but secret diplomacy, inspired nobody knows how, intriguing nobody knows where, often working in close touch with great financial magnates, whose interest is to cause States to incur debts and pay them tribute in a hundred different forms, weaves its net of intrigue and keeps nations in mortal dread of each other." What was urgently needed, Jowett argued, was a House of Commons committee with full access to all the necessary information to explain issues such as "why we should build more Dreadnoughts"—the powerful new battleships that had revolutionized naval armaments since the launching of the first, HMS *Dreadnought*, in 1906. He concluded, "Let us have all cards on the table—the diplomatic cards as well."[26]

Jowett continued to be among the most persistent critics of Grey's foreign policy. The foreign secretary, unsurprisingly, rejected any suggestion of setting up a foreign affairs committee. But Jowett was not easily deterred. Soon after the beginning of the 1914 July Crisis, which would end in the outbreak of war, he wrote in the *Bradford Pioneer* that "what Sir Edward Grey and others cannot prove, nowadays, is that the secret tortuous ways of the old-fashioned diplomatists really succeed in the long run."[27] If a major objective of diplomacy was to avoid a disastrous war, Jowett certainly had a point.

The war reinforced the arguments against secret diplomacy. Whether or not Jowett himself had a hand in drafting the 1916 ILP leaflet *Democratic Control*, it certainly put forward his view. The war had starkly revealed the inadequacy of the existing system of cabinet government, the leaflet declared, and every department had "failed in the current crisis." It continued:

> **If the men who played this disastrous game** at the expense of hundreds of thousands of British lives had been under the necessity of meeting regularly, face to face, at a Committee of Foreign Affairs consisting of members of Parliament representing different parties, ideals and points of view, the criticism of foreign policy during the years preceding the war would have been based on knowledge, and **it would have been almost impossible to carry out the policy which came to such a disastrous conclusion in August 1914. The people would have been warned beforehand, and not faced with a fact accomplished.**[28]

The leaflet concluded with a statement of the ILP's intent to seek a radical change along the lines of the policy it had adopted at its last prewar conference: "The Independent Labour Party seeks to make the system of representative government real and effective by the establishment of Committee Control, not only over foreign affairs but also over all departments of State. Only then will there be a system of Parliamentary Government representative of the will of the people secured by democratic control."

In March 1918, the ILP's weekly paper, the *Labour Leader*, printed the text of the speech that Jowett had delivered during a House of Commons debate on the role of the Foreign Office initiated by Liberal MP Charles Trevelyan. A long-term critic of secret diplomacy and a staunch opponent of Britain's involvement in the war, Trevelyan had been instrumental in the founding of the Union of Democratic Control, set up in December 1914 to campaign for democratic scrutiny of foreign policy.[29] Jowett supported Trevelyan's motion for the establishment of a Standing Committee on Foreign Affairs and emphasized the urgency of democratizing the Foreign Office. Another Liberal dissenter and outspoken critic of the war was MP Arthur Ponsonby, who, like Trevelyan, was among the founders of the Union of Democratic Control.[30] Destined to join the ILP soon after the war, Ponsonby made what Jowett called "a splendid speech" during the debate. Jowett further related that, in 1911, when he asked Grey about commitments to France, he had been referred to the Anglo-French Convention, which dealt merely with maintaining the status quo in Morocco and Egypt.³¹ As he had said a year earlier, in his address as chairman to the ILP's annual conference: "The country had been deceived. I had been deceived."³²

Two ILP pamphlets by J. W. Kneeshaw in the immediate postwar years reinforced the attack on the lack of accountability in foreign affairs. In *The Hidden Hand in Politics*, in 1919, Kneeshaw characterized the Foreign Office as "the last remaining citadel of aristocratic privilege in the country. It secretly and autocratically juggles with the lives and treasure of our whole population, and great as are our democratic powers, we have no power to check its adventures, or even to know in what they consist." Parliamentary sanction should be required for every decision involving international affairs. "To be rid of war, democracy must banish the dark-hand diplomats and establish its complete authority in the Foreign Office as in all other governing departments."³³

The following year, in a second pamphlet, Kneeshaw looked back to the origins of the recent conflict. The "decision that ultimately landed us into the Great War was secretly made in 1904, not by Parliament, but by the Foreign Office," he wrote. He ended by making the more general plea for the extension of accountability in all areas of governance while stressing the particular case of foreign relations. The chief business of democracy was, he argued, "to push out the boundaries of its power" to embrace not only local and national politics but foreign policy as well.³⁴

As for Jowett, he would continue, long after the war, to take every opportunity to remind his audiences of the iniquities of secret diplomacy. In his speech as chairman at the Edinburgh conference of the Labour Party in 1922, which the ILP published as a pamphlet, he drew attention to "the steadily accumulating list of official documents disclosing the pre-war arrangements of the victorious States and Czarist Russia; along with the published statements of one after another of men who filled responsible posts and took part in the events leading to the war." Sir Edward Grey's assurance to the Commons on 3 August 1914 that the House was free to decide whether to go to war or not was true in only the "formal sense," said Jowett. "In reality his assurance was a lie. For in the same speech he disclosed the existence of an agreement with France which bound the Prime Minister and himself along with the Government to which they belonged, in an obligation of honour—or rather dishonour—to go to war."³⁵

Cabinet or Committees? The ILP Debate Continues

In 1917, the ILP's National Administrative Council (NAC) set up a small committee, which included supporters of both the cabinet and committee systems, to report on how best to achieve effective public control of both Parliament and national government policy, as well as to allow MPs greater individual responsibility for choosing how to vote. But this effort seems to have died on the vine.³⁶ Jowett himself returned to the question of parliamentary reform at the 1919 ILP conference, however, moving a motion on behalf of the Bradford branch asking the party to endorse a program that would place the machinery of government on "a sound democratic basis."

The motion demanded both reform of the electoral system so as "to secure Proportional Representation of Parties" and "abolition of the Cabinet system and the substitution of Departmental Committees elected by, and representative of, the various groups in Parliament, the representation being in proportion to the numerical strength of parties in the House of Commons." Jowett's aim was to reaffirm the ILP's policy. Parliament, he charged, was living on its past reputation, bureaucracy was flourishing, and MPs were virtually excluded from administering the affairs of the country and had no contact with the departments of state. "So long as Parliament was organised as a mere debating assembly," Jowett argued, "there was no possibility of the electorate exercising sound judgment because the facts were not disclosed, and the information was not there upon which to base judgment."³⁷

The two proposed amendments to Jowett's motion reflected competing notions of what constituted "real democracy." One advocated for the referendum and initiative approach and was attacked by H. Stenning of the Tottenham branch as "democracy run mad." The second amendment supported the soviet system, a system that Jowett commended as an "experiment" suitable for Russia and Hungary but not appropriate in Britain, with its "deep rooted Parliamentary institutions." He added that the indirect nature of the soviet delegation system meant that electors lost touch with the elected even more than was the case with Parliament. The amendment's seconder, A. J. Thatcher of the Blyth branch, pointed out that the ILP was based on that same system. The amendment was later withdrawn.³⁸

Opposition to the main motion came from C. H. Norman, who would become one of the leading figures of the ILP's Left Wing, a group that pursued affiliation to the Communist International the following year, and—inevitably—from Ramsay MacDonald, who said that the motion was "at least four years old, as far as time was concerned, and so far as the state of mind was concerned, it was 100 years old." He regretted the withdrawal of the soviet amendment, claiming that there was "nothing more critical for the Party to discuss."³⁹ The debate was brought to an inconclusive end through a procedural device that ended it without a vote—a most unsatisfactory outcome from Jowett's point of view.⁴⁰

Yet Jowett was nothing if not persistent, and the following year, at the 1920 ILP conference in Glasgow, he moved that the cabinet system be abolished, now with the support of both the NAC and his Bradford branch. He told the delegates that although some believed that representative government had failed—referring to the enthusiasm for "soviet democracy," then at its height in the ILP—he wanted to "state emphatically that in his opinion representative government had never been tried in national affairs." Formally seconded by John Scurr, the resolution was carried.[41]

It was Jowett's colleague William Leach who moved the Bradford motion at the 1923 conference, declaring that "the Cabinet system demands passive obedience."[42] But whereas in the past, criticisms of cabinet government had been directed at Liberal, Tory, or coalition regimes, a Labour government was now a real possibility. To what extent would Jowett's critique be reflected in, or survive, the reality of Labour rule when its main critic would be the party leader and prime minister? And how would the experience of a minority Labour government influence debates on the issue?

Jowett Advocates for Committees—*and* Cabinet

There were some in the ILP and the Labour Party, even before the defeat of the 1924 government, who sought to radically change the way the Labour Party approached parliamentary politics. Others were determined to resist this. In early October 1924, shortly before the defeat of the government in which he had held the post of under-secretary at the War Office, Clement Attlee, the future Labour Party leader and post-1945 prime minister, wrote a *New Leader* article titled "What Is Democratic Control?" He rejected the ideas contained in motions for the Labour Party conference that sought election of ministerial appointees by the parliamentary party. The government had to be "a team," he argued.[43]

He was even more scathing about the demand "to subordinate the Government and the Party in the House to the fullest control of the Executive Committee of the Labour Party." This was not a move towards greater democracy, he contended, since that committee was "an extreme example of indirect election." Moreover, the "same people who would curb the Parliamentary Party by subordinating it to the General Committee will be found attacking the members of the General Committee. They believe in the dictatorship of the proletariat, but in their own opinion they are the only proletarians."[44] But at least one member of that first Labour government still sought major change in the way the House of Commons operated.

Jowett's advocacy of a radical reform of parliamentary procedure, though endorsed at almost every annual ILP conference, must have sometimes seemed to him like a solitary campaign. This was particularly evident in its lack of support among MPs, who, Brockway tells us, all too often dismissed it as "Fred's obsession."[45] His ideas had more appeal for those who observed the parliamentary scene from outside. In a May 1924 article on proportional representation,

H. N. Brailsford, the editor of the *New Leader* at the time, discussed the likely implications of that electoral system, including the danger that its adoption would lead to "coalitions of the Lloyd George type." He concluded that another possibility existed:

> Place the real power in the hands of Departmental Committees of the House, and it would then be a more bearable evil that party majorities would be rare. Behind P.R. there is a high and difficult ideal of equity. It rejects every impulse of dictatorship. It could work only through a habit of open and fruitful compromise. It would in the end sap the Cabinet system and what is that but dictatorship multiplied?[46]

The debate on the Bradford motion at the 1925 ILP conference generated a pamphlet containing the speeches of the two main adversaries, Jowett and H. B. Lees Smith. Jowett began by saying that it was "peculiarly appropriate" that this debate should follow one on "Labour in Office," a debate that had demonstrates the existence of "a desire that there should be an outlet for expression in Parliament on points of view not held by the Government." He rehearsed the familiar arguments about how the government largely controlled what was debated in Parliament. As he further maintained, MPs often faced the dilemma of whether to vote in support of their government, regardless of the promises they had made to their constituents, or to adhere to their principles by voting against the government and possibly turning it out of office.[47]

His solution was to get rid of the unwieldy committee of the full House and to create much smaller, more viable, House of Commons committees so that MPs could "consider business in detail, the departmental committees reporting their decisions to the full House from time to time at the report stage." But he was no longer advocating the *replacement* of the cabinet by committees. The cabinet should remain, with the role of coordinating the work of the government.[48] He concluded, to applause, that "the nine months of Labour Government have clinched this conviction more than I could have expected it possible to do."[49] Lees Smith, reflecting the views of those who feared that all-party committees might act as a brake on Labour Party initiatives in government, supported the idea of advisory committees that would not have the power "to modify or water-down the policy of the Labour Government." Jowett rejected this as ineffective.[50]

The following year, Jowett dealt in greater detail with the objections to his proposals from both Lees Smith and MacDonald in the pamphlet *Parliament or Palaver?* An introductory note drew attention to Jowett's experience as a long-serving MP and as a cabinet minister, noting his authority and expertise in the area of parliamentary democracy. The pamphlet endorsed the idea of departmental committees, which would "take over for all purposes—legislative and administrative—the committee business of Parliament," carried out by the entire House of Commons sitting as a committee. The threefold purpose was to improve the efficiency of the legislature, enable MPs to take an active part in parliamentary decision-making and permit MPs to be able to take positions on the "merits of the question" rather than as "votes of approval or condemnation of the Government."[51]

The rest of the pamphlet dealt with the objections of MacDonald and Lees Smith. Jowett rejected the former's objection that such a change could only be accomplished after a long drawn-out constitutional conflict. No legislation was necessary, he argued. A Labour majority could simply change the procedure and rules by which the House of Commons carried out its own business. This would take no more than a few days. The "abolition of the farcical and inefficient Committee of the Whole House of Commons" would give more time to members with "personal knowledge and experience" who would be able to "cross-examine responsible officials, elicit facts, and put their proposals" without having to win a private members' ballot or catch the Speaker's eye in order to be allowed to speak.[52]

MacDonald's objection that the Tories would reverse any such reform on returning to power assumed the continuation of "pendulum politics," Jowett argued. Furthermore, there were "rank and file members of other parties as well as of the Labour Party. Is it too much to assume that some of them, too, will want to be something more than mere followers and voting machines? Public representatives, when they have first got powers, do not easily relinquish them."[53]

Similarly, Jowett rejected Lees Smith's contention that the result of applying the policy would be "to destroy the Cabinet system and put every department in the hands of a committee consisting of capitalist representatives as well as Socialist representatives." On the contrary, a Labour cabinet would still provide the driving force. The only power the cabinet would be deprived of under his proposals would be the "threat of resignation to prevent cross-voting in committees." He dismissed the alternative of advisory committees: they would simply add to the existing complexity and would "leave untouched that absurd, futile and time-wasting medley miscalled a committee ... the committee of the whole House of Commons."[54]

A *New Leader* editorial by Brailsford in August 1926 strenuously supported the proposals articulated in *Parliament or Palaver?* He reiterated that the cabinet would remain, with a leadership and coordinating role.[55] This would not be the last time that Jowett's radical idea of parliamentary democracy would play a part in the course taken by the ILP. As we shall see later, his objection to the standing orders of the Parliamentary Labour Party—and, consequently, his support for disaffiliation—was based on the same underlying principle. If MPs were forced to support policies put forward by their party leaders in government, even when these policies were clearly at odds with the platform on which they had been elected, how could democratic representative government become a reality?

Jowett would maintain a defence of parliamentary government throughout the period following disaffiliation, during which the proponents of a "revolutionary policy" aspired to replace it with so-called workers' councils. But even when the ILP began to drift back, slowly and cautiously, towards Labour, he remained opposed to reaffiliation. With a special conference to decide the issue scheduled for September 1939, the NAC—with Jowett among the minority opposing the idea—recommended rejoining the Labour Party. The outbreak of the Second World War, which would delay further consideration of reaffiliation, was just over three weeks away when the *New Leader* featured Jowett's attack on the current system, titled "The Sham of Our Parliamentary Democracy." In his article, Jowett looked back thirty years to the beginning of his "lone agitation" for the committee system reforms that he advocated. He noted that although Labour Party advisory committees on the "Machinery of Government"—made up "mainly of members who were then, or had been, connected with the Civil Service"—had supported such changes, they had been ignored in both 1923 and 1928.[56]

Jowett had been a leading ILP member, serving regularly on the party's NAC not only for the entire interwar period but for the best part of the preceding three decades, beginning with the party's foundation. ILP conferences had approved his proposals on numerous occasions, and, as we have seen, other influential figures such as Brailsford and Brockway had given him their support. One suspects, however, that for many in the party, his advocacy for parliamentary reform had little to do with socialism. The point had been made early on by *Labour Leader* in 1912. "Abolishing the Cabinet system of government," the paper maintained, would require as much effort as "abolishing the capitalist system of industry, and we think it would pay us much better to put our energies into the latter channel."[57]

For Jowett, this was missing the point entirely. The socialist objectives of eliminating poverty, oppression, exploitation, and inequality could only be achieved via the most democratic of means. After all, inequality of power underlay and reinforced so many of inequality's other forms. Jowett's real service to the Left lay not so much in his particular proposals and positions as in consistently arguing this broader case and, by doing so, promoting the cause of democratic socialism at a time when it truly was under siege.

In the next chapter, we return to the years following the First World War. The split in the Liberal Party, formerly the recipient of so many working-class votes; the contrast between Lloyd George's promise of "homes fit for heroes" and the reality of life for the majority in postwar Britain; and the hopes and enthusiasms ushered in by the revolutionary events in Russia all contributed to the emergence of new possibilities. The ILP would face new and intractable problems. The political situation was changing fast in the postwar world, and the continuing existence of the ILP itself was threatened by the Labour Party's new constitution.

2

An Existential Dilemma

Reactions to the Labour Party's 1918 Constitution

One could argue that the fate of the ILP was irreversibly settled early in 1918, when the Labour Party adopted its new constitution. This was the typically summary conclusion of A. J. P. Taylor almost half a century later, although it oversimplified and foreshortened a more complex trajectory. "Ultimately the I.L.P.... was ruined," Taylor wrote. "Socialists could now join the Labour Party as individual members. They no longer needed the I.L.P. as an intermediary and it became a diminishing sect."[1] Only a few years earlier, Ralph Miliband had made a similar observation: "The Labour Party's announcement that it was now a socialist party was to create a serious problem for the I.L.P., which that body was never able to resolve."[2] Until 1918, joining the ILP had been the main route by which committed socialists could become part of the larger Labour Party and attempt to influence its overall direction. With the introduction of the new constitution, however, socialists could now join that organization directly—and, with constituency Labour parties forming in communities all across the country, the ILP seemed destined for superfluity.

The Threat of Redundancy

In his classic study of British political parties, Robert McKenzie characterizes the ILP's response to the Labour Party's 1918 constitution as a "combination of petulance and optimism."[3] Petulance is perhaps rather harsh, and, while there was certainly optimism, much of it seems more like whistling in the dark. Even before the ILP's 1918 conference opened in late March, there were signs of increasing disquiet about the new constitution—which, among other things, certainly strengthened the position of the trade unions in the Labour Party (from which many of the members of the party's National Executive Committee were drawn). Speculating on the probable response of the ILP's National Administrative Council (NAC), a well-informed article in *Labour Leader* reported that "earnest, we might say anxious, consideration was being given to the new constitution."[4] The NAC's report, presented at the conference itself, reminded those in attendance that ILP had "never considered the constitution of the Labour Party to be satisfactory from a democratic point of view," arguing that "a democratic party dependent upon the financial support of powerful and wealthy Trade Unions can never be a democratic party in the true sense of the word."[5] Not long afterward, Ramsay MacDonald would put it more bluntly in the ILP's journal, the *Socialist Review*: "The I.L.P. pays pence, the Trade Unions pay pounds."[6]

Although the NAC report acknowledged that local Labour parties were bound to compete with ILP branches, it tried to see a positive side, predicting that the existence of local Labour parties would "stimulate rather than injure the local branches of the I.L.P." It also expressed the hope that these new constituency parties would be established not by veteran ILP members but by recent recruits to the socialist cause — "by the efforts of men and women whose new-born zest for the Labour Party may be usefully employed in this work."[7] There was, in fact, an element of condescension in this cheerful response. Confronted with the threat of superfluity, the leaders of the ILP sought to justify the organization's continuing existence by pointing to its role as, in Dowse's words, "the intellectual spearhead of the Labour Party."[8] Yet they often did so in a way that put a lot of emphasis on the ILP's past and relatively little on its possible future contributions. In 1919, for example, the Bristol branch published a leaflet that attempted to explain the difference between the two parties. Included was the following summary:

> The I.L.P. supplies the driving force.
> The I.L.P. was founded in 1893.
> Its leaders were amongst the founders of the Labour Party in 1899."[9]

A similar focus on past achievements was visible in another leaflet, published the following year by the party's national headquarters. Titled *The Need for the I.L.P.*, the leaflet sought to face head-on the question of the apparent redundancy of the party, while also casting its new circumstances in as positive a light as possible. It began by acknowledging that, with the advent of individual membership in the potentially more powerful Labour Party, "some persons now wonder why there is a need for a strong I.L.P. as well." It went on to point out that the Labour Party owed its existence to the ILP and that the ILP regarded the larger organization in no "spirit of antagonism." On the home front, much of the Labour Party's work was "concerned with industrial questions," but there was a need for "a wider outlook" on these issues, which the ILP was, its leadership believed, able to supply. In international affairs, no party other than the ILP had "shown up in so convincing a manner the evils of secret diplomacy . . . which brought about the last war." And when it came to the key tasks of publishing, distributing propaganda, and organizing public meetings, the ILP was "able to work for Socialism more effectively than any other body."[10] While these claims were by no means untrue, they tended to look backwards, rather than forwards, and thus did little to resolve the question of the ILP's future. One also thinks of Dowse's comments about the "patronising posture" that the ILP tended to adopt towards the Labour Party at the time, one that combined "a nudging reminder of its past services" with hints of its "moral superiority."[11]

Notwithstanding the NAC's efforts to put a brave face on the matter, among certain elements within the ILP, the Labour Party's new constitution raised serious doubts about both the viability and the wisdom of continued affiliation to the larger organization. Some felt that the ILP's future relationship to the Labour Party should be contingent on evidence of the latter's genuine embrace of socialism. On the agenda of the ILP's 1921 conference was a motion from Lancashire's Chorley branch that sought to "instruct" the Labour Party to finalize a program to be carried out "almost immediately on taking over the reins of Government." This program was to include a commitment to making no secret agreements; an international conference aimed at disarmament; self-determination for all parts of the British Empire; social ownership of land, mines, railways, shipping, and banking; and a new educational system. In addition, the Labour Party was to secure "the repeal of all legislation which is democratically to be considered to be in restraint of human progress," abolish the monarchy and the House of Lords along with "all hereditary privileges," and move quickly towards the "replacement of Capitalism by a saner system of society." This was, to put it mildly, a very comprehensive set of demands, especially in a program to be implemented "almost immediately." Another motion on the agenda, this one from the Glasgow-based Clyde branch, advocated outright divorce, proposing that the ILP declare "the time opportune to sever connection with the Labour Party."[12]

In some respects, it might appear that the ILP had little to worry about. As David Howell points out, despite Labour's new constitution, ILP branches remained significant in many areas because "the early development of individual Labour Party membership was slow and uneven. Especially in the old ILP strongholds such as Bradford, and across much of Scotland, little changed."[13] Matthew Worley makes a similar point, emphasizing local trade unions as a factor: "In areas where trade unionism was weak and fractured, particularly in Scotland and parts of Yorkshire, the ILP effectively was the Labour Party to all intents and purposes."[14] The NAC's Program and Policy Committee—set up in the wake of the ILP's 1920 conference and charged in part with assessing relations with the Labour Party—reached much the same conclusion, reporting in

1921 that "in Scotland generally and in some English districts the local Labour Parties do not compete with the I.L.P."¹⁵ A year earlier, the report of NAC to the party's annual conference had listed 787 branches.¹⁶ But could the party rely on maintaining this number in the longer term, let alone advancing it further, now that constituency Labour parties were entering the field—however slowly in some areas?

The anxiety within the party about its role in relation to Labour is reflected in the fact that, in its report to the party's 1921 conference, the NAC felt it "essential to supplement" the report of its Program and Policy Committee with comments of its own. As the NAC pointed out, the observations were "designed to emphasise the need for the continuation of the I.L.P. as a vigorous organisation consciously Socialist and propagandist in character in home politics and foreign affairs, and with a clear idea of its task in relation to the Trade Union and Co-operative movements."¹⁷

The question was, and would remain, What should the future of the ILP be? One possibility was simply to declare that the party had no future—that it had accomplished its goal. Keir Hardie may have died, but his "Labour Alliance" had been fully realized: socialists and trade unionists were now joined as members of a unified party that had committed itself to socialism. In these circumstances, the ILP could have claimed a victory and gradually wound itself down as the new Labour Party organizations established themselves. But this option attracted very little support among ILP members, for reasons well summed up by Ralph Miliband in his book *Parliamentary Socialism*:

> The I.L.P.'s *raison d'être* after 1900 had been to transform the Labour Party into a party committed to socialism. The Labour Party now said that it was. But, more and more in the course of the twenties, the I.L.P. found itself compelled to carry on its diverse activities on the wholly justified assumption that the Labour Party's conversion to socialism was as much a thing of the future as it had been before 1918. This made for acute conflict.¹⁸

Perhaps the earliest manifestation of this conflict was the campaign mounted in 1920 and 1921 within the ILP to persuade the party to end its affiliation to the Labour Party altogether, in favour of joining instead with the Third (or Communist) International. While such a course of action clearly offered one possible answer to the dilemma posed by the Labour Party's new constitution, support for the idea was driven above all by the atmosphere of excitement surrounding the revolutionary changes in soviet Russia.

The Road Not Taken

The ILP had been a member of the Socialist International, commonly known as the Second International. Founded in 1889, the organization had dissolved in 1916, its members divided over the issue of opposition to the war. There emerged from this division a group of revolutionary socialist parties—the core of the Third, or Communist, International, which convened its first conference in March 1919, in Moscow. The aftermath of the war also saw efforts to revive the Second International, which was formally reconstituted in August 1920, at a conference held in Geneva, drawing its support from groups committed to broadly reformist, rather than revolutionary, policies.

Under the influence of Ramsay MacDonald and Philip Snowden, the Labour Party opted to join the Second International. Within the ILP itself, however, support for the Second International was limited, despite the stance of two of the party's most prominent members. As reported in *Labour Leader*, delegates to the ILP's 1920 conference voted overwhelmingly, 529 to 144, to disaffiliate from the soon-to-be-revived Second International—a decision that served to underscore the anomalous position of the ILP within the Labour Party.[19]

Meanwhile, earlier in 1920, the Scottish Divisional Council of the ILP had voted 158 to 28 in favour of affiliating to the Third International, which had been set up in Moscow the previous year.[20] In spite of the doubts voiced by some divisions, notably Yorkshire, and the hostility of the party leadership, there was certainly a groundswell of enthusiasm in the ILP for Comintern affiliation, and it seemed very possible that, when the national conference met in Glasgow at Easter in 1920, pursuit of such affiliation would become the official policy of the party as the rejection of a revived Second International at that conference suggests.

Reporting on the conference, *Labour Leader* noted that, prior to the opening of the event, some two hundred participants—not all of them conference delegates—had taken part in a "Third International gathering," chaired by C. H. Norman, at which it was agreed to "act together" and "to hold further meetings during the Conference proceedings."[21] Enthusiasm for the Bolshevik revolution was well reflected in a resolution passed unanimously at the conference itself, which resolved to send "fraternal greetings to the Russian Socialist Republic" and desired "to convey to it the sense of rejoicing at the success with which the Russian people have defended the Social Revolution." Its mover, David Kirkwood, said that "Russia had struck such a blow that resounded right throughout the world and they of the I.L.P. had the opportunity of giving expression to that great idea, the ideal of the working class in power."[22] The "Left Wing of the ILP," as it now designated itself, was thus disappointed when a motion for affiliation to the Third International gained only 206 votes. The vote was not outright rejection, however, since the conference resolved that further enquiries and consultations should be undertaken before a definite decision was made. The plan to consider the idea further was approved after Clifford Allen spoke in support of this course of action.[23]

Writing in *Labour Leader* in March 1920, just prior to the party's conference, Allen had firmly rejected "the old Parliamentarianism" and had proposed that the ILP take part in the upcoming "International Conference of Left Wing Socialist bodies."[24] This conference would culminate in the founding, in February 1921, of the International Working Union of Socialist Parties—sometimes called the "2½ International," as it was composed of parties that supported neither the parliamentary socialism of the Second International nor the communism of the Third. In the same article, however, Allen recommended that the ILP also seek affiliation with the Third International, having first set out its own position on three crucial points. The ILP, he argued, should reject violent revolution in the case of Britain. It should, however, accept the "Dictatorship of the Proletariat" because democracy could be meaningful only once economic equality had been achieved. Finally, it should reject the "soviet system" as a "general 'must'" while accepting the "fundamental" idea of "government through working class organisation."[25]

The months that followed found the ILP pursuing its decision to engage in further investigations and consultations on the subject of an international affiliation. The opportunity to explore the possibility of joining the Comintern came when Clifford Allen and Richard Wallhead (who had recently succeeded Snowden as chairman of the ILP) were able to attach themselves, in an "unofficial" capacity, to a group from the Labour Party and the Trades Union Congress that visited Russia on a fact-finding mission in May and June 1920. In his biography of Allen, Arthur Marwick tells us that, at this stage, Allen "hoped to bring the British Labour movement, or at least its vanguard, the I.L.P., into communion with the new Third International."[26]

Allen's companion, Richard Wallhead, had defended the Bolsheviks in 1918 after their suppression of the Constituent Assembly. In a *Labour Leader* article written in August of that year, he praised "the first great Socialist Republic" and asserted that "the Socialist Government of Russia has behind it 85 per cent of the people." While British workers were "demanding the democratic control of industry," he declared, "the Russian workers have it."[27] By the start of 1920, however, he had begun to take a much more cautious view of Russian developments, arguing that while the "dictatorship of the proletariat" was acceptable as a temporary expedient, he was not prepared to accept "exalting it into a philosophy or adopting it as an integral part of a programme."[28]

The twelve succinct questions that Wallhead and Allen had put to the Comintern on behalf of the ILP were reported in the *Labour Leader* in July 1920. They began by asking the Comintern's executive committee how "rigid" was the requirement that affiliates adhere to "the methods outlined in its program." Questions followed on how the dictatorship of the proletariat might apply in Britain, on the use of "Parliamentary methods," on the ILP's affiliation to the Labour Party, and on whether "the soviet system of Government" was a fundamental principle and, if so, to what extent the International recognized "the possibilities of diverse forms of Soviet Government in different countries." Wallhead and Allen, on behalf of the ILP, went on to ask whether parties that left "open" the question of "the use of armed force" to bring about revolution could affiliate and what the International considered to be the difference between communism and other forms of socialism. The list ended with a series of questions aimed at ascertaining whether the Comintern was willing to consider moves to create a united—or more united—international.[29] The following week, the paper announced that *The I.L.P. and the Third International*, the report of Allen and Wallhead, was in press.[30]

By this time, the earlier enthusiasm for Comintern affiliation and for Russian soviet democracy had definitely faded. In a letter addressed to the NAC, Allen was critical of the structure and workings of the new international. It was still an "*ad hoc* body" with "no formal constitution," he reported, and its executive was not elected by the affiliated bodies in "the normal constitutional way." There were, he conceded, representatives of other nationalities on the executive, but it was "first and foremost Russian in character," dominated by Russian leaders and by "the philosophy of the Russian Revolution." As he noted, NAC members would have read the Comintern's "long and rambling reply" to the questions that he and Wallhead had raised, a reply that in fact failed to answer many of these questions.[31]

In his letter, Allen made it clear to the Comintern executive that, were the ILP asked to choose between the Third International and the Labour Party, the ILP would surely choose the latter. With regard to the former, there was no doubt, he stressed, that "at present it is an international of violence." He closed by concluding, with due emphasis, that unless the Comintern were willing to agree that "the method of resorting to civil war as a means of obtaining power" could be left as "an open question," that he would recommend to the next ILP conference that the ILP "should not affiliate to it unconditionally."[32]

Wallhead reported on meetings that he and Allen had had with Mensheviks. "They do not care whether the final political form is Parliament or Soviet; that is unimportant: the chief thing is that it must be democratic and not bureaucratic, as they maintain the present Bolshevik system is." Wallhead's own early optimism about the soviet system had now evaporated. The conditions he observed in Russia, he wrote,

> lead to a devitalising of the democratic basis on which the soviet form is supposed to rest, and makes directly for bureaucracy and autocratic control. The power of the proletariat dwindles almost to vanishing point, and passes to the party that holds power. In Russia at the present time this is the Communist Party and it is very clearly established.

The soviet form, Wallhead concluded, had been "gradually adapted into an instrument of the Communist Party and used to establish the dictatorship of a relatively small minority."[33]

Clearly, these were not the sort of judgments and recommendations that those in ILP's Left Wing were eager to hear. In the interim, the group had established its own biweekly publication, *The Internationalist*, its first issue appearing in June 1920. In it, one of the Left Wing's most prominent members, J. T. Walton Newbold, set out the group's agenda in "The Task Before Us." The Left Wing would, he wrote, have "no mercy" on those, particularly "the younger men and women," who waited "to see how the cat was going to jump" before committing themselves one way or the other to the Comintern affiliation question. The task at hand was the creation of "a united Communist Party in Great Britain, of which the I.L.P. may be, in numbers and influence, the very core."[34]

It was to Newbold that the Comintern sent its "long and rambling" reply, a decision well suited both to annoy the NAC and to reinforce the belief that, from the Comintern's point of view, the object of the exercise was to bring about a schism in the ILP rather than to encourage the party as a whole to pursue affiliation. The Left Wing might claim, in its own published analysis of the Comintern's reply, that "our Russian comrades are deeply concerned to bridge the gulf and overcome the obstacles."[35] But fewer and fewer ILPers were now convinced of this.

The Left Wing had invested some hopes in Allen, who had been very ill in Russia and remained there for some time after the main Labour/TUC party returned home. The second edition of *The Internationalist*, published early in July 1920, noted that "Mr. Clifford Allen is credited with being one of the pioneers of the Communist movement in the I.L.P." and expressed hope that this "augurs well for his propaganda value when he returns."[36] Members of the Left Wing were to be disappointed. In August, readers of the *Labour Leader* learned that Allen could not recommend affiliating to the Third International, unless the latter was prepared to leave the question of violent seizure of power to each affiliated party.[37] This was not something likely to materialize within any foreseeable time span.

One notable opponent of affiliation was E. C. Fairchild, whose article "A Travesty of Communism" also appeared in the Labour Leader that August. Fairchild had, until the previous year, been a prominent member of the British Socialist Party (BSP), which formed the initial core of the Communist Party of Great Britain (CPGB) when the latter was founded in August 1920. Fairchild was also the former editor of the BSP's weekly paper, *The Call*, and, during the summer of 1919, had been one of the protagonists in a heated debate in the pages of the paper that centred on whether there were any real prospects for establishing a soviet system in Britain in the near term. His chief adversary was Theodore Rothstein, who was acting as the representative of Russia's Bolshevik government in Britain. Implicit in Fairchild's criticisms was a muted protest against the subservience of the BSP to Rothstein and to "Moscow."[38] A year later, Fairchild had clearly reached a state of total disillusionment with the entire Communist enterprise.

> The Communists are tired of the endeavour to give knowledge to the slowly moving mass. They ask us to believe they have found the royal path. The Communists propose the revival of aristocracy. It is too dangerous. It is to be an aristocracy of horny hands not of blood. But not every labourer can take part. The privilege may be reserved for those who subscribe to a particular school of opinion.[39]

Towards the end of 1920, the ILP's national office published a pamphlet titled *The Communist International*, which listed the Comintern's famous "21 conditions," translated from the version in the 26 August issue of the Paris-based *Bulletin Communiste*. In a memorandum concerning the publication, Francis Johnson reminded ILP members that "dictatorship means force." He also issued a warning about the fundamentally divisive intentions of the Communist organization: "The tactics of the Third International are to detach from the large Socialist Parties any sections which accept the Bolshevist basis of Dictatorship, Soviet Government and Force."[40] The memo left little doubt as to the opinion of the national office on the subject of ILP membership in the Third International.

Undeterred by the hardening of opposition to their proposal, the Left Wing pressed on. In December 1920, *The Socialist*, the organ of the small Socialist Labour Party (SLP), that was still, at that time, supportive of the Bolsheviks, reported that the ILP's Left Wing was seeking to change the party's official platform so that it would declare the ILP to be a Communist organisation" and would explicitly state that the dictatorship of the proletariat was a "necessary condition for Social Revolution."[41] At the same time, the editor of *Labour Leader*, Katharine Bruce Glasier, announced the paper's intention to publish a "program proposed by the Provisional National Committee of the Left Wing of the I.L.P." as an alternative to the program that had been drawn up by the NAC's Program and Policy Committee. Included in the Left Wing's program, which appeared in *Labour Leader* two weeks later, was an insistence on immediate affiliation to the Third International. In the same issue, a correspondent deplored "the attempt to establish and build up within the I.L.P. an undemocratic and questionable group," namely, the Left Wing's Provisional National Committee.[42]

The Left Wing came under attack again early in the new year, when Ramsay MacDonald—who, like other ILP MPs, had lost his parliamentary seat in the "khaki election" of 1918—lost the Woolwich by-election to the Coalition-Conservative candidate, Captain Robert Gee. The Woolwich seat had been held by the veteran trade unionist and Labour MP Will Crook since 1903, apart from a few months between the two elections of 1910. Ill health—he died later in 1921—led to his retirement and MacDonald then contested the seat for the Labour Party. Many in the ILP blamed MacDonald's failure to win the seat on divisive attacks of the Left Wing and their Communist allies in the newly formed CPGB, as well as on their campaign for voter abstentions. The vicious anti-MacDonald agenda promoted by the vigorous war supporter Horatio Bottomley and his popular *John Bull* magazine may have played a greater part in the defeat, but since MacDonald lost by only 683 votes, it was easy for those opposed to the CPGB and the ILP Left Wing to attribute his loss to their activities. Had Gee won more decisively few would have believed that a campaign by the Communists and their Left Wing allies might have played any significant part in the outcome.[43]

Up to this point, the editor of the *Labour Leader*, Katharine Bruce Glasier, had attempted to steer a middle course between the Bolsheviks' allies and their critics in the ILP. After the Woolwich loss, however, she concluded, with regard to the Left Wing, that the ILP should "give them clear notice to quit."[44] Significantly, MacDonald, in his article "On Woolwich" in the same issue, made no mention of the Left's hostile activities but quoted a correspondent who, writing to commiserate with him on his defeat, commented that for MacDonald to win 13,041 votes "fighting as a 'pacifist' a V.C. who had killed nine Germans with his own unaided hand, and to have chosen an arsenal as a field of battle is a miracle."[45] MacDonald was too canny to risk encouraging support for the Left by attacking them on such a personal issue as their role in his by-election defeat. How much the disloyal activities of the ILP's Left Wing at Woolwich contributed to the growing opposition to the Left Wing within the party is difficult to estimate. But by the time of the 1921 ILP conference that Easter, the writing was clearly on the wall for those advocating Comintern affiliation.

The previously supportive Scottish Divisional Council had, in January, rejected affiliation by 93 to 57, as had Yorkshire, by 64 to 16, and Lancashire, by 114 to 18.[46] As noted earlier, Wallhead's initial optimism about the Bolsheviks had faded, and, reporting to the 1921 ILP conference on the visit to Russia and the Comintern discussions, he took a very different view of the reality of "soviet democracy" and workers' control than he had in 1918:

> It is clear that the idea of occupation and function does not get beyond the mass meeting of the Soviet, since, in the election of the Executive Council, its members are elected for reason and qualities which do not necessarily pertain to them as workers in specific industries, and in election to the Pusidiunes [sic, presumably Presidium] the departure is even greater still.[47]

As regards the Left Wing—which, particularly after Woolwich, many ILP members had come to see as a "wrecking movement"—Wallhead declared in his chairman's address, "There cannot be permitted allegiance to an outside body whose mandates are to be carried out against the expressed will of the Party." The Left Wing should therefore "leave and join with an organisation to which they can honestly give their allegiance."[48]

The Comintern's "21 conditions" provided the focus for opponents of affiliation at the 1921 conference. The discussion turned on a motion moved by J. R. Wilson that the ILP accept Moscow's conditions and thereby commit itself to Comintern affiliation. In rebuttal, George Benson, of the North Salford branch, claimed that their acceptance would "hand over the I.L.P. bound hand and foot, to a foreign organisation" and turn it into "secret conspiracy body."[49] John Paton, who would later become ILP general secretary, delivered a speech in which he offered what *Labour Leader* described as a "remorseless" analysis of the twenty-one conditions. As the paper noted, Paton also argued persuasively that "in the Communist International as at present constituted there was no place at all for freedom of discussion."[50] In the end, the "Moscow amendment" was unequivocally defeated, by a vote of 97 to 521. At this point, members of the Left Wing rose and walked out of the conference.[51] Many of them would join the CPGB.

So the route out of the ILP's dilemma that consisted, essentially, of throwing in its lot with the new Communist Party was closed—at least for the moment. But not all supporters of Comintern affiliation left in 1921, and other enthusiasts for carrying the ILP in that direction would join in later years. The Bolshevik "siege" was only temporally lifted, though it would be more than a decade before it was seriously renewed in a form that would again threatened the continued existence of the ILP.

The rejection of the Moscow amendment was not, however, the only outcome of the 1921 conference. Over the past year, in pursuit of the resolution passed at the 1920 conference to seek an "all-inclusive international" with which to affiliate, the ILP leadership had followed through on Clifford Allen's suggestion that the ILP join in the meeting of "Left Wing Socialist bodies." As a result, in February 1921, the ILP had participated in the formation, in Vienna, of the "2½ International," that is, the International Working Union of Socialist Parties (IWUSP), or the Vienna Union, as it is sometimes called. As the NAC explained in its report to the 1921 conference, an ILP delegation had attended the 1919 meeting in Berne that gave rise to the International Socialist Commission—for all practical purposes, the reconstituted version of the Second International—and had, at that time, "made it clear that they were not empowered to commit the Party" to the new body.[52] Since then, the ILP had taken part in the Vienna meeting at which the IWUSP was founded, and the delegation had submitted a report, which was presented at the 1921 conference. The report was very frank. The IWUSP did not "represent all that the I.L.P. had in mind when it stated its demand for an All-Inclusive International." All the same, war, revolution, and counterrevolution had led to such "sharp differences" that "the gulf between the two extremes is too wide to be bridged." The report concluded by recommending that the ILP should join forces with the other members of the Vienna Union in seeking reconciliation between the Second International and Comintern.[53] Following the rejection of the Moscow amendment, the delegation's report with this recommendation was accepted by a very large majority, in a vote of 362 to 32.[54]

As it turned out, the Vienna Union was short-lived. Its members despaired of reaching an agreement with the Comintern (which, unsurprisingly, had little interest in compromise), and, in 1923, IWUSP merged with the International Socialist Commission to form the Labour and Socialist International. In the meanwhile, another door had also been closed, at least temporarily. What would quickly have become a merger with the new Communist Party of Great Britain—even if, perhaps, the ILP formed the "very core" of the union, as Walton Newbold predicted—had been decisively rejected. But the difficult question of the ILP's future role within the Labour Party remained.

Following the rejection of affiliation to the Comintern, a meeting of the NAC and the chairs and representatives of the divisional councils took place in Manchester towards the end of 1921. The report of the meeting, published in *Labour Leader* under the headline "Position of Party Defined," revealed an ILP that was still attempting to adjust itself to the situation produced by the Labour Party's new constitution. The continued existence of the ILP was necessary in order to maintain the socialist movement in Britain, the report insisted, and, to that end, the ILP should maintain "the closest and most harmonious relationship" possible with the Labour Party. Its most useful contribution to that party would be "the maintenance of its own work." This work should consist, at least initially, in the party's embrace of an educational role, both within its ranks and beyond them, with the latter requiring the party's central office to "systemise" propaganda to a greater degree than had thus far been the case. The report also recommended "new contact" with the trade unions, founded on "an industrial policy which gives the Trade Unions a new conception of their function in the community." The NAC was left to "work out the details."[55]

Ramsay MacDonald, who had headed the poll in the election for the NAC earlier in the year, must have contributed to this report. In view of his success soon afterwards in becoming Labour Party leader and the first Labour prime minister, it is easy to overlook the extent to which MacDonald's position in the larger party was still insecure in the years before 1922. Even though the issue of the role of the ILP within the Labour Party was unresolved, for MacDonald, the support of its members remained crucial. For the first few years following the loss of his parliamentary seat at the end of 1918, one role that the ILP did perform—if not entirely intentionally—was to provide MacDonald with a firm and substantial political base.

3

Ramsay MacDonald and the ILP
A Mutual Ambivalence

Before the 1920s were over, the ILP and Ramsay MacDonald would exasperate and antagonize each other almost to breaking point. Much of the Labour Party, especially many of its parliamentarians, shared its leader's frustrations with the almost constant criticism from the ILP ranks and the behaviour of those MPs who, in pursuing radical socialist objectives, gave their allegiance in the first place to the ILP. The situation had been very different in the years immediately following the First World War, despite the campaign of the ILP's Left Wing for Comintern affiliation. MacDonald, who had written many substantial editorials on international issues for the ILP's *Socialist Review*, could look with some confidence towards the recruits from the Liberals now entering the Labour Party, who fully shared his concerns with peace and international affairs. As Henry Pelling notes, "In more senses than one they were a 'Foreign Legion' as they were dubbed at the time by one of their own number."[1] From MacDonald's point of view, as well as sharing his sense of urgency about international issues, these newcomers might also prove to be an antidote to the more insistently socialist elements among the Labour Party membership.

Liberal and Pacifist Recruits

At the end of July 1914, soon after the outbreak of war, MacDonald had been a signatory of the letter that led to the foundation of the Union of Democratic Control (UDC), which campaigned against secret diplomacy, supported peace on the basis of national self-determination and international disarmament, and wanted the war brought to an end by a just peace. An advertisement for the UDC appeared in the ILP's *Labour Leader* on Christmas Eve 1914. Among the UDC's General Council members list were six MPs, three from the Labour Party—Ramsay MacDonald, Arthur Henderson, and Fred Jowett—and three Liberals—Arthur Ponsonby, Charles Trevelyan, and Richard Denman.[2] The three Liberals listed would all later join the Labour Party.

Among the UDC's other founders, were radical Liberals like Norman Angell and the organization's secretary, E. D. Morel, who were already on their way to coming over to the Labour Party. Most of these men would play prominent roles within the ILP for at least a few years. Indeed, when Morel died in 1924, the NAC report to the annual ILP conference described him as one of the party's "heroes."[3]

Helena Swanwick's 1924 history of the UDC includes photographs of the most active and prominent UDC members, a large proportion of them were already, or were to become, well-known figures in the ILP. They include, in addition to those listed above Philip and Ethel Snowden, J. A. Hobson, William Leach, H. N. Brailsford, and Charles Roden Buxton. "The Independent Labour Party from the first needed no conversion," Swanwick wrote of the party's sympathy for the platform of the UDC. "It had the root of the matter, and from I.L.P. members the Union received some of its best support."[4] Twenty ILP branches had affiliated to the UDC by the time of its inaugural meeting in November 1914, and with the end of the war approaching in 1918, thirty branches joined.[5]

Even before conscription was introduced in 1916, Clifford Allen and Fenner Brockway—both conscientious objectors who would go on to become leading members of the ILP—formed the No Conscription Fellowship, which attracted the support of a broad range of pacifists to enter the ILP, many of whom otherwise had little in common with the party's ideas and objectives. Indeed, some members soon felt the party to be under siege from these newly arriving pacifists. A 1916 letter to the *Labour Leader* from a reader named Herbert Tracy complained that the ILP had become "an annex of the Peace Movement. Its membership has been swollen by an influx of pacifists who have nothing in common with Socialists save their hatred of war, and whose political convictions may be expressed in the formula that whatever any government does is wrong." Tracy may well have felt that his point was borne out by another letter on the same page from "a strong Conservative for 30 years or more" who commended the party for "defending the social ideals of Christianity" by its opposition to the war.[6]

From the standpoint of John Paton, writing years later, ILP members like Tracy were right to be apprehensive about such developments:

> There were scores of wealthy people throughout the country, many of them Quakers, whose implacable opposition to the war had broken their old attachment to the Liberal Party and brought them into sympathy with the I.L.P. They had little real understanding probably of the more permanent Socialist purposes of the I.L.P. but their over-riding concern made them eager to support the Party that had so abundantly proved the sincerity of its opposition to the war.

In general, however, any doubts among other members about this influx were, Paton writes, soon calmed by MacDonald's "soothing accents and sonorous rhetoric."[7] No doubt the fact that many of the new recruits were generous donors also helped.

MacDonald and the ILP: Walking the Tightrope

As we saw in the preceding chapter, the changing balance of forces as regards possible affiliation to the Third International had been signalled early in 1921, when three of the ILP's divisional councils rejected motions in support of the proposal. These included the Scottish Divisional Council, which, despite its initial enthusiasm for the idea, voted against affiliation by a margin of 93 to 57.[8] The radical Scottish socialist John Maclean, a strong proponent of revolutionary communism who contemptuously rejected "reformism" of all varieties, attributed this dramatic change to "the timely and cunning appeals of Ramsay MacDonald."[9]

MacDonald had long been unpopular among the most radical elements of the British Left. In 1895, the year he stood unsuccessfully as an ILP parliamentary candidate, he had been attacked in *Justice*—the weekly paper of the ILP's more purist rival, the Social-Democratic Federation (SDF), which would leave the LRC after its first year because it failed to explicitly adopt a socialist objective. The ILP had been suspect in SDF eyes from the beginning because it called itself "Labour," leaving open the question of whether that necessarily meant "socialist." From this quarter, MacDonald had been attacked for his support of bureaucratic government and his opposition to radical democracy in the shape of the initiative and referendum.[10] Similar criticisms from that quarter continued. The prominent SDF member Ernest Belfort Bax asserted the following year, for example, that MacDonald's commitment to bureaucracy and his weak support of democratic advance meant that "not only all Socialists, but all Democrats and even Radicals with any respect for consistency, must regard Mr. MacDonald as an enemy."[11]

But such attacks did nothing to delay MacDonald's rise to prominence in the ILP, despite some opposition within the party that derived from a similar suspicion of his conservatism. This opposition manifested itself especially strongly after the maverick ILPer Victor Grayson—famed for his unexpected victory in the Colne Valley by-election in 1907—complained in 1909 that the party was effectively controlled by "the familiar quartette," namely, Keir Hardie, J. Ramsay MacDonald, Philip Snowden, and John Bruce Glasier.[12] Indeed, for a vocal minority within the party's own ranks, the prewar ILP was insufficiently radical and only questionably socialist. Such members were more or less continuously debating whether to leave the ILP or remain in the party and struggle to change it.¹³ The war was, however, decisive in salvaging the ILP's radical reputation.

MacDonald's own position on the war may have been more equivocal than that of many of his comrades. Writing in the 1950s, Emanuel Shinwell maintained, dismissively, that "he was neither for the war nor against it." When MacDonald spoke, his audiences "heard a man who loathed past wars, regarded future wars with abhorrence, but carefully evaded giving his opinion on the basic question of the current one."¹⁴ Despite the ambiguity of his position, MacDonald was pilloried as an opponent of the war during the "khaki election" of 1918. But as the mood of the country began to shift a few years after the war, MacDonald's position in the eyes of a significant segment of the public would benefit from his association with the ILP and its pacifist reputation.

At the same time, MacDonald had to contend with the fact that many Labour MPs had supported the war—among them J. R. Clynes, who became the chair of the Parliamentary Labour Party in 1921. In addition, many members of the Labour Party's trade union affiliates were suspicious of ILP "intellectuals," of whom MacDonald was a prime example. Aware that he was "still detested by trades union and other leaders of influence within the Labour Party," as Paton puts it, MacDonald found the support of the ILP "essential" during the early postwar period.¹⁵

Even within the ILP itself, however, not all were prepared to trust MacDonald, especially after MacDonald—despite being a member of the party's NAC—chose in 1920 to accept a position as secretary to the reconstituted Second International after the ILP had voted to disaffiliate from it earlier in the year.¹⁶ As MacDonald's biographer, David Marquand, notes, MacDonald was "censured" by the NAC for accepting the position, although he "persuaded it to rescind its decision without much difficulty." All the same, "he was running a considerable political risk."¹⁷ Since, at the time, the campaign of the ILP's Left Wing for affiliation to the Third International was still attracting support, the risk was undoubtedly substantial. Unsurprisingly, MacDonald's willingness to ally himself with what many perceived as a reactionary organization did little to lessen suspicions among the more radical members of the ILP about his ideological sympathies.

MacDonald as Socialist Theoretician and Constitutional Conservative

No one could say that MacDonald was slow to put forward his own ideas about where the ILP—and the Labour Party—should be heading. Quite apart from his virtually countless speeches and articles, his output of books was truly prolific for so prominent and active a politician. In the decade preceding the outbreak of war, *Socialism and Society* (1905) was followed by *Labour and* the *Empire* and *Socialism* (1907), the two-volume *Socialism and Government* (1909), *The Socialist Movement* (1911), *Syndicalism: A Critical Examination* (1912), and *The Social Unrest: Its Cause* (1913). The most central idea put forward by MacDonald was what became known as his "biological analogy." Socialists should, urged MacDonald, have a positive view of the state and recognize that "communal life" is as real "as the life of an organism built up of many living cells."[18]

MacDonald initiated and edited the ILP's Socialist Library series, of which *Socialism and Society* was the second volume.[19] He was a constitutional conservative, and it was not just Social-Democrat critics, such as the ones quoted earlier from the 1890s, who recognized this trait. In the ILP's own *Labour Leader*, the reviewer of MacDonald's *Socialism and Government* in 1909 had concluded that "where the political democrat insists on popular rights, MacDonald insists on the citizen's duties . . . where the one insists on equality the latter insists on qualifications. In a word, in politics, the advocate of Social-Democracy (using the word in its broadest sense) lays stress on 'Democracy' [while] the author of *Socialism and Government* lays stress on 'Social.'"

The reviewer also saw MacDonald as striking "across the current democratic opinion" in rejecting proportional representation and the referendum.[20] This rejection was a perennial theme in MacDonald's political thought. In the chapter of *The Socialist Movement* titled "The Immediate Demands of Socialism," he begins his discussion of democracy by making it clear that, for him, "the watchword of Socialism is Evolution not Revolution and its battlefield is Parliament."[21] With respect to the institution of Parliament, however, he goes on to disclaim any "abject allegiance to representative government." Rather, representatives need to be "checked"—and it is "the people themselves" who must exercise this function. But, he cautions, while the referendum and proportional representation may "present themselves to the Socialist in alluring garments," these are not appropriate to Britain. "Undoubtedly in countries suffering from corrupt legislators and from gross injustice from an inequality of constituencies," he writes, "these proposals may be entitled to the term 'reforms.' In our country, however, the name cannot be given them." The referendum, he claims, is "clumsy and ineffective" and always more likely to result in a reactionary outcome, while proportional representation would increase "opportunities for the manipulating caucus managers" and make governments' majorities "more dependent upon stray odd men."[22] For MacDonald, the "Socialist machinery of democracy" consisted of "shorter parliaments, payment of members, [and] adult suffrage." Beyond that, checks and safeguards on abuses of power had to rely on "a higher political intelligence on the part of the majority of the electors."[23]

In MacDonald's vision of socialism, the scope of any sort of industrial democracy was also very limited. With regard to the topic of "workshop management," he told readers of *The Socialist Movement* that, under socialism, there would be "an industrial organisation, which will have a very decisive influence on public opinion, and also act as a check upon the political organisation." At the head of this industrial body would be "the ablest business men, economists, scientists, statisticians in the country all having risen through the lower grades of the particular departments to which they belong."[24] Trade unions would, "in all probability, be utilised for advisory purposes by the central authorities," but whether they would "appoint, or have any voice in appointing, workshop managers and business directors" was a matter upon which "no definite opinion can as yet be formed."

When one considers MacDonald's view of democracy, it is not difficult to see why, on the eve of the outbreak of war, *Labour Leader* was able to quote Professor Gilbert Slater's judgment that MacDonald was "on the working of the Constitution the very strictest of Conservatives."[25] During the first few postwar years, however, a seemingly more radical—or at least less conservative—MacDonald emerged. This was nowhere more evident than in the position he took on "direct action" during the debate on the new ILP program in 1920 and 1921.

The Debate on Direct Action

What turned out to be the protracted process of drafting a new ILP program began after the party's 1920 conference, at a time when the Left Wing still enjoyed considerable support. The task of devising this new program fell to the NAC's Program and Policy Committee, which in turn delegated the task to a drafting committee. On the question of direct action—meaning essentially political strikes—its members were divided. One wording of the draft program would have had the ILP saying that it "realised" that because elections "frequently result in false and inadequate representation" and enable governments "to manipulate and thwart the national will, it may be necessary on specific occasions for the organised workers to use extra-political means, such as direct action." This was, however, insufficiently radical for some members of the drafting committee, among them the guild socialist G. D. H. Cole; Leonard Woolf, better known as a member of the Bloomsbury Group; and C. H. Norman, who had chaired the first meeting of the Left Wing. They wished to have the party recognize that "the organised workers" might be driven to secure their aims, as set out in the program, "by extra-constitutional means, such as direct action or revolution."[26]

At the end of 1920, the *Labour Leader* invited readers' comments on these proposals. One correspondent objected in principle to even the more guarded endorsement of direct action. Direct action always led to the use of force by those in a minority, he argued. If the ILP accepted the legitimacy of direct action, then how could the party object to the actions of the paramilitary Ulster Volunteer Force, just prior to the war, or to the more recent activities of the Sinn Fein "extremists"?[27] Here was an argument that one might have reasonably expected such a "constitutionalist" as MacDonald to endorse. But this was far from being the case.

In fact, MacDonald had already distanced himself from such arguments the previous year. In *Parliament and Revolution*, he had been surprisingly blunt. "With some of the statements of those who oppose 'Direct Action' today, I am in profound disagreement," he wrote. "They are false in their conception of democracy and feeble in their conception of Parliament," and their views were "evidence of the blight of political respectability upon the democratic spirit." MacDonald wanted to "offer no hospitality to the views of a Leviathan State whether based upon the will of a monarch or that of a Parliamentary majority." His support for direct action was not without its qualifications, however. In order for direct action to gain popular support, he argued, it must be taken only rarely. "Therefore," he wrote, "the only conditions under which an agitation for 'direct action' to secure political ends can ever become a serious thing are themselves a safeguard against the habitual use, which would be the abuse, of the weapon." And direct action should "only be used to support representative government."[28]

In his brief political biography, Austen Morgan notes that MacDonald "toyed with the idea of 'direct action'" after the Labour Party conference in 1919 but implies that he then became a firm opponent of it.[29] Clearly, though, his "toying" went on for some time. In his 1921 study course for ILP members on the history of the ILP, MacDonald recognizes the danger of armed resistance to socialism by supporters of capitalism and notes that, in view of this possibility, "the idea of a 'dictatorship of the proletariat' crept into Socialist theories of action." However, this "dictatorship" had as its purpose the defence of "a democracy that had declared itself constitutionally" in the face of "a revolutionary capitalist minority opposing, by arms or otherwise, the majority will." The dictatorship of the proletariat, MacDonald continued,

> was never meant to imply that a minority, by seizing political or military power, could force society to become Socialist. Be clear about this (because your Communist sections of the I.L.P. are not at all clear) this is purely the action of a majority wishing to establish Socialism of its

own will, and not a minority forcing it on a country. It has nothing to do with "dictatorship."³⁰

The breadth of MacDonald's interpretation of what was "constitutional" was evident in his defence of the Council of Action set up by the Labour Party and the TUC in 1920, when war with Russia seemed imminent.³¹ "When people talk of the Council [of Action] being unconstitutional they talk nonsense," he wrote in a *Socialist Review* article. "Everything necessary to protect the constitution is constitutional, if constitutional means anything at all except obedience to any outrageous acts done by men who happen to be Ministers."³² As Dowse points out, in this respect, MacDonald shared the nearly unanimous view held in the ILP.³³

A Shift Towards the Left: MacDonald as Tactician

In 1895, *Justice*, the SDF weekly, had referred to MacDonald as "that trimming gentleman."³⁴ There are certainly signs of "trimming"—or, more kindly, of the adaptation of ideas to circumstances—in his pronouncements in the period after the war when he was absent from the House of Commons. As Dowse points out, MacDonald's outlook changed considerably between the "khaki election" at the end of 1918 and his return to Parliament almost four years later, in November 1922. During what Dowse describes as this "brief period of revolutionary grace and virtue," MacDonald voiced ideas that were "quite different from those he held in the prewar period or in the post-1922 years."³⁵

In *Socialism After the War*, published in 1917, MacDonald conceded that socialism "must be rid completely of the idea of the servile political and military State."³⁶ This statement reflected both MacDonald's reaction to the war and his concerns about the concentration of power in the hands of the government. The idea of "the servile state" derived from Hilaire Belloc's book of that title, published in 1912. A strong proponent of distributism, the idea derived from Catholic social teaching that advocates for widespread property ownership, Belloc argued that state-sponsored capitalism or socialism, whereby certain individuals were obliged by law to labour for the benefit of others, threatened a return to slavery. Although Belloc was not a socialist, coming to his views from a very different place on the political spectrum, his book generated much interest among socialists at the time, especially those wary of state-controlled forms of socialism and of the possibility that the nationalization of industry would lead to the loss of workers' control over the terms of their labour.

MacDonald was an opponent of "direct democracy"—the initiative and referendum favoured by many in the British socialist movement—as well as of Jowett's ideas of parliamentary reform. All the same, he favoured strengthening the accountability to MPs of the executive, and, even if he did not share the views of those who wanted to see an end to "cabinet government," he would still go some way in their direction regarding the role of House of Commons committees. "The representative assembly must be the seat of power and not the handmaiden of Ministers," he insisted in *Socialism After the War*:

> For some time Parliament itself has been sinking into a state of feeble servitude to the Cabinet and Executive. It has no real control over finance, it has absolutely no control over the Foreign Office, and about international affairs it does not know enough to suspect when it is being lied to; it cannot introduce its own legislation or express its own mind in the division lobbies.

It might therefore be "wise," he continued, to set up new forms of control by having parliamentary committees attached to "the great departments of State, especially those of Foreign Affairs and Finance."[37] That sounded not unlike the case that Jowett had been making since before the war. Was MacDonald coming around to his point of view?

While he reiterated his opposition to proportional representation, which he saw as the preserve of the "superior oddity," he seemed to modify his position even on this issue. He would never advocate proportional representation, he declared, "but if the tyranny of uniformity and conformity cannot be broken by the intelligence of constituencies, let us have the evil of Proportional Representation, with a chance that a few adherents of independence may be returned to break down the iron ring of party obedience."[38]

MacDonald's *Parliament and Revolution*, written in the summer of 1919, when enthusiasm across the British Left for the Russian soviets was at its height, was reviewed in *Labour Leader* by John Bruce Glasier, the one member of Grayson's "quartette" who was never in Parliament. In Glasier's estimation, "perhaps the most surprising thing in the book" was MacDonald's proposal "for a sort of Soviet Second Chamber of Parliament." This was particularly surprising, he wrote, coming from someone "who has implacably opposed all devices calculated to lessen the responsibility of the popularly elected House of Commons."[39]

In the book, MacDonald defended a territorial system of constituencies based on residential areas and representing individuals as citizens, rather than one based on trade or profession—a system of representation sometimes called "functional" democracy.[40] He also argued against a parliament composed of representatives of constituencies founded on such narrow interests. At the same time, he conceded that Parliament was "moved by class interests and class assumptions" and urged the need for "a reform of the governing machine" that would bring the country's "industrial life" into "more direct and certain contact with its political life."[41] To this end, the House of Lords should be replaced by "a Second Chamber on a Soviet franchise," one that was democratically elected by members of specific groups:

> Guilds or unions, professions and trades, classes and sections could elect to the Second Chamber their representatives, just as Scottish peers do now. It would enjoy the power of free and authoritative debate (no mean power); it could initiate legislation, and it could amend the Bills of the other Chamber; it could conduct its own enquiries, and be represented on Government and Parliamentary Commissions and Committees.[42]

At the time that *Parliament and Revolution* appeared, in 1919, a number of currents, on the Left in general, and within the ILP, were moving in a similar direction. Many on the Left were attracted to the Russian idea of soviets—perceived as councils controlled by the workers and elected in the workplace—and faith in soviets as a brave new form of democracy was central both to the appeal of the Bolsheviks and to the case for ILP affiliation to the Third International. Others, including some of the younger members of the ILP, were drawn to guild socialism, which attempted to combine both "geographic" and "industrial" representation for citizen *and* worker.

David Marquand argues that *Parliament and Revolution* was "in many ways the most effective polemic MacDonald ever wrote."[43] Certainly, MacDonald's apparent change of heart and accommodation to at least *some* of the views that were now so popular on the Left was more likely to win him friends among ILP socialists than a simple reiteration of his commitment to parliamentary government. That commitment still remained, of course, but it was now presented in a way that took account of the attraction of the alternatives now so popular on the Left. He did, however, urge caution: "It is not good enough for us to fly from the State to the National Guilds, or from Parliament to Soviets, because public opinion has so often baffled us and because dishonest men are elected to the seats of princes."[44]

"War is always destructive of the social *status quo*," MacDonald wrote, and "to-day we are in revolutionary times." As a result of the war, "capitalism as the ruling power in Society" had been challenged. The working class had had "to be made a national co-partner," the "national control of mines and railways" had proved necessary, and the "wholesale pillage of national wealth by landlords and capitalists" had been revealed to the public. The question was whether "intelligent labour" could seize the revolutionary moment before it passed.[45]

MacDonald was well aware of the sympathy of most ILP members for the Russian Revolution and the Bolsheviks, a sympathy made uneasy, in many cases, by doubts about the latter's authoritarian methods. In *Parliament and Revolution*, he shrewdly appealed to both these sentiments which can only have helped to take some of the steam out of the "Left Wing" campaign for Third International affiliation:

> We repudiate the right of the capitalist critics of the Russian revolution to condemn the dictatorship of the proletariat in Russia, not only because their speeches show the most idiotic ignorance of the subject, but because their own actions and methods deprive them of the right of criticism. But Socialists ought to maintain a wider and higher view than that of capitalist subjection. A proletarian democracy dependent upon a mass, the political function of which is to receive the stamp of some governing minority is unthinkable. The prospects of such a state are indeed deplorable.

The notion that "capitalist methods of repression and force can be used by socialists" and that "a rule of tyranny is necessary as a preliminary to a reign of liberty" was, he warned, like the "parrot cry" of recent years that the war would put an end to war.[46]

The injustices of capitalism were all too evident but MacDonald went on to point out that the Bolsheviks had "not applied a single principle" other than those that "governing orders all over the world" had themselves applied nor had they "committed an atrocity" that these regimes had not also "committed or condoned." It was merely that the tables had been turned, which capitalist critics of the revolution hypocritically viewed as reason for outrage. "When the masters murdered the slaves," MacDonald wrote, "no one troubled; when the slaves murdered the masters the world was shocked." But only those who rejected all such double standards had the right to criticize: "Those of us to whom murder and starvation are always murder and starvation whoever may be the victims are alone entitled to condemn."[47] A revolution founded on dictatorship could not be sustained. The "Moscow Government" would either fall or, abandoning its inflexible program, would "commence the work of evolutionary revolution and democratic education," MacDonald predicted.[48]

Within the ILP, views on Bolshevik Russia covered quite a wide range. There were, of course, the enthusiasts of the Left Wing of the ILP, some of whom did not defect to the CPGB after the decision in 1921 not to seek Comintern affiliation. There were early ILP critics of the Bolsheviks such as Dr. Alfred Salter, the well-known and distinguished Bermondsey medical practitioner, pacifist, and, as of 1922, Labour MP. After a much more equivocal start, critics also included Philip Snowden and, especially, his wife, Ethel, after her visit to Russia as part of the Labour Party/TUC delegation.[49] But the largest body of opinion in the party was, almost certainly, those who felt that, although Bolshevik methods and institutions might be necessary and worthy of support, at least in the short term, in the case of Russia, they were inappropriate for Britain. MacDonald played to this part of his audience with great skill: "The Russian Revolution has been one of the great events in the history of the world, and the attacks that have been made upon it by frightened ruling classes and hostile capitalism should rally to its defence everyone who cares for liberty and the freedom of thought. But it is Russian."[50] This equivocal attitude was reflected in his judgement on "the dictatorship of the proletariat":

> A dictatorship to maintain the revolution in its critical eruptive stages may be tolerated; but a dictatorship through the period of reconstruction, a dictatorship from which is to issue the decrees upon which the reconstruction of Society is based, is absolutely intolerable. No Socialist worth anything would submit to such a thing. It can be maintained only in such diffused communities as Russia; it can be admired only by Socialists at a distance.[51]

One objection to "soviet" government that was widely voiced at the time concerned its use of a restrictive franchise, which denied the vote to those deemed to be members of the "bourgeoisie." But MacDonald would have none of this criticism. Compared to the British situation, the Russian arrangement had "no reason to be ashamed of itself." The Conservative Party would, after all, "still disfranchise the mass of the workers (except in so far as it has discovered useful tools in them)," while the House of Lords was "frankly a class organ, with power to alter and veto most of the work of the House of Commons." And, he argued, "the special test which our Franchise Law recognises—the educational one—is as great a failure as could well be, for the representatives sent by Oxford and Cambridge to the House of Commons have been mostly undistinguished and unenlightened." The Soviet franchise thus applied "no new principle": it was simply "the disenfranchisement of the rich by the wage-earner," rather than the other way around. Indeed, a "Second Chamber representative of industrial experience and the wage-earning class" was, MacDonald wrote, "a far more intelligent organ of government than one representing the aristocracy of a country."[52]

As his title might suggest, MacDonald did have proposals for parliamentary reform. As an appendix to *Parliament and Revolution*, he included his "Memorandum on House of Commons Business Presented to the Advisory Committee of the Labour Party on the Machinery of Government" of August 1917. Here, he had complained that "a Private Member has become a mere follower and supporter of the Government, with little initiative, little independence, and little power." In addition, there was the time-wasting that resulted from the "notion that it is the business of an Opposition to obstruct," which had "brought subservience to the Cabinet in its train, together with closure rules that destroy discussion." MacDonald proposed a legislation committee that would "take a wider survey of national needs"—a committee able to summon ministers for consultation and liaise with any Commons committees.[53] He criticized the role of the Whips, arguing that there was "perhaps no greater scandal in the whole procedure of the House of Commons," and he argued for a Commons resolution to "put an end to the practice of considering every trifling amendment as a declaration of want of confidence in the Government." Turning to the idea of departmental committees, he considered their possible roles in some detail and concluded that they should consult with ministers and represent Parliament in keeping in touch with departmental policy. But, he added, "these committees will not supplant, but supplement the Cabinet."[54]

In the main text of the book, MacDonald presented other proposals for change, among them devolution, which had very strong support in the ILP. In April 1920, the ILP conference unanimously agreed on the demand for Scottish home rule, while the agenda for the meeting of the Scottish Divisional Council early in January 1921 included motions from twelve branches demanding a constituent assembly for Scotland. Glasgow's Partick branch wanted a Scottish Parliament based on adult suffrage, with elected representatives limited to one session in office and granted "delegate powers only," that would function in tandem with procedures for a "form of initiative" allowing constituents to propose legislation to be decided by referendum.[55] For MacDonald, devolution encompassed the transfer of important powers not only to Scotland and Wales but also to English regional government: "There are many powers which Yorkshire and Durham could exercise without interference from Whitehall, and if greater districts than counties arranged in natural groups determined by old historical differences and more modern economic ones were created which made their Councils really important, new life and reality would be infused into politics."[56]

MacDonald concluded *Parliament and Revolution* with his view of the role of the ILP. It was a product of British history and British conditions, he declared, situating the provenance of the party at a junction of several different traditions: "It found the Radical movement as one ancestor, the trade union movement as another, the intellectual proletarian movement—Chartism and the earlier Socialist thinkers like Owen, Hall, Thompson—as another; the Continental Socialists—especially Marx—as still another." MacDonald did not hesitate to claim the mantle of Marx for the ILP. The party had come into being, he wrote, "after the Liberal political revolution, and it therefore joins democracy to Socialism, carrying on in this respect the work of Marx."[57]

At the same time, MacDonald was adept at wrong-footing would-be revolutionaries in the ILP. In April 1920, in an open letter addressed "To a Young Member of the I.L.P.," he managed to associate them simultaneously with the "cataclysmic" socialism that he claimed had existed in Britain before the ILP came on the scene and with the elitism of the Fabians. "At that time there was no word of 'the Dictatorship of the Proletariat,'" he wrote, "but there was the corresponding Fabian idea that by clever manipulation you could capture the Government and thus give an innocent nation the benefits of the rule of an enlightened Junta."[58] It was this polemical dexterity, no doubt, that led John Maclean to blame MacDonald's "timely and cunning appeals" for turning ILP opinion around on the subject of Third International affiliation. While his comment probably credited even someone as influential as MacDonald with rather too much in the way of powers of persuasion, given that other factors were at work, Maclean did have a point. After all, MacDonald's constitutional conservatism and his preference for gradualism—for "evolutionary revolution"—had been readily apparent even before the war.

MacDonald's *Socialism: Critical and Constructive*, which appeared in the second half of 1921, might seem to include a certain retreat from his support, in *Parliament and Revolution*, for a functional approach to representation, at least in the form of "a Second Chamber on a Soviet franchise." Clement J. Bundock, reviewing the new book for *Labour Leader*, observed that MacDonald's "resistance to the functional theory of the Guildsmen" was noteworthy "at a time when the Sovietists stress it as the ideal form of representation." By way of evidence, Bundock pointed to MacDonald's "assertion that a guild of school teachers controlling education to the exclusion of all other members of the community is 'a vilely reactionary and subversive proposal.'"[59]

In the passage from *Socialism: Critical and Constructive* from which Bundock quoted, MacDonald certainly does express misgivings about democratic structures based on occupational group. But, rather than outright rejecting such structures, he is cautioning against an uncritical embrace of the soviet-style approach to representation, which, in his view, had the potential to undermine the ultimate aims of the socialist movement:

> The Socialist hopes to make mechanical production—the mere toiling part of life—of diminishing relative importance to the cultural part of life, the part that is true living; and as intelligence increases this demand will be made by the workmen with increasing emphasis. Therefore, we must be careful not to construct a political system based on the assumption that workshop differences are to continue to be so important as they

are at present, or that the divisions created by the antagonisms of capital and labour, or the excessive toil caused by capitalist expropriation and inefficiency, are to last."[60]

As he had made clear on the previous page, MacDonald's concern lay with the potential of "functional" democracy to privilege industrial allegiance over citizenship. "He who bases the State on the workshop or the profession," he wrote, "can never expect to create the civic State."[61]

All the same, MacDonald's critical assessment of the limitations of guilds as the basis for democratic representation does not negate the impression that, in his writings of the early postwar period, he was willing to go at least some way towards accommodating the ideas popular among relatively radical ILP members. Indeed, in *Socialism: Critical and Constructive*, he returns to the notion of an "industrial chamber" of Parliament, one that would "act in the capacity of advisor and administrator in the industrial activities of the community" and serve as "the link between the political and the industrial State." Such a body, MacDonald declared, "would meet all the legitimate political requirements of the functionalists and the Guild Socialists," while sparing the community "the confusion which would follow the adoption of their fanciful political structures."[62]

MacDonald's views on a wide range of issues—from parliamentary reform to Russia, from industrial democracy to devolution—might still be far too timid for a Left Winger heading towards defection to the CPGB and, on some points, such as the role of the cabinet or guild socialism, for other radical currents within the ILP. However, from their point of view, he did seem to have moved, and to continue to be moving, in a promising direction. And it was this more apparently radical MacDonald who was to be defeated in the supposedly "safe" Woolwich by-election—the loss that angry members of the ILP and the Labour Party blamed on the Left Wing and their Communist comrades. It was not only the Reverend William J. Piggot who complained about those who "torpedoed their Comrade's work."[63]

In the early 1920s, MacDonald clearly needed the ILP as a sort of political insurance policy, if nothing else. Indeed, he was to remain a member of the party until 1930. That he still had a large degree of ownership of the ILP in the early 1920s is illustrated by his prominent role on the NAC, his frequent speaking engagements, his weekly column in the Glasgow-based *Forward*, and his numerous contributions to *Labour Leader*. It is also evident in his editorship of the ILP's *Socialist Review* and his confidence in attempting to guide the education of members with his *History of the I.L.P.*

In spite of his apparent shift to more radical positions during his exile from the House of Commons a degree of distrust of MacDonald was certainly present within the ILP. However, this suspicion was more than balanced by the optimistic support that he was still able to generate. For Robert McKenzie, writing in the 1950s, MacDonald exemplified Weber's "charismatic leader."[64] Few things seem to date faster, of course, than political charisma. But even though MacDonald's rhetoric might not go down well today, there is plenty of testimony, often from hostile sources, to its effectiveness in its day.

In the aftermath of the war, the Labour Party was swiftly replacing the Liberals as the alternative to the Conservative Party, as well as rapidly approaching the point where it might form a government. At least to a degree, the hard edges of radical socialism within the ILP had been softened by some of the pacifists and former Liberals who had joined the party. And, for a while, the ILP was gaining both prestige and numbers through its association with the Labour Party's electoral advance—and through MacDonald's own close association with the ILP. With its radicalism muted in concession to the Labour Party mainstream, the ILP might have found a role as a support group for MacDonald. It would be the experience of Labour in office that finally closed this route of escape from the ILP's dilemma. Meanwhile, there was one more escape route to be tried and tested—one that did not *necessarily* conflict with the role of providing support to MacDonald.

4

A "Distinctive Program"
Variations on the Way Forward

At the ILP's 1920 conference, not long before he and Richard Wallhead travelled to Russia, Clifford Allen had complained of the similarity between "our program and the program of the Labour Party," which "makes it exceedingly difficult to keep the party alive in the districts." The more Labour gained new members who had no prior experience with the socialist movement, the more imperative it became that there be, within the larger organization, "a nucleus with a program that is distinctive."[1] Allen's complaint did not go unheeded. A resolution passed at the conference had instructed the NAC to set up a committee to consider "the program of the Party, relations with the Labour Party, and the Soviet system of government."[2] This was, of course, the Program and Policy Committee, which was chaired by Ramsay MacDonald.

Over the summer of 1920, the subcommittee charged with drafting a new program held a series of meetings, and the resulting draft was revised and approved by a meeting of the full committee in September.[3] In November, commenting on the draft of the new program, MacDonald would write in *Labour Leader*: "I believe that, in spite of the growth of local Labour Parties and of Communist sections, the I.L.P., in spirit and in policy, remains a companionship which is worth maintaining because it gives one inspiration and faith to go on fighting against Capitalism, and because it is required as a socialist nucleus in the working-class movement."[4] Whether MacDonald's use of the word *nucleus* was a conscious or unconscious borrowing from Allen, or merely coincidental, the ILP was clearly moving towards establishing itself as a party with a "distinctive" program, one that differed from that of the Labour Party overall. Unsurprisingly, precisely what this distinctive program should be was a topic of no small debate.

Guild Socialism and the Question of Industrial Democracy

Allen had argued, at the 1920 conference, that the NAC needed to respond to "the Socialist thought that is coming from Russia" and give more attention

57

to "industrial matters."[5] Allen, who was initially very enthusiastic about the concept of soviets, had wanted to promote some form of industrial democracy since before the end of the war. "To Clifford Allen," his biographer, Arthur Marwick, concludes, "the essential purpose of the I.L.P. was to adopt a thorough-going programme with strong Guild Socialist overtones, completely distinctive from that of the Labour Party." He quotes an entry from Allen's diary for 29 January 1918: "The more I read and think about this new way of getting all the good things of socialism with a minimum of interference by a bureaucratic state, the keener I become about it."[6]

There had long been some support for guild socialism in the ILP. As early as January 1917, a motion asserting that "the principle of Guild Socialism is essential to a democratic state" appeared on the agenda of the No. 9 (Lancashire) Division's conference.[7] In late 1918, the *Socialist Review* published a review of *Self-Government in Industry*, by G. D. H. Cole, the leading guild socialist at the time. This was followed, in the next issue, by an article by Cole himself, and, in 1919, Cole's *Workers' Control in Industry* was published as an ILP pamphlet.[8] Early in 1920, an interview with Cole by Fenner Brockway appeared in the *Labour Leader* under the title "Evolution of Socialist Thought."[9] Robert Dowse is right to stress the influence of Cole at this time: "G. D. H. Cole was practically given the freedom of the I.L.P. press."[10]

In 1919, Cole and his wife, Margaret, became editors of *The Guildsman*, the organ of the National Guilds League (NGL). The life of the NGL was brief, lasting only from 1915 until 1923. But it was productive, generating numerous ideas and initiatives, as well as a certain amount of internal conflict. Essentially, guild socialism—and not all NGL members liked the word *socialism*—was a response to the syndicalist movement, with its rejection of centralized political structures in favour of industrial, or workplace, democracy.[11] It was equally a reaction *against* the state socialism epitomized by the Fabian Society's traditional approach, which was seen by many younger Fabians, like the Coles, as elitist and bureaucratic.

In the ideal guild socialist society all people would be involved in democratic participation as workers, citizens, and—in some versions, at least—consumers. Although advocates of guild socialism varied in matters of emphasis, in essence they all envisioned a "functional democracy," with workplaces and industries under the direct control of those who worked in them and with a democratic national assembly elected by all citizens that would coexist with a second chamber elected on the basis of occupational group. With that goal in mind, in the early postwar years the NGL encouraged experiments with the formation of workers' guilds—essentially producer cooperatives.

There were those in the ILP whose endorsement of the idea of workers' guilds was more cautious. John Scurr, for example was an influential voice in Poplar, where he was a local councillor. He would be elected as a Labour MP for Mile End, another area of London's East End, in 1923. Scurr declared himself to be in favour of industrial democracy. "Yet I must confess," he wrote in the *Socialist Review*, "that I cannot see any way of a brush maker in the East End of London working at home for a paltry pittance controlling her industry, until I have put her in the position whereby she will be able to buy sufficient food to live and have a little leisure to think about something else than mere existence."[12] How could someone in such dire straits, Scurr argued, exercise the sort of control over her industry required by any kind of industrial democracy or be expected to take part in a movement to secure it, he implied. But there was no shortage of enthusiasts for at least *some* variety of guild socialism in the ILP, particularly among the younger members. As Kevin Morgan aptly puts it, "guild socialist sensibilities were *de rigueur* for the coming generation."[13]

Nor was a commitment to some form of industrial democracy out of line with what the leading members of the ILP—who, within a few years, would be the leaders of the first Labour government—were advocating at this time. In his 1920 pamphlet *Socialism Made Plain*, Philip Snowden was at pains to distance the ILP's idea of socialization from any form of bureaucratic nationalization of industry: "Socialists do not propose that the control of industry shall be centralised in a Government Department," he wrote. He then pointed to plans developed by miners for workers' control of that industry, which, in his view, illustrated how to "ensure democratic management." There will, he explained, "be control by representatives of the State and the workers and consumers, through national and regional committees."[14]

In the first part of his 1921 study course on the history of the ILP, MacDonald likewise made his position clear:

> Under State Socialism nationalised industry would have to be managed by a bureaucracy of officials on a highly centralised system. The I.L.P. never was State Socialist in that way. Control will be based upon the workshops, federated into the district, federated into the nation, and finally federated into an international organisation. In this organisation the workers will participate in control according to schemes worked out to meet the circumstances of each industry.

Echoing his remarks in *Socialism: Critical and Constructive*, however, he went on to warn of the potential capacity of guilds to undermine broader civic commitments:

Guild Socialism must be carefully scrutinised. If it is merely to be a series of guilds of workmen, it will cure some evils but will not serve larger social ends and it will not be able to avoid in the end the dangers of "professionalism"; if it be grafted on to a complete social economic organisation, and be merged in the true comprehensive Socialist idea of the civic community, it will be found a social contribution to the problem of nationalised control.[15]

The incorporation of guild socialist ideas into the broader party program was one of several issues that would need to be resolved.

An Uneasy Tension: The Draft of the Program and Policy Committee

At the annual conference in 1921, the version of the program that would have declared the ILP to be "Communist" and endorsed the dictatorship of the proletariat effectively fell by the wayside when most of the Left Wing withdrew from the ILP following the defeat of Comintern affiliation. Ideas from this quarter had, however, influenced the draft program, and there still remained plenty of material to spark disagreement. As noted earlier, in September 1920, the Program and Policy Committee approved an initial draft of the new program, which was put before the annual conference in 1921. The draft proved to be what Philip Snowden, who chaired the conference, would describe as "essentially a compromise between two points of view which were not easily compatible."[16]

Included in the NAC's report to the 1921 conference was a report from the subcommittee responsible for drafting the new program. Fourteen members of the drafting committee agreed that the statement of the party's principal mission should open with the declaration that "the I.L.P. is a Socialist organisation, whose aim is to end the present Capitalist System and its exploitation of Labour, together with all forms of hereditary and economic privilege, and to establish a system by which the community will own, organise, and control resources for the benefit of all."[17] But there were many differences of opinion within the committee itself, which were reflected in debates concerning the wording of certain sections of the program.

Commenting on the committee's report, the NAC noted that the section titled "Control and Management of Communal Property" constituted "a definite change from the traditional State Socialist theory to the more recent theories of workers' control." The committee had been unanimous, the NAC reported, that a greater decentralization of power was the "only way to avoid bureaucracy after the socialisation of industry."[18] Visible in this shift away from state control of industry was the influence both of the Russian system of soviets and of guild socialist models of industrial democracy. Evidently, however, Ramsay MacDonald, was not entirely happy with this new emphasis on workers' control. The previous December, *Labour Leader* had published an alternative version of the draft program written by MacDonald himself. This draft proposed a more equivocal wording, according to which this section of the program should read simply: "The Independent Labour Party believes in Democracy both in its industrial and civic aspects." MacDonald's version also made it clear that industrial democracy meant "more and more control" by wage and salary earners. Tacitly acknowledging the various, sometimes rival, concerns within the ILP, MacDonald wrote that "the Guild Socialist as well as the democrat who suspects that the Labour Government will be sabotaged by bourgeois conspirators ought to find both freedom and room for useful work in the Party, provided they enter as co-operative and not as disruptive members."[19]

According to the NAC, all members of the drafting committee supported "a national representative assembly directly elected by the people." Some, however, including Snowden and Jowett, also wanted provision for a "Co-ordinating Authority," a central body to be composed equally of representatives from the national assembly and from an organization of producers and consumers. Others favoured a system that would provide for "the maximum of decentralisation" and "constant contact" between representatives and their constituents. Again, these proposals reflected both guild socialist hostility to the centralized power of a "sovereign" state and an idealized notion of "soviet democracy," in which delegates are expected to adhere to the mandate given them by those who elected them, who reserve the right to recall the delegate. The NAC took note of the demand for "far more decentralisation" and for "special bodies to deal with education, public health etc." that would be chosen by the methods of election most appropriate to the work that each would have to do.

A further point at issue in this section, the NAC reported, concerned the direct election of the national assembly. Committee member C. H. Norman—a prominent member of the party's Left Wing—wanted the national assembly to "contain representatives of the organised producers and consumers, and of the local authorities, with a view to giving proper representation to the expert knowledge and special views which such representatives could express."[20] There were also differences of opinion on the committee, the NAC said, as to what priority to give to gaining control of "local and national governing bodies." But, despite the lack of consensus on the most contentious question of the role of direct action, the committee did agree that the ILP should aim "to destroy imperialism and render war impossible" and promote the "fullest development of the international working-class movement" and "the liberation of subject peoples."[21]

There was, in short, much debate about the draft program, both among members of the Program and Policy Committee and within the ILP more broadly, coupled with a general awareness that the ILP was in the process of making a significant change of direction. Although need for such a redefinition of the party's platform was widely recognized, nothing would be decided on the subject at the party's 1921 conference, in early April, which was instead dominated by the question of whether the ILP should join the Comintern. This debate left little time for a discussion of the draft program.

This was a relief for some. Near the end of the conference, after the defeat of the Left Wing's "Moscow amendment," Patrick Dollan, who represented the Scottish Division on the NAC, moved that the draft be referred back to the NAC for further consideration. Not only was the time that remained too short to allow for an adequate discussion, he insisted, but now that the party had rejected the idea of membership in the Third International, the "camouflaged Sovietism" contained in the draft program seemed unnecessary. Snowden, who was chairing the conference, accepted Dollan's proposal on behalf of the NAC. According to *Labour Leader*'s report on the proceedings, Snowden told the conference that the NAC had "not sent the programme out to the branches with any enthusiasm," inasmuch as it was, as he pointed out, an uneasy marriage of two incompatible perspectives.[22] So the whole matter was referred back to the NAC.

Towards a Guild Socialist Program: The New NAC Draft

That Dollan should be the one to move for referral was perhaps not surprising. In January, reporting the results of the Scottish Division conference, he had wearily criticized the "long and frequently academic discussion of the draft program" within the ILP, remarking that "the making of programs is not a healthy occupation for normal Socialists, although the theory-weavers and phrase-makers seem to enjoy it."[23] Of course, not everyone in the ILP shared his impatience with the process. Clement Attlee, for one, considered the drafting of a new program a matter "of vital importance." In a letter to *Labour Leader*, written late in July 1921, he offered a number of arguments in support of this proposition, the first relating to the duty of ILP members to promote the party's views. "As a propagandist," he wrote, "I feel the need for a definite statement to which I can relate my arguments." It was also important, he argued, that the ILP have a clear statement of its position for use in the upcoming general election and, especially in view of the recent defeats of the miners and other trade unionists in the industrial field, that the party define its "attitude to the future organisation and control of industry." This would, he argued, demonstrate the value of political action. It was, moreover, "futile" to be debating "the claims of rival Internationals" until the ILP was able to agree on its own program."[24]

In concluding, Attlee strongly recommended that agreeing on a party program be made the "chief item" on the agenda for the party's 1922 conference and that proposals be circulated to branches well in advance of the event itself to ensure ample time for discussion. This plea followed his final argument for the crucial importance of the program. The ILP could live only "by attracting new blood," he wrote, and, to do so, the party needed a "definite programme that will attract the younger men that are coming forward." These "keen souls" would be disheartened by "vague generalities or compromises" and might well be driven to "adopt other programmes which, however impossibilist, are clear and easy to understand."[25] Almost simultaneously, at its biannual conference in early August, the Lancashire Division urged on the NAC the "importance of making a pronouncement on Party policy at an early date."[26]

By late September, the NAC had produced a new draft program, one that had the unanimous support of its members. This new draft appeared in the *Labour Leader* at the end of that month. Perhaps unsurprisingly, given the current flurry of interest in guild socialism, it contained a section headed "Political and Industrial Democracy," which read:

> The I.L.P. believes in democratic organisation both in its political and industrial aspects, for communal ends.
>
> The basis of political democracy must be the whole body of citizens exercising authority through a national representative assembly, directly elected by the people, with a decentralised and extended system of local government.
>
> The basis of industrial democracy must be 1) the organisation of wage and salary earners; and 2) the organisation of consumers.
>
> The exact form of the organisation and the machinery of co-operation between consumers and producers must be determined by experience as step by step is taken towards the achievement of the Socialist Commonwealth.

This new version of the program distanced the ILP from top-down forms of socialism, including the nationalization of industry, insisting instead that socialism must give "workers in the industry an effective share and responsibility for administration." Moreover, should a government or "reactionary class" attempt to "suppress liberty or thwart the National Will," as the ILP believed might easily be the case, "democracy must use to the utmost extent its political and industrial power" to defeat it.[27]

Freed now of the need to try and keep on board the now largely departed Left Wing by including ambiguous phraseology that suggested support for the soviet interpretation of industrial democracy—what Dollan had called "camouflaged sovietism"—the debate on the ILP program began to move in a more definite guild socialist direction.

Yet Two More: The "Allen-Attlee" Alternative and the Bradford Version

Considerable debate about the new program ensued, from the end of 1921 until the ILP national conference the following April. On 8 December, *Labour Leader* published a letter from Clement Attlee that contained what became known as the "Allen-Attlee alternative." Signed by thirteen well-known ILP members, including H. N. Brailsford and Fenner Brockway, it expressed general agreement with the NAC draft, which it declared to be "a good basis." The main criticism of the proposed program, the letter went on, was that it sometimes seemed vague, whereas what was required was "a strong lead."[28]

According to Arthur Marwick, it was Allen who had taken the initiative in producing this alternative version. The NAC left the drafting of the proposed program to NAC members Snowden, MacDonald, Richard Wallhead, Walter Ayles (a Quaker from Bristol), and Emanuel Shinwell, and "none of these men were particularly interested in the theories of Guild Socialism," writes Marwick. Allen therefore formed a group that initially consisted of himself, Fenner Brockway, and "two ex-servicemen of advanced socialist opinions, Clement Attlee and John Beckett," to which others were later added.[29]

Above all, the Allen-Attlee version wanted "clearer recognition" of the "principles of 'workers' control.'" The ILP should take a definite stand "for industrial and political democracy and for devolution by locality and function as against the theory of the all-controlling State." The letter also criticized the omission from the party's statement of objectives "the most important of all, the conversion of the people to Socialist principles." The weak statement on internationalism was also rejected, and the criticism of this last section of the NAC draft was scathing. To call for "a free flow of tropical products in the world's markets" was, the letter said, "a remnant of economic individualism" and quite out of place in an ILP program. The "deliberate organisation of the resources of the world" was what the ILP should be aiming for. The letter was also critical of the reference in the NAC draft to "a relationship between the white and the weaker native peoples, which will tutor the latter in self-government." This it rejected as "not happy" and "likely to be misleading."[30]

The Allen-Attlee alternative retained much of the wording of the section of the NAC draft on political and industrial democracy but made the party's position on the latter more explicit. To the original's call for the "organisation of wage and salary earners," it suggested adding "to whom shall be secured the internal management of industry." To "the organisation of consumers," it called for the addition of a "central body, representative of the people, both as producers and consumers," which "must decide the amount and character of communal production and service necessary." The internal management of each industry "must be in the hands of the workers, administrative, technical, and manual engaged therein, operating in conjunction with the representatives of organised consumers." The Allen-Attlee version was similarly explicit about the party's position on any attempt by reactionary forces to "suppress liberty," stating that "it may be necessary at certain times and for specific purposes, to resort to extra-political methods, such as 'Direct Action.'"[31]

Scarcely a month later, a second revision of the NAC's proposed program entered the fray. Early in January 1922, the new editor of *Labour Leader*—Bertram R. Carter, who had taken over from Katharine Bruce Glasier the previous August—noted the receipt from Fred Jowett of a Bradford branch version of the draft program. Among other things, this version required the party to commit itself to the view "that the kinship the working classes of all nations share should be a stronger tie than the kinship of nation, creed, or colour." Carter expressed skepticism about what he called "Universal Brotherhood." The "bond of nationality" did not seem to be getting any weaker, he wrote, and "the 'colour bar' is hard to get over." A British worker might have "more in common with his own white employer—who, moreover, these days, may not be much further removed from penury than himself."[32]

Strangely, however, Carter made no comment on what now seems like the major difference between the Bradford version and both the draft program of the NAC and the Allen-Attlee alternative—their treatment of industrial democracy. All that the Bradford branch had to say on the subject was: "The I.L.P. will ally itself with and assist in the progress of the Trade Union and Co-operative movements, seeking to impregnate these and other workers' movements with a recognition of the predominating rights of the workers over other interests, and to strengthen these organisations with a view to their participation in the machinery of the Socialist State."[33] Any discerning reader would have been able to predict from this where, at the party's upcoming national conference, opposition to a more elaborate "guild socialist" constitution for the party was likely to originate.

The Bradford draft was presented as an alternative to the NAC's draft at the Yorkshire divisional conference, where the party's new program was the chief theme. Jowett claimed that the Bradford version was "much clearer and more vigorous." In the end, however, the conference decided to "forward" all important amendments to the national conference without expressing any opinion on them.[35] In contrast, across the Pennines at the Lancashire Division's biannual conference, there was a close vote on some of the amendments. At the meeting of the North East Division, the Stanley branch "sponsored" the Allen-Attlee version "in its entirety," but, in a series of votes, many of its clauses were rejected.³⁶ There were, reportedly, fifty-eight amendments to the NAC's draft program on the agenda of the London and Southern Counties divisional conference, at which the NAC draft was "badly mauled." The offending "International" section was completely replaced, and most of the revisions proposed in the Allen-Attlee version were approved.³⁷

Accompanying the lengthy debate on the party's future program was a series of suggestions from *Labour Leader* contributors and readers on how to revive the ILP. Harold Croft, the agent and organizer of the Croyden Labour Party and a former ILP divisional organizer in the Midlands, argued that the ILP divisional councils and federations needed to "reverse the order of their functions" and give priority to propaganda and "educational" activities. He advocated the creation of "an I.L.P. parish" in every area, where such activities would be conducted in the "weekly meeting hall."³⁸

In an article titled "How to Revivify the I.L.P.," W. Randall-Reed saw the rejuvenation of the party as a task for "Young Socialists." He had no doubt of the need to strengthen the party after "three years of industrial trouble and internal dissension," with many branches "hovering on the verge of collapse."³⁹ Shortly thereafter, the Reverend Gordon Lang issued a similar appeal in a piece titled "A League of Young Socialists."⁴⁰ In the same issue, Minnie Pallister, who wrote a number of pamphlets for the ILP during the 1920s, argued that the revival of ILP branches was an urgent matter, one "constantly occupying the minds of all members of the party." She stressed the role of the secretary in building a successful branch. Branch secretaries must be "obsessed with the importance" of the work they are doing, she wrote, estimating that five hundred such men and women were needed to rebuild the ILP.⁴¹

Hopes of revivifying the party were closely bound up with the adoption of a new program, and debate on that subject continued, with, for example, a letter from a *Labour Leader* reader named William Phillips, who was worried that the party might come into conflict with trade union leaders over the legitimacy of "direct action." The ILP "should confine itself to the political sphere," he urged, concluding that "if the I.L.P. would cease discussing issues that are outside the purview of its objects, it would do much to remove the animus existing between Trade Union leaders and I.L.P. bodies."⁴² There was little chance of the ILP following his advice—particularly now that Clifford Allen, with his commitment to industrial democracy, was becoming such a dominant figure in the party. The 1922 conference would be decisive in launching both the new program and what became referred to as the "Allen regime."

5

The 1922 Constitution and the Allen Regime

The adoption of the new ILP constitution, as the new program was often called, was the chief business of the thirtieth ILP annual conference, held in Nottingham on 16–18 April 1922. Within the context of the party's ongoing dilemma created by the changed relationship with the Labour Party, caused by the latter's constitutional changes of 1918, the new constitution was a central part of an attempt to find an escape route that left the ILP intact and still playing a significant political role. This is evident from both the chairman's address that opened the conference in Nottingham and the way it was reported in the *Labour Leader*.

The New ILP Constitution, Debated and Passed

Richard Wallhead's speech included a passage to which the party's weekly gave the subheading "No liquidation of the Party." His words seem to anticipate Ralph Miliband's much later judgment, quoted in chapter 2, that the Labour Party's commitment to socialism was largely lip service. Wallhead said:

> More than once lately, and in somewhat unexpected quarters, the continued existence of the I.L.P. has been invoked. My answer is that there can be no question of the voluntary liquidation of our Party until the principles of Socialism become the accepted economic and political faith of the mass of the people in this country. While it is possible for some of the leaders of the Labour Party to deny the principles for which we stand, our work is far from finished.

The concern for the survival of the ILP was echoed in the editorial comment on the conference in the *Labour Leader* just two days after it ended. Stressing the party's "distinctive mission," the editor noted with satisfaction that "once again it was demonstrated beyond doubt that the I.L.P. is neither to be absorbed into the Labour Party nor intimidated by the Communist Party."[1]

Apart from the debate on the party program, the conference gave particular attention to two issues: opposition to any notion of a deal between the Labour Party and the Liberals and the resignation of Philip Snowden as ILP treasurer. It was the end of his long membership of the NAC. Fulsome tributes were paid, and the *Labour Leader* devoted a full page to reporting them, but it seems highly likely that he was at least one of the "unexpected quarters" referred to in Wallhead's opening address, as Robert Dowse suggests.² He would, however, remain an ILP member until the end of 1928.³

Brockway tells us that it was on Jowett's initiative that the Bradford branch attempted to get the ILP to adopt a simpler "human" constitution. Jowett had felt frustrated when serving as a representative of the Labour Party's National Executive Committee on the commission on socialization at the 1920 Socialist International conference in Geneva. This experience had left him with "a feeling of irrelevance and futility." Fenner Brockway expresses the impatience that Jowett was experiencing: "What was the value of these interminable discussions on the niceties of administration—how much control the State should have, how much the producers, how much the consumers? These were matters for technicians and for experience."⁴ Jowett believed that both the NAC draft and the Allen-Attlee alternative repeated this error.

At the conference, the debate began with an oddly apologetic introduction by Emanuel Shinwell, who presented the NAC's draft. Enthusiasm for a new program was, he claimed, "somewhat subdued." He had anticipated that it might be "a damp squib," and he seemed anxious to divert the blame away from the NAC for "having disturbed the progress of business." It was duty bound, he reminded delegates, to respond to conference resolutions. Even less enthusiasm was shown by Patrick Dollan, the Scottish Division NAC representative, who, once again, attempted to refer the whole issue back to the NAC but was told from the chair that "it must be settled."⁵

The Bradford version was then debated as an amendment. Because of Jowett's position as a member of the NAC, it was moved by Harry Wilson and William Leach. Wilson claimed that the Bradford redraft "emphasised those features of the I.L.P. which formed the very real difference between the I.L.P. and the Labour Party." He criticized the NAC draft because it "dealt with how we should govern the country when we had the chance"; the Bradford draft, in contrast, dealt with how to get that chance. When Wilson expounded at some length on how they must "not allow the standard of life of the common people to sink until we have tried to take the last shilling from the profiteer," John Paton intervened to ask the chairman whether the conference had not too much business to deal with "to listen to propaganda speeches."⁶

Taking the warning to heart, Wilson argued that the clause about setting up "a dual authority of consumer and producer was apparently intended to attract the Guild Socialists without committing the Party to their programme." That was not good enough. "If the Party believed in Guild Socialism it ought to say so." Leach described G. D. H. Cole as "a very brilliant young person who writes a book about every twenty five minutes." Cole had spoken to the NAC, said Leach, in "a new language and they fell down and worshipped. They were afraid of being called old-fashioned fogies." John Beckett, however, claimed that although he had been "filled with joy" when Jowett had called for "a clear programme," Bradford's effort had degenerated into "the kind of thing they saw on a Christmas card with crossed hands and a message of love." It was "one of the flabbiest policies he had ever seen submitted." He defended Cole against Leach, and Bradford's amendment was lost by 127 to 231.[7]

Attlee, successfully moving an amendment from his Limehouse branch calling for a central body representing producers and consumers, insisted on the importance of a central authority:

> The idea of workshop control had been developed steadily; the comrades from Bradford seemed to regard the Socialist State as nothing but a glorified municipality. The whole question was one of incentive to industry, and both Mr R. H. Tawney and J. A. Hobson in their remarkable books had been dealing with it. His branch recognised the need for a central authority. They must not have a number of industrial republics fighting each other, but the great difficulty to-day was that they were overloading the political machinery with industrial matters.[8]

Soon after this, Ramsay MacDonald intervened in the debate to interpret the Attlee amendment as confining the role of the proposed central body to deciding "the amount and character of communal production and service necessary. That does not confer full legislative authority," he claimed. "It would be an administrative body within the political state." As the *Labour Leader* editor saw it, "MacDonald cleared up this point in the wording of the programme to the satisfaction of the Conference."[9]

In the NAC elections, which took place in the middle of the debate on the program, MacDonald came out on top of the poll, with 327 votes. Only Jowett, with the next highest vote of 211, polled well enough to avoid going to a second ballot. MacDonald's influence is plain in some other parts of the report on the conference debate. When Fred Longden, from the Aston branch, wanted to "rule out of citizenship any person deemed to be fit for work who was not willing to contribute," MacDonald asked who was going to do the "deeming." He accused Longden, well-known as a left-winger in the ILP, of espousing an "old-fashioned militarist idea," and Longden's proposal was defeated.[10]

The conference rejected the attempt by the Gateshead branch to add the phrase "on Industrial Union lines" to the part of the "Immediate Objects" section calling for the strengthening of trade union organization. Shinwell characterized this as "a relic of Leftism." After the NAC accepted the amendment—from the Allen-Attlee version—for giving "the workers of the industry effective control," MacDonald once again intervened to insist that the wording should refer to an effective *share* in the administration of their industry. Deferring to MacDonald's argument, the conference then agreed to leave the matter to the NAC, and a wording in line with his view subsequently appeared in the final version.[11]

Brockway would later claim that "the London draft which emphasised workers' control" was adopted.[12] This is not entirely true. When all the debating was concluded and the votes counted, the ILP was left with a mixture of the original NAC draft and the Allen-Attlee (or "London") version. The order and titles of the subsections of the program were as in the original draft, as was the statement of the party's mission, or "Object." The section titled "Political and Industrial Democracy" began with the NAC version, but the detail concerning a "central body" to oversee production and internal management of industry by workers and the "representatives of organised consumers" came from the Allen-Attlee alternative. "Immediate Objects," the section outlining the ILP's shorter term objectives, followed the latter's amended wording—with the first object being the dissemination of socialist principles.

The "Transition period" was as drafted by the NAC but with the words "as defined above" from Allen-Attlee were added to the clause about giving workers an "effective share" in the administration of industry. The wording of the section "Internationalism and Imperialism" came mostly from Allen-Attlee, but with the inclusion of the aim to abolish not only war but also "conscription and militarism." With minor amendments, the Allen-Attlee rendering of the final section, "Method," was accepted—except, significantly, for its endorsement of direct action, where the NAC's more ambiguous wording was accepted. The Bradford version, however clearer and more succinct its supporters claimed it to be, had no direct impact on the final text.

The full 1922 constitution is given as an appendix in Dowse's *Left in the Centre*. The conference was reported in the *Labour Leader* on 20 April, and the following week, the paper devoted much of its front page to an article by Brockway, who lauded the new program as giving a "new confidence" to the ILP while admitting that the party had previously been "a little at sea." He defended the new emphasis on industrial democracy. "The whole trend in modern thought is away from State Socialism," he insisted. "The public has identified nationalisation with State bureaucracy and accordingly dislikes it."[13]

Promoting the Program amid Continuing Doubts

It had taken considerable time and much debate to arrive at the new position, but Allen's aim to create a distinctive program seemed to have been met. Now, the program needed promotion. After the conference, the ILP published a leaflet, *The Independent Labour Party and Its Future Work*, to introduce its new statement of aims and principles to a wider public. This was accompanied by Fred Henderson's pamphlet *Socialism of the I.L.P.*, which sought "to amplify what is set forth in the I.L.P. Constitution," and both of these publications were complemented by a series of pamphlets on the new program, such as F. W. Pethick Lawrence's *Must the Workers Foot the Bill?*[14]

Other efforts at promotion included G. Beardsworth's motion on industrial policy at the Lancashire divisional conference at Blackpool, encouraging "every Branch to make an effort to get inside Trade Union branches" in order to promote discussion of the new constitution, "which points the way to Industrial Democracy, a greater measure of public ownership and a greater measure of public control." The motion countered the tendency of the public to be wary of "public control," Beardsworth argued, by making it clear that "we also stand for workers' control."[15]

In March 1923, almost a year after the ILP conference, a debate began in the *Socialist Review* with an article by William Leach in which, as he had done at the conference, he objected to dividing people into producers and consumers and praised the merits of "public ownership governed by popularly elected committees."[16] This triggered a reply from Attlee, in May, defending the guild-socialist inspiration of the new program and rejoicing that the ILP had "become infected with this heresy." A rejoinder from Leach followed in July.[17]

The influence of the 1922 debates and the program that was then adopted continued in subsequent years. In 1925, ILP chairman James Maxton insisted that "public ownership must be accompanied by workers' control."[18] The following year, Brockway, in setting out the ILP's industrial policy, predicted that "the democratic struggle of the present century will be to supplement political democracy by economic democracy." There should be a "National Industrial Authority" with union representation and with minimal interference from the "State parliament." Internal management, he argued, should be "left entirely to those employed in it." Declaring that, in some industries, it might be possible to "develop self-government by the formation of Guilds."[19]

The 1926 annual conference received the report of the ILP's Industrial Policy Committee, one of whose members was Margaret Bondfield, the future Minister of Labour in MacDonald's second government. The report's detailed consideration of the issues involved was prefaced with the following statement: "The public ownership of industry, without democratic administration by the workers therein, whilst superior to the present system of private ownership and control, would not of itself provide that intelligent co-operation in the new social order or that sense of freedom which Socialism involves." At the end of the report, delegates were assured that though there had been some disagreement among committee members, the report represented "the greatest common measure of agreement."[20]

Yet it is clear that the ILP's move towards guild socialism received nothing like a unanimous welcome. Shinwell's presentation of the NAC's draft at the 1922 conference had been lukewarm, at best. Seven years later, his ILP pamphlet on the nationalization of mines was still less than enthusiastic: "I do not subscribe so generously as some do to the proposal for workers' control, because it is, as yet, somewhat in the academic stage. You must not conceal facts; taking the miners as a whole, they are more concerned about improving wages than about workers' control."[21] Recall, as well, that even at the 1922 conference, the influential Dollan had tried to refer the issue of the new program back to the NAC, several delegates had expressed impatience with the debate, and just over a third had voted for the Bradford amendment. There was clearly much argument and convincing still to be done within the ILP—let alone outside its ranks—if the new policy was to take a firm root. Time alone would test this. And the lack of enthusiasm on the one side was hardly balanced by support for the man who many saw as the true author of the new program: G. D. H. Cole's welcome was less than hearty.

Writing in the journal of the National Guilds League (NGL) soon after the ILP's 1922 conference, Cole declared that the new program incorporated "as much Guild Socialism as can be put in without mortally offending the old stagers." He concluded, "Some commentators are suggesting that the I.L.P. has been converted to Guild Socialism. Perhaps; but I do not hear of any bonfires being ignited by the N.G.L."[22] Nonetheless, after two years of debate, the party now had a new constitution that was generally regarded as guild socialist. Nor was this the only thing that marked the 1922 conference as a watershed in the ILP's history.

"Now for Socialism": The Beginning of the Allen Regime

"For a time I began to doubt whether there was a future for the ILP," wrote Fenner Brockway, looking back to the early post–First World War years from the vantage point of the 1970s. However, he declared, "Clifford Allen ended this defeatism."[23] But there was nothing inevitable in Clifford Allen's election, in 1922, as party treasurer, following Snowden's resignation. In the first ballot at the conference, his main opponent, George Benson, polled 156 votes to Allen's 160. Allen's four-vote lead was halved in the second ballot, which he won by

181 to 179.²⁴ Despite this narrow margin, Clifford Allen became, as Brockway would later write, "in effect the directing head of the Party" until his resignation as chairman in September 1925.²⁵ The fact that he was able to exercise this dominance, initially from his position as treasurer, is significant. Being treasurer of the ILP did not always translate into that sort of power. Allen brought, at least temporarily, a different dimension to ILP fundraising. As John Paton, who joined the headquarter staff early in Allen's reign, put it more than a decade later: "Where previous I.L.P. treasurers had been content to think in terms of half-pence, Allen thought in hundreds of pounds. And he was able to translate his golden dreams into realities."²⁶

Allen was amazingly energetic, especially for someone suffering from so much ill health. Within three days of his election, he was "canvassing for money" in a series of letters to Quakers and other contacts in the No Conscription Fellowship. Stressing the party's stance against the war, he successfully attracted donations.²⁷ The ambitious nature of Allen's plans for the ILP were "given concrete form in an old Georgian building, with an Adam's mantelpiece, in Great George Street," which became the party's London headquarters.²⁸ The week following the report of his election in the *Labour Leader*, a "Message from the New Treasurer" appeared in its columns. Warning members not to expect "any platform work" from him for some time while he concentrated on the party's finances, Allen declared that the problems with the latter were serious. But since success bred success, what was needed was improvement in all aspects of the ILP's work, including "a really first class weekly paper."²⁹

By this time, the weekly *Labour Leader* had become a problem in two ways. First, the circulation had declined from its postwar peak. Dowse tells us that it had fallen to below twenty thousand and that the paper was running at a loss of about £1,200 a year. The second problem related to high-profile conflicts over what attitude to take to the Bolsheviks, which had been fuelling divisions within the ILP. This situation came to a head early in 1921, when the editor of the paper, Katharine Bruce Glasier, and Philip Snowden, who also had some editorial responsibilities, clashed very publicly over the latter's increasingly vehement anti-Bolshevik statements. Ultimately, both resigned from the *Leader*—in Glasier's case, seemingly after a nervous breakdown.³⁰

The arrangements following this conflict were not likely to be sustainable. In April 1921, Tom Johnson, the editor of *Forward*, took over the editorship on a temporary basis, which involved commuting between Glasgow and Manchester. His replacement five weeks later by Bundock, editor of the *Leicester Pioneer*, did away with the very long commute but still left the paper being edited on a "second job" basis. In early July, the NAC announced that Bertram R. Carter had been appointed and would take over the editorship the following month.³¹ But Carter's skepticism about the possibility of "universal brotherhood," noted in the previous chapter, suggests that he was hardly in tune with many ILPers, and his role as editor lasted only a little more than a year.

After becoming treasurer, Clifford Allen persuaded the NAC to transfer the *Leader*'s publication from Manchester to London to change its nature radically, and to give it a new name to emphasize this.³² In early July 1922, it was announced that the move would take place "as quickly as possible" and that a "small limited company consisting of the N.A.C. to give the party direct ownership and control of the paper" was being set up.³³

The desire to begin a new chapter for the ILP was not confined to Allen. In June 1922 the ILP weekly published John Beckett's proposal titled "A Three-Fold Offensive for the I.L.P." This offensive was urgently needed, he argued, in the face of the threat of the Labour Party becoming "another great unwieldy, machine-made, soulless electoral machine, without guiding principles." The ILP needed to organize members to have "access to any Trade Union branch." It also needed to address the danger of Labour being submerged both by "wealthy men . . . who come into the movement one day with a vague idea of helping the poor and become parliamentary candidates the next" and by "pensioned off Trade Union officials" who only took part in debates "when their own industry was under consideration." Beckett said he would hate it if the ILP "became a crew of heresy hunting fanatics" but that it should "oppose the casual selection of candidates." Third, the ILP should play a role in the "reconciliation of wholesale and manufacturing Co-operative Societies with self-government in industry." The party needed to "permeate" the co-ops with "modern Socialist thought, especially relating to workers' control." A special secretary should be appointed for the formation of "industrial and Co-operative nuclei."³⁴

In August, *Labour Leader* readers were alerted to a new initiative that was to take place in November and December. In "The Great I.L.P. Campaign," Fenner Brockway declared that it was the right moment to launch such an initiative: "During the years following the war the position and future of the I.L.P. were a little uncertain, and many members were perplexed. Now our place and function is clear, and the Party is confident." The period of adjustment, he wrote, "was completed at the last I.L.P. conference," and it had become clear that, "despite the letter of its constitution, the Labour Party membership was still very far from Socialist and Internationalist in outlook and spirit." There was a tremendous work of education still to be done within the trade union movement. Brockway stressed that this involved "no spirit of opposition to the Labour Party. We work loyally within it as pioneers."³⁵

In its final weeks, the *Labour Leader* published more details of the new campaign. It was to have three objectives: to reassert the ILP's position in the political life of the country, to renew contact with the unions, and to increase party membership. The key developments were to be the appointment of a national organizer and the launch of a new weekly paper, which would create "an expectant psychology": people would say, "If the I.L.P. can produce a paper like this it is evidently a body to be watched." Three methods would be used to promote the campaign: "special preparatory missions," special conferences for trade unionists "to hear the new I.L.P. Industrial Policy," and big demonstrations with national speakers.[36]

Two or three "Special Missioners" in each ILP division would be tasked to visit lapsed ILP members, to visit ILP branch meetings to consult with members, , and to encourage trades councils and constituency Labour parties to appoint delegates to the conferences that were being planned as part of the campaign. Eleven missioners were listed—all with impressive histories as organizers and activists. The trade union conferences, explained Fenner Brockway, were "to advocate among Trade Unionists the new conception of the revolutionary function of industrial organization, as seen by the I.L.P. I use the word revolution in the sense of denoting a completely new social order: the I.L.P. asserts the real purpose of Trade Unions to be, not improvement of conditions under capitalism, but preparation for direct workers' control under Socialism."[37]

There were to be conferences in every major town to be held in "big halls" and it was hoped that about three hundred demonstrations would take place. "Let no member think that this is an ordinary annual campaign," the *Labour Leader* emphasized. "It is being planned on a scale such as the Labour and Socialist movement of this country has never experienced."[38]

The following week's *Labour Leader* featured a front-page article titled "Us," by Minnie Pallister, the ILP organizer for South Wales, who encouraged ILP members to confidently assert how right the party had been on the issues of the recent past. "We were right on the War. We were right on the Peace. We were right on Reparations. We were right on Russia. We were right on Ireland." She concluded, "From Sinful Modesty, Good Lord, Deliver Us." There were reports in the same issue of plans and speakers from five ILP divisions. Lancashire, Scotland, and London seemed to be most advanced with preparations. Ernest Hunter was announced as honorary director of the campaign.[39]

Brockway encouraged competition between the divisions to see which would contribute the most to the campaign.[40] A story in the *Birmingham Evening Dispatch* claiming that local ILP members were concerned about the cost of the campaign and not at all keen on it was dismissed as a hostile press attack.[41]

The slogan for the campaign—"Now for Socialism"—was announced in the final issue of the *Labour Leader*.[42]

A Great Surge Forward

H. N. Brailsford was appointed editor of the *New Leader*, and he recruited Mrs. M. A. Hamilton as assistant editor.[43] The first issue promised to report week by week on "the big forward movement," for which 365 conferences and about two hundred other meetings had already been planned. Speakers included MacDonald, "whom everyone wants." An early event in the Now for Socialism campaign was to be a weekend rally in Portsmouth, where the main speakers were to be Brockway and Beckett and the central meeting would be a conference aimed largely at union activists under the title "Democratic Control of Industry."[44]

Everything seemed to be going well. Early reports from missioners were "exceedingly encouraging," and there was "a returning pride in the movement which is more valuable than election success, municipal or national, though we want that too."[45] They did not have long to wait. Within a week, the breakup of Lloyd George's coalition government precipitated a general election, in which the number of ILP MPs increased from five to thirty-two. The Now for Socialism campaign was suspended until after the election on 13 January 1923.[46]

Attention now switched to raising a Special Effort Fund for the election. Allen soon announced that the previous record for such a fund had been £2,276 and that this had been surpassed in the first week, with over £2,293 received. His aim was to raise £22,000, but it was not to be. By the end of the year, the total had reached £8,777—only a little more than a third of this ambitious target, though this was a great advance on past efforts.[47]

At the end of 1922, largely under Allen's energetic inspiration, what Dowse aptly calls a "tremendous *élan*" had been created in the ILP.[48] Everything seemed to be surging forward at a very encouraging rate. Twenty-nine new branches had been created since the Nottingham conference, and two more were awaiting NAC approval.[49] The election had immensely strengthened the ILP's parliamentary representation. The *New Leader* gave this assessment:

> Ramsay MacDonald is now at the head of a battalion of incomparable fighting efficiency. Of the Big Five of 1914, Anderson has gone from us, Tom Richardson is in Canada, but Snowden and Jowett are both there, and with them a band of men with the parliamentary experience of Ponsonby, Trevelyan, Wedgwood, Buxton, Spoor, Lees Smith. This is the reward of the hard work and unremitting, unselfish devotion that has rebuilt and extended the organisation of the Party throughout the country in the last two years, and especially since Nottingham.[50]

The circulation of the *New Leader* had also made a very satisfactory start. By mid-November, it was reporting a weekly average sale of 51,292, almost three times that of its predecessor, it claimed.[51] Brailsford explained the paper's aims the following month. The situation had changed, he argued. It was no longer necessary to attempt to substitute for the daily newspaper; the *Daily Herald* was fulfilling that role very well. It was no longer enough to "spread the broad and simple message of the Socialist gospel." While "controversy and fierce denunciation of wrong" was still needed on occasion, "our criticism must be constructive." That, he wrote, was "the conception of our task" which inspired the political style of the paper."[52]

When the Now for Socialism campaign was resumed in January 1923, it ran until the Easter ILP annual conference, at which it was reported that fifty-five conferences and 542 demonstrations and meetings had been held since the campaign's launch.[53] By the beginning of March, the *New Leader* was proclaiming that "the outstanding success of the Now for Socialism campaign is the success of the Trade Union Conferences," while pouring scorn on "a lot of nonsense about the imaginary opposition between ILP 'Intellectuals' and Trade Unionists."[54] There had been a "great revival," and Minnie Pallister was singled out as one of the heroes of the campaign.[55]

A four-page leaflet, *Now for Socialism! The Call of the I.L.P.*, proudly pointed out that thirty-two of the ILP's fifty-five candidates had been returned to Parliament during the election and that "Mr. Ramsay MacDonald, one of the best known members of the I.L.P.," had become "leader of the Official Opposition." The leaflet advocated, as the party's principles, a bold socialist policy, workers' control of industry, and total disarmament.[56] At the annual conference, Wallhead, the retiring chair, noted the deep significance of the new parliamentary situation: "Never before has the official opposition challenged the social system represented by the Government of the day."[57]

Conflicts and Problems Emerge

Not everyone in the ILP was happy with the new arrangements, particularly with regard to the new paper and its editor. The announcement, at the end of 1922, of a monthly *I.L.P. Chronicle*, for "private circulation," to deal with the more mundane aspects of the party's organization could be seen as tacit admission of the *New Leader*'s perceived deficiency in this respect, at least in the eyes of many members.[58] Brailsford's salary was £1,000 a year, which was extremely modest in comparison to what he had been earning previously as a journalist. Allen told the party's 1923 conference that the new editor had taken the job "at tremendous financial sacrifice." But the highest salary prior to this had been £460, and Brailsford's pay was certainly huge compared to the £3.5s a week paid to former editor Katharine Glasier.⁵⁹

During Allen's leadership, the salaries of ILP employees were indeed high.⁶⁰ This seemed outrageous to many ILP members and was criticized at the 1923 conference as being, in the words of the Sheffield delegate, A. Barton, "against the whole tradition of the I.L.P."⁶¹ John Paton mentions the attacks on high salaries, especially from David Kirkwood; he notes, however, that "while it was true that Brailsford was paid more highly than any other official it was also true that he was paid about half what he'd been earning before being persuaded to take on *New Leader*." Paton goes on to give an account of one NAC meeting where, under attack by Kirkwood, Brailsford agreed that "a new and Socialist Franciscan order" would be a "more powerful propaganda agency" than anything else. He pointed out, however, that Kirkwood seemed to be excluding from consideration his own salary as an MP, the fees he received for lectures, and the financial assistance he accepted from trade unions.⁶² More than a decade after he left the editorship in 1926, Brailsford would tell Michael Foot, then the assistant editor at the *Tribune*, that as editor of the *New Leader*, he had had "to face a motion demanding my resignation at almost every Board Meeting."⁶³

As a competitor of the *Nation*, the *New Statesman*, and the *Spectator*, Brailsford's enterprise was a success. It certainly had a wider and more literary feel to it than its predecessor. But, as Marwick writes, "the Party membership did not take too kindly to the new paper."⁶⁴ Dowse sees this as at least partly justified, in that critics were reacting against the "'arty' intellectualism that plagued the I.L.P."⁶⁵

Another cloud on the horizon concerned the core of the new program. G. D. H. Cole may have been dissatisfied with the ILP's half-hearted guild socialism, but the adoption of a stance clearly influenced by it meant that the fortunes of the guild-socialist movement were bound to have some impact on the party's morale and on its standing in the eyes of the Left generally.

In the months following the Nottingham conference, things seemed to be going well. The *New Leader* regularly carried articles by Cole. In October 1922, in a piece consciously titled after the famous prewar pamphlet *The Miners' Next Step*, he was upbeat about the prospects of the "practical Guild movement" spreading beyond the building industry to other areas.⁶⁶ He mentioned an Engineers' guild in London, a national tailoring guild, and a guild being formed by Aberdeen dockers with backing from the Transport and General Workers' Union. The following week, the paper carried an advertisement for the Guild of Clothiers.⁶⁷

Cole extolled the Building Guild in a *Leader* article titled "What We Mean by Workers' Control," concluding that "if a Labour Government comes to power, its first task will be to second the efforts of the workers, through their Trade

Unions to make industrial control a reality. Its chances of success will depend on its understanding that in industrial organisation lie both the source of its power and the means of real social change."[68] With the Labour Party's fortunes clearly reviving with the substantial gains in the general election, Cole urged his readers to "make the Labour M.Ps the political spokesmen of a well-planned and clearly thought-out industrial policy."[69]

But the following week, he had to report that the Building Guild had been forced into receivership by its main creditor, Barclays Bank. The Building Guild was "by far the largest of the experiments in working-class self-government under Trade Union auspices, and its fall," Cole acknowledged, "would inevitably deal a very heavy blow to the whole movement for industrial control." He argued that the episode illustrated how much control the banks had over industry. There is an air of whistling in the dark about Cole's pronouncement the following week that "the working-class movement for industrial control should neither expect, nor desire, a smooth passage. It is challenging the whole basis of capitalist industrialism, and that is a tough job to tackle."[70]

It was indeed, and the task would be even harder with the collapse of not only the Building Guild in January 1923 but also the National Guilds League itself not long thereafter. The NGL annual meeting in May 1923 empowered the executive to wind the organization up without a further conference.[71] Its main organ, the *Guild Socialist*, disappeared in August 1923, while its replacement, *New Standards: A Journal of Workers' Control*, ran for another year.[72] The collapse of the Building Guild and the defection of many of the NGL's most active and prominent members to the CPGB and others to the Distributist and Social Credit movements both contributed to the debacle. This left the ILP as, in effect, the only remaining organized voice for at least a species of guild socialism. How would that very central part of the new program fare in a less encouraging climate?

The ILP leaflet *Now for Socialism! The Call of the I.L.P.* advocated workers' control and made it clear that the party did "not stand for bureaucratic State Socialism." It emphasized that industry was the concern not only of workers but of "the woman in the house and of consumers in general."[73] In the final part of his "Study Course on Economic History," Attlee looked forward to a different society, speculating that another "industrial revolution" might occur in Great Britain: "When the workers, organised as citizens, producers and consumers, resolve to create a new form of economy."[74] But at the end of 1922, the obstacles to be overcome were starting to look even more formidable than before.

The advent of the Allen regime had certainly had a measurable effect in reviving the ILP. Apart from his ability to raise funds and his impressive energy, Allen had other useful characteristics and skills that came to the fore. David

Howell tells us that "some felt that his high-mindedness was combined with, and perhaps in his view justified, utilization of the politician's darker arts."⁷⁵ Certainly, his colleagues all testified to his ability to persuade. He was, says Paton, "most skillful at getting his own way at meetings and conferences" and "a past-master in the art of manipulating men and leading them to his goal."⁷⁶ But, equally, he attributed Allen's success—which made a great, though brief, impact—to his hard work and attention to detail. He always went to meetings fully prepared, and "his look of fragility masked a determined resolution and a great capacity for sustained and careful work. He left nothing to chance."⁷⁷ Allen was, clearly "somewhat autocratic," as Dowse puts it, citing Paton's statement that Allen promised him the job of organizing secretary to the ILP if he simply submitted an application; Brockway was appointed to the same position without even applying.⁷⁸ It is certainly not usual for a treasurer to exercise such patronage in a democratic organization.

Most of the internal changes to the ILP advocated by Allen were intended to increase the ability of the NAC to guide and control the party, but they met with firm resistance. In 1924, having been elected chairman the previous year, Allen attempted to give the NAC greater control over the distribution of funds to the divisional councils.⁷⁹ This included securing agreement from a meeting of divisional representatives. However, he found himself coming up against the commitment to considerable regional autonomy that had characterized the ILP since its foundation. The 1925 conference was extremely critical of Allen's attempts to increase the NAC's power and passed an amendment limiting the powers of the NAC by 283 to 174.⁸⁰ Brockway attributes the "crisis" at the conference to the "growing discontent among working-class members with the middle-class elitist domination of head office."⁸¹ One suspects that this may well have been a rather wider provincial resistance to what was experienced as metropolitan hegemony.

But what of Allen's ambition that the ILP should become a socialist "nucleus" in the Labour Party? He initiated a series of policy reviews and working parties that produced policies, featured in later chapters. But the ILP's pretensions to be the socialist conscience of Labour and that party's "spearhead" annoyed many in the unions. They believed that their numbers and money constituted the real source of the Labour Party's strength, and, as Paton was later to write, they "resented the I.L.P. assumption of superiority."⁸²

Meanwhile, within the ILP, those opposed to Allen were concerned that the organization was becoming what Brockway would much later call "a Fabian society of intellectual compromisers rather than a proletarian confrontation with capitalism."⁸³ There is no doubt that Allen provided, in Dowse's words, "leadership of genius," but his success also masked some "deep tensions and unresolved contradictions" in the party. Much of his success rested on his ability to persuade old No Conscription Fellowship contacts, Quakers, and affluent pacifists to make sizeable donations to the otherwise financially shaky ILP. After his resignation, the "golden flood subsided."[84]

Allen's idea of the ILP's nucleus role might have survived in spite of these hostile pressures if the Labour Party's leadership—and his friend MacDonald, in particular—had shown even a modest degree of appreciation of the policies the ILP was advocating. But this was not to be. Paton and Brockway concur about the irony of Allen's position. According to the former, "the later policies which led directly to open conflict with the Labour Party had their origin in his fertile brain," while the latter notes that "there was a contradiction in Clifford Allen. He stood for a policy rejected by Ramsay MacDonald, and yet he regarded him as the only possible leader of the Labour Party, destined to great achievement."[85] The result was that, by the mid-1920s, the role of the ILP as a support group for MacDonald had collapsed completely, while the problems related to carrying out Allen's nucleus role in relation to the Labour Party had become increasingly acute.

PART II

Socialism in Our Time?

6

The Rise of MacDonald and the First Labour Government

Clifford Allen's short period as the dominating influence in the ILP coincided with the rise of Ramsay MacDonald to the leadership of the Labour Party and, after a relatively short interval, his taking office as prime minister in the first minority Labour government. As we saw in chapter 3, during his almost four years out of Parliament, between December 1918 and November 1922, MacDonald needed the ILP and made efforts to cultivate its support. How much he would continue to need that support after becoming leader—and how much of it would be forthcoming—were not at all clear. One thing, though, was apparent in 1922: MacDonald would have to rely on ILP votes to gain the Labour Party leadership.

There had long been a deep hostility in the socialist movement to the very notions of "leaders" and "leadership." For many, these contradicted their egalitarian and democratic beliefs and smacked of sheep-like behaviour on the part of "followers." In the early days of the ILP, this had been most evident in the pages of Robert Blatchford's *Clarion*, which had exercised a definite but never dominant influence in the party.[1] In the mid-1890s, after the idea of having presidents and vice-presidents in ILP branches had been criticized in the paper by Blatchford himself, several efforts had been made to abolish the national presidency of the party. The nomenclature was changed to "chairmanship" in 1896—and there followed attempts to abolish the role of chairman during the next few years.[2] This effort towards an egalitarian structure was partly motivated by the belief among a significant minority of ILP members that Keir Hardie had come to occupy too dominant a position in the party, although the campaign for the "abolition of the chairman," as the *Labour Leader* called it in 1901, continued after Hardie left the post.[3]

The Labour Party Leadership: Election of 1922

The question of a Labour Party parliamentary leadership arose after the election of 1906, when twenty-nine Labour MPs were elected to Parliament. Interviewed by the *Clarion* soon after the election, J. R. Clynes, who would, much later, lose narrowly to MacDonald in the crucial Labour Party leadership election of 1922, said he favoured "the appointment of a seasonal chairman instead of a permanent leader."[4]

Should Labour fall in with the practice of the longer established political parties and have a parliamentary leader? Jowett, for one, thought not:

> The Labour Party has not and cannot have any leader in the same sense that the ordinary Parties have leaders.
>
> It cannot be too clearly understood ... that in the Labour Group the members all have equal rights when they meet together to decide on all matters affecting their work in Parliament.

Hardie had by this time been elected to chair the Labour parliamentary group, and Jowett conceded that in an emergency situation, when it was not possible to consult the other Labour MPs, the chairman might need to exercise his discretion.[5]

The leadership contest in 1922 involved two crucial meetings: a gathering of ILP MPs and a meeting of the whole Parliamentary Labour Party (PLP), at which the election itself took place. In his 1935 memoir, *My Life of Revolt*, David Kirkwood stresses the support given to MacDonald at this meeting by the left-wing group of MPs from Glasgow's Clydeside, himself among them. He also remembers Arthur Henderson, a leading figure in the early Labour Party, telling him, "You Clyde men are determined to put MacDonald in. Well, if you do, it will only be a few years before you will be trying to put him out." Assuming that Kirkwood's memory is accurate, this was a remarkably accurate prediction.[6]

In his 1953 autobiography, Emanuel Shinwell, another Clydeside MP, gave his own account of the group's support for MacDonald. According to him, at the meeting of ILP MPs, Maxton (already a leading figure in the party) wanted to propose John Wheatley for PLP chairman, but Shinwell dissuaded him, telling him that this choice "would be quite unacceptable to the others." Shinwell then proposed MacDonald, whose candidacy was "opposed by Maxton with all the vehemence at his command" and also by Snowden, with "cold fury." But the proposal was seconded by MacNeill Weir and carried.[7]

Soon thereafter, the meeting of the Labour MPs, now numbering 142, took place to elect the PLP chairman. According to Kirkwood, when the Clyde group proposed MacDonald, the objections of the trade union members soon became clear, and the meeting became "the first real trial of strength between the two sections, the political and the trade unions."⁸ His opponent was trade unionist J. R. Clynes, who had become chair of the PLP the previous year. An MP since 1906, Clynes had been an ILP member prior to 1914, but he had not actively opposed Britain's involvement in the war and had in fact held office in the wartime coalition government. According to Fenner Brockway, who knew him well during this period, he was already known for his "caution and moderation."⁹ But then, most Labour MPs fell into the same category from Brockway's point of view. Clynes lost to MacDonald only by the very small margin of 56 to 61. As Worley writes, "For the first time Labour had a designated leader."¹⁰ Although this was, indeed, the case, MacDonald had been elected formally as the PLP chairman, not as the leader of the Labour Party.

There is, in relation to Labour Party leadership, a tendency to read later states of affairs into the earlier history of the Labour Party and to refer to Hardie and MacDonald as the pre-1914 leaders of the party. While they were undoubtedly often seen and described as such at the time, it is important to understand the change that took place following MacDonald's election. As David Howell points out:

> In electing MacDonald to the Chairmanship of the PLP, this bare majority effectively structured the patterns of Labour politics for almost the next nine years. The metamorphosis from PLP Chairman to Party leader was not instantaneous, but by 1924 and the advent of the first Labour Government, circumstances had ensured that, for many, man and party were almost interchangeable.¹¹

It does seem that MacDonald emerged as leader because of the particular circumstances of the time. Previous chairmen—Hardie, Clynes, and MacDonald himself from 1911 to 1914—had been elected in totally different circumstances. Only in 1922 was it the case that by electing someone to chair the parliamentary party, MPs were in effect appointing a Leader of the Opposition and potential prime minister. It seems likely that MacDonald—much more conscious of and involved with traditional parliamentary procedure and conventions—was a great deal more aware of this than most of those who elected him or, indeed, than most members of the Labour Party and the ILP.

Nevertheless, it seems odd that there was not more debate at the time, especially from those like Jowett who were so concerned that the Labour Party should not become completely entangled in the parliamentary practices and procedures of the past. Marwick does note that "some confusion surrounds the circumstances in which the newly elected Parliamentary Labour Party chose its new chairman—and 'leader,' a new departure in nomenclature as the *Manchester Guardian* (21 Nov. 1922) immediately pointed out."¹² Still, such an important departure from earlier practice might have been expected to generate much more controversy—especially in the ILP.

MacDonald owed his election not simply to the votes of ILP MPs but, given the narrow margin by which he defeated Clynes, to the votes of Clydeside MPs and other left-wingers. An article in *Labour Leader* by Fenner Brockway, which appeared more than a year before the election, illuminates some important aspects of the leadership issue. Brockway was at the time acting as the paper's "London Correspondent," a role that included frequent visits to the press gallery of the Commons. His front-page article "What Is Wrong with the Labour Party?" was a scathing review of the performance of the Labour MPs who had survived the "khaki election" or who had been elected at subsequent by-elections:

> If the seventy-odd members of the Labour Party were all as energetic as Colonel Wedgwood, if they were all as well-informed about some aspect of policy as he is about foreign and colonial affairs, if they all attended as well, if they all put questions and supplementaries as often, if they were all animated by his fighting spirit—how different Parliament would be then.[13]

Brockway went on to claim that as far as speech-making in the Commons was concerned, Labour depended on ILP MPs and that at least fifty out of the seventy Labour MPs "could never be Parliamentary successes." It is not hard to imagine the anger and resentment that such comments would arouse, not only among the rejected MPs themselves but also among their many trade union supporters. It was, demanded Brockway, up to the constituency Labour parties to select "abler men (politically) as candidates."

Before reaching this conclusion, Brockway had damned the chair of the parliamentary group with faint praise, noting that, despite many virtues, Clynes had not "given the Party the invigorating leadership it needs." He was hampered by his physique, being "little in stature," and did not "inspire devotion in his supporters." The Labour Party, Brockway argued, needed to utilize "every Parliamentary opening possible," and the PLP thus needed someone "seeking out these opportunities and thinking out the best means of attack." Brockway added, "It is lamentable that the Party did not invite Mr. MacDonald to do this work as was suggested at the beginning of the year."[14] MacDonald was still out of Parliament at this stage.

Apart from the writer's enthusiasm for MacDonald's skills as a parliamentarian, Brockway's article is notable in at least three respects. First, while Brockway's prescription for greater success demonstrates a realistic appraisal of how parliamentary politics worked, it would have been anathema to those old-time ILPers who were totally dismissive of the very notion of "leadership"—especially any sort that relied on physical magnetism and oratorical skills. Second, it demonstrates the pressures to adapt to existing political culture rather than to mount a root-and-branch challenge to it. Watching from the gallery, even the radical Brockway wanted to see his side scoring well in the existing game. And third, it throws more light on the nature of MacDonald's support—especially within the ILP. It is significant that MacDonald had been making identical criticisms of the Labour Party in the Commons and had praised Wedgwood's aggressive approach to opposition in a *Forward* article in 1920.[15] It remained to be seen what would happen to such support if and when MacDonald reached Downing Street.

Labour's Behaviour in the House: The "Murderers" Incident

Broadly speaking, there were three distinct, though sometimes overlapping, approaches within the ILP to how Labour MPs operated in the House of Commons. The first approach is exemplified by MacDonald. While it is not fair to describe him as being against *any* change in the parliamentary system, he was certainly a constitutional conservative, as we have seen. To his critics, he would soon seem increasingly to be working his way into the established ways of proceeding. Earlier, before Labour achieved office, one of his strongest points—which, as already noted, attracted the support of many, including Fenner Brockway—was in being more adept than most in playing the parliamentary game. But were these not two sides of the same coin?

Jowett, as we saw in chapter 1, stood for root-and-branch reform, but he shared with MacDonald a fundamental belief in the possibilities of representative government and parliamentary democracy; it was just that for him that was something still to be achieved. But in the meantime, while taking every opportunity to challenge what he saw as the defects and absurdities of existing practice, he believed in treating the role of Parliament with seriousness and respect.

The third approach had been exemplified by Victor Grayson, the independent socialist victor in the famous Colne Valley by-election of July 1907. Jowett was one of those who rejected Grayson's propagandist and "scene-making" approach. He had told readers of the *Clarion*:

> I do *not* agree that the House of Commons is the place for propaganda—that it is a debating assembly where rival politicians should discourse at length about their differences, fancied and real. That view has been the curse of Parliament, as I have tried over and over again to explain. If the democracy has any use for Parliament it is to make it work and not talk.[16]

But there were others who *did* take the view—put into words by a *Labour Leader* correspondent, also in 1907—that the role of Labour in Parliament was to "choose a critical moment to defy tradition, to throw respectability to the winds" in support of socialist aims.[17] Unlike Grayson in the prewar days, James (Jimmy) Maxton (1885–1946) had tremendous staying power. After the brief "Allen regime," he quickly became the most dominant figure in the ILP, and he kept that position for the rest of the interwar period. He already had a considerable record of radical activity when he became one of the Clydeside MPs in 1922. This included his work not only as a union organizer but also as an opponent of the war and a conscientious objector, with a conviction in 1916 for sedition as a result of his part in organizing strikes in war industries. Maxton, like Grayson, saw the role of Labour MPs much more in terms of propaganda and was soon to become associated with "scenes" in the Commons. An early example occurred on 27 June 1923.

Maxton had campaigned in the 1922 election with the slogan "Vote Maxton and Save the Children." An election leaflet shows him holding a small child underneath this slogan. The part of his election address under the heading "Education" began with the statement: "The welfare of children is of first importance to me."[18] Not surprisingly, Maxton had campaigned, vehemently and vociferously, against the 1921 Circular 51, which enforced a ruling of the Scottish Law officers that severely limited the ability of authorities to help needy children with meals and clothing.[19] When the Scottish Board of Health proposed further restrictions concerning children's milk and medical assistance, justified by the "need for economy," he was appalled.[20] Nor was he alone. Focusing on a circular of the previous year that had introduced these additional restrictions, Maxton told the Commons: "In the interests of economy they condemned hundreds of children to death. I call it murder. I call the men who walked into the lobby in support of that policy murderers." Challenged by a Tory MP, Sir Frederick Banbury, to withdraw the word "murderers," Maxton retorted that he, Banbury, was "one of the worst in the House."[21]

Maxton resisted calls from Conservative ministers and the deputy speaker to withdraw the word the latter suggesting, rather comically to anyone unfamiliar with the niceties of parliamentary discourse, that he should substitute "no better than murderers." MacDonald also urged withdrawal, arguing that while the results of the legislation might have been "murder," its motives were not homicidal. But first John Wheatley and then two more Clydeside MPs repeated Maxton's charge, resulting in all four being suspended from the Commons in 1923. Some Labour MPs abstained on the suspension vote, though most voted against it.[22]

Gordon Brown, who devotes a chapter to the episode in his biography of

Maxton, quotes the *Times*'s description of MacDonald sitting "white with anger at the folly of his own followers."[23] MacDonald was not the only critic in the Labour Party, but at a special meeting of the parliamentary party, "MacDonald did not directly condemn the Clydeside MPs but said that their suspension was 'prejudicial rather than helpful.'" The "formal decision" of the meeting was to condemn the "fearful infant mortality" and demand a restitution of at least the provision that had existed in 1920.[24]

In retrospect, at least, the episode was significant in two ways. Most obviously, it showed MacDonald's determination to conform to established parliamentary procedures, customs, and accepted behaviour was going to be carried. It was also a harbinger of the trouble he was likely to experience in future from Maxton and his colleagues, especially after Labour gained office. But it also raised questions about how effective Maxton's tactics might be if the incident became a precedent for future demonstrations of a similar kind.

Gordon Brown is probably right to say that "it all amounted to a highly effective publicity stunt."[25] The nature of the subject that Maxton and his colleagues were so understandably incensed about, the way it related to Maxton's own background as a former Glasgow teacher, the prominence he had given to the protection of children in his election campaign, the detail with which he argued the case against the cutbacks in child welfare—all of these factors contributed to the incident's effectiveness. And so did the relative novelty of Maxton's "disruptive tactic."

In an article published in the *New Leader* two days after Maxton's "scene" in the House of Commons, Clydeside MP John Wheatley argued that "what are called 'scenes' in Parliament shock only those who are out of touch with the realities of working class life, and forget the scenes in the homes of the workers."[26] As Dowse points out, this suggests that the "murderers" episode was to some degree premeditated, since Wheatley's defence of "scenes," published only two days after the incident, must have been written and submitted some time before it took place.[27]

Maxton may have seen his controversial tactic as "a method of alerting the working class to the folly of passively accepting the conventions of parliamentary opposition," as Dowse suggests.[28] But how successful was this likely to be if repeated? Brailsford, in his response to Wheatley's article, emphasized that the effectiveness of a strategy based on creating "scenes" depended on a constant dramatic escalation.[29] Furthermore, since the loss of temper in normally placid and polite individuals makes an infinitely greater impression than the ranting of permanently angry ones, there was a danger that, if repeated too often, disruptive tactics and extreme hyperbole would result in Maxton being dismissed as a "good turn" in the Commons. Time would tell whether this danger would actually materialize, but, as David Howell notes, "the continuing controversy over parliamentary behaviour would become entangled with the developing debate about the future direction of the ILP."[30]

Labour in Office: Unexpected and Short Lived

An election was called at the end of 1923 by Baldwin's Conservative government, which hoped to win a mandate for a protectionist policy that it claimed was necessary to alleviate unemployment. It produced an indecisive result. The Conservatives remained the largest single party in the Commons, with 259 seats to Labour's 191 and the Liberals' 159. With a hung Parliament and the rejection of his key policy, Baldwin faced defeat. What should the attitude of Labour be to forming a minority government?

According to Shinwell, there was some opposition within the ILP to taking office and "considerable doubts" throughout the Labour Party about taking on minority government.[31] Willie Stewart, secretary of the Scottish ILP, was opposed, as was everyone who spoke at a meeting of the Clapham ILP.[32] But there was never any real chance that Labour would turn down the opportunity. Brockway says that the matter was "effectively decided" at a meeting of what he calls the "inner leadership"—Snowden, Henderson, Thomas, MacDonald, and Sidney Webb—at the latter's house.[33] Both the Labour Party National Executive Committee (NEC) and the executive of the Parliamentary Labour Party subsequently agreed that the risks of minority government should be taken, as did the TUC's General Council at a joint meeting with Labour's NEC.[34] Baldwin, who had decided not to resign immediately after the inconclusive election of 6 December, left office after being defeated in the Commons in a vote of no confidence, and MacDonald became prime minister on 22 January 1924.

According to Brockway, MacDonald, on Webb's advice, decided to follow the usual practice of the prospective prime minister deciding the composition of the new government and selecting which MPs he preferred for ministerial office. Brockway argues that this revealed "the degree to which the Party was bound by tradition rather than democratic principle."[35] This was part of a divergence that would widen as time went on. MacDonald, unlike most ILP members, saw the choices that had to be made in predominantly parliamentary terms.

A main plank of MacDonald's argument for taking office, which he had put to the various meetings in December, had been the danger that if Labour refused the opportunity to take office there would be a Liberal minority government, which would see Labour having to relinquish the opposition front bench to the Conservatives. If the Liberals were subsequently defeated, Labour would be likely to lose its right to the opposition front bench to them, and its progress of replacing the Liberals as the official opposition would suffer a serious setback.[36] How far MacDonald would go in continuing to adapt to conventional parliamentary procedures and how far this would be paralleled by the pursuit of consensual policies remained to be seen—but the signs were not hopeful from the point of view of radical ILPers.

Would Labour, as A. J. P. Taylor puts it, be "tamed by responsibility?"[37] This seemed all too probable, especially in light of MacDonald's diary note that the members of the "inner leadership" had unanimously supported his view that the party's salvation lay in "moderation and honesty."[38] How would the ILP, especially its MPs and its prominent figures outside Parliament, like Clifford Allen, react? Would the ILP keep supporting MacDonald, or would cracks continue to open up along the fault lines already starting to emerge with MacDonald's cautious and conventionally parliamentary approach to office? Had the likely divergence already been foreshadowed by Maxton's "murderers" incident? With hindsight, these questions are easily answered, but what is now so obvious only gradually became evident.

Marquand tells us that it was widely assumed that MacDonald would "enjoy as much freedom in appointing the rest of the Government as his predecessors had done." He goes on to comment on the lack of awareness in Labour circles that the acceptance of this would inevitably increase the power of the leader of the Labour Party and "bind the party still more closely to the system."[39] For MacDonald, a large part of his problem in forming a government was the limited pool of potential cabinet ministers available to him—or, as he put it, that he was "short of men."[40] In addition, MacDonald was obliged to navigate among divergent views within the Labour Party itself, including those of ILP MPs. Controversy arose after news reached the ILP that MacDonald was considering J. H. Thomas—a Labour MP and trade unionist who had largely supported Britain's involvement in the First World War—for the position of foreign secretary, and, in the end, MacDonald decided to take on the role himself.[41] In retrospect, MacDonald would generally be regarded as more successful in this role than in his domestic policies.

On the face of it, the ILP had a dominant share in the new government. Of the 191 Labour MPs elected, 120 were ILP members, including the prime minister and the chancellor of the exchequer. So with MacDonald doubling as foreign secretary, the three key offices of state were, therefore, held by those who had for decades been the most prominent members of the ILP. Six members of the cabinet, including Jowett and Wheatley—both, like MacDonald, members of the ILP's NAC—were ILPers, as were nine others who had other ministerial posts, including Attlee, Ponsonby, and Shinwell. On paper, at least, this was an ILP government.

From the start, there was a symbolic divergence among members of the new government and their supporters. For MacDonald, conforming to previous practice of ministers wearing court dress on ceremonial visits to Buckingham Palace was following a harmless tradition. But to what Marquand calls the "more Cromwellian sections" of the Labour Party, this was capitulating to an overprivileged and oppressive—as well as, in this instance, ridiculous—established order.[42] In their eyes, this did not bode well for the future, and no doubt many cheered Jowett and Wheatley for refusing to comply.

Almost from the start, MacDonald complained about the lack of support, and even hostility, from ILP backbenchers, and he was not the only member of the government to do so.[43] But Patrick Dollan, in the *Socialist Review*, presented the results of the 1924 ILP conference as refuting any idea of ILP hostility.

> Newspapers had arranged to broadcast the wildest I.L.P. attacks on Ramsay MacDonald in particular and the Government in general. How disappointed they were that the I.L.P. did not give them an excuse to abuse the Government! The Premier, instead of being censured, was the popular hero of the Conference; the Government, instead of being condemned, was awarded a vote of confidence. Even the "wild men" from Scotland were congratulatory of the efforts and intentions of the Government.[44]

But such upbeat assessments quickly became very difficult to maintain. Apart from opposition to specific measures—the services estimates and the Trades Facilities Bill were early examples—there was fundamental disagreement among Labour Party members and supporters about the strategy the government should pursue. Everyone agreed that Labour needed to secure a parliamentary majority in order to proceed, as it hoped, to establish the Socialist Commonwealth. But how was this to be achieved? For MacDonald and the inner leadership, the answer was obvious. Labour must first establish itself as a reliable and responsible government.

From MacDonald's standpoint, this was clearly the way forward. Though Baldwin had been defeated in the January no-confidence vote, the Conservatives remained the party with the most parliamentary seats and the greatest share of the popular vote. Labour had increased both seats and vote share in the 1924 elections—but so had the now reunited Liberals. Labour had replaced the Liberals as the main alternative to the Conservatives, but this might turn out to be temporary. According to the *New Leader*, many ILPers wanted "to restore the two-party system and seal the fate of the Liberals."[45] So, no doubt, did MacDonald. The way to do this, he believed, was to calm the fears of those who saw the advent of a Labour government as almost as threatening as a Bolshevik coup and to win over voters who might otherwise continue to support the Liberals. A demonstration of administrative competence, combined with some progress on the dangerous international scene and cautious moves on the domestic front, was the surest way to achieve the desired result. Encouraging by-election results at Burnley in March and later at West Toxteth seemed to support this view.[46]

But that was not the view of MacDonald's critics in the ILP. Nor, perhaps, was it that of R. H. Tawney, who, at the end of a *New Leader* article anticipating Labour's advent to office, concluded, "If a Government is to drive the engine, there must be steam in the boiler. It is for the rank and file of the movement to supply it."[47] For those who saw themselves as "the Left," any success that Labour might achieve in office was, as Dowse says, "bound up with audacity," particularly in solving the unemployment problem.[48] MacDonald was not going to be able to meet such high expectations—nor was he convinced that being audacious in ways that the Left would have applauded would lead to anything but disaster for Labour.

The ILP, however, was still pledging its full support to the government. H. N. Brailsford, in a *New Leader* editorial following the ILP annual conference, insisted that the party stood "firmly behind Ramsay MacDonald and his colleagues." However, the prime minister might have been wary of the way Brailsford ended the sentence with the words "not by slavish and unhesitating support, but by a comprehension of the difficulties of government."[49]

Clifford Allen, in spite of—perhaps even in part because of—his close personal relationship with MacDonald, took a lead as a critic of the new government. His chairman's address to the ILP conference at Easter 1924, just three months after Labour took office, stressed that the ILP's role should be "maintaining a persistent pressure in favour of 1) an increasingly bold use of power for Socialist measures and administration, and 2) a vigorous preparation of Socialist knowledge in readiness for a further appeal to the nation."[50] Allen, along with other ILP critics, wanted Labour to pursue a radical policy in order to precipitate a polarization between Labour and its opponents.[51] He combined pleas for tolerance of the government's difficulties with a radical view of representative democracy that would be taken up by left-wing critics of Macdonald.[52]

For MacDonald, Snowden, and the majority of members of the Labour government, "bold" measures could only be carried out in the context of a parliamentary majority. A minority government could claim no mandate for radical policies. The first task was to secure that mandate—the policies would then follow. To their critics, this was an excuse for overcautious inactivity. They argued that the government should put forward the policies it really believed in and present its opponents with the choice of either acquiescing or voting it out of office. The Labour Party would then be able to go to the country seeking support for the radical socialist program that its supporters believed would attract sufficient support to give it a majority.[53]

In Brockway's later interpretation, Allen favoured the introduction of a full "socialist programme."[54] James Maxton, already the rising star of the ILP, was another prominent MP urging MacDonald to take a more radical approach. And in the early days of the Labour government, only a few months on from the "murderers" incident, Maxton was involved in a late night exchange of abuse with the Conservative MP Leo Amery and "appeared to take a swipe at him."[55] Such incidents had a dual effect: while they no doubt heartened many committed supporters who were outraged, like Maxton himself, by the injustices of the society in which they were living, they also increased the danger of Maxton being stereotyped as an emotional "rebel" who could be relied on to provide excellent copy for the popular press but would probably make little progress in effective politics.

For most members of the ILP, the core issue was unemployment. By the summer of 1924, the NAC was organizing conferences aimed at bringing "to the notice of the government the immediate improvement that would accrue by the establishment of a 48-hour week."[56] The ILP also pressed for a whole range of other measures thought essential to reduce unemployment, including the raising of the school leaving age. The *New Leader* expressed the disappointment many felt with the government's response, while MacDonald, for his part, complained to Allen about the lack of ILP support.[57] The very ILPers who had secured his election as leader only two years previously now seemed to be ganging up against him. MacDonald took the enmity of the Scottish group in particular as a personal betrayal: "'It's treachery,' he told me," reported Shinwell many years later.[58]

MacDonald's government was always going to be at the mercy of its political rivals. If the Liberals and Conservatives decided the time had come to oust it, there was little that could be done to preserve the minority administration. That said, the issue that led directly to the Labour government losing a confidence vote on 8 October 1924 was not without its almost farcical aspects. The Campbell Case, as it came to be known, turned on the decision of the government's attorney general to drop the prosecution of J. R. Campbell, a Communist journalist. Campbell had been charged with sedition under an antiquated piece of legislation (passed in 1797 during the wars with revolutionary France) after he published an open letter urging members of the armed forces not to shoot fellow British workers. The vote that led to MacDonald's resignation was on this question, but other issues—notably the Russian treaties, which both opposition parties disliked, and a general belief that its opponents might now benefit from an election—also lay behind it.[59]

Given the short time that the party was in office and its precarious minority position, one would expect the achievements of the 1924 Labour government to be relatively modest, as indeed they may have seemed at the time. In retrospect, though, they were not unimpressive. Wheatley's Housing Act, which, over the next decade, resulted in about 450,000 houses built by local authorities, is generally regarded as the high point of its legislative achievements. Brockway notes how MacDonald's "open letters" to Poincaré marked an advance towards ending secret diplomacy, and Marquand has some justification for giving his chapter on MacDonald's foreign policy the title "Foreign Triumphs."[60] But such advances and the efforts of Jowett as First Commissioner of Works and of Trevelyan in his worthy attempt to raise the school leaving age did not prevent a great deal of disappointment among the keenest Labour Party supporters—and above all, in the ILP. Despite Labour being in office rather than in power, there was little appreciation of its minority position. Shinwell sums the situation up succinctly: "The fact that we were really a Government without power ... was ignored by the country and by our own party members. Criticism grew steadily."[61]

With the advantages of twenty-first-century hindsight, it is difficult to dissent from the conclusions of John Shepherd and Keith Laybourn in their 2006 book, *Britain's First Labour Government*. The 1924 government was at least "a useful milestone" for Labour, they argue. It did help to "dispatch the Liberal Party to political oblivion," and it should be judged in terms of its impact over the long term as well as its immediate achievements and failures.[62] But few on the Left, least of all in the ILP, saw matters in such terms at the time. Labour's unexpectedly early advent to office, not even as the largest party in the Commons, had left little time for its leaders to prepare their supporters for the complexities, difficulties, and inevitable disappointments that lay ahead—even if had it wanted to do this. It is doubtful that any members of the new government, even MacDonald himself, fully appreciated the great pressures they would be under from a variety of directions. Expectations remained high, even as MacDonald's government fell.

The ILP approached the general election of October 1924 with optimism. In the *New Leader*, less than two weeks before the election, Allen announced the party's healthy financial state under the headline "Labour's War Chest Already Half Filled," and Dollan reported campaign success in "MacDonald Rallies the North: A Triumphal Tour."[63] But the ILP's hopes were dashed. Amid the hysteria surrounding the *Daily Mail*'s publication of the now famous Zinoviev letter, the Labour Party was resoundingly defeated in the October 1924 election.[64]

Soon after the fall of the first Labour government, the ILP Information Committee reissued MacDonald's pamphlet *The Story of the I.L.P. and What It Stands For*. Originally called *The History of the I.L.P.*, it had been part of the syllabus for socialist study circles published in 1921. The new version began with a preface—unsigned but dated November 1924—which incorporated an apologia for the now defeated administration and an upbeat assessment of the future of Labour and the ILP.

> So well was the work of the Opposition done, that the Election of 1923 gave Labour 191 members instead of 141, and in February 1924, J. R. MacDonald took up the heavy task of forming a Government, although he had behind him less than a third of the total strength of the House of Commons. A Socialist resolution had been defeated by nearly three to one in the House; the country had given no mandate for constructive change; the task was a difficult one—that of doing national work so truly and well, at home and abroad, as to win national consent for Socialist efficiency. That experiment came to an end in October this year when the first Labour Government was defeated by a combination of Tories and Liberals.

This defeat, resulting from "the capitalist pact," should not, the preface continued, obscure the fact that Labour's votes increased by more than a million and that its future prospects were good: not only had many long-standing ILP members been MacDonald's colleagues in government, but socialism and Labour were "winning new adherents every day" and the "growth in membership and branches of the I.L.P. itself goes steadily and rapidly on."[65] The pamphlet ended with a section titled "The I.L.P. Path to Socialism." To the original two subsections, "Programme" and "Methods," was now added a third, "Tactics," which comprised two passages from MacDonald's previous writings. An appendix in the pamphlet reproduced the ILP constitution as adopted at the 1922 conference.

Had the ILP as a whole fallen in line with the approach of this pamphlet, it might have continued its role of providing MacDonald's essential political base. But this was not to be. In Parliament, an ILP-based internal opposition—which, admittedly, did not include anything like the majority of MPs sponsored by the party—had begun to take shape even while the first Labour government was in office. The view of MacDonald's leadership from the emerging ILP "rebels in the parliamentary contingent" was later summed up, dismissively, by David Kirkwood: "The 1924 election was lost—partly because of the Zinovieff letter, which was a swindle, and partly because the Labour Government had accomplished nothing and had challenged nothing."[66]

7

Preparing the Ground for the Living Wage Policy

MacDonald's critics from across Labour's spectrum constituted a distinct minority. Ernest Bevin's attempts to get Arthur Henderson to stand for the leadership against MacDonald failed, as did the attempt by the ILP to get the Parliamentary Labour Party to adopt its policy.[1] Within the ILP group itself, a gulf was beginning to open between what might be termed "nominal" ILP MPs—those who sought and accepted ILP endorsement and support as a matter of course without identifying very closely or exclusively with the ILP—and the small minority of ILP MPs who saw the promotion of the smaller party's policies within the larger one as the essential goal. Though the latter group was increasingly critical of MacDonald's leadership, they had relatively little support in the PLP.

The reluctance of the parliamentarians to participate in an all-out attack on MacDonald's interpretation of Labour politics was, at first, reflected in the attitudes and decisions of the 1925 ILP conference when it refused to oppose what Marquand describes as an "anodyne resolution" from the Yorkshire Division congratulating "the late Labour Government" on its achievements. Singled out for praise were its efforts for peace, improvements for pensioners, and its "comprehensive Housing Act."[2]

One ILP member, Joseph Southall, strongly opposed the motion based on the government's failures in defence and foreign affairs and its continuance of the "policy of Imperialism."[3] The "anodyne" motion was passed, but the vocal opposition to it and the 139 who voted against it were, as Marquand suggests, better guides to the future than the 398 who supported it.[4] Despite the show of support for MacDonald, the conference agenda included critical amendments from a number of branches, including ones opposing Labour MPs wearing court dress or attending "court or ceremonial functions."[5] The section of the NAC report titled "Labour in Office" began by proclaiming that the ILP had "loyally assisted" the Labour government "by every means in their power." It went on to say that ILPers had "exercised constant pressure in favour of a vigorous Socialist policy." No doubt MacDonald would have been more aware of the pressure than of the loyalty.[6]

In retrospect, the 1925 conference came to be seen as one that "repudiated gradualism."[7] At the ILP summer school in August, Clifford Allen told participants that "we were foolishly filled with hopes, and foolishly disappointed" with the 1924 government. He renewed his advocacy of the Labour Party putting forward full-blooded socialist policies, even if it was again in a minority, thus challenging opposing parties to oust it. "We should say that democracy is something which checks rather than initiates," he said. "Democracy should be merely a device to prevent things being done that people do not want."[8] Such radical but risky tactics were clearly never going to be accepted by MacDonald, or by the parliamentary leadership generally. If such tactics were to be ruled out, there was a widespread conviction in the ILP that Labour should never again take office as a minority administration.[9]

Certainly, nothing came of the joint ILP/Labour Party committee in 1925 which considered the ILP's proposition that "the function of the ILP is to bring to the public a realisation of the urgent need for fundamental changes which socialism represents, and to influence the Labour Party in a more complete and rapid direction."[10] But other ILP committees were already hard at work producing policies that they hoped and intended would do just that. Allen's idea of the ILP being a creative nucleus in the Labour Party was being put to the test. Fundamental changes would be demanded in Labour policy and practice.

Clifford Allen: A New Approach to Politics

In September 1925, Allen resigned as chairman of the party—ostensibly because of ill health. His health problems were all too real, but Allen battled on determinedly in spite of them. Certainly, the growing conflicts in the ILP with the critics of his "regime" and, above all, with his eventual successor, James Maxton, was the major factor in his departure, as we will see in a later chapter.

It was some months later that Fenner Brockway paid tribute in the *New Leader* to Allen's crucial role in setting the party on its new course:

> To Clifford Allen more than anyone else we owe the conception or the new approach to politics embodied in this policy. His insistence that it is the duty of the next Labour Government, whether with a minority or majority behind it, to produce its proposals for the redistribution of wealth and Socialist reorganisation, and to stand or fall by them, has had an extraordinary influence on the thought of the Party.[11]

Allen had been instrumental in setting up a number of ILP commissions on a variety of pressing aspects of policy. As F. M. Leventhal maintains, this approach had "sprung from Allen's mind, rather than the NAC."[12] The NAC report for the 1925 conference contained appendices giving the reports of the Empire, India, and Industrial Policy commissions.[13] All were, according to John Paton, "effective documents, with much good material," but they made little sustained impact. The exception was the one that led to the publication of *The Living Wage* report in September 1926, almost a year and a half after the Gloucester conference initiated the inquiry that led to it.[14]

The origins of that report can be traced to at least as early as late 1923. In December of that year, immediately following the election that was to bring the minority Labour government into office the following month, Allen had urged the party to adopt a bold emergency program aimed at addressing two or three urgent questions. Probable defeat at the hands of the Liberals and Conservatives would open the way to an appeal to the country on these issues.[15] A few months later, at the ILP's 1924 conference, in his opening address as chairman, Allen had pressed the minority Labour government to take advantage of its temporary control of the resources of the state to initiate inquiries into all major industries and to "set the enquiring mind of the nation dispassionately to work." He also insisted that "a 'Living Wage' must be enforced as a national policy."[16] At the conference a year later, Allen, in his chairman's speech, expressed regret about the failure of Labour to follow this course and to "set up a national commission to probe the wages question, and by means of impartial enquiry enable a national verdict to be given as to what constituted a 'Living Wage' in a civilised community."[17]

The call for a Living Wage policy was, in fact, nothing especially new. Even before the war, Labour MP Will Crooks had demanded "a 'Living Wage' for all" in a 1911 speech before the House of Commons, which the ILP then published as a pamphlet.[18] In early 1923, Bermondsey's Labour MP, Dr. Alfred Salter, had likewise delivered a speech to the House of Commons, which the Bermondsey ILP branch published under the same title, "A Living Wage for All." Salter went on to contribute an article to the *New Leader* titled "The Cry for a 'Living Wage,'" which appeared in March 1924.[19] Several weeks later, around the time of the ILP's 1924 conference, the paper devoted its front page to a drawing, by "Houynhm," showing a small girl about to discover a large egg labelled "A 'Living Wage,'" with the caption "An Easter Egg for the Worker's Child?"[20]

All the same, that Allen was primarily responsible for initiating the Living Wage policy is supported by much contemporary evidence. This includes a *New Leader* report of the ILP summer school at Scarborough in the summer of 1924. According to the reporter, Allen delivered a keynote address titled

"A Socialist View of Politics," in which he argued for the need for an "entirely different spirit" in politics. Labour should avoid "a phase of 'eternal democratic postponement' wherein the plea 'we are in a minority—we can't do it because we do not have the sanction of democracy' was made." He rejected "this false theory of democracy as the source of power, instead of a check upon the arbitrary exercise of power" and went on to outline his proposed alternative, in which the broad outlines of the policy adopted in 1926 are clearly visible: "A national charter of individual welfare should be prepared, a national minimum of health, food, housing and wages, which would kindle the public imagination, and then we should submit our carefully prepared proposals for the economic re-organisation essential to the achievement of these ends to the decision of Parliament and the nation."[21]

As reported by the *New Leader*, Allen believed the key points in this economic reorganization to be the national organization of finance, the national control of imports, and the national ownership of power and transport. It should be the business of the Labour government to present this program to the nation in such an imaginative fashion that the electorate would become a partner rather than an entity to be exploited to keep one particular party in power. Allen's address was not received without criticism; indeed, Dollan alleged that he was seeking to substitute "the dictatorship of the politician" for "the dictatorship of the proletariat."[22]

When one notes that the same summer school included a talk by Eleanor Rathbone on "Family Endowments," it becomes clear that it marked a significant point in the evolution of the Living Wage policy. Opinion among participants was divided on Rathbone's contribution, "but she had by no means lost the day," according to the *New Leader*'s report. The school also featured a talk by Willie Graham titled "The Minimum Wage" and one by Pethick Lawrence called "Banking and Credit."[23]

The *New Leader* report mentions John Strachey's contribution to the discussion, in which he argued that what was needed was "neither inflation nor deflation but stabilisation."[24] Strachey's view may well have reflected the views expressed by John Maynard Keynes in *A Tract on Monetary Reform*, published the year before, and in the *New Leader* article "Fear and the Business Man," in which Keynes argued for price stabilization, quipping, "I believe that economists have really discovered something thoroughly useful for once." The same *New Leader* issue in which Keynes's piece appeared also featured an article by J. A. Hobson called "Saving and Spending," and both pieces illustrate the quality of economic argument that the ILP paper was capable of producing at this time.[25]

Strachey was by no means alone in stressing the necessity for price stabilization. In September 1923, H. N. Brailsford had advocated it as being both bold and revolutionary, and he ended another article, in August 1924, with the claim that "a steady price level would, at last, make the battle to secure progressively higher real wages a hopeful enterprise. With an expanding market at home, we might then, without fear, throw all our creative powers into the task of increasing production and adding to the nation's wealth."[26]

Allen's speech as chairman to the 1925 conference reiterated the themes propounded at the summer school the previous year. He anticipated that it would rarely happen in the foreseeable future that one party would gain a majority of votes cast; in this situation, he said, it was vital to "reject the notion that it is the function of democracy to *initiate*." He even quoted Edmund Burke's famous defence of the independence of MPs in support of his strategy for Labour governments, even minority ones, to put their full-blooded socialist proposals forward and wait for their opponents to vote them out of office, thus precipitating an election on the basis of Labour's program.[27]

If Allen is, rightly, seen as initiating the process that led to *The Living Wage* report, Brailsford must take the largest part of the credit for popularizing the new policy, both as editor of the *New Leader* and as author of the book *Socialism for To-day*, published in late 1925. As Leventhal says, "Throughout the year and a half of the Commission's deliberations Brailsford was its lynch-pin, reporting its activities to a cautiously approving NAC, propagandizing for the 'Living Wage' in the *New Leader*, expounding its principles at ILP conferences and ultimately incurring the brunt of MacDonald's wrath."[28] What, exactly, was Brailsford advocating that would bring such anger on his head?

H. N. Brailsford: The Living Wage as "Battering Ram"

From the beginning of 1925, Brailsford ran a series of articles in the *New Leader*, under the title "The Socialist Case Restated," that prepared the way for *The Living Wage* report the following year. These articles formed the basis of Brailsford's book *Socialism for To-day*, which Leventhal sees, with much justification, as "trying to put the case for socialism succinctly" in the tradition of Robert Blatchford's *Merrie England*. The latter had made a considerable impact in the 1890s.[29] In a prefatory note (dated October 1925) to his book, Brailsford acknowledges a variety of influences, including the writings of E. H. Lloyd and Otto Bauer, J. A. Hobson and the Webbs, and "three friends": Allen, E. F. Wise, and "Realist."[30] Since Creech Jones is the only fellow member of the NAC's Living Wage Commission not mentioned by name, it seems likely that he was "Realist," a fairly frequent *New Leader* commentator on economic affairs.[31]

Brailsford's book began with six chapters on the development of capitalism before turning to the question of "evolution or revolution." In the mid-nineteenth century, he wrote, the state was seen by socialists as "a capitalist institution which we must contrive to overthrow by revolutionary force." However, by the beginning of the twentieth century, "every Socialist Party in Western and Central Europe knew in its heart that any sudden revolution was impossible and believed it was unnecessary."[32] Although the Russian Revolution had caused this to be reassessed, Brailsford argued that it had only demonstrated what might take place in very particular and unusual circumstances. The civil war in Russia had been "cruel, prolonged, and appallingly destructive," yet it offered "only a faint parallel to the horrors which would attend a similar struggle against the numerous and capable middle-class of any Western country."[33]

Brailsford did not fear that the latter would readily turn to dictatorial methods. "Even in Italy," he noted, "it required a great deal of lawless provocation from the Red side to create Fascism. The Reds disdained Parliament and legal methods. They believed in direct action, and seized not only factories but ships, and above all, great tracts of agricultural land, by tumultuous violence."[34] To succeed, socialists needed the "intelligent consent" not only of manual workers and "the industrial army organised in trade unions" but also of "a part of the professional and managerial class." Even with this support, no one should underestimate the "embittered and unflinching will to resist" that socialism's adversaries would show. This might necessitate "emergency measures and war-time precautions."[35]

Yet, he concluded, "it would be folly to abandon Parliamentary forms." Brailsford invoked the analogy of the 1640s, foreseeing that "Labour in power would repeat the revolution of the seventeenth century, and rally the nation against any Fascist attempt. It is well to start with the constitutional right to call on the obedience of magistrates and soldiers even though we may expect that some of them will disobey."[36] A future Labour government must be prepared for "an effort revolutionary in extent if not in method." Its measures could not be carried out in isolation:

> One change may involve a whole series of changes no less considerable. One could not, for example, impose on industry the obligation to pay a true "Living Wage," without facing at the same time the regulation of credit, the control of prices through the importation, by a National Board, of food and raw materials, and the reorganisation of the more depressed industries.[37]

With what was bound to be interpreted as a criticism of MacDonald and his supporters, Brailsford warned that "the peril of any party which adopts the watchword of evolution is that it may come to imagine that it is playing the ordinary party game." He added, "Talking of 'gradualness,' and deprecating too much zeal, the evolutionary Socialist who sits down to admire the majestic and inevitable march of time may in fact create in others the impatience and despair which hasten the violent catastrophe he dreads."[38]

Turning to the key demand for a living wage, Brailsford makes it clear that this means a "figure which will keep the worker not merely alive, but healthy and efficient; it must allow for a civilised standard of comfort in housing" and for the worker's cultural needs. The notion of "what the industry can pay" must be "ruthlessly disregarded." The proposal was "for a single uniform standard applicable to all trades, below which no wage may lawfully fall, though wages in some trades may and will rise above it." This might hit some export industries hard, but the higher purchasing power of the workers would stimulate the home market. Successful implementation of the policy, he argued, implied the need to control prices of "necessary goods," the reorganization of agriculture to reduce reliance on exports, and the nationalization of "key" industries, with state subsidy of others, in return for a modernizing reorganization.[39]

Brailsford's view on compensation would not have found universal support in the ILP. Certainly, Maxton was unlikely to be persuaded. But Brailsford was quite clear. "From our resolve to avoid civil war and catastrophic revolution," he argued, "it follows that we must pay compensation, at a fair reckoning of its market value, for the property which we nationalise." He wanted such compensation to take the form of "national stock, bearing a fixed rate, or possibly a diminishing rate of interest, or better still, in the form of terminable annuities." At the same time, "graduated taxation" would reduce unearned income "as drastically as public opinion will allow." This would mean that "the owners of property will in effect compensate each other for the socialisation of land and industry. The burden will not fall upon the producers."[40]

Brailsford was cautious about guild socialism. While he believed that it had "started a fruitful discussion," it had "laid salutary but one-sided stress on the interests of the workers."[41] A weakness of the guild idea was its failure to suggest "that the State should be armed with the influence which the control of credit, power and raw materials would confer." Nevertheless, "a free Socialist State" would permit and assist "every form of association for co-operative production." Many kinds of activity, he wrote, should never be nationalized. It was vital, for example, that the press and book publication be independent: "There must be more freedom than there is today for adventure in word and thought and deed."[42]

It is difficult to improve on Leventhal's summary of this aspect of Brailsford's proposals:

> Skilfully navigating between the Scylla of bureaucratic centralisation and the Charybdis of guild structure, he stressed the workers' right to share

in managing the semi-independent Industrial Corporations. While half of the directing board might be chosen by organisations of workers and technicians, an equal number should be selected for their administrative abilities by parliamentary and consumer groups.

Yet there is little doubt that Brailsford's position was a conservative interpretation of the 1922 program. As his biographer says, "More concerned to obtain the best managers rather than satisfy demands for worker control, he was willing to sacrifice participation to professionalism."[43]

As regards credit and banking, Brailsford drew on E. M. H. Lloyd's *Stabilisation* and, "for a brilliant analysis of the theory, and of certain complications in its interpretation," Keynes's *A Tract on Monetary Reform*. The first principle, said Brailsford, should be "to regulate credit in such a way as to keep the general level of prices steady," adding, "Recent theoretical studies leave no doubt that prices are governed much more by monetary policy, and the contractions or expansion of bankers' credit than by the fluctuations of supply and demand for single commodities. It is now realised that a scientific credit policy can, with adequate organisation, prevent any considerable fluctuation in this general level of prices." Bank nationalization and the development of municipal banks would end the situation where banks were "money-lenders whose sole aim is profit." Nationalized banks would have to cover risks and costs but could be used to support agriculture, address the housing shortage, and encourage cooperatives. Another proposal, which followed wartime precedents and would appear in *The Living Wage* report the following year, was the creation of "boards of supply or corporations with exclusive rights to import for bread and flour, wool, flax, jute, oils, iron, nitrates, rubber." These boards would be composed of "business men," rather than civil servants.[44]

"No one in his senses dreams of nationalising every industry at once," Brailsford declared. "To imagine that we can achieve our end . . . by storming the factories and taking them over would be to doom our movement to disaster. Behind the factories we have to cope with the movement of prices, which govern both wages and profits." It was, moreover, "useless to try to intervene at any point in the long processes which end with the finished article in the shop, if you leave raw materials in the hands of price rings, gamblers and speculators." He looked forward to a "few successful experiments in collective contracts" to "pave the way for the formation of manufacturing guilds and the elimination of the capitalist owner."[45] He foresaw also an extension of municipal enterprise with "the right of the workers to share in the control of their activities," as was the case with cooperatives.[46]

As for land, this could gradually be taken into public ownership. A tax levied on urban site values could provide a fund for the gradual purchase of land,

and "in this way the owners would compensate each other." Along with this, agriculture would be reorganized by county-wide or more local committees with a third of representatives from the farmers' union, another third from the agricultural workers' union and the remaining third nominated by the Ministry of Agriculture.[47]

The book ends with several shorter chapters. "The Socialist Road to Peace" includes a proposal for an economic League of Nations controlling credit and raw materials. Then Brailsford turns again to the key question of a living wage:

> To begin by demanding a genuine "Living Wage" would, I believe, be sound strategy. Hitherto Socialists have argued in their propaganda that if industry and the land were nationalised, the consequence would be an increase in our national wealth, and a fairer distribution of the national income. The happy result looked to the average man rather remote, and preliminary processes did not grip his attention. There is much to be said for reversing the order of thought and action. Let us rather begin by demanding the fairer division of wealth; let us insist, first of all, on the elementary human claim to a living wage and then enforce the wide economic changes by which alone it can be realised and secured. The fixing, whether by combined Trade Union action, or by a Royal Commission, of any adequate figure would drive us at once into big political changes. The demand is a battering-ram levelled at the present system.[48]

Brailsford was a member of the commission that produced *The Living Wage* report, and most of the themes and much of the detail of that report had appeared in *Socialism for To-day*. The final months of 1925 and the beginning of 1926 also saw the emergence of a related but separate initiative, described first in a pamphlet and then in a book, both titled *Revolution by Reason*, by two ILP members who were not part of that commission. They were John Strachey and Oswald Mosley.

John Strachey and Oswald Mosley: The Birmingham Proposals

In interpreting the contributions of Strachey and Mosley to the Living Wage policy, it is, of course, difficult to disregard Mosley's later career as Britain's leading fascist. Hindsight can sometimes be a great disadvantage to the historian. Strachey, a Labour MP from 1929 to 1931, followed Mosley into the New Party but broke with him over fascism and instead went on to become a leading apologist for communism (although he never formally joined the party). Mosley and Strachey published two different versions—a pamphlet and a book, respectively—of what came to be known as the "Birmingham proposals"; both were titled *Revolution by Reason*. Hugh Thomas may be correct when he says, of Strachey's version (1925), that "the book reads today like a generously presented amalgamation between Labour 'pragmatism' of the 1960s and fascism."[49]

To be sure, there was some suspicion and resentment at the way the wealthy, aristocratic and glamorous Mosley was able to climb quickly to prominence in both the ILP and the wider Labour Party. As Brockway notes, the usual ILP rule was that parliamentary candidates sponsored by the ILP were required to have been members for a year. This was set aside in Mosley's case. Not everyone would have shared the welcome given to Mosley by the *New Leader*, which featured an article by Mosley under the title "A New Recruit's Defence of Labour," in April 1924.[50] Some may well have suspected that Mosley wished to use the ILP as a base for becoming increasingly prominent among Labour's parliamentary contingent and even, perhaps, that he aspired to eventually become leader of the Labour Party. It seems reasonable to speculate that this might, indeed, have been one of the motives that led to the Birmingham proposals being published—that is, to launch a separate enterprise rather than to respond to the invitation to "assist NAC by submitting memoranda for its consideration" made at the 1925 ILP conference by E. F. Wise, one of the members of the Living Wage Commission.

This invitation was Wise's response to a motion at the annual ILP conference in Gloucester from the Ladywood branch in Birmingham, moved by Mosley. The motion demanded the nationalization of the Bank of England, the bringing of joint stock banks under public control, and the creation of a Banking Advisory Committee to coordinate banking policy. With conference time, as ever, under severe pressure, the motion was subjected to a successful moving of the "previous question," a procedural device that terminated debate on the motion immediately without a vote being taken. Allen, in the chair, hastened to insist that this was not because of any lack of sympathy with what was proposed but because what would emerge the following year as *The Living Wage* report was being referred to the branches. Allen stressed that bank nationalization was already a "traditional" policy of the ILP.[51] The impression of Mosley's self-promotion is reinforced by Strachey's dedication of the book version of *Revolution by Reason*, "To O.M., who may some day do the things of which we dream."[52]

Yet at a time when the NAC was trying to engage the whole of the membership in consultation over the proposals for a Living Wage policy, it was to the ILP's advantage to have as much relevant material in print as possible. And, after all, like Brailsford's *Socialism for To-day*, Mosley's pamphlet—though not Strachey's book—was published by the ILP. Even if Mosley's recruitment of local support for his Birmingham proposals could be seen as an attempt to strengthen his base in the ILP and the Labour Party, it might also be an effective way to involve more ILP members in the debate on economic policy.

The Conservative politician Robert Boothby, in a book written after the Second World War, recalled being a guest of the Mosleys in Venice, where he found his host—Tom Mosley, as he was known in his own circle—spending each morning working with another guest, namely, John Strachey, on proposals that seemed to Boothby at the time to be the "height of political audacity" though "it seems very reasonable stuff today."[53] Following his moving of the Ladywood motion at the ILP conference, Mosley held a well-attended meeting at the Birmingham town hall on 3 May 1925, and in June, he won the approval of his proposals, by 65 votes to 14, by the local Labour Party.

Once more, as with Clifford Allen the previous year, the ILP summer school played an important role in the formation of Mosley's *Revolution by Reason*. As its title page explained, "This pamphlet is founded on the speech delivered by the author to the I.L.P. Summer School at Easton Lodge, August 11, 1925." Mosley claimed that he was seeking the "helpful criticism of the movement" and rejected any notion that the Birmingham proposals were being advanced "in a narrow or dogmatic spirit."[54]

In his biography of John Maynard Keynes, Robert Skidelsky describes Mosley's *Revolution by Reason* as the "first political attempt to apply Keynes's ideas to economic policy." Strachey's book was, Skidelsky maintains, "an enlarged and more muddled version of it."[55] Strachey had indeed acknowledged the influence of "Mr. Keynes and his Cambridge economists, who have brilliantly developed the purely monetary aspect." Others credited included MacDonald, Allen, Brailsford, E. M. H. Lloyd, and, of course "Mr. Oswald Mosley, the originator of these proposals."[56]

Keynes features quite prominently in Strachey's book. The second chapter begins by acknowledging the influence of *A Tract on Monetary Reform*, as Brailsford had done, and Strachey later quotes extensively from *The Economic Consequences of the Peace*. The consequences of underconsumption as outlined by Hobson featured in both versions of *Revolution by Reason*, with Mosley insisting that "the lower wages fall in their mad competition, the smaller becomes the market for which they are competing."[57]

Although Brailsford had stressed the interconnectedness of the policies proposed, a greater sense of urgency is evident in both Mosley's and Strachey's arguments. "We hold that evolutionary Socialism is in itself not enough," wrote Mosley. "Time presses in the turmoil of war's aftermath. The year 1925 holds not the atmosphere of a secluded study where pedants may stroll their way through go-slow philosophies."[58] Strachey emphasized that "*real Socialism, if it is to be quickly effective, must come over the whole productive field simultaneously*" and that "the keys to economic power ... must be acquired, not gradually, but by a single decisive act." He forecasted—accurately enough, as things turned out—"an unprecedented industrial crisis ... inevitable as early as the spring of 1926."[59]

The crucial importance of control of credit was underlined by both Mosley and Strachey. Mosley stressed that banks possessed the power "to give and to allocate purchasing power through the manipulation of price level, which in recent years has been ruthlessly employed in favour of the rentier and against the producer."[60] Skidelsky notes what he considers the most unusual feature of Mosley's *Revolution by Reason*: "Whereas most socialists, even the authors of *The Living Wage* laid the greatest focus on fiscal policy, Mosley focused attention on monetary policy."[61] While Mosley insisted that the proposals were based on "classic and accepted Socialist doctrine," he was, he explained, striving to add to that doctrine:

> Nothing can be more absurd than the suggestion of our opponents that we propose to make everybody rich by printing an unlimited mass of paper money. It is true that we develop modern monetary theory to a further stage where it unites with Socialist theory and can be made the instrument of transferring economic power and effective demand to the workers.
>
> Maybe we over-emphasise the monetary side; if so it is a useful corrective to the neglect it has hitherto incurred. Throughout the ages currency problems have been regarded as the happy hunting grounds of cranks and futile theorists.

Socialist literature contained little on the subject, he continued, and Strachey and he were attempting fill this gap.[62] It was vital that "the increase in the supply of money was accompanied by an increase in the supply of goods" in order to avoid inflation.[63] Noel Thompson, in his "intellectual biography" of Strachey, pinpoints the relative novelty of his subject's position on this. "While, therefore, for Hobson, Brailsford *et al.*, monetary policy facilitated, for Strachey it initiated a rise in living standards and the increased level of economic activity which would follow."[64]

Mosley proposed to campaign with the slogan "The Banks for the People." The two main objectives would be "to expedite Socialism" and "to alleviate the conditions of the workers during the transitional period." What Mosley called "the machinery of the Birmingham proposals" was to be an Economic Council whose role would be to estimate the difference between actual and potential production and "to plan the stages by which that potential production can be evoked through the instrument of working class demand," making sure that demand did not outstrip supply and thus lead to a rise in prices. The Economic Council would, from time to time, fix wages for firms with overdrafts from the state bank until it could be determined that firms could pay. It might establish a minimum wage and or family allowances. What was needed was "a central, disinterested and, in the last resort, democratically controlled Authority which shall control the supply of the national credit."[65]

Strachey stressed that "*the first step must be the creation and maintenance of effective demand.*" He was also keen to "avoid an economic dictatorship under which an all-wise Government provides only those things which it thinks its citizens ought to want. We prefer to let those citizens express their *real* wants by giving them purchasing power." There was, he insisted, "an essential difference between planning to meet a genuine, spontaneously manifested, new demand, and planning to give people what the Government thinks they ought to want."[66]

Both Strachey and Mosley foresaw that one of the consequences of "wealth production directed to working-class uses" might be the "closing down of luxury industry and transfer of labour to useful industry."[67] As things were, firms producing goods for the working class were "few, small and decaying," while luxury firms were "numerous, prosperous and expanding."[68] Skidelsky, in his biography of Mosley, detected a "sharp difference" between him and Strachey in that Mosley attacked the "export fetish."[69] Indeed, he did, noting the paradox that "capitalism searches the world feverously for new markets, while at our own door men, women and children are almost perishing for lack of goods for which we are told that no market exists."[70] Yet Skidelsky's notion of a significant degree of difference in this respect is hard to square with Strachey's inclusion in his book of a section titled "The Foreign Trade Bogey."[71]

Both authors disclaimed any attempt at laying down what Strachey called a "cast-iron policy," with Mosley agreeing that the "collective wisdom of a party and the experience of an expert Civil Service might vastly change and develop these proposals."[72] But the latter did claim for the Birmingham proposals a great advantage over "current Socialist strategy." For many in the ILP that strategy was to "fix a statutory minimum wage and socialise every industry that cannot pay it." The consequence would be that "we should take over first the lame ducks of Capitalism who are too feeble to survive in the new conditions": under his own proposals, Mosley explained further, "we should take over first the strong and vigorous members rather than the dying and obsolescent industries. We should socialise first not the duds but the plums."[73]

Certainly, with Brailsford's *New Leader* articles, condensed into *Socialism for To-day*, Mosley's pamphlet, and Strachey's book, members of the ILP, including the very distinguished member who the year before had been prime minister, had plenty to consider as 1925 turned into 1926. As Skidelsky concludes, "Mosley was the first to break through to a modern economic policy with his so-called Birmingham Proposals of 1925, but the Independent Labour Party was not far behind with its 'Living Wage' policy."[74]

Already in 1925, it was clear that, whether or not the Living Wage constituted a "modern economic policy," there was going to be considerable disagreement over it in the ILP. In the April issue of the *Socialist Review*, John Scurr argued in favour of the idea. "To increase the purchasing power of the bulk of the nation," he wrote, "is the only remedy, and the first and permanent step towards this is the establishment of a basic 'Living Wage.'"[75] Two months later, however, in the same journal, Margaret Matheson posed a critical question in an article titled "'Living Wage' or Socialism?" What was the matter with the ILP, she asked, that they should propose such "a short-sighted policy"? Emphasizing that the party's demand must be for "*Socialism*," she concluded: "Are the leaders of the I.L.P. afraid of this programme and all that it involves? If so, let them be honest and say so; let them make room for others, more courageous, perhaps younger, who will be a race of St. Georges, out for the complete destruction of the Dragon of Capitalism."[76]

St. Georges were slow to come forward, but Arthur St. John responded in a letter printed in the next issue, saying that he was delighted with Matheson's contribution but adding, "though a 'Living Wage' is not a Socialist slogan, *a living income for all is.*"[77] The *Socialist Review* ended the year with Philip Snowden's appreciative, though highly critical, review of *Socialism for To-day*. Though Snowden agreed with Brailsford about gradualism, "judged by the programme he expounds in the later chapters, I should place Mr. Brailsford among the 'moderates' and myself among the 'extremists.'"[78] It was clear that the Living Wage would become ILP policy in 1926, but it was equally plain that this would be far from unchallenged.

8

The Year of the General Strike—and of *The Living Wage*

For the British Labour movement, 1926 would be remembered, above all, as the year of the General Strike. For the ILP, however, it would also be memorable for being the year that the policy variously called the "Living Wage," "Living Income," or "Socialism in Our Time" would at last be officially adopted. During the early months of the year, the policy was debated at all levels of the party, with Dollan reporting its unanimous endorsement by the Scottish divisional conference in January.[1] A few months later, it would be endorsed in outline by the whole party at its Easter annual conference. The commission responsible for the report then set out to produce a final version in time for the Labour Party conference in the autumn.

The Living Wage Commission and Its Critics

Although, as we have seen, Clifford Allen had begun pressing for the adoption of a national Living Wage policy in 1924, he was not formally a member of the ILP commission.[2] The authors of *The Living Wage* report were H. N. Brailsford, J. A. Hobson, A. Creech Jones, and E. F. Wise. They were all, as Paton later insisted, "men with a high sense of responsibility, wide knowledge, a good practical sense."[3] Wise's background was that of a Cambridge-educated senior civil servant. During the First World War, he had been assistant director of Army Contracts and, later, second secretary to the Ministry of Food. He was the British representative on the Allies' Supreme Economic Council. A committed cooperator, he was instrumental in re-establishing trade with Russia through the soon-to-be Bolshevized union of consumer cooperatives, or Centrosoyus, for which he worked for a period.[4] In 1929, the Manchester Co-operative Union would publish his *Consumers' Co-operation in Soviet Russia*. He would be a Labour MP from 1929 to 1931.

Arthur Creech Jones shared with Wise both his civil service background and a later—but much longer—career as a Labour MP. His stance as a wartime conscientious objector precluded his return to the civil service. In 1926, he was a national officer of the Transport and General Workers' Union, formed a few years earlier by the amalgamation of several smaller unions. Hobson was, of course, well-known chiefly for his economic writings, while Brailsford, a distinguished journalist and writer since before the war, was still the editor of the *New Leader*.

The novelty of the commission's report would lie not in its individual features but in their combination into a coherent strategy that the ILP, as the forward-looking nucleus, could offer to the Labour Party. Allen thought that the ILP should adopt the distinctive program, insisting that it could be pursued by the next Labour government—whether majority or minority.

Writing in the *New Leader* on New Year's Day 1926, Brailsford was clear that there was nothing new about the main objective of the Living Wage project. It was only the proposal for children's allowances that was not already "part of orthodox Labour doctrine."[5] This part of the Living Wage, or Living Income, policy was to become the most controversial issue for the trade unions.[6] But it was not a new idea either. Eleanor Rathbone's book *The Disinherited Family* had appeared in 1924. Brailsford, characterized by Rathbone's colleague and first biographer, Mary Stocks, as a "pioneer advocate of family allowances," had worked with Rathbone during the war as part of what became her Family Endowment Committee.[7]

Labour MP Hugh Dalton mentioned her book approvingly when he wrote to the *New Leader* disclaiming any intention of getting involved in the wider debate on the Living Wage issue but praising the advocacy of children's allowances as a "bold proposal towards 'distribution according to need' on a vaster scale and over a wider range than we have hitherto attempted."[8] Rathbone herself contributed a long letter a few weeks later in which she registered her disagreement with both Dalton and the ILP for rejecting what she saw as "necessary stepping stones towards a State scheme." Brailsford devoted that week's editorial to discussing her views on a contributory system while supporting "Miss Rathbone's plea for partial experiments, *e.g.* in supplementing teachers' salaries."[9]

The children's allowances proposals were to be incorporated in the new policy if separately approved by the ILP conference. In his article "Socialism in Our Generation: The 'Living Wage' as Lever," in the New Year's Day edition of the *New Leader*, Brailsford had explained that the allowances "varying with the number of persons in each household," were to be seen as a means of supplementing working-class incomes," through direct taxation. He suggested that the Labour Party should propose a commission to fix a living wage as "the minimum standard of civilised existence." It should not be deterred by its minority position; the responsibility for rejecting the socialist measures proposed should be placed on Labour's opponents. As well as Brailsford's article, the first *New Leader* of 1926 featured an article by the Labour MP for Penistone, Rennie Smith, called "How Capitalism Kills Markets: The 'Living Wage' Means Work."[10]

The paper also marked the new year by publishing an ILP manifesto demanding what its title declared: "A Frontal Attack on Poverty." The manifesto explained that "the I.L.P. sees in the 'Living Wage' a first demand for justice." But logic, the manifesto argued, would lead rapidly to a socialist state. Prices must be controlled if any increases in money wages were not to be worthless. That meant a national banking system controlling credit, the nationalization of the import of raw materials and food, and, given the needs of industry for cheap transport and "mechanical power," the "nationalisation as coordinated services of railways, mines and electrical generation." This was to be accompanied by the reorganization of agriculture, the "public ownership of land," and the "national organisation of the building industry and of the production of building materials."[11]

Promotion of the Living Wage policy relied not solely on words. From time to time, it would be the theme of a cartoon by "Flambo" on the front page of the *Leader*. In January, Flambo featured a picnicking family, threatened by black clouds marked "Hunger and Poverty," taking shelter under a "Living Wage" umbrella, with the words "And we want it now" at the bottom. In April, the paper featured another Flambo cartoon, captioned "A 'Living Wage' Is So Bracing"—a play on the classic railway poster that promoted an English east coast resort town with the tag line "Skegness Is So Bracing." Yet another, headed "The Living Wage Keeps the Wolf from the Door," appeared in October.[12]

But not everyone in the ILP was braced by the Living Wage proposal. An early critic was Ellen Wilkinson. The ILP may have intended the policy to be an "energising myth," she wrote, but once it came to fixing it in "definite figures," it would be equated with union-weakening trade boards that set rates in some low-wage industries and "set everyone quarrelling about the details of something that is a myth, and, as I believe, not even an energising myth." Brailsford's editorial response argued that the "chief novelty" of the policy was the "reversal of the usual order of thought." The orthodox method was "to preach and enforce nationalisation first, trusting to its effects to bring about a better distribution of wealth." Why, as Wilkinson's page-long article had asked, "go to Birmingham by way of Beachy Head" like Chesterton's "rolling English drunkard?" Responded Brailsford, "For the sound psychological reason, that to the average man the landscape of

Beachy Head is more attractive than Snow Hill"—one of the Birmingham railway stations.[13]

Nationalization was not the only means to a "good life" for which a living wage would provide a minimum basis, Brailsford continued. "We propose the 'Living Wage' partly because it makes a concrete appeal to the average man, partly because it would bring stimulus to industry, above all, because the effort to secure it must direct our attack to the keys of economic power."[14]

Ellen Wilkinson was a formidable critic. Once a founding member of the British Communist Party, she was by this time a Labour MP. But a critic with an even higher profile was the leader of the Labour Party himself.

MacDonald and Brailsford: Locking Horns over the Living Wage Policy

Ramsay MacDonald's wrath was directed not merely at the report *The Living Wage* but, even more fundamentally, at the role that the ILP had assumed—or so it seemed to many ILPers. At the end of February 1926, the weekly editorial in the *New Leader* responded to MacDonald's recent criticisms in the *Socialist Review*. Brailsford complained that the party leader had not criticized *The Living Wage* or other, specific, ILP policies: "His case is that no group within the Labour Party has the right to suggest any programme at all. That, in his view, is the prerogative of the Parliamentary Party." The ILP was not trying to give orders to the Labour Party, Brailsford protested. If the ILP approved *The Living Wage* report, the next step would be to submit it to the Labour Party conference. Was the ILP to have no role in setting Labour's program? In a direct challenge to MacDonald's leadership style, Brailsford declared, "It is not great leadership which seeks to check the initiative and arrest the thinking of a democratic party."[15]

Brockway would later recall the beginning of this conflict between MacDonald and Brailsford. He had "never quite understood" MacDonald's haste in rushing to condemn the Living Wage policy: "MacDonald's reaction was a cruel disappointment to Allen. Allen always held MacDonald in high esteem and I believe he really hoped that Britain's first Labour Prime Minister could be won to acceptance of his socialist philosophy and programme. Brailsford and MacDonald got into bitter conflict over the report, but never Allen and MacDonald."[16] The issue of MacDonald's attitude would not go away. On 16 March, the *New Leader* featured "The Transition to Socialism: A Reply to Mr. MacDonald by the Editor," in which Brailsford complained about the "unpleasant surprise" of the tone of MacDonald's attacks on *The Living Wage* in recent editions of *Forward* and the *Socialist Review*. MacDonald appeared to be claiming that policy was the province only of "those who exercise executive responsibility in Parliament. That is a claim which the two older parties might allow. It is a novel doctrine in the Labour Party."[17]

Brailsford's interpretation seemed to be confirmed by MacDonald's article "The Work of the I.L.P.: Its Relation to the Labour Party" in *Forward* a fortnight later. The scope of the ILP was, the Labour Party leader insisted, "wide and fertile." But it should not "strive to be ahead of the Labour Party in its manifestoes and resolutions upon Parliamentary tactics." And, in what was bound to look like an attempt to divide the potential opposition, MacDonald praised "those who have been working at the Birmingham financial programme, or the stabilisation problem."[18]

At the beginning of April, Brailsford began his *New Leader* editorial "Mr. MacDonald as Critic" by expressing regret that MacDonald had not accepted the *New Leader*'s invitation to state his case but had instead renewed his attack on *The Living Wage* in *Forward*. He denied that the authors of the report intended that the Living Wage policy was to be brought about by simple "statutory enactment" or that it proposed to nationalize "all the decrepit failures of industry," as MacDonald was claiming. The role of the "suitably constituted authority" to determine the level of the wage would often be "persuasive rather than coercive." Neither "prosperity nor poverty" should determine nationalization, which should be directed at industries that "control the life and shape the development of every other industry—banking, the import of raw materials and staple foods, coal, electricity and the railways."[19]

He could, however, "warmly agree" with MacDonald's praise of Hobson. "His economic teaching is the starting point of our policy," wrote Brailsford; "he has given it his support in these columns, and is an active member of the Commission which is working it out in detail." But the most "startling thing" about MacDonald's comments," he continued, was the "commendation of the 'fine work' of those who have drafted 'the Birmingham financial programme.' To the extent of four-fifths, or thereabouts, this programme is identical to our own," he concluded. "It differs only in taking a view of the uses of credit which, to our more conservative minds, seems a little reckless. Is it really possible that by taking a less orthodox view of credit we could win Mr. MacDonald's approval for our policy?"[20]

Nor did MacDonald have it all his own way in the pages of *Forward*. The day after Brailsford's editorial came out, Dollan, who was not destined to be one of the rebels of the ILP, as we shall see in later chapters, was clearly not at all happy with MacDonald's position. "Does he mean us to infer that the I.L.P. has no right to make comments on the actions of the Labour Party in Parliament?" he asked.[21] By this time, the ILP annual conference was about to open at Whitley Bay. In its report on the conference the following week, *Forward* noted, "MacDonald, perhaps wisely, chose to stay away."[22]

The 1926 ILP Conference: "A New Chapter in Our Party's History"

Jowett, acting as temporary chairman following Allen's resignation, addressed the Whitley Bay conference. His speech was later published as *Socialism in Our Time*, which was how the proposed new policy was coming to be known.[23] It was under this title that Brailsford moved approval for *The Living Wage* report, expressing regret that Allen, "who inspired the policy," was not there to do so. Brailsford used the same title for his editorial the week following the conference, which had, he said, "opened a new chapter in our Party's history." A "Socialism in Our Time Campaign Fund" was then announced and donation slips distributed, to be completed and returned with cheque or postal order.[24]

At the beginning of the conference, Jowett, like Brailsford in his mover's speech, paid tribute to Allen. He insisted that the ILP was fulfilling its purpose; it was doing "pioneer work, work for Socialism." Turning to *The Living Wage* report, he went on:

> We propose that the Labour Movement put its whole power behind this demand and make it the supreme issue both in the political and the industrial worlds. We suggest that the Labour Party and the General Council of the T.U.C. should unite in declaring that they will not tolerate the standard of existence of the workers, whether they are employed or unemployed, remaining below a definite measure of human needs.

The "first big step" would be children's allowances, but later measures must include "national control of banking, money, transport, land, electrical power, and the importation of foodstuffs and raw materials." He ended with an exhortation: "Let us go boldly forward, Socialism in Our Time! Internationalism in Our Time! That is our aim."[25]

The proposals in *The Living Wage* report, presented as work in progress to be finalized in detail by the commission, were carried by an "overwhelming majority," with only two delegates voting against the addendum on children's allowances.[26] Both Strachey and Mosley took part in the debate. Strachey intervened on the question of banking and imports, having withdrawn an amendment in exchange for a guarantee that he would be allowed to speak. He complained that no real credit policy was outlined by the NAC, and until that was done, it was useless to go on with a Living Wage policy.[27]

For his part, Mosley stressed that the proposed commission to establish the policy was the "key," along with the issue of demand. *Forward* reported that Mosley had urged a "more drastic financial policy" and had suggested that "a crisis might come in which the slogan of the Socialist Movement might have to be changed from 'Socialism in Our Time' to 'Socialism Today.'"[28] Indeed, a crisis was nearer than even Mosley may have anticipated. Less than a month after the ILP conference at the beginning of April, the General Strike had begun.

The ILP and the General Strike

The General Strike of 1926 arose out of the seemingly interminable conflicts of the coal industry. It was triggered when the mine owners decided to impose new terms involving longer hours of work and major reductions in pay. When negotiations broke down, the General Council of the TUC called its affiliated unions out on strike in solidarity with the miners. The strike lasted from just before midnight on 3 May until 12 May, when it was called off by the TUC, leaving the miners to struggle on for six months and eventually to be forced to accept the harsh conditions imposed by the employers. Many on the Left believed that the strike had been gaining ground when it was terminated, and some thought that it had had revolutionary potential.

Because the print unions had been asked to join the strike, the *New Leader*, along with all other newspapers, including the Labour-supporting *Daily Herald*, was not published during the strike. Later, Brockway concluded that calling out the print unions was a "big tactical mistake" by the TUC, since it essentially silenced the press and gave the government a monopoly in how the strike was reported. Indeed, the government immediately established and distributed its own bulletin, the *British Gazette*, which was used as propaganda against the strike. The TUC, in response, produced its own strike bulletin, the *British Worker*, but the government managed to block the TUC's paper supply, thus reducing the bulletin from the planned eight pages to one.[29]

Like the rest of the Left, the ILP was actively involved in the strike. Brockway tells of his efforts to keep the *British Worker* going. He is critical not only of the TUC leadership, saying that his "first reaction was that the T.U.C. General Council had become either demoralised or corrupted," but also of some other labour movement bodies.[30] He recounts how he phoned the TUC to put the ILP's printing works at its disposal, only to be told that the Typographical Society, one of the print unions, was "raising difficulties." He asks, "Was this a general strike or a general do-as-you please?" and says that he was shocked to learn that the directors of the Co-operative Printing Society had refused to help because the strike had halted their regular business.[31] How much of this reflects later hindsight and how much his views during the conflict is difficult to assess.[32]

The first edition of the *New Leader* following the strike was, as one would expect, largely devoted to news, commentary, and analysis of the event. It appeared on 21 May and included both an article by Brockway, "The I.L.P. Does Its Bit," and Bertrand Russell's rejection of the "unsound" government argument that the General Strike was "undemocratic." The following week, the paper featured "The I.L.P. in the General Strike," which was followed in the next two editions by the two-part "The Secret Story of the Strike," written by A. J. Cook, general secretary of the miners' union and an ILP member.[33] Near the end of the year, the paper published a letter from Cook, which began "We Shall Never Forget the Generosity of the I.L.P." The same issue reported that the ILP Miners' Relief Fund had reached £8,672.[34]

What effect the strike had on the ILP in general and the promotion of the Living Wage/Socialism in Our Time policy is very difficult to determine. The collapse of the TUC's resolve and the appalling suffering of the locked-out miners and their families were demoralizing for the Left and added to the sense of frustration with a Labour Party seen to have stood impotently on the sidelines.

But did failure on the "industrial" side focus attention back onto the "political"? As ever, there was a wide range of reactions to the strike, but certainly for many, the experience had demonstrated the limits of direct action and reinforced the belief that *some* variety of political action, be it reformist or revolutionary, was a much more promising way forward. Having played its minor part in the strike, the main task set by the ILP was to propagate its new policy and, above all, to persuade the Labour Party to adopt it. From the standpoint of the ILP, the General Strike had been caused precisely by the mineowners' refusal to pay a living wage.

Controversy over the Living Wage Continues

Even before the General Strike, arguments over MacDonald's attitude towards *The Living Wage* report had rumbled on. Emrys Hughes's *Forward* article, "The Lost Leader," asked what the Labour leader's alternative policy was. A week later, a *New Leader* letter from Frank Hall of the Southall ILP branch criticized MacDonald for "ridiculing all our efforts in *Forward*" instead of arguing his case at the ILP conference. Mary Sutherland struck back the very next day in *Forward*. She complained about the tendency she detected in the ILP for "snarling at MacDonald."[35]

MacDonald's critics were at least as focused on his dismissive tone as on the substance of his rejection of *The Living Wage*. The Labour leader had told *Forward* readers that he was "grieved to the quick that the poor old I.L.P. seems to be making itself ridiculous, and I am too good an I.L.Per to keep silent. These tactics will never be pursued whilst any Parliamentary Party cares twopence about socialism. And that's that." Hughes, on the same page of the paper, described this as "a caustic and contemptuous attack on the I.L.P." in "one short superficial paragraph."[36]

Brailsford was not impressed with "Mr. MacDonald's Alternative," and in a *New Leader* editorial that appeared in August, Brailsford welcomed MacDonald's proposal for workers' control of separate industries. However, he added, "one might entrench workers firmly within the governing body of each organised industry only to then realise that "a stronger power must control the masters of their masters." The socialization of banking and of the import of raw materials was vital.[37]

In July, *Forward* published an article under the headline "A Half-Way House to Socialism: The Admissions of J. M. Keynes." In the *New Leader*, Brailsford was just as keen to claim at least a degree of support from the radical Liberal economist whose *The End of Laissez-Faire* he welcomed. He noted that Keynes was aligned with the ILP in advocating "the deliberate control of currency and credit by a central institution." No one's support would be more welcome, Brailsford continued. "The more clearly we define our own aims to include this directive use of intelligence for the common good, the more surely we shall rally men who believe in the positive tasks of civilisation."[38] In a lecture at the ILP summer school that year, however, Keynes showed that he was certainly not entirely at one with ILP thinking. Brockway's report notes that his characterization of the subsidizing of declining industries as "reactionary" generated much debate.[39]

The first extracts from the final version of *The Living Wage* report appeared in the *New Leader* at the beginning of October, and a week later, Brailsford described his anticipation of the policy's reception at the Labour Party conference in Margate the following week:

> We feel confident, in spite of the curiously ill-tempered and careless criticism with which our plan was first received, that Conference cannot dismiss it as a suggestion unworthy of study. The name of J. A. Hobson among the signatories should alone avail to save it from that fate. We believe we have met, by slight modifications, the able criticisms which Miss Ellen Wilkinson made, while it was still a draft sketch. The people who dismiss it as "mere Liberalism" will doubtless be undeceived when the Liberal Press unmasks its batteries.

The report's proposals were not "catastrophic" and would destroy nothing but poverty, he added. "It aims at the general good; its purpose is to trace a path through prosperity to Socialism."[40]

Ironically, in light of events still a few years in the future when he was again Chancellor of the Exchequer, the most prominent leveller of the charge of "mere Liberalism" was Philip Snowden. Brailsford took on his argument in "Socialism and the 'Living Wage': A Reply to Mr. Snowden." He conceded that the "transfer to social ownership and control" of banking, the import of raw materials, the "direction of the flow of new capital," and the rest did not amount to socialism. Yet he insisted that the "conquest of economic power" meant that though private enterprise "might survive for a generation, the general direction of industry and the ability to control it, even to dictate to it, would be in the hands that governed the key services." But he agreed with Snowden in rejecting Maxton's proposal of demanding a 20 percent all-around wage increase:

> Apart from the impossibility of getting so much in one instalment without inflation, this plan sets up no standard of civilised human life. Worse still, it leaves uncorrected the shocking inequalities that now obtain in the wages of different trades. It is not a general percentage increase we should demand, but rather the levelling up of the wages of the depressed trades to some standard based on human need.[41]

Brailsford, at least, was not entirely dejected by the Labour Party conference's failure to support the ILP policy. His first report on the proceedings was headlined "Drifting Back to Politics," and the following week, he noted that there had been considerable support for the ILP's proposals for an inquiry into children's allowances. At the same time, his antagonism towards MacDonald was very evident. "Mr. MacDonald shrugged his shoulders and contrived in words, gestures, and tones, to convey something of the disdain he feels for our proposals," he reported.[42]

Plainly, there was a significant personal element involved in the conflict between MacDonald and Brailsford. Leventhal cites the former's criticisms in *Forward* and Brailsford's *New Leader* comments in April, in which he accused MacDonald of interpreting the ILP policy in a distorted way. He concludes, "MacDonald had begun to denigrate the ILP programme. Despite his sympathy for Hobsonian economics—and affection for Hobson—he resented efforts by the ILP to foist its visionary policy on the Labour Party as a whole and immediately perceived Brailsford as the culprit."[43] MacDonald's antagonism reinforced his determination to have nothing to do with *The Living Wage*. Marquand quotes an April 1926 letter from MacDonald to Paton in which the former declares, "I can speak at no conference to popularise absolutely meaningless phrases and to mislead the whole Socialist movement."[44]

There were, of course, other critics of the Living Wage—or, as it was increasingly called, the Living Income—policy on the Left. Hugh Dalton, as a former student of Keynes might have been expected to be supportive, but he thought that, like the Mosley-Strachey proposals, it would prove to be inflationary if implemented.⁴⁵ *Labour's Northern Voice*, the organ of the Lancashire ILP, showed little enthusiasm for the new policy. After the national ILP conference in April 1926, its regular columnist, "Vox," had praised its "stirring introduction," which had "reflected the opinion of every thoughtful member of the working class." But the paper's editor expressed doubt about putting "the living income in the forefront of the programme." Presumably, he surmised, the NAC believed that "the living-income slogan" would be "the inspiring cry which will solidify the working class and drive it forward to take power in its own hands." However, there would have to be "yet another Commission to define *what is* a living income," and this would "leave the working class cold." The ILP would do better to keep pushing for "the full Socialist policy." At the end of the year, in the paper's "Comments and Criticisms," it was argued that the policy was helpful only "if we intend to legislate for Socialism in earnest at the first opportunity. We do not want to admit bankruptcy of ideas by resorting to a 'stunt.'"⁴⁶

So, in spite of the endorsement of the Living Wage proposals at the national ILP conference in the spring of 1926, the policy remained controversial within the Party. In time it would become clear that even those who supported it had radically different interpretations of its meaning and its implications. Before exploring this, however, we need to take a closer look at *The Living Wage* report.

9

Pursuing the Living Wage Policy

The main elements of *The Living Wage* report, those we saw developing in the last two chapters, are succinctly summarized by Marquand in his biography of MacDonald:

> It advocated a system of family allowances paid for by taxation, the nationalization of the Bank of England, to secure state control of credit and monetary policy, and Government bulk purchase of foodstuffs and raw materials. But these were only the trimmings. The core of the report was a proposal to introduce a national minimum wage and to set up an Industrial Commission to reorganise the industries unable or unwilling to pay it. The resources needed to finance the higher wages, the report emphasized, could not come from taxation. They would come instead from the increased production which higher wages would call forth. For higher wages would lead to higher consumption; and the "pressure of higher consumption" as Hobson called it, would force industry to produce more wealth and employ extra labour. With one blow, the "Living Wage" would solve the unemployment problem and raise working class living standards to a tolerable level.[1]

A "New Development"

James Maxton was, of course, quite correct when he told the 1926 Whitley Bay conference delegates that there was nothing new about the proposals made in *The Living Wage*. The individual elements that made up the report were indeed familiar. They had been "outlined in Clifford Allen's address at York, and came up for discussion at Gloucester," he said, referring to the 1924 and 1925 ILP conferences.[2] But a lack of real understanding seems evident in Maxton's comment in *Forward* that though Brailsford, in his motion to accept *The Living Wage*, had said that it marked "a new development," in practice the ILP had "always taken the main ideas for granted."[3] This missed what was essential.

As we have already seen, the individual constituents of the policy may have lacked novelty; what was new was the degrees of emphasis placed on them and, above all, the way they were linked into a seemingly coherent strategy. As noted in chapter 7, Brailsford claimed that the significance of the policy lay in "reversing the order of thought and action."[4] His article, "Socialism in Our Generation: The 'Living Wage' as Lever" had developed this point in early 1926. "Strangers who watch our movement often liken it to 'religion,'" he wrote. "The analogy is dangerously true." The Living Wage policy was "a simple human demand, which must carry with it, if we can stir the ambitions and stimulate the thinking of the average worker and his wife, assent to all the rest." The reaction of those working-class families to proposals for giving priority to, for example, bank nationalization, were likely to be cold, bewildered, and skeptical.[5] This point was reiterated in *The Living Wage* report itself:

> We have dealt rather with the economic plan than the politics of this transition. But it is evident that this policy has the merit of making a simple and concrete appeal to the average worker and his wife. Family Allowances and a "Living Wage" touch them in their daily experience of life. Once their attention is concentrated on these things, the rest of the scheme will enlist their defensive instincts.[6]

The idea was to begin with this "simple and concrete" appeal, which would have had a much wider constituency than socialist ideology. The report began with a section under the subheading "The Place of Wages in Labour Strategy." We should note here, especially, the word *strategy*. The widespread acceptance of the claim that industry should pay a living wage to all engaged in it was the report's starting point. This has, it said, "become in our generation an ethical principle, accepted as one of the foundations of our civilisation. Neither of the capitalist parties venture to dispute it." The principle was implicit in all wage disputes; the General Strike had been against employers who "defied" it and, however inadequately, the principle also lay behind the setting up of trade boards for "sweated" industries.[7]

The Contents of *The Living Wage* Report

Although the report assumed that securing the goal of an adequate income for all would eventually lead to the public ownership of major industries, this was not an immediate objective. Nationalization in conditions of economic depression would result in Labour facing either the subsidizing of "uneconomic" railways and mines or a great increase in unemployment in a time of low wages and mass unemployment. "If, on the other hand, it were possible by any means to promote an upward movement in wages generally and so to stimulate trade, the problem of nationalisation would be immensely simplified."⁸ For successful nationalization, the report argued, either a "boom" or "some expedient" to create general prosperity was essential. Raising wages by industrial action would mean short-term price increases, and unions would soon discover that even if they were able to control individual industries, they would find standing behind them "the mechanism of banking and credit control." Price increases, if left uncontrolled, could quickly cancel out wage increases. Nevertheless, strong unions were essential, and Labour must bring about an understanding between "the two sides of the movement." That accomplished, the demand of four or five million voters would be reinforced by the "organised will of the Trade Unions."⁹

The second chapter of the report, on underconsumption, acknowledged its basis in Hobson's economic thought. The ethical considerations previously highlighted converged with economic necessities. Low wages meant a limitation of the home market and prevented the realization of the full benefits of mass production. Market expansion depended on the extension of "credit and currency" and the wider distribution of purchasing power, chiefly to the wage-earning class, in order to ensure that money was spent rather than saved. At the same time, the control of credit and "stabilisation of the general price level" were imperative, lest wage increases be cancelled out by rising prices. But the "surest way" to expand markets was "to increase the output of essential goods and services, through the reorganisation of industry for higher production."¹⁰

The next chapter dealt with credit and banking. Much work remained to be done "on the Quantity Theory of Money," but the aim must be "to abolish the Trade Cycle, or at least to limit it to harmless and barely perceptible oscillations." It was vital to choose the right point in the trade cycle to pursue stabilization of prices. The report referenced "the well-known books by Mr. Keynes and Mr. Hawtrey," as well as E. M. H. Lloyd's International Labour Organization report, *Stabilisation* and *Unemployment in Its National and International Aspects*. The ILO report proposed the nationalization of the Bank of England with a charter committing it to the achievement of a stable price level on the model of the Federal Reserve Board in the United States.¹¹

Eleanor Rathbone's *The Disinherited Family* featured in the chapter on family allowances, as did J. L. Cohen's *Family Income Insurance* on estimating the annual cost of "a State scheme to be financed by direct taxation." The Australian experience was cited as a relevant precedent. The report rejected the notion that children's allowances would encourage a rise in the birth rate: "Reckless breeding is in fact a phenomenon of abject poverty. Every increase in comfort and self-respect makes for prudence and self-restraint."¹²

The fifth chapter urged the Labour Party's National Executive Committee and the TUC's General Council to set up a commission "to formulate in precise terms and figures the vague claim which is in all our minds." The result should allow for at least two weeks of holiday per year, and once again, the need for as wide a consensus as possible was stressed:

> Our purpose, then, is not to enforce by legislation a universal statutory minimum. We propose to start with the authoritative declaration of a minimum—a figure which the whole community formally accepts, and intends, within a measurable period to attain by the reorganisation of industry. When the official enquiry has resulted in the fixing of a figure, the next step might be the passing of a resolution by the House of Commons declaring that it is the nation's purpose to base its economic life on this figure.

The economic effect of the new purchasing power would be considerable and immediate. The trade unions were understandably concerned lest a minimum wage become a maximum in practice, so it was vital that they would "retain their freedom to bargain and their traditional functions." The Living Wage policy would not be imposed by the state, but the state would create the conditions in which unions could demand it "with every prospect of success." The report envisaged its regular upward revision. This might take place every five or ten years, increasing the wage level until it reached the point "at which an increase of leisure, and a deepening of its cultural life seemed more important than the effort to increase material prosperity."[13]

The final four chapters, preceding the conclusions, were titled "The Re-Organisation of Industry," "Prices and Raw Materials," "The Provision of Capital," and "The Export Trade." It was essential that "banking, coal mining, electrical supply and railways should be nationalised," but this needed little more explanation, since it had already been covered, in the case of mining by the Labour Party's *Coal and Common Sense* plan. As for other industries, an Industrial Commission should be appointed to reorganize them to increase efficiency. The commission's chief and possibly only power would be to "enforce the amalgamation of businesses."[14]

On imports of raw materials and food, the report clearly drew on the wartime experience of E. F. Wise. The authors envisaged buying agencies "appointed by state but with close links to the industry concerned," which would enjoy a monopoly for the import of the materials concerned. There might also be a "National Industrial Bank" of a decentralized kind, which would claim representation on governing boards where it invested. It would "become one of the most powerful means by which the penetration and control of industry can be promoted." The Industrial Commission and the councils of nationalized services would become "the planning and directive centre of the nation's industrial life." As regards exports, the report stressed the importance of arriving at international agreements and pointed out that underconsumption "operates beyond our own island" in, for example, India and Kenya.[15]

The report concluded by urging that the difficulties of carrying out the plan should not be underestimated and that the parliamentary tactics were the province of the Parliamentary Labour Party. Earlier points about the priority to be given to stimulating prosperity were re-emphasized:

> We advance our policy as an alternative and antithesis to a catastrophic strategy. It aims at creating general prosperity, and only in this atmosphere of well-being would a party that embraced it attempt large constructive changes. Taking care before it joined the hotly-contested issues of nationalisation, to stimulate the nation's trade, it would then approach its more contentious work with the public in a mood of optimism and good temper.[16]

Prosperity was, in other words, an essential prerequisite to winning support for a more far-reaching socialist program.

The Significance of *The Living Wage*

The Living Wage report would stand the test of time relatively well. During the nine decades since its publication, few have echoed MacDonald's contemptuous dismissal. From Keith Middlemas, who referred to it in the 1960s as "probably the strongest weapon in the whole ILP armoury," to Andrew Thorpe, who, in 2001, called it "a useful contribution to a wider debate," to Matthew Worley, who discusses it in *Labour Inside the Gate* (2005), historians have taken the idea seriously.[17] The revival of the report's central demand in the Living Wage campaign of early twenty-first-century Britain also suggests a continuing political relevance.[18]

Brockway, whose enthusiasm for *The Living Wage* waned considerably in the 1930s, still saw it as a work in progress when he was writing his memoir *Towards Tomorrow* in the 1970s. "The report was a notable document," he declares, "extraordinarily relevant as I write fifty years later. It included a national minimum wage for all, the socialisation of what Nye Bevan afterwards termed 'the commanding heights of the economy,' workers' participation in management, national control of investment and import and export boards to balance foreign exchanges."[19] Marquand, in his 1977 biography of MacDonald, published the same year as Brockway's memoir, declared it "a milestone in the history of the British Left," going on to explain its significance:

> In spite of oversimplifications and gaps in the argument, it pointed the way to the managed welfare capitalism which was to transform most of the western world after 1945: in approach, if not in detail, it offered the Labour movement at least the basis of a reformist alternative, both to revolutionary Marxism and to its existing unhappy mixture of utopian aspiration and fiscal orthodoxy.[20]

There are certainly features of the report that point in the direction that Marquand indicates. The authors were always keen to cite precedents—not from the postrevolutionary USSR but from distinctly prerevolutionary sources. Some have already been noted, such as the Australian example of child endowment, which was an issue in that country in the mid-1920s, especially in New South Wales. Other references in the report include the suggestions that the wartime Excess Profits Duty might be revived, that the German model could serve in some respects as a guide for the proposed National Industrial Bank, and that the recent Samuel Commission on the coal industry was a Tory precedent "for the re-organisation of a defaulting industry."[21]

The proposal for state agencies to buy essential raw materials and foodstuffs was similarly supported by recalling the "notable success during the war in the case of wool, edible oils and other important raw materials." The report added that Switzerland had continued "on permanent lines since the war" in the case of wheat.[22] The backwardness of British industry was another theme. In a *New Leader* editorial in April 1926, Brailsford had cited the Balfour Commission's finding that real wages in New York were double those in Britain.[23]

The "inevitability of gradualism" had already acquired a bad name in the ILP, but the party was adamant, at this stage at least, about rejecting cataclysmic change. *The Living Wage*, having called for the nationalization of the Bank of England, conceded that other banks might be difficult to nationalize. "Some intermediate solution might be considered, which would assimilate them to public utility corporations, and give the Government some representation on their governing bodies." And it noted as one of the gains attendant on successful price stabilization that the small investor's savings would become less risky.[24]

David Howell says of the ILP commission that produced *The Living Wage* that the group "epitomized the blend of progressive liberalism and ILP ethical socialism that characterized Allen's hopes for the Left."[25] There was certainly support for *some* openness towards Liberals in Hobson's *New Leader* article "Liberals and Labour: The Acid Test" in early 1926. He saw no reason why what he called the "anti-imperialist wing" of Liberalism should not support *The Living Wage* based upon family needs, "which is the true foundation of a sound economic Socialism." The acid test was the nationalization proposals.

But why, he asked, "should a modern Liberal prefer to leave these services to be organised by private trusts or combines for profiteering instead of organising them for the gain of the community?"[26]

Brailsford, too, was open to at least a degree of co-operation with Liberals and others outside the labour movement. As noted earlier, he supported Jowett's proposals for parliamentary committees and proportional representation. This was to come to the fore again in 1929, nearly three years after the publication of *The Living Wage*. At that time, Brailsford was still a fairly regular contributor to the *New Leader*, although he had resigned as its editor in October 1926. This 1929 episode is quite a revealing one. It began after the Labour Party had achieved minority government office once more, and there was considerable speculation about possible deals with the Liberals. While Brailsford was at pains to reject the idea of any formal agreement with the latter, he advocated Labour's participating in an open "conference" with them and offering support for proportional representation or at least the alternative vote. He noted that what he called the "genuine party man" hoped, by refusing "this elementary measure of justice," to "crush the Liberals." This seemed to him "to be deeply immoral and anti-democratic," for it denied about five million voters parliamentary representation. Brailsford also wanted "informal and friendly consultation of men outside our ranks who command respect by their knowledge and experience" on a wider range of issues. "We might," he insisted, "avoid making many a mistake by listening to Mr. Keynes on questions of currency and credit." However, a *New Leader* editorial note registered disagreement with much of Brailsford's argument.[27]

A few weeks later, a front-page *New Leader* article by Ellen Wilkinson praised MacDonald for rightly rejecting "the discredited imbecilities of proportional representation." In the same issue appeared Brailford's "Crush or Convert?" in which he returned to his earlier argument and claimed that opposing proportional representation meant returning to the "two party system." This would mean "the gradual approximation of the two parties, for it means the liberalising of both of them."[28] He again made his argument for proportional representation and for an "open conference" with Liberals at the ILP summer school at Welwyn. The conference took place, but Brailsford seems to have gained little support.

Brockway supported Brailsford on electoral reform, but Maxton "frankly expressed his disappointment that the main author of the 'Socialism in Our Time' programme should now be urging a Labour-Liberal agreement." Maxton caused some amusement by defining his attitude to proportional representation with the simple statement "I agree with Mr. Ramsay MacDonald," while Shinwell concluded, "Two years ago H.N.B. was the intellectual leader of the

Left; now he wants an understanding with the Liberals!"[29] On these issues, Brailsford was very much in the minority within the ILP.

A "Living Wage" or "Socialism in Our Time"?

Hobson's and Brailsford's positive attitudes towards exploring possible common ground with Liberals was just a particular instance of a wider divergence—or, at the very least, of an important difference of emphasis—within the ILP. This was summed up by the alternative titles of the ILP's new policy. Calling it the "Living Wage" or, as it soon came to be preferred, the "Living Income" stressed Brailsford's "reversing the order of thought and action" by emphasizing the wide appeal of the demand. True, the belief was that the logic of events would mean that serious pursuit of an adequate income for all would trigger all the other changes outlined in the report. As A. J. P. Taylor puts it, underlying the Living Wage policy was the agenda that "the attack on poverty should be accelerated, though with the hope that capitalism might be ruined in the exertion."[30]

"'Socialism in our time.' How the phrase thrills one," wrote Sydney R. Elliott at the beginning of his ILP pamphlet *Co-operation and Socialism*, published at the end of 1926.[31] Certainly, it made a stirring slogan—for socialists. But if the Living Income policy was to be seen simply as a device to justify translating private ownership into public ownership, the wider appeal was likely to be diminished. Soon the policy became, as David Howell puts it, "blurred." He notes that Maxton and others interpreted it in a way that pushed their own agendas. Maxton also added, as Worley says, a "sense of urgency and militancy."[32]

Marquand notes the ambiguity of the living wage notion in terms of its political and economic underpinnings:

> Before the commission had finished its work ... the concept of the "Living Wage" had acquired political overtones, which were, at bottom, incompatible with the economic assumptions on which the report was based. As Hobson saw it, the point of the "Living Wage" was to eliminate the "under-consumption" which he had always regarded as the root cause of unemployment. Once that had been done, the system would operate in the old way (though with the help of new machinery), and obey the old laws. Implicitly, if not explicitly, the report's economic proposals were based on the premises that capitalism could be made to work, that the extra resources that were needed to raise the standard of living of the wage earner could, and would, be produced by the normal processes of capitalist economics once the capitalists knew that there was a market for their products.[33]

The key word here is "implicitly." Leventhal seems much closer to the mark when he concludes, "Whether managed welfare capitalism could provide a 'Living Wage' or whether it was feasible only under socialism was never settled. Brailsford himself alternated between the two, depending on his audience, but seemed increasingly disposed to maintain that the 'Living Wage' need not await a complete socialist transformation."[34]

Brailsford certainly thought that divisions within capitalism should be exploited by the Left. In 1928, he wrote that "it should be our task to bring into the open the continuous secret struggle between the entrenched forces of the *rentier* interest, with the banks as their leaders, and the scattered and ignorant forces of industry."[35] His own interpretation of the policy he had done so much to devise and to propagate became clearer in a series of articles titled "From Chaos to Order," which appeared in the *New Leader* towards the end of 1930. Essentially, they amounted to a restatement of *The Living Wage* report. He acknowledged that he, and the ILP generally, had encountered more opposition than expected. "When we drafted our programme, now many years ago," he wrote, "we may have over-estimated the agreement within the Movement of these fundamentals. We supposed that everyone accepted what is called the 'Under-Consumptionist Theory.'" The program proposed "a conscious and deliberately-planned transition to Socialist order." Brailsford tried to refine the rejection of gradualism: "we, too, are gradualists," he declared, if gradualism meant rejecting "a sudden cataclysmic rush" to socialism. Yet he rejected the gradualism that meant "a slow, unconscious, drift towards Socialism, down the sluggish stream of history, without rudder or oar."[36]

In the second instalment of "From Chaos to Order," which dealt with underconsumption, Brailsford cited Hobson's "valuable little book, 'Rationalisation and Unemployment.'"[37] "The Masters' Master," the third article (31 October), carried as a subheading "Socialise the Banks." This was followed in the next five weeks by articles revisiting the other areas of *The Living Wage* program; titles included "The Money Trust" (7 November), "Raising the Standard of Life" (14 November), "The Children's Share" (28 November), and "A National Food Service" (12 December). Brailsford's own view emerges most clearly in "The Seats of Power," the final article of the series, published on 19 December:

> For my part I would rather talk of socialisation than of nationalisation, and while I want to see fundamental things owned by the nation, I hope for great elasticity and a wide latitude for experiment in devising many methods by which production and exchange shall be carried out. There is room in my Utopia for Mr. Cole's Guilds, for the Liberals' 'public concern,' even for privately managed workshops and farms, provided we

maintain a firm, yet friendly, framework of control, stop the accumulation of wealth, and approach equality of income.

Socialism was "an historic struggle for the redistribution of power," he explained. Ownership and wealth mattered "chiefly because they confer power." He ended the article, and the series, by stressing again the practicality of a strategy that began from what he perceived to be the standpoint of the ordinary worker:

> It is, we believe, a workable programme; not merely because it has based itself on the economic realities of to-day, but also because it takes account of the daily needs and habitual thinking of the average worker. It summons him to struggle for a "Living Wage," but it teaches him, while he forms his ranks, that this goal can be won only by capturing the seats of power.[38]

This would not, however, be the ILP's direction of travel in the new decade. By the middle years of the 1930s, some of the once keenest supporters of *The Living Wage* were to insist that there had been an undesirable shift in its interpretation. They included its initiator, and now a peer and a supporter of MacDonald's National Labour Organisation, Clifford Allen. Marwick quotes a passage from Allen's 1934 book *Britain's Political Future*: "I once ventured to say," he recalled, "in a daring moment from the chair of the Independent Labour Party that we could see the end of extreme poverty and the foundation of a new social order during our lifetime. This statement has since become the slogan 'Socialism in our Time.'" What was "a well-founded scientific hope," he wrote, had been "wrecked by those who made a battle cry of what should have been a spiritual and intellectual development." Allen concluded by presenting his book as a "plea that we should resort to the task and method originally intended."[39]

Two years later, the former ILP general secretary, John Paton, arrived at a very similar judgment. "The original, balanced and carefully planned 'Living Income Programme' . . . had disappeared under the accretions with which it had been loaded (each more extreme than the last)," he wrote, "and now was embodied in the slogan 'Socialism in Our Time.' This represented now little that was stable or recognisable as a programme but expressed really an ever-fiercer impatience and an extreme militancy of spirit."[40]

"Socialism—with Speed": Revising the Living Wage Policy

In the meantime, the Living Income policy faced much criticism from those who saw themselves as guardians of the Left. In a 1927 pamphlet, W. T. Symons attacked the "adopted child of the vigorous, theoretic brain of the editor of 'The New Leader,'" asserting that "if the enemies of a good life for all had sat down to devise the destruction of the Socialist Movement in this country, they could not have hit upon a more perfect plan." Why had the authors of *The Living Wage* come to "abandon Socialism for this narrow objective?" The Living Wage proposals were "not revolutionary" but simply "a grandiose recital of ameliorative proposals." Symons emphasized how far short they had fallen: "They have forgotten that socialism came into being to supersede the wages system."[41] And as expected, the CPGB, now entering its most sectarian phase, was contemptuously dismissive of the Living Wage proposals.[42]

Within the ILP, greater emphasis was being put on the need to move rapidly forward, as is suggested by the title of Brockway's *Socialism—with Speed: An Outline of the I.L.P. "Socialism in Our Time" Proposals.* "Speed depends on the human will," he declared, combining this with the pessimistic assertion that "spiritual death is creeping upon the Labour movement."[43] Later, in July 1928, Brailsford was more in line with wider ILP opinion than he was over attitudes towards the Liberals when he expressed the party's disappointment with the *Labour and the Nation* policy statement of the Labour Party aimed at the coming election. He criticized the "trust in the Mond Conference"— the discussions with employers initiated by the TUC aimed at finding less confrontational resolutions to disputes. To "renounce by silence the weapon of State action—that is negligent timidity," he declared. As for *The Living Wage*, Labour's position seemed to be that "wages are the concern of the Trade Unions." In the same issue, while Ellen Wilkinson warned against division in the ranks, Brockway complained that the new Labour program included what he called "no plan for socialism" or for "the 'Living Wage.'"[44]

For the ILP, 1929 opened with plans to revise the Living Income policy so as to speed up its implementation—an entirely distant prospect given the failure of Labour to adopt it in the first place. As Brockway explained to *New Leader* readers, the revised policy would require a future Labour government to bring about a living income for all within two years. Such a government would determine the standard to be reached, immediately impose it throughout the public sector, and insist on adherence to it of all organizations with government contracts. There would be, Brockway emphasized, no toleration of "*less than a Living Income in any industry which is doing public work or receiving public assistance.*" Other industries would be given two years to fall into line.[45]

Criticisms of the Living Wage policy appeared in the letters to the paper in February and March. E. F. Wise, one of the original signatories of *The Living Wage* report, replied with the claim that "the Living Income policy as now worked out holds the field as a plan of campaign which will unite in one co-ordinated effort the fighting spirit and the resources of the Political, the Trade Union, and the Co-operative Movements."[46]

On the eve of the 1929 annual conference, Brockway, in a *New Leader* article, included *The Living Wage* report among the issues he wished to see discussed at the ILP conference. The party, he said, could be divided into two groups: those members who saw the policy as a "spearhead of the demand for the Socialist reorganisation of industry" and those who were prepared to settle, for the time being, for a lower "practical minimum."[47]

Opening the conference as chairman, Maxton told delegates that the Socialism in Our Time policy laid down three roads to be taken. The first, he said, was "the road of public ownership of Land, Mines, Transport, Banks"; the second was "lifting up the standards of life of the people"; and the third was the demand that "the working people of this country, through the Trade Union and Co-operative Movements should assume an increasing share in the control of and direction of industry." This was a rather different order of priorities from the ILP's position in 1926. It looked very much as though, for Maxton, Brailsford's "reversal of the usual order of thought," if it had ever meant anything to him, had now gone by the board. This raises the question of how well Maxton understood the significance of the strategy outlined in the Living Income/Socialism in Our Time policy as originally conceived or, if he understood it, to what extent he actually supported it.[48] These doubts are reinforced by some of Maxton's later statements. In what was described as his "Presidential Address" the following year, he outlined how, after 1923, a new policy "finally crystallised under the slogan 'Socialism in Our Time,' and was embodied in a series of practical steps which came to be known as the 'Living Income Policy.'" Maxton went on to distance himself from the original proposals:

> These plans were made before I became Chairman. I was not asked to discuss whether the I.L.P. should go on or not, I was not ask to define slogans for it or to lay down proposals for the speedy realisation of Socialism. I was asked to use my chairmanship to spread the idea of "Socialism in Our Time" by propaganda, to urge its acceptance, through the wider Labour Party, and to get it accepted by the nation. That is the task that I have tried honestly and sincerely to fulfil.

No doubt that was true. No one could fault the energy and sincerity of his endeavours, but the essence of the Living Income policy was its strategy; to Maxton it seemed to be simply a matter of slogans.[49]

In contrast to the Whitley Bay conference of 1926, where the original draft of the policy had been approved with virtually no opposition, the delegates at the conference three years later were split on the updated version, with substantial minorities favouring critical motions and amendments. Dollan had failed some weeks earlier, at the NAC meeting, in his motion that *The Living Wage* report be referred back for further consideration, losing the vote by 3 to 7. He did rather better at the conference: although he still lost, it was only by 131 to 183. There was less, but still significant, support for the motion by Allen Skinner of the London Central branch to reaffirm the original Whitley Bay version, which lost by 102 to 182. The amended report was finally accepted by 183 to 134.⁵⁰

Just how confused the evolution of the Living Wage, Living Income, or Socialism in Our Time policy was becoming is brought out well by Emrys Hughes, who, following the 1929 conference, attempted to explain the situation to readers of *Forward*:

> The original "Living Wage" proposals became mixed up with P. J. Dollan's advocacy of a £4 a week legal minimum and the Cook-Maxton campaign, while H. N. Brailsford, one of the drafters of the programme, in a fit of despair gave up hope of it being accepted by the Labour Party and came to the conclusion that the only thing left was a Labour agreement with Lloyd George. At the Norwich conference last year Dollan succeeded in carrying an amendment making the establishment of an immediate all-round minimum wage the first plank of the programme, whereas the Whitley Bay resolution had laid it down that this could only be achieved by the Socialist reorganisation of industry.
>
> As a result the National Council was instructed to present another report. This report, a twelve-page pamphlet, was presented to the conference by E. F. Wise who explained it had the unanimous support of the National Council, with the exception of Dollan.⁵¹

The ILP rejoiced in its openness, tolerance of dissent, and internal democracy—features that contrasted vividly with the state of affairs within the CPGB. There were always plenty of disagreements about all aspects of the ILP's work, but not since the departure of many of the members of the Left Wing group back in 1921 had there been such pronounced divisions within the party. At the same time, and intimately connected with these divisions, the tension between the ILP and the rest of the Labour Party seemed to be increasing inexorably.

By no means can all the responsibility for this be laid at the door of the ILP. MacDonald seemed to go out of his way to respond to the growing hostility from the Left by being as offensive as possible in return. It was his dismissal of ILP policies as "flashy futilities" in 1928 that caused the most—and longest lasting—offence. Once again, as with his earlier rejection of the Living Wage report in 1926, the tone and context offended as much, if not more, than the substance. MacDonald's column in *Forward* was an ostensibly light-hearted "diary." On this occasion, he described an encounter during a train journey with "a sprightly damsel, armed with field glasses and racing calendars," who expressed great appreciation for "Shaw's glorious book"—presumably The

Intelligent Woman's Guide to Socialism and Capitalism. MacDonald regretted that Shaw's "plain declarations of ultimate purposes are taken to support such absurdities as Socialism in our Time and its attending programme of flashy futilities." As the editor of *Forward* commented in the same issue,

> It is not difficult to understand outbursts of irritation at Party leaders when Mr. MacDonald in his article in this week's *Forward* calls the I.L.P.'s programme of "Socialism in Our Time" a "programme of flashy futilities" when nine-tenths of the alleged futilities have already been endorsed by the Labour Party conferences, and the whole lot of which he commended very warmly when they appeared under the pen of Sir Oswald Mosley.[52]

The disparaging term was greatly resented by ILPers and it seems to have stuck in many minds. Three years later, *Labour's Northern Voice* used "Flashy Futilities" as the title for an article.[53]

The Living Wage Bill of 1931—and After

In 1931, with the ILP seriously at odds with the second Labour government, Maxton was successful in the House of Commons ballot for the right to move a private member's bill. With the support of the ILP parliamentary group, this bill was introduced at the beginning of February 1931. "The I.L.P. 'Living Wage' Bill" proposed a committee comprising three working-class housewives, three trade union representatives, and three cooperative movement representatives; the committee was to determine what should constitute a living wage. It was to report within three months, setting a suitable figure.

There was never the remotest possibility that MacDonald's government would take up the bill or arrange for it to be given the parliamentary time needed to progress beyond the initial stage, let alone that a Commons majority could be secured. But Brockway reported that those voting for the bill included "many who desired to register support for the principle without any belief in its immediate application. No Cabinet minister voted, but the Chief Whips, five junior Whips and five Under-Secretaries voted with the I.L.P."[54] *Forward*, so often critical of Maxton and the ILP rebels, republished Maxton's speech moving the Living Wage bill verbatim from *Hansard*.[55]

But such a moment of unity was not to last. Soon *Forward* would forsake an ILP disaffiliated from the Labour Party, while Maxton would be searching for a "revolutionary policy" to replace Socialism in Our Time. His early biographer, Gilbert McAllister, was, in 1935, totally dismissive of the earlier ILP policy. It was, he wrote, a policy as remote from revolutionary idealism as anything could well be. It was, in fact, a programme of reformist policy akin in many respects to the New Deal with which President Roosevelt was later to rouse America. It advocated Family Allowances and a "Living Wage"—both desirable things but neither of them Socialism or instalments of Socialism. The man who invented the slogan, then the battle-cry of the left-wing, was one Clifford Allen, a former Chairman of the I.L.P., who was later to sit in the House of Lords, a staunch supporter of Mr. MacDonald's National Government, hardly recognisable under the title of Lord Allen of Hurtwood.

Socialism in Our Time was, he concluded "a kind of advanced Liberalism masquerading as revolutionary Socialism." It was "flashy, showy, and cheap," and "the slogan itself was an unhappy one."[56]

10

James Maxton and Increasing Tension with Labour

Although Fenner Brockway, in his summary of events under James Maxton's leadership, exaggerates more than a little, he is accurate enough in terms of the general direction of the ILP: "Under Maxton's chairmanship the I.L.P. became aggressively socialist and proletarian. The middle-class experts and careerists disappeared from Head Office overnight and those who were satisfied with Labour Party policy either resigned or retained a nominal membership only."[1] Yet as late as the end of 1930, of the four signatories of *The Living Wage*—surely the most prominent "middle-class experts"—only Hobson's "political habitation" seemed "to be a little doubtful," as J. Allen Skinner put it in his *New Leader* review of the economist's *Rationalisation and Unemployment*. In the same issue, Brailsford drew on Hobson's "valuable little book" in one of his "Chaos to Order" articles.[2] We have already seen that Wise was still active on the Living Income policy in 1928, and, after he was elected MP for Leicester East the following year, he published an article—"Banking and Finance: The Socialist Approach"—in the *New Leader*, in June 1930. In October, he demanded the socialization of food supplies, while Creech Jones wrote on the future of trade unionism the same month and reviewed Tawney's *Equality* in the paper in May 1931.[3] Brailsford, under pressure, especially from Kirkwood, over his relatively high salary, had resigned from the *New Leader* editorship in October 1926, but he was still a fairly frequent contributor to the paper in 1931.[4] Like Creech Jones and Wise, Brailsford would remain active in the ILP until it disaffiliated from the Labour Party in 1932.

By the beginning of 1928, the very different direction of the ILP was evident to John Strachey, now editing the *Socialist Review*. In the February edition that year, prompted by Snowden's resignation from the ILP, he noted how the war had brought about "a large influx of middle-class pacifists, bringing with them considerable money, ability and devotion to the cause of pacifism." All three of these had been useful, but Strachey now welcomed what he saw as the departure of the "Right Wing" with the always risky slogan "Better Fewer but Better." He returned to this theme in his "Notes of the Month" in August. The pacifist entrants of the war period were, he said, now "reverting to their natural position of Left Wing Liberals."[5]

Maxton and Allen, both dominant figures in the ILP at different times, had much in common, for all their differences of background, temperament, and political approach. Both had exhibited the greatest determination, commitment, and courage as conscientious objectors during the war. Both had degrees of personal integrity that even their most inveterate opponents recognized. Both suffered from ill health and neither lived to anything like a ripe old age: Maxton died in his early sixties, and Allen did not even see his fiftieth birthday. But in other respects they were very different. Maxton had none of Allen's organizing ability—or, indeed, his skill in tapping contributions to the ILP from wealthy sympathizers. But Maxton was a superb orator, and there is so much testimony, both during his lifetime and after his death, to his magnetism that it impossible to doubt his effective charisma. John Paton, a critic of Maxton as a "false prophet," still noted "the almost hypnotic charm of a unique personality."[6]

Maxton's personal popularity extended far beyond those who were inspired by him to become committed socialists. It even took in his political opponents in the House of Commons. Brockway records that "every Member spoke to him and he spoke to every Member, usually parting from them with an anecdote which left them chuckling. Yet he never compromised himself politically."[7] According to another colleague, David Kirkwood, he was the "most popular man in the House of Commons" and was "called 'Jimmie' by friend and opponent alike."[8]

Gilbert McAllister, writing in 1935, spoke of Maxton as "in a large sense the conscience of the British nation to-day," adding, though, that he went wrong when he attempted "to combine his idealism with a bungling meddling in practical affairs."[9] Some of the same characteristics that made him inspiring to—and even loved by—his most fervent supporters also made him all too easy to caricature. As David Howell says, "James Maxton seemed the Tory cartoonist's model of a socialist revolutionary—cadaverous features, lank dark hair, an emotional disrespect for bourgeois niceties."[10]

What Maxton could have done about his personal appearance was limited, but the stereotyping was reinforced by dramatic confrontations in Parliament. In the end, he was in danger of becoming what a later generation would call a "national treasure," universally admired for his outspoken sincerity, courage, and firm principles but not able to make a breakthrough beyond the already converted when it came to the realities of politics. And in any representative capacity, he was all too often inclined to follow his own beliefs and instincts rather than be guided by those he was representing.

The Divide Between Maxton and Allen

Maxton's tendency towards independent action proved to be the final straw for Clifford Allen. There was also increasing tension between the two men over Maxton's growing criticism of—and Allen's continuing support for—MacDonald. Brockway mentions the dispute over the proposed reappointment of MacDonald as editor of the ILP's *Socialist Review* as the "final issue" between them on the eve of Allen's resignation. MacDonald's removal was certainly opposed by Allen, and it contributed to his decision to go.[11]

However, as Arthur Marwick makes clear, Allen was even more concerned about Maxton's very questionable behaviour in representing the ILP at the 1925 Labour Party conference.[12] Maxton had been a member of the ILP's Finance Policy Committee, whose majority decided in favour of paying compensation in the case of nationalization. The committee's report, which was accepted by the ILP conference, was introduced by Hugh Dalton, who explained that the proposal of the committee was that compensation would be "paid off through the taxation of accumulated wealth." Before this statement, Dalton had reported that there was "a dissenting minority of two, and my friend Maxton who is one of them, will be able to bring a fresh mind to bear upon this matter as he was only present at two of the twenty-four meetings of the Committee."[13] This led, Marwick tells us, to "a brisk exchange of letters" between Allen and Maxton over the latter's attendance record.[14]

In October 1925, at the Labour Party conference in Liverpool, Maxton was the ILP representative on the Standing Orders Committee. In that role, he agreed to a composite motion, one that combined an ILP amendment on land nationalization with other amendments that opposed compensation. This, as Marwick says, "committed the I.L.P. to a policy which was the exact opposite of that hammered out by Allen's committee of experts and endorsed by the Party as a whole."[15] Both Marwick and Martin Gilbert quote the whole of Allen's letter to Maxton written a few days later. In it, significantly, Allen refers to his correspondent as "the future Chairman of the Party."[16] It had become customary for the office to be held for a period of three years, and Maxton had been a candidate for the office before. Clearly, Allen saw him as his almost inevitable successor who would take over the following year. Allen accused Maxton of "political irresponsibility, which fell not far short of political untrustworthiness." He went on: "When I saw the future Chairman of the Party revealing that he considered himself entitled to pledge the Party to Land Nationalisation without compensation in flagrant defiance of the recorded decision of the Annual Conference at York, I realised that the future of the Party was destroyed."

The letter makes it clear that even more than Maxton's own behaviour, it was the support for his actions at the subsequent NAC meeting that finally convinced Allen to resign. There is a pattern here that would be repeated on at least two occasions over the following years: Maxton would say or do something that was questionable for one holding a high-profile position in the ILP; there would be condemnations from some and misgivings among many in the party, but in the end, he would escape official criticism and have his position endorsed retrospectively.

The immediate result of what happened in Liverpool was Allen standing down, though he insisted that the "one or two incidents during that week" were decisive only because "they were the culmination of a long period of despair and unhappiness."[17] Two weeks after writing the letter to Maxton, Allen explained his resignation to MacDonald in similar terms. A "series of disgusting events concerned with the Liverpool Conference and the *Socialist Review*" had brought matters to a head and convinced him that it was "useless going on with these people."[18] Years later, after he too had broken with Maxton's ILP over Labour Party affiliation, Brailsford, in a letter to Allen, would refer to "that wretched Labour Party conference" when "Maxton behaved so ill" and to Allen's "irritation against Maxton and the Glasgow gang (for which you had very good grounds)."[19]

Maxton's message to the ILP on being elected as chairman was exemplary. He disclaimed any intent to "try to exert a great personal influence" and stressed that responsibility must be "distributed throughout the movement, rather than concentrated in the National Chairman." He ended with a plea for tolerance and unity. "The temptation to quarrel with the Rights or with the Lefts," he wrote, was great but must be resisted.[20] It remained to be seen how far these good intentions would be reflected in the future progress of the party.

Whatever his intentions, Maxton was increasingly seen as the leader of the ILP opposition to MacDonald. Writing on the front page of the *New Leader* in early 1927, he claimed he was not competing for the position of leader of the movement. He also denied that he had attacked MacDonald, but this failed to divert criticism.[21] The year ended with Maxton's suspension on 23 November after calling the Tory chairman of a Commons committee "damned unfair."[22]

In the meantime, the *New Leader* reported on "The MacDonald Debate," as the article was titled, at the 1927 annual conference of the ILP, which the writer described as the "outstanding" issue of the conference.[23] The NAC's decision not to nominate MacDonald for Labour Party treasurer had engendered a more intense version of the conflict of two years earlier over the *Socialist Review* editorship, which had contributed to Allen's resignation. This time, Brockway, who was at the centre of the conflict, tells us of the "protest signed by a formidable list of members, including MPs and leading officials throughout the country, and branches began to object in numbers which appeared disturbing." Brockway's "trump card," as he referred to it, during the conference debate was to read a letter from MacDonald in which he said that it would be better for him not to be nominated by the ILP in view of his differences with the party.[24] A motion, by Hill, to refer the issue back to the NAC for further review was rejected by a vote of 312 to 118.[25]

The debate seems to have been rather more divisive and acrimonious than Brockway's later account might suggest. Before moving for referral, Hill, from the Leicester branch, had tried to get the NAC simply to withdraw the proposal not to nominate MacDonald, but he abandoned the attempt after Maxton made it clear that the NAC stood by its decision. Hill claimed that MacDonald had "worked for 'Socialism in Our Time' like no other man," while Crockett from Stirling "pleaded for a reversion to the old outlook" and insisted that "gradualism was the quickest and best method of getting better social conditions." The Living Wage policy itself was long and gradual, and MacDonald should not be condemned for refusing to subscribe to a policy that he conscientiously believed would not expedite the "slow and steady development towards Socialism."[26]

Brockway, who spoke for nearly forty minutes, argued that it was not a matter of MacDonald disagreeing with ILP policy on "one or two occasions" but that his "whole attitude of mind is wholly different from the mind of the I.L.P." He pointed out that MacDonald would be nominated as Labour Party treasurer by other groups within the Labour party and that the ILP would regret it if he were not elected. But Brockway triggered protests when he went on to say that those circulating the "Memorial"—that is, the document complaining about the NAC's refusal to nominate MacDonald—were not motivated solely by loyalty to the Labour Party leader but "in some cases by definite opposition to the militant Socialism and Internationalism of the I.L.P."[27]

The cause of Labour Party unity was not assisted by a predominantly hostile press. Following the 1928 ILP conference, the *New Leader* protested that at least two Sunday papers, *Reynold's News* and the *Sunday Times*, "stated that Mr. Maxton referred to the demand of Mr. Ramsay MacDonald that the I.L.P. having finished its work should cease to exist as an impudent proposal. The facts are that Mr. Maxton did not even mention Mr. MacDonald, nor ascribe to him a proposal he has never made."[28] But the great issue of 1928 for the ILP, the Cook-Maxton (or Maxton-Cook) "manifesto," could not be dismissed as misreporting by an antagonistic and mischief-making bourgeois press.[29]

The Cook-Maxton Manifesto

As it appeared in the 22 June 1928 edition of the *New Leader*, the manifesto was a modest letter of five paragraphs. It announced that the signatories were intending to launch a campaign involving a series of "conferences and meetings." Best known as the leader of the miners' union during the General Strike, Arthur Cook was also an ILP member, though he was perceived as being close to the CPGB at this time. The unease that this campaign announcement caused in leading ILP circles was immediately apparent in the editorial note that followed: "We are authorised to state that the above letter is a purely personal communication, and in no way commits anyone but the two signatories."

Maxton and Cook called for an "unceasing war against poverty and working class servitude" and "against Capitalism." Only by their own efforts would be workers "obtain the full product of their labour," since the Labour Party had abandoned the founding principles of "Hardie and the other pioneers who made the Party." Moreover, readers of the manifesto were now being asked to believe that the ILP "is no longer a working-class Party, but a Party representing all members of the community." At the proposed conferences, "the rank and file" would be given the opportunity to state whether they "accept the new outlook, or whether they prefer to remain true to the spirit and ideals which animated the early pioneers."[30]

The manifesto also appeared in *Daily Herald*, whose editor at the time, William Mellor, rejected the Cook-Maxton analysis under the title "Socialism and Capitalism." The manifesto's authors, he argued, were not at all explicit about the claimed "serious departure from the principles which animated the founders." As might be expected from a paper owned by the TUC the *Herald* dismissed Maxton and Cook's criticism of that organization's participation in the Mond-Turner talks with employers: did not Cook participate in negotiations with the mine owners? Both Cook and Maxton had fought hard for improvements for workers *within* capitalism. The manifesto's reference to militant socialism being "crushed" by the Labour Party raised the question of whether the authors were referring to the CPGB. If so, they should understand, said Mellor, that the Labour Party was "a 'constitutional' democratic party; the Communist Party stands for dictatorship."[31] While the *Herald* agreed that there could be "no peace with Capitalism," the Cook-Maxton proposals would "enfeeble solidarity." The paper quoted Dollan's condemnation of the formation of "new wings and new cliques," while one of its editorials rejected as unhelpful "*ad hoc* conferences outside the aegis of the Labour Party."[32]

The initial reaction in the *New Leader*'s letters section was not much more encouraging for the new campaign. A number of critical letters appeared under the title "Maxton-Cook Manifesto: Views of Our Readers—A Split or a Revival?" The paper reported that of the first ten letters received, six were critical. "Fidelis" criticized the timing, believing that the manifesto would be good provender for the enemies of the Labour Party as the election approached. The ILP would be accused of the "fomenting of class war." S. Lever of Hackney asked, "Does Maxton think that by propounding a militant programme he will enlist the support of the Communist Party?" If this was so, he would be disappointed. Jack Swan, a member of the Executive Committee of the Miners' Federation and of the ILP, thought that if Maxton and Cook had found a "shortcut to Socialism," they would get a hearing. But he noted that "both comrades have had the opportunity of putting forward a policy in the Councils of the Miners' Federation and the I.L.P." In the same issue, Brockway defended the radical approach of the manifesto authors while accepting that members of the NAC had a strong case in asserting that Maxton should not have taken this action when chairman—or at the very least, not without having consulted them.[33]

Brockway, writing in the 1940s, said that "the Cook-Maxton campaign was planned in a good deal of secrecy and announced to the world without any consultation with the National Council of the I.L.P. or with its Head Office officials, despite the fact that Maxton was chairman of the Party." He believed that the "real instigator" was John Wheatley, who was widely regarded as one of the very few successes of the 1924 government. He would die suddenly in 1930, leaving Maxton without the person who many regarded as his guru.[34]

John Paton, political secretary of the ILP at the time of the Cook-Maxton affair, would also later explain his reaction to the manifesto in some detail in *Left Turn!* He had not, he said, had any real warning: "There had been a preliminary announcement in the Press of its coming, but since Maxton had not troubled to inform me of its contents nor seek to consult the National Council I'd concluded it was something of no special importance." The significance of the Cook-Maxton initiative, for Paton, lay in the series of public meetings that would "create an *ad hoc* organisation which inevitably must be recruited from the I.L.P." This meant that the campaign was indirectly an attack on the ILP. Paton had, he insisted, no quarrel with the intentions of the manifesto. Maxton and Cook were great assets to the party.

> As a combination they were an immensely popular attraction everywhere; if they'd placed their dates with me I could have organised their campaign through the I.L.P. with immense effect, both for its immediate aims and for the I.L.P. as well. It was doubly galling to think that my chairman had made this move without a word to me as Party secretary and had done it in a way which would almost certainly ensure its failure.[35]

Paton initially believed, like Brockway, that Wheatley was behind the move, especially since Wheatley seemed to be dissatisfied with the ILP and to wish to form a new party. But Paton later came to the conclusion that the origins lay in Maxton's "quixotic desire" to rush to the aid of Cook, whom he believed to be in danger of being expelled from the TUC General Council for refusing to treat its discussions as confidential. This, according to Paton, led to a meeting at the House of Commons involving—in addition to Cook and Maxton—the MPs Wheatley, Buchanan, Kirkwood, and Campbell Stephen; John Scanlon, a journalist closely associated with the Clyde MPs who was to help organize the campaign; and the CPGB's William Gallacher.[36]

Controversy over the Cook-Maxton Campaign

Paton's reaction was not unlike that of Allen at the time of his resignation, and the same pattern was to follow. By early July, *New Leader* letters were running in favour of the Cook-Maxton program by a margin of four to one.[37] Gilbert McAllister, in his biography of Maxton, says that the NAC was "rent in two" over the manifesto.[38] The division within the ILP is nowhere better illustrated than in the contrasting responses to the Cook-Maxton agenda of *Forward* and *Labour's Northern Voice*, the former very critical and the latter generally supportive. The Glasgow-based *Forward*, edited by Tom Johnston, a close associate and supporter of Dollan, criticized Cook-Maxton under the title "Socialism or Confusionism."[39] The editor of the Lancashire Division's own *Labour's Northern Voice* complained of not having been sent a copy of the manifesto though it was "inserted in the dope papers" even before it appeared in *Forward* and the *New Leader*. He found the comments in *Forward* "not very helpful" and saw Cook-Maxton not as "an outburst of irritation" against MacDonald but as a "trumpet call" that might bring people to "perceive how they are being led up the garden."[40]

In the following week's issue of *Labour's Northern Voice*, Mrs. H. M. Mitchell was equivocal about "Maxton Cookery." "To older stagers of the I.L.P. who have never felt it necessary to run about with the red flag in one hand and a volume of Marx in the other," she wrote, "the manifesto seems remarkably mild." But she believed that the "consternation" generated showed the need for it." A week later, the paper reported that at the Lancashire divisional conference, the feeling had been "in favour generally" and the reception of Maxton, who attended the conference, was enthusiastic. He declared himself amazed at the uproar that he and Cook had caused in the party and excused himself from going into detail about the manifesto. He had, he said, already spent six hours explaining himself to the NAC and four with the Scottish Divisional Council.[41]

Meanwhile, in an interview in *Forward*, Maxton denied "the faintest intention" of either starting a new party or drafting a program. Asked about the claim that those who remained true to the ideals of the labour movement were being "crushed," Maxton complained of "a steady but relentless attempt to smother and obliterate the I.L.P." since he had become chairman. "We are told it has outlived its purpose and is no longer necessary," he said. "Philip Snowden ostentatiously resigns from it on that ground. And all our efforts at translating our propaganda into Socialism in our time are persistently opposed and ridiculed." The same issue of *Forward* raised doubts about the "Rank and File conference" planned in Glasgow. Could such an event really be called a conference? Those attending would represent only themselves. There were an estimated 200,000 trade unionists and cooperators in the city, and St. Andrew's Hall had a capacity of about 4,000. If only a fraction of the "rank and file" turned up, it would be necessary to adjourn to Glasgow Green.[42]

The next edition followed this with an appeal to avoid fracturing the ILP and a plea that the manifesto authors' future meetings "be arranged under the auspices of the Party of which they are both members." While some letters commended the manifesto for sounding an alarm, Dollan attacked not the content of the manifesto but its constitutional impropriety and political folly. He had worked with Maxton longer than most, he wrote, and no one had more regard for him, but Maxton was wrong to promote "unofficial campaigns," especially in view of the planned ILP Socialism in Our Time autumn campaign. Moreover, "no other Chairman of the I.L.P. found it necessary to go outside the organisation to hold conferences and meetings to consult the rank and file on questions of party policy, and Maxton had no need to break this unwritten rule."[43]

Dollan was becoming as much a thorn in Maxton's side as Maxton was in MacDonald's. He had repeated his criticism of Maxton's lack of consultation at the NAC meeting where Maxton's calm presentation had, he said, "captivated the members of the Council even if it did not convince all of them he did right." Seconded by John Scurr, Dollan had attempted to persuade the NAC to reject ILP participation in the campaign while endorsing "the spirit and aim of the document." The vote was lost by 8 to 5, even though Scurr disclaimed any intention to censure Maxton. Frank Wise and Dorothy Jewson then moved what became the NAC's statement. It was endorsed by 7 votes to 6 after the failure by the same narrow margin of an amendment from Shinwell and Mosley to leave out the encouragement of branches to support the Cook-Maxton campaign.[44] It was accepted that the manifesto was not "intended to disrupt" and that it expressed the "distinctive policy of the I.L.P. which rejects ... both the inevitability of gradualness and the inevitability of violent revolution."[45]

Somewhat cynically, Mosley maintained that differing appeals to sections of the electorate helped win elections and that "Maxton and Cook appealed to the working class as no one else could." Jowett, who opined that the party had never experienced an internal debate conducted at "such a high level of sincerity and seriousness," criticized the timing of the campaign. He argued that Maxton and Cook should have waited until after the publication of the Labour Party's Labour and the Nation policy. But Brockway's *New Leader* headlines "The I.L.P. Burns Its Boats" and "Maxton Endorsed" told their own story. According to Brockway, Maxton was thinking in terms of "a 'Moody and Sankey' campaign" by Cook and himself, which "would reach a wider circle than an I.L.P. campaign."[46]

As far as *Forward* was concerned, hostilities were only just beginning. Dollan detected "major inaccuracies" in an article by Cook criticizing the Labour and the Nation policy in the CPGB's *Sunday Worker*. Dollan reported the Scottish Divisional Council's decision not to support the "unofficial campaign," adding that Cook had told him that the Scottish Council's decision did not represent the branches or the members.[47]

In the meantime, three to four thousand people attended the first of the Cook-Maxton meetings in Glasgow. The *New Leader* reported Maxton's concession that "if a vote were taken of the working classes as between 'Socialism in Our Time' and the 'Inevitability of Gradualism' the latter would get a majority. That was why he and Cook were conducting their campaign."[48] Predictably, *Forward*'s account was much more negative, reporting that the most successful aspect of the meeting was the chairing by David Kirkwood, who dealt impressively with the considerable amount of heckling. The rest of the report was highly skeptical. "Was this conference the beginning of a great 'revival'?" the writer asked. "Let us hope so. There was no attempt by anybody to outline a constructive programme."[49]

Once again, this contrasts sharply with the way *Labour's Northern Voice* headlined the Manchester event that soon followed: "The Maxton-Cook Campaign: Huge Meeting at Free Trade Hall."[50] It is true that the *Voice* did not *entirely* ignore the charges of constitutional impropriety against Maxton. A small item in September reported that the Miles Platting ILP branch had protested against Maxton and dissociated itself from the support given to the "unofficial meetings" by the Lancashire Division.[51]

Meanwhile, another front had opened in *Forward*'s anti-Cook-Maxton campaign. On 21 July, the paper had carried on its back page an advertisement headed, in all caps, "Socialist Revival: Cook-Maxton Campaign," in which Kirkwood sought donations to finance further activities, with a goal of "100,000 shillings." Reacting like a bull to this red flag, Dollan attacked Kirkwood the following week. Here was a member of the ILP's National Council, whose priority should have been to address the current £1,553 deficit of the party, appealing for £5,000 to finance the Cook-Maxton campaign, he complained indignantly.[52]

In the *New Leader*, Dollan reiterated his objection to Kirkwood's attempt to promote a "private" socialist revival. It was, he insisted, "an even more violent breach of democratic procedure than was the issue of the manifesto." He rejected "this individualism under a guise of Socialism." Those who found the Labour Party too reactionary should leave. If they chose to stay, then "let us accept the difficulties of membership as honourably as we accept the privileges." He ended with the declaration that "the special function of the I.L.P. within the Labour Party is to educate rather than to dominate."[53]

A very different view was to be found in the *Socialist Review*, where Strachey, in the August edition, declared that he saw the Cook-Maxton campaign as "undoubtedly a political event of importance." In essence, he argued, it asked whether Labour was a socialist party, and the NAC's support of Cook-Maxton seemed to show that the socialist elements within the ILP were "again in the saddle." Later, in October, he concluded that its agenda implied both "combined international action, at least with the workers of the rest of Western Europe, and . . . a dictatorship of the proletariat, i.e., the complete scrapping of parliamentarianism for at least a transitional period." But none of this, he concluded, was faced explicitly by Cook and Maxton.[54]

Maintaining the Pressure: More "Maxton-Cookery"

Maxton and Cook then produced a twenty-four-page pamphlet titled *Our Case for a Socialist Revival*, which was summarized for *New Leader* readers on 9 September. It was published not by the ILP but by Workers' Publications Ltd., and readers were asked to write to Kirkwood or Cook for copies. It was a response, its introduction said, to requests for "a more detailed account of what is wrong with the Labour Movement." Current moves towards "capitalist rationalisation" were no more likely to succeed than previous remedies to that system. What was needed was a class struggle for emancipation and "the defeat of the capitalist class."[55]

Both "the Mondist policy" of the TUC and the new program of the Labour Party, the pamphlet said, reflected the "abandonment of Socialism," as did "the measures of intimidation and suppression of those within the Labour Movement who are opposing these policies." Acceptance of capitalist rationalization of industry meant working for "the hell of robotry" instead of for "nationalisation and workers' control."[56] The alternative, as Cook and Maxton saw it, included the revival of the union militancy of 1921–22 in organizing the unemployed, the "crushing defeat of Mondism," and the election of leaders prepared to pursue "a conscious Socialist trade union policy." With all of this accomplished, there should be a centralization of power in the General Council of the TUC in order to enable it to pursue "a militant class policy," while unions should carry out studies of their industries and work out detailed schemes of nationalization and workers' control.⁵⁷

The Labour Party, too, was in need of urgent rescue. The new Labour program had completed the party leadership's move towards the right: the program "must be regarded not as a Socialist programme but as an enlightened Liberal programme." The authors demanded the "staffing [of] the main departments of government with consistent Socialists" and the speedy nationalization of manufacturing industries, with "proper provision for adequate participation of workers in control and management of public services and industries." Compensation for nationalization was rejected lest this enable capitalists to "take the wealth received in compensation to other countries in the world and there develop exploitation anew." An exception might be made for the aged or disabled, but there must be no chance of society "burdening itself with a *rentier* class."⁵⁸

The pamphlet stressed the importance of both the cooperative movement and a "powerful Trade Union Movement prepared to support a Socialist Government in its struggles for the expropriation of the capitalist class." A real socialist policy in relation to the cooperatives would, while drawing them closer to the trade unions in the immediate struggle to defend the wages of the working class, "put before a Socialist Government the task of expropriating the big multiple stores . . . and transferring their control to the Co-operative Movement." A socialist government would also have to assist the co-ops "to oust the remaining capitalists from retail and wholesale distribution."⁵⁹

The "struggle against Imperial domination and the menace of war" must be supported, Cook and Maxton insisted. The short section "Barriers of Capitalism" was, in the context of the rest of the pamphlet, rather restrained. Of the House of Lords and the monarchy, it confined itself to a statement supporting their abolition. But there was no restraint about urging the defeat of the new program being proposed at the coming Labour Party conference and "declaring war against capitalism." In a final section, Cook and Maxton complained of the intolerance of dissent within the Labour Party before concluding that "the fight within the Labour movement to-day is a fight between the forces of Socialism and those who have fallen under the influence of capitalism."⁶⁰

Cook-Maxton: The Fallout

There is little doubt that most ILP members saw the manifesto and the follow-up pamphlet as, in Brockway's words, "a popular statement of the

'Socialism in Our Time' programme."⁶¹ This underlines the point made in the previous chapter that the subtlety of *The Living Wage* report's strategy had not taken as much root as it might have seemed in 1926. Aimed almost entirely at labour movement activists, the strategy of *Our Case for a Socialist Revival* was simply to replace the unsatisfactorily "reformist" policies and leaderships of the trade unions and Labour Party with an uncompromisingly militant alternative while simultaneously pursuing the entire spectrum of the most radical policies. At the very least, this was an extremely tall order. The response of the *New Leader* was lukewarm. "Notes of the Week" simply listed all the headings and demands of the pamphlet and noted that it was all covered by existing ILP policy.⁶²

The criticism from "Watchman," a columnist for the Birmingham weekly *The Town Crier*, was more scathing. Watchman was skeptical about what he called Maxton's "orgy of oratory." Jimmy Maxton was "a lovable personality," he said. One could not quarrel with him. "Nor can one argue with him; Jimmy doesn't argue—he tells you." Reference was then made to Brailsford's response to Snowden the previous year:

> Mr. Brailsford is not arguing that because great changes can come about only a step at a time we should sit down and wait for them to come of their own accord. On the contrary he urged that all good Socialists should hasten the changes by effective propaganda among the masses of the people. When Maxton rages against those who want to trust the coming of Socialism to "some mysterious force raging outside ourselves" he is raging against people who do not exist in the ranks of the Socialist movement.⁶³

Maxton and Cook did not fare much better at the hands of their more revolutionary critics either. In December's *Socialist Review*, Strachey reiterated the case he had made in the summer: Cook and Maxton did not admit how little a Labour government could do without "declaring itself a revolutionary Government, establishing a dictatorship of the proletariat, abolishing the Parliamentary system and imprisoning opponents." He went on to say that he agreed with Palme Dutt's similar criticism in the October issue of the Communist-aligned *Labour Monthly*.⁶⁴

By early 1929, Maxton seems to have taken the advice of those critics who urged that his campaigns should be carried out from within the ILP. In February, *Labour's Northern Voice* carried an advertisement for a special conference for the local labour movement, where delegates would discuss proposals regarding a living wage for all workers in an effort to win "socialism in our time."⁶⁵ Dollan was now disposed to be conciliatory. Reporting on the annual

Scottish divisional conference held in January, he wrote, "It would be idle to pretend that the Cook-Maxton enterprise did not disturb the I.L.P. in Scotland but none of us who know the I.L.P. believed the disturbance would be more than temporary." It had been, he concluded, a "tolerant conference" with no "personalities," and "Maxton was at his best."[66]

The Cook-Maxton campaign was not a success. Paton, as might have been anticipated, later claimed that "it left behind it nothing but sharpened resentments and fresh difficulties for the I.L.P. in its relations with the Labour Party."[67] One notable result was the resignation, not only from the NAC but also from the ILP itself, of MP John Scurr. Once a prewar member of the Social-Democratic Federation, he had long been very active in the ILP. As a member of the Poplar Borough Council, he had been jailed for contempt of court in 1921, when, in hopes of mitigating the plight of the local poor, Poplar councillors took part in a protest against an increase in property taxes.[68] He was not, in short, the sort of member that the ILP would expect—or, arguably, could afford—to lose.

Scurr's resignation letter, dated 14 November, was included in the NAC's report to the 1929 annual conference. It made quite clear what had triggered the severing of his relationship with the ILP: "The recent action of the Chairman, the enunciation by him of a new programme, and the endorsement of him by the majority of the N.A.C. and a considerable body of the membership, especially in my own London division, has in my judgement entirely altered the basis of the I.L.P." He attacked the "new spirit" and "new outlook" in the party, which he believed "much more in accord with impossibilism" than with the legacy of Keir Hardie. He did not doubt the sincerity of Maxton and his supporters, but in his opinion, rather than bring about Socialism in Our Time, they would "postpone its realisation for many years." With an election approaching and Labour "on the threshold of power," ILP members were "being led to believe that the Labour Party will not make good. It is heart-rending. It is worse. It is the acme of foolishness." He ended with the hope that "the temporary aberration of the I.L.P. will speedily pass away." This was not something that Scurr, who died in 1932, would live to see.[69]

If Scurr's departure was evidence of the alienation felt by what was now seen as the Right of the ILP, there was little compensating support from the CPGB, which was entering its most sectarian "class against class" years of the "third period."[70] Palme Dutt, writing in *Labour Monthly* in April 1929, ridiculed the "final self-exposure of Cook and Maxton." The "final swan-song of Maxton was sung at the Scottish I.L.P. conference," he concluded, and the "funeral of the Clyde Brigade was solemnised at the Glasgow united meeting of Henderson, Wheatley and Kirkwood, at which the police kept order by the arrest of seventeen workers."[71]

The general election of 1929, which resulted in another minority Labour government under Ramsay MacDonald, followed at the end of May. Sometimes referred to as the "flapper election," it was held under the terms of the Representation of the People Act 1928, which removed the discrimination against women under age thirty of its 1918 predecessor. The travails of both Maxton and Cook continued in this new political situation. By September 1929, the *New Leader* was reporting Maxton's expulsion from the Communist-dominated League Against Imperialism. He had taken risks in trying to establish friendly relations with the Communists, the *Leader* noted, but his efforts had not been reciprocated: "The whole episode throws a brilliant searchlight on the almost total failure of Communist propaganda in this country. When the Third International decreed, against the advice of its most level-headed adherents, that Labour must be fought at the polls, it signed the death warrant of the British Communist Party."[72] Cook was not spared either, but *Forward*'s critical attitude to Cook underwent a sea change after he condemned CPGB's tactics in the Miners' Federation. Successive headlines in March 1929 tell the story—"Communists Attack Cook," "Another Attack on Cook," and then an article by Cook titled "Stop Squabbling and Work for a Labour Government: Advice to Scots Miners."[73] On the Communist side of the dispute, the June 1929 *Labour Monthly* published "Cook's Break with the Revolutionary Working Class."[74]

In the midst of all this, Maxton remained undeterred and continued to win support among ILP members. In early 1929, an editorial in the *New Leader* had commented on press reports that Maxton had decided to accept another nomination as chairman. There was nothing in the constitution that limited the term of office, although no one since Hardie, who held the position from 1893 to 1900, had served more than three years in that capacity.[75] At the 1929 ILP annual conference, Maxton was re-elected with 284 votes; Shinwell received 39 and Dollan 38.[76]

Maxton would remain chairman until 1931 and would again hold the position from 1934 until 1939. This final tenure was not foreseen. At the Scottish ILP conference in early 1931, Maxton announced that he was addressing them for the last time as national chairman. He said that "he would be glad to get back to his work as a Socialist agitator without the constraints of office." After the Cook-Maxton episode, there must have been some who wondered what these constraints could possibly have been.[77]

The frustration of active ILPers with the Labour Party went far wider than Maxton and his most fervent supporters. At least part of the responsibility lay with the larger party—and above all, with MacDonald himself, in his dismissive response to *The Living Wage*. Serious consideration well short of endorsement and adoption might have been sufficient to reduce at least some of the alienation that many were coming to feel towards the "official" movement. The growing tensions are not attributable to Maxton alone. His popularity on the Left was, in large part, due to the way he articulated and dramatized the frustration already felt by so many activists. That said, the way he pursued the ILP case was bound to exacerbate rather than conciliate.

At an ILP meeting at the Brighton Dome during the 1929 Labour Party conference, Maxton declared, "I am a Socialist agitator. My function is to stir up discontent and keep it hot and strong. And it is more necessary with a Labour Government than at any other time."[78] A minority Labour government had then been in office since the beginning of June. It was to end with MacDonald's formation, in 1931, of a National Government. This set in motion a train of events that led to the ILP's ill-fated, and later often much regretted, decision to disaffiliate from the larger party that it had done so much to create.

---------- PART III ----------

Leaving Labour

11

The Second Labour Government

The beginning of 1929 brought more signs of the increasingly recalcitrant stance that was coming to characterize the ILP's relationship with the Labour Party. On the agenda for the London divisional conference was a motion from the Clapham branch critical of what it saw as Labour's tendency to compromise with opponents and temper its policies in hopes of attracting wider support. The branch recognized "the necessity of converting the masses of the people to our point of view" but felt that Labour could best achieve this goal by advocating a "bold and uncompromising policy." In an amendment to the motion, the Marylebone branch pressed for clarification of the ILP's position on the Labour Party's "Disloyalty clause." These rumblings of discontent in London were symptomatic of things to come. Indeed, many within the ILP were growing impatient with what they saw as the Labour Party's half-hearted promotion of socialist policies and its efforts to impose this tepid approach on MPs—including, most notably, ILP MPs.

The Lead-Up to the 1929 Election

Two months later, Brockway included in his list of issues for the upcoming ILP conference the demand for "revolutionising Parliament" by means of the committee system. He also noted the need for the ILP MPs to urge the Labour Party to pursue the Socialism in Our Time program endorsed by the ILP at three consecutive annual conferences.[1]

Reporting on the 1929 annual conference, the *New Leader* praised Roden Buxton for his courage and sincerity in arguing for "what was unquestionably an unpopular view." According to Buxton, the ILP was "sowing suspicion" of the labour movement and, as a result, "was becoming increasingly disliked." Buxton went on to argue that "overlapping with the Labour Party" was a mistake. Instead, the ILP should abandon all connection to "legislative and administrative work" (including the nomination of candidates for Parliament) and stick to its traditional role of promoting socialism, focusing exclusively on education and propaganda. Buxton's views were not utterly without support. One delegate thought it would be "better for Maxton to come out of Parliament and be a John the Baptist for the I.L.P." But all of this was overwhelmingly rejected. "The I.L.P. has never been satisfied with advocating principles only," Brockway explained in his report on the conference for the *New Leader*. Opposition came from across a very wide spectrum. Patrick Dollan said that 95 percent of Scottish ILP members would reject Buxton's view, while Trevelyan insisted that the ILP "must be all it is or nothing."²

At the conference, the demand for the reform of parliamentary procedure as advocated by Jowett—"who," Brockway reminded his readers, "has made the subject of Parliamentary Reform his life-work"—was once more agreed upon without dissent. The new regulations for the selection of ILP parliamentary candidates based on their acceptance of the party's policies were approved. The successful NAC motion, moved by Kirkwood, insisted that candidates should have a satisfactory record of membership and service in the ILP and should undertake to accept "in general" ILP policy and give effect to it in the House of Commons if elected.³

An amendment to the NAC motion, put forward by London Central on behalf of four other branches as well, would have enabled the NAC to end the ILP membership of those MPs who "consistently opposed party policy." Although the proposed amendment was defeated by a vote of 214 to 124, it clearly had the support of a significant minority of delegates. The amendment would also have instructed ILP MPs to vote against war credits. The following week, the *New Leader* concluded that, on the war credits issue, the ILP's policy should be "to work within the Labour Party for the acceptance of our views, but to acknowledge the authority of majority decisions when they go against us." However, acceptance of dissent on "issues of principle upon which minorities feel so keenly" was essential.⁴

With the general election campaign underway, the *New Leader* editor reiterated that the ILP regarded socialism as an "urgent vital necessity" and complained that the Labour Party had no "transitional programme." Yet the paper also put out a four-page "MacDonald Special" supporting the Labour leader and stressing his "work for peace."⁵ After the election, at which Labour, while failing to gain a majority in the House of Commons, became, for the first time, the largest party in terms of seats won—a total of 287, as compared to 191 in the election of December 1923—the NAC and the *Leader* remained supportive. But how long would this last?

Another Minority Labour Government

The first NAC meeting following the election passed a resolution congratulating MacDonald "on his great personal triumph." It was, the resolution said, an opportunity for his government to begin the "reorganisation of our society on Socialist lines." In that work, he would be "assured of the loyal and whole-hearted support of the Independent Labour Party."[6] At least for a while, the support continued. "A promising beginning has been made with the two chief objects of the Government—Employment and Peace," declared the *New Leader* in June, while an editorial headline the following month recognized that the government had put forward a "Good Reformist Programme."[7]

But ILP support for the government was not to last. By the time of the Labour Party conference in the autumn of 1929, the *New Leader* was complaining of "timidity and feebleness" and predicting that "unless within a reasonable measure of time it is possible to do something substantial for the workless the Government will fall with a crash."[8] In the House of Commons, Maxton had responded to the King's Speech laying out the new government's proposed legislation by saying that he hoped "not to make difficulties for the present Government." He would, he said, be "very patient." But Maxton's speech, reproduced verbatim from *Hansard*, was headlined in *Forward* as "Maxton and the Labour Government: Terms on Which He Will Give His Support," hardly suggesting the stance of a Labour MP patiently disposed to support his own government.[9]

Brockway had been elected as MP for the London constituency of East Leyton. In his 1942 memoir, *Inside the Left*, he recalled the first meeting of the Parliamentary Labour Party, at which Wheatley argued that it was wrong to accept office as another minority government, while Brockway himself urged that "the Government should introduce its socialist programme and stand or fall by it," much as Allen had suggested years before. MacDonald, of course, rejected both of these proposals. Brockway's account continues:

> He turned towards the I.L.P. Group and warned the Party that the one thing which might destroy the Government was "sniping" from within. A roar of cheers resounded through the room. There was no misunderstanding the threat in MacDonald's voice or in the cheers; so early in the life of the second Labour Government the battle between MacDonaldism and the I.L.P. was joined.[10]

From the standpoint of its Labour adversaries, who were seeing the ILP increasingly as a "party within the party," the very fact that MacDonald was physically able to turn "towards the I.L.P. Group," whose members were presumably sitting together as a distinct bloc, was itself significant.

The ILP Parliamentary Group and the Insurance Bill

Unemployment and provision for the unemployed had always been crucial and emotive issues for the entire labour movement. Labour came to office having pledged to repeal the "not genuinely seeking work" provision of the existing legislation, which was used to disqualify some of those seeking unemployment benefits. The minister of Labour, Margaret Bondfield, had appointed the Morris Committee to recommend changes, but the members of the committee who represented employers' organizations were unwilling to accept what came to be known as the Hayday Formula. This took its name from Labour MP Arthur Hayday, one of the two Labour Party representatives on the committee. The Hayday Formula would have disqualified only those who had definitely refused suitable employment. Instead, the Morris Committee recommended that disqualification should also take place when employment was available and the claimant failed to prove "reasonable efforts to obtain such work." There seemed to be little or no difference between what was now proposed and the old formula that Labour had opposed.[11]

Opposition to the Insurance Bill, as it became known, was widespread in the trade unions as well as in the ILP. Even before the bill was published on 15 November 1929, a front-page editorial in the *New Leader* vehemently objected to it under the headline "Stop the Persecution: An Appeal to Miss Bondfield." The Labour Party's Clynes, the editorial said, had been entirely right the previous weekend when he had said, "Better that some shirkers should receive money than that thousands of honest men should be deprived of benefits to which they are justly entitled."[12] A special meeting of the ILP parliamentary group, attended by thirty MPs, less than a quarter of those entitled to attend, took place at the NAC's request. The MPs were unanimous in appointing a subcommittee to draw up proposals that became known as the "I.L.P. Minimum Demands," which were approved at a subsequent meeting of the parliamentary group.[13] But by now the alarm had sounded among those ILP MPs who saw themselves, first and foremost, as government loyalists.

Aspects of the Insurance Bill constituted some improvement, from the Labour Party's point of view, and, as *Forward* reported, publication of the bill had unleashed "a storm of hostile criticism from the capitalist press."[14] Two significant meetings took place on 19 November. In the morning, the Parliamentary Labour Party (PLP) heard MacDonald ask for support for the bill "not as something they desired, but as the best they could get under the circumstances."[15] The PLP overwhelmingly approved the bill and insisted that there should be no amendments unless the entire PLP agreed to them—something that Maxton made clear he refused to accept.[16]

In a meeting that evening, the ILP parliamentary group carried a motion, moved by Shinwell, supporting the bill. Only fourteen opposed.[17] William Leach, the MP for Bradford Central, had collected the signatures of sixty-six MPs who were members of the ILP in a "memorial" that declared, "Our principal work in Parliament is to help the Labour Government in the purposes it has set itself. We refuse to embarrass its ministers in their work." At the meeting, however, Maxton and his supporters rejected the attempt to make the decision of the ILP parliamentary group binding on all its members, arguing that although the practice of the group had always been "to reach the greatest measure of common agreement," it had "never been held that Group decisions bound every member."[18] Like Maxton, the *New Leader* was far from accepting the PLP view: "Amend! Amend! Amend!" was its front-page demand. While the paper recognized that the majority of ILP MPs would support the bill, it accused those who had signed the memorial of "losing all sense of proportion and taking party loyalty to impossible lengths." The pro-Labour *Daily Herald* also noted that a minority group within the ILP, "led by James Maxton," were determined to press for amendments.[19]

The divisions within the ILP between those supporting Maxton's line and those who regarded the Labour Party as having the first claim on their support now widened. Leach, in a letter to the *New Leader*, made this quite clear. "I regard this as *my* Government," he wrote. "Perhaps you don't regard it as *yours*." It is doubtful that he was convinced by the editorial note that followed his letter, which emphasized that the paper gave *"general support to the Government."* Another MP, Mary Hamilton, insisted the following week that "those of us who propose to support the Government have searched our consciences as sincerely as Maxton and his friends have done."[20] The Maxton group pressed ahead with the amendments, none of which garnered more than thirty-nine votes. For Brockway, writing more than a decade later, "This was the first step in the course which led to the disaffiliation of the I.L.P. from the Labour Party."[21]

The NAC supported the Maxton group's actions on the Insurance Bill, with three members voting against. One was Dollan, who blasted Maxton on successive days in the *New Leader* and *Forward*. His *New Leader* article, "The Clydesiders: What I Think of Them," was scathing. Maxton was not as popular on the Clyde as many people seemed to think, Dollan wrote:

> Clydeside and Scotland did not follow him in his demand for the affiliation of the Communists to the Labour Party; in his Cook-Maxton campaign; nor in his League Against Imperialism adventure. Mr. Maxton is a great favourite and appreciated for his devoted service to the I.L.P. and Socialism but Clydesiders do not regard him as the best leader in tactics and policy.

There was sympathy for Maxton's position on the Insurance Bill, but Dollan rejected the "general attitude of critical hostility adopted by some of them [ILP MPs] to the Labour government since its formation."²²

As early as August, Dollan continued, Maxton had said that the government was not benefiting a "single working-class member of the community." Criticism was legitimate but there should be "some regard for team work."²³ The headline of Dollan's article in *Forward*, just one day later, asked "Should I.L.P. Support Maxton? The National Council's Blunder." The antagonism of "certain Clydesiders" and others towards the Labour Government was being exploited by "hostile critics," he said.²⁴ In the final 1929 edition of *Forward*, under the headline "A Plea for Loyalty," Dollan asked ILP members to support the Labour Party and criticized both Maxton, for violating the ILP constitution, and the NAC, for endorsing his action. He complained, "It is a case of 'my hero right or wrong.'"²⁵

As with Cook-Maxton the year before, the division of opinion in the ILP was clear, once again, from the contrasting reactions of *Forward* and *Labour's Northern Voice*. While Dollan was making his criticisms in the former, the latter was reporting the Lancashire Divisional Council's unanimous congratulation of Maxton and his supporters for their "fight to obtain justice for the unemployed" and making a front-page plea urging members to "rally to the rebels."²⁶

Dollan had now clearly emerged as the major critic within the ILP of Maxton and the Clydesiders, though by no means the only one. The *New Leader*'s report of the Scottish divisional conference in early 1930 noted "Wheatley's formidable speech" in support of Maxton and the other rebels. But this was not enough to achieve majority support for their actions. Shinwell, in reply, questioned whether there was any point to debating the matter any further. Maxton had said that whatever the conference decided, he would "do it again," so why "hold a Conference at all?" asked Shinwell. Dollan then left the chair and attacked "the formation of the Left Group in the House of Commons," which, he argued, had no justification in ILP policy. "On the question of mandate," wrote the reporter, "he challenged Maxton to produce a resolution from the N.A.C. justifying his conduct." Support for the actions of the Maxton group was defeated by 103 votes to 94. An editorial comment in the *New Leader* concluded:

> The narrow defeat of Mr. Maxton and his immediate associates at the Scottish I.L.P. Conference is not so astonishing as it may appear on the surface. Those who are closely in touch with affairs north of the Tweed have always been quietly amused at the popular myth so firmly held in the south that Scotland was a great stronghold of the rebel Left. Mr. Maxton has always held, and events may prove him to be right, that the main strength of his support lay outside his native land.²⁷

This judgment was supported at the end of January by reports of "support for the Rebels" at three of the other divisional conferences. The Welsh conference included a significant exchange involving W. G. Cove, MP, who had taken over MacDonald's former constituency of Aberavon. When Cove said that "the Labour Party was their child, and they had the right to slap it," one delegate shouted, "Yes, but not to kill it." Nevertheless, a card vote endorsed the actions of "the Rebels" by 47 to 37, and their supporters sang "The Red Flag" after the vote. David Mort, the division's NAC representative, resigned on the spot.[28]

There seems to have been less division and less acrimony at the Yorkshire and Midlands conferences. Support for the NAC statement endorsing the Maxton group's actions on the Insurance Bill was unopposed at the latter, though it rejected, by 52 votes to 6, a motion moved by Joseph Southall calling for disaffiliation from the Labour Party. Yorkshire approved without dissent the NAC statement supporting the rebels. This approval was advocated by the formidable Jowett.[29]

Three weeks later, after the Southern regional conference had endorsed Maxton's initiative, the *New Leader* noted that this brought it into line with the "rest of the country (Scotland excepted)." In the same issue, Ernest E. Hunter, the paper's editor until John Paton took over in April, announced "The End of a Chapter": MacDonald had resigned from the ILP. Differences had built up over a long period, Hunter wrote, after summarizing appreciatively the Labour leader's contribution. However, "when the I.L.P. inscribed on its banners 'Socialism in Our Time,'" he continued, "the rumbling of the storm became louder and louder." The ILP had embarked on a course "alien" to MacDonald's "mind and mood," he concluded.[30]

In April 1930, at the ILP conference in Birmingham, Dollan—expressing the desire that "the old fellowship of the I.L.P. would return"—made a last ditch attempt to refer back to the NAC the section of its report that supported the rebels. Once again, he argued that they had had "no mandate from the party."[31] But he was, as he anticipated, defeated by 367 votes to 53, and the conference endorsed the actions of the Maxton group by, in Brockway's words, "an overwhelming majority." The conference also decided to "reconstruct" the ILP group in Parliament to include only those who accepted ILP policy as determined by its national conference.[32]

"Discipline Run Mad": The Struggle over Standing Orders Begins

The new Labour MP for Wolverhampton, W. J. Brown, would turn out to be something of a maverick's maverick. Since he was the long-time general secretary of the Civil Service Clerical Association, this may well have surprised those addicted to stereotypes. Before long, he would fall out permanently with the Labour Party; be tempted for a short while by Mosley's New Party, though not sufficiently to join it; and, after losing his seat in the disastrous (for Labour) general election of 1931, return to parliamentary politics as an independent during the Second World War, retaining his seat at Rugby from 1942 until 1950. His indignation and contempt towards the Labour establishment is clear in a *New Leader* contribution, "Discipline Run Mad," in April 1930.

In his article, Brown noted a Downing Street lunch attended not only by Labour ministers but also by representatives of the Liberals, finance, and industry, which was probably bad enough in itself from the standpoint of most ILPers. Worse was to come. The following day, "23 Labour Members of Parliament were 'carpeted' for having, a day or two earlier, voted in favour of the abolition of the Air Force." At a Parliamentary Labour Party meeting, they were told they "must either obey or get out."[33]

The PLP had begun to tighten up its standing orders in 1929, returning to the issue in March the following year.[34] By the time Brown's article appeared, the alarm had already been sounded from the ILP side by Jowett. For him, what was at stake was the radically robust interpretation of representative government for which he had vigorously advocated for more than two decades. Jowett's article "Labour and Cabinet Rule," which appeared in the *Bradford Pioneer* at the end of 1929, spelled out his concerns once more and related them to the course being pursued by MacDonald's government. "If the present Labour Government succeeds in gaining this power to suppress minority action in the House of Commons," he wrote, "then Labour will have established a system of dictatorship over colleagues in Parliament never before known."[35]

The cabinet already had "immense power," wrote Jowett. The previous Monday, the minister in charge of the Unemployment Insurance Bill had moved to close the debate on the bill while John Wheatley was waiting to speak. Jowett doubted that this would have happened had Wheatley—who had served as a cabinet minister himself in the 1924 Labour government—been a Tory or a Liberal. Although, in principle, all MPs should have an equal right to speak, Jowett argued, it was objectionable when the usual practice of giving priority to former cabinet ministers was ignored simply to silence opinions that the government found "disagreeable." Jowett denied that, in voting against the closure of the debate, he had "voted against the Government." He had voted against the decision of the chairman, he insisted.[36]

Jowett ended by reminding readers of the ILP's long-held Bradford policy and reproduced (in bold type) the resolution carried at the ILP conference on the eve of the Great War:

> The famous Bradford Resolution, passed at the Coming of Age conference in Bradford in 1914, is quite clear and still stands. It is the answer to

any charge that might be made against an I.L.P. member of Parliament who voted to increase unemployment benefits this week. I will end by quoting it in full:

> That Cabinet rule, which involves the suppression of the rights of the private member to any adequate voice in the policy of his Party, and which implies the resignation of the Ministry and the dissolution of Parliament when proposals of the Cabinet are negatived, besides making almost impossible the free consideration of proposals which have not received the Cabinet hall-mark, is inimical to the good government of the country; that with a view to ultimately break up this system, the Parliamentary Labour Party be asked to take no account of any such considerations and to vote on all issues in accordance with the principles for which the party stands.

This motion was move by Wm. Leach and seconded by J. H. Palin.[37]

The fact that Leach, Jowett's fellow Bradford MP, had moved the motion in 1914 and was now, as we have seen, a staunch supporter of the government and an active opponent of ILP rebels would not have been lost on many who read this—as, no doubt, Jowett intended.

The reports of ILP conferences and the weekly comments and debates in the *New Leader* suggest that while the vast majority of ILPers were, as conference delegates, happy to nod through motions reaffirming support for Jowett's policy of either replacing or augmenting the cabinet system with House of Commons committees, few were prepared to give such a procedural or constitutional issue the kind of priority it needed if it was to make any real impact. But the growing conflict over Labour Party discipline and the standing orders of the parliamentary party triggered a period when other ILP members emphasized the desirability, even the crucial necessity, of supporting Jowett in his efforts towards "constitutional" change. Indeed, the ILP submitted to the 1929 Labour Party conference a motion demanding that "departmental committees in association with the Minister and composed of members of all parties in proportion to their numbers" should be established. It had the usual negative fate.[38]

In January 1930, the *New Leader* called again for "drastic reform" of parliamentary procedure. The cabinet system, it claimed, had gone from bad to worse. J. Allen Skinner revived Jowett's "Parliament or Palaver?" title in an article claiming that the proposals in the original pamphlet provided "the means of making Parliamentary working tolerable for the self-respecting Back Bench man."[39]

Then came what R. T. McKenzie calls the "culminating absurdity" of the ILP revolt. On 17 July, Brockway was suspended from the Commons, on the motion of MacDonald, for "disregarding the authority of the Chair," as *Hansard* records, when he attempted to initiate a discussion of the critical situation in India. He claimed that over five thousand men and women were in prison there as a result of political activities. In a vain attempt to prevent his colleague's suspension, John Beckett, who would soon follow Mosley not only into the New Party but into fascism and eventually into internment during the Second World War, tried to remove the mace. Its presence at the clerk's table was deemed essential, by long parliamentary tradition, for Commons business to be conducted. Beckett, too, was suspended.[40]

The following week, the *New Leader* editor, John Paton, made a plea for a "sense of proportion" and complained of the "reduction of the private member" to a "mere vote-recording machine." He continued with a reiteration of the call for parliamentary reform: "A method of procedure which *compels* a conscientious member to resort to active revolt is self-condemned. Every citizen who cares for effective democratic government must join in the effort, to which Mr. F. W. Jowett has long given the lead, to reorganise the Parliamentary machine and fit it for the business of a modern State."[41]

Earlier, at Easter, the ILP conference had rejected the demand of Labour's National Executive Committee that MPs pledge not to vote against the official view. Brockway commented in his report on the conference that if this demand were not modified, the relationship of the ILP to the Labour Party would be in serious trouble. He claimed that the Maxton group had voted independently of the official Labour line only ten times out of a possible two hundred. All the same, it was vital for the ILP to have "a coherent group" that was required to support ILP policies.[42]

From the ILP's standpoint, Labour's disciplinary regime was objectionable in principle. In the House of Commons, policy was ultimately decided not by the PLP but by senior cabinet ministers. If PLP decisions were binding on the government, that would be acceptable, but, Brockway insisted, "the 'Left'" could not possibly accept a discipline that imposed "a policy often out of harmony with the decisions of the Labour Party Conference, and in determination of which the Parliamentary Party has no real voice."[43] However, he also argued that Labour's standing orders denying MPs any right to vote against government policies were unenforceable. "Some Labour M.Ps may enjoy the prospect of disciplining the Left Wing," he said, but others, such as Catholics in relation to the Education Bill, would also find themselves coming into conflict with the rigid discipline that was being imposed.[44]

For the ILP, a particular decision of the Labour Party NEC ratcheted up the tension. The national executive committee refused endorsement to Tom Irwin, the ILP candidate adopted in East Renfrewshire, who had made it clear that he intended to accept the statement requiring its candidates to adhere to ILP policies. The NEC's decision, wrote Brockway in the *New Leader*, marked "a new outbreak of disciplinary measures." Of the episode, Paton would later write, "This was really a declaration of war by the Labour Party, and was so regarded by the I.L.P. It came at a time when negotiations for a settlement were still nominally proceeding."[45] Other similar conflicts would follow in constituencies where ILP candidates were initially adopted by Labour, and these would culminate in the general election of 1931 following the collapse of the Labour government, when nineteen ILP candidates were refused endorsement by the Labour Party.[46] If the problem from the viewpoint of the ILP was the unreasonable discipline now being insisted upon by the Labour establishment, from the other side of the conflict, the new arrangements for the ILP parliamentary group and the seemingly unremitting hostility it pursued towards the government were just as objectionable.

The ILP Parliamentary Group: The Fissure Widens

Seven or eight years after the unravelling relationship between the ILP parliamentary group and the Labour government, which most Labour MPs felt duty bound to support, became visible to all, John Paton described the situation in the 1929–30 Parliament as follows:

> In effect the I.L.P. became a permanent opposition within the Labour Party. Its members ignored the official "whips" and took their instructions now solely from the I.L.P. At "Question Time" they shot at the Labour Ministers just as relentlessly as they'd done at their Tory predecessors; their amendments to the Government's proposals became a regular feature of the Order Paper; in every debate it was their speeches which were felt to be the most deadly in exposing the Government's weakness and timidity.[47]

The response of those Labour MPs who believed it their duty to support the Labour government and still belonged to the ILP was almost a mirror image of the attitude of the rebels to the attempts of Labour to impose discipline. At a meeting attended by thirty-nine ILP MPs on 16 July 1929, Maxton had been elected chairman of the group, and his close ally Campbell Stephen its secretary.[48]

If the rebels were outraged by demands for what they saw as blind obedience, those MPs who were now excluded from the ILP parliamentary group because they refused to commit to following ILP policy were equally incensed. The tone of the conflict between these two groups had already been set by Maxton. In answer to a delegate's question at the 1930 ILP conference, he said that the reconstruction of the group could only be carried into full effect after the general election. But he went on to make it clear that the NAC did "intend to exclude from the I.L.P. Group in the House, members who declare themselves I.L.P.ers but have never accepted the policy of the I.L.P. and in public and in private have been hostile to I.L.P. policy."[49] As Ralph Miliband says of the reorganization of the group, "The rebels thus became a more tightly-knit body. But they also became more isolated from their parliamentary colleagues, who deeply resented their activities."[50]

Meanwhile, the NAC still held out hopes of finding a compromise with Labour over the standing orders issue. The dispute had led to certain ILP parliamentary candidates not being selected or, when selected, not endorsed. But the NAC insisted that, at a meeting with Labour's National Executive Committee in July 1930, it had become clear that the objections of the Labour Party were apparently based on a misinterpretation of a clause in the "Regulations for I.L.P. Candidates" adopted by the Carlisle conference in 1929. It had been "mutually agreed" that the standing orders question was "capable of amicable settlement." In the meantime, the NAC said, "the work of reforming the Parliamentary Group was being carried through."[51] This process was by no means uncontested. One of the most outspoken of the internal critics was, predictably, Patrick Dollan.

Dollan made a contribution to the 1930 ILP summer school under the title "A Rebel Against the Rebels," which is how he saw himself. As the *New Leader* reported, he expressed "disbelief in sectional groups working in the House of Commons, and asked that I.L.P. Members in the House should not just be fault-finders."[52] He was not alone. According to the NAC report to the 1931 ILP conference, Shinwell had raised the position of those ILP MPs who, like himself, first as financial secretary to the War Office and then as secretary for Mines, had accepted office under MacDonald. The NAC had conceded that having raised no objection to members joining the government at the time, it could not do so in retrospect. But if they wished to join the ILP's parliamentary group, they should be asked for an assurance that if an occasion arose on which the NAC believed that they should resign their offices, they would be prepared to do so, and they should also give assurances that they were "advocating the policies of the I.L.P. within the Labour Party." Moreover, in future, they should consult the NAC before taking office.[53] These were not conditions that Shinwell or any of the other holders of governmental office were likely to find remotely acceptable.

Shinwell was tenacious in his objections to the changes in the ILP's parliamentary group. This triggered an exchange that spread over two editions of the *New Leader* in November 1930. In a piece headlined "Shinwell and the I.L.P.:

Light in the Darkness" on 14 November, Shinwell was reported as arguing that members of the Parliamentary Labour Party would be "compelled to leave the I.L.P." if the NAC enforced the policy that had been adopted. He asked: "Am I to assume that, if the I.L.P. minority can flout the Parliamentary Labour Party, then the minority in the I.L.P. can flout the N.A.C.?" Surely "the right to flout" was not a monopoly of the ILP group.[54] Paton replied the following week, insisting that "few subjects have been more fully discussed by the I.L.P." and that Shinwell must accept that the decisions reached would be enforced.[55] In the same issue, Dollan complained that "a membership of 142 I.L.P.ers ... had been reduced to a fragment which exercised political anarchy instead of Socialist discipline" and pleaded for more tolerance of party members with differing views.[56]

At the 1931 ILP conference, Dollan was supported by George Hardie, "brother of the pioneer." No ILP MP disagreed with ILP policy, Hardie claimed. "The disagreement was in method." He declared that he hated dictatorship, and he urged toleration "so that the Party might again become the mainspring of the Movement." An altercation involving Stephen and Dollan became so heated that they were admonished from the chair.[57] Tensions were continuing to grow in the ILP, but neither was MacDonald's government itself free of them.

Mosley's "National Policy" and the ILP: From Fissure to Chasm

The most dramatic dissent from within government centred on Oswald Mosley's "memorandum," his resignation, and the sequence of initiatives that moved him and some of his supporters to fascism. This would indelibly colour the political atmosphere of the 1930s.

MacDonald had appointed J. H. "Jimmy" Thomas as Lord Privy Seal and had charged him with unemployment policy. One of those given the task of assisting him, as the Chancellor of the Duchy of Lancaster, was Mosley. Skidelsky summarizes Thomas and the response to his appointment as follows: "Totally devoid of constructive ideas, intimate with the City and big business, the boon companion of half the House of Commons, the jingoistic upholder of imperial and national unity, his appointment gladdened conservatives and dismayed radicals."[58] If this was really how Thomas was seen, it is hardly surprising that Mosley found his subordinate position frustrating.

With support from George Lansbury and Tom Johnston, once the editor of *Forward*, who had been given similar roles in addressing unemployment, Mosley drew up and submitted his memorandum. It called for a much more co-ordinated governmental and administrative response to unemployment and for long-term economic reconstruction. It included short-term measures put forward by himself and his two colleagues and a financial and credit policy that owed something to advice sought from Keynes.⁵⁹ When the document was rejected by the cabinet in May 1930, Mosley resigned from the government. For the rest of 1930, he pursued his demand for an interventionist policy within the Labour Party.

Mosley had little success with the PLP but rather more at the Labour Party annual conference in October. Brockway's later account records that he had "never seen or heard such an ovation at a Labour Party conference" than the reaction to Mosley's speech.⁶⁰ The motion was narrowly defeated by 1,251,000 to 1,046,000, with most of the votes, of course, being the "block votes" of affiliated unions. The vote showed, Michael Foot writes in his biography of Bevan, that Mosley had "the overwhelming majority of the constituency parties behind him."⁶¹

It looked as though Mosley's intention was to secure the Labour Party leadership. A new version of the memorandum was produced. Supported by seventeen Labour MPs in February 1931, it proposed a national economic planning organization tasked with producing a national plan, an investment board to rationalize and reorganize British industry, and a mixture of protection and imperial preference. It also included, notes Foot, "some startling additions affecting the reform of Parliament."⁶² Noel Thompson sees John Strachey, still one of Mosley's closest supporters at the time, as largely responsible for the idea that the government, reduced essentially to a small cabinet of five, would have sole right to initiate legislation by Orders in Council, with parliamentary debates on its proposals only taking place if more than two hundred MPs petitioned the Speaker.⁶³ The revised memorandum, *A National Policy: An Account of the Emergency Programme Advanced by Sir Oswald Mosley*, whose main authors were Aneurin Bevan, W. J. Brown, Strachey, and Allen Young, was published. Meanwhile, Mosley and some, but by no means all, of his supporters—Bevan being the most notable exception—had resigned from Labour and set up the New Party.⁶⁴

Mosley's plan "partly accorded with the earlier analysis of the I.L.P. devised by Hobson and Wise," notes Foot.⁶⁵ Mosley had some support in the ILP, with some ILPers following him into the New Party, and some—like Beckett—even into fascism. But most had major objections to Mosley's scheme, seeing it as an emergency program to prop up capitalism rather than a blueprint for advancing socialism; it was also imperialistic, authoritarian, and, at least prospectively, anti-democratic.

In early December, the NAC rejected Mosley's proposals because they placed otherwise desirable goals in the context of an emergency cabinet system and the British Empire rather than of the "Socialist organisation of world trade." The following week, W. J. Brown, one of the signatories of the revised memorandum, denied that it was anti-democratic.[66] *Forward*'s comments on Mosley's proposals were scathing. It had, it said, expected something better, after his resignation speech, than the "political cocktail" Mosley delivered. His advocacy of "Export Trade and the Commonwealth" was "dangerously near Beaverbrook bunk."[67]

In the new year, John Paton complained that Mosley had misrepresented the ILP's Socialism in Our Time policy in claiming that it meant a "twenty five year delay" before any decisive action would take place. On the contrary, he insisted, it meant "*immediate* large-scale operations immensely greater in intention and scope than anything Sir Oswald proposes."[68] At the ILP's London divisional conference, Allen Young, now seen as Mosley's "first lieutenant," had given an "excellent speech," reported the *New Leader*. He made the case for "the short-term policy of setting capitalism on its feet, at the same time securing a measure of control over wages, prices and general economic conditions." But Dr. C. A. Smith, who would chair the ILP at the end of the 1930s, argued against the "Imperial ideas" being advocated, and a restatement of ILP policy was approved with overwhelming support.[69]

After the resignations from the Labour Party, Brockway, in the *New Leader* article "Running Away from Socialism," accused the Mosleyites of abandoning the cause.[70] For E. F. Wise, Mosley was "the discreet buccaneer." Ten days before, his talk had been of "a New Labour Party"; now, it was just the "New Party." Wise observed that the bold spirit of Mosley's Birmingham program of five years before had gone. There was "no talk now of 'the banks for the people.'" As Wise saw it, Mosley was "adroitly angling for the support of disillusioned elements in all the old Parties." It was also noticeable that dictatorship had "receded to the last chapter." While the ILP shared "his ardent desire" for the reform of parliamentary procedure, "of Mussolinis and Pilsudskis we are suspicious."[71]

Hot on the heels of the defection of the Mosleyites came the resignation, as Minister of Education, of Sir Charles Trevelyan. He was frustrated by the reappearance of the old issue of religion and the schools and despairing of being able to get the school leaving age raised, which was one of the short-term measures proposed by the Mosley memorandum to reduce unemployment. Trevelyan was also, very explicitly, totally disenchanted with MacDonald's leadership. The reactions of the Parliamentary Labour Party and the *Daily Herald* were hostile, but the *New Leader* was supportive. It published the resignation speech made to his constituents, emphasizing Trevelyan's declaration: "I want to see a Labour Government cease from the mere effort to keep office and just govern decently, and turn to an effort to break through to Socialism and establish a new Society."[72] It also carried an article by the former minister under the title "Break Through to Socialism," in which, the paper noted, "he advocated the Socialist plan embodied in the 'Socialism in Our Time' policy of the I.L.P."[73] The gulf between the Labour government and its supporters and the ILP continued to widen apace.

Divisions *within* the ILP would continue to increase, but the extent of these was partially masked by the more general dissatisfaction of ILPers with MacDonald's government, unhappiness that covered a wide political spectrum within the smaller party. One of the rebel ILP MPs was Elijah Sandham, who complained that "a sense of Socialism seems completely lacking in some of our Cabinet Ministers."[74] He would later support disaffiliation from the Labour Party but then soon find himself at odds with those attempting to commit the ILP to a "revolutionary policy." In February 1931, a front-page *New Leader* article by Wise denounced Snowden's "stiff-necked financial orthodoxy."[75] Wise would soon be one of the most persistent and outspoken opponents of disaffiliation.

The dispute over discipline and the standing orders of the PLP rumbled on interminably. A NAC statement on relations between the ILP and Labour, in June 1931, listed the eight occasions when the ILP group had voted against the government and emphasized that "no fewer than 126 out of the 280 Labour M.Ps have, on one occasion or another, voted against the Government." From their Labour critics' point of view, this statement totally failed to recognize any difference between an individual rebellion and an organized opposition within the party. The NAC complained, emphatically, that new standing orders sought to "impose constraints on the Members of Parliament hitherto unknown in the Parliamentary history of this country."[76]

The following month, Brockway reported the ILP's response to the latest letter on the issue from Arthur Henderson, the Labour Party secretary, under the headline "The Crisis Before the I.L.P." Agreement might still be reached, he argued. The ILP recognized the need for the parliamentary party to have standing orders, but it could not accept rules that prohibited Labour MPs from "voting against the Official Whip when their Socialist convictions and pledges" compelled them to do so. Brockway urged the ILP to press forward with the Socialism in Our Time campaign. A week later, the *New Leader* made a point of listing the "Actual Offences" of seven MPs reported to the PLP and published a letter from Jowett detailing occasions when MacDonald, Snowden, and Lansbury had voted against the official line in earlier years.[77]

The arrival of a National Government was anticipated some weeks before it became a reality. Brockway tells us in *Inside the Left* that in June 1931, he heard that "MacDonald was entering into secret negotiations with representatives of the Conservative and Liberal Parties to scuttle the Labour Government and form a National Government" and that he sounded a warning in the *New*

Leader. Brockway is referring to his front-page piece "Towards A 'National' Government," published near the end of July 1931, in which he alleged that British capitalism had "quivered on the edge of a precipice for two days" the previous week and that "influential feelers for formation of National Government had been put out."[78]

Meanwhile, the ILP's final parliamentary revolt against the MacDonald government had ended, after "one of the longest sittings of Parliament on record," with the passing of the Anomalies Bill. Promoted by Margaret Bondfield, this bill limited the right to unemployment benefits of casual and seasonal workers and married women. The seventeen members of the ILP group sometimes had the support of other Labour MPs and of a solitary Liberal, Frank Owen, but for the most part, the ILP group was "left to maintain the fight alone."[79]

12

The Road Towards Departure

Four days after Ramsay MacDonald replaced the Labour government with the kind of coalition Fenner Brockway had anticipated, Brailsford, still very much an active contributor to the *New Leader*, struck what now seems a surprisingly optimistic note: "the second Labour Government has fallen," he wrote, "and all of us feel relief." He roundly denounced what he called "the Bankers' Government." From first to last, MacDonald had been "in the grip of the City," which had been covering up its own "reckless profiteering by an attack upon the unemployed." The new situation left the ILP with questions about its own future. "May I add an entirely unofficial suggestion of my own?" Brailsford asked. "It is that the I.L.P., while it flings itself into this struggle, should aim at restoring the unity of the liberated Labour Party. We do not want to recall the differences of recent months."[1]

From the National Government to Labour's Defeat

For a brief moment, it seemed as though the ILP might take Brailsford's advice to heart and attempt to let bygones be bygones as far as its relationship with the Labour Party was concerned. *Forward* urged its readers to avoid "personal bitterness" and to demand the nationalization of banks and a "constructive financial and economic policy."[2] The same issue of the *New Leader* that carried Brailsford's article quoted above called on the Labour Party and the General Council of the Trades Union Congress to rally the troops for resistance.[3] But though some in the ILP—notably, Brailsford and Wise—were to make the case for restarting relations with Labour with a clean slate and would continue to argue along the same lines right up until disaffiliation, this was not to be the dominant mood.

A week after Brailsford's appeal for unity, the *New Leader* featured a front-page article calling for a "new revolutionary outlook" and a "new revolutionary tactic." There was no sign that the Labour Party recognized that these were needed, the writer said. In ousting MacDonald and electing its new leader,

Arthur Henderson, the party had made "no attempt to find out whether Mr. Henderson's views on the economy were substantially altered from what they were a fortnight ago." Elsewhere in the issue, Clynes was reported to have said that "the I.L.P. are against us as they are against the Government and against everybody else. They are irreconcilable." His conclusion was hardly challenged by the *Leader*'s assertion that the PLP standing orders were "only the superficial manifestation of a fundamental difference in point of view, which was the real thing that divided the I.L.P. Group from the rest of the members of the Parliamentary Labour Party." The paper confirmed that the ILP would continue to attack gradualism.[4]

The rejection of gradualism was common ground for both supporters and opponents of disaffiliation, though what exactly was meant by the term was not clear. Certainly, Brailsford's "The 'City' or the Nation?" series, soon to be published as an ILP pamphlet, pulled no punches. It had "always been evident that the City would mobilise against socialism, and it was now clear that it had done so against the mild quasi-Liberal reformism for which the late Government stood." Labour was inevitably faced with a decisive break with its reformist traditions, he concluded.[5]

Brailsford focused on the City of London. "For many years," he wrote, it had "been a commonplace among Socialist thinkers and writers in this country that the balance of power among the forces of Capitalism was slipping. Since the war it has passed unquestionably from the industrialist to the financier. It is no exaggeration to say that for ten years the bankers have governed us." In the crisis, the governor of the Bank of England had refused to borrow from the United States without the imposition of cuts in the "dole"—the unemployment benefit. The way the issues had been presented to the public turned on what he called the "Misuse of 'We.'" Brailsford argued that "we" were being shouldered with the responsibility for what had happened: "We are not a handful of moneylenders who make a profit of 5 per cent by lending other people's money with a recklessness which ought to destroy their singular reputation as experts. But to this unsavoury profiteering interest the entire life of the nation is about to be sacrificed."[6] He ended with a challenge. "On this question the Labour Movement must make up its mind promptly," he declared. "We have to settle this issue of the City versus the Nation. Until we settle it this will not be an independent country, and Labour must renounce all hope of power."[7]

In his *New Leader* article "What Should the I.L.P. Do?" Brockway attempted to answer the question posed by his title. This edition of the *Leader* featured advertisements for his own *The I.L.P. in Crisis* pamphlet, as well as Brailsford's *The 'City' or the Nation?* and Maxton's *A "Living Wage" for All*. Like Brailsford, Brockway believed that "gradualism is dead," but otherwise, his emphasis was very different. Capitalism was "tottering." There was, he insisted, a real possibility of the "collapse of Capitalism in chaos." So, he pleaded, "let us make it the final fight."[8]

In early October, in an "Open Letter" to delegates to the Labour Party conference, Brockway acknowledged the difficulties of Labour MPs, even the "heroism" of "those who faced misunderstanding by voting against their convictions because of a sense of loyalty to the Party." But the ILP could not accept the present standing orders. The paper promoted a "One Hundred Thousand Shillings Fund for Socialism," invoking Socialism in Our Time and featuring photos of former chairmen of the party from Hardie onwards—with the notable exception of Clifford Allen, who was now supporting MacDonald's National Labour Organisation, the group formed to organize the activities of the small number of MPs from the Labour Party who now supported the National Government.[9]

John Strachey had now broken with Mosley and was rapidly realigning himself as a supporter—though not a member—of the CPGB. In the same October 1931 issue of the *New Leader*, in "Where Does the I.L.P. Stand?" he declared gradualism bankrupt. He then asserted that the ILP should call for the return at the election of "only revolutionary Socialist candidates" and adopt a program that would include working to "establish a workers' Dictatorship capable of destroying Capitalism and laying the foundations of Socialism."

In contrast to both Brockway and Strachey, Wise declared himself encouraged by the Labour Party election manifesto, which called for the public ownership of banks together with other features that he saw as being close to the Socialism in Our Time program.[10] But the ILP chairman's message the following week centred on the refusal of the Labour Party to endorse ILP candidates who refused to accept the PLP standing orders. "The real issue is not rules and regulations," Brailsford insisted, "It is policy. The Standing Orders are only the test of policy." The real question was whether Labour would "go all out for Socialism."[11]

The refusal of endorsements made Brailsford's position more difficult, as he was the first to recognize. Like Wise, he saw Labour's program as "a frontal attack on the very centre of the British capitalist system." It was nothing less than declaring "class war." To commit "to nationalise banking, or even to control it effectively (if that could be done without full public ownership) is to strike at the seat of power." The problem was that it was difficult to believe that the Labour Party was "in earnest": had it not, "while adopting this apparently revolutionary programme, in effect banished the I.L.P. from its ranks"? Was the Labour Party, he asked, "so strong, and so sure of victory, after these desertions, that it can afford to lose a regiment before it enters the battle?" The issue of discipline had only become acute because the party had been "led into strange courses by the three deserters who now direct the enemy." There had been rebels only because the leadership had "fallen into false hands," and the remedy lay "not in tight discipline, but in honest leadership."[12]

One member—indeed, a senior officer—in Brailsford's regiment was Fenner Brockway. Refused endorsement like the other ILP candidates, he made clear in a letter to Labour Party leader Henderson, published in the *New Leader*, that he was not prepared to say that he would never vote against the party whips. He could not break pledges "authorised by the Party programme." He asserted that for the previous twenty-five years, the course Labour had pursued in Parliament had not been decided by the Parliamentary Labour Party. Instead, Brockway wrote, "it was dictated by Mr. MacDonald and Mr. Snowden."[13]

This was one of the most volatile—arguably *the* most volatile—periods in the history of the Labour Party. As Ben Pimlott points out, there were three splits in eighteen months: first the Mosley/New Party breakaway, then MacDonald's National Labour Organization, and, still to come, the disaffiliation of the ILP from Labour.[14] Initially, the National Government presented its role as short-term: it was "to deal with the national emergency only."[15] But the various pressures within its constituent parties resolved themselves into the decision to go to the electorate as a coalition.

The 1931 general election took place on 27 October. In September, when it became evident that MacDonald was about to call an election, *Forward* headlined Maxton's forecast with "A Smashing Workers' Majority."[16] This was not to be. On the contrary, it was a disaster for Labour. In 1929, Labour had been the largest single party in the House of Commons. Now, it was reduced to double figures, only twenty more than the once more divided Liberal Party. Even the new leader of the party, Arthur Henderson, failed to secure election, with the result that George Lansbury was elected to chair the PLP.

Those who followed MacDonald and became the National Labour Organisation could muster only 13 seats, while the Conservatives soared to a dominating position with 470. This made even more daunting the task of those like Clifford Allen who believed MacDonald had made the best of the awful choices available in August. Allen still hoped, as Martin Gilbert tells us, that MacDonald would be able to "maintain some degree of Socialist activity in what was a predominantly Conservative government."[17]

Exactly how many seats were held by the Labour Party after the 1931 election depends on how one counts the ILP MPs. They were in an anomalous position in that though the ILP was still part of the Labour Party, the unendorsed ILP MPs were excluded from the Parliamentary Labour Party.[18] But however one does the counting, the Labour contingent had shrunk to around fifty. In *Inside the Left*, Brockway lists five surviving members of the ILP parliamentary group, but two of those soon left: Kirkwood did not follow the ILP when it disaffiliated, and Richard Wallhead, a former chairman of the ILP, returned to the Labour Party in September 1933. The remaining trio of Maxton, Buchanan, and McGovern were to be augmented by the success of Campbell Stephen in 1935. As Gidon Cohen says, however, there was no sign of the ILP being able to look forward to electoral success outside of a very few local strongholds—above all, Glasgow.[19]

Andrew Thorpe, in his study of the 1931 election, sees Labour poised "on the verge of a great transition" but lacking the "detailed policy work" that would have made its offer to the electorate credible in the way that it was to become in 1945. In fact, he says, its manifesto was "little more than an article of faith from an already doomed and pessimistic party."[20] But the extent of the defeat was a great shock to many, including the ILP. At the *New Leader*, Paton was about to hand over the editorship to Brockway. His final editorial appeared in the edition following the election. "Not in their most pessimistic moments," he wrote, "did anyone imagine the Labour Party was fated to receive the crushing blow which has befallen it in this election." It undermined democracy and made it difficult to argue against those who questioned the utility of "the democratic method."[21]

A "New Era" in ILP-Labour Relations?

In the week after the election, Maxton took stock of the new situation in the *Leader*. He argued that had Labour adopted the Socialism in Our Time policy, it would have meant refusing to lead a minority government in 1929 and developing a militant opposition. In future, he wrote, the ILP "must think of itself again more as a Movement of the people and less as a political party with Parliamentary skills."[22]

In the same issue, which also reported the death of A. J. Cook, Brailsford returned to his plea for a new era in ILP-Labour relations. "It is possible," he wrote, "that like all pioneering movements, the I.L.P. thinks too much of recording protests and registering dissent. History does not move in that way. It moves by the common action of great masses. We shall best serve the workers by contributing with all the fire and intelligence we can command to the creation of a massive unity." Labour should clear up "the needless tangle in the House" and the ILP should cooperate in considering how best to help it. Labour had now broken with "reformist tradition." It aimed at economic power.[23]

Moreover, no one should underestimate MacDonald, Brailsford warned. He was "skilled in all the arts of evasion, negation and delay" and, as prime minister, had the right to call another election whenever he chose. It was perfectly possible that he might "attempt yet another essay in national heroism" and try to form an anti-Tory coalition. This was best combatted from inside the Labour Party. The ILP must not have a half-hearted approach towards Labour: "We are in or out. If we are in, let us stay in with graciousness and loyalty. If we go out our fate will be such impotence as has befallen Mosley's group." For his part, however, Brockway remained skeptical. The standing orders dispute was a symptom of a much wider conflict, and the question remained whether Labour was going "to break with gradualism."[24]

Among the minority of Labour MPs who had survived the 1931 election was Dr. Alfred Salter. He thought Brailsford's *New Leader* article "the first common-sense pronouncement" in the paper for months. As someone who had been a member of the ILP for twenty-five years, he had been "terribly distressed by the impossibilist attitude" in recent years. There were now, Salter insisted, "three 'musts'" for the ILP. First, it must show "a *whole-hearted declaration of loyalty to the larger Movement*"; the "bitter, treacherous and malevolent attacks which have made the I.L.P. loathed amongst Labour Party members must stop for good." Second, ILP MPs must accept the PLP standing orders "*just as the rest of us have done*"; they were aimed not at suppressing individual dissent but "at *organised* opposition to majority decisions." Finally, the ILP must give up "toying with revolution."[25]

Salter was critical of Maxton, who, he wrote, had "leaned more and more of late to the Communist outlook and tactic." There was no way that the chasm between the ILP and the CPGB could be spanned. Democrats could never accept the notion of a dictatorship of "a conscious minority." He was scathing about the standing of the ILP: "The I.L.P. appears to outsiders as a negligible body and a spiteful rump, daily dwindling in numbers and hardly of more account than the Mosleyites." If the changes he urged were not made, Salter predicted, the ILP would degenerate into "a mere nuisance and irritant, like the Communist Party."[26]

An editorial note rejected completely Salter's interpretation of the standing order issue, and the *New Leader* was able to cite some support outside ILP ranks for its opposition to the standing orders. The following week, Josiah Wedgwood—another surviving Labour MP and, like Salter, a former member of the ILP—was praised for his "manly refusal to accept the tyranny of the present Standing Orders."[27] But the breach with Labour was widened when that party's executive committee instructed constituent Labour parties to select only candidates who accepted the standing orders.[28] By this time, a *New Leader* editorial had lambasted the Labour Party for its failure to adopt "a revolutionary Socialist policy to meet the rapidly declining condition of Capitalism and the desperate plight of the working class." In the same issue, Maxton emphasized this failure under the headline "Labour Has Not Learned."[29]

The debate on possible withdrawal from the Labour Party was now underway in earnest. *Forward* was totally opposed and supported Brailsford, claiming that he had done "more than anybody else to outline the Socialism in Our Time policy." The ILP would have no future outside the Labour Party. "If it takes the last stupid step of leaving the Labour Party and going into isolation that will be the end of the I.L.P. as an organisation with the slightest influence in British politics," it predicted.[30]

As in the preceding years, *Labour's Northern Voice* was heard mainly on the pro-disaffiliation side of the debate, though in December 1931, Ellis Smith made the argument that disaffiliation would lead to isolation. In the same issue, as part of the series "Should the I.L.P. Leave the Labour Party?" Bob Edwards argued for disaffiliation. The election of Labour's shadow cabinet indicated no change in the party's policies, he maintained. "A disaffiliated ILP would give us a new lease of life by attracting into our ranks hundreds of conscious Socialists" who had been driven out of the Labour Party by its shameful compromises.[31]

At first glance, especially from the distance of the twenty-first century, it is difficult to understand why, faced with an appalling political earthquake, both sides in the dispute were not more ready to compromise, as Brailsford and a few others were urging. With its parliamentary representation so reduced and its standing so undermined by near electoral wipeout, surely Labour could not easily contemplate losing such a core of active members as the ILP constituted. Yet Salter's outspoken attack on the course taken by the ILP in the preceding period gives us a good indication of why, in spite of this, the hardening of attitudes on the ILP side was complemented by the continuing intransigence of the Labour Party leadership. As Pimlott says, Labour Party leader George Lansbury had "little sympathy for the rebellious ILP. When Maxton gave trouble, Lansbury was as firm as Henderson that ILP members must subscribe to Labour Party Standing Orders or get out." Pimlott asserts persuasively that "MacDonald's departure made little difference to the quarrel; if anything it made the NEC and PLP leadership more insistent on a rigid adherence to Party decisions."[32]

As 1932, the crucial year for the ILP, approached, it was striking how spread across almost the entire political spectrum were so many who had played prominent roles in the party at various times in the previous decade. The disaffiliation of the ILP would extend this even further before the end of that year. Strachey, as already noted, was moving rapidly towards uncritical support of the Communist Party. A few years earlier, his inspiration had been Mosley, who he had once hoped would "some day do the things of which we dream." But after the complete failure of the New Party at the 1931 election, Mosley was about to launch the British Union of Fascists, an enterprise in which he would be joined by two former prominent ILPers—John Beckett and Dr. Robert Forgan. MacDonald and Snowden, who a decade earlier had been almost synonymous with the ILP, were now at the head of a government reliant on the Conservatives. Supporting them was Walton Newbold and the former ILP chairman Clifford Allen. Ten years or so earlier, Newbold had been successively a leader of the ILP's Left Wing, a committed Communist, and even, briefly, a Communist MP.[33] Others, like Salter, were still unequivocally committed to Labour.

The Disaffiliation Debate Heats Up

In the *New Leader*, in early 1932, E. F. Wise made a case against disaffiliation, while John Paton reported that the East Anglia Division had supported disaffiliation in light of Labour's "continued adherence to 'gradualist' policies and failure to learn the lessons of the election." Wise argued that not only would the standing orders be of little importance while Labour was in opposition, but that they could be changed at any time. The ILP should put forward "reasonable modifications."[34] At the very beginning of the year, Brockway had argued that it was difficult to "look at the world without reaching the conviction that we are approaching a revolutionary epoch." His conviction was growing that the Labour Party was "so distant from the realisation of Socialist duty at this time" that continued association with it was becoming a handicap for the ILP.[35] It was, he added two weeks later, hard to avoid the conclusion "that Capitalism is approaching a series of crises which must eventually lead to a complete economic breakdown."[36]

The idea that the collapse of capitalism was imminent was widespread, though by no means universal, in ILP circles. Even the philosopher—and future star of the BBC "Brains Trust"—C. E. M. Joad, believed that "a revolutionary situation may be upon us at any time during the next few years." Many of his friends, he told readers of *Forward*, had joined the Communist Party. He had not, and his reasons for not doing so were also reasons for remaining a member of the ILP. He believed that violence unleashes "forces of evil which have effects unforeseen and unforeseeable." He saw the Labour Party as torn between its professed policy of superseding capitalism and its actual policy of getting the best deal possible for workers within it. It was "no more a socialist party than Britain a socialist country." The task was still to make it one; therefore, the ILP should remain affiliated, work to transform the outlook of the Labour Party's members, and "seek to remould it from within."[37]

Wise would have concurred with Joad's conclusion, but he dissented from the notion that capitalism was close to extinction. "There is much talk in some quarters of the imminent collapse of Capitalism," he noted. But what did this collapse entail: a sudden, complete stop or "a long drawn-out process of increasing trade difficulties?" How could the ILP hope to exercise any power against the organized labour movement, and was it not "the very worst moment" to split the movement? Letters critical of Wise's support for continued affiliation with Labour soon followed, including one from Joseph Southall asking, "Where is the evidence of any change of heart in the Labour Party?" There was no doubt that the leadership of the ILP agreed with Southall rather than with Wise and Brailsford. As Maxton saw it, Wise seemed to believe that when MacDonald and Snowden formed the National Government "the Labour Party was born again." On the contrary, he argued, Labour was "not now an instrument working for unity, but for disintegration and disillusionment."[38]

Brockway, reconsidering the Socialism in Our Time policy in an article with the title "After the Revolution," concluded that it had relied on "Socialism through prosperity; a series of measures speedy but successive, to secure a redistribution of the national income and the control of the key sources of economic power." It was now clear that it was "not speedy enough" and that a "much more drastic policy" was needed. On another page, Paton reported the "overwhelming weight of support" for disaffiliation at the South West divisional conference.[39]

It was clear that the party was seriously divided on disaffiliation. At the end of January 1932, Paton noted that, "contrary to what had been expected," five divisional conferences had rejected disaffiliation, with only three—London and South, East Anglia, and the South West—supporting it.[40] One of the divisions that had rejected disaffiliation was the largest—Scotland. *Forward* reported the Scottish Division's vote of 88 to 49 under the headline "Decisive Vote Against the Break with Labour Party."[41]

In his chairman's address at the Scottish divisional conference, Dollan had expressed regret that "the Party was divided by theoretical differences in a kind of civil warfare." Three of the Clydesiders—Maxton, Buchanan, and McGovern—had spoken for disaffiliation, but Kirkwood had echoed Dollan's complaint that the movement was "split from top to bottom." He claimed to have been "victimised" for his stance in favour of remaining within the Labour Party. He had been invited to open the Leeds ILP bazaar but was then told that he was not wanted: "That's the tolerance of the I.L.P.!" he declared emphatically.[42]

The Scottish conference did not confine itself to decisively rejecting disaffiliation. An addendum to its motion for the coming ILP national conference instructed the NAC to approach Labour to discuss moving "towards a common policy" in the House of Commons. This policy was to be based on a future

Labour government rejecting "Cabinet Rule" and having its ministers elected by and responsible to the PLP, which was, in its turn, to promote policy "in accordance with conference decisions." Labour should also revise its standing orders to "allow a greater measure of freedom." The addendum was passed by 101 to 5, with Maxton apparently voting with the minority.[43]

The Scottish—and other anti-disaffiliation votes—gave hope to those who wished to remain with Labour. In the *New Leader*, Wise commented that it was plain from the divisional conferences that the branches wanted to stay inside the Labour Party. This claim was echoed the following day by Emrys Hughes, writing in *Forward*. In the same issue of the Scottish paper Paton argued that there was no "observable tendency" towards compromise by the Labour Party and that remaining affiliated could therefore "only lead, **so long as the I.L.P. maintains its militant policies**, to renewed irritation, confusions, and mutual frustrations." Nevertheless, Hughes noted, there had been an "overwhelming decision of the I.L.P. Divisional Conferences against disaffiliation."[44]

Maxton rejected these arguments, along with any notion that the ILP had made itself unpopular in the broader labour movement. "However unpopular we have made ourselves with Labour Leaders and Trade Union Officials," he argued, "that unpopularity does not extend far beyond that somewhat limited circle of the elect of the Labour Aristocracy."[45]

A week after Maxton's article appeared, Wise made it clear that he was pleading for consideration of the ILP staying in the Labour Party "at the moment when this Party has accepted Socialism as its policy and is within measurable distance of having the opportunity of putting it into effect." But—ominously, from Wise's point of view—in the same issue of the *New Leader*, Paton reported support for Maxton's point of view in "Packed Halls for Maxton."[46] The tide seemed now to be turning in favour of disaffiliation.

The most fervent and uncompromising supporters of disaffiliation were to be found in the London-based Revolutionary Policy Committee (RPC), formed in 1930, at the instigation of Dr. Carl Cullen, chairman of the Poplar branch, who had already established a committee to work for disaffiliation. In early 1932, Cullen's branch published a "Memorandum on the Present Political and Economic Situation in the I.L.P." It assumed the imminent collapse of capitalism and saw the possibility of a revolutionary crisis developing from a general strike. The ILP should disaffiliate on the basis not of rejection of the PLP's standing orders but in order to clear the ground for a revolutionary policy that recognized the need for a "dictatorship of the proletariat," with the setting up of workers' councils as a preparatory step.[47]

As the ILP annual conference approached, the Poplar branch's March program included, as one of the speakers for its Tuesday meetings, Jack Gaster, another leading RPC member. There was also to be a speaker from Friends of the Soviet Union, whose talk was titled "The Soviet System of Government." As for the coming ILP conference, it was absolutely essential, according to the Poplar branch, to disaffiliate from what was now "a reformist party." That accomplished, the ILP must "adopt and propagate a definitely revolutionary policy."[48] The RPC's initial support lay in London, but even there, branches were divided. Poplar, Clapham, and Marylebone were among those pressing for immediate disaffilation, while Golders Green, Leyton, and the North West London Federation were in favour of remaining in the Labour Party and continuing to press for socialist policies.[49]

The NAC was clearly concerned that divisions in the party were becoming fraught. Wishing to avoid or at least minimize a split, it insisted that, contrary to impressions given by press reporting, there was no one in the ILP who was in favour of gradualism. The issue was simply whether or not to stay in the Labour Party. The NAC had decided to make no recommendation on this and to leave it "to the free decision of the Conference," which was now approaching rapidly.[50]

The arguments of both sides were given plenty of space in the *New Leader*. In March, under the heading "A Non-Member Remonstrates," Louis Anderson Fenn, the prospective Labour candidate for Handsworth, recommended that ILPers try to "see ourselves as others see us." He felt that the ILP had "during the last ten years provoked psychological reactions which have prevented the adoption of its often quite sound ideas." ILPers did not realize "the sort of exasperation which their rather 'superior' attitudes provokes among good Socialists who are members of the Labour Party." The ILP had "become a sort of rival show which claims to have custodianship of the ark of the covenant of Socialism." It should "stop trying to be a political party." This last recommendation was likely to be contemplated by few on either side of the disaffiliation debate.[51]

Firmly on the pro-affiliation side of the argument, *Forward*, and above all Dollan, buoyed by the Scottish conference result, remained optimistic both about the final outcome of the debate and the possibility of making peace with Labour. At the end of February, Dollan, in "A Move Towards Peace," wrote that he had detected the potential for conciliation when the NAC agreed to approach the Labour Party again on the standing orders issue. He was convinced that there was "no outstanding difficulty." He complained of "Communist tactics" by the Left involving a "secret meeting" in Glasgow the previous Sunday, and he chided those responsible with a failure to accept defeat "in a sporting spirit"—a notion that would seem to many very odd later in the year when Dollan failed to accept the disaffiliation decision in a like manner. He had wanted the NAC to recommend support for the Scottish pro-affiliation motion at the coming

ILP conference, but the supporters of disaffiliation, he alleged, "evaded the issue by voting for no recommendation."[52]

As the annual ILP annual conference at Blackpool approached, Paton once more insisted that there was no division within the party on gradualism. As for the dispute with Labour over the standing orders, while this was immediately important to MPs, the issue had a wider significance as "the Parliamentary expression of the challenge presented to 'gradualism' by the I.L.P. conception of a planned and speedy advance to Socialism." In "A Personal Plea," Brailsford made an appeal to the party to remain affiliated to Labour. "It would be ridiculous, if it were not painful, that our tiny group should stand apart when a mere remnant of a Labour Party faces overwhelming hosts." He wanted the ILP to fling itself with "ardour and generosity" into the "general work of the Labour Party." The ILP was still an important factor in the larger party. "I think that the chance came last August for a dramatic reconciliation," he wrote, "and I regret that the leaders of the I.L.P. did not seize it then." But it was not too late. At the general election, Labour had "boldly challenged the City." By "declaring for the social control of banking and finance, it struck at the seat of power of British Capitalism."[53]

But other contributors in the same issue suggested that the tide was still flowing in the direction of disaffiliation. While the NAC announced that it would be presenting "a revolutionary policy" to the conference, Jennie Lee, who had already made a reputation as a militant ally of Maxton in the 1929–31 Parliament, took the view that Labour's commitment to socialism was only theoretical.[54] Firmly committed to the ILP, she argued that it would be a good thing if the party was expelled by Labour for pursuing a militant policy. But if the ILP split in two "over a vaguely understood and seemingly abstract issue, such as Standing Orders, then the Labour Party will have won one more round in the struggle to decide whether the organised working-class movement is to remain a pillar of the existing order, or to become a battering-ram for Socialism." She concluded that although it would be best if the ILP reached an agreement over the standing orders with Labour, "on each practical issue of the day-to-day class struggle it must take an uncompromising stand, thus presenting the broader party with the choice of either accepting such a stand, or fighting us on concrete bread-and-butter issues, where the average worker will know which side to take and what he is taking sides about."[55]

The ILP might have been united against gradualism, but when it came to what to do about it, there was nothing approaching a consensus. It would take the two conferences of 1932 to decide the affiliation issue—at least for the time being. The question of what should replace gradualism would then divide it further.

13

Disaffiliation Wins the Day

Two crucial ILP conferences took place in 1932. The first was the party's annual conference, held in Blackpool in April, and the second a special conference in Bradford, convened three months later. The central issue at both was, of course, the continued affiliation of the ILP to Labour. Given the essential role that the ILP had played in the creation of the Labour Party—and given the iconic status of the late Keir Hardie, invoked by advocates on both sides of the disaffiliation debate—the idea of severing ties was not one that ILP members took lightly. Opinion was divided at the Blackpool conference, and no decision was taken, but tensions deepened in the months to follow, as Labour refused to give ground on the question of standing orders. By the time Bradford conference opened at the end of July, its outcome seemed to some foreordained.

Easter in Blackpool: A Three-Way Division

The *New Leader* report on the Blackpool conference featured portraits of some of the most prominent speakers with labels that indicated how the delegates had divided into three camps: the photograph of Cullen was labelled "Disaffiliation," C. G. Garton represented "Conditional Affiliation," and Dollan, "Unconditional Affiliation." A photo of MP George Buchanan was tagged "Urging Disaffiliation," while one of Wise was captioned "E. F. Wise Pleads for Unconditional Affiliation."

The paper reported that Cullen, on behalf of the Poplar branch, had argued for disaffiliation in "a cool and detached way" and had denied press reports "that the unofficial left-wing were intending to form a new party."[1] Dollan, by contrast, had made an "impassioned speech" that generated both laughter and anger as he ridiculed the ILP divisions and branches supporting disaffiliation. He pictured them carrying out insurrections against the cathedrals of Truro, Winchester, Norwich, and Westminster. He insisted that the standing orders issue was of "minor importance." What mattered was policy. He argued that the long-term work of the ILP had borne fruit at the Labour Party conference at Scarborough the previous autumn, when Labour had accepted socialist policies that the ILP ought now to help the party work out in greater detail. Garton told the conference that "if the Labour Party was wedded to gradualism then the conditional affiliationists would be ready to go outside." He urged that after negotiations with the Labour Party had been concluded, a special conference be held to make the decision on whether to accept whatever result emerged. This proposal was later adopted by the conference.[2]

Both Maxton, "after much mental turmoil," and Paton supported disaffiliation. After what was called the "most intense debate ever held in the I.L.P.," unconditional affiliation was defeated by 214 to 98 votes. Immediate disaffiliation was also rejected but a relatively large number of delegates voted in favour of it: 144 compared to 183 against. Eventually, it was agreed by a large majority to reopen negotiations with the Labour Party on the standing orders issue.[3]

Before the debate, the tone had been set by Brockway's speech from the chair. He was not, he would claim later, "greatly excited over the disaffiliation issue." Instead, he had "placed emphasis on the development of a revolutionary policy and regarded the issue of the Standing Orders as important only in so far as they prevented the expression of such a policy."[4] At the time, the *New Leader* reported that in his address, Brockway had told delegates, "Decide upon your revolutionary policy, express the new Socialist spirit, in life as well as word, and the issue of affiliation and disaffiliation will settle itself."[5]

The most significant feature of the conference, according to the *Leader*, was "the practically unanimous realisation of the necessity for a revolutionary policy." In his report, Paton emphasized that "no voice in the Conference from beginning to end uttered a word in support of the policies of 'gradualism' which the I.L.P. unitedly challenges and which was the real issue underlying the Standing Orders dispute." He went on to note, "One section of those who supported disaffiliation did so, as they quite clearly stated, because they believed that the methods of political democracy had no relevance to the new situation." Their view centred on "the world breakdown in Capitalism" and they called for a "quickening up to meet the new situation of the basic proposals of the 'Living Income Programme.'"[6]

Paton shared the belief, expressed by a significant number of ILPers, that the economic crisis would lead to authoritarian rule in Britain, as it had elsewhere. There were signs that the National Government was moving in this direction. "By almost its first act—the institution of legislation by Orders in Council—it struck at the roots of British constitutional and democratic practice," wrote Paton. "It was the British equivalent of the German pseudo-fascism—of government by Presidential decree."[7]

The emphasis of *Forward*'s reporting of the conference was quite unlike the *Leader*'s presentation of a three-way division. It focused instead on the rejection of immediate disaffiliation and the upcoming meetings with Labour, which, it was hoped, would lead to an acceptable resolution of the standing orders issue.⁸ In his conference report the previous year, Emrys Hughes had accused those criticizing the Labour Party for "cowardice" of being inconsistent. On a critical amendment to Trevelyan's Education Bill, the ILP group had decided to give itself "a free hand," and Beckett voted with the Tories while Maxton, Stephen, and Buchanan abstained.⁹ Now, in 1932, *Forward* revived this criticism, but this time, the focus was more squarely on Maxton and the standing orders controversy. He had said that abstaining was not good enough, but was he being consistent? asked Hughes. "If Maxton takes up the attitude that he is justified in abstaining in order to conciliate Catholic opinion on questions of education he should be equally ready to take the same attitude when there is a difference with the Labour Party on other issues." *Forward* asked what the ILP parliamentary group planned to do now that a motion supporting secular education had been passed by 111 to 20 at the ILP conference, noting that "Maxton, McGovern, Stephen and Buchanan have all pledged themselves at the last election to the 'Catholic Observer' to uphold the Catholic schools."¹⁰

In his chapter titled "The Split," Gidon Cohen contends that the Blackpool conference was simply "postponing the inevitable." But was it as inevitable as hindsight seems to suggest? Clearly, a large group among the conference delegates favoured instant disaffiliation, yet they were by no means the majority. Nearly a third of delegates were even prepared to retain unconditional affiliation, and one of the most prominent supporters of this view, Wise, had been re-elected as a national member of the NAC by the conference. He and other opponents of disaffiliation, notably Brailsford, must have felt they were struggling against a strong and rising tide. However, the fact that they continued to make the argument for remaining with Labour as forcefully and frequently as they did suggests they had not entirely given up hope of persuading a majority of ILPers. After all, relatively swift changes of policy stance were not unknown in the party.

The most obvious example of such a turnaround is the issue of affiliation with the Third International that arose at the start of the previous decade. As we saw in chapter 2, at the beginning of 1920, a strong surge of opinion was working in favour of seeking Comintern affiliation, but, rather like the 1932 conference in Blackpool, its 1920 predecessor had postponed the decision pending further investigation or negotiation. Over the following year, the firm—and, from the ILP point of view, totally unreasonable—stance of the Comintern itself had played a large part in turning the tide. Had the Labour

Party leadership adopted a somewhat less intransigent approach in the summer of 1932, the balance might have been tipped in favour of those who wished to preserve the ILP's relationship to Labour. Signs of flexibility were not forthcoming—although intransigence was by no means confined to one side in the dispute. One cannot, of course, rely uncritically on Brockway's account of the ILP's discussions with Labour, both before and after Blackpool, but it does offer some interesting insights.

One such insight concerns a conversation with Labour's Arthur Henderson, whom Brockway met at the Geneva Disarmament Conference in early 1932. To Brockway's surprise, he found that Henderson did not concentrate on the standing orders and took the view that organizational difficulties could be overcome. His concern was rather about where the ILP was going in terms of policy:

> He challengingly raised the issue as to whether we had any real faith in Parliament. He had gathered that we believed that ultimately the transition from Capitalism to Socialism would be made not through Parliament but by a direct struggle for power between the working-class and the possessing class. Did this mean that we stood for Socialism by revolution?

Brockway recalled that Henderson was not satisfied with his reply that the ILP would "use Parliament as long and as fully as it could be used."[11] Given how much evocation of a revolutionary policy was going on in the ILP, Henderson's concerns are not at all surprising. As we shall see in the next chapter, a good deal hung on what exactly—or even approximately—was meant by "revolution" and "revolutionary."

As for the final talks with the Labour Party, Brockway remained convinced a decade later that "it was the obstinacy of the Labour Party Executive which closed the door to agreement." But it is also true that, referring to earlier discussions with Labour, he commented, "I have the impression that Maxton deliberately permitted things to take their course."[12] This was very much in line with the view that *Forward* took at the time, with Dollan, as usual, setting the pace. In April, he wrote that Maxton had been "one of the chief obstacles to an agreement."[13]

Much water had flowed under the political bridges by the late 1930s, when both the ILP and Labour were edging towards a compromise that seemed likely to lead to reaffiliation—until the outbreak of war intervened. This movement towards agreement suggests that those who opposed disaffiliation in the early years of the decade were not facing an inevitable defeat, though the odds were against them. At Easter 1932, the final decision—whether inevitable or not—still lay ahead. The Poplar branch expressed regret that the Easter conference had adopted a policy of leaving the door open to continued affiliation, which was not what that branch had been hoping for.[14] The fate of the ILP was still to be decided. The debate continued—and would go on even after disaffiliation.

Tensions Prior to Bradford

Brailsford's continuing campaign for the retention of the Labour Party affiliation sometimes took less direct routes. In April, two weeks or so after the Blackpool conference, his article "Is Keynes a Socialist?" appeared in the *New Leader*. In Keynes's article "The Dilemma of Modern Socialism" in the *Political Quarterly*, the economist had advocated "central control of investment and the distribution of income in such a way as to provide purchasing power." This showed, Brailsford wrote, that "Mr. Keynes marches pretty closely with our own Living Income Policy. In so far as I had a hand in drafting and defining it, it was this aspect of it which chiefly attracted me. We used to insist it was a prescription for economic health." Brailsford then turned to the role that he wanted the ILP—and Keynes—to play: "It is our job (and his) to indoctrinate the Labour Party with the firm and reasoned belief that an expansion and equalisation of consumption is the first step to economic health."[15]

In early May, the *New Leader* reported the NAC proposals for the coming meeting on standing orders with Labour.[16] The month also began optimistically for Dollan, who still anticipated a positive outcome from the negotiations with the Labour Party. Successive headlines of his *Forward* contributions proclaimed "Now For Unity" and "Nearing Unity: Labour Party Ready—ILP Willing."[17] But then his focus shifted to the efforts of the Glasgow and West of Scotland Disaffiliation Committee, which had held a meeting, with Maxton and McGovern on the platform, attended by three hundred people. He dismissed the two speakers as "the advocates of working class disunion."[18]

At the beginning of June, it was reported that Labour had refused to revise the standing orders as "a condition precedent to the admission of I.L.P. Members" but that the PLP would be reviewing them.[19] This generated some mild hope for a successful resolution of the long-running dispute, but it proved a very temporary moment of optimism. The following week, Brockway's statement as chairman began by noting the *Daily Herald* report of 2 June, according to which the PLP had decided that any reconsideration of the standing orders would be postponed "until prior to the creation of the next Labour Government." Brockway's account was supplemented by Paton's "Full Story of the Negotiations," which concluded with the NAC's decision to call a special conference. The decision of the PLP was confirmed by Labour's national executive. A "satisfactory revision" of the standing orders, Paton concluded, was indispensable if ILP affiliation was to continue.[20]

Dollan dissented passionately from the NAC's recommendation to support disaffiliation at the coming Bradford conference. He was supported by *Forward*. "To wreck the Labour Socialist alliance on a minor issue like that of Standing Orders is a calamity," the editor of the Scottish ILP paper concluded. With Labour in opposition, the standing orders were "practically non-existent," and the ILP MPs could join the PLP "without sacrificing an iota of their enthusiasm and anxiety to achieve Socialism in Our Time." *Forward* noted that many of the Left had said that they expected the ILP to return to Labour within two or three years, which made the idea of disaffiliation even odder. The paper appealed to the "rank and file" to oppose the move.[21]

The *New Leader* issue of 24 June is particularly helpful in gauging the point that relations between Labour and the ILP had reached by that time. It included a letter from Labour Party Assistant Secretary J. S. Middleton confirming that the ILP must accept the party's constitution and its MPs must be members of the PLP. That meant accepting the standing orders. An editorial comment followed claiming that if there had been "a real desire" on the part of the Labour Party to reach a settlement, "such Constitutional difficulties could have been overcome."[22]

Most revealing, however, is Hilda Lane's account of the situation in "Why We Left the Women's Conference." The ILP had been represented at the Labour Party women's conference by four delegates—Dorothy Jewson, Dora Russell, Annie Hambley, and Lane herself. There had been, Lane conceded, two "bright intervals." But she complained of problems created over Russell's credentials and the hostile chairing during Jewson's and Russell's speeches, which led to 105 delegates voting in their support "as a protest against the treatment meted out to them by the Chairman." Faced with what they saw as unrelenting hostility, the ILP delegates decided to withdraw from the conference. "As we got to the door," Lane recounted, "some delegates shouted good-bye and applauded." For Lane and the others, this experience was decisive:

> We realised that it's not only a question of Standing Orders which makes the difference between us and the Labour Party, but the outlook towards vital things. In our wildest dreams we did not imagine a Labour Women's Conference giving a great ovation to an ex-Minister responsible for an Act which operates so unjustly and harshly against women; that they would turn their backs on Socialism at the bidding of the same Minister; that they would uphold the Chairman in her very unfair treatment of one section.[23]

The ex-minister was, of course, Margaret Bondfield. Labour Party hostility towards the ILP was not confined to the women's conference. As George Hardie put it in an anti-disaffiliation letter to *Forward* a week later, "It is unfortunate, but true, that many of the trade unions and other sections of the Labour Party are hoping the I.L.P. will get out."[24]

At the beginning of July, a statement was issued by Maxton and Brockway as the chairmen, respectively, of the ILP parliamentary group and of the ILP itself. Labour had rejected the party's proposal to meet for the purpose of "settling the differences" and was insisting there could be no further discussion until the ILP accepted the current standing orders. Brockway and Maxton maintained that the real source of the difficulties was "the compromising policy of the Labour Government and its betrayal of working-class interests and the Socialist cause." The ILP had no course open to it but to leave the Labour Party. A special conference was announced for 30 and 31 July in Bradford. It was to plan for "reorganisation as a completely independent political force." Paton reiterated the belief that responsibility for the breach did not lie with the ILP, emphasizing his claim that "*had the will to peace existed in the Executive of the Labour Party, the technicalities could have been surmounted.*"[25]

Not all of those favouring disaffiliation were prepared to wait for the Bradford conference. Some rejected the idea of remaining with the ILP while it debated disaffiliation. In early July, the CPGB's *Daily Worker* published a letter from J. Corbett, who had been secretary of the West Bromwich ILP branch. He was now joining the Communist Party. By concentrating on Parliament, he declared, the ILP was "damping down the struggle" when what was needed was a "soviet system."[26] Corbett's views would be echoed in the ILP in the years following disaffiliation.

The opponents of disaffiliation had not yet conceded defeat. *Forward* published a long pro-affiliation letter from E. Haydn Jones, preceded by an editorial statement that noted that the correspondent's branch, Briton Ferry ILP, was the biggest branch in Wales and one of biggest in the entire United Kingdom. Briton Ferry had unanimously opposed disaffiliation.

A final summation of the cases for and against affiliation appeared in the *New Leader* on 15 July—which may have been in time for branches to take the rival arguments into account before mandating their conference delegates. The arguments of Brailsford and Stephen appeared on facing pages. Brailsford insisted that the standing orders issue was relatively unimportant: "History moves on a broad front, with masses of men as its counters. If the whole body advances, it matters not at all that at some moment in the march our little platoon may have felt some restriction on its pace, or enjoyed something less than the full luxury of self-expression."[27]

Brailsford went on to say that outside the Labour Party, the ILP would find, as the Communists had, that it was "difficult to fight on two fronts." Contesting parliamentary elections would be, he argued, difficult in the absence of proportional representation—which, as we have seen, he supported. It was probable, in the actual circumstances in which the disaffiliated ILP would find itself, "that its efforts will lessen the total representation of Labour." As he saw it, Labour had a real chance of advancing towards socialism, but that window would not stay open forever: "Tides do not stir history daily, as they move the sea. The chance that offers to-day, while the capitalist system swoons and staggers, may not return in our lifetime."[28]

The ILP had been right to rebel against the MacDonald government, Brailsford continued, but when MacDonald, Snowden, and Thomas left and Labour "challenged the City, ought we not to have seized the moment for reconciliation?" Neither side had "behaved with the bigness and generosity that our ideals should inspire." Yet the fact remained that "at the last election the Labour Party executed a remarkable change of front. It abandoned the old gradualist, reformist tactics. It made a frontal attack on the City, the central seat of the power of British Capitalism. On this it has not gone back." Its program for the coming Labour Party conference in October concentrated on "four strategic keys: banking and investment, electricity, transport and the land." Finally, Brailsford asked, why should the ILP, "feeling hopefully within itself the force to attract the millions to its banner, doubt its ability to achieve this end within the existing Party?"[29]

On the other side, Stephen dismissed out of hand those favouring affiliation unconditionally. Not only had they been "absolutely out of sympathy with the policy of the I.L.P. in recent years," but they had also been "contemptuous of the 'Socialism in Our Time'" policy and should have left the ILP with Snowden and MacDonald. He turned to the conditional affiliationists, some of whom had "become fainthearted and are ready to advocate a complete surrender" when faced with the prospect of disciplinary action. "A Labour Party which rebuffs the approaches of an I.L.P. anxious for a settlement will not prove a stronghold for any section of the working class in the day of trouble, whether nationally or internationally," he insisted.[30]

Stephen invoked the example of Lenin, who had not feared splits in the movement. He had been reading Trotsky's *History of the Russian Revolution*, which had featured in a *New Leader* article the previous week. "Is there any Socialist to-day who does not realise, as Trotsky makes plain, that we owe a Socialist Russia to the courage and independence of Lenin and his associates?" he asked. The Labour Party might have lost MacDonald "for the time being as its titular leader, but the doctrine of which he was the most notable spokesman is still the philosophy of the Party, in spite of the brave words of a leader here and there regarding the futility of gradualism." His conclusion was predictable and uncompromising: "disaffiliation is the only way."[31]

Elsewhere in the same *New Leader* issue, it was announced that Jowett's pamphlet *The I.L.P. Says "No"* was now available. Jowett was able to draw on his experience as a founding member of the ILP, a long-serving Labour MP, an opponent of the war, and a member of the 1924 government. His argument began with the ILP's role in the formation of the Labour Party: "Without full liberty of its M.Ps in the House of Commons to give effect to its propaganda, within the limits of Labour Party Conference decisions, the I.L.P. as a Socialist organisation could not have become affiliated to the Labour Party."[32]

This right had been unchallenged for more than twenty years. "Over and over again since the Parliamentary Party was formed in 1906," Jowett argued, "this right has been asserted and maintained by I.L.P. Members of Parliament." He rehearsed the many occasions when the ILP had opposed the prewar unofficial alliance with the Liberals and when it had been "a dissentient minority"—which included MacDonald and Snowden throughout the war years. Snowden's "historic Socialist resolution" would have been impossible under the standing orders they were now being asked to accept.[33]

Jowett maintained that, when it was free of the restrictions now being insisted upon, the ILP had played a crucial role throughout the time that Labour had been in Parliament. A great misfortune had been the absence of "a militant I.L.P." from the House of Commons between 1918, the year of the khaki election, and 1922. This had been a disaster, "for in those four years, the vast accumulation of national property, machinery and plant owned by the nation when the war ended was deliberately pillaged for fear it would be used as effectively for peace as it had been for war." Then came the first Labour governments. The turning point followed. The party leaders were "determined that a future Labour Government must not be hampered by a dissenting minority under any circumstances." The 1929 government had pursued a course of compromise, fishing for Liberal support, which culminated in "the last big compromise"—giving in to the bankers. This and the gulf between Labour's propaganda—with its promises on pensions, housing, school maintenance, and unemployment insurance—and its parliamentary practice accounted for the huge decline of support at the previous year's election.[34]

It is not possible to gauge the influence of Jowett's pamphlet on the views of members and the stance taken by branches. It was published shortly before the crucial Bradford special conference, which may have been too late for some members to consider its arguments. What is crystal clear is that for Jowett, his position on the standing orders dispute was of a piece with his critique of the "cabinet system" and his commitment to a representative democracy that maximized the accountability of the government to Parliament and of MPs to their constituents. He summed it up in one statement: "We of the I.L.P. who refuse to be bound by the present Standing Orders of the Parliamentary Labour Party refuse because the present Standing Orders empower the Parliamentary Party, at its own discretion, to prohibit Labour members from acting in the House of Commons in accordance with their platform propaganda." The 1914 ILP conference had, Jowett continued, determined in passing the Bradford Resolution that ILP MPs should vote "on all issues in accordance with the principles for which the Party stands," and that remained official policy. The ILP had "distinctly repudiated the mischievous pretence that Labour Members of Parliament may act and vote in the House of Commons contrary to the policy and principles of the Party purely to keep in step with a Cabinet." Consequently, Jowett concluded, "The answer to those who demand that it must surrender the freedom of its M.Ps to fulfil their pledges honestly made in accordance with the principles and policy advocated officially by the Labour Party for election purposes is—No—No—**Never**."[35]

By this time, the attention of other key figures in the ILP was already turning away from the pros and cons of disaffiliation and towards the "revolutionary policy," the search for which was to become the ILP's distinctive feature once it had abandoned the Labour Party. Paton referred to the new constitution that the NAC would propose. Its basis would be "definitely Marxist," and it would embody "the new thought and spirit with which the I.L.P. is surging."[36] A *New Leader* editorial the following week amplified this. The ILP, it said, would frankly accept "the Marxian philosophy of class struggle" and restate socialist policy "in the circumstances of the breakdown of Capitalism." A change of emphasis was now needed: "First power—then a Socialist Plan is the slogan required." The draft constitution to be submitted to the conference rejected "methods of gradual reform" and sought to concentrate its activities "upon achieving the decisive change from Capitalism to Socialism." In the same issue, an article by John Lewis, titled "Goodbye to All That," attributed the mistakes of the past to Fabian influences: "The Fabian tide flowed well up to the highest councils of the I.L.P. It is going out, and it must not return."[37]

The following day, *Forward* featured Dollan's final appeal against the "mischievous policy" of disaffiliation, the responsibility for which he placed squarely on the "Maxtonites." Apart from Maxton, he maintained, no one on the NAC had "any following in the country." As for Maxton himself, he had "no disposition or ambition" to lead a revolution. "But thanks to the admiration of unthinking admirers he would rather be the leader of a small party in Parliament than a co-operator in the Labour Party."[38] Two days later, the Communist Party's

Willie Gallacher, in a *Daily Worker* article headlined "The I.L.P.'s 'Gentlemanly' Revolution," mocked the ILP for advocating "revolution without struggle."[39]

According to a front-page article in *Labour's Northern Voice*, written two days prior to the start of the conference, the Blackpool branch was firmly of the opinion that unless the "obnoxious Parliamentary Standing Orders" were modified, the ILP should not remain affiliated. The Blackpool branch urged the party to "preach revolutionary Socialism."[40] In the issue of the *New Leader* published the day before the special conference, John Lewis urged the ILP to "prepare to take whatever steps are necessary, when the time comes, to ensure that the express will of the people shall prevail, and not be thwarted by Fascist Dictatorship, the inevitable alternative to Democratic Socialism." In another article in the same issue, readers were also informed that branch amendments to the NAC's motion calling for disaffiliation fell into four categories. Five branches supported disaffiliation but wished to "strengthen the wording." Two wanted the ILP MPs to rejoin the PLP and press for changes to the standing orders. Two others demanded a "plebiscite of members," and six were in favour of delaying the decision. But, the article pointed out, there was common ground in the demand for policies recognizing the need for "revolutionary change."[41] About a week earlier, the *Daily Herald* had reported the demand for a plebiscite and had identified the Gorbals ILP branch, whose local MP was the "disaffiliationist" Buchanan, as the source of the demand. A few days later, the *Herald* published an article under the headline "Many Branches to Oppose I.L.P. Leaders."[42]

But if the ILP's desire for "revolutionary change" was distasteful to gradualists within the Labour Party, neither did it satisfy the appetite of the Communists. On the opening day of the conference, the CPGB's *Daily Worker* carried a manifesto addressed to ILP members under the heading "No Middle Policy Possible." In addition to disparaging the record of the ILP leadership in the fight against cuts to public expenditures, the manifesto criticized as ineffectual ILP policies that attempted to steer a middle course between revolution and reform. A few days later, the newspaper presented the outcome of the ILP conference as a "game played by Maxton, Brockway and Co.," the goal of which was merely to "prevent the decline in membership." Clearly, from the Communist standpoint, not only was the ILP's leadership cynical and manipulative, but the party's initiatives were essentially useless.[43]

In the meantime, the opening day of the conference saw Kirkwood's defiant declaration in *Forward*, headlined "Why I Refuse to Leave the Labour Party." The same issue included Dollan's statement favouring a referendum of ILP members irrespective of the decision to be made at Bradford. It was, he argued, the only fair method on such an important decision.[44] From the time that disaffiliation was first mooted, however, almost everyone who made any statement about it (with the exception of Jowett) had insisted that the issue of the PLP's standing orders was only the most immediate cause of the breach with Labour. Yet it was clear at the Blackpool conference that the majority of delegates, and presumably of the membership, wished to stay with Labour if the standing orders issue could be resolved. It was this issue that had, as Gidon Cohen puts it, "the pivotal role in the decision to disaffiliate."[45]

For London supporters of the Revolutionary Policy Committee, which had pressed hard for disaffiliation since its inception, the Bradford result was a foregone conclusion. Months earlier, the committee had predicted that 30 July would be "an historic day for the British Working Class Movement." The ILP would decide that it could "no longer work within the Labour Party or with the leaders who betray the workers."[46] By the time of the Bradford conference, the outcome did appear inevitable, yet the most prominent opponents of disaffiliation certainly carried the fight to the very end.

Bradford and Its Aftermath

At Bradford, Dollan attempted to refer back the crucial section of the NAC's report recommending disaffiliation. He argued that the conference was not sufficiently representative to make such a momentous decision and called for a direct vote of the membership on the issue. Defeated by 252 to 115, he warned of "civil war in the Branches." Wise was the main speaker opposing the disaffiliation motion, which was passed by 241 to 142. The *New Leader* reported the reaction: "'The I.L.P. is now disaffiliated from the Labour Party,' said the Chairman. Immediately the cheers swept the hall and delegates sprang to their feet and sang the 'Red Flag' whilst the Guild of Youth 'red shirts' on the platform held their flags over the platform, waving them excitedly from side to side." Red shirts and banners were a feature of the conference, and Brockway told the *New Leader* that he "hoped that red shirts would soon be a common sight in every part of Britain." Within a few weeks, an advertisement appeared in the paper for red shirts and blouses.[47]

Both Dollan and Wise left on the second day of the conference. Wise had resigned from the NAC. In his letter of resignation, which Brockway read from the chair, Wise said that "secession from the Labour Party when it is more Socialist in outlook, intention and opportunity than at any time in its history seems to me to be an act of treachery to the Labour Movement and of suicide for the I.L.P."[48] The decision had been made, but there were immediate, as well as longer-term, consequences—and recriminations.

Dollan, Brailsford, and Wise were scheduled to be speakers at the ILP summer school in August.[49] Wise actually made his contribution, arguing that there would be "no complete collapse" of capitalism.[50] The fact that they had agreed, before the disaffiliation decision, to speak at the summer school suggests that these leading advocates of continued affiliation had not regarded the result at Bradford as inevitable, as does Brailsford's angry, rather than resigned, response to the conference's decision. He would not, he said in a letter to the *Manchester Guardian*, be lecturing at the summer school since he would have "nothing to do, whether as writer or speaker, with an organisation which has behaved with such conspicuous silliness."[51]

The following week, Maxton responded to Brailsford's comments in a *New Leader* article headed "After the Great Decision." Regarding Wise and Brailsford, he said that "the I.L.P. has been a good friend to both of them for some years, has given them the status in the public life of this nation that they possess." A "certain restraint," he said, "would have been 'more in keeping with the ordinary decencies." He preferred to believe that Wise was "not himself," but he made no mitigating plea for Brailsford's "contemptuous phrase" about the "conspicuous silliness" of the Bradford decision in a letter "to a well-known Capitalist journal." Maxton added, "These sentences are the only harsh personal things I want to say of anyone."[52]

In the editorial that same week, Brockway said he was puzzled by Brailsford's response to the disaffiliation decision. "After all, it was only a year ago that Mr. Brailsford said at the I.L.P. Summer School that 'Socialist honour' demanded that the I.L.P. should leave the Labour Party." But, he concluded, many of those members not accepting the decision had been out of step with the ILP for many years.[53]

Brailsford proved quite capable of defending his decision to cancel his summer school lecture, and the *Leader* published his letter a week later. According to his account, the *Manchester Guardian* had approached Paton, as ILP secretary, to inquire whether he, Brailsford, was still intending to take part in the summer school. He claimed that he had already made his position clear in case the Bradford decision was to leave the Labour Party. Following the letter was a long note in which Paton conceded that Brailsford had indicated that he would withdraw from the ILP if it disaffiliated, but Paton pointed out that there were many precedents for nonmembers addressing ILP summer schools. He had assumed that Brailsford would attend. Brailsford also dismissed the charge concerning "Socialist honour." The political situation had been transformed since he had made the statement, he explained:

> At that point the Labour Government under MacDonald and Snowden was the abject servant of the City. A month later the Labour Party was free, and began the frontal attack on the Bank, in which it is still engaged. The root of our difference of opinion is that your watch stopped twelve months ago. Have you sworn an oath never to wind it again?[54]

Immediately following Bradford, Dollan questioned whether the ILP had truly been represented at the Bradford conference. He doubted whether a third of the 250 Scottish branches had been represented and believed that at least half of the Lancashire branches were opposed to disaffiliation, which was supported by the "most backward" areas. No one would be more delighted, he insisted in a variant of his Blackpool conference speech, "if Mr. Maxton succeeds in creating such intense feeling in the South of England that the Red Flag will soon be hoisted over the town halls of Bournemouth, Eastbourne, Exeter and Chelsea."[55]

Despite the negative response from prominent ILPers, support for the Bradford decision seemed solid. Successive issues of the *New Leader* carried headlines proclaiming "Branches Back Bradford: Overwhelming Support for Disaffiliation" and "Solid for Disaffiliation: More Support for the Bradford Decisions." The same editions reported the expulsion of Dollan and fifteen other Scottish members for "organising openly to wreck the I.L.P." The London Division was asking for expulsion of ten members including Brailsford, Wise, and Creech Jones for "actively opposing" the special conference decisions. All three authors of the original *Living Wage* report still active in the ILP had clearly reached a parting of the ways.[56] On the eve of the Bradford conference, the *Daily Herald* had quoted Wise as saying: "Not one of the authors of the 'Socialism in Our Time' pamphlet . . . is in favour of disaffiliation."[57]

The *New Leader* dismissed as "just bubble and bluster" press reports of resignations from the party. More than a third of delegates had voted against disaffiliation but "only the merest fraction" had left.[58] From outside the ILP—and very much on the Labour Party side of the fence—the *Daily Herald*, on 1 August, headlined its front page with "I.L.P. Cuts Adrift," while its editorial expressed regret for the loss to Labour of Maxton and Brockway, "two able and sincere men." The ILP leadership had clearly "determined beforehand on severance."

"The I.L.P. has marched off, a little contingent on its own, with a loud beating of tom-toms," wrote the Labour MP for Woolwich East, George Hicks, in the *Workers' Monthly*.[59] The *Herald* predicted that membership losses would be great, particularly in Scotland, and that after a time, ILPers would either return to the Labour Party or accept the logic of their "revolutionary phrases" and join the Communist Party.[60] Neither fate was what most supporters of disaffiliation in the ILP intended or foresaw in the summer of 1932. The party was now embarked on a career based on a revolutionary policy—but whether there was any agreement about what this actually meant remained to be seen.

14

What Is a Revolutionary Policy?

Those who supported disaffiliation expected it to begin a new and positive era for the ILP. Freed of the straitjacket of Labour Party standing orders and Labour's commitment to gradualism, the ILP would mobilize the British working class to move towards socialism by adopting a "revolutionary policy." But what did this mean? Some time after disaffiliation, at the beginning of 1934, one of the leading proponents of such a policy, Dr. Carl Cullen, explored the ILP's identity in the *R.P.C. Monthly Bulletin*: "It is customary now for members of all shades of opinion in the I.L.P. . . . to claim they are revolutionaries and that the I.L.P. is a revolutionary party. But what is a revolutionary party?"[1] Even before the Bradford conference, it had become apparent that ILP members had varying ideas about what such a party would look like and what constituted a revolutionary policy.

The years immediately following the disaffiliation decision of July 1932 would see rival versions put forward by a number of different individuals and groupings. The sequence of accompanying events is quite bewildering in retrospect and must have been even more so for many ILP members at the time. The year 1933 saw the resignation of John Paton, the ILP's general secretary, and of Richard Wallhead, a former chairman and one of the few ILP—or even Labour—MPs to survive the 1931 election. Then, in addition to those members who had already left as a consequence of disaffiliation, the party lost members to the newly formed Independent Socialist Party after the 1934 ILP annual conference. The following year, in October 1935, most of the Revolutionary Policy Committee left to join the Communist Party of Great Britain, leaving behind a remnant in the shape of the Communist Unity Group. Add to that the brief period of Trotskyism in the ILP, between 1934 and 1936, leaving in its wake a residue of activists influenced by its doctrines, and it is easy to see that many ILP members might have found it difficult to keep up with what was happening in the party during these years. Such people were likely to be among those who let their memberships lapse.

The Revolutionary Policy Committee

The earliest and most uncompromising calls for a new policy came from the Revolutionary Policy Committee (RPC), the body that had been established in 1930, at the initiative of Dr. Carl Cullen, chairman of London's Poplar branch, with the express intention of bringing about the adoption of such a policy by a disaffiliated ILP. The RPC called for a new revolutionary policy based on an interpretation of Marxism quite close to that of the Communist Party.[2]

In January 1932, Cullen had circulated a memorandum based on the Poplar branch's deliberations that was intended as a basis for discussion of the need for a revolutionary policy. The first two sections, "The Approaching Collapse of Capitalism" and "The Success of Soviet Russia," contrasted those two scenarios. The document went on to call for the establishment of "workers' councils" in preparation for revolution.[3] In London, its main stronghold, the RPC began to hold meetings just before the national and divisional ILP conferences. It also began publishing a monthly bulletin. These activities soon led to disquiet among other members of the London Division.

In March, the London divisional organizer, John Aplin, questioned the RPC's activities at a meeting of divisional representatives and the NAC. His divisional council, Aplin said, "was anxious to have an expression of opinion as to the new development of the 'unofficial movement.'" He complained that the RPC had two financial appeals operating in London that were bound to have an impact on the divisional council's own fundraising effort; the council, he said, "would be glad to know how far this movement could be permitted to go." When asked what action he had taken, Aplin said he had taken none because he believed it to be "a matter for the national movement."[4]

The NAC and the national secretary were clearly reluctant to become involved. Brockway, who was chairing the meeting, thought that such movements could be made unnecessary if more provision were made in the party for "general discussion." Paton also urged caution, maintaining that it was better "to drift for a while" while keeping "a watchful eye." The real problem, he went on, was not "discussion" but the "desire to organise a Conference vote."[5] Such concerns were to resurface later in the year and began to generate attacks on the RPC's policy as well as on its tactics.

The writers of an article in the July 1932 *R.P.C. Monthly Bulletin* expressed little doubt that disaffiliation was on the way. They were scathing about the NAC's failure to make a recommendation on this key issue to the Blackpool conference, attributing the "weakness" of the ILP largely to "the failure of the N.A.C. to do its job—that is to lead the party, in a period of crisis, without waiting for Conferences and decisions some months after the break of events." RPC members were, they said, "communists in all but C.P. membership and the tactics of the C.P." Signed with the initials of Cullen and Jack Gaster, another leading RPC figure, the article complained that policy proposals from branches had been thwarted by the standing orders committee at the Blackpool conference: "Resolution after resolution was slaughtered by the S.O. committee." Cullen and Gaster urged the ILP to work for "the full revolutionary objective by revolutionary action" while attempting to "understand the psychology of the militant or potentially militant workers." Nothing should be done which might "be a barrier to the ultimate formation of a united revolutionary movement."[6]

While the RPC welcomed the disaffiliation outcome of the special conference at Bradford, it was frustrated in its attempts to convince conference delegates to support its own version of a revolutionary policy. Gaster moved an amendment that sought to reorganize the ILP "on the basis of creating a revolutionary movement comprised solely of active workers organised, so far as possible, on an industrial basis." It proposed a limited role for ILP MPs, one that would be "planned and definitely controlled by the N.A.C." after consultation with the appropriate division. These MPs would be subordinate to the ILP members who were concentrating their efforts on the revolutionary struggle outside parliament. The amendment was lost on a show of hands. Speaking for the NAC, Stephen "thought Gaster's idea of trying to make Parliament only a propaganda field was nonsense," while in a later debate, Paton warned that the Communist Party was "trying to detach the left-wing of the I.L.P."[7] He might have been tempted to add "again."

Immediately after disaffiliation, at the ILP summer school, J. Allen Skinner, the London Division representative on the NAC, complained that the policy of the RPC of London was little different from that of the Communists. He went on to say that the real issue was "that the I.L.P. are democrats and the C.P. are not." Members of the RPC would, no doubt, have preferred to read the article "Lenin Can Teach Us!" by Maxton, published in the same issue of the *New Leader* as the report of Skinner's comments. Maxton praised the Bolshevik leader's "sound theoretical basis," his "firmness of character," and his insistence that "the desire always to be in the majority should be killed." The emphasis, said Maxton, was on "always."[8]

At a NAC meeting in early October, Skinner complained about the RPC's "permanent form" and its appeals for funds, which were not allowed under the party's constitution. Brockway, attempting a peacemaking role, reported informal contacts with the RPC and expressed his belief that its observance of ILP rules would be improved. It was agreed that Paton and Maxton would make clear the illegitimacy of such financial appeals.[9] But Skinner had already resigned the month before from chairing the London Division and representing it on the NAC, to be replaced in the latter capacity by the RPC's Gaster.[10]

Support for the RPC's version of revolutionary policy was spreading. In early 1933, there were motions in favour of workers' councils—a core RPC demand—on the agendas not only of the London divisional conference but also, in the name of the division's executive, at the earlier Scottish one.¹¹ But opposition to the RPC was also becoming more evident.

John Middleton Murry and *The Necessity of Communism*

The RPC's opponents already included John Middleton Murry (1889–1957), a prolific writer and critic. Murry is now best remembered as the husband of Katherine Mansfield and the editor, after her death in 1923, of much of her work, but his influence in wider literary circles of the interwar period was significant. Offering a completely different interpretation of "revolutionary policy," he was to play an important role in the ILP over the next few years.

"My evolution into revolutionary Socialism has been unusual," Murry told the participants in ILP's summer school in 1932. "I was hardly interested in politics."¹² The editor, until 1930, of the literary journal *The Adelphi*, which he had founded in 1923, he remained closely involved with the journal and its new editor, his friend Sir Richard Rees. An early sign of the beginning of Murry's "evolution" was his review in March 1931 of R. H. Tawney's "brilliant book" *Equality*, a trenchant critique of the inadequacy of the notion of "equality of opportunity" and a powerful argument for a truly egalitarian society. A few months later, in a review of several books on contemporary Russia, Murry declared that "the English Revolution, if it comes, will assuredly not follow the pattern of the Russian, which was prescribed by conditions fantastically remote from our own." It was therefore "ridiculous for an Englishman to become a Communist," he concluded, "if by that we mean an active believer in the armed prosecution of class warfare and the dictatorship of the proletariat."¹³

The key words here are "if by that we mean." In December 1931, in an *Adelphi* article titled "Towards a Marxian Revolution," Murry described Marx as "the great prophet of the modern world." Tackling the question of why workers in Britain nonetheless continue to resist revolutionary ideas, Murry went on to argue, in January, that "it is not the Marxism of the Communist Party in England that repels, instinctively, the working-classes; it is the rigidity and stupidity of its Marxism." Announcing the coming publication of his book, *The Necessity of Communism*, the following month, Murry explained to *Adelphi* readers that "by Communism I *do* mean the economic revolution that has taken place in Russia; I do *not* mean the political forms in which that revolution has taken place in Russia."¹⁴

Murry was particularly scathing about Communist intellectuals, as he made amply clear in a March 1932 article in *The Adelphi*. Writing under the title "The Moral Basis of Revolution," Murry was dismissive of what he took to be mere fantasies of violence. "The Communist intellectual in this country," he wrote, "*always has the gun. And that I call play-acting.*" While they might enjoy imagining themselves "doing the shooting" and "giving the orders," the ultimate vacuousness of their revolutionary posturing was affirmed by the lack of concern it provoked. "In England," Murry noted, "the intellectual can talk the rankest Communism in a London restaurant with the Chief of the Metropolitan Police at the next table, and nothing will happen to him—absolutely nothing."[15]

Murry established himself as an important voice in the ILP at the very beginning of 1932. Described editorially in the *New Leader* as "one of the foremost literary critics" and the author of the forthcoming *The Necessity of Communism*, he was given front-page prominence, complete with a photo. In "Why I Joined the I.L.P.," he explained his decision: "Because I am a Communist. Not a member of the Communist Party. That is a different thing." For an "English Marxist," he declared, the ILP had "more of the true faith within its ranks—the absolute will to revolution, but not to bloodshed for its own sake—than any other Labour organisation in England." A contribution in the same issue by another writer, the popular novelist and travel writer Ethel Mannin, largely endorsed Murry's views. She described herself as "an extreme Left Socialist" who believed that "*we are even now witnessing the beginning of the slow but inevitable decline of private Capitalism.*"[16]

A few years later, after he had left the ILP, Murry recalled how his discovery of Marx through his reading of *Capital* had been "one of the most revolutionary events in my life," an event that necessitated political commitment. He had quickly discarded the possibility of joining the Communist Party, as it "seemed to me rather childish." He went on: "I chose the I.L.P. precisely because it seemed to have no backbone at all. Neither of course had the Communist Party—it had a backboard from Moscow instead. But the I.L.P. had neither backbone or backboard: therefore, in a negative way, it seemed to me flexible. Something might be done with it, and in it."[17] It was in this spirit—which must have seemed extremely arrogant to many members—that Murry began his short but eventful participation in the ILP.

A series of Murry's articles under the collective title "Fundamentals of Marxism" was published in the *New Leader* at intervals throughout 1932.[18] A very positive review of his book by Felix Grendon appeared in the paper in early April. Grendon summed up the author's approach: "The gist of his exposition is contained in a warning not to take the fatalistic or deterministic element in

Marx's teaching more seriously than Marx, in practice, took it himself."[19] The firmly affiliationist *Forward* was also, rather surprisingly, supportive of Murry, calling him "one of the leading literary figures of our time," and its review of *The Necessity of Communism* supported his contention that the spiritual and economic revolutions would stand or fall together. The review concluded, "This is a book to buy."[20]

In the book, Murry claimed to be a "proletarian in bourgeois clothing." He was an example of a comparatively rare phenomenon—"a board-school boy who, by dint of a lucky scholarship at the age of nine, had been thrust neck and crop into the machine for gentleman-production."[21] Murry, whose father was a clerk in the civil service, had indeed won a scholarship to Christ's Hospital, a leading "public school," and had continued his education at Brasenose College, Oxford. By 1932, Murry was living in Norfolk and was active in the Norwich branch and the East Anglian Division of the ILP. In *Forward*'s report on the Blackpool conference, he was mentioned, in passing, in a comment about secret meetings of "Left-wing delegates"; they were alleged to have organized a slate of candidates for the NAC, but Murry "wasn't thought red enough to get on the Left Wing list."[22] At Bradford, he opposed Gaster's proposals. The ILP should, he said, "reject false rigidity."[23]

After the ILP had broken with the Labour Party, the *New Leader* featured an account of the Bradford conference by Murry, who described himself as a "hardened Marxist Socialist" and "a very new member of the I.L.P." Murry was very much in favour of the break with Labour and of a revolutionary policy. "Dare we let it go into history as a simple conflict over Standing Orders?" he asked, insisting that the underlying issues of disaffiliation were much deeper. But his version of Marxism and his notion of a revolutionary policy were very different from those of the RPC, whose proposals, he noted with satisfaction, had been rejected on three occasions by the conference. The ILP had "become Marxist," he concluded. "But precisely because it has become truly Marxist, it has remained British, wary of rigidity."[24]

Without "the inward necessity of becoming English, Communism will never gain a hold in this country," Murry maintained in *The Necessity of Communism*. But Russian communism was not a model to be followed. "To create in this country a 'revolutionary situation' such as existed in Russia in 1917 would require that the complete economic collapse against which Communism is our one real safeguard should actually have occurred," Murry declared emphatically.[25] The positive results of the Bolshevik revolution needed to be recognized, but "let no irresponsible sentimental sympathiser with the U.S.S.R. delude himself about conditions there." While in Britain, Marxism had been "quietly emasculated," in Russia it had been "noisily coarsened." Murry was convinced that "the author of the *Thesen über Feuerbach* would have been astonished at the crudity of Lenin's *Materialism and Empirio-Criticism*."[26]

For Murry, it was Marx's "ethical passion" that had made him "the mightiest spiritual force in the modern world." With him, "suddenly the values of Christianity were real." In a footnote, Murry quoted Engels, from the preface to the English translation of *Das Kapital*, to the effect that in Britain, revolution might be carried out peacefully and by legal means and without triggering a "pro-slavery" rebellion.[27]

Insisting that "class warfare" should not lead to "class hatred," Murry suggested a short-term practical program that would have been broadly in line with what one of the more radical supporters of the Socialism in Our Time policy might have advocated. Murry proposed an *immediate* minimum wage at least 10 percent above unemployment benefit level, the nationalization of banks under direct political control, and taxation designed to reduce all incomes to a maximum of £1,000 a year.[28]

In "The Danger of Orthodoxy," the fourth instalment of his "Fundamentals of Marxism" series in the *New Leader*, Murry rejected the stance of Maurice Dobb, a member of the CPGB then emerging as a leading authority on Marxist economics and known for his fidelity to the Communist Party line. For Murry, Marxism rested on "the ethical postulate that the man who understands the historical process . . . will make himself the willing instrument of the process." Without this, it was "a mere armchair theory of revolution." In support of this idea, he invoked William Morris. Morris was not a utopian, he insisted, but "a professed Marxian Socialist—and a better one even than Mr. Dobb."[29]

For most people in Britain, Marxism was equated with the Communists, and if the Communist Party represented Marxism, there was obviously, according to Murry, "no hope for Marxism in this country." The Communist Party had no room for morality, he argued, "but the British working-man Socialist insists upon it." Murry's claim that "revolutionary Socialism is the modern form of the Christian religion" predictably generated some debate in early 1933. In February, in his review of an "important new book"—*Moral Man and Immoral Society*, by the American theologian Reinhold Niebuhr—Murry insisted that Niebuhr, like Marx himself, was not only a Marxist but "something more."[30]

Murry's papers, archived at Edinburgh University, include a "Memorandum on Organisation of the New I.L.P.," which, though not dated, was probably written towards the end of 1932. In it, Murry explains that he started "from the postulate that the adoption of the Marxist philosophy and a revolutionary programme and policy" must mean "real change" in ILP's activities and that "Brockway's admirable slogan 'first power, then a plan' . . . is to be incorporated into action." Since the path to revolution in Britain was not clear, the ILP must "create a revolutionary party" and take every opportunity presented by "the steadily deepening crisis" to pursue "revolutionary action." His definition of this latter phrase, however—as action that "permanently advances the cause of the Social Revolution"—shed little real light on the question of precisely what this action would entail.[31]

Invoking the "theory and practice of Lenin" and the "one successful revolutionary Socialist organisation," the Bolshevik Party, Murry argued that the ILP should focus on putting the Bolsheviks' three "guiding principles" into practice. In fact, despite a few "decorative deviations," the ILP had already achieved the first: "constant contact with and penetration of the working-class." It therefore needed to concentrate on the other two principles: a "clearly apprehended Marxist theory animating a nucleus of dedicated men" and "an inwardly apprehended necessity of discipline." It must not, however, make the "fatal mistake" of the CPGB, which, lacking a clear sense of the "dynamic of Marxism," had failed to appreciate the need to present Marxism "in a form that is native in the British character and in harmony with the deep-rooted ethical tradition of British Socialism." The ILP alone had the "moral quality" to make Marxism a "living doctrine" in Britain.[32]

Although Murry did not wholly reject Parliament, he argued that the ILP needed to "outgrow the 'parliamentary mentality.'" The party should be "consciously *non*-parliamentary," he urged, "which is not the same as *anti*-parliamentary." For Murry, the ILP needed a broad vision that centred on bringing about revolutionary change throughout society as a whole, rather than one that confined itself to parliamentary activities. He also noted a strong tendency in some ILP branches to concentrate narrowly on local politics: this tendency should be "extirpated."[33] In a "Memorandum of Comments" appended to his "Memorandum on Organisation," Murry further suggested that, following disaffiliation, the ILP should pursue the policy of the early CPGB and encourage its members to remain individual members of the Labour Party, where they could "unceasingly" promote ILP policies from within it.[34]

Murry was not overly concerned about maintaining the party's membership numbers. "One indoctrinated and dedicated man," he asserted, "is worth twenty vaguely sympathetic members." Rather, ILP branches must concentrate discussion on the "fundamental revolutionary Socialist principle" and must not "lose sight of the revolutionary wood in the political trees," as the ILP had tended to do when it was part of the Labour Party. To this end, he proposed that the following year's summer school be devoted to the "intensive study of Revolutionary Socialism," with the "best of the potential local leaders" in attendance. This should have the effect of producing "a veritable text book for branches for the ensuing year."[35]

Murry argued that branches should be allowed to develop along individual lines, with some in London and the South evolving into "fine theoretical" branches able to attract "young middle-class intellectuals." A "very careful overhaul of literature" was also needed; Murry recommended including Morris's *Commonweal* essays. Indeed, the ILP should emphasize the cultural essence of the movement: "Nothing is more disheartening to the young convert to Socialism than to attend a branch meeting where one hour is taken up with the reading of correspondence from H.Q. and the next on a debate on the candidates for the local council. Would the Catholic Church treat a convert thus? Never."[36]

With regard to recruits, one of the more surprising of Murry's recommendations was for physical training for the ILP's Guild of Youth. "A young revolutionary Socialist should feel he is capable of taking care of himself in a street-fight," he insisted. "Physical courage and moral courage make the true revolutionary combination. A red shirt is a little forlorn without a straight left to implement it." He also suggested (unsuccessfully) "The Straight Left" as the Guild's new slogan.[37] Murry also felt that the party's heroic revolutionaries should be properly celebrated: "Maxton," he suggested, "should be persuaded to write that life of John Maclean." In addition, a short history of the Bolsheviks should be written and circulated.[38]

There should be a "frank recognition" that "the acceptance of the class-war as a principle means the acceptance of the ideology of war." Many of those recruited into the new ILP would be "men who served in the Great War, the surviving remnant of the idealistic volunteers of 1914." As Murry went on to argue, "Any suggestion that these men were in any respect inferior to the pacifists must be strenuously avoided. Individualistic pacifism may have consorted well enough with the 'evolutionary' Socialism of MacDonald and Allen; it does not consort with revolutionary Socialism." An appendix to the main text of the memorandum concluded that both pacifists and those prepared "to fight, in the literal sense" might be reconciled on the basis of training for "*disciplined non-resistance.*"[39]

With his emphasis on "discipline" and his invocation of the Bolsheviks, Murry might have seemed, especially to an observer new to the ILP's discourse, to have much in common with the RPC, especially as regards his "non-parliamentary" approach. The RPC also called for the tightening up of discipline at the 1933 conference and emphasized that the "first essential" was "to acquire a sound knowledge of theory."[40] Of course, the RPC meant something radically different from what Murry had in mind. However much Murry admired the Bolsheviks, he was clear that their methods should not and could not be applied in Britain, and his attitude towards ethics and, especially, his sympathy for religion was completely at odds with the commonplace understanding of Marxism.

If the RPC proffered one version of what constituted a revolutionary policy, and Murry quite a different one, this by no means exhausted the interpretations available to members of the ILP. Moreover, the RPC was still a fairly marginal group within the party, and Murry was a newcomer. Would a version of revolutionary policy put forward by the general secretary of the ILP prove more persuasive to party members?

Paton's Alternative Revolutionary Policy

After disaffiliation, Brockway and Maxton were keen to avoid any further splits within the ILP. Faced with the emerging disagreements about what exactly should constitute the revolutionary policy for which the ILP was searching, they took a conciliatory position. As we saw earlier, so did the party's general secretary, John Paton—at least initially. Interestingly, he makes no mention of Murry in his 1936 memoir, *Left Turn!* But he has much to say about his own version of the revolutionary policy, which was, like Murry's, totally at odds with that of the RPC. While the RPC sought eventual unity with the CPGB, Paton wanted the ILP to *replace* it. Later, he reflected back on that time:

> I was perfectly aware that there was no room in Britain for two revolutionary parties with similar programmes. It was clear to me that the success of the new I.L.P. could only be achieved at the expense of the Communist Party. The new policy would consolidate within the I.L.P. those elements which tended to be attracted to Communism; it might hope to draw from the Communist Party those of its adherents who were dissatisfied with its constant failures; and it would stand a good chance of drawing fresh support to the I.L.P. from the considerable numbers of people of Left views but attached to no party. It was a policy, in my view, which would set the I.L.P. not only in definite competition with the Communist Party, but in active and determined opposition to it in a struggle from which I believed the I.L.P. would emerge victoriously.[41]

Paton wanted to disaffiliate only at the national level, leaving "the onus on the Labour Party of taking action to break the innumerable *local* links between the two bodies." He was frustrated when the annual conference insisted on a "clean break," cutting individual members off from any participation in the Labour Party. This resulted, he said, in driving out of the ILP "every single member of local influence and weight," with the exception of a "tiny minority."[42] Clearly, he was far from sharing Murry's wish to see the end of local concerns.

Paton also opposed "the creation everywhere of brand new bodies called 'Workers' Councils.'" After his departure from the ILP, he was scathing about this policy:

> The few thousand of our members who were left after our purge were expected to create this "state within a state" in the teeth of fierce opposition not only from the Labour Party and the trades unions, but of the Communist Party, as well, which looked with extreme disfavour on this attempt to poach on their preserve. The R.P.C. was nothing if not ambitious. I found to my dismay, quite early on, that Fenner Brockway, with his usual susceptibility to an attractive phrase, had incorporated "Workers' Councils" in the speeches he was making all over the country (without, of course, attempting to define them), and was unwittingly doing much to make the path of the R.P.C. easy. It was already clear enough that the revolutionary policy I'd so desired was very different from the one I was likely to get.[43]

It is plain that Paton completely underestimated the support the RPC could generate and the wider appeal of the workers' council policy. This is evident from the fact that, as noted earlier, he would resign from the ILP within a year of disaffiliation.

Parliament or Workers' Councils?

Workers' councils were indeed at the core of the RPC's notion of a revolutionary policy, though support for them was much wider. But not all supporters of such bodies saw them in exactly the same way; the arguments of their advocates had different emphases. Supporting the setting up of workers' councils "wherever possible to deal with immediate problems of the struggle," the Scottish ILP executive, in early 1933, insisted that the councils should be open to every section of the working-class movement. "Such Workers' Councils will break down the dominance of those Trades Councils that are tied to the Labour Party and will become Councils of Action whenever opportunity arises," it predicted.[44] The experiences of similar bodies in 1920 and 1926 were much invoked.

The belief that the collapse of capitalism was imminent but that its beneficiaries and supporters would resort to fascism to ward off a socialist revolution was widespread in the ILP—and beyond—at this time. As *Revolt*, then the organ of the Chelsea branch of the ILP, made clear in May 1932, workers' councils and soviets were the same thing: "In the cotton districts of the North of England the workers have set up their own committees to deal with the situation. These are British Soviets."[45]

But the RPC's view of workers' councils went beyond support for them in a "revolutionary crisis" or as a response to particular eventualities, as in the case of the cotton industry. A more full-blooded notion was that of workers' councils as the instruments of government once the crisis had swept capitalism away. This vision was reflected soon after in the London Division's proposal for a new ILP constitution, which would be debated at the upcoming annual conference in April 1933. In a section titled "Democracy," London wanted the ILP to recognize that "the instruments of government, national and local, are mere covers for capitalist exploitation" and to repudiate "capitalist democracy." This was to be replaced by workers' councils. "To this limited democracy, a democracy of the working class only, the I.L.P. subscribes."[46]

Gidon Cohen sees the position that the 1933 ILP conference was to take, under considerable RPC influence, as "based on a neo-syndicalist workers' council programme."[47] Certainly, there are echoes of syndicalism—and, even more, of the syndicalist-influenced "Left Communists" of the immediate post-1917 years—in the ILP debates of the 1930s. But there was at least one significant difference with the latter. More than any other far Left grouping, Sylvia Pankhurst's Communist Party (British Section of the Third International) had committed itself to a "soviet democracy," which it saw as more genuinely democratic than any parliamentary system.

When councils of action were being set up in 1920, while the CPGB had sought direct representation, its Left Communist rivals wanted to "sovietise the councils of action." This, in their view, meant excluding any representation from *political* organizations. Only representatives of workshop bodies—and those of other social groupings including, especially, housewives—should be included in the councils of action. Any input of political parties would be strictly confined to the base level of the workshop or local group, where they might legitimately seek to achieve some influence. Eventually, via the coming revolution, a complex system of soviets would take over all state functions, local and national, with recallable delegates elected on a strictly proportional basis and mandated not by any "political" organization but by the meetings they were representing.[48]

In the ILP debates of the 1930s, there may have been a general commitment to "working class democracy as the highest form of democracy," as the 1934 annual conference agreed, but when the composition of workers' councils was discussed, it seems always to have been in terms of more or less ad hoc representation of whatever groupings—industrial, social, or political—were willing to take part. This might have been acceptable for the essentially defensive councils of action of past years. But could it possibly be, even in theory, a democratic basis for, as the 1934 conference maintained, "the attainment of power and the foundation for the dictatorship of the working class necessary to maintain that power"?[49]

What did support for workers' councils imply about the need—or lack of need—for ordinary parliamentary and local government electoral activity? For the most determined advocates of workers' councils, such as the London Division's C. A. Smith, who was not a member of the RPC, there was no possibility of achieving the socialist goal via Parliament.[50] In its February 1933 edition, *Labour's Northern Voice* had asked, "Can Socialism Come the Parliamentary Way?" to which Elijah Sandham's answer was "Yes." "No," responded Smith the following month.[51]

At about the same time, *Revolt* (in its new, expanded version, now subtitled *The London Workers' Paper*) carried the same message from Smith: "We are forced to the conclusion that Parliament, the instrument created by the capitalists to give legal sanction to their exploitation ... cannot become the means by which their power is overthrown." What was needed was for workers' councils, along the lines of the 1919–20 councils of action and the strike committees during the 1926 general strike, to take a "consciously built up permanent form," as was being done, Smith reported, in Camberwell.[52] The third issue of *Revolt* would report, two months later, that Wimbledon had followed Camberwell's lead when its Unemployed Workers Committee resolved, by 16 votes to 3, to rename itself Wimbledon and District Workers' Council.[53]

Another advocate of workers' councils was RPC member William Warbey, who, also in March 1933, presented them as having a unifying role in his *New Leader* article "The Workers Way Out?" The *"unification of resistance,"* Warbey emphasized, *"involves a UNIFYING ORGANISATIONAL FORM."* He envisaged, in a second article, that the councils would unite trade union rank-and-file committees; Co-op Guilds; housewives' committees; NUWM branches; Labour Exchange councils; estate and street committees; and ILP, CPGB, and even Labour Party branches.[54]

Jowett responded to Warbey the following week, on the eve of the Derby conference, in a *New Leader* piece with the title "Not by Civil War: A Parliamentary Majority Must Be Won." Like Wallhead a little later, he saw in the proposals for workers' councils the advocacy of preparations for civil war. This was wrong and dangerous, he declared: wrong because war is "a beastly and inhuman thing" and dangerous because "it incites and gives welcome excuse for organised force to forestall the working class."[55]

Jowett rejected councils "composed of a diverse admixture of producers, consumers, householders, anti-war councils, workers' sports and social organisations." There were two reasons why workers' councils, all very well in themselves, could not substitute for parliamentary activity, he argued. It would take longer to get them organized across the country than to achieve a parliamentary majority, and only such a majority could give a "nation wide mandate." But the same issue of the *New Leader* reported, under the title "The I.L.P. in Scotland," a demonstration by the Johnston Workers' Council. There was considerable enthusiasm for the workers' council idea, however vague and ambiguous it often appeared to be.[56]

Attempts to formulate a revolutionary policy for the post-disaffiliation ILP would continue. In particular, the focus would soon fall on the role that was to be sought for the largely hypothetical workers' councils and what the existence of such councils would imply for the party's parliamentary and electoral activities. As the 1933 annual conference would confirm, moreover, support for workers' councils was by no means confined to the RPC.

15

Turbulent Waters
A United Front—or a United ILP?

As became evident in 1933, central to debates surrounding the ILP's revolutionary policy was the issue of relations with the Communist Party of Great Britain. The key question was whether forming a united front with the CPGB would culminate in undermining the unity of the ILP itself. Neither the party's 1933 conference nor the NAC would succeed in resolving the differences on this question, and a decision on the respective roles of Parliament and workers' councils remained equally elusive. Indeed, by July, the national leadership had become a cacophony of different voices.

With the 1933 conference approaching, the London Division, which was by now dominated by the RPC, protested when John Paton, the party's national secretary, refused to circulate to all branches a pamphlet explaining the new ILP constitution that London was proposing. In a letter to the London divisional organizer, John Aplin, Paton argued that to distribute the pamphlet would "establish a most undesirable precedent" and would mean that branches would be "faced with a deluge of opposing statements." At the same time, Paton insisted that he was personally "in sympathy" with the London proposals, even though they were "exceedingly badly and loosely drafted." He wanted the coming conference to adopt a constitution that would, in the most explicit way, express "the Marxist conceptions" that both he and London wanted the ILP to endorse.¹ Yet the partial but considerable success of the RPC at the coming annual conference would soon lead to Paton's resignation. As we saw in the previous chapter, his idea of "Marxist conceptions" was, like Murry's, totally at odds with that of the RPC.

The assurance of personal sympathy was missing from the letter to branches in which Paton reported the rejection of the London proposal. He could not, he said, circulate a one-sided statement to branches unless the same opportunity was extended to opponents of its position. Such a "printed paper debate" would, he said, "usurp the function of Annual Conference itself." To the plea that branches might mandate conference delegates without having heard London's proposal, the secretary replied that it appeared to him that London's pamphlet was "an attempt to secure the mandate" by "an ex parte statement to which their opponents have no opportunity of effective reply."[2]

An attempt to reverse Paton's decision at a meeting of the NAC's Consultative Committee at the House of Commons on 30 March failed.[3] At the next NAC meeting, held on the eve of the conference, Paton criticized the RPC's *Bulletin No. 8*, whose "tendencies seemed to him to be dangerous to the Party." The NAC agreed to emphasize "loyalty to the Party," but Sandham's motion to ask the London Division "to take steps to put to an end the activities of this association" was lost by eight votes to two.[4]

Though prevented from circulating its pamphlet, the RPC had enough success at the 1933 ILP conference at Derby to increase the alarm felt by its opponents in the ILP. Gaster, representing the London Division, had emphasized the need to make clear "not merely that they were out to bring a complete change, but that the change was to be made by the seizure of the power of the machine from the capitalist class by every means in their power." The party needed to "clear up the ambiguities" left by the special conference at Bradford, he argued. Was power to be sought through Parliament or through workers' councils?[5]

The NAC had made its own attempt to clarify the party's position on parliamentary activity in a statement drawn up by Maxton, Brockway, C. A. Smith, J. Allen Skinner, and Paton. It is notable that Jowett, who was both the most experienced former parliamentarian still in the ILP and the party's acknowledged authority on the reform of parliamentary procedure, was not a member of this subcommittee. In its report, the NAC claimed that the conference at Bradford had placed the ILP on a "definitely revolutionary Socialist basis."[6] The statement drawn up by the subcommittee further declared that the struggle for socialism would depend on effective "industrial and class organisations" such as workers' councils. The working class must "discard the belief that Socialism can be achieved simply by voting power exercised through Parliament." Parliament was "an instrument of government of the Capitalist State" and could not be the main instrument of its destruction.[7] The statement went on to list seven advantages to parliamentary activity, mostly variants on Parliament as a highly visible platform for "agitation." However, a revolutionary party must realize that these activities were "only ancillary to the creation outside Parliament of a working-class organisation based on industrial power." In addition to being the chief instrument in overthrowing capitalism, this would be "the embryo organisation for the economic and political administration of the subsequent Socialist Society."[8]

The Derby Conference: The Role of Parliament and the New Constitution

At the Derby conference, Brockway, in his chairman's speech, began by asserting that "the old policies of the Labour and Socialist Movement are utterly useless and must be scrapped." Capitalism was "crumbling" and the only way forward was "to pull down the ruins and rebuild on new foundations." He insisted that the "quality of a revolution is not to be measured by the degree of violence that accompanies the change but the degree of the change itself." The workers would take control of workplaces with a National Workers' Council to "co-ordinate all industries and plan their operation according to needs." While he rejected Parliament as "inadequate for administering the new system," he believed that it could still be useful in the period leading up to the revolution.[9] In concluding, he argued that the historic role of the ILP was to act as "a bridge to join the divided forces of the working class movement" and that its "special duty" was to "build a united front in the international field."[10]

At the conference, Maxton put forward a motion to accept the NAC's statement on the place of parliamentary activities within the party's new program. In his opening comments, however, he insisted that the delegates be under no illusion as they voted on the NAC's proposal. As he pointed out, the statement "did not throw away the Parliamentary weapon—it retained it as one weapon to use in the struggle to revolutionary Socialism." At the same time, it gave Parliament "diminishing importance in the struggle as compared with what had been the general view in Labour Party circles."[11]

Following Maxton's speech, Murry moved that the statement be referred back to the NAC. Paying due attention to "traditions, customs and political habits" was fundamental to Marxism, he argued, and the downgrading of Parliament ran contrary to the "essential psychology of the British working-class." Every revolutionary socialist "knew instinctively that they must do all in their power to preserve to the last possible moment those democratic methods because if they threw them over their opponents were ready to use them." Murry was opposed by McLaughlin from the Sheffield branch, who cited Lenin's view of the state and said he believed that the NAC statement expressed "the new feeling" growing within the ILP.[12]

Murry's motion was also opposed by Jennie Lee and by William Warbey, with the latter arguing that the choice was either "the Capitalist State machine or the development of the workers' alternative." The workers' seizure of power must be based on industrial power and on "all that has been built up on the traditions of the people, the Trades Unions, the Guilds, the N.U.W.M., Tenants' defence organisations and other bodies thrown up by the struggle." Workers' councils would be simply "a co-ordination of all forms of struggle developed by the workers in their attack upon the system."[13] Although the unanimous approval that Maxton had requested was not achieved, the NAC's statement was eventually endorsed later in the conference.[14]

For the RPC, the most important part of the conference deliberations took place on a proposed new constitution, which appeared on the agenda in the name of the London Division and eleven of its branches.[15] Cullen moved the London proposal as a "complete alternative" to the party's existing consitution. The division's desire for a single vote on the constitution was frustrated by the decision of the Standing Orders Committee that constitutional proposals should be debated and voted on in separate sections.[16] Cullen would complain the following month that, in the debates that followed at the conference, the London Division's efforts had repeatedly been sabotaged by the Standing Orders Committee, which had exhibited a "damnably silly (*or* damnably knavish) attitude," and that Brockway, in chairing the debate, had excluded many London delegates from speaking.[17]

Of a possible 195 votes, only 37 were made against the least contentious section of the London proposal, "Responsibilities of Membership." Given that membership would require "full acceptance" of the constitution's principles and strict adherence to the party's rules, it was presumably the same 37 votes that were recorded against the final acceptance of the constitution after all its constituent parts had been decided.[18] Rather more contentious was the section titled "Development of World Socialism." This section committed the party to opposing "imperialist domination over subject races," to seeking "affiliation or association" with most effective international movements, to resisting war, and to supporting the USSR as "the first workers' republic." It was passed by 91 votes to 68.[19] The section titled "Objective" was yet more divisive. Here, the aim of the ILP was declared to be a "classless society" in which all would perform "work of social value." All economic resources were to be "communally owned and controlled," and there would be an end to "rent, interest or profit" and to "all forms of monarchical or hereditary government." Even after some amendment, this section passed only by a vote of 87 to 80.[20]

The London Division was narrowly defeated, by 90 to 87, on the central and most contentious part of the proposed constitution—the section that dealt with method.[21] This sought to commit the party to developing "the militancy of the workers" with "the objective of seizing power." The ILP should make use of "any critical situation arising out of the breakdown of capitalist economic machinery or war." It would develop a "powerful organisation of the unemployed" and would work for the creation of workers' councils to prepare for "a workers' dictatorship . . . for the carrying out of working-class measures necessary in the transitional period."[22]

The debate was intense. Cullen declared that the Bradford conference had left the party "in a state of confusion." It was "a mixture of idealist conceptions which completely ignored the facts of capitalist democracy." Real democracy was possible only in a classless society: in a stratified society, there "was no such thing as democracy as the machine was biased in favour of the monied and propertied classes." Skinner, speaking for the NAC, pointed out that what was now being referred to as "the old Constitution" was in fact "formulated at Bradford six months ago." The ILP was, he said, "going through a feverish time and suffering from a number of infantile disorders." Gaster's proper place was in the CPGB, Skinner maintained, inasmuch as he and his comrades were "making the I.L.P. into a receptacle for petit bourgeois anarchism."[23]

For Jowett, another NAC speaker, the whole debate had an air of unreality. He recalled the 1922 Nottingham conference, which had accepted the "guild socialist" constitution. Conference delegates, like those involved in the current debate, had also attempted to put "doctrinaire theories into the constitution," theories in which "two Parliaments were postulated, one the political Parliament the other a parliament of consumers. Their theories had no more relation to the man in the street than playing with toy bricks." He then made his usual declaration that "representative Government had never been tried. Instead they had the antiquated system of Cabinet rule." Now, he said, there were those who wanted "to get power by civil war." He expressed his total opposition to this, but he also predicted that it was unlikely to happen in a country where you needed a licence to hold a gun.[24]

The result of the debate was only a partial success from the point of view of the RPC. The ILP, according to its new constitution, now rejected all forms of "collaboration with the capitalist class," and though electoral activity was declared to be "essential," it was "only one aspect of the general struggle." The party predicted that capitalist interests would "offer resistance" and resort to "some form of dictatorship." But though the constitution now committed the party to "prepare the minds of the workers" for such a situation and for the "capture of power," it made no mention of workers' councils.[25]

In spite of some setbacks, particularly on the issue of workers' councils, the conference was, as Cohen says, "a considerable victory for the RPC."[26] In the *New Leader*'s report on the Derby conference, the section dealing with the debate on the constitution was headlined "The Marxists' Field Day." The RPC's *Bulletin* declared that "the rank and file were looking to us for a lead" and went on to report that the RPC held two "conferences" of its own at Derby, the first attended by about fifty people and the second, towards the end of the main conference, by even more. At these meetings, "Comrades Cullen and Gaster outlined the views and organisation of the London Committee."[27]

Yet if, as we shall see, RPC members were far from satisfied with the results of the Derby conference, on the other side of the debate were those who were even less satisfied. Richard Wallhead, one of the five ILP MPs elected in 1931 and a veteran ILPer who had chaired the party between 1920 and 1922, resigned from the ILP in protest soon after the conference. Following his departure, the *New Leader* carried an article expressing appreciation of his work for the party. At the same time, it explained that Wallhead interpreted the conference result as "relegating the use of Parliament to a minor place and substituting for it a physical force revolution through Workers' Councils," adding that the decisions at the Derby conference did not "justify this interpretation."[28]

No doubt Wallhead's resignation letter reflected his true estimation of the direction in which the ILP was heading and its dangers. However, it seems likely that his decision, or at least the timing of it, was also influenced by his failure to be re-elected to the NAC, albeit in circumstances that remain somewhat murky. Four national members of the NAC were to be elected by the conference delegates. After no candidate secured a majority in the first round of voting, the conference held a second vote, with the field consisting of the eight candidates who had gained the most votes in the first round. Maxton, who had initially polled the highest and now gained a clear majority, was declared elected, and then a third round was held, in which the four next highest scoring candidates took part. This resulted in the election of C. A. Smith, Campbell Stephen, and Jennie Lee, with the last garnering 115 votes to Wallhead's 107.[29]

When the newly elected NAC met the following day, close to the end of the conference, Brockway, who had been returned unopposed as chairman, proposed that Wallhead "be informed of the statement made that day at the Conference with regard to the unfortunate hitch in the ballot proceedings," as well as told that "the Parliamentary Group was to be recommended to appoint him as liaison member to the N.A.C."[30] This proposal was accepted, though Wallhead did not take up the offer. The *New Leader*'s report on the conference three days later indicated that there had been a "mistake in the method of counting." According to the conference report itself, during the final session the three successful candidates had offered to resign so that the vote could be held again, but the NAC had decided against this after consultation with the Standing Orders Committee—and with Wallhead himself.[31]

Proposals for workers' councils could be dismissed as simply hot air by the likes of Jowett, but Wallhead and Paton clearly did not take the matter so lightly. However, the aspect of revolutionary policy that would provoke yet further internal conflict—and, eventually, a significant loss in membership—was "Co-operation with the Communist Party," an item that appeared on the agenda for the final day of the conference. On the eve of the conference, at a meeting of the NAC, Wallhead had asked "that his dissent should be recorded to co-operation with the Communist Party in any form."[32]

Cooperation with the CPGB: The Derby Conference Debate

More than a decade earlier, the Left Wing of the ILP had tried to bring the ILP into the Comintern fold. Now, having parted with Labour, the party was once again under siege from the same quarter, with Comintern affiliation again on the agenda. The Affiliation Committee, inspired by the CPGB leadership and particularly by writer and editor Palme Dutt, sought to propel the ILP into unconditional Comintern affiliation—an effort that proved to be counterproductive. The RPC was embarrassed when two of the Affiliation Committee members were revealed to be undercover members of the CPGB and were duly expelled from the ILP. This was followed by the temporary suspension from the party of two other committee members after they paid a visit to Moscow, "to try to clarify the Comintern's twenty-one conditions and alleviate the fears of some ILPers about what fulfilling those conditions would really mean," as Cohen explains. One of those suspended was Bob Edwards, who would play a very prominent role in the ILP in later years. The suspicion was that their visit had been at least partially Communist-funded.[33]

As before, in spite of such clumsy efforts at intervention by the Communist Party itself, the issue was fought out in the ILP and in the minds of its members. Those with an interest in the left-wing politics of the day who believed the adage that "the spectator sees more of the game" might have taken note of *Forward*'s headline on the coming ILP annual conference a few days before it began. "Will the I.L.P. Join the Communists?" it asked, with the commentator concluding that "it looks as if the I.L.P. is going to meet the usual fate of ultra Left organisations and split up into more Lefts and Rights." Those now regretting disaffiliation would "find their way back" to the Labour Party.[34]

That the eventual fate of the "revolutionary" ILP would be to be taken over by the CPGB seemed all too obvious to those in the party who feared such an outcome. The fact that a conference convened by *Labour Monthly*, which took place on 11 March 1933, not long before the ILP's annual conference, was well attended by members of both the Communist Party and the ILP could only reinforce this belief. Later revelations about the activities of the Communist-led Affiliation Committee and the undercover role of CPGB members in the ILP simply confirmed such suspicions.[35]

The fears of those ILPers who were alarmed at the prospect of working with the Communists began to be realized right at the start of the Derby conference during the debate on the NAC report. The debate focused on the stance that the party should adopt towards organizations of the unemployed. Reports gathered by the NAC from across the country revealed a very patchy pattern of support among ILPers for the National Unemployed Workers' Movement (NUWM), a pattern that was attributed to the "sectarian" and "partisan" tactics of the Communists.[36] A resolution recognizing the Communist-led body as "the only national body of the unemployed" was moved by the London Division. This was accepted after an amendment pledging support for "all organisations" working for the unemployed was lost by 65 to 100. During the debate, Berriman from the Bristol branch put forward the case for the National Federation of Unemployed Workers, while Murry objected that the NUWM "was controlled by the C.P."[37]

This debate was followed by a motion to "approach the Secretariat of the Communist International with a view to ascertaining in what way the I.L.P. may assist in the work of the International." Moved by Warbey, with Gaster supporting it, the motion generated opposition from the Bootle, Edinburgh, and Sheffield branches—and not least from the NAC. Opposing it for the NAC, Paton maintained that "the failure of the Comintern had been even more spectacular and colossal" than that of the Labour and Socialist International. He claimed that in several cases, the "Left" parties associated with the ILP had larger memberships than the Communist parties of those countries. The NAC wanted an "all-inclusive International which must be formed from constituents of both the present Internationals." Nevertheless, in spite of the NAC's opposition, the motion was narrowly passed by 83 to 79.[38]

The debate on cooperation with the Communist Party was concluded in a "private session," which excluded the press and everyone who was not a delegate, indicating how sensitive and potentially divisive the issue was. Only the final—amended—NAC proposals were reported. It was confirmed that "further co-operation" with the Communists was desirable for resisting fascism, defending the Soviet Union, and opposing capitalist attacks at home and abroad. The ILP would continue to seek a united international. Cooperation should be on the basis that "the co-operating parties will refrain from intersectional attacks in the united action campaign."[39]

The NAC proposals, now adopted by the conference, went on to comment on the use by the CPGB of the word "strikes" in its suggested program for cooperation. The ILP did not believe in advocating strikes indiscriminately "but only where there is a prospect of such action being effective." Also, in the ILP's view, "the agitational method of 'demonstrations' should not be carried to the extent that familiarity with them destroys their effect," nor should they be "used ineffectively or needlessly to expose the demonstrators to police attack."[40]

After the Conference: Trying to Shape a Revolutionary Policy

The ambiguities of the positions adopted by the ILP at the Derby conference are to some extent evident in the *New Leader*'s front-page article headlined "How Workers Can Unite," appearing soon after the conference. While at a national level, only the ILP and the CPGB were cooperating, the writer claimed that a wider "united front" was being formed in many areas.[41]

Meanwhile, on the NAC, Elijah Sandham was unsuccessfully pressing for divisional councils to report on RPC activities at the next NAC meeting.[42] From the sidelines, *Forward* saw the ILP now "divided into two almost equal sections": one supported the "Moscow International" and the other was "hesitating to throw over completely the traditional theories and practices of British Socialism." The "vague declarations" of the leaders of the party, Maxton and Brockway, made it difficult to know where they stood, the writer concluded.[43]

Just how difficult the ILP was already finding its attempts to cooperate with the Communists was already evident. At the beginning of the year, the *New Leader* had scorned "the pitiful futility of the Communist Party leadership of the Hunger March to London" and maintained that Communist sectarianism had "destroyed the possibilities of effective organisation."[44] In early February, B. Grooms, a member of the Stapleford-Sandiacre ILP branch, spanning the border between Nottinghamshire and Derbyshire, wrote to the *Leader* complaining that at a Communist meeting in Stapleford, Harry Pollitt, the CPGB's general secretary, had "implied" that the ILP had failed to assist striking cotton workers and the recent hunger march, among other similar damaging accusations.[45] A debate between Pollitt and C. A. Smith, speaking for the ILP, took place in Stapleford in the spring. "The red-shirted Guild of Youth were vividly in evidence," reported the *New Leader*, going on to say that Pollitt had announced that his party would "wage a merciless war on the conception that there can be two parties" committed to revolutionary socialism. For his part, Smith insisted that the ILP was "the most democratic political party in the country in the way in which its policy is formulated, as well as in the way its finance is raised." The implication that the CPGB was not democratic in either respect was very clear.[46]

Concerns about the RPC also continued. The same issue of the *Leader* carried a letter from J. Allen Skinner under the titled "Is the R.P.C. a Danger?" Skinner, who had resigned as chair of the London Division, asserted that an RPC conference prior to the London divisional meeting had agreed on the constitutional proposals that were then "carried without a single amendment" at the subsequent ILP divisional meeting. The divisional council had become "a redundancy."[47] But at a NAC meeting the following week, only Sandham dissented from "no action" in response to a letter from another member protesting against "the operations of the R.P.C." Maxton deplored what seemed to him to be "the development of rival factions."[48]

The NAC also discussed cooperation with the CPGB. Sandham was again alone in proposing that the council dissociate itself from the report of the representatives negotiating with the Communists. Both Jennie Lee and Campbell Stephen expressed worries about the danger of being "absorbed." Paton and Jowett also voiced concerns, while Sandham called for negotiations to be discontinued.[49]

Responding to questions from readers soon thereafter, Brockway, as editor of the *New Leader*, tried to clarify ILP policy. Revolution meant "fundamental change" from capitalism to socialism. The party had not "thrown over Parliamentarism" but doubted whether a parliamentary majority was enough to avoid revolution, since the ruling class was likely to turn away from democracy if faced with socialism. Fascism was a real danger, but the ILP did not favour physical force insurrection.[50]

If this was meant to calm the internal conflicts, it failed. The *Leader* soon published a piece headlined "The R.P.C. a Danger? Should Sections Within the I.L.P. Be Tolerated?" This featured three letters. Skinner dismissed Maxton and Brockway's defence of "general discussion" as "a wilful blinding of one's eyes." He charged that the RPC's avowed aim was to capture all the divisional machinery and achieve a "United Communist Party." Skinner was supported by Fred Howard, whose letter attacked the "subversive pseudo-Communist tactics" of the RPC, which, he maintained, was "not an honest organisation" but a "parasitical group." The third letter, from Cullen, defended the RPC as an organization that would "continue to be a danger to tradition and convention," which clearly did nothing to reassure members who were uneasy about the RPC's activities.[51]

This discussion in the *Leader* was followed later that month by an exchange between Jowett and Maxton. The former's article, explicitly repudiating any idea of violence, was headed "Towards Revolution, Parliament Must Be the Instrument." He again dismissed the notion of workers' councils composed of an "intermixture of unrelated and discordant bodies." Maxton's reply reiterated that Parliament was not being rejected, but it was "only a small part of the fight." The essential task, he concluded, was to build workers' councils. "I have pushed the United Front proposals," he added.[52]

The day after Maxton's article appeared, the NAC met. Sandham insisted that branches had complete autonomy: if they did not carry out united front activities, the divisional council could not make them. A united front including Labour was fine; one with only the CPGB was "all wrong." On this, the Lancashire Divisional Council executive was unanimous, he said. He attributed a fall in membership in the division—from 9,000 to under 2,000—to the United Front policy.[53]

Sandham was not alone on the NAC in questioning that policy. Jennie Lee was, as Cohen says, a "vocal advocate of the new revolutionary policy."[54] But she agreed that continuing to pursue a united front with the Communist Party alone was "harmful" and that too much attention was being given by the ILP to the Communists. In mining areas in Scotland, she argued, the policy had done the ILP infinitely more harm than disaffiliation had. It had "killed some of the branches and halved the membership in others. This was not a loss of ineffective members but of real revolutionary fighters." Where there was no tradition of Communist activity, she thought a united front was possible, but where the CPGB had been active, the long-standing bitterness and antipathy made it impossible. In such areas, the combination of the ILP and the Communist Party was "a weaker thing than the I.L.P. alone."[55]

Stephen added that the general view from reports from the localities was that the United Front policy had gained nothing for the ILP but had led to membership losses. While Gaster insisted that the NAC could not vary conference decisions, Percy Williams, the Yorkshire representative, said that it should act when a policy was found to be "disastrous" and that the participation in the united front should be confined to "concrete proposals." Five different motions were then debated at some length, culminating in the one moved by Smith, calling for the United Front policy to be continued "in conformity with the decisions to be reached on general policy," being passed by 7 votes to 3.[56]

Much of the final day of the NAC meeting was devoted to a long discussion of "general policy," which again revealed deep divisions. C. A. Smith wanted a "Marxist view of the class struggle and the State": the real fight was "not so much against Capitalism as against the State," he maintained. The ILP needed to occupy key positions in all parts of the working-class movement and to turn its attention to the civil service, the armed forces, the docks, and munitions works. Socialism could not be won by industrial force alone: there would be a "final determination by physical struggle." Meanwhile, more power should be concentrated in the ILP's executive committee, with "no nonsense about local autonomy." They should "organise the branches on a semi-military basis." For her part, Jennie Lee was looking forward to "the formation of a new revolutionary party." The ILP could make a contribution to that goal, but she believed that the CPGB-like methods of Gaster and his associates were "really only possible for a party that is heavily subsidised and not dependent on the resources of its own members." However, she did agree that parliamentary activities should be "secondary."[57]

Gaster insisted that the ILP needed "a sound theoretical basis," but his view of the membership did not suggest much confidence that this might be achieved. He urged the NAC to face the fact that the ILP "was largely composed of second-rate brains and a large percentage of its members were incapable of consecutive and logical thought." For Sandham, the entire discussion had been "poisoned" by the idea of reliance on force. Stephen, citing the failure of "the anti-parliamentary party led by Guy Aldred," believed that the weakness of the ILP was that it was widely perceived as an "insurrectionist" party—a view encouraged by Labour. For him, the goal should be to capture Parliament and turn it into a workers' council. McGovern thought that "their activities must centre round Parliament," a view shared by Paton.[58]

As usual, Maxton and Brockway attempted to play a peacemaking role, which carried the very considerable danger of satisfying no one on any side. ILPers were "idealists," said Maxton, and "for such people crudities such as war, even class-war, were repellent." The workers' council issue should not be allowed to "get on top of the Party" and sow strife, he argued. Brockway stressed that despite claims to the contrary there was considerable agreement within the party. He therefore supported the idea, put forward at the beginning of the discussion, of setting up a subcommittee to produce an "agreed statement" on ILP policy. Other NAC members might submit "documents on the matters arising" to the subcommittee, which would be made up of Brockway, Paton, Williams, Garton, and Gaster. When such a resolution was passed, Sandham immediately asked for his dissent to be recorded.[59]

With opinions so divided among members of the NAC, there was little sign of any agreement on policy among the wider membership in the pages of the *New Leader*. At the end of June, a few days after the NAC meeting, letters to the paper debated the question "Should the R.P.C. continue?" Skinner charged the RPC with disloyalty to the ILP, claiming that the great majority of its adherents gave "their first organisational loyalty to the R.P.C." Richard Rees, now an active ILPer in the London Division, maintained that in the capital, the movement had always been too much influenced by "intellectual theoreticians." From the other side of the argument, T. K. Frienensen, of Sheffield, maintained that Skinner and "the Right Wing 'democrats'" were simply "disgruntled" about the results of the annual conference.[60]

"A Clear Lead": The NAC Policy Statement

As Cohen says, the decisions made at the Derby conference "did not resolve the central ideological disputes within the ILP."[61] Indeed, if anything, it intensified them. The RPC had moved the party only some way towards what it regarded as a revolutionary policy. Its opponents, with their own conceptions of what should constitute such a policy, were determined to reverse the resolutions adopted at the conference. To complicate matters further, the positions put forward were often less than crystal clear. Could the newly established policy subcommittee, or the leadership generally, arrive at a clear statement of a policy that would suffice to restore unity to the ILP? The subcommittee's deliberations would demonstrate just how difficult that would be.

The first meeting of the Subcommittee on General Policy took place at the very beginning of July. As originally proposed, its members were Brockway, Paton, Williams, Garton, and Gaster. It was agreed that, while the ILP's position must be sufficiently flexible to cope with other possibilities, the most "probable developments" included the decline of British capitalism with a lowering of the "standards of life." In such circumstances, the "capitalist class" would abandon democracy for fascism. Complications might include war against Russia triggered by the threat posed by that country's "example of socialist construction," the clash of imperialisms in the Far East, or the "struggles of subject peoples," especially in India.[62]

The subcommittee concluded that parliamentary institutions were "an instrument of capitalist domination" and that parliamentary activities must be linked to a "united working class organisation" that would be prepared to act against "capitalist dictatorship and war" in a revolutionary crisis. These conclusions were described as "tentative" and were to be the basis for "private discussion": NAC members could express their own views and, if necessary, submit supplementary reports, but meeting minutes would be circulated only to subcommittee members. Meanwhile, Garton, Brockway, and Williams, who appeared to be in near agreement on both the constitution and the role of workers' councils, should seek to produce a joint statement prior to the next meeting.[63]

In the initial draft of its report to the NAC, the subcommittee declared "the most important task of the Socialist Movement" to be the creation of "a united working-class organisation."[64] Paton, however, submitted a supplementary report, in which he registered his "complete opposition" to this draft, including the "relegation of Parliamentary activities" to a subordinate role. In addition, Paton wrote a longer piece, titled simply "Party Policy," in which he outlined his own views on the subject. In it, he commented that, although the ILP was united in its "desire for revolutionary socialism," judging by the various interpretations of decisions made at the 1933 annual conference, there were "at least half-a-dozen definitions of what that means."[65]

As if to illustrate Paton's point, Brockway submitted his own statement on party policy. He dismissed the possibility of achieving socialism by the "gradual transformation of Capitalism" and presented the gaining of parliamentary seats as "an incidental part of our general socialist agitation and organisation." Furthermore, he wanted to reverse a decision made at the Derby conference to the effect that ILP members in trade unions should not pay the political levy—which normally went to the Labour Party. He also argued that, as a general rule, workers' councils should not be set up in areas where they would rival existing trades councils, which were already well-established in many localities and served to represent trade union branches in the area.⁶⁶

Brockway was equivocal on relations with the Communists. Although cooperation with the CPGB was "natural" because both parties had "a revolutionary outlook," he urged caution. "Two months ago," he pointed out, "the British C.P. changed its policy, and even, apparently, its temper, over one week-end. Sudden conversions of that kind are not reliable." Moreover, this reversal of CPGB policy had been "artificially imposed from outside." While the ILP did want to cooperate with the Comintern, he argued, it would not accept "subservience."⁶⁷

The Subcommittee on General Policy met again, roughly three weeks later. The minutes cover a single page and list only three items. Brockway presented a "revised draft" of the report which reflected discussions between Brockway and Garton that had taken place between the meetings. After "full consideration," the subcommittee agreed to submit the revised draft to the NAC. According to the minutes, Williams was to be asked whether he agreed with their conclusions. In the meantime, Paton, who was "opposed to the basic assumptions of the document," and Gaster, who registered his "dissent from several sections," were asked to submit minority reports to the NAC.⁶⁸ When the NAC met two weeks later, it was faced with resolutions against the RPC from six ILP branches. Once the NAC turned to the subcommittee report, there was unanimous agreement on the recommendation to reverse the political levy decision—but on very little else. Gaster's minority report viewed the policy statement as still too favourable to parliamentary action: in his view, the main job of the ILP was to "initiate Workers' Council work outside Parliament." The party should pursue "*one* line rather than half-a-dozen," he argued, and it should also seek "daily co-operation with the C.P. and other revolutionary elements with a view to the definite formation of united leadership of the mass movement (finding ultimate expression in Workers' Councils) in a united revolutionary party." There must be no "cutting down" of the Derby conference decisions, Gaster concluded.⁶⁹

For his part, Paton insisted that he stood by the ILP's rejection of reformism and was committed to "an absolutely revolutionary outlook and policy." However, many of the "frothy utterances" of the "majority" report, as the report drafted by Garton and Brockway had come to be called, were "mere romantic posturing and mock heroics from people who lived in a dream world of illusions." While it was totally impracticable to build up a mass movement divorced from existing organizations, he argued, the alliance with the CPGB was "disastrous." Instead, the ILP should seek to "fill the place the Communist Party had never been able to occupy by becoming the first really revolutionary party in Great Britain, an achievement which would mean the extinction of the Communist Party." Not only should cooperation with the Communists be ended, Paton reiterated, but the ILP should "proceed to open attack on their disruptive influence."[70]

Percy Williams, E. B. James, and Campbell Stephen supported Paton, while C. A. Smith declared himself "appalled" that matters decided at the annual conference were being regarded as "open questions." The conference had decided that parliamentary activities were "ancillary," Smith said, but members of the NAC were going against the ILP's policy and "putting forward Parliament as the main instrument." They were "ridiculing" workers' councils and trying to get out of the agreement with the CPGB. Smith claimed that membership had held up better in areas where cooperation with the Communists was most "enthusiastically" carried out, and he threatened to resign from the NAC and force a by-election for his replacement.[71]

It was left to Garton to defend what was still called the majority report. It had put forward an outline of "comprehensive policy," of which the United Front policy was "only an incidental part," he insisted. The subcommittee agreed, on Gaster's suggestion, to take the majority report as the motion and vote on the minority reports as amendments. Although Elijah Sandham insisted that a vote should first be taken on whether the "association with the Communist Party should be maintained," he was alone in supporting this idea, presumably because Paton, as an ILP official, had no vote. A motion to accept Paton's minority report was then lost by a vote of 10 to 5, Gaster's was rejected by 14 to 1, and the majority report was carried by 10 to 5, with Sandham, Jowett, Stephen, Williams, and James in the minority. Gaster than asked for his dissent on the section "The Place of Parliament" to be recorded.[72]

It now fell to the *New Leader* to report to the membership the results of the NAC's deliberations, which it did on 11 August. According to the paper, the statement released by the NAC provided a "clear lead." Cooperation with the CPGB was to be regarded as the first step in realizing a real unity of working class forces for revolutionary socialist purposes." On the contentious issue of workers' councils, the statement read:

> Workers' Councils should be formed only when the organisations prepared to co-operate represent the power of effective working-class action in the locality. The Councils should represent not only such existing organisations as are prepared to co-operate (Trade Union branches,

Co-operative organisations, the I.L.P. the C.P., N.U.W.M. etc.) but even more importantly, factory committees, street and estate committees which definitely represent the workers where they are employed and live.

As immediately became evident, if this was a clear lead, it was not one that all members were prepared to follow. The same *New Leader* issue announced that Paton was resigning because of a "difference on policy" and that, in December, Brockway would take his place as secretary, with Maxton again becoming party chairman.[73]

Maxton and Brockway would continue to do their best to reconcile the irreconcilable. In a pamphlet titled *A Clear Lead*, they took a wary position on the United Front policy, stressing crucial differences with the CPGB:

> The temper of the two parties is different. The tactics are different. The I.L.P. believes in democratic control by the party membership. Its members would never be willing to obey orders, from either a national or an international executive, which they had no voice in determining.
>
> Under present conditions the amalgamation of the I.L.P. and the Communist Party is impossible. The Communist Party is not prepared to break from the rigid organisational and financial control of Moscow.[74]

They confirmed, however, that where cooperation was possible, the ILP would pursue it. Even before this declaration, however, it had become clear that the ILP stronghold of Lancashire was not—for the most part—willing to go along with even this qualified version of a united front.

PART IV

Unity Remains Elusive

16

Lancashire Revolts
Continuing Conflict over the United Front

At the end of July 1932, at Bradford, the ILP made the momentous decision to leave the Labour Party in order to pursue a new revolutionary policy. In the year following that decision, it swiftly became apparent that party members, including the ILP's most prominent leaders, held radically divergent views—some of them outright incompatible—as to what this policy should be. Paton's desire to see the ILP "open attack" on the "disruptive influence" of the CPGB, with the goal of ultimately stepping into that party's place, could hardly be reconciled with the vision of those who favoured cooperation with the Communists, with whom the ILP should join in a united front. Debates also swirled around the nature and function of workers' councils and the place of parliament and electoral activities under this new, more radical dispensation. Although the ILP had always prided itself on being more decentralized and democratic than most political organizations, in the face of internal discord, it fell to the NAC to provide the party with a clear sense of direction—provided, of course, that it could arrive at some measure of consensus itself.

The Lancashire Revolt

Among the members of the NAC, Elijah Sandham was the most outspoken and unyielding opponent of new ILP policies. As we saw in the previous chapter, despite sitting on the NAC, Sandham was a strong supporter of divisional autonomy, in keeping with the ILP's tradition of decentralization. In April 1933, his Lancashire Division—pleading a weak financial situation—refused to contribute to the ILP's recently established Power for Socialism Fund, which all branches were expected to support, thereby directing a proportion of divisional resources towards the party's central operations. Sandham and his circle of associates were especially incensed by the costs associated with the ILP's national publication, the *New Leader*.[1] At the NAC meeting the following month, Sandham opposed paying the editor of the *New Leader* on the grounds that such work should be performed as a "voluntary service," as was the case with his division's own paper, *Labour's Northern Voice*.² While Sandham's opposition to centralized authority was doubtless grounded in principle, it also reflected his dissatisfaction with the direction in which the ILP seemed to be moving—namely, towards a closer relationship with the Communists.

Sandham was implacably hostile to the RPC, an attitude in which he was not alone. In June 1933, a *Labour's Northern Voice* article by J. Allen Skinner—the London Division's former representative on the NAC, whom Gaster had replaced—urged the ILP to take the necessary "steps to safeguard the Party." Despite what Brockway and the NAC seemed to believe, Skinner declared, the RPC was not some sort of discussion group but "an internal caucus aiming at placing those members who are not so organised at a disadvantage in the Councils of the Party." He suggested that, "regrettable as is the necessity," ILP members opposed to the RPC should form their own "protective caucus." It should have no policy other than "the purely negative aim of protecting the Party against the danger of becoming further caucus-ridden by the R.P.C.," and it should "go out of existence as soon as the R.P.C. caucus is brought to an end and the Party reverted to the normal healthy functioning of a democratic movement." In the following month's edition of the paper, Richard Rees and his close associate from *The Adelphi*, John Middleton Murry, wrote in support of Skinner's position.³

These anti-RPC sentiments led to the formation of the "Unity Group," in which both Sandham and the Lancashire Division organizer, Tom Abbott, played leading roles.⁴ By late July, *Forward* was reporting on developments within the Lancashire Division under the headline "The United Front with Communists: An I.L.P. Breakaway in Lancashire." According to the paper, on 17 June, a circular from the Lancashire executive committee had recommended that branches withdraw from any collaboration with the Communist Party. The article went on to say that CPGB's *Daily Worker* was devoting two or three of its columns every day to attacking Brockway, and it looked as if the Communists were now demanding that the NAC expel the Lancashire Division's executive.⁵

When the NAC next met, in early August, Gaster attacked Lancashire's "disloyalty to the Party" while Sandham defended branch autonomy. After Brockway ruled that conference decisions had to be applied by the party as a whole, Sandham insisted that the party was "falling to pieces" and that his executive was struggling to cope with this situation. Three different motions were discussed, after which it was agreed to send Paton, himself now close to resignation, to the Lancashire Division to demand that the offending circular be withdrawn.⁶ A few weeks later, the *New Leader* reported that the Lancashire Divisional Council had, by a vote of 10 to 5, refused to withdraw the circular and was insisting that united front activities were "killing our identity as a Party." Meanwhile, in *The Adelphi*, Skinner continued his critique. Was the RPC and the urge for a revolutionary policy "revolution or romance?" he asked.[7]

Lancashire was supported by the Welsh Division and the Bradford, Norwich, Hutchinsontown, and Clydebank branches, the latter suggesting that "a plebiscite of the members" should be taken on the United Front policy. But many others supported taking a firm line with Lancashire, including, within that county, the Liverpool Federation, which dissociated itself from its divisional conference's decisions and asked for the formation of a new divisional council. Only by a narrow vote had it agreed to continue to pay fees to the divisional council until a new organization was formed. When, at the September NAC meeting, the chairman ruled that the NAC could replace the Lancashire council, Campbell Stephen maintained that "no Law Court would allow such a ruling," and Sandham supported him. Gaster's motion of censure was carried by 8 votes to 6, while Garton's proposal that the *Northern Voice* should be regarded as an "opposition organ" if it continued publishing articles "contrary to Party policy" was passed with an even smaller majority of 7 to 6.[8]

Meanwhile, the September 1933 issue of *Labour's Northern Voice* was defiant. Its front page was headlined "Lancashire I.L.P. Says 'No' Because It Believes in a Real United Front." Claiming that there was little support for the NAC's policy in the division, the paper charged that the London Division had been "the consistent advocate of an alliance with the Communists," with its representatives openly proclaiming their objective to be "*the absorption of the I.L.P. in the Communist Party*." The RPC, it claimed, dominated the "vacillating" NAC. The Lancashire Division and the *Voice* were diametrically opposed to the CPGB's policy of "a bloody catastrophic revolution" and did not want to be "tarred in the minds of the public with the same brush." A key part of "Our Credo" followed the article which insisted that it was simply "traditional I.L.P. policy":

> In this country we believe that Socialism cannot be established except by the will of the ordinary wage-workers of this country. That to establish Socialism we have to use *all* the organisations built up by the workers, including Parliament. That it is equally important to organise class-conscious workers at the point of production as it is to organise them at the ballot box.

If the NAC as a whole was "vacillating" in the eyes of the *Voice*'s editor, Jowett was clearly seen as an exception, since the same issue carried his article "Why I Disagree with the I.L.P.'s. New Policy." He was against any idea of trying to seize control without majority support and any limiting of parliamentary and municipal activity; he was also against "day-to-day" cooperation that could involve association with the CPGB in "mutinous and purely explosive industrial and insurrectional activities." He concluded by quoting John Middleton Murry on the "real issue" of the Derby conference: it was not a question of being "for or against the Parliamentary weapon as such, but for or against the futility with which the Parliamentary weapon has been used."[9]

Those who expected the Lancashire Division to fall into line after the NAC had censured it were immediately disappointed. Crisis in the ILP had been brought nearer, said Murry in *The Adelphi*, by the NAC policy statement that relegated Parliament to "a mere platform for propaganda," endorsed the continuation of "the discredited 'united front,'" and insisted on creating workers' councils—"on paper."[10] Murry then appeared in the October edition of *Labour's Northern Voice*. In "Our Task as Revolutionary Socialists," he praised the previous issue of the paper for giving a lead and predicted that workers would "reject with contempt" the policy now advocated by "the disruptive element in the I.L.P.," which wanted them to ignore their traditional methods and organization "in favour of semi-military Workers' Councils and go into training for a life-and-death struggle with the forces of the State." The real task, said Murry, was to ensure that the Labour Party went into the next election with "a thorough-going Socialist policy" before it was too late. "History will not wait while our left-wing intellectuals draw up their plans for the revolution," he warned.[11]

The following month, the *Voice* carried a long letter from Arnold Higginson of Preston defending the role of Parliament and objecting to its "degradation" while demanding radical reform. But T. W. Sudlow from Blackpool could not "see where Middleton Murry's revolution comes in" and mocked those afraid to cooperate with "those terrible people, the Communists."[12]

From the sidelines, *Forward* continued to pour scorn on the ILP. Robert Calderwood, who had been the Labour Party election agent at the Kilmarnock by-election, charged that "Kilmarnock was the first victim of Maxton's new methods of achieving Socialism." The ILP had helped to lose the election for Labour, he argued. He blamed Maxton personally: "Without Maxton the I.L.P. in Scotland would not live to see another by-election." In the same issue, John J. Fraser, the former ILP organizer for Yorkshire, explained why he had left the ILP. There had been nothing but confusion since disaffiliation, he said. He had no sympathy with violence, thought workers' councils impracticable, and was totally opposed to dictatorship "either in a Capitalist or a Socialist State" and to a united front with the CPGB.[13]

At the end of the year, few ILPers, whatever their views on the United Front policy and the RPC, were happy with the state of affairs in the party. The second edition of *Controversy*, the new internal discussion organ, addressed the situation in "The Basic Problem of the I.L.P. To-day." The approaching

1934 annual conference would have to face up to the party's problems, the editorial said. The Derby conference decisions and NAC statement had not solved the party's problems. While the ILP had broken with "the old reformist and Social-Democratic basis," opponents of the "present revolutionary policy" would try to reverse the Derby decisions.[14]

Meanwhile, the crisis in the Lancashire ILP showed no signs of abating. The writer of a *New Leader* report in February 1934 on the division's recent council meeting detected the existence in the divisional council of two distinct forces—one supporting the NAC, the other "rejecting root and branch its interpretation of party policy on co-operation with the CPGB, workers' councils and the relegation of Parliamentary activities to a secondary place in the struggle for power." The latter group significantly outnumbered the former. At the Lancashire meeting, a motion calling for ILP policy to revert "in every detail prior to Derby" was passed by 29 to 16, and another one insisting that socialism "must be presented as a constitutional end" was adopted by 29 to 14. Sandham's report on the NAC meeting was accepted by 30 to 12, and its condemnation of divisional officers rejected by 34 to 9.[15]

Much of the February edition of *Labour's Northern Voice* was, predictably, devoted to the triumph of the Lancashire majority. "Lancashire Stands Firm," proclaimed its front page. The article warned that the "philosophy of violence of the Communist Party" had "bored its ruinous way into the I.L.P." and sought to destroy the only socialist force that stood between the CPGB and the reformism of the Labour Party. But in Lancashire, "the wreckers"— the RPC and other supporters of unity with the Communists and CPGB—had failed. Lancashire wanted a "real revolutionary policy" that was "acceptable to the majority of the British people." Socialism must be presented as "a constitutional end to be sought by constitutional means," and a socialist government would have to make every effort constitutionally available to it against any "anti-democratic and unconstitutional opposition by the King, the House of Lords, or by capitalists, or by financial revolutionaries."[16]

The editor of the *Voice* jokingly proposed putting out a pamphlet with the title "How Not to Do It," to be offered at a reduced price to RPC branches. He looked forward to another to be published after the York conference, to be called "How Lancashire Did It," with, he hoped, a "congratulatory foreword by Maxton and Brockway and a minority foreword by Comrade Jack Gaster."[17]

Lancashire was not entirely alone in its opposition to the new policy. At the beginning of the year, the NAC had decided to conduct a survey of members on the United Front. The questionnaire was drawn up by Brockway and Campbell Stephen.[18] The results revealed that Yorkshire, East Anglia, and Wales had majorities of respondents opposed to continuing cooperation with the Communists. In addition, surprisingly, thirteen London branches showed majorities opposing it, though the individual responses from the London Division showed a narrow majority of 96 to 92 for the United Front policy. Some went further. The Stapleford-Sandiacre and New Ferry branches wanted "disciplinary action against the R.P.C."[19]

For its part, *Labour's Northern Voice* looked forward with optimism to the coming ILP conference. The NAC had been "insulted and smacked enough by the Communist Party to have learned, what everyone else knows, that 'united front' with the C.P. means *absorption*." It was hoped that the party would "tread anew the democratic Socialist path."[20]

The York Conference: Disagreement, Division, and Defections

As had been the case the year before, few in the ILP were satisfied with the outcome of the 1934 annual conference. That it would be extremely divisive had long been clear. While the Sheffield branch had submitted a motion supporting cooperation with the Communist Party Murry's East Anglian Division declared both the workers' council policy and association with the Communists "disastrous." It demanded instead a "real" united front of workers' organizations rather than "the pretence that goes by the name of the 'United Front.'" The Norwich branch argued that in a country with a working-class majority, socialism could only be based on the "enlightened democratic consent of the majority of people" and that it was essential not only to propagate "Collectivism"—which fascists and Nazis also did—but "Socialism as an ethically superior social system." In contrast, the motion from the London and Southern Counties Divisional Council demanded that the party concentrate on "the economic and industrial struggle." Workers' support could not be secured by "idealist and utopian propaganda," the council maintained.[21]

The NAC report to the conference noted that the Lancashire Division had opposed the policy adopted by the previous year's conference. It recognized the right to try changing the policy, but the division had encouraged branches to refuse to carry out the policy decided upon at the national conference, and it had used "its organ the 'Northern Voice' publicly to attack the policy of the Party."[22]

The policy statement adopted by the York conference was alarming for those wanting to revert to pre-Derby positions, while at the same time being far too cautious and lukewarm from the point of view of RPC supporters. The ILP, the statement said, would "associate with the Communist International in all efforts which, in the view of the I.L.P., further the revolutionary struggle of the workers." The goal of seeking a united socialist-communist international was reaffirmed, as was the United Front—though on a significantly limited basis:

"After surveying the results of co-operation with the Communist Party over the last year," the NAC now recommended that "the national co-operation of the two parties be based on specific objects as agreed upon by the representatives of the two parties from time to time." While the ILP looked forward to the ultimate creation of a single revolutionary party, said the statement, the "fact must be faced . . . that in other areas, co-operation with the Communist Party has tended to estrange sections of the 'official movement.'"²³

As the *New Leader* reported, Sandham was successful in defeating a particular clause in a motion, a clause that he attributed to a "London complex" that sought, he maintained, to turn the ILP into "an insurrectionary organisation." The rejected clause had called for the planning of party work "during a period of illegality." The ILP paper commented, "Evidently a majority of the Conference was convinced of the tactical error of including references to illegal work." This was not an interpretation of the decision that Sandham would have welcomed or accepted.²⁴

On the advice of the NAC, a London Division motion that called for "real democracy" via workers' councils and insisted that "a Parliamentary representative must be drawn from the working-class struggle in the locality" was defeated by 85 to 66. This was after Brockway had argued that it "subordinated Parliament to a greater degree than was desirable." But the attempt by Murry's Norwich branch to commit the party to the idea that "constitutionalism was the only real line of activity for a revolutionary party in this country" was also rejected by 101 to 61. A similar move by the Manchester City branch to adopt a "real revolutionary policy" that was "constitutionalist" suffered the same fate.²⁵

If the outcome of the conference was disappointing to the opponents of the United Front and workers' councils, it was a great deal less than a success from the RPC point of view. The *London R.P.C. Bulletin* rejected the *Leader*'s claim that the York conference had "cleared up" ILP policy and "reaffirmed the revolutionary policy adopted at Derby. There was no plan of action and not even a recognition that revolution involved a struggle."²⁶

Just how divided the ILP had become, even at the level of its national leadership is evident from the continuing controversy after the 1934 conference. Almost all the energy of the party seemed to be absorbed in the internal conflict. Reaching any agreement on what constituted the revolutionary policy that the disaffiliated ILP was committed to pursuing seemed less and less achievable.

One campaign in which Gaster had been successful was in securing Sandham's removal from the list of ILP parliamentary candidates by a vote of 88 to 71.²⁷ He had attempted this earlier at the January NAC, arguing that since candidates were required to accept party policy "in general," Sandham's opposition to the August statement disqualified him.²⁸ At the NAC meeting on the final day of the conference, Maxton tried to conciliate with suggestions that the NAC might recommend restoring Sandham to the list "if Lancashire would now co-operate wholeheartedly." He did not want, he said, to "drive out Lancashire."[29]

Sandham agreed on the basis that "the York Conference had reversed the decision of the Derby Conference on C.P. co-operation and that had been the mainspring of the difficulty in Lancashire." This was the proverbial red rag to a bull. Gaster denied that the conference had "reversed" Derby policy and insisted that Lancashire must show that it was "in line with revolutionary policy and not reformism."[30]

The confident and jocular tone of the pre-York *Labour's Northern Voice* had now gone. "Lancashire Under the Hammer! The Last Round-Up?" it asked, focusing on the rejection of Sandham as candidate for the Liverpool constituency of Kirkdale, which he had represented as MP between 1929 and 1931. "Here was a chance to down Sandham, and up rose the bold Gaster, moving that his name be deleted from the list. Away with him!" Maxton, the writer went on, had played a Pilate-like role, insisting that "Sandham was a just and honourable man and had done no constitutional wrong." This made no difference. "Vengeance was theirs," concluded the article, "and off the list goes Sandham's name, and at the same time is recorded one of the most discreditable episodes in the history of the I.L.P."[31] Some might well have recalled the circumstances of Wallhead's resignation the previous year.

By the middle of April 1934, the *New Leader* was reporting further "dissension" in Lancashire in the form of a Unity Group meeting at which the topic of discussion was—rather ironically, in view of its name—the formation of an Independent Socialist Party. Others advocated joining the Socialist League as an alternative.[32] The new National Executive Committee, elected at the York conference, was sufficiently alarmed to send Campbell Stephen to talk to the Lancashire ILP. He and John McGovern met the divisional council on 12 May.[33] Their report to the Inner Executive—another innovation of the recent conference, examined later in this chapter—on 26 April showed that they still hoped to keep the dissident Lancashire members on board. Demands from the Wigan branch and the Liverpool Federation for official recognition of a recent conference of "revolutionary" ILPers was rejected. They were told that "the N.A.C. was negotiating with the Divisional Council with a view to securing that national policy is applied in the Division."[34] But it was too late. The divisional organizer, Tom Abbott, who had already resigned from the ILP, called a conference on 13 May, the day after Campbell Stephen and McGovern's visit. It was there that the Independent Socialist Party (ISP) was founded.[35]

Abbott's letter of resignation had already appeared in full in *Forward*, headlined "Veteran Lancashire Organiser Leaves I.L.P." Abbott claimed that "the

York conference had taken away every bit of autonomous freedom which members and branches have enjoyed since the Party came to life in 1893." Workers' councils would "sabotage the Trade Unions." For him, York seemed to have been the next step in allowing the absorption of the ILP into the CPGB. This was the result, he said, of tolerance of the RPC at its inception by the national leadership. Now, it dominated "the central control and the new Executive."[36] The RPC, almost equally dissatisfied with the results of the York conference, drew some comfort from noting that the "extreme Right element" had been "defeated so decidedly that the majority of it has retreated from the struggle."[37]

For Abbott and others—including Murry, who also left the ILP at this point—the decisions made at York were clear evidence of an RPC conspiracy to deliver the ILP membership to the Communists. But this is far from how it seemed to the supposed head conspirator. "John Middleton Murry—you need not have resigned!" began Gaster's article "On Leadership," published in the June edition of *Controversy*. "Sitting on the fence," he went on, "may be an uncomfortable position for ordinary people like you and me: it is the normal position of the professional politician." Murry "need not have feared that the wild revolutionaries of London" would dominate the ILP. The result of York had not been a triumph for the advocates of a revolutionary policy. On the contrary, the party was "left bitterly disillusioned with the failure to clarify anything, realising that that failure was due to the timidity and cowardice of the platform."[38]

The July–August edition of *Controversy* featured responses to Gaster. The lead piece was by George Johnson, who represented East Anglia on the NAC. He agreed with Gaster's "long wail" to the limited extent that ILP policy had been left in mid-air. Even a "harmless resolution" from Norwich, which was only a plea that "the ethical side of our propaganda should not be neglected," had been rejected.

> It is certainly true to say that we are sick and tired of wrangling with the C.I. [Communist International], and I am certain that there is a real majority of us who are sick of our futile association with the C.P. and all that it entails. We are sick of the "high falutin" on Internationals and consider it would be more profitable to leave them entirely alone for some time.

The break with the Labour Party had not been primarily about the standing orders issue, Johnson maintained. Rather, it was "the culmination of a long dispute on the difference between promise and performance." There was no question of a new policy. Johnson defended the "Parliamentary and Trade

Union tradition" as something "in the blood and bones of the British working man." He wanted the ILP to "repudiate all the half-baked Communist and Syndicalist notions that go by the name of the new policy" and to return to the policies of the immediate post-disaffiliation period. The same edition of *Controversy* also carried Aplin's article "The 'Infantile Disorder' in the I.L.P."[39]

Meanwhile, in June, *Labour's Northern Voice*, which was to align itself with the ISP, published a long letter from the former ILP secretary, John Paton, in which he expressed regret about the opportunity lost by the ILP after disaffiliation. Not only should the party have rejected the "pseudo-revolutionary tactics" of the CPGB, but it should have mounted a "consistent and informed attack" on it. Instead, it had "succumbed to the fatal lure of revolutionary romanticism and become a pale imitation of the discredited Communist Party." In the same issue, an editorial on the basis of the founding principles of the ISP declared that the new party would represent "not merely 'collectivism' as an economic system, but Socialism as an ethically superior social system."[40]

The following month's edition included the full text of Elijah Sandham's letter of resignation. After twenty-six years of membership in the ILP, he specifically addressed Maxton in an open letter: "My friends have been defeated ... by the unexpected fact that the leadership of the party, yourself especially, have been on the side of the Communistically-minded elements whose object has been to so identify the I.L.P. with the Communist Party that the I.L.P. will be rendered redundant."[41] Sandham's letter was applauded by Katharine Bruce Glasier in her regular *Voice* column. "Let us Socialists cease to apologise for believing in democracy," she urged.[42]

Remaining opponents of the United Front would not have been reassured by what the ILP's executive called the "disruptive tactics" of the Communists in inviting ILP divisions and branches to send fraternal delegates to the coming Comintern conference while not extending that invitation to the national ILP. The NAC would have been glad to send a "fraternal delegate," but its members believed that since they had been "deliberately excluded," it was not in the party's interest that other sections of the ILP should attend. The view taken in the *New Leader* was optimistic—outwardly, at least—about the losses of members to the new ISP. "There is no doubt," he wrote, "that within a short time the I.L.P. in Lancashire will be in a stronger position to do effective work for Socialism than it has been for many years."[43]

More than any other factor, it was the United Front policy that had caused defections from the ILP in 1934. Yet for those who favoured such cooperation, the prospects by the end of the year were still far from encouraging. At the NAC meeting in November, Brockway reported that he had indicated in discussions with the CPGB that "an extension of joint action would be difficult if the

C.P. continued to disintegrate the I.L.P. from within by contacts acting on its behalf."[44] This theme was repeated in more detail in the report, the following month, of a meeting of the ILP's Inner Executive with Communist representatives. Brockway referred to the statement by Harry Pollitt, the CPGB general secretary, that his party had refused applications for membership "and advised applicants to remain inside the I.L.P. with a view to securing the affiliation of the I.L.P. to the Communist International and the unification of the two parties." From the ILP side, this seemed anything but innocent, as the minutes of the meeting make clear: "Brockway said it was legitimate for a loyal member of the I.L.P. to advocate this policy within the Party, but when an I.L.P. member applied for membership of the Communist party it showed that his real loyalty was to the C.P. and he only remained in the I.L.P. to carry out C.P. purposes. The I.L.P. could not permit this tactic." For his part, Pollitt claimed that there were no organized Communist factions in the ILP.[45]

Another factor that was to increase the alienation between the ILP and the CPGB had made its appearance in 1934. The ILP was being caught up in the Stalin versus Trotsky conflict. In June, Gaster alerted the NAC to a statement made by former members of the Communist League, a Trotskyist organization, that had appeared in *Controversy*.[46] The RPC's own *Bulletin* warned of the League "attempting to use the I.L.P. as a medium for propaganda in favour of a Fourth International."[47] Then, at the December meeting with the CPGB, Pollitt referred to the "Marxist Group" claiming, not without foundation, that "these Trotskyists were organised as a group within the I.L.P. to oppose any united action with the Communist Party." Maxton responded by pointing out that "the rules of the I.L.P. permitted groups within the party to advocate particular policies," adding that "the Marxist Group had been preceded by the Revolutionary Policy Committee which advocated affiliation to the Communist International and the objective of the unification of the I.L.P. and the C.P."[48] A few months later, following the 1935 annual conference, Brockway claimed that the conference had proved that the vast majority of the ILP accepted the "'Revolutionary Socialist' line, and only fractions the 'Communist' and 'Trotsky' lines."[49] However, both Communists and Trotskyists would continue to feature in the ideological struggles within the ILP in the mid-1930s.

The Move to "Democratic Centralism"

One feature of the ILP since its earliest days had been its maintenance of a strong form of internal democracy. This can be seen as a weakness. Dowse, for instance, identifies a critical problem in the ILP as being "the almost complete lack of political discipline in the party." But it was also a source of strength in maintaining the party's independence and commitment to a distinctive form of democratic socialism. This went back, as Dowse says, to the decision, at the time the ILP was founded, to establish a central body—the National Administrative Council—with relatively weak executive powers.[50]

The decentralized approach was confirmed towards the end of the First World War. In defining the duties of the NAC, the 1918 conference resolved that the council should not "initiate any new departure or policy between Conferences without first obtaining the sanction of the majority of branches."[51] In 1920, it was established that, "subject to the general constitution of the Party, each Branch shall be perfectly autonomous."[52] By this time, the party was operating with a smaller executive committee drawn from the NAC. Then, in 1924, delegates were told that "the N.A.C. decided at their first meeting to abolish the Executive Committee and to meet more frequently itself."[53]

A decade later, those wishing to promote a revolutionary policy and transform the ILP into a real revolutionary party believed that the commitment to decentralization and branch autonomy to be yet another symptom of what was wrong with the party. At least in principle, they were successful in introducing a form of Leninist "democratic centralism."[54] In early 1934, the NAC agreed, by 7 votes to 4, to propose changes designed to improve efficiency and to create "a real leadership for the party." This was to be achieved by re-establishing an Executive Committee, as well as by setting up an even smaller group, which came to be known as the Inner Executive, with the power to make emergency decisions. The changes were proposed with the possibility in mind that the party might have to function underground, as an illegal body, after an authoritarian government suppressed dissent.[55] At the York conference that April, it was agreed that the new Executive Committee should meet at least once every six weeks and the full NAC not less than once every twelve weeks. Changes to rules were no longer to be solely the prerogative of the annual conference. If two-thirds of the NAC's members supported a proposal, the council could now make a change unless either one-third of the branches or two-thirds of the divisions objected within two months of its circulation.[56]

Alarm bells rang instantly, especially for those already disenchanted with the direction in which the party seemed to be travelling. Looking forward to the soon-to-be-inaugurated Independent Socialist Party, J. T. Abbott, the former Lancashire Division organizer, cited, in his letter of resignation, what he saw as the crushing of autonomy: "The Dictatorship is now in possession of what I think will prove a corpse, but its spirit and intention, to my mind, is by implication the desire to dictate through a political party to the whole community."[57]

Following the 1934 conference, the *New Leader* changed in both appearance and substance. It adopted a tabloid format and attempted to become a simple source of propaganda for agreed ILP policy. It would no longer feature internal debates; that function would be confined to the ILP's "internal" organ, *Controversy*. Elijah Sandham objected strongly to the changes in the *Leader*. "No controversy is allowed in the *New Leader* in case the workers hear something which *is not fit for their ears*," he wrote. "*Everything in the party has to be designed by the select few supermen at the head of affairs, then told in simple language to the humble rank and file*."[58] Sandham had hesitated to join the ISP—though once he did so, he was elected as its chairman by the first of its annual conventions.[59] For him, the direction the ILP was heading in was clear; it was following "the Communist and Russian model."[60]

But if anything along the lines predicted by Sandham had been the intention, it failed to work out in quite that way in practice. One contender for the position of chief offender was the new national secretary, Fenner Brockway. His articles critical of Soviet foreign policy, which will be examined in a later chapter, led to protests and accusations of breaching ILP policy from the most determined proponents of democratic centralism—notably, Gaster. But more than any other issue, the notion of a highly disciplined and united democratic-centralist party would be tested, almost to destruction, by the Abyssinian crisis of 1935.

— 17 —

The Abyssinian Crisis and the Fate of Democratic Centralism

Abyssinia, as Ethiopia was commonly known in Britain at this time, was the sole survivor—if one discounts Liberia as a special case—of the late nineteenth century "scramble for Africa."[1] The country had successfully fought off a previous Italian invasion in 1896 but continued to face potential threats from Italian colonial territories on its borders. In early 1935, following a border incident the previous November, it became obvious that Mussolini was preparing for another attempt at conquest. The crisis was a significant test of the League of Nations and collective security.

For the ILP, the crisis, which became inextricably bound up with the party's desire to prevent another war into which Britain would inevitably be dragged as it had been in 1914, led to sharp differences. The resulting internal conflict ultimately led to a unique situation whereby the Inner Executive, composed of ILP MPs, effectively overturned the decision of the party's annual conference and had its action endorsed by a referendum—or "plebiscite," as it was referred to at the time—of ILP members. The two most prominent members of the party, Chairman Jimmy Maxton and General Secretary Fenner Brockway, found themselves on different sides of the debate; rather strangely, this division was reflected in the leadership of the RPC, with *its* two leading figures, Gaster and Cullen, also taking opposing sides.

A Three-Way Split on Abyssinia

The *New Leader* first reported on the issue towards the end of February 1935. In contrast to two of the positions adopted later, the paper placed some hope in the fact that, with the USSR now a League of Nations member, "enemies of Imperialism look to Litvinov to champion the rights of an ancient nation even in the corrupt courts of Capitalism."[2] Further developments were reported by the paper in March. In June, in "Musso Still Mobilising," the paper warned of the Italian threat, and, in July, an article headlined "War in the Autumn" predicted the imminent outbreak of conflict. Arguing that it was "up to the workers to do everything in their power to stop war supplies going to Mussolini," the author of the article called for an "organised refusal to handle arms for Italy." This call was repeated the following week with a plea for the "common people of all countries" to "hamper and obstruct" war preparations. If threatened with a mass movement at home, the author reasoned, France and Britain would think again before "vouchsafing open or camouflaged support to Italian Fascism."[3]

"We Must Stop the War!" the *New Leader* declared on its front page in August, going on to argue that, rather than relying on capitalist governments, workers should take action themselves. An equal duty rested "upon the Communist International," the paper opined, and particularly upon Maxim Litvinov, the Soviet representative to the League of Nations and also the chairman of its Council.[4] Faith in Litvinov seemed limited, however. Two weeks later, a front-page article headlined "Workers, Beware! You Are Being Led into War" warned the workers in question not to leave the taking of action to "the Capitalist-controlled League of Nations." Opposition to war, the *New Leader* maintained, had been weakened by the Labour Party, the CPGB—now well advanced with its "popular front" policy—and the Trades Union Congress, all of which supported League sanctions against Italy. The threat of war was real. "This is July, 1914, over again," the paper declared.[5]

The policy of rejecting calls for action by the League and relying instead on "workers' sanctions" had now taken political shape. A September ILP leaflet titled *Abyssinia—Crisis Faces the Workers* warned that the conflict might be "the spark to the world war." No reliance should be placed on the League or on a British government hypocritically "posing as a defender of the liberties of Abyssinia." Rather, the British labour movement should "follow the magnificent example of the Trade Unions in South Africa who are refusing to handle goods" and get their local trades council to set up "an all-inclusive Workers' Committee of Action."

The London Division's leaflet *Workers' Action Can Stop the War!* made the same plea, invoking the 1921 Councils of Action and the *SS Jolly George* episode in 1920, when a strike of London dockers had prevented the dispatch of munitions to Poland during the war with Russia. The leaflet described the British government's motives in the new crisis as aggressive and devious in the extreme. The government had, it said, "assisted the war-like Fascist powers to arm." It had encouraged Germany, Italy, and Japan. Its talk of peace was "so much hypocrisy." Though protecting its African imperialist interests against Italian encroachment, the government wanted peace so that it could "unite with Germany and Japan in preparation for war on the Soviet Union."[6]

The Abyssinian Crisis and the Fate of Democratic Centralism

Under the headline "Dangerous Policy of Labour Party and T.U.C.," the *New Leader* claimed that the British government wanted "a share themselves" in Abyssinian territory. It cited the ILP Inner Executive's resolution in declaring that "the struggle between these rival imperialisms is not worth the loss of a single British life." But the wording of the Inner Executive's resolution—reported in the same issue—hardly lent itself to the interpretation offered here. The resolution spoke not simply of rival imperialisms but insisted that "the difference between the two rival dictators and the interests behind them are not worth the loss of a single British life." Rival *imperialisms* suggested actual or potential conflict between British and Italian empire builders. Rival *dictators* meant Mussolini and Haile Selassie, the Ethiopian emperor. The Inner Executive resolution went on to call "upon its members and the working class of Britain to offer the maximum opposition by holding mass demonstrations in their area, by refusing to bear arms, and in every other way possible to show to the Government their determination that they are not going into another blood bath under the false cry of a small defenceless nation."[7]

There was now a three-way split in the ILP. There were those who saw the imminent conflict in terms of the two rival dictators—Mussolini and Haile Selassie—and who believed that the ILP should support neutrality. The second group, wanting to oppose Mussolini, supported the League of Nations' action, and the third rejected the League's action and favoured trying to support the "small defenceless nation" by means of "workers' sanctions." Maxton and the parliamentary group favoured the first approach; the RPC, with the exception, notably, of Gaster and Hilda Vernon, took the second line; and Brockway, the general secretary and editor of the *New Leader*, supported the third. Outside the ILP, most of the Left supported the demand for serious action by the League.

As the crisis grew, that erstwhile ILP stalwart, *Forward*, came out in support of League action, but it gave some front-page support to Brockway's alternative policy of "workers' sanctions"—action by trade unionists, mainly dockers and seamen, to deny war materials to the aggressor.[8] Clearly, though, like many on the Left, it doubted whether such sanctions could be an effective alternative rather than an additional support for action by the League.

To complicate matters further, within the RPC leadership, Cullen backed the CPGB's support for League sanctions. He argued that, with the adherence of the USSR, the character of the international organization had been transformed. Meanwhile, Gaster sided with Brockway. At an ILP Executive Committee meeting in September, it was reported that the membership was "overwhelmingly opposed to a War or sanctions" and that antiwar meetings had taken place in many areas.⁹ But despite the *New Leader*'s insistence, in an editorial, that the ILP had a "clear line," the reality was very different.¹⁰

Within the London Division, Cullen and most of the RPC membership were faced with opposition from a strange alliance of Gaster, Aplin, and the Trotskyists of the Marxist Group. One group of Trotskyists had joined the ILP in February 1934. Others arrived later that year. Together, they formed the Marxist Group, which included the Trinidadian-born intellectual C. L. R James.¹¹ In October 1935, as the long-anticipated Italian invasion of Abyssinia began, the *New Leader* gave front-page prominence—complete with a photo and full-cap headline—to James's denunciation of the League of Nations' "imperialistic plot" against Abyssinia. James decried the "League's scheme to rob Abyssinia of its independence," anticipating a deal along the lines of the stillborn Hoare-Laval plan unveiled a few weeks later. Instead, he argued, the ILP should stand for "independent organisation and independent action."¹²

Cleavage in the RPC: League Sanctions Versus Direct Action

Italy was condemned as an aggressor by the League of Nations, of which both it and its victim were members. The League's imposition of sanctions followed, but the process was long-winded, half-hearted, and partial, omitting oil and other crucial war materials. On 7 October, the RPC held a special conference of "London supporters," which approved a "Statement of Objectives." The *New Leader* having refused publication, the statement appeared in the *R.P.C. Bulletin*. It declared a "complete lack of confidence" in the ILP's policy and insisted that the Abyssinian crisis had exposed the "delaying tactics of the major imperialist powers" in contrast to the "consistent stand" of the USSR. It expressed support for an economic and financial boycott of Italy via the League and claimed that the *New Leader* had deliberately thrown doubt on "the honest endeavour of the Soviet Govt. to check Italian aggression and preserve world peace."¹³ At the NAC meeting two days later, Gaster managed to win only four votes—including his own and Brockway's—for a motion to support "in principle the Abyssinian opposition to Italian aggression." Maxton was one of the nine voting against.¹⁴

Shortly thereafter, the *New Leader* was reporting the "tremendous activity" throughout the country generated by the ILP's antiwar campaign, which followed the issuing of a manifesto by the NAC.¹⁵ The National Government was not concerned with Abyssinian independence, the manifesto claimed. The real issue was not between Italy and Abyssinia, but between Italian imperialism and British imperialism: "The Report of the Committee of Five, in which the British representative took a leading part, would place the economic, financial and political control of Abyssinia in the hands of European Governments (with

Britain no doubt dominant). British Imperialism would sacrifice Abyssinia no less than Italian Imperialism." By demanding League sanctions, the Labour Party, the Trades Union Congress and the Communists were lining up the workers behind British imperialism, the manifesto concluded. Sanctions would lead to war—which the advocates of sanctions would then have to back. The government had already made full preparations for a naval blockade of Italy. Its "War policy" had to be opposed.[16]

An article in the October issue of *Controversy*, written by Jack Gaster on behalf of the London Emergency Committee, addressed the stance of the ILP on Abyssinia. Gaster rejected Maxton's "two rival dictators" position, claiming that a defeat for Italy might mean "the collapse of Italian Fascism." His main point was that Abyssinia, though "feudal," represented "a small force *in opposition* to imperialist expansion." Rejecting the "Imperialist line of the T.U.C." and the "wrong but completely different line of the C.P.," Gaster called for "*workers' action under workers' control*."[17]

An editorial note explained that the London Division had appointed the Emergency Committee, composed of Aplin, Cullen, Gaster, Matlow, and Vernon. As Cohen points out, the editor's statement that all members of this committee except for Cullen had approved Gaster's article masked what the RPC's own *Bulletin* called a "sharp cleavage" within the RPC, with Cullen leading the majority who supported the CPGB's line urging effective League sanctions.[18]

Cullen chaired the RPC but his two colleagues from that group, Jack Gaster and Hilda Vernon, found themselves making common cause in supporting "workers' sanctions" with both Bert Matlow of the Marxist Group and that implacable opponent of factionalism, John Aplin. The October *Bulletin* contained statements of the two competing views within the RPC leadership. The introduction to the statements was headlined "Crisis in the R.P.C.?" and the response below this question was "Yes, there is a crisis in the R.P.C."[19]

Cullen's piece, "The War Crisis," denied that there was any parallel with 1914 or any real danger of a war between Britain and Italy in spite of the bellicose language being used on both sides. The League was—now that the USSR had joined—a possible "stalking horse" for the workers, since "we have our own powerful representative leading and consolidating the opposition to the designs of the Imperialist Powers." He went on to endorse the Popular Front policy of the CPGB, arguing that there was a "limited and temporary community of interest amongst the general mass of the population including the middle classes."[20]

Unless animated by "sectarian prejudice," no socialist really believed that the USSR was "betraying the workers" or lining up with capitalist powers, Cullen asserted. Was not the British capitalist press complaining of "the subversive

Communist influences at work in the League?" The fight of the Abyssinian people, he insisted, was "the fight of the Italian workers, our fight, the fight of the workers of the world." If the ILP persisted in its "ultra-left sectarian line" it would lose "the last shred of respect that still clings to it."[21]

The case for "effective direct working class action" was made by Jack Gaster and Hilda Vernon, who believed that the League was "finished." Even those who supported action by it, they wrote, knew that this could only be "an auxiliary to direct working class action." The *Bulletin* made it clear in a foreword that it was Cullen rather than Gaster and Vernon who spoke for the RPC on this issue.[22]

The next issue (November) of the *R.P.C. Bulletin* announced itself as the final one. The issue's foreword noted that meetings of the NAC and regional representatives and of the London Division had brought about an entirely new situation and that a conference of the RPC had decided, by an "overwhelming majority," to leave the ILP. The foreword called upon "all revolutionary socialists" to apply for CPGB membership. It is clear that although the Abyssinian crisis was not the underlying cause of the RPC's departure, it was certainly the catalyst.[23]

The foreword of the *Bulletin* explained that differences over Abyssinia were completely overshadowed by other urgent issues, and it stressed that the RPC had the "full support" of Gaster and Vernon. The minority of six who had opposed leaving the ILP was "led by members who for some time past have been trying to make use of the R.P.C. for the propagation of the policy and views of the 'Communist Opposition' and for the formation of an 'Opposition' grouping."[24] The RPC had dissolved itself but the "tiny opposition group anxious to inherit the 'goodwill' of the R.P.C. within the I.L.P." was continuing and "attempting to take the title to itself."[25]

The main article in the final issue of the *Bulletin*, "Why We Left the I.L.P.," was signed with Cullen's initials. He wrote that the "Fascist onslaught on Abyssinia started a chain of consequences" and opened "a new phase of working-class struggle." Hostility to the USSR, Comintern, and the United Front policy by the ILP leadership had been a bone of contention for the RPC for some time, he continued. It had been hoped that a serious crisis would bring about unity; instead, the Abyssinia crisis had given a "death-blow to that hope." The ILP leadership had "laid it down that there is no difference between the rival imperialisms of Italy and Abyssinia" and had rejected "even the encouragement of working-class action in support of the Abyssinian people."[26]

Gaster's resignation letter also appeared in this final issue of the *Bulletin* and his leaving was reported in the NAC minutes at the end of the month. He made no mention of Abyssinia. But if the departure of the RPC simplified the ILP debate, it certainly did not curtail it.[27]

Democratic Centralism Stumbles: An Internal Clash over Abyssinia

The *New Leader*, under Brockway's editorship, may not have directly repudiated the "rival dictators" approach of the Inner Executive, but certainly the way in which it reported the progress of Mussolini's aggression was far from neutral. "Abyssinia Sacrificed" was its front-page headline in December 1935 at the time of the abortive Hoare-Laval deal, with the subtitle "National Government Offers Half Its Territory to Italy." The following week, the front page drew attention to the "important article by C. L. R. James" in that issue. James concluded with the statement "If Abyssinia is to be saved it will be by her own exertions and the help of the International working class." The final issue of the paper for that year called for "working class action to end the Italo-Abyssinian war."[28]

At the beginning of 1936, a *New Leader* editorial titled "Socialists and Sanctions" declared that the only aim of the British government was to maintain the interests of British imperialism. The Labour and Communist parties had "made a profound mistake in urging the operation of Government sanctions." Instead, "the workers must act through their own organisations." Opposition to Italian aggression was, then, to be pursued by means of sanctions imposed by workers. An editorial in March ended by quoting a note to the League from the Abyssinians to the effect that they "seldom met foreigners who did not desire to possess themselves of Abyssinian territory and destroy our independence." Abyssinia was clearly portrayed by the *New Leader* editor as a victim of imperialism.[29]

Moreover, when the ILP divisions met in the run-up to the annual conference, dissent from the stance of the Inner Executive was evident. Yorkshire supported the Sheffield branch's rejection of the Inner Executive's position, while the Midlands Division congratulated the *New Leader* editor "on the early line adopted by him with regard to the sanctions policy of the League of Nations."[30] The minutes of the NAC meeting in February also noted a protest from the Hull branch against the official policy.[31] With just over a week to go before the start of the conference, the *New Leader* headlined an article with "League Betrays Abyssinia: Knew Poison Gas Was to be Used." It reiterated support for workers' sanctions, adding that "workers must trust themselves and their own actions."[32]

The NAC's report to the 1936 conference at Keighley included the letters sent to other organizations explaining the ILP's opposition to "reliance on the League of Nations" and urging "united action to resist war." Five thousand letters and forty-eight thousand leaflets had been distributed via branches, it said.³³ The report also included, in an appendix, the text of a resolution of the International Bureau for Revolutionary Socialist Unity (IBRSU) from August 1935, which supported the "workers' sanctions" rather than the "rival dictators" line.³⁴ The IBRSU resolution made the Bureau's position quite clear: "The International Bureau for Revolutionary Socialist Unity unconditionally takes the side of suppressed peoples against Imperialist rulers and declares openly that it wishes for the defeat of Italian Fascism and the victory of the Abyssinian people." It called for the "liberation of Italy's slaves" and for the prevention of sending arms to Italy and troops to Africa by the "International Working-Class."³⁵

The Sunday morning session of the ILP conference began with C. L. R. James's successful reference back of the "Activity Against War" section of the NAC report on the grounds that the Inner Executive had "adopted a do-nothing policy on the Abyssinian war." Jones, for Lancashire, with Aplin seconding, then moved a motion congratulating Brockway "on the line adopted by him on the sanctions issue" and declaring that the conference was dissociating itself "from the declaration of the Inner Executive of the N.A.C. as published in the 'New Leader' of September 13 1935." This declaration, the motion asserted, conflicted with party policy and contradicted Party discipline. Jones's motion was carried by 70 to 57, and James's reference back won by the narrowest of majorities—66 to 65.³⁶ It seemed as though the authority of the annual conference as the policy-making body of the party had been vindicated—if only by a single vote—and the "rival dictators" position of the Inner Executive repudiated, along with its interpretation of "democratic centralism." But the following day was to be one of the most dramatic for the party during the whole period covered by this book—and indeed during its entire existence.

The Revolt of the Inner Executive and the Plebiscite

The day after these crucial votes, Maxton made a statement from the chair. They were all, he said, united against capitalist and imperialist war, but they differed on their positions on "working class action against Italy." Then came the bombshell: "The Chairman of the Party, the three members of the Inner Executive, the Parliamentary Group, and other members of the National Council are unable conscientiously to operate the decision reached yesterday." Maxton reported that the NAC had decided, in light of the narrowness of the majority, to refer that matter to a "ballot vote" in three months' time. In the meantime, there would be "liberty of expression for different views," and the conference was asked to express its confidence in the NAC—which it agreed to do by 93 to 39.³⁷ Before the conference ended, the NAC had met once again; agreed on arrangements for the plebiscite, as it was referred to; and appointed Aplin, Johnson, and McGovern as scrutineers.[38]

The Abyssinian debate was the main topic in the *New Leader*'s report of the conference at the end of that week, with Brockway giving his summation of the different responses to the Italian aggression by the *Leader* and the Inner Executive and the NAC:

> The *New Leader* took the line that as International Socialists the I.L.P. must ally itself with the Abyssinian people in their struggle against Imperialism. It was urged that the form of support should be working class action against Italy by refusal to handle munitions, oil, and war materials for Italy.
>
> This line, maintained by the *New Leader* for several weeks, was changed by a decision of the Inner Executive (later endorsed by the National Council), that the Party should be neutral and should regard the Italo-Abyssinian conflict as one between "two rival dictators."

The *Leader*'s report explained that Brockway, fearing the resignations of the whole of the Parliamentary group, and especially Maxton, had supported the NAC's plebiscite proposal. It had been fiercely opposed by the London Division, with C. A. Smith maintaining that the NAC was "wrong strategically, tactically, psychologically, and morally, and that the Party had missed a great opportunity for giving a clear and courageous lead to the workers of this country who were ready to respond."[39] From the political sidelines, *Forward*, which had supported the ILP before disaffiliation, published "I.L.P. Revolt Against Maxton," by Emrys Hughes. He described how, when Maxton had threatened to resign, "the conference performed another somersault." He then asked how long the party could last without Maxton.[40]

Severe internal conflict was still far from over. The Executive Committee declined, by a narrow vote of 7 to 6, to circulate a document stating the London case. According to meeting minutes, the committee decided that it was "undesirable" to circulate more than the "pamphlet stating both sides." The way the Inner Executive had behaved became an issue in itself. The Larkhill branch, it was reported at the Executive Committee meeting, "condemned the I.E., the Parliamentary Group, and the N.A.C. for their refusal to accept Conference decisions." The Executive Committee agreed to pose "alternative questions" in the plebiscite, though, as we shall see, this by no means placated all the critics of the wording.[41] An issue of *Controversy* published Maxton, McGovern, and Southall making the case for neutrality versus James, Brockway, and Bob Edwards, who advocated "workers' sanctions."[42] In spite of the prohibition on discussion of "inner organisational matters," the *New Leader* published both a letter from McGovern complaining about the content of *Controversy* with respect to Abyssinia and one from its editor, C. A. Smith, defending it.[43]

The plebiscite scrutineers reported at the end of June. The vote itself was now controversial. The Ilford branch "decided to return the ballot papers unmarked because there was no opportunity for expressing support for workers' sanctions." From Salisbury, it was reported that the branch, "as a protest, feels unable to take part in the Plebiscite, owing to the questions, as put, do not cover the issues as raised at Annual Conference." There were thirteen individual protests and seven branch resolutions complaining about the wording.[44] More were reported at the NAC meeting a few days later: twenty-four additional branches and guilds had protested about the form of the questions, including the Swindon branch. The Gateshead and Watford branches had refused to vote because of their dissatisfaction with the questions.[45]

No wonder the Dundee branch resolved that "in view of the strong feelings aroused members of the Party should preserve a sense of proportion and recognise that Party unity should take precedence over all differences." For his part, Maxton insisted that "not a single speech had been delivered in Parliament by members of the I.L.P. Group which had not advocated revolutionary working class action in relation to the Italo-Abyssinian War." As if to add further to the confusion and conflict, the NAC agreed that a policy statement by Brockway should be circulated to the branches and published in the *New Leader*, but "without giving majority figures in the Plebiscite."[46] One result of this decision seems to have been that when the NAC reported to the 1937 annual conference, the appendix dealing with the plebiscite gave only the wording of the two questions, without any indication of the result.[47]

The "ballot vote" was supposed to establish clearly the view of at least the majority of ILP members and to draw a line under what, as we have seen, was a difficult, divisive, and confusing issue. But if this was the intention, it was hardly the result. Of the 3,751 ballot papers sent out, only 1,442 were returned. The first question "Should the I.L.P. have declared against Italy and in favour of Abyssinia by advocating the refusal of War Materials to Italy?" was answered "yes" by 576 compared to 734 votes for "no," and the second one, "Should the I.L.P. have refused to back either Italy or Abyssinia and opposed the sending of War Materials to either side" received 809 votes for "yes" and 554 for "no."[48]

By this time, as Cohen points out, the war was over. Haile Selassie had been forced out and Mussolini was triumphant—for the time being. In June, the *New Leader* had used the headline "The League Is Dead" and had concluded, "Italy has got away with it."[49] But the problem within the ILP remained, with the NAC "attempting," as Cohen says, "to square the circle."[50]

The NAC statement following the vote explained that "the National Council does not regard the vote of the Party on the Italo-Abyssinian War as laying down a policy to be applied under all circumstances" and acknowledged the need for clearer policy as regards wars that did not involve the United Kingdom. The ILP opposed "unity" with capitalist governments preparing for or prosecuting war and rejected any support for a war authorized by the "Capitalist-dominated League of Nations," the policy statement said, emphasizing "class struggle," the "seizure of working class power," and "the special duty of defending the Soviet Union."[51]

When the NAC reported to the 1937 conference at Glasgow, it included the statement that if a "subject people" was attacked by an "Imperialist Government," it would be the duty of the British working class "to take all possible action in support of the subject people, including organised action to refuse materials to the Imperialist Government." This was exactly the policy that the Inner Executive and the plebiscite had rejected, in the case of Abyssinia. The NAC statement allowed the leadership some wiggle room by giving it a degree of discretion in how the policy might be applied in particular cases. But it was evident that, as Cohen says, "the plebiscite was a short-term measure to keep the Parliamentary Group within the Party."[52]

This was a strange state of affairs for an organization that, a few years previously, had embarked on the construction of a revolutionary policy, one of whose tenets was the downgrading of the importance of parliamentary representation. The whole episode also suggests that—for better or worse—the idea of the ILP practising democratic centralism was a nonstarter. This seems borne out by criticisms made within the party.

Democracy and Party Discipline in the 1930s

It would be wrong to imagine that the NAC, in earlier years, had always strictly confined itself to administrative matters. For one thing, it is seldom easy to distinguish such issues from those of policy. Opinions on what fell on either side of the dividing line were always likely to vary considerably. It would also be naïve in the extreme to imagine that in the ILP, everything that was said was dutifully minuted and that factional manoeuvres and individual intrigues were unknown. But policy debates in the NAC certainly became more frequent in the post-disaffiliation years.

A noticeable feature of NAC meetings at this time is the number of issues where the voting of each member was recorded in the minutes. In most of the NAC meetings of 1933 and 1934, there was at least one such instance, something that would normally only take place when it was insisted upon by a participant. The largest number of such votes was in September 1933, when nine were recorded in the minutes of the meeting. During the following year, after two in January and four in April, the number of roll call votes rose to seven at the March–April meeting and six in both the June and August meetings. On the latter occasion, no fewer than five dealt with alternative methods of dealing with the case, mentioned earlier, of the two members suspended for participation in the "unofficial" deputation to the Comintern in Moscow under the auspices of the Affiliation Committee.[53]

The increased number of such votes was not the only unusual feature of the post-disaffiliation ILP. The Inner Executive was decidedly odd in certain respects. Apart from its rather sinister-sounding title, it seems strange that, at a time when the role of Parliament was being presented as less central than it had been previously, the body at the top of the ILP hierarchy should be composed predominantly of MPs and that it met most frequently in a House of Commons committee room. If the object was to achieve an effective central leadership whose writ would run throughout the party, it was clearly not very successful. One possible exception to this is the Abyssinian issue, given the way the plebiscite majority fell in line behind the Inner Executive. But was the key factor in that issue the democratic centralist structure or the unrivalled charismatic leadership of Maxton and the *real* importance of the parliamentary group, despite the party's declared policy about MPs taking a back seat?

The *New Leader* certainly became almost opaque as far as internal debates were concerned, with the exceptions already noted. But the emergence of a monolithic party line was undermined by the existence of *Controversy*—and later, *Between Ourselves*. In 1935, the editor of *Controversy*, C. A. Smith, said that the paper's circulation was confined to ILP members because of what was hoped to be a temporary lack of agreement within the party. He looked forward to its distribution, following the resolution of the policy issues, to "*all progressive students of politics.*"[54] The 1936 annual conference accepted Smith's proposal to make it "available to the public."[55] An order-form leaflet described *Controversy* as "the only open forum for all Socialists and Communists" and listed G. D. H. Cole, J. R. Campbell, Harold Laski, Ignace Silone, and Stafford Cripps—as well as Jimmy Maxton—as contributors.[56]

In 1937, the NAC report to the annual conference in Glasgow confirmed that, as its name suggested, *Controversy*'s role was to "maintain a genuine open forum, with the regular presentation of I.L.P. policies and also of opposed policies." It was now in a printed form and internal discussion was to be "continued through a Bulletin ... issued to Party members who take '*Controversy*.'"[57] In November of that year, in "A Survey of the Party Position," Fenner Brockway requested that lists be prepared of "Lefts" outside the party who might be sympathetic to the ILP so that they could be sent specimen copies of *Controversy*, accompanied by "a persuasive letter." He suggested as suitable targets the Workers' Educational Association and the National Council of Labour Colleges, university socialist societies, and the Labour League of Youth, as well as trade union and branches of the Co-operative Party.[58]

By 1939, a virtue was made of the fact that *Controversy* was being sold to "serious students of politics in the Communist, Labour, and Co-operative parties."[59] But if the idea was to show a united front to the world and keep internal disagreements within the party, it was no more successful than such attempts usually are. In 1936, the Perth and Govanhill branch protested against the wider circulation of the ILP pamphlet that gave competing arguments on the Abyssinia policy in preparation for the plebiscite—but how was it possible to keep such controversies out of the public gaze?[60] As we will see in a later chapter, this was certainly not possible in the case of another internal controversy—the disagreement over Maxton's response to the Munich Agreement in 1938.

C. A. Smith, the former editor of *Controversy*, became chairman of the party in 1939. Soon after this, he contributed a piece to the new internal forum, *Between Ourselves*, headlined "Re-establishing Party Discipline." His title, in itself, suggests that the democratic centralism enterprise had been far from successful. Smith began by declaring that "the I.L.P. has suffered severely because of a deplorable lack of discipline." The ILP claimed to be a democratic party, he said.

> But democracy does not mean anarchy. Democracy means majority rule. And when the majority has declared its will, or when a decision has been given by the appropriate elected authority, then opposed minorities or individuals must obey or leave the Party. That is a simple statement of the theory of democratic centralism and it is the lack of central control which is one of the I.L.P.'s chief weaknesses.

Smith went on to trace the "succession of episodes" since 1934 that he regarded as abuses of ILP freedom and even as "flagrant treachery." In 1934, "the Sandham-Abbot group, controlling the Lancashire Divisional Council, tore away an important section of members, premises and press." The following year, the RPC left to join the CPGB "four months after denying my charge that they were preparing that very step." In 1936, Trotskyists carried out "similar manoeuvres and a smaller breakaway."[61]

Smith identified four species of "indiscipline" that had undermined the ILP in the previous five years: the use of "party platforms" to advocate policies not accepted by the ILP; the occasional actions, in conjunction with outside bodies, of groups with their "own policy and discipline"; attacks on the party and its leadership; and the refusal to perform specific duties such as the distribution of the *New Leader*. "All such anti-Party conduct must cease," he concluded.[62]

One obvious response to Smith's plea is to conclude that, in itself, it amply illustrates that the attempt to adopt democratic centralism had been a total failure, despite the recent increased stress on discipline. Smith himself, as editor of *Controversy*, had written to the Inner Executive in 1936 drawing attention to criticisms of the NAC made in that publication and asking whether a reply could be authorized. The Executive's response was to agree that McGovern should respond "in his individual capacity," hardly exemplifying the iron fist of centralized control.[63]

Was democratic centralism in the ILP any more than part of the attempt to be revolutionary by adopting a Leninist vocabulary that had little correspondence to the party's reality? If democratic centralism meant avoiding the four kinds of indiscipline mentioned by Smith, it is difficult to see anything very novel about it. Their rejection and avoidance is part of the usual pattern of behaviour expected in any internally democratic organization—even if honoured, not infrequently, more in the breach than the observance. In any event, the idea that the ILP was actually operating according to any notion of democratic centralism was hardly made credible by the party's three-way split over the Abyssinian question. Few, if any, would argue with Cohen's conclusion that "factionalism remains central to understanding the ILP in the 1930s."[64]

As Brockway reported to the NAC following the 1935 annual conference, though an amendment "for the abolition of groups" had been passed, the motion to which it was attached had been defeated, and "consequently the matter had fallen." Maxton commented that while there was a "strong majority feeling in the Party against the existence of groups that take permanent form and carry on permanent activities," the majority of delegates were not prepared to support the expulsion of group members.[65]

As we have seen, the London ILP organizer, John Aplin, had been concerned about the activities of the RPC since at least 1932. He resigned from his position following the 1935 annual conference, telling the Inner Executive and the NAC that he had done this because "the Divisional machinery was being used by the R.P.C. for group purposes and in order that he might have freedom to mobilise opinion in that Division against the group system."[66] The NAC reported that an investigation by the Inner Executive had failed to prove Aplin's allegation, but the Inner Executive had put forward, and the NAC had endorsed, the recommendation that rather than resort to group activities, members should argue their case at ILP meetings or in *Controversy*.[67] "Just prior to the General Election," said the NAC's report to the 1936 annual conference, "a majority of members of the R.P.C. resigned from the Party, but the existence of other unofficial groups has persisted." The NAC declared its intention of bringing a motion to outlaw such groups to the 1936 annual conference.[68] Brockway reported to the NAC a few weeks later that "despite the N.A.C. statement that membership of unofficial groups involves disloyalty to the Party, the minority of the R.P.C. had decided to maintain itself as the Communist Unity Group and the Marxist Group still continued."[69]

Whatever one makes of the ILP's democratic centralism, the protracted controversy over Abyssinia threw significant light on how its internal democracy actually worked during these years. Abyssinia was the final straw for the RPC and marks the effective end of the possibility that a united Communist Party might be achieved by a CPGB-ILP merger. Abyssinia in 1935, much more than Czechoslovakia three years later, was what Neville Chamberlain would eventually infamously call "a far away country" that ILP members, along with the rest of the population, knew little about. There was no recruitment of volunteers to fight against fascism there. But there would be in Spain, whose civil war was well underway by the time the convoluted tale of the ILP's response to the Abyssinian crisis had come to an end. Spain would put the seal on the party's breach with the Communists and mark a vital stage in its disillusionment with the USSR. This very hesitant process began earlier in the 1930s, however, with criticisms of Soviet foreign policy and continual difficulties with maintaining a united front with the Communists.

18

Soviet Foreign Policy and the League of Nations

Growing Criticism in the ILP

There had always been some in the ILP who were less than starry-eyed about the USSR. In his biography of Orwell, Bernard Crick mentions, for example, Myfanwy Westrope. A writer herself, Westrope ran the Booklovers' Corner bookshop in Hampstead, where she worked part-time in 1934 and 1935. She had visited the Soviet Union in 1931 but had returned "profoundly disillusioned" and "plunged into ILP activity even more heartily on her return."[1]

The CPGB and the USSR: Contrasting Views Within the ILP

Anyone reading the publications of the ILP in the interwar period is bound to be struck by the very different ways in which the USSR, on the one hand, and the Communist Party of Great Britain (CPGB), on the other, were perceived by many in the party. In spite of the attempts to achieve campaigning unity with the latter—and the efforts of the ILP's Left Wing and, a decade later, the RPC—relations between the ILP and the Communists were never very good. Just after disaffiliation from the Labour Party, Brockway, while praising the "achievement of the Russian working-class," had little time for homegrown Communism. He felt that the CPGB's "rigidity of mind and method" made it incapable of appealing to the working class in Britain. Nor was it prepared to cooperate with others on the Left. As Brockway noted of the Communist Party, "It speaks of a united front of revolutionary Socialists only to destroy it in practice."[2]

At about the same time as Brockway's comments, in 1932, the Chelsea ILP branch published a glowing account of life in "Socialist Russia." There were fifty children's theatres in the USSR, it reported, and "in all Soviet plants and factories the seven hour day will generally be introduced by the end of 1932, and the conditions in which the WORKERS work keep them healthy."[3] This was not so different from the sort of thing that appeared in the Communist press. "Soviet Prisoners Get Fortnight's Holiday," declared a headline in the *Daily Worker* around this time, followed by another that claimed the existence of ten million walkers ("ramblers") in the USSR.[4] A few months later, a *New Leader* headline asked, "What About Political Prisoners in the British Empire?" and the paper attacked critics of the USSR in "The Hysteria Against Russia."[5]

The contrast in attitudes towards the CPGB, on the one hand, and the Soviet Union, on the other, could hardly be plainer. Of course, this contrast can, in large part, be explained by the fact that British Communism lived, so to speak, next door and its behaviour could be directly experienced, unlike the USSR, which for most on the Left existed only as an idealized entity in the imagination. Then there was the emotional investment in what seemed the only successful example of socialism and the demand for solidarity that this required. This was made more intense by not-so-distant memories of armed intervention against the Bolsheviks and fears that this might soon be repeated. Another factor was, no doubt, that so much of the reporting and criticism of Communist Russia could be dismissed as hostile propaganda from "bourgeois" politicians and a "capitalist" press. Both were noted neither for factual accuracy nor fair play.

We have seen examples of distrust and criticism of the CPGB in earlier chapters. Even the members of the RPC, most of whom left the ILP for the CPGB in 1935, had not been uncritical of some aspects of the Communist Party—and even of Soviet policy and behaviour. In his article "On Leadership" in the June 1934 edition of *Controversy*, Gaster's criticisms were blunt and outspoken: "The C.P.G.B. has lamentably failed to offer sound revolutionary leadership to the workers of this country. It is to a large extent discredited. It is criminally sectarian."[6] Nor was the RPC completely trusted by the Communists—hence, the CPGB-sponsored Affiliation Committee and undercover infiltration by Communist Party members.[7]

But until the mid-1930s, there was, in the ILP, little criticism at all of the USSR and only in the later part of the decade did critics become outspoken. There was, of course, nothing peculiar to the ILP in this. One has only to call to mind the Webbs' *Soviet Communism: A New Civilisation?* of 1935 and its even less critical edition, without the question mark, in 1937.[8] When John Evans reviewed the book over two issues in the *New Leader* in early 1936, in the midst of the internal conflicts over Abyssinia, he recommended it enthusiastically. It was "no mean feat" for the authors "to shake free in their eighties from the mental habits of a lifetime," he wrote. "Yet the Webbs have done no less." He saw this as part of "the leftward swing within the Labour movement." Any notion that Russia might be living under an authoritarian regime was quickly dismissed in the first part of the review: "To the question 'is Stalin a Dictator?' the Webbs reply that he is 'not the sort of person to claim or desire such a position even if it were possible, which it is not, for him to achieve it.'"[9]

It is difficult now to fully appreciate the magnetic attraction for almost the entire British Left of the Russian Revolution, both before and after the Bolshevik takeover. In the earliest days and until some time after the end of the First World War, even MacDonald and Snowden maintained at least a "benefit of the doubt" view of the Bolsheviks.[10] And even those fiercely opposing Third International affiliation would often go on to maintain very uncritical views about what was happening in the USSR, even long after the advent of Stalin.

The memoirs of prominent members of the ILP confirm this long-lasting attraction. John Paton, national secretary for many years, was a firm opponent of the British Communist Party, as we have seen. The disaffiliated ILP would, he hoped, replace it as a revolutionary alternative to Labour. In contrast, he records in *Left Turn!* that for him, "as for most Socialists, the fate of World Socialism was bound up with the success or failure of the Russian Revolution." He later refers to "the immense Socialist achievements in Soviet Russia."[11]

Fenner Brockway succeeded Paton after the latter resigned as secretary at a time when it looked to many as though the pro-Communist faction in the ILP was going to carry all before it. Brockway, like his predecessor, was also late in becoming a critic of Communist Russia. Rather more surprisingly, Fred Jowett, that quintessentially democratic socialist whose ideas on radical parliamentary reform were examined at the beginning of this book, had, according to Brockway, "unbounded" admiration for the USSR in spite of his fundamental rejection of the CPGB and of the Comintern. "Jowett was a fervent and almost uncritical admirer of the Soviet Union," writes Brockway. "There was a tendency among many British Liberals and even among some Labourists, to identify the dictatorships in Germany and Russia. Fred devoted much of his writings at this time to countering this case."[12]

There had, however, long been critics of Bolshevism in the ILP. The earliest one to appear in *Labour Leader* was Dr. Alfred Salter, later the Labour MP for Bermondsey West. Salter, in March 1918, praised the Bolshevik Party's "uncompromising devotion to the ideal" but went on to conclude that "we must definitely dissociate ourselves from its violence, its suppression of opposing criticism and its disregard for democracy."[13] Ethel Snowden's negative views, based on her visit to Russia as part of the Labour Party/TUC delegation, were expressed in her book *Through Bolshevik Russia* and in press interviews and brought a storm of criticism from the Left in 1920, which contributed to her husband dropping out of ILP activity.[14]

In 1926, the *New Leader* did publish an attack by the Menshevik Raphael Abramovitch on the "present terrorist dictatorship" in Russia, and Brailsford, the editor at the time, conceded that "on this subject we must accept the literal truth of the Menshevik indictment." But Brailsford nevertheless stressed the need for "socialist unity" and the acknowledgement of the achievements of the revolution.[15] In 1927, the *New Leader* reported, under the headline "The Soviet Prisoners" on critics of the regime being held by the Soviet Union, explaining that, in protest against the suppression of critics, Fenner Brockway "regretfully felt he must decline the kind and courteous invitation to attend the recent 10th anniversary of the Russian Revolution. The reason still stands."[16] But such criticism was exceptional. Praise and celebration were far more usual.

Included in the NAC's report to the 1924 annual conference was an obituary of Lenin, who was described as "unquestionably one of the greatest figures in the history of the Socialist movement." Cablegrams had been sent to "Madame Lenin" and the Council of People's Commissars expressing the ILP's "profound sympathy" and its "deep admiration for Lenin's great work for world Socialism."[17] In 1930, Emrys Hughes, the editor of *Forward*, defended the USSR in "How the Press Lies About Russia," while a few months later, the *New Leader* published an article by Karl Radek under the title "Capitalism Attacks Russia: The Truth about the Moscow Trial." Radek defended the trials and, in some cases, executions of engineers "for industrial sabotage instigated by foreign and Russian capitalistic interests."[18] Seven years later, he would himself be a victim of one of Stalin's show trials.

The articles by Hughes and Radek appeared in the middle of Comintern's "class-against-class" period, during which organizations like the ILP were denounced as "social fascists." At the beginning of 1929, *Forward* had warned of the attack on the ILP in "New Ideological Attack on Left Wing: Sinister Strategy of the C.P.G.B." *The Communist*, the article reported, had attacked Maxton and the ILP leadership as "the most dangerous enemies of the working class" and had called for "a persistent ideological campaign," which, the writer commented sarcastically, was just "the way to rouse the masses and take their minds off the football coupons."[19]

When, later that year, Maxton was expelled from the Communist-dominated League Against Imperialism, a *New Leader* writer noted that "the whole episode throws a brilliant searchlight on the almost total failure of Communist propaganda in this country. When the Third International decreed, against the advice of its most level-headed adherents, that Labour must be fought at the polls, it signed the death warrant of the British Communist Party." The CPGB's decline in membership and influence, the article concluded, was a "reflection of that dictatorship and domination which are entirely alien to the spirit of the British Labour Movement."[20]

The ILP thought no better of the CPGB when, in the mid-1930s, the Communists became advocates of the "popular front," urged workers to vote Labour, and renewed its attempt to be allowed to affiliate to the Labour Party. In the October 1935 issue of *Controversy*, Edward Conze mocked the CPGB in "The Communist Party's Last Somersault." He recalled that in 1928, the Comintern had adopted standing orders requiring biennial world congresses, yet because such democratic procedures were disliked by "the more dictatorial-minded Communists," none had been held until the current year. The result had then been that Communist parties, with the British being a little slower than most, had "swung round to a policy of extreme 'right-wing reformism.'"[21]

At the beginning of 1936, John McGovern, fresh from being returned to the House of Commons as a Clydeside MP, one of the four successful ILP candidates, all in the Glasgow area, asked what the ILP's reaction would be "if Willie Gallacher is admitted to the Parliamentary Labour Party." Gallacher was the sole Communist returned in the 1935 election. He represented another Clydeside constituency. McGovern compared the uncompromising socialist policies of the ILP with those of CPGB: "Three years ago the crime of the I.L.P. was that we were inside the Labour Party. Our crime to-day is that we are not following the C.P. in a wild scramble to get inside and place ourselves under the heel of the T.U.C. and Labour Party bosses." Gallacher and the CPGB, McGovern noted sarcastically, were trying to demonstrate to Labour that "the I.L.P. are bold, bad boys, and the C.P. are good little lads who will help, if admitted to the Labour Party, to put the I.L.P. in its place." He mocked the swings in Communist policy: "When Bertram Mills requires turns for his circus he should apply to the C.P. It has a leadership that can turn every kind of somersault ever recorded." The ILP's members were not "robot enough to turn right about when ordered." On the contrary, he concluded, "we retain our rights as a democratic organisation and intend to defend them against all comers."[22]

But such disdain for the homegrown Communists and even for the Comintern had little impact on the ultraoptimistic views of the USSR. Throughout 1931 and into the following year, *Labour's Northern Voice* devoted much space to the Five-Year Plan adopted in the Soviet Union, as did *Forward*, while the *New Leader* published its praise under the headline "Russia's Second Five Year Plan: Amazing Details."[23] At about the same time, the ILP's Welsh Division carried a motion congratulating "the Soviet Union upon the titanic effort it is making to reveal to the Workers of the World that Socialism is the only escape from the chaos of Capitalism and pledge ourselves to do all in our power to expose the abusive and lying campaign now being waged against the U.S.S.R."[24] Soon after this, the party published a Commons speech made by Fenner Brockway in a no-confidence debate on the Labour government, which included the following confident prediction:

> Tory members sneer at Russia, but, sooner or later, we shall have to face the fact that the five-year plan which Russia is putting through is a quite deliberate plan to raise the standard of her people by 100 per cent, a quite deliberate plan to rationalise and modernise her industry on the basis of Socialist principles, which will become a competitive factor in the world.[25]

Beginning in April 1932 and running throughout the year and into the following one, the *New Leader* included more than a dozen well-illustrated "New Russia Supplements." Titles included "The Soviet System Explained" in May and "Russia is Wonderful—But Don't Be Expecting Too Much!" the following month.[26] At the 1933 annual conference, Brockway included in his chairman's address the statement "We declare to the workers of Russia that if any conflict develops between the British Government and Soviet Russia our stand will be with them and not for the capitalist and imperialist Government of this country." The conference went on to carry unamimously a motion moved by the Sheffield branch and the Edinburgh Federation, which pledged resistance "to any attempt to strangle the progress of Soviet Russia" and "to agitate for a general strike to restrain the Government in the event of any attempt to make war on Russia." The constitution adopted by the conference stated, in the section "The Development of World Socialism," that "the I.L.P. supports the U.S.S.R., the first workers' republic."[27]

Later that year, Brockway and Maxton's "Clear Lead" statement, though pledging cooperation where possible, stressed the differences between the ILP and the CPGB, charging that "the Communist Party is not prepared to break from the rigid organizational and financial control of Moscow."[28] The difference in attitude towards "Soviet Russia" and "Moscow," which were somehow perceived as independent of each other, is again clear. The NAC's statement to the 1935 annual conference, "A Socialist Policy for Britain," once again underlined the contrast in perceptions of the Soviet Union and the CPGB. It concluded that "the Soviet Union is a Socialist citadel in a hostile Capitalist world and must be defended at all costs." But in Britain, the statement went on, the Communist Party frequently pursued tactics that hindered the development of an effective revolutionary movement. It was sectarian in its attitude and actions, which prejudiced its work in the trade unions and tended to make united action difficult. "Its organisational basis prevents freedom of discussion and decision within the Party and tends to create an automatic mind among its membership. Its financial dependence upon the Communist International involves a control of policy detrimental to the development of a revolutionary policy suited to British conditions."[29]

However, the sudden changes in Soviet foreign policy and in Comintern attitudes towards those not so long before despised as "social fascists" began a prolonged and very hesitant process of change in attitudes towards the Soviet Union. This change began when Brockway criticized the USSR's recent positions on international issues.

Brockway's "Anti-Soviet Slanders" and Relations with the Comintern

Hostility towards Brockway from the Communists and, prior to its departure from the ILP, the RPC, had been building since 1933. A straw in the wind appeared in May 1933 in an article that was part of the *New Leader* series "The New Russia Supplement." Under the title "Russia's Peace Policy," it was as uncritical and laudatory as was the rest of that series. It complained about the exclusion of the USSR from the "Four-Power Pact" that MacDonald was promoting, commenting that "Russia obviously cannot be excluded from any pact whose object is to maintain peace in Europe. Her exclusion clearly meant her isolation."[30] This suggested the direction that Soviet policy was now taking—trying to avoid isolation by seeking international agreement. Brockway would soon make himself very unpopular in parts of the Left—especially the CPGB and the RPC—by his criticism of the USSR for joining the League of Nations and attempting to achieve alliances with "bourgeois" states.

A few weeks later, Brockway's article "Workers Prepare: The Bankruptcy of the Internationals" appeared in the *New Leader*, spread over the paper's two middle pages and adorned with photos that were eye-catching if not particularly relevant. In it, Brockway maintained that the Comintern was sacrificing the interests of the workers, citing two actions as evidence: first, its resistance to calls for an international workers' boycott of German goods and, second, the "Russian acquiescence in Japanese Imperialism in the Far East, by its recognition of Manchukuo and its offer to sell Japan the Chinese Eastern Railway." He went on: "Russia does not want war. That is understandable. But international working class opposition to Imperialism must not be sacrificed even to the interests of Russia." The following week, a letter from a member of the Stepney branch alleged that Brockway's comments ran contrary to the ILP's policy of support to the USSR, a policy adopted little more than a month earlier at the Derby conference. The writer, who was not alone in his complaints, asked for "a definite statement from the Party Chairman. Does he want Russia to go to war with Japan?"[31]

In the next four issues of the *New Leader*, Brockway developed his arguments further. On 30 June, he noted that his article published two weeks earlier had caused "considerable controversy"—as he had anticipated—but went on to repeat his criticisms, adding that Russian trade agreements with Germany would "help to stabilise Hitlerism." He returned to these allegations the following week, in an article that began, "I shall ignore the hysterical Communist charges that I am a 'cheap publicist of the hounds of War and Fascism,'" before he proceeded to engage with them.[32] In his third article, Brockway reiterated his criticism of the Communist International's failure to support a working-class refusal "to handle or transport goods for Germany," speculating that such an action might have sufficed to bring the Hitler regime down. He rejected Communist charges that he was colluding with Paton and others to avoid carrying out the pro-USSR policy of the Derby conference.[33]

By now, the ILP was committed to exploring the possibility of cooperation and even—once again—affiliation to the Third International. In the early part of 1934, the party published correspondence arising from Brockway's letter of inquiry about the conditions of affiliation to the Communist Internatonal. The reply, signed "O. W. Kuusinen, for the Political Secretariat of the E.C.C.I. (dated Moscow, February 20th 1934)," began with the greeting "Comrades" and then immediately went on to characterize Brockway's letter as consisting for the most part of "anti-Communist and anti-Soviet slanders." It referred to his "notorious articles last summer against the Communist Party of the Soviet Union and the Communist International," which were in "full conformity with the anti-Soviet slanders of the counterrevolutionary traitor, Trotsky." Brockway's reply, dated 12 March 1934, stressed that the views he had expressed were not just his own but also those of the NAC and that they were borne out by the "history of Communist Parties both in Europe and America."[34]

Brockway saw the changes in Russian foreign policy as predicated on the Soviet Union's fear of Nazi Germany and consequent wish to draw capitalist countries—above all, Britain and France—into cooperation against the growing threat it represented. The Comintern's official adoption of the Popular Front policy, at its Seventh World Congress in the summer of 1935, was a corollary. The policy was dismissed by the ILP, in a one-page leaflet titled *What the I.L.P. Stands For*, as "the surrender of the class struggle and the fight for Socialism."

The USSR and the League of Nations

The ILP had always been, at best, highly suspicious of the "bourgeois" League of Nations, and never more so than during its period of revolutionary policy in the 1930s. There were persistent reports that the USSR was intending to join the League, which it finally did in September 1934. Those hostile to the League were bound to be critical of the Soviet Union's action. Brockway had already refused, in May, to withdraw criticism of the direction in which the USSR appeared to be heading.[35]

Editorial comment followed over the summer. In July, the *New Leader* argued that "in entering 'pacts' and 'alliances'" with capitalist governments, soviet Russia was in danger of taking on obligations that might conflict with "the interests of revolutionary action by the working class." In September, while acknowledging the circumstances that had brought about the Soviet decision, the ILP paper declared that "whatever may be said for Soviet Russia entering the League from a Governmental standpoint, nothing can be said for the International Working-Class Movement entering the League either in mind or action."[36]

At the end of November 1934, Brockway's article "Soviet Russia's Foreign Policy: An Issue Socialists Must Face" appeared in the *New Leader*. It was prompted, he explained, by reports from the French Chamber of Deputies about a secret Franco-Russian alliance. Fear of attack by Germany and Poland, in the west, and Japan, in the east, had led the USSR "entirely to reverse her foreign policy." Previously, the Soviet Union had managed to combine the aims of the preservation of peace, "so that the great work of Socialist construction might proceed in Russia," with that of encouraging social revolution in capitalist countries and nationalist revolt in their empires. It had relied on action by the working class to prevent war rather than on pacts with capitalist countries or the intervention of the League of Nations. But now it had joined the League and accepted the "collective system" of peacekeeping.[37]

What if, asked Brockway, "a British Government fights side by side with Soviet Russia against Germany and Japan in the next war, not because of any regard for Russia, but because it wishes to maintain the Versailles Treaty and the British Empire. Will Socialists be expected to enlist?" If they did so, they were likely, among other disastrous outcomes, to end up having to "crush a revolution in India."[38]

Brockway explicitly connected the change in Russian foreign policy to the new popular front line of the Comintern and the CPGB. Everywhere, Communist parties were moderating their policies. In Britain, the Communist Party was clearly preparing the way for a changed attitude towards the Labour Party. As he explained, his article had been prompted not only by recent events but also by Gore Graham's *War and Peace and the Soviet Union*, which had, he maintained, misrepresented "a former warning which I wrote on ... Soviet Russia's foreign policy, as I anticipate this warning will be misrepresented." It was an issue of "first importance" to all socialists, he concluded.[39]

The December meeting of the Inner Executive noted a complaint about Brockway's article from Gaster, who maintained that a position on Russian foreign policy was "a matter definitely decided by Annual Conference." The

IE's April meeting rejected a motion from the London Division "strongly protesting against the Editor's article on the diplomacy of the Soviet Union." The Inner Executive insisted that there was no divergence from ILP policy. When it reported this to the NAC, however, it added that a number of resolutions and letters had been received about the issue."[40]

Soon thereafter, Gaster was supported by A. H. Hawkins, now chair of the London Division, in a bid to get his own article, critical of Brockway, published in the *New Leader*. But he was reminded by the Inner Executive "that the principle had been accepted that inner-Party controversy should be excluded from its columns."[41] Undeterred, Gaster attempted to refer the Inner Executive minutes back at the next NAC meeting.[42] Gaster was by no means alone in protesting against the line being taken on the issue of Soviet foreign policy, although opposition was concentrated in his own London Division. Another NAC meeting a few days later, at the annual conference, noted protests from the London Divisional Council, five London branches, and fourteen individual London members.[43]

International Alignments

"Make 1934 Historic!" Maxton had demanded on the front page of the first *New Leader* of the New Year.[44] A month earlier, *Controversy* had predicted that at the 1934 annual conference, the "real alternatives" would be affiliation to the Communist International, or the creation of a new united international.[45] When, in keeping with the resolution passed at its 1933 conference, the ILP had approached the Comintern with an offer of cooperation, the initial response had been encouraging: the Comintern welcomed "united front activity" with the ILP and expressed its "readiness to commence negotiations with the N.A.C. of the I.L.P."[46] However, the later exchanges over Brockway's "anti-Soviet" articles in early 1934 made this seem less and less likely, in spite of determined efforts of supporters to bring the ILP around to this position.

February 1934 saw the RPC-dominated Affiliation Committee protesting to the NAC against the London Division's exclusion of its members from holding office. The committee went on to request the circulation of its statement favouring affiliation with the Comintern. The NAC instructed Maxton to investigate and refused to circulate any material from such "unofficial bodies."[47] The next NAC meeting endorsed the London Division's action on the understanding that the rights of members who had signed the Affiliation Committee would be restored "when satisfactory guarantees of Party loyalty were given."[48]

In the meantime, the ILP had been busy exploring other possibilities for international cooperation. The previous March, Paton had written to the Socialist and Communist Internationals on behalf of the "International

Committee of the 'Left' Independent Socialist Parties," which represented a number of left-wing parties spread across Europe and hoped to achieve "real proletarian unity."⁴⁹ Paton had now left the party, but the ILP remained committed to a wider form of unity. Brockway, his successor as general secretary, presented a draft statement of ILP objectives. Its first aim was "to bring about the unification of all genuinely revolutionary sections of the working-class in one International." The ILP would oppose any new international being formed but would work with "independent Revolutionary Parties" to bring them to support an "inclusive revolutionary international." This was approved after the defeat, by 9 votes to 4, of a motion by Gaster calling for "sympathetic" affiliation to Comintern.⁵⁰

"Is a New International Necessary? Revolutionary Parties of Ten Countries Meet in Paris" was the headline of a *New Leader* report in February 1935 by "our own correspondent." The report gave details of the meeting of parties supporting the International Bureau. The ILP was firmly opposed to the formation a new international, and that view won the day in Paris, the writer explained. At the Paris meeting, Brockway spoke of the need to bring together three elements of what he and the ILP regarded as the political side of the working-class movement: the "revolutionary sections" of the Socialist International, the "independent revolutionary parties" represented at the meeting, and the Communist International. He insisted that "there can be no real revolutionary international without the Russian Communist Party" and other Communist parties. Although he conceded that there were "no prospects for reform" of the Comintern in the immediate future, the time for a unity conference would arrive at some stage.⁵¹

The difference between an international bureau and an "international" seems extremely difficult to discern—and evidently was so at the time. "Is not the Bureau in fact if not in name, an International?" asked the *London R.P.C. Bulletin* in June. It rejected the idea that the other participants were "genuinely revolutionary." The claims to this status of Norwegian, Dutch, and German supporters of the Bureau were duly trashed in some detail. As to "revolutionary unity between the C.I., the Trotskyists and other 'revolutionary' sections and parties," it concluded, "we fear the N.A.C. lives in dreamland." This is a conclusion from which it is difficult, with the benefits of hindsight, to dissent.⁵²

Nevertheless, in the summer of 1935, the NAC decided that if the ILP was invited to send fraternal delegates to the Comintern's upcoming World Congress in Moscow, it should send two members plus one from each divisional council.⁵³ But when Brockway reported that the CPGB's J. R. Campbell had indicated that it was unlikely that such an invitation would be forthcoming unless the ILP specifically requested it, the Inner Executive agreed that "the decisions of the annual conference and of the N.A.C. did not entitle it take such action."⁵⁴ The following year, 1936, the NAC reported that it had told the Communist Party that it was willing to send fraternal delegates to the Seventh World Congress of the Comintern on the understanding that the ILP was not committed to the decisions of the congress and was free "to express the Party view." The ILP annual conference was told subsequently that "no invitation was received and fraternal delegates were not sent."⁵⁵

Meanwhile, in April 1935, the Inner Executive responded to a resolution from the London Division "protesting against the political line of the Editor's article on the diplomacy of the Soviet Union." The Inner Executive insisted that there was no divergence from party policy. It also noted letters from the Harrow branch, which had refused to distribute the *New Leader* containing Brockway's article until instructed to do so by the divisional council.⁵⁶ How divisive the issue had become in the London Division is clear from the minutes of the NAC meeting two weeks later. In opposition to the London divisional statement, as well as other resolutions critical of the articles from London already noted, Brockway's line was supported by eight London branches as well as by two letters from members outside the capital.⁵⁷

Still operating within the ILP, the *London R.P.C. Bulletin*, in July 1935, had taken issue with Brockway's "Final Rejoinder" on the USSR foreign policy issue in that month's *Controversy*. The RPC complained that though the Inner Executive and the Derby conference had eventually backed "Brockway's line," he had been propagating it in the *New Leader* long before this, while other points of view were "suppressed." Had as much space been given to "an explanation of the Soviet Union's foreign policy," the *Bulletin* argued, the voting at Derby would have been different. Whatever Brockway's intentions may have been, his articles "hindered the closer unity of the I.L.P. and the C.P."⁵⁸

Moreover, Brockway was "fundamentally pacifist" rather than revolutionary.⁵⁹ Under his editorship, the departing RPC alleged in its final *Bulletin*, the *New Leader* had "come out with insinuations, questions and innuendos about the good faith and revolutionary integrity of the Soviet government." This was not "comradely criticism but the cautiously deliberate encouragement of anti-Communist sentiment." Under the subheading "The *New Leader's* Crooked Line," the "mountebank" Brockway's article of 30 November 1934 was particularly singled out for denunciation: "Unscrupulous hostility to Communism could go no further," the *Bulletin* article concluded.⁶⁰

In his 1938 book *Workers' Front*, Brockway set out to demonstrate succinctly how Hitler's rise to power and the USSR's consequent fear of Germany had brought about a "complete turn" in Communist foreign policy:

> When Mussolini established his dictatorship in Italy, the Communist International called on the working class to organise a boycott of goods to Italy, to refuse to handle or transport any articles destined for Italy. When Hitler established his dictatorship, Soviet Russia immediately renewed its trade agreement with Germany. At the moment when Hitler was rounding up the German Communists, imprisoning them, herding them in concentration camps, inflicting indescribable tortures on them, executing them, the representatives of Soviet Russia were putting their pens to an extended agreement for mutual trade between the two countries.[61]

This account was even more dismissive of the USSR's foreign policy changes than Brockway's *New Leader* articles of earlier years had been. It reflects the growing disillusionment with the USSR that was taking place, albeit in a very uneven way, within the ILP.

Conflicts over Russian foreign policy and Abyssinia were as nothing compared to the divisions that were opened up by the Moscow trials between 1936 and 1938 and, above all, by the Spanish Civil War during the same period. The earlier gap between the way the CPGB, and even Comintern, were dismissed and the laudatory view of the Soviet Union was narrowing rapidly. Unlike the criticism of Soviet adhesion to the League of Nations and the reorientation of its foreign policy, this time there would be implications for the way the state of affairs in the Soviet Union itself was regarded.

19

The ILP and the USSR
From Doubt to Disillusionment

Conflicts over Russian foreign policy and Abyssinia were qualitatively different from the divisions that were opened up by the Spanish Civil War and the show trials that marked the height of what would become known as Stalin's Great Terror. With the earlier issues, the argument had been about the wisdom of the road taken and the perceived lack of revolutionary principle involved. This time, they were literally about life or death issues. Questions were raised about Soviet ethics—not just about political judgment and policies. The trials and purges instituted by Stalin coincided with the Spanish war. In the three years leading up to the outbreak of the Second World War, the attitude in the ILP towards the USSR would shift considerably.

Spain and the Moscow Trials

In early 1936, the *New Leader* was cautious about recent events in Russia. It was not, Brockway wrote, prepared to accept Trotsky's charges of "persecution of Opposition Communists" without an "impartial investigation." But he noted that the Comintern response was "not reassuring."[1] Then, in August, a few weeks after the outbreak of civil war in Spain, the same issue that headlined "Spanish Workers Fight for Soviets" featured Brockway's article "Doubts Caused by the Moscow Trial." He concluded that "Stalin may make a purge of his critics; but this trial has been a bad day's work for Soviet Russia." The first of the three main show trials, this one known as the "Trial of the Sixteen," had finished a few days earlier with death sentences for the defendants.[2]

The same issue of the paper also reported that John McNair, the assistant secretary of the International Bureau, was going to Spain as the ILP's envoy. The following week, McNair reported on what he had found in "Workers Control Everything in Catalonia."[3] This marked the beginning of intense ILP involvement with Spain. In contrast to the rather theoretical conflicts over Abyssinia, this involvement would be highly practical and would lead to actual participation in the fighting by members of the ILP.

Political turmoil was nothing new for interwar Spain. But when Franco's July 1936 military revolt against the democratically elected Republican government developed into full-scale civil war, Spain was seen by most on the Left, not the least by the ILP, as another European state in grave danger of falling into fascism. This apparent threat was reinforced by the support for Franco, including significant armed intervention, that quickly came from Fascist Italy and Nazi Germany. Britain and France followed a policy of non-intervention, however, leaving the Republicans increasingly reliant on Russian support and armaments. Thousands of foreign supporters of the Republic, by no means all of them Communists, fought in the International Brigades organized by the Comintern, although, as we shall see, a different path was followed by most ILP volunteers.

In spite of these efforts, the war ended with the installation of Franco, who would act as dictator until his death in 1975. For the ILP, the war marked a distinct turning point in its relationship with the Communists. For later generations, the ILP's experience of the war has been most often understood via George Orwell's *Homage to Catalonia*. As we shall see, Orwell served with some of the ILP contingent, though he was not an ILP member at the time.

In its report to the 1937 annual conference in Glasgow, the NAC gave an account of what had been done in response to the Spanish events. Within a month of the "Fascist putsch," the council had sent John McNair to Barcelona. The ILP had raised over £2,000 to support the struggle, and after the news—which later turned out not to be true—that the leader of the Partido Obrero de Unificación Marxista (POUM), Joaquin Maurin, had been shot by Franco, the ILP equipped a military ambulance named after him.[4] A pamphlet by McNair titled *In Spain Now!* had been published in 1936, along with the "undelivered speeches" of Julián Gorkin, another of the POUM's leaders.[5] Early the following year, the London Division had published Jack Huntz's *Spotlight on Spain*, and, in another fund-raising effort, Edward Fletcher and Roland Penrose had visited Spain to gather materials for an exhibition of Spanish art, which opened in February 1937.[6]

In addition, the report noted that McGovern had also visited Spain in order to get information about the attitude of the Catholic Church, with the resulting pamphlet, *Why Bishops Back Franco*, selling twenty-eight thousand copies.[7] But most significant of all for what followed, the report mentioned that an ILP contingent, "on the initiative of Bob Edwards," had joined the POUM militia and that Bob Smillie was among those who had "enlisted."[8] The grandson of the Scottish miners' leader Robert Smillie, Bob Smillie was prominent in the ILP's Guild of Youth. His death in Spain in ambiguous circumstances would become a *cause célèbre* for the ILP later in 1937.

"The Moscow Trial: An International Investigation Required" headlined the *New Leader* in January 1937. The article reported the execution of the sixteen defendants in the show trial, including the prominent Bolshevik leaders Zinoviev and Kamenev.[9] The NAC maintained its cautious position, confining itself to a resolution calling for the setting up of an "impartial investigation by representative Socialists who have the confidence of the working class." In the meantime, the party was instructed to refrain from coming to any premature judgment. That this was still a divisive issue in the ILP, even though the RPC had decamped to the CPGB nearly eighteen months earlier, is evident from the postconference reports in the *Leader* in early April.[10]

The NAC's motion, while acclaiming the October revolution as "the greatest event in working-class history," focused on "causes of disquiet," which included the Moscow trials, the growing differentiation of income, the reintroduction of the right of inheritance, and foreign policy. The NAC, said the *Leader*, was, "assailed from both sides—from those who wanted no criticism of Soviet Russia and those who wanted severer criticism." The trials were defended by Jack Huntz and Bill Jones but attacked as "frame-ups" by Patterson of the Clapham branch, who "did not hide his support of Leon Trotsky," and Cund, of Liverpool. Amendments from both sides of the issue were defeated, and the conference overwhelmingly endorsed the NAC's report.[11]

The POUM, the ILP, and Trotskyism

The NAC report included this statement, in bold: **"The Party has identified itself with the political line of the P.O.U.M. and has energetically repudiated the attacks which have been made upon the P.O.U.M. by the Communist International."**[12] Though the ILP was still attempting to achieve unity with the Communists, as well as with the rest of what they regarded as the working-class movement, its efforts were complicated and ultimately doomed, as far as the Communists were concerned, by the overriding context of the Stalin-Trotsky conflict. As we have seen, as early as 1934, the Comintern was associating Brockway's criticisms of Russian foreign policy with the "anti-Soviet slanders of the counterrevolutionary traitor, Trotsky."[13] The ILP's relationship with the POUM, a fellow affiliate of the International Bureau, became the focus for ferocious Communist criticism.

In February 1937, the *New Leader* had reported on the "Agreement Against Calumny" put forward in Spain by the POUM and the Iberian Anarchist Federation (Federación Anarquista Ibérica, or FAI). The *Leader* printed the text in bold: **"We undertake not to make use in our political campaigns of defamation or calumny against other anti-Fascist organisations. We agree to avoid all actions which may ferment discord in the anti-Fascist front."** But, ominously, the paper also reported that the Spanish Communist Party had not signed this agreement.[14]

The ILP's identification with the POUM was total. "We Are Proud of P.O.U.M." declared the headline of a *New Leader* article by John McNair.[15] Orwell's biographer, Bernard Crick, describes the POUM as "the ILP's ideal self-image."[16] Some historians seem to have accepted the Communist view that the POUM was a Trotskyist organization, though they are not always consistent in the way they describe it. On at least one occasion, Paul Preston refers to it as "quasi-Trotskyist."[17] In the list of organizations in Hugh Thomas's classic account of the Spanish Civil War, the POUM is described simply as "Trotskyist," while in the text itself, it is referred to as "the semi-Trotskyist Marxist party," a label that is also used by Ian Slater in his book on Orwell.[18]

Such designations raise questions about their possible meanings and implications. In his book *Workers' Front*, Brockway writes that the POUM might "be described as a Leninist Communist Party," which goes some way towards explaining why some find it difficult to differentiate it from a Trotskyist organization.[19] Crick, in his Orwell biography, notes that the POUM leader Andrés Nin had been an early follower of Trotsky but, having found him "too egocentric and dogmatic," had broken off any contact with him in 1934.[20]

At the time, Brockway was adamant about the matter:

> The P.O.U.M. is not a Trotskyist party. In its own official statement, published on May 11th, it said: "We do not hold a point of view in common with Trotsky." There is a Trotskyist group in the P.O.U.M. as there is in other sections of the working class, but it is small and has no representatives on the Executive Committee. Andres Nin [sic] and a section of the Party used to belong to a Trotskyist organisation, but when Trotsky issued orders that they should join the Socialist Party, they refused and joined with the Workers' and Peasants' Bloc, led by Joaquim Maurin [sic] and Julien Gorkin [sic] to form the P.O.U.M. Since then there has been a complete break with Trotsky and "La Batalla" has quite recently carried articles attacking Trotskyism.

Brockway then added—in bold: "**It is the custom now of the Communist Party to denounce any Socialists who maintain a revolutionary attitude as Trotskyists. This is only to cloak the departure of the Communist Party itself from a revolutionary policy.**"[21]

The ILP itself certainly included some Trotskyists, though they were neither numerous nor united. C. L. R. James, as mentioned earlier, had been prominent in the debates over Abyssinia. Most belonged to the Marxist Group, whose members joined the ILP in February 1934 but left in October 1936, with

James taking the initiative in successfully arguing for abandoning the allegedly "centrist" party. In itself, this would seem sufficient to refute any suggestion that the ILP was Trotskyist.[22] Earlier in 1936, the *New Leader*, in an editorial, had rejected Trotsky's criticism of the International Bureau for Revolutionary Socialist Unity for having no common policy; he should be using his prestige, the editor wrote, to "bring all Revolutionary Socialists together" instead of "exaggerating differences from the sectarian angle of his own collection of groups."[23]

Whether the ILP was democratic centralist or not, there was always a considerable range of views within the party, as the three-way split over Abyssinia had amply demonstrated. Insofar as one can identify a mainstream position in the ILP, it had at least as much in common with the "Left Communism" of the early 1920s, with its idealized notion of soviet democracy, as with the "Bolshevik-Leninism" of Trotsky's followers.[24] Regardless of the divisions in the party, in 1937, ILP concerns about events in Spain and Russia grew. So did the hostility of the Communists with whom it aspired to achieve "unity."

The Barcelona Events and the Death of Bob Smillie

When the 1937 ILP conference met in Glasgow, tensions were already building between the Communists in Barcelona and the POUM and its anarchist allies. Fighting broke out on 3 May. Even before this, the *Daily Worker*, in the article "Destroying Its Name and Tradition," had accused the ILP conference of sabotaging itself through association with the "treacherous record" of the POUM. As for the ILP debate on Russia, the party had, said the *Worker*, "boiled down to passing lip-service to the great triumphs of the past 20 years with all the emphasis laid on criticisms based on Trotskyite fictions."[25]

At first, the *New Leader* called for judgment to be suspended on events in Barcelona pending clarification, adding, "The I.L.P. has supported P.O.U.M. in its stand for the Workers' Revolution as the answer to Fascism, but we have also used our influence to maintain Workers' unity in the anti-Fascist struggle."[26] Then, a week later, the front page was devoted to the POUM's official reply: "The Truth About Barcelona."[27] This was followed by Brockway's pamphlet under the same title that maintained and even strengthened the close identification of the ILP with the POUM. In the list of organizations at the beginning of the pamphlet, the POUM was described as the "I.L.P. of Spain." Brockway linked the difficulties of the USSR in revolutionary Catalonia directly to the Soviet foreign policy he had been criticizing for the previous four years, one that "aimed at securing an alliance with France, Britain and the 'democratic capitalist' countries." But, as he went on to point out, "These countries would never enter such an alliance if Russia encouraged revolutions. It was therefore a matter of importance to Russia that its arms should be used in Spain only for parliamentary democracy." With this end in view, the Soviet Union had imposed conditions on the military aid it was giving to the Spanish republic, Brockway said. These included the exclusion of the POUM from government and administration and the "separation of the war from the revolution."[28]

After the POUM's exclusion, "the Government began to assume an openly counter-revolutionary character," Brockway argued. He dismissed the charge that the POUM was responsible for the uprising in the Catalan capital, instead blaming the anarchist group Friends of Durrutti, which had been immediately disowned by the anarchist leadership. According to Brockway, the POUM leadership had faith that "in time the workers would protest against the counter-revolution which the Government was carrying through." As a working-class party, the POUM thus had to "associate" itself with the spontaneous movement in Barcelona once it began. Brockway compared the POUM's support for the uprising to that given by Lenin and the Bolsheviks to the July 1917 uprising in Petrograd against what he described as Kerensky's version of a "popular front" government. He quoted a paragraph from John Reed's account of the events in Petrograd in *Ten Days That Shook the World*, as well as a recent judgment by the former *New Leader* editor H. N. Brailsford. Brailsford maintained that the POUM "represented the older and now heretical position," adding that "the Communist Party is no longer a party of the industrial workers or even a Marxist Party."[29]

The ILP had often made even harsher comments about the CPGB, as we saw earlier, and these had been reciprocated. But only in May 1937 did anyone in either party come close to calling for the deaths of members of the rival organization. Palme Dutt, citing a *New Leader* report by McNair, wrote in the *Daily Worker* that the ILP volunteers in Barcelona had "served under the P.O.U.M. in this armed rising against the Spanish People's Front and its constituted authorities—an act of treason which in any war would be punishable by death."[30] "Spanish Trotskyists Plot with Franco" proclaimed a headline in the *Worker* a month later, again underscoring the CPGB's allegation that members of the POUM were engaged in a full-scale "fifth columnist" conspiracy with the fascists.[31]

But, despite such accusations from the CPGB, the *New Leader* denied that disagreements over Spain were wrecking the unity movement in Britain. The objective was not to unify the ILP and the CPGB, the paper reminded its readers, but to promote united action on issues on which the two parties agreed. The paper soon reported, however, that the *Daily Worker* had, unsurprisingly, refused to take an advertisement for Brockway's *The Truth About Barcelona* and had published its own dismissive response to the book.[32]

The reliance of the Republican cause on Soviet support enabled the Communists to play a more dominant role, and they used the opportunity to suppress their allegedly Trotskyist opponents in the POUM. These included the ILP volunteers, who were soon forced to flee Spain. It was in this context that, in June 1937, news arrived of the death of Bob Smillie. His arrest and imprisonment—"entirely unjust" in Hugh Thomas's words—had taken place as he was about to leave Spain. He had subsequently died, apparently of appendicitis.[33] The 18 June issue of the *New Leader* carried an obituary written by John McNair, and the ILP also published an eight-page booklet, *We Carry On: Our Tribute to Bob Smillie*, written by Dan McArthur, the chairman of the Scottish ILP Guild of Youth, with a foreword by Maxton.

Neither McNair nor McArthur offered any explanation of Smillie's death, although Brockway investigated the circumstances, along with ILP member and freelance journalist David Murray and Julián Gorkin of the POUM. They concluded that Smillie had not been provided with the medical attention he needed while in prison but that there was no evidence that his death was due to other circumstances.[34] And, with that, the ILP leadership seemed content to let the matter rest. Writing about Smillie's death, Tom Buchanan suggests a number of reasons why the ILP refrained from attempts to politicize the incident, foremost among them a wish to protect the reputation of the Spanish Republic, to avoid jeopardizing the situation of other prisoners held in similar circumstances, and to preserve its relations with the CPGB.[35] As far as one can judge, these factors certainly played a large part. But at least one additional factor was almost certainly at work, namely, a desire on the part of the ILP's leaders to protect both themselves and the POUM against renewed charges of Trotskyism and alleged collaboration with Franco.

As Buchanan notes, at its meeting in December, the NAC received a resolution from Yorkshire's Dewsbury branch expressing "dissatisfaction regarding the 'mystery' surrounding the death of Comrade Bob Smillie." By way of response, the NAC chose simply to endorse the results of the investigation conducted by Brockway, Murray, and Gorkin.[36] Evidently, then, the leaders of the ILP had no interest in reopening the question. The next item in the minutes, which also concerned the Dewsbury branch, sheds light on their possible motives. Percy Williams, who represented the Yorkshire Division, reported that, under the influence of one P. J. Barclay, "a programme of lectures had been arranged including a number of Trotskyist speakers who were not members of the Branch." The NAC duly warned the Yorkshire Division, as well as the Lancashire and North East divisions, not to acquiesce to Barclay's Trotskyist "advances."[37]

As, in combination, these two items suggest, the ILP leadership must have suspected that any further probing of the "mystery" of Smillie's death would be used by the Communists as proof of Trotskyism not only within the ILP and its Spanish counterpart, the POUM, but also within the other affiliates of the International Bureau for Revolutionary Socialist Unity. This interpretation is strengthened by the fact that another item on the agenda of the same NAC meeting concerned efforts to secure amnesty for all "anti-Fascist prisoners."[38] In pursuit of this goal, a delegation from the International Bureau, led by the French human rights advocate Félicien Challaye, visited Spain; Maxton and McGovern gained an interview with the British Foreign Secretary; and a group of ILP MPs paid a visit to the Spanish embassy. Suspicions of Trotskyism would have helped none of these initiatives.

All that said, the NAC did publish a report that concluded, "We consider that Bob Smillie's death was due to great carelessness on the part of the responsible authorities, which amounted to criminal negligence," repeating this statement in its annual report to the 1938 conference. As Brockway would write forty years later, "A strong boy should not have died of appendicitis."[39]

Meanwhile, in August 1937, the *New Leader* had reported the murder of the POUM leader Andrés Nin.[40] The NKVD, the Soviet Union's central intelligence agency, under its chief operative in Spain, Alexander Orlov, was suspected as being responsible, although that had not yet been proven.[41] In spite of the ILP's desire to support a united front, both in Britain and Spain, the party was increasingly riven with doubts not only about the activities and policies of Comintern and its affiliates in Spain but also about the realities of the situation in the Soviet Union itself.

Growing Doubts About the Soviet Union

Along with outrage over the Soviet role in Spain and the use of the Comintern as "an instrument of the foreign policy of Soviet Russia," as Brockway charged in his pamphlet on Barcelona, more criticism of the state of affairs in the USSR was starting to appear in the *New Leader*. A magazine section included a review of Max Eastman's *The End of Socialism in Russia*. The reviewer, William Warbey, conceded that its author was "unbalanced by hatred of Stalinism" but went on to cast doubt on the claims made in Pat Sloan's *Soviet Democracy*, recently published by Gollancz as part of the Left Book Club series:

> It is precisely on this question of democracy, of the extent to which the dictatorship of the proletariat is, in fact as well as in theory, a democracy for the vast majority of the people, or is, on the other hand, the dictatorship of a small section of the proletariat over the rest, that Sloan is most

unsatisfactory. He is particularly shaky on the fundamental question of the right to the expression of opposition opinion."[42]

Yet just how difficult it was for at least some in the ILP to appreciate the real state of affairs in the USSR is illustrated by Maxton's June 1937 review of Trotsky's *The Revolution Betrayed*. Maxton was willing to concede that "though Trotsky has not justified his title, he has made out a case that deserves the earnest consideration of every active Socialist and Communist in Russia and elsewhere. Stalin should weigh it carefully and consider whether some parts of the criticism are not justified."[43] Ironically, Maxton's display of optimistic faith in the power of reasoned critique was published just days before the CPGB's *Daily Worker* ran the banner headline "Red Army Traitors Executed," shortly followed by an article by Page Arnot titled "The Trial of the Eight Traitors—And Why."[44]

At the same time, though, signs of the emergence of a much more critical view of Russia had already begun to appear. In the issue of the *New Leader* that reported Smillie's death, an issue published the same day as Arnot's article in the *Worker*, Brockway's editorial "Something Wrong in Russia" asked how the trials could be explained. Did the Russian leaders understand "the setback which has been given to the cause of Socialism in all countries?" It seemed that all who were critical of the Popular Front policy "must be treated like fascists" and "dismissed as Trotskyists," he complained. "And this in the name of 'democracy'!"[45] The following week, denouncing the charges being brought against leaders of the POUM as a "frame-up," Brockway emphatically predicted that "**the repetition of the tactic in Spain will destroy what little authority the Communist Parties retain.**" He went on to note that Brailsford, whose name was again appearing from time to time in the *New Leader*, had once been "sympathetic to the Communist line in Spain." Now, disillusioned, the former editor was writing of the Soviet purges that what had really happened would never be known "because in Russia there is neither honest justice nor free discussion."[46]

While in mid-July, the *Daily Worker* greeted the new electoral law in Russia as a guarantee of democracy, Brockway, writing in the *New Leader*, continued to denounce both what he saw as the "Communist conspiracy against P.O.U.M." and the shooting of the Russian generals. He concluded, citing the *New Statesman*, that "**it is the vice of dictatorship that there is no definite line between a difference of policy and treason, and no way of pressing one's policy except by plotting against the head of the State.**"[47]

In November, responding to claims about what were said to be the first democratic elections in Russia since the revolution, the *New Leader* commented:

The unreal "democracy" of these elections is not the democracy which Russia needs. Russia needs proletarian democracy—democracy, first, within the organisation of the Communist Party so that freedom of expression in determining policy will be permitted; democracy, second, within the State so that the working masses may freely read and discuss the issues of Socialist policy and decide the line to be followed.

In the same issue, Maxton urged the Soviet leaders and "their representatives in this and other lands" to consider whether their "present tactics of ruthless suppression and unrestrained slander of those who dare to offer even friendly criticism is in the best interests of World Socialism, the working-class movement, or the Soviet Union itself."[48] And, on the eve of Christmas, the *Leader* concluded that "it is time that the Working Class Movement made clear to the Soviet authorities the opinion of the mass of workers in all countries."[49] Criticism along the same lines continued into the new year, with Brockway asking: "Does anyone believe . . . that if real proletarian democracy existed in Russia, or even real democracy in its Communist Party, it would be possible for any dangerous movement of sabotage against the Social Revolution to lift its head there?"[50]

Six weeks later, C. A. Smith made one of the most outspoken attacks on the Russian dictator to appear in the *New Leader*. It was, he said, "curious that the Communist Party should support two men each of whom have killed more communists than any other man who ever lived; Chiang-kai-Shek it supports 'critically'; Stalin it supports entirely uncritically."[51] When another trial, with Bukharin among the accused, began, the *New Leader* editor expressed the belief that "few Socialists who know the prisoners and their records will be able to believe that they have been guilty of the charges made."[52]

On 11 March, a letter to Stalin was dispatched signed by the four ILP MPs and Brockway. It was published in the *Leader* on the same day under the headline "STALIN—STOP! A Powerful Appeal to Moscow from the I.L.P. M.Ps." Brockway would later explain that the letter was written following a discussion with "Jay Lovestone, the leader of the Communist Opposition in America, and he urged me that the duty of issuing a supreme appeal to Stalin to save the honour of Socialism by stopping the 'terror' rested with the I.L.P."[53] The letter began by asserting that the signatories were among the first British workers in 1917 "to hail the victory of the Russian workers." They were now shocked by the recent trials in the U.S.S.R. and "compelled to protest." They could never be convinced of the charges; "the inconceivable character of the alleged crimes not only fail to convince—they have the opposite effect."[54]

Were the charges true, the letter continued, they should have to conclude that "there was something inherently wrong with the Russian Revolution to attract such degenerate types to the top of the ladder of leadership"—a notion they unreservedly rejected. The trials were not examples of "working-class justice" but "an outrageous travesty on the most elementary human rights and a bestial crime" resulting from "the system of bureaucracy which has grown up since the time of Lenin." Stalin was urged to "stop these trials and killings" and to "empty the Soviet prisons of the workers now languishing in them—and restore U.S.S.R. to its rightful place—the vanguard of humanity." As well as appearing in the *Leader* and as an appendix to the NAC's annual report, the letter was published as a leaflet titled *The Moscow Trials: Text of a Letter Written to M. Stalin by the Independent Labour Party's MPs.*[55]

In the *New Leader*, Brockway wrote that "the question mark over Russia is whether the Socialist economic basis beneath will succeed in expressing itself politically, or whether the bureaucracy will destroy the Socialist basis first." The following month, he took note of a motion, submitted by one branch of the ILP for consideration at the upcoming annual conference, proposing that, on the basis of "the information available," the party endorse the results of the Moscow trials. Brockway predicted that such a motion was likely to find little support among delegates, who were bound to "find it difficult to believe that six thousand persons, many of them with revolutionary records of undoubted sincerity," had all managed to become "the tools of the Capitalist class."[56] It is not surprising, then, that in its report on the 1938 annual conference, the *New Leader* noted that "one voice was raised in the Conference for silence about Russia when we cannot praise. One voice was raised in defence of the Moscow Trials. There were only two votes in 111 for this view." The report continued, "Nevertheless, an overwhelming majority held that the basis of a Workers' and Socialist State remains in Russia and demands working-class action to defend it against Imperialist aggression."[57]

Coming on the heels of a resounding condemnation of the Moscow trials, this opinion reflected a gap that had long existed within the ILP, namely, that between the suspicion and often hostile disdain in which the CPGB and, to a lesser extent, the Comintern were held and the esteem that the Soviet Union itself enjoyed. Yet the combined effect of Stalin's show trials and the experience of the Spanish war—above all, the implications of the events in Barcelona and what followed—had shifted attitudes in the ILP. While no doubt the trials and the events in Spain were the major catalysts for the growing disquiet about the Soviet Union, there were other causes for concern as well. In his 1938 volume *Workers' Front*, under the heading "The Sickness of the Labour Movement," Brockway wrote: "Even in Soviet Russia where workers' power was gloriously won in 1917, the increased differentiation of income and the reintroduction of the right of inheritance indicate a retreat from the classless society of Socialism rather than an advance towards it."[58]

At the same time, as long as the civil war in Spain continued, the ILP faced a dilemma. With the British and French governments pursuing policies of "non-intervention" and Fascist Italy and Nazi Germany showing no restraint in their support of Franco, the Soviet Union was the sole supplier of military resources to the Spanish Republic. Any criticism of it could therefore be presented as an attempt to undermine the only powerful friend of those resisting fascism in Spain. At the same time, how could the purges and show trials be ignored? The ILP could not be seen as condoning such appalling actions.

As events in Spain unfolded, it also became ever harder to maintain a line of separation between the USSR, as an exemplary workers' state, and the Comintern—a gap that, for some, had narrowed almost to the point of extinction. The cover of John McGovern's 1938 pamphlet *Terror in Spain* carried as a subtitle "How the Communist International Destroyed Working-Class Unity, Undermined the Fight Against Franco, and Suppressed the Social Revolution." In it, McGovern attacked "Cheka Limited," calling it "the vicious machine of Comintern." (Although the Russian secret police had not been called the Cheka since 1922, the term was still widely used in this sense.) McGovern explicitly linked Cheka-style activities in Spain to the Soviet Union. "Russia has bought her way into Spain," he wrote. "In return for Russian assistance in arms, Comintern has been given this tyrannical power and she uses it to imprison, torture, and murder Socialists who do not accept the Communist line." His pamphlet concluded: "If Socialism means what Moscow imposes, I would not want it. The Socialism I work for must give freedom, not tyranny, to the workers. All tyrannies I will denounce."[59]

McGovern was a particularly outspoken critic of the Soviet Union. Following the Munich crisis of late September 1938, however, when Fenner Brockway addressed the Holborn and St. Pancras Group of the Peace Pledge Union on pacifism as it related to the Left, he left no doubt about his views. He told the participants that, as regards the Moscow trials, "every allegation which could be tested because it related to some incident supposed to have taken place outside Russia has been found to be false on thorough investigation." In Spain, the Communists had engaged in "lying, forgery and assassination against another working-class party, the P.O.U.M., because of a disagreement in policy." He repeated his contention that in Russia, there was a conflict between "the socialist economy" and the "system of bureaucracy."[60] His assessment was perhaps indebted, at least in part, to Orwell's *Homage to Catalonia*.

Orwell in Spain and in the ILP

Perhaps more than anyone else in the twentieth century, George Orwell came to personify the left-wing rejection of Stalinism. There would be no more powerful support for the ILP's position on the Spanish Civil War than his classic account, *Homage to Catalonia*. Within days of its publication in April 1938, it was advertised in the *New Leader* as "the most exciting of any book that has yet come out of Spain." The following week, it was reviewed by John McNair, who quoted extensively from the book and said of the author, "So far as I know he is a member of no political party."[61]

Orwell had, of course, served with ILP volunteers in the POUM militia, under his real name, Eric Blair. According to his biographer Bernard Crick, Orwell was under the impression that papers from a left-wing organization were needed in order to enter Spain. Orwell declined to join the International Brigade until he had seen the Spanish situation for himself, and Pollitt, the CPGB's general secretary, to whom he had been introduced by John Strachey, refused to help him. Orwell then rang the ILP, with which he claimed "some slight connections, mainly personal," and Brockway gave him letters of introduction to John McNair, the ILP representative in Barcelona. Orwell was also put in touch with ILPers who were waiting to depart for Spain, but he went on ahead, reaching Barcelona on 26 December 1936. (The ILP contingent arrived two weeks later.) Once in Spain, he accepted McNair's offer to join the POUM militia.[62]

Orwell's *The Road to Wigan Pier* was published in March 1937, several months after his departure, and was reviewed for the *New Leader* by Ethel Mannin under the heading "Sense and a Lot of Nonsense." While critical of Orwell's "particular aversion" to the ILP, which he regarded "as middle class and snobbish," she declared the book "worthwhile for its first part," in which Orwell documents the appalling conditions of the working class in England's industrial north. Mannin felt that Orwell was "a good Socialist," despite his "curious fixed ideas" that socialists were all too often "'bearded fruit-juice drinkers,' 'sandal-wearers,' nudists, sex-maniacs, and heaven knows what." She went on to tell *New Leader* readers that "he is at this moment fighting with P.O.U.M. (in Bob Edwards' contingent) on the Aragon Front, and it may well be that he has already outgrown the confused and contradictory ideas set forth in the second part of this book."[63]

Evidently, George Kopp, who commanded ILP volunteers on the Aragon Front, was pleased with Orwell's service. In a letter written on 16 April 1937, he mentioned "Eric Blair," along with Bob Smillie and Paddy Donovan, as those "who behaved exceptionally well."[64] The 1937 ILP summer school, held in Letchworth, opened on 5 August with a two-minute silence for Smillie, who had died in June. Then both Orwell and Donovan spoke, Orwell with some difficulty because of a bullet wound he had sustained in the throat. Other former members of the ILP contingent in Spain were also in attendance.[65]

Reporting on the summer school session, the *New Leader* noted that one of its features had been

> the mounting revelation of the reactionary character of Communist Party policy in Spain. Most of the I.L.P. students were aware of the position in broad outline, but the piling up of facts, first by John McNair and then by Jeanne Antonino, supplemented by the simple direct statements of the members of the I.L.P. contingent, have produced an overwhelming effect.[66]

These revelations were both reflected and reinforced in *Homage to Catalonia*, with its sometimes trenchant criticisms of the Spanish Communists. As Buchanan points out, even if *Homage to Catalonia* was Orwell's "least successful book" in his own lifetime, it was for the ILP, a vindication—from an independent source, at least at the time it was written—of the anti-Stalinist position the party had adopted.[67]

When, in September 1937, the *Leader* published an account of what had happened in Barcelona, based on the recollections of some of the members of the ILP contingent, the writer emphasized that Orwell was "not a member of the I.L.P."[68] Crick speculates that it was the positive response of the ILP to *Homage to Catalonia* that prompted Orwell to join the party, rather than remaining "an ILP fellow-traveller." Orwell became an ILP member on 13 June 1938, and his "Why I Joined the ILP" appeared in the *Leader* on 24 June. It was, he said, the only British party that "aims at anything I should regard as Socialism," although he emphasized that he also hoped for the electoral success of Labour.[69] Two weeks later, Orwell reviewed Frank Jellinik's *The Civil War in Spain*, describing it as "an excellent book" in spite of its unfairness to the POUM and the fact that it was written from the perspective of "a Communist or Communist partisan."[70]

Orwell's membership in the ILP was not to last long: he left the party over its stance after the outbreak of war.[71] By that time, at least some in the ILP had abandoned any hope that the Soviet Union could be portrayed as some kind of exemplary "workers' state," and there was little appetite within the party for more attempts at cooperation with the CPGB. In September 1938, the *New Leader* carried a report of a visit to the CPGB congress, whose writer said that he found "the unifomity of the speakers absolutely terrifying":

> The C.P. is evidently as much an automaton as any Nazi party. The delegates acted as one man, sang the "International," clapped, shouted "Hurrah," stood up in respectful show of admiration, waiting for signals to cheer or sing, just as you would expect a trained corps of Nazis to do.
>
> There can be no hope that a party of this kind can bring human liberty.[72]

Of course, disillusion triggered by the Moscow trials and the executions that followed extended far beyond the ILP. No doubt Brockway was right when he said that "reaction has gone wide and deep into the ranks of the working class."[73] In October 1938, another trial took place, in Barcelona—this one of prominent members of the POUM. In April 1939, in its report to the ILP's annual conference, the NAC declared that the trial had "disproved the infamous slanders made against our brother-Party by the Communist International," which had claimed that POUM members were agents of Franco and had "treacherously deserted the front." The report went on to note that, although those tried had been convicted for their part in "the Barcelona May 1937 resistance to the attacks ... on the workers' rights," they had subsequently "found refuge in France."[74] In a letter to Raymond Postgate, written on 21 October 1938 from Marrakesh, Orwell left no doubt about his own view of the proceedings. "The accusations against the P.O.U.M. in Spain are only a by-product of the Russian Trotskyist trials," he stated, adding that "from the start every kind of lie, including flagrant absurdities, has been circulated in the Communist press."[75]

Other ILP Critics of the Soviet Union

The Moscow trials and, above all, the events in Spain were the major issues that began to generate criticism of the USSR. Although most members of the ILP continued to regard the Soviet Union as "a Workers' State in which the foundations of a Socialist Society have been laid," notions that all was not as ILPers thought it should be were beginning to be expressed increasingly in the final three years of the 1930s.[76] As Jennie Lee put it in a review of Walter Citrine's book *I Search for Truth in Russia*, "Sensible people have a healthy scepticism of the 'pure sugar-candy' versions of the Soviet Union that the Communist Press and propagandists pour forth."[77]

In May 1936, for example, there was a letter in the *New Leader* from Mrs. G. Carling of Perth who was "uneasy" about new divorce law proposals in Russia, which seemed in danger of worsening the position of women.[78] Six months later, the *New Leader* carried a review of John Strachey's *The Theory and Practice of Socialism*. The reviewer, William Everett, conceded that the book had some good features but noted that it made three false assertions: that socialism had been established in Russia since 1928; that effective democracy now existed there; and that socialism did not necessarily entail economic equality, which was neither practicable nor desirable. He also criticized the "careful suppression of the facts about the C.P. in Catalonia" and regretted Strachey's "degradation" into "a C.P. Yes-man."[79]

The USSR still won plenty of support and admiration in the *New Leader*, but critics were beginning to be much more prominent. One early critic was

Ethel Mannin, whose articles and reviews appeared fairly frequently in the *New Leader*.[80] After a seven thousand-mile "unconducted tour" of Russia, she reported her conclusion that it was "not yet the Promised Land," though still a "Promising Land." She did, however, note inequalities, poor living conditions, and the privileges of commissars, and concluded, "Taking all these things into consideration, not excluding its militarism and its foreign policy, it is impossible not to see Russia to-day as a gigantic question mark, and anxiously ask concerning it—Quo Vadis?"[81]

Mannin's criticisms triggered complaints. One letter in the *New Leader* urged her to "leave this sort of unfairness to anti-Socialist propagandists." Mannin defended herself in the same issue. That "a skilled engineer or great artist" should enjoy superior living conditions, she argued, was something that would not happen in "a true Socialist State (which the U.S.S.R. is to my mind considerably short of)."[82]

The *Leader* reported criticism of her article in a Moscow radio broadcast. The paper rejected the charge that it was "anti-Soviet" and revealed that the top official Mannin criticized for living in luxury was Litvinov, the Commissar for Foreign Affairs, whose country home she had visited during her trip. A week later, Brockway defended her in an editorial, rejecting the allegation that the paper was "giving vent to all kinds of anti-Soviet propaganda." This was nonsense. Since Mannin's article, the *New Leader* had included "columns extolling Russia." Brockway insisted that "we respect Russia as a powerful Workers' State, the greatest thing that has happened in history, strong enough to be criticised as well as acclaimed."[83]

The USSR might have still been a "workers' state" at the beginning of 1936, but by the time the 1940 ILP conference met, the Soviet government had become, in the words of a NAC motion attacking the Russian invasion of Finland, "the Stalinist regime."[84] Yet a residual belief in the USSR remained for many. In the preface to the postwar (1947) edition of *Inside the Left*, Brockway would deny being "unsympathetic to Russia." Though a critic of "the part it has played in international affairs and its repression of liberty at home," he had "never lost sight of the overriding consideration that private Capitalism has been ended there." His "criticism of Russia's foreign policy and its denial of liberty" were, he went on, "if anything, stronger now than when this book was written." However, reflecting a time when the beginning of the Cold War, as it is seen today, seemed all too likely to result in a "hot" one in the near future, he added,

> I feel that the supremely important duty of Socialists today, both as a matter of justice and for the sake of the peace of the world, is to retain an objective international attitude towards the power-politics struggle which threatens to bring war again, and not allow themselves to accept

without unprejudiced examination the case against Russia which the politicians, the press and the wireless broadcasts are piling up.[85]

Perhaps the best illustration of the still starkly divided attitudes within the ILP towards Soviet Russia is to be found in the October 1939 edition of the new internal discussion organ, *Between Ourselves*. By this time, Stalin's pact with Hitler had, in many ILP eyes, further discredited the standing of the USSR. Nevertheless, David Thomas, who claimed an ILP membership extending over forty years, wrote a laudatory account with the title "What Russia Means." In the same issue, Don McGregor responded to Thomas's article in "Russia—Reflections." Rejecting Thomas's idealization of the USSR, McGregor concluded: "If Russia is a 'Socialist State' then Marxism must find another name to define what is really meant by 'workers' democracy' (which does not exist in Russia) and most of us will be pleased to renounce the label 'Socialist.'"[86]

By the time this edition of *Between Ourselves* appeared, the war that the ILP had warned about for so long had broken out, and, once again, the party was taking a stand against it—opposition that provoked yet a further decline in membership. In the next chapter, we return to 1935 to explore the ILP's attempts to develop a united front both with the CPGB and with the Labour Party.

20

Calls for Unity as War Approaches

Despite the arguments of Jowett and other opponents of the new revolutionary policy, many in the ILP had come to view Parliament as inextricably bound up with a hostile capitalist state. In their eyes, the role of Parliament in the struggle for socialism had been downgraded. This did not, however, mean that electoral politics no longer had any significance. After all, if the party could not secure substantial support in the ballot box, which simply required supporters to take a few minutes every so often to cast a vote, what prospects were there for the success of an extraparliamentary policy requiring sustained commitment and active participation? All the same, the results of the party's electoral efforts were not at all encouraging—a circumstance that was the source of no small concern.

The 1935 General Election

The only general election falling between the ILP's disaffiliation from Labour and the outbreak of war in 1939 (or indeed until 1945) took place on 14 November 1935. Prior to this, the ILP had contested three by-elections, none of which it managed to win. On two occasions, the Labour Party candidate was returned, while in the case of the Kilmarnock by-election, the Left's vote was split between Labour and the ILP, which allowed the return of a supporter of the National Government with a minority of the vote.

The NAC policy statement delivered at the ILP's 1935 annual conference had foreseen the party putting up candidates in the upcoming general election, not only in areas where the ILP was strong but also in several constituencies regarded as "special circumstances," including one in which "a notoriously reactionary Labour Party candidate" had been adopted as that party's candidate.[1] In the end, the ILP ran candidates in just seventeen contests.

In the weeks preceding the election, with the Abyssinian crisis at its height, the ILP actively pursued its antiwar campaign. On Sunday, 15 September, London's St. Pancras branch held a march from Mornington Crescent to a rally in Regent's Park under the slogan "Abyssinia! Workers' Action or World

War?"[2] On Thursday, 26 September, the London Divisional Council held a meeting at Memorial Hall at which Brockway, Maxton, and Gaster, among others, gave speeches.[3] The party produced a four-page election manifesto that attacked the "war-minded Government," which, it predicted, would return to "warlike measures" if the negotiations with France and Italy over Abyssinia failed to "recognise British Imperialist interests." The manifesto made it clear that the ILP rejected League sanctions and rearmament, describing them as "futile schemes to reconstruct or patch-up Capitalism" by the National Government and by Labour. Anticipating workers' resistance, it also warned of the possibility that a fascist dictatorship could come "to maintain class privilege against the revolts and amidst the ruins of the present system." In places where no ILP candidate was running, workers were advised to vote for any Labour Party candidates prepared to pledge consistent support "by vote as well as by voice" for "Peace and Justice for the Unemployed—as well as the fundamental objective of Socialism."[4]

Some ILP parliamentary candidates—like Brockway, who ran in Norwich—emphasized the party's wider objectives, while others placed much greater stress on domestic issues such as unemployment benefits.[5] Although Jowett, running in Bradford, announced himself as "an anti-war candidate," his election address concentrated on bread-and-butter questions. Jowett also devoted about a third of his address to explaining why he was not an "official" Labour Party candidate. He reiterated his well-established objections to the pledge required by Labour since 1931. This meant, he said, that as a Labour candidate, he would not have been able to "honestly make a promise to the electors to support any proposal."[6]

The final issue of the *R.P.C. Bulletin* presented the ILP's election strategy as hopelessly sectarian. Having cooperated with the CPGB in developing a united front, the ILP should have been working for "the only immediate alternative," namely, "the return of a Labour Government." Instead, the *Bulletin* concluded, its tactic had been to undermine and demoralize the mass resistance to the National Government "on a pretext of putting forward a revolutionary line."[7]

The ILP was successful only in four constituencies, all in Glasgow. Maxton, Buchanan, and McGovern were re-elected, with Campbell Stephen as the only new MP. In both North Lanark, contested by ILP candidate Jennie Lee, and East Bradford, where Jowett was the candidate, the Labour Party took enough votes to deny the ILP a victory.[8] Despite this decidedly tepid electoral performance, there was no sign of repentance from the ILP. The following month, the *New Leader* made it clear that the party was "not prepared to follow the Communist Party in surrendering [its] liberty to voice, vote, and act for its principles in order to join the big battalions," arguing that "such big battalions tied to a policy of compromise would melt away in a crisis."⁹ It seems very unlikely that anyone reading this in December 1935 would have anticipated that, within only two years, the ILP would be contemplating rejoining the Labour Party. First, however, the ILP had to exhaust its attempts to bring about a united front that included both Labour and the CPGB.

The ILP Calls for a United Front

Several months before the general election of November 1935, Brockway and Maxton, for the ILP, and Pollitt and Gallacher, for the CPGB, had agreed on electoral cooperation, which would include joint meetings designed to generate "mass feeling to bring pressure to bear on Labour Party candidates in favour of the united front and a militant policy."¹⁰ While many Labour Party members favoured such cooperation, there was very little chance that Labour would agree to any activity that involved working with the Communists.

In 1933, the National Joint Council of Labour, which represented both the Labour Party and the TUC, had responded decisively to proposals for a united front. Its policy statement *Democracy Versus Dictatorship* "stated the case against Communism and Fascism with equal vigour," as Jupp succinctly puts it. The following year, the Labour Party conference banned any united action with the CPGB or with Communist "front" organizations without the National Executive Committee's approval—a very remote possibility.¹¹ Not that any of this deterred the ILP.

The NAC's report to the 1936 conference took heed of outcomes in the recent general election, in which the presence of rival candidates on the left had worked to the advantage of the Conservatives. The NAC recommended that, in the future, the ILP should "make the United Front proposals to other working class parties with the objective of eliminating the danger of a split vote and lessening the chances of the ruling class candidate." But this recommendation did not mean that the party leadership had any long-term hopes for Labour. "The sooner a Labour government with a working majority is returned," declared the NAC, "the sooner will the workers lose faith in Reformism."¹²

In August, the ILP wrote to the Labour, Communist, and Co-operative parties, a letter that was subsequently published as a leaflet titled *Get Round the Table*. In it, the ILP leaders claimed that there was "an overwhelming demand for united action among the rank and file of all sections of the working class." The letter urged the formation of a joint committee, which would draw up plans for united action and make arrangements to ensure that only one "working-class" candidate ran in each constituency. Such "an immediate alliance of all working class Parties," it noted, had taken place in France and Spain, although there the alliance had been extended to include "non-working class elements."¹³

This last remark represented a very muted rejection by the ILP of the "popular front" approach. And when, around the same time, Eleanor Rathbone, speaking at the ILP summer school, called for "a Popular Front from Harry Pollitt to Winston Churchill," the *New Leader* confined itself to commenting that "Miss Rathbone's faith in Winston Churchill was the most surprising feature of the lecture."[14] In any event, the NAC was obliged to report to the 1937 annual conference that the Labour Party had rejected the *Get Round the Table* proposal. The Co-operative Party had simply not replied, while the CPGB had "put forward the alternative course of affiliation to the Labour Party."[15]

Meanwhile, "critical support" was given to Labour candidates in by-elections at Derby and Balham. The Communist Party's pursuit of Labour Party affiliation, doomed as it turned out to be, left the NAC in the rather odd position of agreeing, by 10 votes to 2, to support the Communists' right to affiliate while urging ILPers to explain that their party could not follow the same course because of the "restrictive conditions involved."[16] The prospects for the ILP's United Front initiative looked anything but promising.

As ever, outwardly at least, the ILP remained optimistic that a degree of unity could be achieved. Back in March 1933, Brockway had given his *New Leader* editorial the title "Hope for Unity at Last," and three weeks later, on the paper's front page, he announced, in another headline, "United Action Is Coming!" All sections of the working-class movement could agree on resistance to fascism, war, and wage cuts and could campaign for the abolition of the means test for unemployment benefits.[17] Yet, three years later, there was still little to justify such optimism. As we have already seen, the ILP was struggling to maintain its own unity in these years—and not with any great success.

Brockway would, in retrospect, write that "the most impressive co-operation between the I.L.P and the Communist Party" occurred in connection with the organization of counterdemonstrations against the provocative attempt by Oswald Mosley and his British Union of Fascists to march through London's East End—then an area with a large Jewish population—on 4 October 1936.[18] But how far what happened can accurately be regarded as a clear example of cooperation between the two parties is debatable.

For most of the Left, the episode was seen in the context of the war in Spain—particularly the siege of Madrid and the "¡No pasarán!" ("They shall not pass!") speech of the iconic Communist orator "La Pasionaria."[19] As Robert Benewick puts it in his study of the British fascist movement, the East End was "transformed into an expectant Madrid."[20] This interpretive parallel is evident in the way that the "Battle of Cable Street"—which subsequently became such an emotive reference point for so many on the British Left—was reported in the press at the time. The day after the march, the Communist Party's *Daily*

Worker headlined its report "Mosley Did Not Pass: East London Routs the Fascists," an allusion that was echoed at the end of that week by the *New Leader*'s "Mosley Did Not Pass! What Happened in East London and Why."[21] Similarly, when the ILP published what was described on its cover as a "Souvenir of the East London Workers' Victory over Fascism," it did so under the title *They Did Not Pass: 300,000 Workers Say No to Mosley*.[22]

The ILP did not hesitate in taking a large share of the credit for the protest. According to the *New Leader*, "A great demonstration organised by the I.L.P. in East London sent a telegram to the Home Secretary demanding that the march should be stopped. But the I.L.P. was prepared for refusal. It announced in the Press that it had called the East London workers to mass in Aldgate in such numbers that the march would become impossible."[23] The *Leader* did at least mention, however, that the Communist Party had made the same call. In contrast, the *Daily Worker*'s report ignored the ILP, stating simply that "the Communist Party had appealed to the workers to throng Aldgate and Cable Street."[24]

The ILP's "souvenir" pamphlet began by celebrating the way in which "East London workers irrespective of their race, or creed, irrespective of their political affiliations, Jews and Gentiles, Communists, Socialists and Labour Party supporters demonstrated to the whole world that the best traditions of East London's militant past were safe in their hands." It again gave equal credit to the Communist Party for the call for the counterdemonstration, while noting that neither the opposition of the Labour Party nor the advice of the Jewish Board of Deputies, which had recommended that people stay away, had deterred the "rank and file."[25]

Mentioning both "the I.L.P. and Communist sections," the local *East London Advertiser* reported that a large number of men "had met at Aldgate to take part in the I.L.P. demonstration." But it also reported on the representations made the previous week by mayors of East London to the Home Secretary calling for the march to be banned.[26] Benewick likewise draws attention to the "quieter forces at work," including the efforts of J. H. Hall, the MP for Whitechapel, and George Lansbury, the mayor of Poplar (and, until the previous year, the leader of the Labour Party). He also notes that the Jewish People's Council had collected one hundred thousand signatures on a petition demanding that the BUF march not be allowed to go ahead, describing the ILP as "more active" than the Communists in organizing the resistance to the march.[27]

Barricades had been erected in and around Cable Street, and there was considerable violence when the police attempted to clear them. But, in the end, the five-thousand-strong fascist march, which posed the near-certainty of serious bloodshed had it been allowed to proceed, was diverted away from the East End by the commissioner of the Metropolitan Police. Brockway later wrote, in *Inside the Left*, that even though the Communist Party was stronger in East London than was the ILP, "by chance our propaganda had the bigger effect" because *The Star*, a London evening newspaper, had run an article headlined "I.L.P. Call to Workers."[28]

Up to this point, it had been the ILP that took the lead in calling for a "united front," but soon there was an initiative from another quarter. It came just a few weeks after the Cable Street incident.

The Socialist League's Unity Campaign

Encouraged by the significant vote for unity at the 1936 Labour Party conference, the Socialist League now took up that cause. It had been formed in 1932, largely by former ILPers who chose to remain with Labour, including Brailsford and Wise. Four years later, the League's most dominant figure was Stafford Cripps. Appointed Solicitor General and knighted by Ramsay MacDonald in 1930, as well as one of the few Labour MPs to survive the 1931 general election, Cripps had refused to serve in the National Government. Subsequently, he had moved swiftly to the radical Left. Meetings of the Socialist League with the CPGB and the ILP took place. It was agreed to join negotiations in early November 1936 and the League's executive committee endorsed the Unity Campaign. A joint statement with the other two participants called for "facilities for the provision of arms" to the Spanish Republic to be made available.[29]

The *New Leader* greeted the venture with its usual optimism on New Year's Day 1937, in "Unity of the Left?" This was soon followed with the front-page article "Unity Move This Week-End?" and the hopeful headline "Campaign by Socialist League, I.L.P. and C.P. Proposed: Mass Support Certain." News of "The Unity Manifesto," the joint statement put out by the three parties, and an article by Aneurin Bevan explaining why he supported unity followed.[30] At this point, the optimism seemed fully justified. Meetings were well attended and enthusiastic, with the most important of them including addresses by the three leading figures of the Socialist League, the ILP, and the CPGB—respectively, Cripps, Maxton, and Pollitt. This seemed, as Cohen says, "a signal of hope."[31] But from the start, the Socialist League's initiative faced major problems, which only grew with time.

The Communist Party was hoping to achieve its goal of Labour Party affiliation. This was supported by the Socialist League—but it set off alarms in the Labour Party, especially in the highest echelons. Whether Ben Pimlott is right to say that "Cripps, ever open to the influence of a new *guru*, especially a conspicuously working-class one, had indeed fallen under Pollitt's spell," there is little doubt that this was how most of the Labour Party leadership saw it.[32] The CPGB had wanted to base the campaign on the participating organizations seeking Labour Party affiliation and on support for a popular front. The ILP would accept neither. The Labour Party would need to change in a radical and democratic direction before the ILP could consider reaffiliation, the party's leaders argued. As for the popular front, "we are not prepared to become allies with the Liberal Party, Tory 'democrats' or other sections of the Capitalist class."[33]

There was some support for unity from *Labour's Northern Voice*. Reporting the Manchester launch of the campaign on 24 January, the *Voice* gave front-page support under the headline "Unity for Attack! Close the Ranks for the March to Socialism." The former ILP-supporting and now Scottish Socialist Party paper, *Forward*, was much more skeptical. Dollan, expressed his doubts about the campaign in "Maxton's Latest Move." The Scottish Socialist Party had been invited to participate in the campaign but wanted "more assurances" about real unity. This would best be achieved, Dollan said, if the ILP were to reaffiliate with Labour. "But," he concluded, "can anyone tell me why it should be made a condition of a scheme for working-class unity in Great Britain that the contracting parties refrain from any general criticism of the policy of the Soviet Union or its government?"[34]

The huge differences between the ILP and the CPGB over events in Russia—and especially over the war in Spain—made it difficult for them to subordinate these issues to the interests of domestic unity. But the ILP certainly wished to do so. Already by February 1937, Brockway was urging that Spain must not be allowed to undermine the unity campaign. He cited a letter from McNair, the ILP's representative in Barcelona, who wrote, "We must use the unity in Britain to bring unity in Spain rather than allow the disunity in Spain to bring disunity to Britain." McNair had suggested unity meetings in Valencia, Barcelona, and Madrid with Maxton, Pollitt, and Cripps, "but I fear that it is not yet practical politics," wrote Brockway.[35] In this area, things could only get worse for the Unity Campaign. One has only to recall the mutual recriminations, and especially the content and tone, of *Daily Worker* attacks on the ILP later in 1937 to appreciate how difficult it was for these two advocates of unity to maintain a semblance of it in practice.

The third constituent of the alliance, the Socialist League, soon had its own troubles. On New Year's Day, William Mellor set out the League's objectives in "What We Stand For in the Struggle for Socialism" in the first issue of the *Tribune*, which he edited. The paper was set up by Cripps and fellow Labour MP George Strauss to back the League's Unity Campaign. The first issue also included a review of books on Spain by Brockway—which might have seemed a promising start in the direction of unity.[36] Much less promising was the fact that a substantial minority of members voted against supporting the Unity Campaign at a special Socialist League conference in mid-January.

When added to the abstentions, they slightly outnumbered those approving the Unity Manifesto.[37]

Soon thereafter, the Labour Party NEC announced that the League was to be disaffiliated from the party. This proved to be the beginning of the end for the Socialist League. It tried to continue the campaign by relying on individual members to promote its aims in the Labour Party, but Labour's NEC was determined to prevent any further moves to achieve unity with the Communists. It announced that from 1 June, League membership would be incompatible with remaining within the Labour Party.[39]

The *New Leader*'s optimism still continued: "Unity Can Win," it insisted at the beginning of April. But the following month, the League's conference was faced with a difficult decision. Could the organization survive not only its disaffiliation but the expulsion of its members from the Labour Party? On the eve of the conference, the *Tribune* expressed the hope that the conference would not abandon the Unity Campaign, but only a week later, it carried an article by Cripps on why the League had decided to dissolve.

Reassessing Unity

By the summer of 1937, a number of things were becoming increasingly apparent. The ILP was not on the way to replacing the CPGB as a "revolutionary socialist" party. Still less were supporters of Labour going to abandon "reformism" and come over en masse to the ILP. The fate of the Socialist League's Unity Campaign confirmed that Labour had no intention of allowing affiliation by the Communists or of taking part in any sort of united action with them. The notion that the ILP could cooperate with the CPGB while retaining its own independent policies on matters outside a unity agreement was increasingly difficult to maintain in light of the extreme discord over Spain.

It was also evident that it was working with the Communists that Labour objected to. Cooperation with the ILP was quite a different matter. So much was clear from the NAC's report to the annual conference during Easter 1938:

> The failure of the Unity Campaign was due to (a) the retreat by the Socialist League and the Labour Party participants when threatened with disciplinary action (b) the political conflicts between the I.L.P. and Russian policy, the persecution of the P.O.U.M. and other questions, and (c) the antagonism within the Labour Party to the C.P. arising from the Moscow Trials and the "purge" in Russia.

This, the report continued, "points to the desirability of the I.L.P., when the occasion arises, approaching the Labour Party for united action independent of the Communist Party."[40]

The previous November, Brockway had submitted "A Survey of the Party Position," marked "Confidential," to the NAC. He began by maintaining that the ILP had been right to disaffiliate five years earlier. Before disaffiliation, he wrote, ILP policy and membership had been "vague." In recent years, the party had become "a conscious political unit" with a "clearly defined political line." In these new circumstances, affiliation was now "a tactical question." Weighing the pros and cons of reaffiliation, he saw the advantages of a return to Labour as threefold: it would bring greater contact with and influence on a larger organization, provide a chance to increase membership, and lead to a larger circulation for the *New Leader* and other ILP literature.[41]

It would be necessary, Brockway continued, to insist that the ILP be able to continue as an "organised unit" with its own newspaper and other publications, to voice its own policy on platform and in Parliament, and to criticize official policy "in a comradely spirit." He conceded that the party would have to forego the right to *vote* independently in Parliament, but this was something he would be prepared to accept. He stressed that the voting issue must not lead to another split in the ILP. On the contrary, possibilities for unity with other small socialist parties—including the Independent Socialist Party—should be pursued. "We have to convince these of the role of the I.L.P. as *the* Revolutionary Socialist Party in this country," he emphasized.[42]

Towards the end of the document, Brockway turned to the best way to approach the reaffiliation. The ILP must challenge Labour's policy aggressively, but "at the same time we must keep before ourselves and the workers the aim of Working Class Unity." Before making any further moves towards Labour, the ILP should seek an "electoral understanding" with it. The party had, said Brockway, little hope of defeating Labour candidates anywhere other than in Glasgow. He proposed seeking an agreement for the next general election whereby, in return for not contesting elections elsewhere, Labour would leave the four Glasgow seats—as well as North Lanark, East Bradford, and one of the Norwich seats—to the ILP.[43]

In December 1937, the NAC unanimously agreed that "the first necessity at the present moment is to concentrate on strengthening the I.L.P.," and it endorsed a motion to be put to the annual conference reiterating its desire for socialist unity with "a permanent structure for common action by the working class on class issues." This was approved by the 1938 conference, whose resolution on ILP policy read, in part: "An essential step towards securing the unity of the working class on a federal basis, either within the Labour Party or by a Workers' Front including the Labour Party is for Revolutionary Socialists to unite in one Revolutionary Socialist Party." The immediate task, the resolution concluded, was to "strengthen the I.L.P. as *the* Revolutionary Socialist Party of Britain."[44]

The ILP would continue to support the idea of a "Workers' Front." Brockway's lengthy book of that title was published in 1938. Here, he qualified the opposition to the Popular Front, including bourgeois parties. In his chapter titled "The Popular Front in France," Brockway maintained that the first step should have been the formation of a "Workers' Front Alliance between all the working-class forces, Socialist, Communists and Trade Unionists." This could have been followed by an "electoral understanding" with the Radical-Socialists to support each other's candidates in the second ballot without committing to any longer-term alliance. Though clearly, as Brockway pointed out, the French approach could not be applied in Britain with its simple plurality electoral system, the experience in France seemed sufficiently important to warrant a summary of its advantages in italics: "*This tactic, from the Workers' Front point of view, would have combined the advantages of obtaining the maximum vote against the reactionaries and Fascists without surrendering the right to carry on the class struggle and to seize any opportunity to carry through the social revolution.*"[45]

Meanwhile, the threat of war was growing.

The Approach of War and the Munich Agreement

Recalling the attitudes of the 1930s in her autobiography, Simone de Beauvoir wrote: "To sum it up in a nutshell, everyone on the Left, from Radicals to Communists, were simultaneously shouting 'Down with Fascism!' and 'Disarmament!'"[46] This was as true of the ILP as of the Left more generally. No one in the ILP was anything but an opponent of war, but only a minority were pacifists. For some, Spain had provided the crucial test. Brockway's account, written just a few years after that war ended, was clear: "The Spanish civil war compelled me to face up squarely to the pacifist philosophy which I continued to cherish." Faced with the proposal by Bob Edwards for an ILP contingent to fight against Franco, he knew that "this would have the support of the great majority of the membership" and realized that his support for it meant "a final break with pacifist traditions." He recalled that he "did not hesitate."[47]

Total distrust and rejection of British imperialism, whose record seemed to the ILP to differ hardly at all from that of fascism, was a hugely important factor in the approach of the ILP towards the coming war. A *New Leader* editorial in early 1937 could hardly have been clearer on this point:

> British Imperialism is as great a menace as German Fascism. It is a menace because British ownership of one-third of the earth's surface is a continual challenge to other nations, and we must not forget that within the British Empire, and particularly in India, the worst practices of Fascism are being applied to keep the peasants and workers in subjection.

Underlying both imperialism and fascism was the capitalist system: both were "an expression of capitalism."[48]

The ILP was critical of Labour Party support for—or failure to oppose—rearmament. This, the *New Leader* said, was "compelling thousands of Socialists to reconsider their position." On Christmas Eve 1937, the *Leader* ran an article under the headline "Last Xmas Before War?" By the following summer, it seemed as though that might well be the case, given Hitler's move against Czechoslovakia. In July, the paper highlighted the threat that this could lead to general war. At the beginning of September, its front page demanded, under the headline "Stop War!" that the brakes be applied, and by the month's end, the paper was attacking European leaders in "Betrayers All! Chamberlain, Hitler and the Whole Capitalist Gang" and was urging readers to "resist war."[49]

The Munich Agreement, which ceded part of Czechoslovakia to Germany, was signed by Britain, France, Germany, and Italy on 29 September 1938. Gidon Cohen has described how the Munich Agreement and the response of the ILP Parliamentary Group—and, more specifically, of Maxton and McGovern, to Chamberlain's role in it—led to "perhaps the most public controversy within the ILP during the 1930s."[50] The NAC, with Maxton chairing as usual, had met on 25 September and unanimously agreed on a statement, which was issued as a leaflet titled simply *Resist War!* The one-page statement called for opposition to a war that "would not be fought for Czechs, but for Capitalist profits" and would "immediately bring the destruction of those democratic liberties that now exist in Britain." Whereas, in 1914, resistance to war had been limited to only a "relatively small minority of the working class," the ILP now recognized the existence of "a widespread opposition both to war and to commitments leading to war."

The initial *New Leader* report, by John McNair, of Maxton's speech of 4 October, less than a week after the Munich Agreement was signed, gave little hint of the divisions that were to follow. Three days after the Commons debate, the paper headlined "Maxton's Great Speech in Parliament." Maxton had said that "the Prime Minister did something which the common people wanted to be done," though he had made it clear, wrote McNair in his report in the same issue, that "whilst he had congratulated the Prime Minister, he accepted neither the political nor social philosophy of the Prime Minister." Congratulations on the speech from the Bradford branch were also reported, but not all ILP members saw the speech in that light.[51]

Inevitably, the BBC and the press concentrated exclusively on Maxton's congratulation of Chamberlain, which seemed to suggest ILP endorsement of the Munich Agreement. According to Brockway, prior to the speech, he and Aplin had urged Maxton to avoid any such impression. Maxton made no such a commitment. A hastily convened Inner Executive meeting supported Maxton, with only Brockway and Aplin dissenting. But it was agreed that the Inner Executive would "put no obstacle" in the way of the dissenters making public statements critical of Maxton's—and McGovern's—speeches. Refusing to accede to Maxton's request for a delay, Brockway did exactly that. He later regretted his haste. In his 1955 biography of Maxton, John McNair would write of his subject's state of mind at the time of this incident: "To be misunderstood by some of his friends was more than he could bear and he had what amounted to a physical breakdown."[52]

The episode remained an issue at the 1939 conference the following April. A motion from the Greenwich branch began: "This Conference repudiates the congratulations offered to Mr. Chamberlain by Comrades J. Maxton and J. McGovern at the time of the 'crisis' in September 1938. It condemns their failure to use the opportunity they had to put forward a clear revolutionary analysis of events, and their consequent misrepresentation of Party policy." The quotation marks around "crisis" seem to reflect the belief that "the Government Propaganda deliberately created a War scare in September 1938," as Joseph Southall put it in an open letter to ILP members a few weeks before the conference.[53]

After also repudiating an "Imperialist speech" on Palestine by McGovern, the Greenwich motion demanded that "immediate steps be taken to bring the Parliamentary Group within the discipline of the Party." Amendments showed the depth of disagreement among the membership. While Bradford's proposed amendment sought to completely reverse the motion, turning it into one congratulating the two MPs, Croyden's demanded the expulsion of the whole Parliamentary Group. Clapham wanted the Group "entirely subjugated to the authority of the Party."[54] All three proposals, supportive and critical alike, were defeated, but a large minority, 43 to 45, voted in favour of referring back the Parliamentary Group's report. Brockway—whose contribution to the debate was conciliatory, stressing common ground—records Maxton's comment to him that while members "did not like what we did," they were not prepared to "chastise us for it." Brockway agreed. But, as Cohen concludes, it was "a very uneasy vote of confidence after a very public spat."[55]

In the meantime, during the post-Munich weeks of 1938, Brockway tried to make the ILP's position clear so as to distance it from pacifists without alienating them. He gave a speech, subsequently published as a pamphlet, to the "After the Crisis" conference organized by a London group of the Peace Pledge Union, in which he put forward the ILP's stance on war:

> We would oppose a war between the "democratic" states and the Fascist states. We would oppose a League of Nations war. We would oppose a collective security war. We would oppose them because we recognise

that they are all still capitalist and imperialist wars, arising not from any struggle for democracy and liberty against tyranny, but from rival imperialist interests.

At the same time the I.L.P. is not pacifist. Pacifists and the I.L.P. may join in opposing rearmament and war, but the I.L.P. does not believe that the transition from capitalism to socialism will be made by the pacifist method. If war occurred the I.L.P. would not merely resist passively, but would prepare for the moment when the war could be ended by the overthrow of the capitalist and war-making governments across the frontiers.[56]

There was a belief, in the ILP and elsewhere on the Left, that just as the war that began in 1914 led to the Russian Revolution, any new conflict would produce a similar upsurge of revolution on a much wider scale. But this was not a welcome scenario. Brockway again summed up the prospect from the ILP perspective in *Workers' Front*: "One may be confident that the war will end in social revolution, but that will only be at the cost of millions of lives, victims not only of Capitalism, but of the failure of the working-class movement to destroy Capitalism before it moves on to its final disaster."[57]

It was against this background of the growing threat of war and the ILP attempts to find a credible position that reconciled its hatred of war and its opposition to both fascism and capitalism that serious moves were initiated to bring the party back into the Labour fold.

Feeling a Way Back to Labour

By the late 1930s, it had become extremely difficult for any of the supporters of disaffiliation to retain the hopes they had had in 1932. Like Brockway, they could cling to the idea that disaffilation had made the ILP "a conscious political unit," but this was far from any of the disparate futures for the party that they had hoped for. Members of the RPC and others who wished to see a merger with the CPGB to create a united revolutionary party had either postponed their dream to an indeterminate future or left the ILP altogether. Efforts to at least cooperate in a united front had finally broken on the growing hostility over events in Russia and, above all, in Spain. Even the majority of the Trotskyists who had "entered" the ILP had given up and gone their own way. Nor had the ILP been able to make any discernible progress in weaning the working class away from the reformist and gradualist Labour Party. Gidon Cohen estimates that ILP membership declined from 16,773 in 1932 to 2,441 in 1939.[58]

Even so, by the standards of groups that were self-consciously to the left of Labour, in the 1930s as well as before and after that decade, the ILP was still a formidable force—still, says Cohen, "relatively strong."[59] But while the

CPGB was enjoying a modest upsurge, thanks to Comintern's adoption of the Popular Front policy, whose most effective instrument in Britain was the Left Book Club, the ILP was struggling to keep up. In his survey of the party's position, Brockway had noted the great disadvantage the ILP endured because of the absence of books in tune with ILP philosophy and policy. "The 'Left Book Club' is a powerful instrument for the C.P. in this respect," he acknowledged. The ILP's limited financial resources were the problem; the best it had been able to do was "to encourage Messrs. Secker and Warburg to publish a number of books."[60]

The failure to form a second United Front had confirmed that there was no prospect for a united front—or "workers' front"—that included the Communists as well as Labour, but there were clearly plenty of erstwhile members of the Socialist League—including former ILPers—whose politics were not too distant from those of the ILP. The prospect of a reaffiliated ILP being able to recruit many of these, or at least to work with the emerging "Labour Left," must now have seemed more promising than any of the other routes towards some sort of socialist unity.

The atmosphere in which reaffiliation began to be considered was very different from that of the earlier years of the decade. There was little real enthusiasm for Labour on the part of advocates of rejoining the larger party; Brockway, for example, would continue to reiterate that it was a "tactical question." And although determined opposition continued, a resigned acceptance that reaffiliation seemed inevitable is readily detectable in the statements of some who argued against it. The direction in which the ILP was now heading—and the doubts and difficulties that that entailed—became evident in 1938.

In July of that year, the *New Leader* reported that talks were taking place with the Labour Party on the ILP's relationship with it. There were, it said, different views in both the NAC and the party generally. The guiding principle was "the need for contact with the mass movement and at the same time the need for freedom to maintain the Revolutionary Socialist policy of the Party." At a NAC meeting two weeks later, the council agreed to continue negotiations. Only John Aplin dissented.[61] More references to ongoing discussions appeared in the *Leader* in subsequent weeks, and in September, the paper published a letter from Joseph Southall opposing reaffiliation. The *New Leader* was not supposed to be a "discussion paper," it said, but it wanted to avoid any appearance of unfairness.[62] It is clear, though, that Brockway, at least, had made up his mind. "I reached the view," he would later write, "that some sacrifice of freedom was justified in order to function within the mass political movement of the workers."[63]

The NAC annual report for 1939 explained that a meeting with Labour had taken place on 14 June and that, ten days later, a letter was received from Labour's NEC stating its view that the only "satisfactory basis" of association between the two parties would be the affiliation of the ILP. The NAC decided to try again for a "united action and an electoral agreement" and, if this was rejected by Labour, to ask for clarification of conditions of affiliation. Brockway's letter to James Middleton, the Labour Party general secretary, was included in an appendix to the NAC report. It began with a friendly "Dear Jimmy" and went on to rehearse the ILP's desire for cooperation, noting that Labour's NEC "thought the best method for co-operation between our two Parties would be the affiliation of the I.L.P. to the Labour Party." As Brockway also noted, he appreciated the fact that the PLP's standing orders—such a matter of contention during the previous five years—were being "liberally interpreted," with Lansbury and others allowed to vote against rearmament.[64]

The NAC assumed, wrote Brockway, that if the ILP were to rejoin Labour, the party would "enjoy the rights which it held when previously affiliated," but it wanted to know what limitations the party would need to accept. The Munich crisis delayed Labour's response, but a reply was finally received at the end of February 1939. In Labour's view, there was no need to discuss conditions of affiliation since these were already laid out in the party's constitution and were "not negotiable." By this time, the NAC had set up a subcommittee to consider the future of the ILP, including the possibility of Labour Party affiliation.[65]

How divided the ILP remained on this crucial issue was evident from the motions submitted for debate at the annual conference. The Alexandria branch wanted to instruct the NAC to terminate the negotiations, believing that a return to Labour "under any conditions would discredit the I.L.P." The Guild of Youth was also, predictably, opposed, but Nottingham supported conditional reaffiliation and the Welsh Divisional Council welcomed the negotiations. There was support, too, from the East Anglia Division, and its motion attracted a long amendment from Clapham, which concluded that "seeing there is no possibility of Soviets in this country at the present time," the "correct tactic" was to apply for Labour Party affiliation.[66]

The ILP's final annual conference of the interwar years opened on Saturday, 8 April 1939, in the Yorkshire seaside resort of Scarborough. The day before, Brockway's editorial in the *New Leader* had acknowledged the doubts about Labour Party affiliation but concluded that "the duty of working within rather than against the mass Working Class Movement persists, even if we reject affiliation."[67]

Although the report of the NAC subcommittee did not support formal reaffiliation, it did recommend that ILPers join the Labour Party as individuals—a compromise that was defeated by 68 votes to 43. Among the more vocal opponents of affiliation, Jowett was still arguing that the standing orders of the PLP were unacceptable, as was Labour's stance on rearmament and the possibility of war. Jennie Lee similarly rejected the prospect of affiliating "at the moment when the Labour Party is disintegrating and lining the workers up behind the Government for war." Others, however, feared the prospect of the party's increasing isolation and diminishing membership, while the Glasgow-based Tom Taylor was concerned that the ILP might become "a second SPGB." The Socialist Party of Great Britain (which still exists) had, like the Socialist Labour Party, broken away from the Social-Democratic Federation at the beginning of the twentieth century. An "impossibilist" party, it was sometimes known derisively by members of other left-wing groups as the "Small Party of Good Boys," the idea being that its purist approach had rendered it totally ineffective.

The need to avoid such a fate for the ILP was a major factor in generating support for reaffiliation. Yet the 1939 conference was not ready to embrace "unconditional" affiliation, which it rejected by 68 to 43 while supporting the pursuit of a "conditional" variety by a very similar, though reversed, margin of 69 to 40.[68] C. A. Smith, who opposed reaffiliation, was elected as chairman of the party. The ILP lost one of its four MPs soon thereafter when George Buchanan rejoined the Labour Party.[69]

When the Executive Committee met following the conference, it appointed a negotiating committee comprising Brockway, Maxton, Smith, and McNair to attempt to implement the "conditional affiliation" decision.[70] The debate within the party continued. In mid-July, the *New Leader* reported a letter from Middleton on behalf of the Labour Party NEC, which simply stated that the NEC would not "vary its position."[71]

Nothing better sums up the dilemma of the ILP in 1939, as well as the party's predicament throughout the interwar years, than an article by Douglas Moyle, "The Outlook for the Party," in the July edition of the internal discussion journal *Between Ourselves*. The ILP would, Moyle began, "feel relieved to shelter within a larger organisation which would ease us of some of the strain." The Labour Party could "comfortably absorb us." This was clear, since "entry can only be accomplished in accordance with the arrangements made by the Executive and the T.U.C. to render us ineffective." The normal functioning of the Labour Party machine would "do the rest." It would not matter much to the British working class whether the ILP was "inside or outside the Labour Party." There was no "fundamental gain" in rejoining Labour. But to remain outside was "to court the danger that threatens the existence of our party as we know it." The strength of the ILP would be "further minimised," and, sooner or later, the ILP might be supressed. At least one member, Moyle said, had told him that that "would be the best thing that could happen to us." Much greater effort would then be made by the active members "to build and expand on an industrial basis—for which our party cries out at this moment." Without this, there was "no hope for our party."[72]

If the ILP rejoined Labour, members of its parliamentary group would be known as ILP MPs. But, Moyle cautioned, since "the legislature is more or less completely controlled by the ruling class, and becoming more so, it correspondingly ceases to be a useful channel through which the workers can put right those things which are wrong." Therefore, in spite of the best intentions of the parliamentary group, "we can expect no good results in this sphere." The press only reported the parliamentary group's "mistakes" and "the Party and Group cannot afford to make many more 'mistakes.'" It was to be hoped that in the future, the ILP would not "bank so much on Parliamentary work. If we do not go into the Labour Party the I.L.P. might consider the possibility of withdrawing from Parliamentary activity."[73]

NAC members who had not already expressed their opinions on the affiliation issue at an earlier Executive Committee meeting were asked to do so at the NAC meeting on 5 August. There were still voices both for and against, but a sense of inevitability is palpable in some of their comments, such as Tom Stephenson's statement that he was against affiliation—but would accept whatever was decided. Or that of Trevor Williams, who declared himself for affiliation—reluctantly. After all had spoken, Brockway proposed a special conference and a motion supporting affiliation subject to maintenance of "organisational independence" and the right of ILP MPs to abstain from support of PLP policies on matters of principle.[74]

Brockway was opposed by Jowett, who stressed the impossibility of amending the PLP's standing orders and predicted that they would be "smothered at the Annual Conference by the block vote" if they returned to the Labour Party. He urged that any decision be postponed until the 1940 annual conference. Surveying the ILP's experience since disaffiliation, Maxton said that they "had not had the success we expected." In the Labour Party, he added, the ILP could "make its distinct personality felt," but whatever they decided, they "must carry the Party with us." That this would be particularly difficult in the event of war was stressed by both Smith and Bob Edwards. The former thought that in a war, "there would be no place for us inside the Labour Party, and we should realise this before applying for affiliation." But Edwards maintained that in that eventuality, the Labour Party would split and "our place should be inside to rally the anti-war elements."[75]

A vote in favour of seeking affiliation was narrowly carried by 8 votes to 6, with Smith and Jowett among the minority. It was agreed that a conference would take place on 17 September in or near Leeds, with just the one motion for discussion.[76] The next edition of the *New Leader* dedicated its front page to the story, under the headline "National Council of the I.L.P. Recommends Affiliation—Special Conference to be Held." The report emphasized that formal affiliation did not imply ideological absorption: as it insisted, there would be "no going back on the international revolutionary Socialist convictions which we hold." The same issue featured an article by Fred Jowett under the title "The Sham of Our Parliamentary Democracy." In it, Jowett looked back thirty years to the beginning of his "lone agitation" for the committee system as a replacement for the existing parliamentary structure. As he noted, Labour Party advisory committees on the "Machinery of Government," composed chiefly of members "who were then, or had been, connected with the Civil Service," had supported such changes, but their advice was ignored in both 1923 and 1928. Jowett's opposition to renewed affiliation remained implacable.[77]

On 23 August, little better than two weeks after the NAC agreed to seek affiliation, Stalin signed the notorious alliance with Hitler. Two days later, the *Leader* carried a piece on its front page headlined "Capitalism Marches on Towards War," as well as an article by John Aplin with the title "No Good Can Come of the Soviet-German Pact."[78] On 3 September, only a fortnight before the ILP special conference was scheduled to take place, Britain declared war on Germany. The following spring, the NAC reported to the annual conference: "The outbreak of War on 3rd September led the N.A.C to suspend the special conference. The N.A.C. takes the view that under present War circumstances it is not desirable that the Party should apply for affiliation to the Labour Party."[79]

One can only speculate about what might have occurred had the special conference been scheduled for a few weeks earlier. Clearly, there would have been considerable opposition to affiliation, but it seems most likely that the NAC majority would have carried the day, possibly at the expense of another split, which all were so anxious to avoid. Then again, the NAC's 1940 annual report opened with the observation that the outbreak of war had "completely dominated all other events." It could thus be that, even if the special conference had taken place and had voted to pursue reaffilation, the overriding issue of the war would have brought the process to an end before it had been completed. As it was, however, Britain had embarked on a "capitalist and imperialist" war to which the ILP quickly affirmed its opposition: "I.L.P. Takes Historic Stand" proclaimed the headline in the 8 September 1939 issue of the *New Leader*.

21

The Ex-ILP
A Case for Continuity

For many decades it has been a standing joke to point out that "ex-Communists" far outnumbered existing Communist party members. By the end of the 1930s, this was also true of the ILP, but with a significant difference. Typically, ex-Communists rejected their former beliefs, in some cases becoming fervent denouncers of the "God that failed." For many of the people who left the ILP, however, the story was rather different. Of course, those who followed Mosley into fascism, on the one hand, or joined the CPGB, on the other, repudiated their former beliefs, which they came to see as a great error. We must also assume that there were those who, after a youthful dalliance with the ILP, became Conservatives or Liberals later in life or simply became alienated from politics altogether. But of the fourteen thousand or so ILPers who left the party in the 1930s, a very significant proportion of those who had been among the most active members believed that they, rather than those who remained in the party, constituted the "real ILP." As Robert Dowse says, "Who was 'really' the I.L.P. was a question nobody could answer."[1]

The Scottish Socialist Party

We have seen the efforts made in the months before disaffiliation by, especially, Wise, Brailsford, and Dollan to divert the ILP from what they regarded as a path doomed to end in self-destruction. The first ex-ILP organization to be formed, in late August 1932, was the Scottish Socialist Party (SSP). This title had real resonance in the labour movement, since it had first been used as the name of the party founded by Keir Hardie some years before the formation of the ILP. There is not the slightest doubt that the SSP saw itself as the "real" ILP in Scotland. Ben Pimlott quotes the statement made by Dollan to the founding conference, as reported in the *Morning Post*. "Whoever may claim to be the ILP, we in this hall are the ILP."[2] His audience would have regarded that as a statement of the obvious.

As we have seen, Dollan's immediate response to disaffiliation from Labour was to question whether the Bradford conference had been representative of the ILP membership, especially of its larger and most active divisions, Scotland and Lancashire. That was at the beginning of August 1932. Then, in the 14 August edition of *Forward*, there appeared a statement whose signatories included Dollan and Keir Hardie's brother David. It announced that "those who believe in affiliation have formed a National Committee representative of every area in Scotland, to organise the I.L.P. to maintain its historic purpose." A delegate conference in Glasgow was announced for 21 August. The same issue carried a long reply from Paton to what he called Dollan's "unscrupulous arguments." The ILP secretary denied that the Bradford conference had been "rigged."[3] Two weeks later, the short-lived *New Clarion* reported that the Scottish "expellees" from the ILP had included two founding members of the ILP, George Hardie and Martin Haddow, "who helped start the Scottish Socialist Party in 1888."[4]

In spite of threats of expulsion from the ILP's NAC, hardly a deterrent for those already determined to leave, *Forward* was able to report that 170 delegates were planning to attend the Glasgow conference. The previous day, the *New Leader* had reported that "the I.L.P. wreckers"—Dollan and fifteen other Scottish members—had been expelled for "organising openly to wreck the I.L.P."[5] The 1932 conference was attended by 220 delegates. *Forward*'s lengthy report claimed that, had he lived, Keir Hardie would have been among the expelled. But, "unable to ex-communicate Keir Hardie, they ex-communicate his relatives." The paper also discussed the ownership of buildings and other property in "Property Rights in the I.L.P.: The Legal Position."[6] This would be an ongoing issue for some time.

In September, *Forward* reported that the new Scottish Socialist Party formed at the conference was gaining more branches than the now disaffiliated ILP, that the SSP was in the process of setting up federations of branches, and that it had adopted a municipal program. Two months later, the SSP claimed a steady increase in membership, as compared with the "Dilps"—disaffiliated ILPers. Early in the New Year, eleven branch reports appeared in *Forward*. Property disputes continued, and the paper blamed the ILP for repudiating a provisional agreement.[7]

As we saw in earlier chapters, sniping at former comrades in the ILP continued in the Scottish paper. When the Scottish ILP conference took place, *Forward* quoted a Motherwell delegate as saying that the ILP was "divorced from the Labour Party and courting the Communist Party." It did not take much foresight to predict that if this was so, it would be a course strewn with difficulties. The same issue of the paper reported that an ILP meeting at Glasgow's

Metropole Theatre had been disrupted by Communists. Maxton had "challenged a persistent interrupter to a fight." A few weeks later, the paper was even-handed enough to praise Maxton's speech on poverty in Britain—which, it said, "created a sensation"—and to publish a "practically complete" version.[8]

The SSP seems to have done reasonably well, at least in its earliest years. A hundred branches and a membership of more than two thousand was reported following its first annual conference at Easter 1933, and two years later, *Forward* reported an attendance of more than 220 delegates.[9] *Forward* became the party's official organ in 1934, and the paper continued to propagate the doctrines of democratic socialism for the rest of the decade.[10]

Probably the majority of the pre-disaffiliation activists, and certainly a sizable proportion, went with the SSP rather than the "Dilps." But the SSP's very existence did raise the question of whether, since the entire enterprise had been based on staying within the Labour Party, a separate organization—particularly one confined to Scotland—was necessary. For the moment, that was answered in the positive. An SSP monthly meeting in January 1933 confidently predicted that negotiations with the Labour Party would quickly lead to affiliation.[11]

Labour Party initiatives featured prominently in *Forward*. After Labour gained control of Glasgow City Council towards the end of 1933, the paper published a celebration of the party's successes in "What Labour Has Done in Four Weeks." This was soon followed by Dollan's article "What Labour Has Done in Three Months."[12] Arthur Woodburn, the secretary of the Scottish Labour Party, made fairly frequent contributions to the paper. In November 1935, he claimed that the overwhelming majority of the pre-disaffiliation ILP members remained in the Labour Party. Two years later, *Forward* carried his "Open Letter to Stalin: Stop the Executions and Wind Up Comintern." In 1938, he reviewed Brockway's *Workers' Front*, which he considered "a deadly indictment of the Communist Party in Britain, Russia and Spain." But he concluded, "A great silence settles on the I.L.P. It is the silence of the politically dead." On the same theme the following month, he wrote, under the headline "Where Is the I.L.P.? The Present Caretakers of a Once Great Party," that he detected "a steady flow of what remains into the Labour Party."[13] The veteran former ILPer Minnie Pallister reported on the Labour Party women's conference in *Forward* in 1938.[14]

The SSP was not immune from the ideological conflicts of the decade, however. In early 1938, *Forward* headlined "Trotsky Found 'Not Guilty,' International Commission Reports on Moscow Trials." This was followed a few weeks later by an article on the current state of affairs in Russia by the famous exile himself.[15] This sort of thing did not go down well with all SSP members.

After the party's annual conference the following year, we find Dollan complaining of intolerance on the part of some younger delegates who denounced *Forward* editor Emrys Hughes, "as if he were a traitor" for allowing different views to appear in the paper and for permitting Trotsky to state his case.[16]

From the start, the SSP was close to the other anti-disaffiliationists in England and Wales in what became the Socialist League, although it declined to enter the Unity Campaign that ultimately led to the League dissolving. Amalgamation of the two bodies was discussed but never finalized.[17] But relations were good. Trevelyan represented the Socialist League at the SSP's 1934 conference, and William Mellor brought the League's greetings the following year.[18]

Though not neglecting wider British and international issues, the SSP was focused to a large extent, as one would expect, on Scottish and, above all, Glasgow politics. This was particularly true of Dollan. Gidon Cohen relates how Dollan's autocratic behaviour led to his being sacked as treasurer, in 1937, by the "unholy alliance" of ILP Glasgow councillors and the Moderates.[19] But by the end of the following year, *Forward* was able to welcome "Lord Provost Dollan."[20]

By this time, the argument that there was no need for an SSP separate from the Scottish Labour Party was gaining ground, though a motion to dissolve was rejected by the 1938 annual conference. This was repeated the following year, but the conference heard that membership was declining, and in 1940, the SSP was wound up.[21]

The Socialist League

The Socialist League began in 1932 as a merger between the Society for Socialist Inquiry and Propaganda (SSIP) and the ex-ILP affiliationists in England and Wales. The SSIP, known informally as "Zip," had been founded by G. D. H. Cole and Margaret Cole the previous year. A vital link with the trade union movement, soon to be lost, was made when Ernest Bevin, a dominant figure in the Trades Union Congress during most of the interwar period, agreed to become chairman.[22] The inside back cover of *The Crisis*, a *New Statesman* pamphlet written in 1931 by Bevin and G. D. H. Cole, advertised the new organization, declaring its object to be "the development and advocacy of a constructive Socialist policy."[23]

During its brief existence, the SSIP published an impressive number of pamphlets, with such titles as *Anglo-Soviet Trade* and *Facts and Figures for Labour Speakers*, along with G. D. H. Cole's *National Government and Inflation* and Colin Clark's *National Planning*. It also published a series of study guides, the first six of which, all written by Cole, dealt with matters such as banking, credit, and the gold standard, as well as capitalism (addressed in *How Capitalism Works*, published in May 1932). Others in the series included Michael

Stewart's *Forms of Public Control*, whose aim was to suggest "reasons why we must devise new forms of control."²⁴ The SSIP established local branches, one or two of which also published material (such as the pamphlet *Housing in Stoke on Trent*, which appeared from the North Staffordshire branch). The Socialist League took over all these publications, together with the attractive uniform cover design used by the SSIP. Beginning in 1934, it also published the *Socialist Leaguer*, which, in September 1935, became *The Socialist: [Socialist: Journal] Journal of the Socialist League*, which espoused similar positions. Early in 1937, an independent publication—the newly founded *Tribune*, which adopted similar positions—began to gain growing influence.²⁵

The *New Clarion* of 13 August 1932 included a letter from the SSIP secretary, E. A. Radice, urging anti-disaffiliation ILPers and like-minded others to join the SSIP, as well as the article "Why We Remain Loyal to Labour" by Wise. Two weeks later, the paper reported that the former ILP affiliationists were holding a meeting to precede the Labour Party annual conference at Leicester, while on the same day, *Forward* reported their London conference, which had been chaired by Wise.²⁶

An advertisement in the *New Leader* in late September declared that the inaugural conference of the Socialist League would take place on 2 October. It was being organized by the former ILP affiliation committee "in co-operation with S.S.I.P." Its aim, the advertisement said, was "to establish a Socialist educational and propaganda organization affiliated to the Labour Party." The ILP's *New Leader* noted that the new organization was appealing to ILP branches to support it, and an editorial note predicted, "None will."²⁷

The Leicester conference duly took place and was followed by a meeting in London two weeks later. A significant division immediately occurred, with Cole wishing to retain Bevin as chairman and the former ILPers insisting on Wise.²⁸ At this point, the latter group was clearly in the ascendant. As James Jupp notes, "Even the Socialist League, which inherited the outlook of the Fabians through the Society for Socialist Inquiry and Propaganda, soon succumbed to the more sweeping philosophy of the former ILP members who led it." Or, as Patrick Seyd puts it, "A faction of the left had been formed to take the place of the ILP."²⁹

The League scored its greatest success in influencing Labour Party policy during its first week. Leading League members, especially Wise and Charles Trevelyan, played a prominent part at the Labour conference, which adopted commitments to nationalize the Bank of England and the joint stock banks. A future Labour government would, the conference agreed, introduce socialist legislation immediately. "Never again in the 1930s," says Pimlott, "was the Left so successful at Conference in the face of NEC opposition." Nor was anything comparable to take place again until the 1960s.³⁰ This heady moment of success is nicely captured in an account of the Labour Party conference by Charles Trevelyan in an early Socialist League pamphlet:

> At Leicester the resolution was passed, which I moved myself, hoping for agreement but finding to my surprise and satisfaction a hurricane of approval which swept the assembly. That resolution has put the leaders who may be at the head of the Labour Party in the event of another Labour Ministry under a definite mandate to introduce Socialist measures at once and to drive them through Parliament.³¹

The merger with the SSIP was by no means straightforward. Although thirteen members of its executive had signed the letter inviting Labour Party members to the inaugural Socialist League conference, there was significant opposition within the SSIP.³² According to a *Manchester Guardian* report, there was a "distinct reluctance to go into partnership with the ILP affiliationists" among SSIP members.³³ When the final SSIP conference met on 6 November, the supporters of the Socialist League failed to achieve the necessary two-thirds majority for the merger of the SSIP with the League and had to resort to the expedient of dissolving the SSIP, which was achieved with a majority vote of 70 to 27.³⁴ Cole withdrew from the League's National Council in June 1933—ostensibly because of the pressure of work, but he would later refer to political disagreements.³⁵

The Labour Party NEC was divided about how welcoming it should be to a Socialist League application for affiliation. The decision to approve this in anticipation, subject to the League's constitution being "in harmony" with that of Labour, was only passed with the chairman casting a vote.³⁶ The League, with a membership of two thousand, was able to affiliate to Labour in 1933.³⁷ As we saw in the preceding chapter, Sir Stafford Cripps was to become the dominant figure in the Socialist League. Yet, in spite of Cripps's dominance, sufficient evidence of the influence of former ILPers remained for the League to qualify, at least partially, as an "ex-ILP" organization. A sort of backhanded confirmation of this can be found in a 1935 issue of the Comintern's magazine, the *Communist International*, which commented that the Socialist League continued the "traditional I.L.P. role in the working-class movement under a pseudo-Marxist cloak."³⁸

The two leading figures of the anti-disaffiliation forces in the ILP—Wise, until his untimely death in 1934, and Brailsford—remained active and influential. Wise's pamphlet *Control of Finance and the Financiers*, part of the League's London Socialist Forum series, continued a focus that went back to at least the days of the Living Wage policy. Faced with a Labour government intent on establishing financial control, "many British 'patriots' would certainly have a shot at transferring their money to foreign capitals," Wise predicted. But the financial situation in the previously favourite destination, the United States, was "not encouraging." Meanwhile, the existence or possibility of fascism or governments of the Left in many European countries "diminishes their attractiveness," Wise concluded.[39]

Brailsford remained a frequent contributor to League publications. In early 1935, we find him expressing a very ILP-like concern with India, first in his article "The Labour Party and India." A few months later, he complained bitterly that "every attempt that the Labour Party has made in committee to render the Indian Bill a little less undemocratic, has, of course, been defeated by the automatic working of the National Government's majority." The next issue included his article "Facing the Next War."[40]

By this time, it was clear that the League was going to find it extremely difficult to repeat its initial but fleeting success in rallying Labour Party support on the scale necessary to influence policy. The "decisive moment," as David Howell identifies it, was at the 1934 Labour Party conference, where "the conference platform backed by the votes of the major unions overwhelmingly defeated the League's challenge."[41] The policies the Socialist League was attempting to promote were reminiscent of the Living Wage, or Socialism in Our Time, policy of the ILP in earlier years, particularly in Maxton's version.

The League's national council proposed, as immediate objectives, factory legislation to ensure the safety of miners; the raising of the school leaving age to fifteen, and to sixteen within two years with maintenance allowances; and noncontributory pensions of £1 per week from the age of sixty. These measures were to "constitute the first fundamental requirement of the transition from Capitalism to Socialism." Prior to the 1934 Socialist League conference, the document "Forward to Socialism," to be debated at the conference, was circulated to members. Marked "Private and confidential," it was accompanied with a request that the "greatest care" be taken by branches and members to avoid it being seen by nonmembers. It listed as measures "already given" the socialization of finance, transfer of land ownership to the community, control of overseas trade, and "Emergency Social alleviation." This was all intended to lead on to a five-year plan for the socialization of transport, mining, energy, munitions, chemical, textile, iron and steel industries, shipbuilding, and agriculture. There would be only limited compensation.[42] "Forward to Socialism" was duly endorsed by the conference.[43] Following a special conference on 25 November 1934, the *Socialist Leaguer* proclaimed, "We have passed out of the realm of programme making into the realm of action."[44]

Further echoes of earlier ILP policies and attitudes can be found in the article "Our Challenge to 'Gradualism,'" which appeared in one of the early issues of *The Socialist* (the new incarnation of the *Socialist Leaguer*). The writer insisted that the League was determined to win over the Labour Party. In order to "further this end and to challenge most clearly and boldly the reascendency of 'gradualist views' within the Party and the whole Labour Movement, and all schemes which can classified under the heading 'Capitalist Reconstruction,' the National Council has decided to launch a national campaign of propaganda and recruiting for the League." There would be forty to fifty conferences or mass meetings in towns across the country, from north (Jarrow) to south (Portsmouth) and from east (Ipswich) to west (Bristol).[45]

The League soon acquired a similar reputation in wider Labour Party circles to that of the ILP at the end of the previous decade. It was, Pimlott says, a "successor left wing body to the ILP." Jupp notes that the League found itself "in the same critical relationship with the Labour Party which had forced its predecessor, the I.L.P. to disaffiliate."[46] Even more than the ILP, the Socialist League was perceived by many in the wider labour movement as a factional body comprising intellectuals. After Cripps became so dominant in 1937, Hugh Dalton dismissed the League as a "rich man's toy."[47] For many in the Labour Party, the League was seen, says Pimlott, as "a disruptive body of middle-class intellectuals grinding a left-wing axe."[48] Patrick Seyd is probably right to point out that while the ILP, in the 1920s and even beyond, had been able to retain the loyalty of many, "irrespective of political stance," this was not something that was inherited by the League.[49]

The Independent Socialist Party

That other "successor" to the ILP, the Independent Socialist Party (ISP), differed from the Scottish Socialist Party and the Socialist League in a number of ways. Unlike them, the ISP was not composed of affiliationist ILPers but of those, particularly in the Lancashire Division, who, though they had supported disaffiliation in 1932, soon came to fall out with what they took to be the ILP's version of revolutionary policy. To the future members of the ISP, this seemed to be leading more and more to cooperation with—and possibly absorption by—the Communist Party.

The Independent Socialist Party had nothing like the public prominence or impact of the Socialist League or the Scottish Socialist Party. But like those organizations, it was led by people, notably Sandham and Abbot, who had previously played important roles in the ILP and saw themselves as being the "real" ILP. In chapter 16, we left the ISP shortly after its foundation in May 1934, with Sandham's open letter of resignation from the ILP appearing in *Labour's*

Northern Voice two months later. As if to reinforce the appearance of continuity with the ILP, where summer schools had long been a notable feature, the same issue of the *Voice* carried an advertisement for the "*Adelphi* Socialist Summer School," at which Middleton Murry and Sandham were to be lecturers.[50] The impression of continuity with the past was reinforced in the following issue by Sandham's article explaining why he had now joined the ISP, in which, he insisted, "the spirit of the I.L.P. must be kept alive." Once again, he castigated his former party for departing from its authentic ethos of former times in favour of "the Communist and Russian model."[51]

A month later, *Labour's Northern Voice* reported on the arrangements for first annual convention of the ISP, which began with a reception at the Clarion Club in Manchester. Speakers at the demonstration during the conference were Murry, Sandham, and Abbott. The conference remained wary of the Labour Party. "As Socialists," the *Voice* declared in October, "we do not desire to see a Labour majority gained at the forthcoming election unless it is given by electors desiring *Socialist* reconstruction." Cohen quotes an earlier edition of the paper (June 1934) to demonstrate that the ISP, believing that the Socialist League would eventually be forced out of the Labour Party, saw itself as "a live Independent Socialist Party to which they can turn."[52]

But any branch or member could join the Labour Party if they wished. Murry moved a motion on the ISP's political aims, which ended with the declaration that "the Convention asserts that the will of working-class democracy must prevail."[53] The constitution adopted was based on that of the ILP in 1922; this move, as Cohen tells us, led the *New Leader* to brand the breakaway organization as backward-looking, a criticism that Murry was to take up within the ISP, as we shall see.[54]

The ISP manifesto did not set out any principles or policies that many ILP members would not have endorsed. The party stood for "publicly owned and democratically controlled" industry and "economic equality." It believed in revolution but only "by enlightened democratic consent of the majority" and the "full use of the political, industrial, and co-operative strength possessed by the British democracy."[55] The manifesto was divided into three sections headed "Recognises," "Advocates," and "Proposes." One assumption about the nature of politics in the first section would have certainly been rejected by most of its ILP contemporaries. It stated that "the future welfare of the community depends on the establishment of economic classlessness to correspond with the political classlessness which has already been achieved." It is extremely doubtful that many in the ILP believed that "political classlessness" had been achieved.[56]

"Economic classlessness," however, was a shared aim. Also shared with the ILP was the belief that "the decline of capitalism would involve "the whittling away of former concessions gained by the people." The two parties also held in common an uncompromising rejection of all "'remedies' such as 'New Deals,' Fascism, Social Credit, class collaboration, evolutionary 'socialism,' and 'national' government or state capitalism." All of these, the ISP declared to be futile and likely to divert the working classes from "their common advance towards Socialism." Murry's influence is apparent in the declaration that other "working-class political parties" had "not succeeded in suiting their methods to English political traditions."[57]

Nor would there have been much that ILPers would have opposed among the eleven policies "advocated" by the ISP. These included the "equality of women with men," abolition of the House of Lords, reform of the Commons, and "democratisation of the armed forces, police, civil service and judiciary." Like the ILP, the party proposed "to resist war by every means at its disposal."[58]

The ISP pamphlet *Behind Rearmament: Preparing for Fascism in Britain!* conceded that there would be "an absorption of some unemployed by reorganising on a war basis, but not on the scale that some folk imagine." Those in control did not intend to produce a situation where wages would be forced up. The ISP General Council perceived a sinister domestic threat behind the government's decision to rearm: "Our view is that the war preparations are deliberately intended to consolidate industry in Britain under corporate control, and to deprive ordinary folk of their democratic organisations for resisting the will of capitalism." The council asked, "Can this coming of British Fascism be averted?"[59]

One key objective for preventing this fate was that the hoped for "repudiation" of rearmament by the Labour Party should be "carried on to the industrial field, as it will be suicidal for democracy if Trade Union leaders decide to collaborate in forwarding rearmament which their political colleagues have denounced." The ISP needed to get its message across: "The danger of British Fascism involved in war reorganisation should be explained and re-explained to organised labour." The pamphlet ended with a stirring call for a "vocal, stubborn refusal to operate the Government plan. It is your job to run all risks to help in the struggle to preserve democracy."[60]

The ISP's membership was not confined to Lancashire. There were branches in Nottingham, Aberfan, Hastings, and Maidstone, and even in the British colony of Sierra Leone. Yet there is no doubt that the old ILP Lancashire Division formed the core of the new party, with Abbott as general secretary and Sandham as chairman. The other big influence, early on, was Murry, who took the lead in forming a London branch. How dependent it was on him is amply evidenced by the fact that it collapsed soon after Murry resigned and joined the Labour Party in May 1936.[61] In the meantime, Murry's influence was largely exercised through what *Labour's Northern Voice* referred to as the "London unit" and the *Adelphi* summer school. The 1936 summer school was to be opened and closed by Murry; other speakers included J. Allen Skinner and Herbert Read.[62]

There was a crucial difference between the former ILPers of Lancashire and Murry and his London branch. It was not just that the latter were intellectuals. Even more significant was that so many in Lancashire, not least its leading members, had spent many years, even decades, in the ILP, whereas Murry was, as he often reminded his audiences, a new recruit not just to the ILP and, later, the ISP but to socialism itself. The Middleton Murry Papers contain the draft of a speech to be made to the ISP convention. It is not dated but internal evidence suggests that it was to be delivered to the 1935 meeting. Murry's warning of the dangers of focusing too much on the past was potentially applicable to the rest of the ex-ILP, but the danger was greater with the ISP, which had much less to concentrate on in the way of "practical politics" than did the SSP or the Socialist League.

Murry began his draft by acknowledging that he had been a socialist for only a few years and that, during this time, he had found himself "more and more drawn towards the Lancashire comrades." He had come to believe that "what they meant by Socialism was fundamentally the same thing as I meant by it myself." Then he turned to criticisms of the direction that the ISP seemed to be taking. He declared himself disappointed by "various prominent members" of the ISP who seemed to assume that "whole hearted support of and belief in the I.S.P." was the only possible attitude for a "convinced and sincere Socialist." Many people in Britain would "admit the need and the necessity of a new organisation of Socialists which left every member free to be a member of the Labour Party or even the I.L.P." Yet there was "a pretty complete lack of response at present" to the idea that the time had come for "a new Socialist political party that arrogates to itself the right of being by nature infallible, and treating sincere Socialists outside its ranks as a sort of moral lepers."[63]

It was quite mistaken, wrote Murry, to believe that the simple solution was "the recreation of the old I.L.P." That party had been "continually putting on pedestals men whom I had met and judged and in whom I had no faith at all." It had done this with MacDonald, Allen, and Snowden, the latter of whom "dares to confess even now that he never could read a word of Marx." If the notion of reviving the "old ILP" was meaningless to a middle-aged forty-five-year-old like himself, how much more so to younger socialists? They might favour the creation of a "new Socialist organisation," but "heaven preserve them from a return to the old, still more from a return to the old with an odour of sanctity, a new assumption of past infallibility. In their eyes it is a preposterous claim, rejected beyond appeal by history."[64]

Murry advised those who felt loyalty to the old ILP "to cherish this loyalty in your hearts, and not proclaim it from your platforms." Otherwise, the ISP would become "a party of old men, brooding on their bitter stories of a past of failure." He was, he said, "through sheer circumstances . . . in the position of being one of the chief propagandists of the I.S.P. to the Gentiles." What was needed was an organization that would "unite and deepen the mutual understanding of Socialists active in all sections of the present Labour movement and also among the large and I believe increasing number who are unattached." He concluded with a plea for a "new kind of political party."[65]

Murry complained that the right of individual ISP members to join the Labour Party was only "grudgingly conceded from headquarters." But Labour was soon to proscribe the ISP, a "huge blow" to the new organization, as Gidon Cohen says, and one that dashed Murry's version of the way forward for the party. Murry and the London group soon decided to urge the ISP to apply for affiliation to the Labour Party, and disputes between London and the Lancashire ISPers followed. Murry himself resigned from the General Council in March 1936, and, following the rejection by the party's third convention in May of a motion calling for affiliation to Labour, he resigned from the ISP and joined the Labour Party.

Rather sadly, the ISP soldiered on in much the sort of political isolation of which Murry had warned. Like the ILP, it opposed the war in 1939. Sandham died in 1944 and the party continued, chaired by Abbott until his death in 1951. Soon thereafter, it dissolved itself. Of the three ex-ILP organizations that claimed to be the "real ILP," the most successful, in immediate terms, was the SSP, which did, largely via Dollan, make an impact on Scottish—and particularly Glasgow—politics. All of these organizations, in one way or another, veered back towards the Labour Party, though the ISP's ambition to achieve a species of half-in-and-half-out status was thwarted by Labour's NEC.[66]

The Later Clifford Allen: A Limiting Case?

The SSP, the Socialist League, and the ISP could all make a reasonable case that, in one way or another, they were continuing what they saw as the ILP tradition. In this, they were different from the other groups that left the party in the 1930s—the RPC and the Trotskyists—who made no such claim. Can any sort of a case for ILP continuity be made for the former treasurer and chairman of the party Clifford Allen? He certainly retained a degree of respect and affection on the part of at least some of his former ILP comrades. Jennie Lee remembered the way he had been "the very embodiment of the martyrdom that some of our members had suffered during the war." She recalled his visit to her home early in the early postwar period: "I shall never forget the tall, ascetic face and figure of Clifford Allen framed in our doorway with half a dozen squat dark-looking miners grouped around him. I should not have been surprised if he had suddenly sprouted wings and a halo."[67]

True, this was written a few years after Allen's death in 1939, a few months before his fiftieth birthday. Yet even just after he followed his friend MacDonald into National Labour, there had been those on the Left prepared to defend him—at least to some extent. National Labour was, as Kenneth O. Morgan says, "an exotic breed," but he tells us that MacDonald still "insisted, to impressionable young aesthetes like Kenneth Clark, on his socialist convictions."[68] That Allen held similar convictions is without doubt: he had always regarded the case for socialism as self-evident—a matter of scientific rationality.

Allen had been approached by MacDonald in early December 1931 and asked, "Would you like to be a Lord?" Martin Gilbert tells us of Allen's determination to maintain a socialist voice in the new government by giving it support in the House of Lords.[69] The reaction in ILP circles to this former chairman's decision to accept lordship was always likely to be extremely negative. Murry, as we have seen, dismissed him, along with MacDonald and Snowden, as someone he had "no faith in."[70]

The immediate reaction to Allen's "elevation" was a mixture of lighthearted humour and mild spitefulness. A *New Leader* editorial noted the advent of "Baron Clifford Allen" and commented, "One past Chairman of the I.L.P. is a Viscount and another is a Baron. A third is the Prime Minister of a 'National' Government. We begin to shudder even for James Maxton and the present Chairman of the I.L.P.... Maxton's phrase remains: We have no giants!" Inset in the middle of the piece was a twenty-line poem, the final stanza of which read:

> The Viscount Snowden earned his noble place,
> But why does Allen such an "honour" reap?
> Has then apostasy become so cheap
> That one with ease towards a Peerage climbs
> By writing two short letters to the "Times"![71]

Mild enough stuff, perhaps, but the following week, it drew an immediate rebuke from Helena Swanwick, the first chronicler of the Union of Democratic Control, in which Allen had played such a prominent role. The "attack on Clifford Allen made my heart sink," she declared, deploring the "cheap cry of 'traitor.'" A week later, Brailsford, by this time already engaged in what turned out to be his unsuccessful struggle to keep the ILP affiliated to Labour, acknowledged the sincerity and good intentions of "Clifford Allen (as we may still call him)." However, he rejected the defence of MacDonald that Allen had made in his pamphlet *Labour's Future at Stake*, with its "plea for reunion under his leadership within some centre Party coalition, which he seems to contemplate." Brailsford concluded:

> With much else in the pamphlet we may agree. We need this exhortation to think clearly and talk persuasively. We did not find the right "tone of voice" in the emotional stress of last year. It is true that millions of voters could be won for a Socialist policy if we ceased to frighten them and cared only to convince them. But no conviction will lead to action which ignores the fact that there is in the society of to-day a fundamental cleavage of interest between the owning and the working classes.[72]

There was nothing so conciliatory in Maxton's response. He denounced Allen's desertion as "wicked" and, in reply to Brailsford, concluded that instead of making him "Lord Allen of Hurtwood," MacDonald should have made Allen a bishop. Yet Brailsford was not entirely alone in taking a more measured view of Allen's latest position, though Wise felt it necessary to make it clear in a proaffiliation letter to the *New Leader* in February 1932 that he was not supporting Allen.[73]

One example of a more conciliatory view appeared in the Guildford-based *Workers' Monthly*, which was published in local editions in various parts of southern England. The February 1932 issue carried a correspondent's appreciation of Allen's wartime role and his "good service to Socialism" as chairman of the ILP. It continued, "Again he takes an independent course. Will the future justify the attitude he now takes? Will he succeed in his endeavour to bring back Ramsay MacDonald as the leader of the Labour Party? I think the answer is decidedly in the negative." A few months later, Allen contributed an article entitled "Socialism in Our Time" to this organ of the Southern Counties Workers' Publications. He argued, "If when public opinion urgently demands proposals for a more common sense organisation of finance and banking we advocate our cure in a tone of hatred and arouse terror, we shall miss our chance."[74]

The *Workers' Monthly* editorial response was polite but firm. "We ourselves have always appealed to reason," the editor insisted. He welcomed Allen's contribution. If it indicated that he was "beginning to realise the wrongness of his support for the 'National' Government we are glad." But he was "doomed to disappointment" if he hoped to persuade the Labour movement that "anything Socialistic will ever come out of this collection of reactionary elements" that constituted the National Government.[75]

The Ex-ILP

Allen was not entirely neglected by the ILP during the period when the party was preoccupied with the debate on disaffiliation. In May 1932, the *New Leader* carried an advertisement for a talk by him under the title "The Crisis—And the Result." It was to be given at a meeting organized by the Marylebone ILP branch, which was also mentioned in passing in the paper.[76] Then, in August, soon after the fateful Bradford conference, the paper devoted an editorial to Allen's position, asking, with emphasis, "*Do we believe that social order and design can replace the present world chaos without a catastrophic break?*" It ended on a note of incredulity: "Lord Allen thinks that not only it can, but that the National Government is doing it!"[77]

For his part, Allen was still sufficiently concerned about his old party to comment on its demise in "The End of the I.L.P." in the monthly publication of the National Labour Party. None of the "fragments" into which the ILP had "shattered itself" could possibly survive, he predicted. It was "a lamentable end to a great and at times romantic history." The ILP had been right about the war. But it, and now the Labour Party also, had succumbed to "a minority mind" that dallied "with the wish to shock and frighten with revolutionary words a public that is now willing to be convinced and led into the promised land of social order of which we have told them." It was better, Allen argued, to combine efforts. "Of course we know—whether we be enlightened Labour, Conservative, or Liberal men and women—that we shall encounter in the last ditch an insignificant group who cling to vested interest." But this should deter no one. Those who had led for the previous thirty years were now "nearing the end of their journey." Allen asked: "Are we, who are younger, to keep apart from each other when we could combine to express the new common will of the twentieth century?"[78]

Allen's approach was to lead to one of the last of his political initiatives in the shape of the Next Five Years Group, which included the future Conservative prime minister, Harold Macmillan, and the Liberal and editor of *The Economist*, Walter Layton, as well as Norman Angell.[79] Inspired in part by Roosevelt's New Deal, this group was founded at an Oxford Union meeting in early February 1935, though there had been preparatory informal discussions during the previous year.[80]

As many political "realists" predicted, the group's life was a very short one. It declined steeply after Macmillan abandoned it the following year. Yet it did produce *The Next Five Years: An Essay in Political Agreement* and two manifestos, which were published as appendices to the book. The first manifesto warned of the trend towards political violence: "Organisations of a semi-military character, exacting a strict discipline from their adherents, displaying a uniform of coloured shirts, employing common symbols and a new form of salute, have grown in some countries into vast private armies." Even in Britain, there were "parades of Fascist blackshirts." The second manifesto noted that "Fascists and Communists alike pour scorn on democratic institutions and advocate their replacement by dictatorial method," while they called for "speeding up the machinery of government."[81]

The foreword to *The Next Five Years* listed 152 signatures, including 33 marked as having attended at least one of the preliminary conferences. The "drafting committee" was identified as Allen; W. Arnold Forster; A. Barratt Brown, Principal of Ruskin College, Oxford; Geoffrey Crowther; Harold MacMillan, MP; and Sir Arthur Salter. In all, seven signatories registered dissent with one or other section of the program proposed. The book was substantial, running to 320 pages including the appendices. Part 1 comprised eight chapters on economic policy, and the second part dealt with international relations.[82]

Very few of the signatories were associated with Labour, and none were leaders of the party, but the book contained some distant echoes of *The Living Wage*. The introduction declared there to be "a challenge to develop an economic system which is free from poverty and makes full use of the growing material resources of the age for the general advantage, and a challenge to safeguard public liberty and to revitalize democratic government." Approaches relying on "muddling through" had to be rejected. The community could "and must deliberately plan, direct and control—not in detail but in broad outline—the economic development to which innumerable activities contribute."[83]

The chapter on economic planning favoured "planning coherently" and declared optimistically, "The *motive* of profit-making has already, to a greater extent than is commonly realised, ceased to be the mainspring of economic activity in this country." Prompted by the "principle of developing resources for common good," the future would see an extension of "public ownership or control." There should be a "Government Planning Committee" and an "Economic General Staff" of "persons with more specialized expert knowledge, with more permanent tenure," both of which would include "members drawn from the Trades Union and Labour movement." The book's epilogue argued that "the principle of government by consent and free discussion must be made much more fully operative through the extension of education—that cardinal function of a democratic State; through improvement of the system of representation, and through the further breaking down of barriers of class."[84]

Though most on the Left were, understandably, wary of Allen's initiative, some spoke up for taking *The Next Five Years* seriously. In the *Daily Herald*, Francis Williams observed that "the unanimity they have been able to reach is significant, for it is a unanimity not simply of pious hopes but of positive proposals." But he went on to declare that it was "in almost all respects the immediate programme of the Labour Party, as I believe of any body of men and women genuinely seeking economic improvement must be. The Conservative and Liberal supporters of The Next Five Years should be in the ranks of the Socialist movement."[85] Yet, insofar as there really was a "Butskellite consensus" in the 1950s, Allen's initiative can surely be seen as foreshadowing it.

To those of us who grew up with the idea that 1931 saw an unforgivable "great betrayal," what is pleasantly surprising is the relative lack of personal animosity directed at Allen, and not at Allen alone. When the first volume of Snowden's memoirs appeared in 1934, dealing with the years up to 1919, *Forward* confined itself to the comment that it must have made "happier writing" than the next volume would be. A week after the former chancellor of the exchequer's death, the same paper announced, "Had he been a younger man he would have once again returned to the Socialist Movement for one of his last messages was to wish success to the Socialist candidate at Greenock." The writer quoted from Snowden's last letter, sent to his friend Martin Haddow on the day he died: "In quieter moments I go back to the old faith in which I believe as firmly as ever."[86]

Conclusion
The Legacy of the ILP's Interwar Years

Like any political organization, and perhaps more than most, the ILP was never quite "one thing" at any point in its history. In the period in question, its stance and its leadership, as well as its size and potential political influence, was almost continually changing from the end of the First World War in the final weeks of 1918 to the outbreak of the Second in the late summer of 1939. One of its most prominent early leaders, Philip Snowden, was already showing definite signs of disenchantment with the party by 1920. This was reinforced after the critical reactions of many in the party, as well as elsewhere on the Left, to his wife Ethel's outspoken criticisms of the Bolsheviks after her visit that year to Russia with the Labour Party delegation.[1] Rapid change and, especially after disaffiliation in 1932, internal controversy, would continue for the rest of the interwar years.

It could plausibly be argued that by 1939, the ILP was an entirely different sort of organization than the one that had operated twenty years previously. In the early 1920s, it was still the main route for individuals to become members of the Labour Party and was therefore still part of the political mainstream. Its position in this respect was already threatened, and seen to be threatened, by the provision in the new Labour Party constitution for individual party membership in local branches. Twenty years later, the ILP was a much smaller entity on the political fringe, yet there were also continuities. It was throughout—in spite of all its diversions, crosscurrents, and contradictions—a residuary legatee of the pre-Leninist radical democratic currents of the Left, including guild socialism, with its emphasis on workplace democracy.

It is an almost universal judgment that the 1932 disaffiliation was a huge mistake. It is difficult to find any grounds on which to disagree. Many in the ILP itself had already reached the same conclusion by 1939. Only the outbreak of war prevented the holding of a special conference to decide whether to follow the NAC's recommendation to seek reaffiliation. Peter Thwaites pinpoints the choices and the consequences for the ILP when it decided not to go ahead with this in his thesis on the ILP between 1938 and 1950:

> When the ILP hesitated on the brink and then took a step back from reaffiliation to the Labour Party in 1939 it unwittingly doomed itself to virtual extinction. Inside the Labour Party the ILP might have replaced or united with the infant Tribune Group to become the voice of the Labour Left. Or it might have become submerged within the mass party within a short time and ceased to be a coherent group, but at least the individual ILPers would have been in contact with the mass of the labour movement and they might have been able to exert an influence, no matter how small, on the direction the Labour Party took.[2]

The danger of being submerged in the Labour Party and thereby losing its radical identity was one side of the siege that the ILP experienced—mainly from forces within it and in the minds of its members—throughout the interwar period. On the other side, the besiegers were the ideas and emotions drawing the party either into a merger with the CPGB or towards trying to set itself up as its own version of a Bolshevik-style revolutionary party in a context where there was little sign of revolution, though some believed that revolution might have ensued with a more determined leadership in the General Strike of 1926.

A few years later, after the Great Crash of 1929, it looked to many as though capitalism really was on its last legs. But it turned out that there was little prospect of revolution—and if there had been, it is doubtful that the ILP could have reached any clear position on how a revolution should be conducted. The post-disaffiliation policy conflicts over revolutionary policy were to show this rather conclusively.

But this does not necessarily mean that the experience of the ILP—both before and after it left the Labour Party—was without value. There is little doubt that the core of the interwar ILP contributed more than most forces on the Left to the preservation of the traditions of democratic socialism in Britain. It was, throughout that time, both more radical than mainstream Labour and infinitely more democratic than were the Communists or their later adversaries in the fragmented Trotskyist movement.

This account began with Fred Jowett's long involvement as a consistently prominent figure in the ILP. He was a leading member from the party's foundation until his death during the Second World War. His continued commitment, together with that of others who stayed with the ILP through all the crises and conflicts of the period, gives a sense of continuity to an organization that saw many great changes.

But we must always remember that Mosley and John Beckett, who departed to fascism; MacDonald, Snowden, and Allen, who ended up with National Labour; and Brailsford and Wise, who opposed disaffiliation and became leading figures in the Socialist League were all once leading ILPers. Other influential figures in the ILP, for at least some of the period, included people as diverse as Fenner Brockway, Katharine Bruce Glasier, Patrick Dollan, Bob Edwards, George Orwell, Edith Mannin, John Middleton Murry, Jennie Lee, Minnie Pallister, John Paton, Jack Gaster, Dorothy Jewson, and Elijah Sandham. Yet Jowett's tenacious stand on reforming parliamentary procedure in order, as he saw it, to make representative democracy more genuinely democratic can stand for wider trends in the ILP. The party resisted—in the end—all attempts either to depart from the democratic principles of the party or to jettison its radicalism.

The ILP was surely right to wish to expand the boundaries of democracy. Democracy, of course, has its own problems, including those of definition. As Dennis Pilon says in *Wrestling with Democracy*, what "democracy is or should be in the west has never been settled" in spite of the fact that "political scientists often carry on as if democracy is obvious."[3] For left-wing democrats, the aspiration has always been to establish some significant degree of democratic control and accountability over the economy. How they have proposed to do this and the nature and extent of the desired control has varied greatly from time to time and place to place, but that goal has always been present.

Democracy always requires defending, deepening, and expanding. The ILP support for Jowett's proposals, albeit not as robust as he would have liked, meant that the party never accepted the complacent constitutional attitudes that were found so often in the Labour Party, nor, in the end, did it enter a would-be revolutionary cul-de-sac—although it came alarmingly close to the latter. Yet it is not without significance that in 1939, Jowett felt that he had been a lone voice. It reflects the way in which concern with issues of parliamentary reform, like Parliament itself, had been sidelined by the ILP during the post-disaffiliation years.

With the new Labour Party constitution in operation, it was, and still is, easy to conclude that the ILP was doomed from the beginning of the interwar period. Certainly, its position in the new dispensation *could* be regarded as anomalous, but there is no shortage of anomalies in British constitutional and political practice. And it is worth noting that the initiative to leave Labour came from the ILP. Its position was certainly made difficult by the unbending insistence by the larger party on its parliamentary standing orders and refusal to endorse candidates who would not agree to accept them. But neither under MacDonald's leadership nor subsequently was there any move by Labour to expel the ILP, and at the end of the 1930s, when it looked as though it was returning to the fold, the attitude from Labour's NEC seems to have been relatively welcoming. That reaffiliation did not take place at the end of the 1930s was, once again, the decision of the ILP.

Some in the party suggested that the ILP should adjust to the new situation in the party brought about by Labour's 1918 constitution by following the pattern of the Fabian Society, concentrating exclusively on research, the promotion of policies, and "making socialists." There was never much likelihood of that happening during the interwar years. A very wide spectrum of ILP opinion was determined to retain a more active role of participation in local and national electoral politics. This continued after disaffiliation, though there was bitter conflict over the place of such activities, as well as over the attempt to put forward workers' councils as an alternative.

At the beginning of 1920, it looked as though the ILP was going to resolve the question of its future role by throwing in its lot with the Communist International. But this was rejected the following year at the expense of losing some members to the new Communist Party of Great Britain, though not on the scale of a major split. For the time being, the siege from that side was lifted—or at least eased to the extent that it no longer threatened the very existence of the ILP, which would have surely been rapidly absorbed into the CPGB had the ILP's Left Wing carried the day in 1921.

Given the mutual hostility that developed from 1924 onwards between MacDonald and the ILP "rebels" inside and outside Parliament, it is easy to overlook both the earlier support for the soon-to-be Labour leader and the degree to which he was dependent on the ILP. Without its backing, MacDonald would not have become the first fully established leader of the Labour Party, nor would he have been prime minister in the two minority governments. Had Clynes secured just another handful of votes, he might well have interpreted the role of chairman differently. One can only speculate about the impact that Clynes's success might have had on the development of the Labour Party and British politics more generally.

There is no doubt that in his "wilderness" years, when he was out of Parliament following the war, MacDonald was clearly dependent on the ILP—and made efforts to present himself as concerned with the issues that animated the party. Without repudiating his earlier, more conservative views, MacDonald made a real effort between 1918 and 1922 to signal a degree of support, or at least respectful consideration, for the more radical views and policies the party was debating. This is true of the questions of industrial democracy, the role of MPs, and direct action. MacDonald's position during the war may have been more equivocal than those of some other prominent ILPers, but it was a dominant factor in his support in the party. The positions he took in the immediate postwar years can only have helped to consolidate his position as its leading figure and candidate for the leadership among both ILP parliamentarians and the wider membership. This would be in great contrast to his later dismissive, even contemptuous, response to ILP policies—especially the *Living Wage* report—in the second half of the decade.

The five or so years that followed the rejection of Comintern affiliation were the most creative and productive period for the ILP between the two wars. No longer internally besieged by the "Left Wing," it still had reasonable relations with the rest of the Labour Party, although experience of the first Labour government soon put this under severe strain. Allen's notion of the ILP as a "nucleus" carried the implication that it would be leading the way as Labour's most "advanced" element. This was bound to be resented, to at least some extent, in other parts of the Labour Party.

If these parts were going to be won over to the ILP's "distinctive program," a great deal of tact and patience would be needed. The same qualities were required of the Labour Party and its leadership if the ILP was not to evolve into a permanent internal opposition. Such qualities were in short supply on both sides. In the end, Allen's personal loyalty to MacDonald would overcome his criticisms of Labour's approach under the latter's leadership, as the position he took in 1931 and subsequently demonstrated. But this was not remotely true of the vast majority of ILPers.

The party had taken a long time to arrive at its "guild socialist" 1922 constitution, but that constitution played relatively little part in subsequent internal discussion. This is surprising given the long and passionate debates that had taken place in 1921 and 1922. The collapse of the broader guild socialist movement seems to have been reflected in the declining focus on the subject within the ILP. But throughout the interwar period, the ILP did remain hostile to "state socialism" and in favour of "industrial democracy."

Allen clearly believed that socialism was simply the most rational and most "scientific" way of both running the economy and becoming a socially just society. In line with this belief, he proposed, in early 1924, that MacDonald take advantage of the government's control of resources to begin inquiries into major industries and "set the enquiring mind of the nation dispassionately to work."[4] His view of democracy entailed a minority Labour government proposing radical policies and then, following a parliamentary defeat, fighting a subsequent election on those policies—rather than waiting until it could acquire a prior mandate. When considering this, we should note that in his address to the 1925 ILP conference, Allen was concerned with the unlikelihood of Labour, or any other party, obtaining a majority of *votes* rather than of parliamentary seats. "It is doubtful," he said, "whether British politics will long continue to be limited to two great Parties. If that is true, then it is unlikely for some time to come that any one Party will be able to secure a majority of votes polled."[5]

The short period of the "Allen regime" constituted the most successful and significant of the interwar years for the ILP. In part, this was because of Allen's ability to obtain donations from, largely, the more prosperous pacifist associates with whom he had worked during the war. But there was also a determined energy during this period of organizational changes, including the replacement of the *Labour Leader* with Brailsford's *New Leader*. Along with this went more energetic, organized, and confident campaigning.

While all of that was important, surely the major achievement of the period was *The Living Wage* report. In its initial form, especially as promoted by Brailsford, the report sought to devise and promote a policy that would attract popular support and be difficult for political opponents to counter. It was, at the same time, intended to open up the prospect of winning democratic backing for more radical socialist policies. However, for it to be adopted by the Labour Party, the concerns of trade unionists, fearful that the political side of the movement was trying to seize its territory, would have to be conciliated. This, again, would require great tact and patience, both so conspicuously lacking in the ILP.

The rejection of a more patient, long-term approach soon became evident, as the Living Wage policy quickly became Socialism in Our Time and the step-by-step and flexible strategy of the original document was abandoned in favour of the demand for speedy implementation of a comprehensive program of radical socialist measures. More than with any other individual, Jimmy Maxton exemplified the restless and relentless pursuit of the socialist commonwealth. It is difficult to understate his impact on the ILP. From the mid-1920s, it was increasingly Maxton who was most likely to come to mind whenever the ILP was mentioned.

Even those who disagreed with him most strongly always testified to Maxton's extraordinary qualities. The notion of "charisma" is overused, but he was certainly an orator who could generate enthusiasm and support that was little, if anything, short of devotion. His sincerity was beyond question. He was liked and respected even by political opponents. The problem for the ILP was that, however contrary to his own declared belief that the ILP had "no giants," he was in danger of turning the party into a one-man band. This was particularly true in the post-disaffiliation years. Above all, he appealed to those committed to the uncompromising pursuit of left-wing goals. His political purism is best exemplified by his "two dictators" stance in the Abyssinian crisis.

Conclusion

One thing that Maxton clearly was not was what would now be called "a good team player." That he was unlikely to fulfill this role in a Labour Party context was already suggested by the "murderers" episode early in his parliamentary career. Nor was this his forte within the ILP, as his behaviour as ILP representative at the 1925 Labour Party conference and in the 1928 Cook-Maxton campaign revealed. But just how much the party came to revolve around Maxton is evident in the episode of his threatened resignation and the subsequent plebiscite over Abyssinia.

The tendency to turn individuals into unchallengeable icons is not confined to organizations of the Left, but it sits very awkwardly there because of their egalitarian values. Maxton was not the first iconic figure in the ILP. Long before, Keir Hardie had been granted this status as had, to a lesser extent, Snowden and MacDonald, as Murry was keen to point out to the ISP. Maxton's near-iconic status helped to take the ILP out of the Labour Party, with a consequent loss of membership. In what direction would it now turn?

One possibility that was immediately ruled out was the path taken by Oswald Mosley. For a few years, he had seemed likely not only to begin to rival Maxton in ILP circles but even to claim the leadership of the Labour Party. His Birmingham Proposals and *Revolution by Reason* had been taken very seriously, though it was not clear to what extent they were an alternative to *The Living Wage* or simply a contribution to the debate around that report. But as the authoritarian and nationalistic strains in Mosley's thinking became clearer, they were rejected by the ILP, although it is true that some former ILPers, most notably John Beckett, followed him not just into the New Party but into the British Union of Fascists.[6]

What of a move to the supposedly revolutionary Left? By the 1930s, circumstances appeared to favour a new attempt to work with, and eventually merge with, the CPGB. The departure, in different ways and in different directions, of two former chairmen of the ILP—Wallhead and Allen—helped to clear the ground for this. Wallhead, like Allen, had started as a supporter of the Bolsheviks but had come back from the 1920 visit to Russia critical of the regime. One of the few Labour survivors of the disastrous 1931 election, Wallhead had initially gone along with disaffiliation but had returned to the Labour Party in 1933. He died the following year. In 1931, Allen had put himself well beyond the pale in ILP eyes by siding with MacDonald and accepting a peerage.

Things now looked very different to many still in the ILP. The apparent success of the Five-Year Plans in the USSR contrasted with the disasters of the stock market crash and depression in the capitalist world. A younger generation of ILPers were keen to show themselves to be authentic revolutionaries, and many rather older members, like Brockway, were equally keen to turn their backs on "gradualism."

The party embarked on what it believed to be a revolutionary course. But, while many could support the *need* for a revolutionary policy, relatively few were agreed on what that actually meant. It is probably true to say that for most ILPers, their conception of revolution was of a transformative growth of socialist values and attitudes among an overwhelming majority of an inclusively defined working class leading to radical social, economic and political change. Precisely how this might be translated into political action was far less clear. It would quickly become evident that any attempt to prescribe a strategy would lead to fundamental disagreement and conflict. In particular, there was no way to bridge the gulf between the Revolutionary Policy Committee, which sought eventual merger with the CPGB, and those like Paton who aspired to replace it completely.

Fear of being merged with the CPGB powered the opposition to the United Front policy, which seemed so essential to the RPC. This apprehension led to substantial defections from the ILP in Lancashire and to the formation of the Independent Socialist Party. Yet not long afterwards, with the differences over Abyssinia as the catalyst, as well as its long-nurtured hostility to Brockway's criticism of Soviet foreign policy, the RPC gave up what had come to seem like a hopeless attempt to bring the party at least into alliance with the Communists. Most of the Trotskyists who had joined in the post-disaffiliation years also soon abandoned their attempts to convert the ILP into the sort of organization they envisioned.

It is ironic, particularly for a party routinely seen as "in the centre" or centrist, that by the later 1930s, the ILP and the CPGB had effectively swapped places on the conventional political spectrum. True, the attempt to apply democratic centralism was even more of a failure in the case of the ILP than it usually is. Yet in the "class against class" period at the beginning of the 1930s, it had been the Communists who rejected any sort of alliance with so-called social fascists, let alone with any political forces outside the working-class movement. By the later years of the decade, it was the ILP that dismissed the notion of a "popular front" intended to include not only the CPGB and the Labour Party but also elements of the "bourgeois" parties. Instead, it favoured a much more exclusive "workers' front." It was now the ILP rather than the CPGB that pursued a form of "class war." It was the ILP that regarded the League of Nations as an irredeemably bourgeois and imperialist entity, while the CPGB supported it once the USSR had joined. And it was the ILP that supported the revolutionary policy of the POUM during the Spanish War in opposition to the Communists.

Conclusion

The way the CPGB was regarded by ILPers—a spectrum ranging from the benevolence of the RPC and some others through mild suspicion to outright contempt—contrasts with the much more unanimous ILP commitment to the USSR as the "first workers' republic." The Moscow trials and especially the experience of the Spanish Civil War began to undermine this commitment, yet many ILPers clung to the idea that somehow, as Brockway asserted in 1938, there was a socialist economic basis in the Soviet Union that might be salvaged. Uncritical views of aspects of Soviet reality still persisted.

Sometimes, the statements relating to Stalin's Russia of some of those who were, or had been, ILP members seem truly shocking with the hindsight that the twenty-first century gives. One example comes from Jennie Lee's 1942 book *This Great Journey*, where she attributes the USSR's famine of ten years earlier to a "war" in which

> peasants who killed their livestock and refused to cultivate the land rather than conform to Soviet methods of farming and land-holding trapped themselves into famine. It was famine from such causes that I had seen in the Ukraine. But the plus factor added by Russia was not poverty, or disease or illiteracy. It was exactly the reverse. It was the fight *against* these barbarities.[7]

Jennie Lee was, as noted earlier, by no means one of the more credulous figures on the British Left as far as communism and the USSR were concerned. No doubt, too, we should recall the wartime alliance with Stalin. And, as Tony Judt says of the Soviet Union,

> many people needed to believe in its self-definition as the homeland of revolution—including quite a few of its victims. Today, we do not know what to make of the many Western observers who accepted show trials, minimized (or denied) the Ukrainian famine, or believed everything they were told about productivity and democracy and the great new Soviet constitution of 1936.[8]

The blindness and wishful thinking involved in left-wing perceptions of the USSR even at the height of Stalinist atrocities were not, of course, confined to the ILP. The best-known example of this is the Webbs's *Soviet Communism: A New Civilisation*. But they were anything but alone. We might be tempted to discount as overly partial the publications of the Friends of the Soviet Union such as *The New Democracy: Stalin's Speech on the New Constitution* or *Spies, Wreckers, and Grafters: The Truth about the Moscow Trials*. Nor is it surprising that the Anglo-Soviet Parliamentary Committee published the 1933 pamphlet *More Anti-Soviet Lies Nailed*, by its secretary, W. P. Coates.[9] What is rather startling is that the latter contained a foreword by the then leader of the Labour Party, George Lansbury, which hailed the "wonderful experiment" of the USSR and declared that "we are not called upon to judge or accept all the means they adopt to attain their ends."[10]

Yet few would challenge Lansbury's credentials, in the domestic context, as a radical democratic socialist. The same is true of Charles Trevelyan, though some might find his baronetcy and position of monarch's representative in the county, as Lord Lieutenant of Northumberland, a little anomalous. We have already encountered him a number of times. He first appeared in chapter 1 as a radical Liberal MP before the First World War, initiating a House of Commons debate on secret diplomacy in which Fred Jowett made a "vigorous speech." In chapter 3, he appeared as one of the new postwar recruits to Labour and the ILP, and in chapter 5, he was briefly mentioned as one of the MPs who strengthened ILP parliamentary representation in 1922. His admirable attempts to raise the school leaving age featured in chapters 6 and 11 with, in the latter case, his resignation as the Minister of Education of the second Labour government after the failure of his Education Bill. He was also noted there for his support for continued ILP involvement in electoral politics and his declaration that the Labour government ought to aspire to do more than just "govern decently" and should make an effort to "break through to Socialism and establish a new Society." Finally, as a leading member of the "ex-ILP", we saw him experiencing a moment of triumph as, in effect, a Socialist League spokesman at the 1932 Labour Party conference and bringing the League's fraternal greetings to the Scottish Socialist Party in 1934.

In 1935, Trevelyan was, he told readers, "in Soviet Russia for quite a long time," and on his return, Gollancz published his account of the visit as *Soviet Russia: A Description for British Workers*. Trevelyan recommended "the great book being written by Mr. and Mrs. Sidney Webb." His own chapter headings include "Russian Democracy," "A Classless Society," and "The Holidays of the People." He claimed that in the sphere of economic life, "the Russian worker is a free man indeed compared with the workers in our own capitalist lands" and that the introduction of secret ballots would make the "mechanism of Russian Soviet Government as completely democratic as our own." He told his readers that the "Communist Party as such does not direct government either in the village or the factory or the Kremlin" and that "the most vigorous debating organisation in the country is the Communist Party," with "no curb on the frankness of discussion or the vigour of opinions."[11]

With even people like Lansbury and Trevelyan successfully persuaded of the benevolence of Stalin's Russia, it is hardly surprising that reports that went further than to suggest that the Soviet Union might be still a little way short of socialist perfection were dismissed as hostile propaganda and that even mild criticism was challenged. Hobsbawm captures the attitude towards Russia of many on the Left—including ILPers: "Whatever its weaknesses, its very existence proved that socialism was more than a dream."[12] Furthermore, so much hope was invested by the Left because, as Kevin Morgan says, "over time the revolution in Russia came to function as a surrogate for its absence elsewhere."[13] The best that can be said for the ILP was that by the late 1930s, it was less uncritical than much of the rest of the Left.

Many in the ILP subscribed to the myth of soviet democracy, believing that genuine control of Russia lay, or at least had lain in the earliest days of the revolution, in the hands of the largely workplace-based grassroots. All could qualify as "workers" by making a positive contribution to society, and the Communist Party's role was confined to voluntarily accepted intellectual guidance. Even those who saw the practice of Stalin's regime as a cruel parody of soviet democracy still clung to the hope that the genuine article could still be established—or restored—as long as the state remained in control of the economy. Such a notion did not then seem so incredible as it does today.

Versions of soviet democracy on the British Left varied in theoretical consistency, if not in practicality. In the early days of the CPGB, when it demanded representation on councils of action, it was fiercely opposed by the "Left Communists" of its erstwhile rival, Sylvia Pankhurst's Communist Party (British Section of the Third International). This challenge was on the grounds that such bodies should be made up entirely of delegates from shop-floor "industrial" bodies. Political organizations must be entirely excluded from direct representation.[14] This may have been utopian, but it was consistent with the ideals that had informed syndicalism and similar demands for "workers' democracy." But, though the ideal of soviet democracy was shared by many in the ILP, the workers' councils advocated in the party in the 1930s for immediate implementation were to be ad hoc bodies made up largely of "political" representatives rather than delegate bodies proportionally representative of groups of actual workers. Such bodies could satisfy neither the criteria for pure soviet democracy nor those of advocates of (reformed) parliamentary democracy like Jowett.

Everyone in the ILP was familiar with delegate democracy as practiced in British trade unions, political parties—including the ILP itself—and other voluntary organizations. The tendency of such a system to favour the objectives of the most active participants could lead to allegations that it produced results unrepresentative of the opinions of the membership. In the ILP, this was the case argued for a referendum on disaffiliation by those who claimed that the decision of the Bradford conference of 1932 did not truly reflect the views of the majority of members. Many trade unions have provision for the requisitioning of special conferences or members' referendums as a safeguard. In all voluntary organizations, like the ILP, the tendency for the "militants" to push it too far in a direction not favoured by less active members is and was balanced, ultimately, by the ability—much employed in the ILP of the 1930s—to leave the organization. Delegate democracy as a structure of state power would be very different in that it would lack any such an option. Believers in the reality of soviet democracy in Russia or of the possibility of bringing about a more authentic version in Britain seem to have given little consideration to the ways in which practice might fall short of the utopian ideal.

What can be said to sum up the nature of the ILP in the two decades between the wars? One cannot, logically, insist that throughout the period, the ILP included a range of different beliefs that were generally tolerated—at least until the existence of the party seemed to be threatened—and then go on to argue for its possession of uniform ideology. Can any valid generalizations nevertheless be made?

The ILP did more than most organizations of the Left, in practice as well as in theory, to support the equal status of women. The party is sometimes described as adhering to "ethical socialism." Certainly, most ILPers had a strong sense of moral purpose. Thwaites calls it "a libertarian party, with a respect for the freedom of political units which was reflected in its own ultra-democratic structure and constitution."[15] That is true enough. Anything that smacked of authoritarianism was always going to meet with opposition from the vast majority of ILPers—once it had been clearly identified as such. The socialism that the party hoped to see accomplished "in our time" was definitely to be democratic and egalitarian, with a much greater liberty for the individual than capitalism could deliver.

The ILP included pacifists. More broadly, it was consistently antimilitarist and antiwar. Yet in its response to the Spanish Civil War, the party showed a willingness to support the use of force when used defensively against fascism. Did ILPers, as uncompromising revolutionary socialists, foresee a violent revolution? This was never clear. For some, force would have to be used, again defensively, when the predicted violent revolt of supporters of capitalism faced with the prospect of socialism took place. In such circumstances, force might be legitimately needed to resist the imposition of fascism.

In his book *The Totalitarian Enemy*, written during the early months of the "phoney war" in 1939, Franz Borkenau noted that "in Russia the old landowners, bankers and industrialists have been killed or driven into exile." He went on to say that "in Republican Spain, on the contrary, the OGPU [Soviet secret police] killed and drove into exile those who wanted to kill or drive into exile landowners, bankers and industrialists."[16] The ILP would have endorsed the comment on the role of the Russian secret police, but most of its members would have indignantly disclaimed any desire to kill adherents of capitalism. In the Spanish context, the ILP would have defended the POUM against any such allegation. It did not see support for revolution and solidarity in the fight against Franco as in any way contradictory.

In the ILP utopia—or at least the "workers' democracy" version of it—far from being exterminated or expelled, members of the former "capitalist class" would be rapidly converted into useful members of the socialist commonwealth, helping in one way or another to advance the cause of humanity. As "workers," they would have the right to take part in the election, mandation, and, if necessary, recall of workplace delegates, who would faithfully pursue the policies laid down by their constituents. Those unable to work would, of course, also be accommodated with similar rights.

As a general rule, the ILP shared many of the beliefs and assumptions of the wider Left. It is often difficult now to understand why they were accepted so uncritically. Marx and Engels gave a brilliant sketch in the *Communist Manifesto* of the development of societies through different socioeconomic stages in the past and the predicted future. This was often interpreted not as a sequence of ideal types revealing the essence of feudalism, capitalism, and socialism but as something close to an actual historical account. The French Revolution could be trimmed and moulded into an unambiguous bourgeois revolution, while Britain's Industrial Revolution of the eighteenth century could become something close to the beginning not just of modern industrial capitalism but of capitalism *tout court*. The achievement of socialism would be a similar sudden and once-and-for-all transition. The resulting conclusion was all too often that "come the revolution," everything would be possible, but without it, nothing could be achieved. Yet if, in some ways, the bar was set very high, in other respects, what was deemed to constitute socialism was much less demanding.

As with others on the Left, socialism for the ILP was in danger of being seen mostly in negative terms—as an absence of capitalism. Public ownership and control of the economy, however nominal, seemed all that was required to meet the basic criteria for a socialist society. That a socialist society was supposed to be infinitely more democratic and egalitarian than anything in the present or past, that the mission of socialism was to enhance as far as humanly possible the well-being and happiness of humankind was not lost sight of in the ILP. But it had to struggle with the notion that—essentially—socialism equalled public ownership. This was so even though the party always rejected "state socialism" and supported "industrial democracy."

The shortcomings of the ILP during the interwar period are easy to detect. Murry had some justification for criticizing the tendency to grant iconic status to leaders later found wanting, such as MacDonald and Allen. The easy acceptance of Maxton's seeming inability to play a representative role showed that this had hardly become a thing of the past. Yet it is reasonable to ask whether the ILP was any more confused and inadequate than any other part of the British Left.

If we seek signs of a lasting impact of the interwar ILP, we should look at the postwar Labour Party rather than at the disaffiliated ILP of later years. So many of the ILPers who have appeared in these pages contributing to the debates and controversies of the period went on to play roles in the Labour Party—as Labour MPs in some cases, such as Paton, Brockway, and Bob Edwards. As David Howell points out, whether they stayed with the ILP, like Brockway and Jennie Lee, or sided with the Labour Party at the time of disaffiliation, like Emrys Hughes, "all the ex-ILPers were insistent that the breach should not be repeated."[17] One of the main advocates of disaffiliation in 1932, Fenner Brockway, would rejoin the Labour Party after the war and become active in the Tribune Group on the Labour Left, a prominent proponent of the Campaign for Nuclear Disarmament as well as the chair of the Movement for Colonial Freedom and a founder of War on Want. He would take part in many other campaigns, including those mentioned in the introduction. He would die, still active on the Left and as a Labour peer, just a few months short of his century, in 1988.

Another firm supporter of disaffiliation had been Jennie Lee. She returned to the Labour Party and was elected again as an MP in 1945. She became the first Minister for the Arts in Harold Wilson's government from 1964 to 1970. In this role, she played a crucial part in what Wilson would later claim as the greatest achievement of his government—the creation of the Open University. Losing her parliamentary seat in 1970, she became, like Brockway, a Labour member of the House of Lords.

For Labour, the inheritance from the ILP—and the ex-ILP—was a mixed one. It contributed to the radical and democratic aspects of the Labour Left. At the same time, it is not hard to see the factionalism that characterized the ILP's participation in the larger party in the later 1920s, reproduced in later episodes. To be fair, the art of pursuing critical questioning and radical proposals while avoiding degenerating into unity-undermining sectional activism is a particularly difficult one that is rarely adequately practised. The post-1945 history of the Labour Party illustrates this abundantly. This should not obscure the ILP's positive role.

Apart from this general, but not to be underestimated, contribution to the preservation of democratic socialism or radical social democracy, some significant questions need to be asked about the ILP's legacy. Do any of the ideas debated and adopted by the ILP in the 1920s and 1930s still have any relevance for those who aspire to revive Labour in Britain, or to social democracy or democratic socialism more generally, after the neoliberal decades? Some of the values of the ILP are timeless but need to be constantly reasserted—notably, its internationalism, anti-imperialism, and antimilitarism. The egalitarian aims of the ILP, as well as its suspicion of all warlike activities, seem more urgent than ever at a time when, both at a global level and within so many countries, the gap between rich and poor seems ever widening and the first decades of the century have demonstrated the all-too-often negative consequences of even well-intended military intervention. All of these were certainly values cherished by the ILP, but they were also widely shared by much of the rest of the political Left and sometimes far beyond.

There are at least three more candidates for contemporary relevance that are more particular to the ILP. They are Jowett's campaign for "real" representative government; the guild socialist, or at least guild socialist–influenced, constitution of 1922; and the Living Wage policy adopted four years later. The relevance in each case lies more in the general thrust and underlying aims of these policies than in their specifics. It is not necessary to revive Jowett's particular formula to pursue his aim of making elected representatives accountable to their constituents and the executive accountable to the people's representatives. At a time when the public regard for politics and politicians, never that high, is at a very low point, this goal is surely more relevant than ever.

The twenty-first century may be unlikely to see a revival of the elaborate blueprints of guild socialism. Yet achieving at least a degree of representation for employees in both the public and private sectors and creating effective forms of social management that go at least some way to reconcile the interests of producers, users, consumers, and the community at large are still relevant aspirations for any social democratic party.

The same is true of the ILP's living wage policy, the continuing relevance of which has been evident in the new Living Wage campaign in Britain. Even more generally relevant is the principle that Brailsford, Creech Jones, Hobson, and Wise advocated: the need to make "a simple and concrete appeal to the average worker" and to take goals that are widely supported as a starting point for policies to advance equality and social justice. That the general thrust, if not the specific details, of these three ILP policies remains current the better part of a century later suggests that the party should not be relegated to the status of a "centrist" body floating uncomfortably during the 1920s between the remainder of the Labour Party and the British Communists.

The merit of the post-disaffiliation ILP lies in the fact that it tested the notion of a "revolutionary policy" to destruction. Whether or not gradualism was inevitable, it became clear that there would be no serious support for a Lenin-style revolutionary party in Britain—even one detached from the edicts and the embrace of Moscow—at any time that could be foreseen. The democratic and ethical values of the ILP were under siege in the 1920s and 1930s not so much from outside forces as from the conflicting ideas in the heads of its members. That, despite contentious debates within the party ranks, these values were for the most part upheld may not be the most impressive of the ILP's achievements, but their survival surely counts as at least a modest success.

Notes

Introduction

1. Evelyn Waugh, *Vile Bodies*, 52.
2. Hugh Thomas, *John Strachey*, 26, 40. Strachey (1901–63)—about whom we will hear more in chapter 7—served for some time as the editor of the ILP's *Socialist Review*.
3. Robert E. Dowse, *Left in the Centre: The Independent Labour Party, 1893–1940*, 47.
4. The report of the party's National Administrative Council to the 1930 annual conference listed the last four of these as "Papers Associated with the Party," also reminding delegates that the *Northern Voice* was "directly under the management and control of the Lancashire Divisional Council." NAC *Report*, 1930, 29. (Note: The reports of the ILP's National Administrative Council, which were presented at the party's annual conferences, were often published as separate documents, rather than as part of the main conference report. In such cases, their original, very long-winded, titles have been abbreviated to NAC *Report*.)
5. Gidon Cohen, *The Failure of a Dream: The Independent Labour Party from Disaffiliation to World War II*, 1.
6. Fenner Brockway, *Inside the Left: Thirty Years of Platform, Press, Prison, and Parliament*, 145.
7. In the wake of this vote, a special conference of the party was scheduled for 17 September. As Gidon Cohen suggests, had the outbreak of the Second World War not led to the suspension of plans for this conference, the NAC's recommendation would probably have won the day. Cohen, *Failure of a Dream*, 161.
8. On Communist efforts to infiltrate the ILP, see ibid., chap. 7.
9. Kevin Morgan, *Bolshevism, Syndicalism and the General Strike: The Lost Internationalist World of A. A. Purcell*, 17.
10. *Labour Leader*, 4 August 1921.

Chapter 1: Democracy, Foreign Policy, and Parliamentary Reform

1. Robert E. Dowse, *Left in the Centre: The Independent Labour Party, 1893–1940*, 5.
2. J. B. Priestley, preface to Fenner Brockway, *Socialism over Sixty Years: The Life of Jowett of Bradford*, 12. Priestley was a prominent novelist, playwright, social commentator, and broadcaster.
3. Arthur Marwick, *Clifford Allen: The Open Conspirator*, 86.
4. Brockway, *Socialism over Sixty Years*, 211.
5. *The Clarion*, 2 November 1906, 4 December 1908. On "direct democracy" in British socialism before the First World War, see Logie Barrow and Ian Bullock, *Democratic Ideas and the British Labour Movement, 1880–1914*.
6. See Ian Bullock, *Romancing the Revolution: The Myth of Soviet Democracy and the British Left*.
7. F. W. Jowett, *What Is the Use of Parliament?* 3, 16.

8. *The Clarion*, 3 August 1906. *The Clarion* was edited by Robert Blatchford, a major propagandist for socialism in Britain, especially in the 1890s. It was broadly supportive but often critical of the ILP at this time.
9. H. M. Hyndman, "Our Republic," *Justice*, 14 June 1884. For longer extracts from this article, see Barrow and Bullock, *Democratic Ideas*, 14–15.
10. *Labour Leader*, 20 July 1901.
11. *The Clarion*, 3 March 1905.
12. *The Clarion*, 23 March 1906.
13. *The Clarion*, 10 July 1908.
14. Jowett, *What Is the Use of Parliament?* 16, 29.
15. Ibid., 3–4.
16. Ibid., 24–25.
17. Ibid., 12.
18. Ibid., 13.
19. Hansard, HC Deb, 14 March 1913, vol. 50, cc588–89, 620, 622.
20. *Labour Leader*, 31 May 1912; Barrow and Bullock, *Democratic Ideas*, 271.
21. On the Bradford Resolution, see Barrow and Bullock, *Democratic Ideas*, 207–17, 271–74.
22. *The Clarion*, 17 April 1914.
23. *The Clarion*, 17 July 1908. The Triple Entente, following on from the "Entente Cordiale" with France of 1903, had ended Britain's period of "Splendid Isolation," during which it had avoided alliances or "understandings" with Continental European powers.
24. Hansard, HC Deb, 8 March 1911, vol. 22, cc1190–91.
25. *The Clarion*, 7 August 1908.
26. *Bradford Daily Telegraph*, 14 August 1908, quoted in Brockway, *Socialism over Sixty Years*, 121–22. Jowett was not alone in advocating such a committee. According to F. M. Leventhal, Brailsford had put forward the idea of a parliamentary committee analogous to the Senate Foreign Relations Committee in 1909. *The Last Dissenter: H. N. Brailsford and His World*, 109–10. Leventhal cites the *English Review* 4 (December 1909): 122–31.
27. *Bradford Pioneer*, 10 July 1914, quoted in Brockway, *Socialism over Sixty Years*, 128.
28. Unless otherwise indicated, emphasis (whether boldface or italic) is in the original.
29. More will be said about the Union of Democratic Control in chapter 3. Sir Charles Trevelyan (1870–1958) hailed from an aristocratic family, becoming 3rd Baronet of Wallington in 1928. After graduating from Cambridge, he entered politics, serving as a Liberal MP from 1899 until 1918, when he stood and lost as an ILP candidate. He returned to the House of Commons as a Labour MP in 1922, where he remained until defeated, like most Labour candidates, in the 1931 election. Throughout his career, he was active in promoting educational reform, including the raising of the school leaving age. He served as the parliamentary secretary to the Board of Education from 1908 to 1914 and then as its president in 1924 and again from 1929 to 1931, in MacDonald's Labour governments. He will appear from time to time in later chapters, particularly in connection with his role in the Socialist League after 1932.
30. The son of Sir Henry Ponsonby, Queen Victoria's private secretary, Arthur Ponsonby (1871–1946) began his career in 1882, as a Page of Honour in the royal

household. Educated at Oxford, he joined the diplomatic service before turning to politics. He was elected to the House of Commons in 1908, as a Liberal MP, but switched his allegiance to the Labour Party after the war, returning to the House of Commons in 1922 as a Labour MP and serving in both of Ramsay MacDonald's Labour governments. Raised to the peerage in 1930, he went on to become the Labour Party's leader in the House of Lords and a founder of the Peace Pledge Union. He resigned from the Labour Party in 1940, when it joined Churchill's wartime coalition.

31. *Labour Leader*, 28 March 1918.
32. *Labour Leader*, 17 April 1917.
33. J. W. Kneeshaw, *The Hidden Hand in Politics*, 7–8.
34. J. W. Kneeshaw, *Democracy "Done Brown,"* 5, 8.
35. F. W. Jowett, *"Down with the Parasites": Jowett's Chairman's Address to the Labour Party Conference at Edinburgh*, 5.
36. *Report of the Annual Conference Held at Leeds, April 1917*, 79. After their first mention in each chapter, titles of annual conference reports are shortened to *Report of the Annual Conference*, followed by the year.
37. *Report of the Annual Conference Held at Huddersfield*, April 1919, 81.
38. Ibid., 82. See Bullock, *Romancing the Revolution*, 114–15, for more on the notion of the Russian soviets as "an experiment."
39. Ibid., 83.
40. Ibid., 84.
41. *Report of the Annual Conference Held at Glasgow, April 1920*, 91–92.
42. *New Leader*, 6 April 1923. As we shall see, Leach was later to change his mind on this issue. William Leach (1870–1949) started out in local Bradford politics like Jowett, served as Bradford Central MP in 1922–24 and 1929–31, and from 1935 until he retired in 1945. He was Under Secretary for Air in MacDonald's 1924 government.
43. *New Leader*, 3 October 1924. Clement R. Attlee (1883–1967) had joined the ILP in 1907, but he did not share the party's opposition to the war, in which he served and was wounded. In his account of Attlee's early political career, Ben Pimlott perhaps downplays his involvement with the ILP. While acknowledging that Attlee took an active part in establishing the party's Stepney branch, he writes that, "in 1914, Attlee rejected the pacifism prevalent in the ILP" and joined the war effort. He goes on to mention that Attlee was mayor of Stepney after the war and was elected as the MP for Limehouse in 1922, but he gives no hint that Attlee returned to the ILP and, for a short while, played a very active role in it. Ben Pimlott, *Labour and the Left in the 1930*, 24; see also Kenneth O. Morgan, *Labour People: Leaders and Lieutenants, Hardie to Kinnock*, 137. In fact, Attlee was sufficiently close to the ILP to have reported to the party's 1923 conference on the activities in Parliament during the preceding year. Although he was often known, according to the custom of those times, by his wartime rank, as Major Attlee, in ILP literature of the period he generally appears as C. R. Attlee.
44. Ibid.
45. Brockway, *Socialism over Sixty Years*, 232.
46. *New Leader*, 9 May 1924. H. N. (Henry Noel) Brailsford (1873–1958) had already established himself as a leading political journalist and commentator before the First World War. He edited the *New Leader* from 1924 to 1926.

47. F. W. Jowett and H. B. Lees Smith, *The Reform of Parliament: Speeches by F. W. Jowett and H. B Lees Smith at the* ILP *Conference*, 2. Hastings Bernard Lees Smith (1876–1941) was a lecturer at the London School of Economics and later a professor of public administration at the University of Bristol. A Liberal MP from 1910 until 1918, he joined Labour in 1919 and was Labour MP for Keighley in 1922–23 and 1924–31, and from 1935 until his death. He was postmaster general in MacDonald's 1929 administration and briefly succeeded Trevelyan at the Board of Education in 1931.
48. Ibid., 3.
49. Ibid., 6.
50. Ibid., 8.
51. F. W. Jowett, *Parliament or Palaver? Answers to Objections to Proposal for Reform of Parliament*, 3. Jowett's biographer characterizes this publication as "one of the most effective political pamphlets ever printed." Brockway, *Socialism over Sixty Years*, 237.
52. Jowett, *Parliament or Palaver*, 4, 6.
53. Ibid., 11.
54. Ibid., 13, 16, 22.
55. *New Leader*, 6 August 1926.
56. *New Leader*, 11 August 1939.
57. *Labour Leader*, 31 May 1912.

Chapter 2: An Existential Dilemma

1. A. J. P. Taylor, *English History, 1914–1945*, 131.
2. Ralph Miliband, *Parliamentary Socialism: A Study in the Politics of Labour*, 61.
3. R. T. McKenzie, *British Political Parties: The Distribution of Power Within the Conservative and Labour Parties*, 482.
4. "Forecast of the N.A.C. Report," *Labour Leader*, 14 March 1918.
5. NAC *Report, 1918*, 16.
6. J. Ramsay MacDonald, "The I.L.P. and the Labour Party," 120.
7. NAC *Report, 1918*, 16–17. For the changes in the Labour Party constitution, see Henry Pelling, *A Short History of the Labour Party*, 43.
8. Robert E. Dowse, *Left in the Centre: The Independent Labour Party, 1893–1940*, 35.
9. *The I.L.P. and the Labour Party: What Is the Difference?* No doubt the 1899 date refers to the founding of the Labour Representation Committee, which actually took place at a conference held late in February 1900—although the call to convene the conference was issued in 1899.
10. *The Need for the I.L.P.*
11. Dowse, *Left in the Centre*, 47.
12. *Resolutions and Nominations to be Submitted to the 29th Annual Conference of the I.L.P., Southport, 27th, 28th, 29th March 1921*, 31.
13. David Howell, *MacDonald's Party: Labour Identities and Crisis, 1922–1931*, 238.
14. Matthew Worley, *Labour Inside the Gate: A History of the British Labour Party Between the Wars*, 10.
15. "Report on Policy and Relations with the Labour Party," in NAC *Report, 1921*, 59.
16. NAC *Report, 1920*, 18.
17. NAC *Report, 1921*, 8.

18. Ralph Miliband, *Parliamentary Socialism: A Study in the Politics of Labour*, 61.
19. *Labour Leader*, 8 April 1920.
20. *Labour Leader*, 8 January 1920. For more on the whole episode of the ILP's seeking Comintern affiliation, see Ian Bullock, *Romancing the Revolution: The Myth of Soviet Democracy and the British Left*, chap. 8.
21. *Labour Leader*, 8 April 1920.
22. *Report of the Annual Conference Held at Glasgow, April 1920*, 18. Kirkwood was the former treasurer of the Clyde Workers' Committee, formed in the Glasgow area in 1915. It was a key part of the wartime upsurge of the shop stewards' movement. See Walter Kendall, *The Revolutionary Movement in Britain, 1900–21: The Origins of British Communism*, chaps. 7 and 8; and James Hinton, *The First Shop Stewards' Movement*.
23. *Labour Leader*, 8 April 1920.
24. *Labour Leader*, 25 March 1920.
25. *Labour Leader*, 25 March 1920.
26. Arthur Marwick, *Clifford Allen: The Open Conspirator*, 195–96.
27. *Labour Leader*, 8 August 1918.
28. *Labour Leader*, 29 January 1920.
29. *Labour Leader*, 22 July 1920.
30. *Labour Leader*, 29 July 1920. The report's full title was *The I.L.P. and the Third International: Being the Questions Submitted by the I.L.P. Delegation to the Executive of the Third International and Its Reply, with an Introductory Statement by the National Council of the I.L.P.*
31. "Clifford Allen's Letter on the Third International and Visit to Russia," in NAC *Report, 1921*, 36–37. "Long and rambling" was indeed an apt description. The Comintern reply began with the eighth question—the broadest of the twelve—on the difference between communism and other forms of socialism. This gave the Third International executive the opportunity to spend more than twenty pages on a didactic version of the history of the socialist movement from a Leninist perspective. This was the longest of the replies, but others were far from short. According to Brockway, Harry Pollitt, long-time secretary of the CPGB, told him that the reply to the ILP had been written by "Lenin himself." Fenner Brockway, *Inside the Left: Thirty Years of Platform, Press, Prison, and Parliament*, 138.
32. "Clifford Allen's Letter," 38.
33. "Report of the Chairman, Councillor R. C. Wallhead, on his Visit to Russia and Meeting with the Executive of the Third International," in NAC *Report, 1921*, 55.
34. *Internationalist*, 19 June 1920. Newbold's wife, Marjory, had an interview with Comintern officials in Moscow. A report of this appeared, together with her photo, in the *Internationalist*, 17 July 1920.
35. *Moscow's Reply to the I.L.P.*, 1.
36. *Internationalist*, 3 July 1920.
37. *Labour Leader*, 19 August 1920.
38. On the debate in *The Call*, see Bullock, *Romancing the Revolution*, 135–45.
39. *Labour Leader*, 5 August 1920.
40. Francis Johnson, *The Independent Labour Party and the International: A Memorandum for Members*, 3–4. Though always maintaining the lowest of profiles politically, Johnson ran the ILP's national office for nearly four decades.

41. *The Socialist*, 9 December 1920.
42. *Labour Leader*, 23 December 1920.
43. David Marquand, *Ramsay MacDonald*, 274–75. MacDonald would return to the House of Commons the following year, as the MP for the Welsh seat of Aberavon.
44. *Labour Leader*, 10 March 1921. On the conflict between Snowden and Glasier, see Bullock, *Romancing the Revolution*, 346–52.
45. *Labour Leader*, 10 March 1921. In another article on the by-election, MacDonald complained, with much justification, that, "My private life was soused in a sewer bath, widows and mothers who had lost sons were told of my night club kind of orgies throughout their racking sorrows!" *Socialist Review*, April–June 1921, 103.
46. *Labour Leader*, 13 January 1921 (Scotland); 27 January 1921 (Yorkshire and Lancashire).
47. *Report of the Annual Conference Held at Southport, March 1921*, 55.
48. *Labour Leader*, 31 March 1921.
49. *Report of the Annual Conference, 1921*, 115.
50. *Labour Leader*, 31 March 1921. As Paton recalls in his autobiography, he responded to a heckler in the audience by declaring that he would "sooner go to hell with Ramsay MacDonald than to paradise with some of the leaders of our own Left wing." John Paton, *Left Turn! The Autobiography of John Paton*, 86. Paton's speech was not soon forgotten. In an article on the twenty-one points that appeared in the January 1933 issue of the ILP internal discussion organ *Controversy*, John Robson noted that the seventh point "even denounced Ramsay MacDonald by name." This, he wrote, "was too much for us in 1921, and so, led by John Paton who was prepared to follow Ramsay to hell, the I.L.P. set out for the promised land of Socialism by the road of Constitutionalism." Paton (1886–1976) supported disaffiliation but had resigned from the ILP by the time the *Controversy* article appeared. He was a Labour MP from 1945 until he retired in 1964.
51. *Labour Leader*, 31 March 1921. The eventual loss of membership to the ILP—and the gain to the CPGB—was not, however, on the scale that the Left Wing defectors and the CPGB had wished. Walter Kendall estimates the actual number of CPGB recruits at about five hundred or, "at the absolute maximum, one thousand." Kendall, *Revolutionary Movement in Britain*, 276.
52. *Report of the Annual Conference, 1921*, 11.
53. *Report of the Annual Conference, 1921*, Appendix 1, "Report of the Delegation to the Vienna Conference, February 22–27, 1921," 36.
54. *Report of the Annual Conference, 1921*, 12.
55. "Report of the Manchester Consultation," *Labour Leader*, 1 December 1921.

Chapter 3: Ramsay MacDonald and the ILP

1. Henry Pelling, *A Short History of the Labour Party*, 47. The "one of their own number" was evidently George Young, one of the Liberal recruits to the Labour Party.
2. *Labour Leader*, 24 December 1914.
3. NAC *Report, 1925*, 36. The *New Leader*, 21 November 1924, had devoted its front page to a picture of Morel, and the same issue featured his "last message" and a commemorative piece by Ponsonby.

4. H. M. Swanwick, *Builders of Peace: Being Ten Years' History of the Union of Democratic Control*, 50–51.
5. Ibid., 34, 52.
6. *Labour Leader*, 2 March 1916.
7. John Paton, *Left Turn! The Autobiography of John Paton*, 153–54.
8. *Labour Leader*, 13 January 1921.
9. *The Socialist*, 13 January 1921. John Maclean (1879–1923) was, in Walter Kendall's estimation, the "greatest of the Clydeside socialists." *The Revolutionary Movement in Britain, 1900–21: The Origins of British Communism*, 334n45.
10. *Justice*, 29 June 1895.
11. *Justice*, 21 November 1896. See also Logie Barrow and Ian Bullock, *Democratic Ideas and the British Labour Movement, 1880–1914*, 40–42.
12. *The Clarion*, 9 April 1909. See also Barrow and Bullock, *Democratic Ideas*, 184. John Bruce Glasier (1859–1920), who always appeared in print as J. Bruce Glasier, was the editor of *Labour Leader* until 1916, when illness forced him to resign. It was then that his wife, Katharine Bruce Glasier (1867–1950) took over as editor of the paper. She remained very active in the ILP, until its disaffiliation from the Labour Party, and subsequently in the Labour Party itself.
13. The ILP's more left-wing members were also instrumental in the attempt, in 1911, to forge a union between the ILP and the SDF (or the Social-Democratic Party, as it had then become). The main outcome of the 1911 "unity conference" was the birth of the British Socialist Party. Only thirty-six branches of the ILP took part in the conference, however, with members of the Social-Democratic Party forming the core of the new organization. See Walter Kendall, *The Revolutionary Movement in Britain, 1900–21: The Origins of British Communism*, 38, and, on the search for "socialist unity" before 1914, Keith Laybourn, "The Failure of Socialist Unity in Britain, c. 1893–1914."
14. Emanuel Shinwell, *Conflict Without Malice: An Autobiography*, 115. This rather ungenerous comment may cause some to wonder about the appropriateness of the title of Shinwell's memoir.
15. Paton, *Left Turn!* 84.
16. Ibid., 78.
17. David Marquand, *Ramsay MacDonald*, 262. For Paton's view of the episode, see Paton, *Left Turn!* 78.
18. J. Ramsay MacDonald, *Socialism and Society*, 133.
19. Minutes of NAC meeting, 3 April 1905, 21.
20. *Labour Leader*, 26 November 1909.
21. J. Ramsay MacDonald, *The Socialist Movement*, 150.
22. Ibid., 153.
23. Ibid., 154.
24. MacDonald, *Socialist Movement*, 190.
25. *Labour Leader*, 9 July 1914. By "Conservatives," Slater almost certainly meant not members of the Conservative Party per se but conservatives in general.
26. "Report on Party Program," in NAC *Report, 1921*, 53.
27. *Labour Leader*, 2 December 1920. A militia organized in 1912 by Edward Carson, the Ulster Volunteer Force (originally the Ulster Volunteers) threatened to use violence to oppose the Liberal government's efforts to impose Home Rule in Ireland.

28. J. Ramsay MacDonald, *Parliament and Revolution*, 78.
29. Austen Morgan, *J. Ramsay MacDonald*, 85.
30. J. Ramsay MacDonald, *The History of the I.L.P.*, 15.
31. See Stephen White, "Labour's Council of Action 1920."
32. *Socialist Review*, October 1920, quoted in Dowse, "Note on Ramsay MacDonald and Direct Action," 307.
33. Robert E. Dowse, *Left in the Centre: The Independent Labour Party, 1893–1940*, 61.
34. *Justice*, 23 November 1895.
35. Robert E. Dowse, "A Note on Ramsay MacDonald and Direct Action," 307.
36. J. Ramsay MacDonald, *Socialism After the War*, 11.
37. MacDonald, *Socialism After the War*, 43, 47.
38. Ibid., 49.
39. *Labour Leader*, 16 October 1919.
40. In his 1920 volume *Guild Socialism Re-stated*, G. D. H. Cole succinctly laid out the theory of functional democracy. An individual "should be called upon, not to choose someone to represent him as a man or as a citizen in all aspects of citizenship, but only to choose someone to represent his point of view in relation to some particular purpose or group of purposes, in other words, some particular *function*. All true and democratic representation is therefore *functional* representation." Consequently, "there must be, in the Society, as many separately elected groups as there are distinct essential groups of functions to be performed" and individuals "must therefore have, not one vote each, but as many different functional votes as there are different questions calling for associative action in which they are interested" (32–33).
41. MacDonald, *Parliament and Revolution*, 50–52.
42. Ibid., 54.
43. Marquand, *Ramsay MacDonald*, 257.
44. MacDonald, *Parliament and Revolution*, 3–4. "National Guilds" refers to the guild socialist movement, which, as we shall see in chapter 4, was to be very influential for a time in the ILP.
45. Ibid., 11–13.
46. Ibid., 15, 18.
47. Ibid., 19, 20.
48. Ibid., 17.
49. See Ian Bullock, *Romancing the Revolution: The Myth of Soviet Democracy and the British Left*, 202–5. Dr. Alfred Salter (1873–1945) was the subject of a biography by Fenner Brockway, *Bermondsey Story: The Life of Alfred Salter*. Ethel Snowden's book *Through Bolshevik Russia* raised considerable criticism and hostility in left-wing circles as did her public statements.
50. MacDonald, *Parliament and Revolution*, 98.
51. Ibid., 32.
52. Ibid., 34–35. It is interesting that MacDonald gave university representation as the example of the way in which the British system fell short of the benchmark of "one person one vote of equal value." At the time he wrote the book, franchise rules were governed by the Representation of the People Act, 1918, which, though it enfranchised some women for the first time, still completely excluded those under thirty years of age. University graduates, not just of Oxford and Cambridge, could vote for university representatives in twelve separate

constituencies, as well as voting for those running for office in the constituency where they lived. There were also other forms of plural voting—notably, where property was owned that enabled people to register in more than one parliamentary constituency. This remained so until 1948.
53. Ibid., 107–9.
54. Ibid., 111, 114.
55. *Report of the Annual Conference Held at Glasgow, April 1920*, 97; "Preliminary Agenda, [Meeting of the] I.L.P. Scottish Divisional Council on 3 and 4 January 1921," 5.
56. MacDonald, *Parliament and Revolution*, 66.
57. Ibid., 102–3.
58. *Labour Leader*, 1 April 1920.
59. Clement J. Bundock, review of J. Ramsay MacDonald, *Socialism: Critical and Constructive*, in *Labour Leader*, 8 September 1921 (the quotation is from p. 241). Bundock's review prompted a reply from Horace Miles, the secretary of the Coventry ILP branch, who noted that Bundock was "a little behind the times," since the "Soviet idea of representation and the functional theory of the Guildsmen are entirely different as he would find out if he examined them." Miles also remarked that MacDonald was "still hopelessly in the mire of Herbert Spencer's 'biological sociology.'" Horace Miles, letter in *Labour Leader*, 15 September 1921.
60. MacDonald, *Socialism: Critical and Constructive*, 240–41.
61. Ibid., 240.
62. Ibid., 259.
63. *Labour Leader*, 10 March 1921.
64. R. T. McKenzie, *British Political Parties: The Distribution of Power Within the Conservative and Labour Parties*, 350.

Chapter 4: A "Distinctive Program"

1. *Labour Leader*, 8 April 1920 (quoting Allen's remarks at the conference).
2. *Labour Leader*, 11 November 1920.
3. *Labour Leader*, 28 October 1920.
4. *Labour Leader*, 11 November 1920.
5. *Labour Leader*, 8 April 1920.
6. Arthur Marwick, *Clifford Allen: The Open Conspirator*, 57, 48.
7. *Resolutions for the No. 9 Divisional Conference to Be Held . . . on 20 January 1917, at Stockport*, 1.
8. *Socialist Review*, October-December 1918, 365–72; G. D. H. Cole, "National Guilds and the State," *Socialist Review*, January–March 1919, 22–30. G. D. H. Cole, *Workers' Control in Industry*.
9. *Labour Leader*, 5 February 1920.
10. Robert E. Dowse, *Left in the Centre: The Independent Labour Party, 1893–1940*, 66.
11. The use of the term *guild* reflects the contemporary interest in a revival of the medieval guild system as advocated in Arthur J. Penty's *The Restoration of the Gild System* (1906) and in the writings of A. R. Orage, editor of the *New Age*. A more definitely socialist interpretation of guilds was made by S. G. Hobson in his 1914 publication, *National Guilds*, and a little later by some of the younger Fabian intellectuals, notably the Coles.

12. John Scurr, "Thoughts on I.L.P. Policy," *Socialist Review*, October–December 1919, 362. Scurr (1876–1932) served as a Labour MP from 1923 to 1931. We will learn more about his role in the ILP in chapter 10.
13. Kevin Morgan, *The Webbs and Soviet Communism*, 101.
14. Philip Snowden, *Socialism Made Plain*, 14.
15. J. Ramsay MacDonald, *The History of the I.L.P.*, 20.
16. *Labour Leader*, 7 April 1921.
17. "Report on Party Program," in NAC *Report*, 1921, 50.
18. NAC *Report*, 1921, 67.
19. *Labour Leader*, 23 December 1920.
20. NAC *Report*, 1921, 47.
21. Ibid., 73.
22. *Labour Leader*, 7 April 1921.
23. *Labour Leader*, 13 January 1921. Patrick Dollan (1885–1963) was a leading figure in the ILP until the time of its disaffiliation from the Labour Party. At that point, he rallied many Scottish ILPers and formed the Scottish Socialist Party, which affiliated to Labour.
24. *Labour Leader*, 28 July 1921.
25. *Labour Leader*, 28 July 1921.
26. *Labour Leader*, 4 August 1921.
27. *Labour Leader*, 29 September 1921.
28. *Labour Leader*, 8 December 1921.
29. Marwick, *Clifford Allen*, 75. See also Roy Jenkins, *Mr. Attlee: An Interim Biography*, 94, and Brockway, *Towards Tomorrow*, 63.
30. *Labour Leader*, 8 December 1921.
31. Ibid.
32. *Labour Leader*, 5 January 1922. Carter's remarks appeared in "At the Sign of the I.L.P.," a regular column in *Labour Leader* at the time that contained commentary from the editor on current issues.
33. Quoted in ibid.
34. *Labour Leader*, 2 February 1922.
35. *Labour Leader*, 9 February 1922.
36. *Labour Leader*, 16 February 1922.
37. *Labour Leader*, 23 February 1922.
38. *Labour Leader*, 8 December 1921.
39. *Labour Leader*, 26 January 1922.
40. *Labour Leader*, 9 February 1922.
41. Ibid. Directed mainly at women, Pallister's pamphlets included *The Candle and the Pumpkin*, *Mrs. Smith of Wigan*, and *Socialism, Equality, and Happiness*, as well as *Socialism for Women*, which the ILP published in 1925 both as an ordinary pamphlet and as "ILP Course No. 8: 8 Short Talks for Study Circles and Discussion Classes."
42. *Labour Leader*, 2 March 1922.

Chapter 5: The 1922 Constitution and the Allen Regime

1. *Labour Leader*, 20 April 1922.
2. Robert E. Dowse, *Left in the Centre: The Independent Labour Party, 1893–1940*, 48.

3. Keith Laybourn, *Philip Snowden: A Biography, 1864–1937*, 88; Colin Cross, *Philip Snowden*, 174.
4. Fenner Brockway, *Socialism over Sixty Years: The Life of Jowett of Bradford*, 178.
5. *Labour Leader*, 20 April 1922.
6. Ibid.
7. Ibid.
8. Ibid.
9. Ibid.
10. Ibid. Fred Longden had clashed with MacDonald over his attitude to the Bolsheviks in 1919 and criticized "stupid statements" about Russia in the *Labour Leader* in the same 1922 issue that reported the conference. Described by David Howell as "an old-style ILP propagandist," Longden had been imprisoned as a conscientious objector during the war. He became a full-time lecturer for the Workers' Educational Association in the 1920s and a Labour MP for a Birmingham constituency in 1929–31 and 1945–52. David Howell, *MacDonald's Party: Labour Identities and Crisis, 1922–1931*, 244.
11. Ibid. Robert E. Dowse, *Left in the Centre: The Independent Labour Party, 1893–1940*, 210.
12. Brockway, *Socialism over Sixty Years*, 204.
13. *Labour Leader*, 27 April 1922.
14. *The Independent Labour Party and Its Future Work*; Fred Henderson, *Socialism of the I.L.P*, 3. The *Independent Labour Party* leaflet, which is undated, evidently appeared in 1922, although it is catalogued in the ILP Collection under 1920.
15. *Labour Leader*, 20 July 1922.
16. William Leach, "Guild v. Municipal Socialism," *Socialist Review*, March 1923, 107, 113.
17. C. R. Attlee, "Guild v. Municipal Socialism: A Reply," *Socialist Review*, May 1923, 214–15; William Leach, "Guild v. Municipal Socialism: A Rejoinder," *Socialist Review*, July 1923, 35–40.
18. James Maxton, *Twenty Points for Socialism*, 15.
19. Fenner Brockway, *"Make the Workers Free!" The Industrial Policy of the I.L.P.*, 6, 9–10.
20. ILP Industrial Policy Committee, *Trade Unions and Socialism: A Report to the I.L.P. Conference, 1926, on the Industrial Aspect of Socialism*, 2, 16. Margaret Bondfield (1873–1953) was the first woman cabinet minister in Britain, having been a junior minister in the 1924 government.
21. Emanuel Shinwell, *Nationalisation of the Mines: A Practical Policy*, 6.
22. *Guild Socialist*, June 1922.
23. Fenner Brockway, *Towards Tomorrow: The Autobiography of Fenner Brockway*, 63.
24. *Labour Leader*, 20 April 1922.
25. Fenner Brockway, *Inside the Left: Thirty Years of Platform, Press, Prison, and Parliament*, 142.
26. John Paton, *Left Turn! The Autobiography of John Paton*, 153.
27. Arthur Marwick, *Clifford Allen: The Open Conspirator*, 77.
28. Paton, *Left Turn!* 183.
29. *Labour Leader*, 27 April 1922.
30. On the clash between Snowden and Glasier and its implications for the *Labour Leader*, see Ian Bullock, *Romancing the Revolution: The Myth of Soviet Democracy and the British Left*, 346–50.

31. *Labour Leader*, 14 April, 20 May, and 7 July 1921.
32. Marwick, *Clifford Allen*, 77.
33. *Labour Leader*, 6 July 1922.
34. *Labour Leader*, 8 June 1922.
35. *Labour Leader*, 17 August 1922.
36. *Labour Leader*, 24 August 1922.
37. Ibid.
38. Ibid.
39. *Labour Leader*, 31 August 1922.
40. *Labour Leader*, 7 September 1922.
41. *Labour Leader*, 14 September 1922.
42. *Labour Leader*, 28 September 1922.
43. *Labour Leader*, 24 August 1922. Leventhal tells us that Mary Agnes Hamilton was "imposed" on Brailsford at MacDonald's insistence. F. M. Leventhal *The Last Dissenter: H. N. Brailsford and His World*, 176.
44. *New Leader*, 6 October 1922.
45. *New Leader*, 13 October and 20 October 1922.
46. *New Leader*, 27 October and 15 December 1922.
47. *New Leader*, 3 November and 29 December 1922.
48. Dowse, *Left in the Centre*, 89.
49. *New Leader*, 6 October 1922.
50. *New Leader*, 24 November 1922.
51. *New Leader*, 17 November 1922.
52. *New Leader*, 22 December 1922.
53. *Report of the Annual Conference Held at London, April 1923*, 19.
54. *New Leader*, 2 March 1923.
55. *New Leader*, 16 March 1923.
56. *Now for Socialism! The Call of the I.L.P.*
57. *New Leader*, 6 April 1923.
58. *New Leader*, 29 December 1922.
59. *Report of the Annual Conference, 1923*, 98–99. See David Marquand, *Ramsay MacDonald*, 277, and Leventhal, *Last Dissenter*, 175, for Brailsford's salary, and, for Glasier's, Laurence Thompson, *The Enthusiasts: A Biography of John and Katharine Bruce Glasier*, 230.
60. Brockway, *Inside the Left*, 143.
61. Marwick, *Clifford Allen*, 79–80.
62. Paton, *Left Turn!* 242–43.
63. Quoted in Leventhal, *Last Dissenter*, 257.
64. Marwick, *Clifford Allen*, 79.
65. Dowse, *Left in the Centre*, 83.
66. *The Miners' Next Step* was the title of a syndicalist-influenced pamphlet of 1912 published by the Unofficial Reform Committee, of which Noah Ablett was a leading member.
67. *New Leader*, 13 October and 20 October 1922.
68. *New Leader*, 3 November 1922.
69. *New Leader*, 24 November 1922.
70. *New Leader*, 1 December and 8 December 1922.

71. W. H. Greenleaf, *The British Political Tradition*, 437; Kendall, *Revolutionary Movement in Britain*, 282–83; John S. Peart-Binns, *Maurice Reckitt: A Life*, 62.
72. I am grateful to Anthony Carew for this reference. For later rival attempts in the 1930s to revive guild socialism by Cole, Mellor, Hobson, and others, see David Blaazer, "Guild Socialists After Guild Socialism: The Workers' Control Group and the House of Industry League."
73. *Now for Socialism!*
74. C. A. Attlee, *Economic History—with Notes for Lecturers and Class Leaders*, 32.
75. Howell, *MacDonald's Party*, 239.
76. Paton, *Left Turn!* 32, 33.
77. Ibid., 193, 33.
78. Dowse, *Left in the Centre*, 84, citing Paton, *Left Turn!* 179. See also Brockway, *Towards Tomorrow*, 64.
79. A total of 280 delegates had voted for Allen compared to 161 for Maxton and 25 for Morgan Jones. *Report of the Annual Conference, 1923*, 108.
80. Dowse, *Left in the Centre*, 80–81.
81. Brockway, *Towards Tomorrow*, 69.
82. Paton, *Left Turn!* 156.
83. Brockway, *Towards Tomorrow*, 69.
84. Dowse, *Left in the Centre*, 75, 78.
85. Paton, *Left Turn!* 192; Brockway, *Towards Tomorrow*, 68.

Chapter 6: The Rise of MacDonald and the First Labour Government

1. For socialist attitudes to "leadership" in the 1880–1914 period in Britain, see Logie Barrow and Ian Bullock, *Democratic Ideas and the British Labour Movement, 1880–1914*, 45–50, and, in the trade union context, 89–92.
2. *The Clarion*, 10 November 1894; Barrow and Bullock, *Democratic Ideas*, 80.
3. *Labour Leader*, 23 March 1901; Barrow and Bullock, *Democratic Ideas*, 81.
4. *The Clarion*, 26 January 1906; Barrow and Bullock, *Democratic Ideas*, 183.
5. *The Clarion*, 23 February 1906; Barrow and Bullock, *Democratic Ideas*, 184.
6. David Kirkwood, *My Life of Revolt*, 195. Arthur Henderson (1863–1935)—"Uncle Arthur" to many Labour MPs—chaired the parliamentary party from 1908 to 1910. After MacDonald's resignation as chairman of the parliamentary party in 1914, he held the position again until October 1917. Having been the first Labour cabinet minister in Lloyd George's wartime coalition, he was Home Secretary in the first and Foreign Secretary in the second Labour government in 1924 and 1929–31. After its fall, he was leader of the Labour Party until October 1932. Henderson was awarded the Nobel Peace Prize in 1934.
7. Emanuel Shinwell, *Conflict Without Malice: An Autobiography*, 83. Emanuel Shinwell (1884–1985), another—though temporary—"Red Clydeside" MP, held ministerial positions in both of MacDonald's government and as Minister of Fuel and Power, then Secretary of State for War and later Minister of Defence in Attlee's postwar governments.
8. Kirkwood, *My Life of Revolt*, 195–96.
9. Fenner Brockway, *Inside the Left: Thirty Years of Platform, Press, Prison, and Parliament*, 26. J. R. Clynes (1869–1949) had begun his career in labour politics in 1892, as an organizer for the Lancashire Gasworkers' Union. He was appointed

Leader of the House of Commons in MacDonald's 1924 government and was Home Secretary in the 1929–31 administration.
10. Matthew Worley, *Labour Inside the Gate: A History of the British Labour Party Between the Wars*, 26.
11. David Howell, *MacDonald's Party: Labour Identities and Crisis, 1922–1931*, 28.
12. Arthur Marwick, *Clifford Allen: The Open Conspirator*, 81.
13. *Labour Leader*, 1 September 1921. Colonel Josiah Wedgwood (1872–1943) was another former radical Liberal MP who, unlike some of the other recruits to the Labour Party and the ILP from that quarter, had fought in the war, winning a DSO in the ill-fated Dardanelles campaign. His colonelcy dated from 1917, when he became Assistant Director of Tank Warfare. Later, he served as a cabinet minister without portfolio in the 1924 Labour government but was critical of MacDonald and not given office in the latter's second administration.
14. *Labour Leader*, 1 September 1921.
15. David Marquand, *Ramsay MacDonald*, 271–72; *Forward*, 10 July 1920.
16. *The Clarion*, 6 December 1907.
17. *Labour Leader*, 28 June 1907.
18. "Vote for Maxton and Save the Children, 15 Nov 1922," http://gdl.cdlr.strath.ac.uk/maxton/redcly145.htm, and "Election Address of James Maxton, Labour Candidate for Bridgeton, 15 Nov 1922 (page 3)," http://gdl.cdlr.strath.ac.uk/maxton/redcly146c.html, Maxton Papers, 1921–30, Glasgow Digital Library.
19. Gordon Brown, *Maxton*, 130–31.
20. Ibid., 132.
21. Ibid., 133.
22. Ibid., 133–34.
23. Ibid., 134, quoting *The Times*, 28 June 1923.
24. Ibid., 136–37.
25. Ibid., 138.
26. *New Leader*, 29 June 1923.
27. Robert E. Dowse, *Left in the Centre: The Independent Labour Party, 1893–1940*, 94.
28. Ibid., 95.
29. *New Leader*, 6 July 1923.
30. Howell, *MacDonald's Party*, 248.
31. Shinwell, *Conflict Without Malice*, 94.
32. For Stewart, see Dowse, *Left in the Centre*, 102, citing *Forward*, 15 December 1923; for Clapham, see Marquand, *Ramsay MacDonald*, 297, quoting Brailsford, letter to MacDonald, 10 December 1923, MacDonald Papers, Public Record Office 5/33.
33. Fenner Brockway, *Socialism over Sixty Years: The Life of Jowett of Bradford*, 206. This is the meeting that is mentioned in MacDonald's diary on 10 December 1923, quoted in Marquand, *Ramsay MacDonald*, 298.
34. Marquand, *Ramsay MacDonald*, 298.
35. Brockway, *Socialism over Sixty Years*, 207.
36. Marquand, *Ramsay MacDonald*, 298.
37. A. J. P. Taylor, *English History, 1914–1945*, 280.
38. Marquand, *Ramsay MacDonald*, 298.
39. Ibid., 299.

40. MacDonald to Henderson, 22 December 1923, MacDonald Papers, Public Record Office 5/35. Quoted in Marquand, *Ramsay MacDonald*, 302.
41. Marquand, *Ramsay MacDonald*, 302. In a letter to MacDonald, Ponsonby protested: "The incredible seems about to happen. We are actually to be allowed by an incredible combination of circumstances to have control of the F.O. [Foreign Office] and to begin to carry out some of the things we have been urging and preaching for years. To give this job to J.T. is simply to chuck the opportunity away." Ponsonby to MacDonald, 12 December 1923, in MacDonald Papers, Public Record Office, quoted in John Shepherd and Keith Laybourn, *Britain's First Labour Government*, 57.
42. Marquand, *Ramsay MacDonald*, 313.
43. Marquand quotes from Ponsonby's diary as well as MacDonald's: MacDonald, 2 March 1924, and Ponsonby, 17 April 1924, in Marquand, *Ramsay MacDonald*, 320.
44. Patrick Dollan, "Forward from the Annual Conference," *Socialist Review*, May 1924, 227.
45. *New Leader*, 14 December 1923, quoted in Dowse, *Left in the Centre*, 103.
46. Marquand, *Ramsay MacDonald*, 319, 326.
47. *New Leader*, 11 January 1924.
48. Dowse, *Left in the Centre*, 104.
49. *New Leader*, 18 April 1924.
50. Marwick, *Clifford Allen*, 86. Allen's speech was later published as the ILP pamphlet, *Putting Socialism into Practice*.
51. *New Leader*, 11 February 1924, cited in Dowse, *Left in the Centre*, 102–3.
52. David Howell, *A Lost Left: Three Studies in Socialism and Nationalism*, 265.
53. Dowse, *Left in the Centre*, 110–11.
54. Brockway, *Socialism over Sixty Years*, 214.
55. Brown, *Maxton*, 155–56.
56. Minutes of NAC meeting, 17 May 1924.
57. Dowse, *Left in the Centre*, 107, citing *New Leader*, 8 August 1921, and Allen to MacDonald, 16 September 1924. Allen's collected correspondence is now in the Clifford Allen (Lord Allen of Hurtwood) Papers, Irvin Department of Rare Books and Special Collections, University of South Carolina Libraries.
58. Shinwell, *Conflict Without Malice*, 94.
59. Shepherd and Laybourn, *Britain's First Labour Government*, chap. 7, gives a full account of the Campbell case and the end of the first Labour government.
60. Brockway, *Socialism over Sixty Years*, 217; Marquand, *Ramsay MacDonald*, chap. 15.
61. Shinwell, *Conflict Without Malice*, 94.
62. Shepherd, and Laybourn, *Britain's First Labour Government*, 199.
63. *New Leader*, 17 October 1924.
64. The Zinoviev letter, now believed to be a forgery, was published just four days before the election. Purportedly written by Comintern leader Grigory Zinoviev, the letter instructed the CPGB to mobilize the support of those in the Labour Party sympathetic to Soviet objectives. It was widely believed in Labour circles, both at the time and subsequently, that the publication of the letter contributed substantially to Labour's election defeat, although this argument is no longer widely accepted. The most exhaustive investigation of the affair is the 1999 report by the chief historian of the Foreign and Commonwealth Office, Gill Bennett, "A

Most Extraordinary and Mysterious Business": *The Zinoviev Letter of 1924*. For a useful summary and discussion, see Richard Norton-Taylor, "The Zinoviev Letter Was a Dirty Trick by MI6," *The Guardian*, 4 February 1999.
65. J. Ramsay MacDonald, *The Story of the I.L.P. and What It Stands For*, 2.
66. Kirkwood, *My Life of Revolt*, 228.

Chapter 7: Preparing the Ground for the Living Wage Policy

1. Robert E. Dowse, *Left in the Centre: The Independent Labour Party, 1893–1940*, 118, citing *New Leader*, 11 December and 18 December 1925.
2. "Resolutions to Be Presented to the 33rd Annual Conference, 12–14 April at Gloucester: Final Agenda, 1925," 19.
3. Joseph Southall (1861–1944) was a Birmingham-based Arts and Crafts movement painter active in the ILP. A Quaker, he was an uncompromising opponent of militarism and war preparations.
4. *Report of the Annual Conference Held at Gloucester, April 1925*, 125; David Marquand, *Ramsay MacDonald*, 419.
5. *Resolutions to the 33rd Annual Conference*, 20.
6. NAC *Report, 1925*, 10.
7. Peter James Thwaites, "The Independent Labour Party, 1938–50," 28.
8. Clifford Allen, *The I.L.P. and Revolution: Chairman's Speech to* ILP *Summer School, Easton Lodge, August 1925*, 3, 10.
9. Dowse, *Left in the Centre*, 114.
10. Ibid., 124, quoting NAC statement in *Report of the Annual Conference Held at Whitley Bay, April 1926*, 28.
11. *New Leader*, 2 April 1926.
12. F. M. Leventhal, *The Last Dissenter: H. N. Brailsford and His World*, 189.
13. NAC *Report, 1925*. The appendices were "Socialism and the Empire" (48–52); "India To-day, and the Duty of British Socialists Towards It" (52–56); "The Industrial Aspect of Socialism" (57–59).
14. John Paton, *Left Turn! The Autobiography of John Paton*, 233; Henry Noel Brailsford et al., *The Living Wage: A Report Submitted to the National Administrative Council of the* ILP.
15. *New Leader*, 14 December 1923.
16. *Report of the Annual Conference Held at York, April 1924*, 98–100. Marwick quotes substantially from this speech. Arthur Marwick, *Clifford Allen: The Open Conspirator*, 86–88.
17. *Report of the Annual Conference, 1925*, 88–89.
18. Crooks, Will. *"A Living Wage for All": An Appeal for a Weekly Minimum Wage of 30 Shillings—A Speech Given to the House of Commons, 26 April 1911*.
19. *New Leader*, 7 March 1924. See also Alfred Salter, *"A Living Wage for All": Dr. Salter's Speech in the House of Commons on 7 March 1923*. When a bronze statue of Salter sitting on a park bench was stolen in November 2011 from Cherry Garden Pier, Simon Hughes, Liberal-Democrat MP for Bermondsey, expressed outrage in his blog of 21 November 2011 and described Salter as "the greatest of our MPs in the last century." The statue was replaced in November 2014 after a local campaign raised about £60,000.
20. *New Leader*, 18 April 1924. There is no shortage of other examples of early usage of "Living Wage" in the *New Leader*. In 1924 alone, these include George Dallas's

article "A Living Wage on the Farm," *New Leader*, 25 July, and the debate initiated by "Historicus" the following month on "What Is a Living Wage?"
21. *New Leader*, 22 August 1924.
22. Ibid.
23. Ibid. An article by "Historicus" cites Rathbone at the summer school and makes a footnote reference to her "able and informative" book, *The Disinherited Family*. The article led to a number of letters the following week, including one from Rathbone herself. In it, she asked when "adjusting the income of the worker to the number in the family dependent on it" was going to become "an immediate question of Labour politics" and contrasted attitudes in Britain to the more positive ones of the Belgian and French trade unions. *New Leader*, 29 August 1924.
24. *New Leader*, 22 August 1924.
25. *New Leader*, 20 June 1924.
26. *New Leader*, 21 September 1923 and 29 August 1924.
27. *Report of the Annual Conference*, 1925, 88–89 (emphasis in original).
28. Leventhal, *Last Dissenter*, 189.
29. Ibid., 190.
30. Henry Noel Brailsford, *Socialism for To-day*. The note appears on an unnumbered page.
31. For example, "Realist" contributed "How to Stop the Wheat Gambler" in August 1923 and "The Cotton Trade" in March 1924.
32. Brailsford, *Socialism for To-day*, 63.
33. Ibid., 64.
34. Ibid., 66.
35. Ibid., 67.
36. Ibid., 67–68. It is notable that, even in the 1920s, Brailsford was already interested in the English revolution of the 1640s. After retiring from journalism, Brailsford (1873–1958) wrote *The Levellers and the English Revolution*. Incomplete at his death, it was edited by Christopher Hill and published in 1961.
37. Brailsford, *Socialism for To-day*, 68–69.
38. Ibid., 69.
39. Ibid., 77, 79–80.
40. Ibid., 82–83.
41. Ibid., 84, 88.
42. Ibid., 111–12.
43. Leventhal, *Last Dissenter*, 190, 238.
44. Brailsford, *Socialism for To-day*, 120–21, 97, 99, 102.
45. Ibid., 103–4, 109.
46. Ibid., 112.
47. Ibid., 112–15.
48. Ibid., 119.
49. Hugh Thomas, *John Strachey*, 51. Note that Thomas was writing in the 1970s, so the emphasis should be on "today." Michael Newman writes that although both versions were nationalistic, Mosley's was "overtly racist in one passage and full of declamatory rhetoric," which raises the question of what would have been seen as racist, even by socialists, at the time. Michael Newman, *John Strachey*, 8. In any case, it is very doubtful that anyone in the ILP had an inkling in the

mid-1920s of the surprising future political trajectory of Mosley—or indeed, of Strachey, who returned to the Labour Party in the 1940s and was again elected as an MP, serving in the postwar Labour government. Certainly, G. D. H. Cole had no reservations about citing both pamphlet and book in *Industrial Policy for Socialists: Ten Outline Lectures for Study Classes, 1925*.

50. Fenner Brockway, *Inside the Left: Thirty Years of Platform, Press, Prison, and Parliament*, 209; *New Leader*, 11 April 1924. For the ease and something bordering on adulation with which Mosley and his wife, Cynthia, were received more generally in the Labour Party, including a substantial quotation from Egon Wertheimer's 1929 *Portrait of the Labour Party*, see Kevin Morgan, *Labour Legends and Russian Gold*, 133–34.
51. *Report of the Annual Conference, 1925*, 158.
52. John Strachey, *Revolution by Reason: An Account of the Financial Proposals Submitted by Oswald Mosley at the Thirty-Third Independent Labour Party Conference, and Endorsed by the Birmingham Borough Labour Party and the I.L.P. Federation*.
53. Robert J. G. Boothby, *I Fight to Live: Autobiography*, 24. Boothy added that, at this time, "Mosley saw himself as Byron rather than Mussolini" and, like the poet, spent much of the rest of the time in Venice swimming.
54. Oswald Mosley, *Revolution by Reason: An Account of the Birmingham Proposals Together with an Analysis of the Financial Policy of the Present Government Which Has Led to Their Great Attack upon Wages*, 5.
55. Robert Skidelsky, *John Maynard Keynes*, 246.
56. Strachey, *Revolution by Reason*, x–xi.
57. Mosley, *Revolution by Reason*, 9. Hobson's version of "underconsumptionist" economics can be traced back at least to his 1909 book *The Industrial System*, and the underlying idea can be traced back much further.
58. Mosley, *Revolution by Reason*, 7.
59. Strachey, *Revolution by Reason*, 119, 126, 251.
60. Mosley, *Revolution by Reason*, 7.
61. Robert Skidelsky, *Politicians and the Slump: The Labour Government of 1929–1931*, 64.
62. Mosley, *Revolution by Reason*, 6.
63. Ibid., 12.
64. Noel Thompson, *John Strachey: An Intellectual Biography*, 16.
65. Strachey, *Revolution by Reason*, 7–8, 14–15, 18, 138, 158.
66. Ibid., 150, 79.
67. Mosley, *Revolution by Reason*, 17.
68. Ibid,; Strachey, *Revolution by Reason*, 111.
69. Robert Skidelsky, *Oswald Mosley*, 146.
70. Mosley, *Revolution by Reason*, 20.
71. Robert Skidelsky, *Oswald Mosley*, 146; Strachey, *Revolution by Reason*, 188.
72. Strachey, *Revolution by Reason*, ix; Mosley, *Revolution by Reason*, 27.
73. Mosley, *Revolution by Reason*, 20.
74. Skidelsky, *Oswald Mosley*, 15.
75. John Scurr, "A Basic 'Living Wage,'" *Socialist Review*, April 1925, 153.
76. Margaret Matheson, "'Living Wage' or Socialism?" *Socialist Review*, June 1925, 242–44 (emphasis in original).

77. *Socialist Review*, July 1925, 41.
78. Philip Snowden, Review of *Socialism for To-day*, *Socialist Review*, December 1925, 284–85.

Chapter 8: The Year of the General Strike—and of *The Living Wage*

1. *Forward*, 16 January 1926.
2. Allen's influence is no doubt reflected in the fact that Dowse includes him in his account of the committee's composition. Robert E. Dowse, *Left in the Centre: The Independent Labour Party, 1893–1940*, 130.
3. John Paton, *Left Turn! The Autobiography of John Paton*, 234.
4. For Wise's involvement with cooperatives and Russia, see Kevin Morgan, *The Webbs and Soviet Communism*, 189–93.
5. *New Leader*, 1 January 1926.
6. Not, of course, among *all* trade unionists. See, for example, Arthur Creech Jones, "A Family Income—a Trade Union View," *Socialist Review*, August 1926, 27–31.
7. Mary D. Stocks, *Eleanor Rathbone: A Biography*, 100. For a report by Stocks on the 1923 Labour Party women's conference in York, which emphasized the discussion of "child endowment" policies, see *New Leader*, 11 May 1923.
8. *New Leader*, 15 January 1926. Dalton claimed that Rathbone had recently joined the Labour Party. This appears to be quite wrong. Although, as Johanna Alberti puts it, Rathbone was "willing to speak the language of ethical socialism," she "could never have worked closely with the Labour Party." Johanna Alberti, *Eleanor Rathbone*, 71.
9. *New Leader*, 19 February 1926. The blue Greater London Council plaque on the house where Eleanor Rathbone once lived in Tufton Street, Westminster, describes her simply as "Pioneer of Family Allowances." She was also a very prominent early-twentieth-century feminist and, later, an independent MP.
10. *New Leader*, 1 January 1926. Rennie Smith (1888–1962) was Labour MP for Penistone from 1924 to 1931.
11. Ibid.
12. *New Leader*, 8 January, 2 April, and 15 October 1926. The series continued into the following year. A cartoon in the 7 October 1927 issue of the *Leader*, titled "The Living Wage Unlocks the Gate," showed a man with a key approaching a set of gates labelled "Socialist Commonwealth."
13. *New Leader*, 8 January 1926.
14. Ibid.
15. *New Leader*, 26 February 1926.
16. Fenner Brockway, *Inside the Left: Thirty Years of Platform, Press, Prison, and Parliament*, 149.
17. *New Leader*, 12 March 1926.
18. *Forward*, 27 March 1926.
19. *New Leader*, 2 April 1926.
20. Ibid.
21. *Forward*, 3 April 1926.
22. *Forward*, 10 April 1926.
23. *Report of the Annual Conference Held at Whitley Bay, April 1926*, 78; F. W. Jowett, *"Socialism in Our Time": Address of the Chairman to the ILP Annual Conference, Whitley Bay, April 1926*.

24. *New Leader*, 9 April 1926.
25. Jowett, "Socialism in Our Time," 6–8, 13.
26. *Report of the Annual Conference, 1926*, 87.
27. Ibid., 86.
28. Ibid., 83; *Forward*, 10 April 1926.
29. Brockway, *Inside the Left*, 187–93.
30. Ibid., 191.
31. Ibid., 188, 190.
32. Ibid., 191.
33. *New Leader*, 28 May, 4 June, and 11 June 1926.
34. *New Leader*, 29 October 1926.
35. *Forward*, 17 April 1926; *New Leader*, 23 April 1926; *Forward*, 24 April 1926.
36. *Forward*, 17 April 1926.
37. *New Leader*, 13 August 1926.
38. *Forward*, 17 July 1926; *New Leader*, 23 July 1926.
39. *New Leader*, 13 August 1926.
40. *New Leader*, 1 October and 8 October 1926.
41. *New Leader*, 29 April 1927.
42. *New Leader*, 15 October and 22 October 1926.
43. F. M. Leventhal, *The Last Dissenter: H. N. Brailsford and His World*, 191.
44. David Marquand, *Ramsay MacDonald*, 454. The original source is the MacDonald Papers, Public Record Office 6/29.
45. Ben Pimlott, *Hugh Dalton*, 155.
46. *Labour's Northern Voice*, 16 April and 17 December 1926.

Chapter 9: Pursuing the Living Wage Policy

1. David Marquand, *Ramsay MacDonald*, 452–53.
2. *Report of the Annual Conference held at Whitley Bay, April 1926*, 84.
3. *Forward*, 10 April 1926.
4. Henry Noel Brailsford, *Socialism for To-day*, 119.
5. *New Leader*, 1 January 1926.
6. Henry Noel Brailsford, John A. Hobson, A. Creech Jones, and E. F. Wise, *The Living Wage: A Report Submitted to the National Administrative Council of the Independent Labour Party*, 53.
7. Brailsford et al., *Living Wage*, 1.
8. Ibid., 4.
9. Ibid., 6–7.
10. Ibid., 8–12.
11. Ibid., 13–18.
12. Ibid., 20–24.
13. Ibid., 30–36.
14. Ibid., 37.
15. Ibid., 42–43, 46, 49–50.
16. Ibid., 54.
17. Keith Middlemas, *The Clydesiders: A Left Wing Struggle for Parliamentary Power*, 237; Andrew Thorpe, *A History of the Labour Party*, 58; Matthew Worley, *Labour Inside the Gate: A History of the British Labour Party Between the Wars*, 100–101.

18. Arguably, a further milestone was reached when, following its success in the 2015 election, the Conservative government announced that a "National Living Wage" would replace the existing minimum wage of £6.50 per hour. The initial increase, to £7.20 per hour, was accompanied by a four-year freeze on most working-age benefits, the elimination of government support for students from low-income households, and a number of other cuts, prompting Labour MP Harriet Harman to comment that the budget left "working people worse off." For details, see "Budget 2015: Osborne Unveils National Living Wage," *BBC News*, 8 July 2015, http://www.bbc.com/news/uk-politics-33437115.
19. Fenner Brockway, *Towards Tomorrow: The Autobiography of Fenner Brockway*, 64.
20. Marquand, *Ramsay MacDonald*, 452.
21. Brailsford et al., *The Living Wage*, 29, 46, 38, 46.
22. Ibid., 43.
23. *New Leader*, 9 April 1926.
24. Brailsford et al., *Living Wage*, 19, 44.
25. David Howell, *MacDonald's Party: Labour Identities and Crisis, 1922–1931*, 264.
26. *New Leader*, 15 January 1926.
27. *New Leader*, 7 June 1929.
28. *New Leader*, 5 July 1929. In a letter that appeared the following week (in the issue of 12 July), R. J. P. Mortishead, assistant secretary of the Irish Labour Party, took Wilkinson to task and made the case for proportional representation.
29. *New Leader*, 16 August 1929.
30. A. J. P. Taylor, *English History, 1914–1945*, 303.
31. Sydney R. Elliott, *Co-operation and Socialism*, 3.
32. Howell, *MacDonald's Party*, 265–56; Worley, *Labour Inside the Gate*, 101.
33. Marquand, *Ramsay MacDonald*, 452.
34. F. M. Leventhal, *The Last Dissenter: H. N. Brailsford and His World*, 189.
35. *New Leader*, 18 May 1928.
36. "The Spirit of the I.L.P. Programme," *New Leader*, 10 October 1930.
37. "Under Consumption," *New Leader*, 17 October 1930.
38. *New Leader*, 19 December 1930.
39. Marwick, *Clifford Allen*, 129, quoting *Britain's Political Future: A Plea for Liberty and Leadership*, 176.
40. John Paton, *Left Turn! The Autobiography of John Paton*, 311.
41. W. T. Symons, *A Living Wage or a Living Income: An Attack upon The Living Wage and an Alternative Policy for the Independent Labour Party*, 3, 5, 6, 7. In the original, the final quotation in this paragraph was entirely in capital letters.
42. See, for example, T. H. Wintringham, *Facing Both Ways: The I.L.P. and the Workers Struggle*.
43. Fenner Brockway, *Socialism—with Speed: An Outline of the I.L.P. "Socialism in Our Time" Proposals*, 4.
44. *New Leader*, 13 July 1928.
45. *New Leader*, 15 February 1929.
46. *New Leader*, 22 March 1929.
47. *New Leader*, 29 March 1929.
48. James Maxton, *"Roads to Socialism": Chairman's Address to the I.L.P. Conference 1929*, 5–6. In light of this, it might seem a little ironic that in Gordon Brown's biography of Maxton, one of the four sections of the book is titled "Socialism in Our Time."

49. James Maxton, "Where the ILP Stands": Presidential Address of James Maxton to the ILP Conference, Together with a Declaration on the Relation of the ILP to the Labour Party, 4–5.
50. New Leader, 5 April 1929. The Cook-Maxton campaign will be examined in chapter 10.
51. Forward, 6 April 1929.
52. Forward, 23 June 1928.
53. Labour's Northern Voice, June 1931.
54. New Leader, 6 February and 13 February 1931.
55. Forward, 14 February 1931.
56. Gilbert McAllister, James Maxton: The Portrait of a Rebel, 183–84.

Chapter 10: James Maxton and Increasing Tension with Labour

1. Fenner Brockway, Inside the Left: Thirty Years of Platform, Press, Prison, and Parliament, 185.
2. New Leader, 17 October 1930.
3. New Leader, 20 June and 24 October 1930; 10 October 1930, 22 May 1931.
4. Brockway, Inside the Left, 187.
5. Socialist Review, February 1928, 3, 5; August 1928, 3.
6. John Paton, Left Turn! The Autobiography of John Paton, 287–88. Paton, who insisted that he had "known and liked Maxton for nearly twenty years" (292), gave the title "False Prophet" to the chapter in his book that dealt with the advent of Maxton. He was particularly critical of the Cook-Maxton episode and, later in the book, of what he saw as Maxton's excessive toleration of the Revolutionary Policy Committee (whose ideas and activities will feature in later chapters).
7. Brockway, Inside the Left, 223.
8. David Kirkwood, My Life of Revolt, 209.
9. Gilbert McAllister, James Maxton: The Portrait of a Rebel, 20.
10. David Howell, MacDonald's Party: Labour Identities and Crisis, 1922–1931, 223.
11. Brockway, Inside the Left, 157.
12. Marwick, Clifford Allen, 100.
13. Report of the Annual Conference Held at Gloucester, April 1925, 147. Hugh Dalton (1887–1962) played little part after this time in the ILP. There are few references to the party in the first volume of his memoirs, though he does tell us about his joining the Cambridge branch as a student and later losing interest in it before the outbreak of the war, in which he served as an artillery officer. He also mentions his nomination by the ILP as a Labour candidate. Hugh Dalton, Call Back Yesterday: Memoirs, 1887–1931, 46–47, 70, 139. In a July 1923 diary entry in which he refers to a letter from Brockway informing him of the nomination and asking whether he was an ILP member, Dalton wrote, "I thereupon join or rather rejoin after a lapse of years." Ben Pimlott, ed., The Political Diary of Hugh Dalton,1918–40, 1945–60, 35. See also David Howell, "Traditions, Myths and Legacies: The ILP and the Labour Left," in Alan Mckinlay and R. J. Morris, eds., The ILP on Clydeside, 1893–1932: From Foundation to Disintegration, 210. Dalton was later a key figure in the postwar Attlee governments and is remembered for promptly resigning as Chancellor of the Exchequer in 1947 as a result of unintentionally leaking some details to a journalist on his way to the House of Commons about an hour before making the budget speech.

14. Arthur Marwick, *Clifford Allen: The Open Conspirator*, 98.
15. Ibid., 100.
16. Allen to Maxton, 21 October 1925, Allen Papers, quoted in Marwick, *Clifford Allen*, 100–101, and also included in Martin Gilbert, *Plough My Own Furrow: The Story of Lord Allen of Hurtwood as Told Through His Writings and Correspondence*, 194–95.
17. Ibid.
18. Allen to MacDonald, 2 November 1925, MacDonald Papers, Public Record Office, quoted in David Marquand, *Ramsay MacDonald*, 430.
19. Brailsford to Allen, undated but ca. 1934, quoted in Gilbert, *Plough My Own Furrow*, 297.
20. *New Leader*, 9 April 1926.
21. *New Leader*, 7 January 1927.
22. Gordon Brown, *Maxton*, 204.
23. *New Leader*, 22 April 1927.
24. Fenner Brockway, *Inside the Left: Thirty Years of Platform, Press, Prison, and Parliament*, 185.
25. *New Leader*, 22 April 1927.
26. Ibid.
27. Ibid.
28. *New Leader*, 13 April 1928.
29. To begin with, "Maxton-Cook" was favoured by the *New Leader* and other ILP sources, but in the long run alphabetical correctness won out and it is now usually known as Cook-Maxton and will be referred to as such in this account—except when Maxton-Cook appears in quotations.
30. *New Leader*, 22 June 1928. It is not completely clear whether Cook *was* an ILP member at this time. He is referred to as such on several occasions, but Dollan asserted, in *Forward*, 28 July 1928, that he was not a member.
31. *Daily Herald*, 22 June 1928.
32. Ibid.; *Daily Herald*, 25 June 1928.
33. *New Leader*, 29 June 1928.
34. Brockway, *Inside the Left*, 194–95, 276. See *New Leader*, 16 May 1930, for Paton's tribute to Wheatley at the time of his death.
35. Paton, *Left Turn!* 297–98.
36. Ibid., 300–301. McAllister lists the same eight "left-wingers" in his 1935 biography of Maxton, *James Maxton*, 184.
37. *New Leader*, 6 July 1928.
38. Gilbert McAllister, *James Maxton: The Portrait of a Rebel*, 190.
39. *Forward*, 23 June 1928.
40. *Labour's Northern Voice*, 6 July 1928.
41. *Labour's Northern Voice*, 13 July and 20 July 1928.
42. *Forward*, 30 June 1928.
43. *Forward*, 7 July 1928.
44. *New Leader*, 6 July 1928.
45. *Forward*, 7 July 1928.
46. *New Leader*, 6 July 1928.
47. *Forward*, 14 July 1928.
48. *New Leader*, 13 July and 20 July 1928.

49. *Forward*, 14 July 1928.
50. *Labour's Northern Voice*, 3 August 1928.
51. *Labour's Northern Voice*, 21 September 1928.
52. *Forward*, 21 July and 28 July 1928.
53. *New Leader*, 27 July 1928.
54. *Socialist Review*, August 1928, 3; October 1928, 6.
55. A. J. Cook and J. Maxton, *Our Case for a Socialist Revival*.
56. Ibid., 3–6.
57. Ibid., 9–10.
58. Ibid., 19–20.
59. Ibid., 10–11, 12, 19, 20.
60. Ibid., 21–22.
61. Brockway, *Inside the Left*, 195.
62. *New Leader*, 7 September 1928.
63. *Town Crier: Birmingham's Labour Weekly*, 14 September 1928. Watchman was referring to Brailsford's "Socialism and the 'Living Wage': A Reply to Mr. Snowden," *New Leader*, 29 April 1927.
64. *Socialist Review*, December 1928, 7. Rajani Palme Dutt (1896–1974) was a member of the CPGB and the founder of *Labour Monthly*, which he edited from 1921, when it began publication, until his death. The paper survived him by seven years: its final issue appeared in 1981.
65. *Labour's Northern Voice*, 8 February 1929. The conference is reported in the edition of 22 February.
66. *Forward*, 19 January 1929.
67. Paton, *Left Turn!* 304.
68. On the Poplar episode, see Noreen Branson, *Poplarism, 1919–25: George Lansbury and the Councillors' Revolt*. Scurr's wife, Julia Sullivan Scurr, was also a Poplar councillor and was likewise jailed for her role in the rebellion. A well-known suffragist and a long-time activist on behalf of working women, she had died in April 1927, at the age of only fifty-seven.
69. *Report of the Annual Conference Held at Carlisle, March–April 1929*, 38. For the Poplar episode, see Noreen Branson, *Poplarism, 1919–25: George Lansbury and the Councillors' Revolt*. On "impossibilism," see Walter Kendall, *The Revolutionary Movement in Britain, 1900–1921: The Origins of British Communism*, chap. 1.
70. See Matthew Worley, *Class Against Class: The Communist Party in Britain Between the Wars*. "Third period" refers to an analysis of the postwar years as consisting, first, of an upsurge in militancy, followed by a second period of capitalist consolidation, ushering in a revolutionary "third period"—a schema adopted by the Sixth Congress of the Comintern in the summer of 1928.
71. *Labour Monthly*, April 1929, 203–4.
72. *New Leader*, 27 September 1929.
73. *Forward*, 2, 16, and 23 March 1929.
74. *Labour Monthly*, June 1929, 342.
75. *New Leader*, 4 January 1929.
76. *Report of the Annual Conference Held at Carlisle, March–April 1929*, 67.
77. *New Leader*, 16 January 1931.
78. *New Leader*, 4 October 1929.

Chapter 11: The Second Labour Government

1. *New Leader*, 1 February and 29 March 1929.
2. *New Leader*, 5 April 1929.
3. Ibid.
4. *New Leader*, 5 April and 12 April 1929.
5. *New Leader*, 4 May 1929.
6. NAC resolution, 9 June 1929, as reported in NAC *Report, 1930*, 45.
7. *New Leader*, 14 June and 5 July 1929.
8. *New Leader*, 4 October 1929.
9. *Forward*, 13 July 1929.
10. Brockway, *Inside the Left: Thirty Years of Platform, Press, Prison, and Parliament*, 198–99.
11. Robert Skidelsky, *Politicians and the Slump: The Labour Government of 1929–1931*, 133–35.
12. *New Leader*, 25 October 1929. The sentence was italicized in the original.
13. "N.A.C. Report," *Report of the Annual Conference Held at Birmingham, April 1930*, 5.
14. *Forward*, 23 November 1929.
15. Skidelsky, *Politicians and the Slump*, 147.
16. Ibid, 151.
17. Robert E. Dowse, *Left in the Centre: The Independent Labour Party, 1893–1940*, 157.
18. "N.A.C. Report," *Report of the Annual Conference, 1930*, 6.
19. *New Leader*, 22 November 1929, *Daily Herald*, 20 November 1929.
20. *New Leader*, 29 November and 6 December 1929.
21. "N.A.C. Report," *Report of the Annual Conference, 1930*, 6; Brockway, *Inside the Left*, 208.
22. *New Leader*, 13 December 1929.
23. Ibid.
24. *Forward*, 14 December 1929.
25. *Forward*, 28 December 1929.
26. *Labour's Northern Voice*, 6 December and 13 December 1929.
27. *New Leader*, 13 January 1930.
28. *New Leader*, 31 January 1930.
29. Ibid.
30. *New Leader*, 21 February 1930.
31. *New Leader*, 25 April 1930.
32. Brockway, *Inside the Left*, 208.
33. *New Leader*, 11 April 1930.
34. R. T. McKenzie, *British Political Parties: The Distribution of Power Within the Conservative and Labour Parties*, 436.
35. F. W. Jowett, "Labour and Cabinet Rule," Reprinted from the "Bradford Pioneer," December 6th, 1929, 1.
36. Ibid.
37. Ibid. In the original, the text of the resolution was printed in boldface.
38. "N.A.C. Report," *Report of the Annual Conference, 1930*, 54.
39. *New Leader*, 24 January and 13 June 1930.
40. McKenzie, *British Political Parties*, 439.

41. *Hansard*, 17 July 1930; *New Leader*, 25 July 1930. Brockway gives his account of this episode in *Inside the Left*, 204–6, and, surprisingly given the course Beckett had taken during the intervening years, records his "friendly memory of earlier association" with him (206).
42. *New Leader*, 25 April 1930.
43. *New Leader*, 9 May 1930.
44. *New Leader*, 6 June 1930.
45. *New Leader*, 5 December 1930; John Paton, *Left Turn! The Autobiography of John Paton*, 339.
46. Gidon Cohen, *The Failure of a Dream: The Independent Labour Party from Disaffiliation to World War II*, 20.
47. Paton, *Left Turn!* 322–23.
48. "N.A.C. Report," *Report of the Annual Conference, 1930*, 60.
49. *Report of the Annual Conference, 1930*, 79.
50. Ralph Miliband, *Parliamentary Socialism: A Study in the Politics of Labour*, 166.
51. NAC *Report, 1931*, 4–5.
52. *New Leader*, 15 August 1930.
53. NAC *Report, 1931*, 6.
54. *New Leader*, 14 November 1930.
55. *New Leader*, 21 November 1930.
56. Ibid.
57. *New Leader*, 10 April 1931.
58. Skidelsky, *Politicians and the Slump*, 87.
59. Ibid., 195–207.
60. Brockway, *Inside the Left*, 211.
61. Michael Foot, *Aneurin Bevan: A Biography, vol. 1: 1897–1945*, 125.
62. Ibid., 128.
63. Noel Thompson, *John Strachey An Intellectual Biography*, 66.
64. *New Leader*, 27 February 1931.
65. Foot, *Aneurin Bevan*, 120.
66. *New Leader*, 12 December and 19 December 1930.
67. *Forward*, 13 December 1930. The press baron Lord Beaverbrook, owner of the *Daily Express* and other large circulation papers, was a lifelong campaigner for the unity of the British Empire/Commonwealth.
68. *New Leader*, 30 January 1931.
69. *New Leader*, 13 February 1931.
70. *New Leader*, 27 February 1931.
71. *New Leader*, 6 March 1931. Poland's Marshal Józef Pilsudski was certainly a dictatorial figure, though not a fascist. He did have in common with Mussolini that he was a former socialist.
72. *New Leader*, 20 March 1931. In the original, Trevelyan's remark was set in bold type.
73. *New Leader*, 24 April 1931.
74. *Labour's Northern Voice*, 17 April 1930. Elijah Sandham (1875–1944) was a Labour MP for the Liverpool constituency of Kirkdale in the 1929–31 parliament. As we will see in chapter 16, he would break with the ILP in 1934, chiefly over the issue of a united front with the Communists.
75. *New Leader*, 20 February 1931.

76. *New Leader*, 12 June 1931. In the paper, these words were set in boldface, as were "no fewer than …"
77. *New Leader*, 10 July and 17 July 1931.
78. Brockway, *Inside the Left*, 216; *New Leader*, 24 July 1931.
79. Brockway, *Inside the Left*, 214; *New Leader*, 24 July 1931.

Chapter 12: The Road Towards Departure

1. *New Leader*, 28 August 1931.
2. *Forward*, 29 August 1931.
3. *New Leader*, 28 August 1931.
4. *New Leader*, 4 September 1931.
5. *New Leader*, 11 September 1931.
6. H. N. Brailsford, *The "City" or the Nation? Reprinted from the New Leader*, 3, 5.
7. Brailsford, *The "City" or the Nation?* 8.
8. *New Leader*, 18 September 1931.
9. *New Leader*, 2 October 1931.
10. Ibid.
11. *New Leader*, 9 October 1931.
12. Ibid. The "three deserters" were, of course, MacDonald, Snowden, and Thomas.
13. *New Leader*, 16 October 1931.
14. Ben Pimlott, *Labour and the Left in the 1930s*, 11.
15. *The Times*, 25 August 1931, quoted in Andrew Thorpe, *The British General Election of 1931*, 94.
16. *Forward*, 19 September 1931.
17. Martin Gilbert, *Plough My Own Furrow: The Story of Lord Allen of Hurtwood as Told Through His Writings and Correspondence*, 204. See *Manchester Guardian*, 7 September 1931, for Allen's initial defence of MacDonald, which is quoted in full in Arthur Marwick, *Clifford Allen: The Open Conspirator*, 112–14.
18. Some sources give the Labour total as 52, others as 46: see, for example, Marwick, *Clifford Allen*, 115.
19. Brockway, *Inside the Left: Thirty Years of Platform, Press, Prison, and Parliament*, 219; Gidon Cohen, *The Failure of a Dream: The Independent Labour Party from Disaffiliation to World War II*, 80.
20. Thorpe, *British General Election of 1931*, 164.
21. *New Leader*, 30 October 1931.
22. *New Leader*, 6 November 1931.
23. *New Leader*, 6 November 1931.
24. Ibid.
25. *New Leader*, 20 November 1931.
26. Ibid.
27. *New Leader*, 27 November 1931.
28. *New Leader*, 18 December 1931.
29. *New Leader*, 11 December 1931.
30. *Forward*, 7 November and 12 December 1931.
31. *Labour's Northern Voice*, December 1931.
32. Pimlott, *Labour and the Left in the 1930s*, 22–23, 43.

33. On Newbold, see Ian Bullock, *Romancing the Revolution: The Myth of Soviet Democracy and the British Left*, 364–65.
34. *New Leader*, 15 January 1932.
35. *New Leader*, 1 January 1932.
36. *New Leader*, 15 January 1932.
37. *Forward*, 9 January 1932.
38. *New Leader*, 15 January 1932.
39. *New Leader*, 22 January 1932.
40. *New Leader*, 29 January 1932.
41. *Forward*, 30 January 1932.
42. Ibid.
43. Ibid. Hughes reported Maxton's vote in the next issue (6 February).
44. *New Leader*, 5 February 1932; *Forward*, 6 February 1932.
45. *New Leader*, 12 February 1932.
46. *New Leader*, 19 February 1932.
47. "Memorandum on the Present Political and Economic Situation in the I.L.P.," cited in Cohen, *Failure of a Dream*, 81–82.
48. *Independent Labour Party, Poplar Branch, March Programme*, 1932, 1–4.
49. "Final Agenda for the Divisional Conference to Be Held 23–24 January 1932," 3.
50. *New Leader*, 26 February 1932.
51. *New Leader*, 18 March 1932.
52. *Forward*, 27 February 1932.
53. *New Leader*, 25 March 1932.
54. Lee was the youngest MP in 1929 but lost her seat in the 1931 debacle. As she put it in the introduction to her memoir, "At twenty-four I was thrown into Parliament.... Three years later I was thrown out again." Jennie Lee, *This Great Journey*, xiii. The book, written when Lee was working for Beaverbrook's Ministry of Aircraft Production, was partly concerned with presenting the "people's war" to Americans and Canadians.
55. *New Leader*, 25 March 1932.

Chapter 13: Disaffiliation Wins the Day

1. *New Leader*, 1 April 1932.
2. Ibid.
3. *New Leader*, 1 April 1932.
4. Brockway, *Inside the Left: Thirty Years of Platform, Press, Prison, and Parliament*, 239–40.
5. *New Leader*, 1 April 1932.
6. Ibid.
7. Ibid. The Brüning government, which had been in power in Germany since the indecisive election of 1930, relied on presidential decrees to implement its policies. The Weimar constitution gave President Hindenburg considerable emergency powers, which he used until May 1932 to support Brüning.
8. *Forward*, 2 April 1932.
9. *Forward*, 11 April 1931.
10. *Forward*, 2 April 1932.
11. Brockway, *Inside the Left*, 238–39.

12. Ibid., 241, 238.
13. *Forward*, 2 April 1932.
14. *Independent Labour Party Poplar Branch, April Programme*, 1932.
15. *New Leader*, 15 April 1932.
16. *New Leader*, 6 May 1932.
17. *Forward*, 7 May and 14 May 1932.
18. *Forward*, 21 May 1932.
19. *New Leader*, 3 June 1932.
20. *New Leader*, 10 June 1932.
21. *Forward*, 18 June 1932.
22. *New Leader*, 24 June 1932.
23. Ibid. The NAC report the following year praised the ILP's women's conference delegates for "putting forward the I.L.P. point of view on the various subjects discussed," adding that "their fight was all the more praiseworthy in that it was made against obvious attempts by the platform to limit their freedom in debate which ultimately led to their withdrawing from the Conference as a protest." *NAC Report, 1933*, 27. The "ex-Minister" was Margaret Bondfield, and the "unjust" Act for which she was held responsible was the Anomalies Act, against which the ILP parliamentary group had fought a determined rearguard action.
24. *Forward*, 2 July 1932.
25. *New Leader*, 1 July 1932.
26. *Daily Worker*, 4 July 1932.
27. *New Leader*, 15 July 1932.
28. Ibid.
29. *New Leader*, 15 July 1932.
30. Ibid.
31. Ibid.
32. F. W. Jowett, *The I.L.P. Says No to the Present Standing Orders of the Labour Party*, 3.
33. Ibid., 4, 8, 10. The "historic Socialist resolution" refers to what had happened nine years earlier. In March 1923, Snowden, back in the Parliament as MP for Colne Valley since the previous year's general election, had moved a motion in the House of Commons calling for "the gradual supersession of the capitalist system by an industrial and social order based on the public ownership and democratic control of the instruments of production and distribution." It had, of course, been rejected. *Hansard*, HC Deb, 20 March 1923, vol. 161, cc2472.
34. Jowett, *I.L.P. Says No*, 9, 11, 15.
35. Ibid., 7–8, 11, 16. Jowett ended his pamphlet emphatically with these final three words all in bold and increasing in size.
36. *New Leader*, 15 July 1932.
37. *New Leader*, 22 July 1932.
38. *Forward*, 23 July 1932.
39. *Daily Worker*, 25 July 1932. A few days earlier, the paper had published "The Swindle of I.L.P. Disaffiliation," in which it compared disaffiliation from Labour to the time when the ILP had broken with the Second International and flirted with the Third, only to end up back in the Second again. "No worker," the paper declared, "should allow himself to be deceived by this gang." The ILP leadership was accused of "holding back the rank and file." *Daily Worker*, 20 July 1932.

40. *Labour's Northern Voice*, August 1932. (Formerly a weekly, the paper had switched to monthly publication.)
41. *New Leader*, 29 July 1932.
42. *Daily Herald*, 21 July and 25 July 1932.
43. *Daily Worker*, 30 July and 2 August 1932.
44. *Forward*, 30 July 1932.
45. Gidon Cohen, *The Failure of a Dream: The Independent Labour Party from Disaffiliation to World War II*, 27–28.
46. *Revolt*, 14 May 1932.
47. *New Leader*, 5 August 1932. The red shirts advertisement first appeared on 19 August.
48. *New Leader*, 5 August 1932.
49. In the *New Leader*, 8 July 1932, Wise was listed to speak on "Is Capitalism Breaking Down?"; Dollan, on "Is the I.L.P. Right or Wrong?"; and Brailsford, on "Democracy and the Revolutionary Problem."
50. *New Leader*, 19 August 1932.
51. *Manchester Guardian*, 8 August 1932, quoted in F. M. Leventhal, *The Last Dissenter: H. N. Brailsford and His World*, 225.
52. *New Leader*, 12 August 1932.
53. Ibid.
54. *New Leader*, 19 August 1932.
55. *Forward*, 6 August 1932.
56. *New Leader*, 19 August and 26 August 1932.
57. *Daily Herald*, 29 July 1932.
58. *New Leader*, 2 September 1932.
59. *Workers' Monthly*, November 1932.
60. *Daily Herald*, 1 August 1932.

Chapter 14: What Is a Revolutionary Policy?

1. C. K. Cullen, "The Function and Organisation of a Revolutionary Party," *National R.P.C. Monthly Bulletin (with London R.P.C. Bulletin)*, January 1934, 3.
2. Gidon Cohen, *The Failure of a Dream: The Independent Labour Party from Disaffiliation to World War II*, 812.
3. C. K. Cullen, *Memorandum on the Present Political and Economic Situation of the ILP*, 1–2.
4. "Summary of Discussion at Meeting of Divisional Representatives with the N.A.C. Held in the Labour Hall, Blackpool, on Friday March 25th, 1932, A. F. Brockway Presiding."
5. Ibid.
6. *R.P.C. Monthly Bulletin*, July 1932, 1, 2, 3.
7. *Report of the Special National Conference Held at Bradford, 30–31 July 1932*, 33, 42.
8. *New Leader*, 19 August 1932.
9. Minutes of NAC meeting, 8–9 October 1932, 8.
10. Cohen, *Failure of a Dream*, 96.
11. "Final Agenda for the Independent Labour Party Scottish Divisional Conference, 28–29 January 1933, in Glasgow," 4; "Final Agenda for Divisional Conference to Be Held on Saturday and Sunday, February 11th and 12th 1933, in London."

12. "The Return to Fundamentals: Marx and Morris," draft of an address to the ILP's summer school in Caerleon, August 1932, John Middleton Murry Papers, MS 2508.12, p. 1. Murry's address formed the basis of a two-part essay published later that year in *The Adelphi* (October and November 1932).
13. *The Adelphi*, March 1931, 520; July 1931, 353.
14. *The Adelphi*, December 1931, 142; January 1932, 203; February 1932, 260.
15. *The Adelphi*, March 1932, 367.
16. *New Leader*, 1 January 1932. Ethel Edith Mannin (1900–1984) had begun her career in copywriting and journalism. Having been a Labour supporter earlier, she had become disillusioned with that party and played an important role in the ILP in the 1930s.
17. "Community," John Middleton Murry Papers, MS 2508.32b, pp. 1, 2.
18. The first three articles, "Historical Materialism," "The Class War," and "More About the Class War," appeared in the *New Leader* on 1 March, 15 April, and 20 May 1932, respectively.
19. *New Leader*, 8 April 1932.
20. *Forward*, 2 April 1932.
21. John Middleton Murry, *The Necessity of Communism*, 50. Board schools were primary schools—or as they were then called, elementary schools. Set up by the 1870 Education Act, they were run by directly elected school boards until control was passed to the general local authorities by the 1902 Education Act.
22. *Forward*, 2 April 1932.
23. *Report of the Special National Conference Held at Bradford on 30–31 July 1932*, 39.
24. *New Leader*, 5 August 1932.
25. Murry, *The Necessity of Communism*, 9; the sentence was italicized in the original.
26. Ibid., 107, 9, 11, 15.
27. Ibid., 20, 29, 127.
28. Ibid., 120–22.
29. *New Leader*, 2 September 1932.
30. *New Leader*, 23 December 1932; 15 January and 10 February 1933.
31. "Memorandum on Organisation of the New I.L.P.," n.d. [1932?], John Middleton Murry Papers, MS 2508.15a, p. 1.
32. Ibid., 1, 2.
33. Ibid., 9.
34. "Memorandum of Comments," John Middleton Murry Papers, MS 2508.15a, p. 15. Murry anticipated much opposition from within the ILP to the proposal that its members attempt to infiltrate the Labour Party, but he appears to have overlooked the probable reaction of Labour Party leaders themselves.
35. "Memorandum on Organisation," 3.
36. Ibid., 4, 5, 6.
37. Ibid., 6.
38. Ibid., 9.
39. Ibid, 11.
40. *R.P.C. Monthly Bulletin*, March–April 1933, 1; *National R.P.C. Monthly Bulletin* (with *London R.P.C. Bulletin*), January 1934, 4.
41. John Paton, *Left Turn! The Autobiography of John Paton*, 393.
42. Ibid., 396–98.
43. Ibid., 399–400.

44. "Final Agenda for the Independent Labour Party Scottish Divisional Conference, 28–29 January 1933, in Glasgow," 4.
45. *Revolt*, 14 May 1932.
46. "Final Agenda for Divisional Conference to Be Held on Saturday and Sunday, February 11th and 12th 1933, in London," 7.
47. Cohen, *Failure of a Dream*, 12.
48. See Ian Bullock, *Romancing the Revolution: The Myth of Soviet Democracy and the British Left*, chap. 9.
49. *Decisions of the 42nd ILP Annual Conference, Together with the Statement of ILP Policy Endorsed at the Conference Held 31 March–3 April 1934 in York*, 14.
50. Cohen, *Failure of a Dream*, 111.
51. *Labour's Northern Voice*, February and March 1933.
52. C. A. Smith, "Workers' Councils," *Revolt: The London Workers' Paper*, March 1933, 7, 8.
53. *Revolt: The London Workers' Paper*, May 1933, 8.
54. *New Leader*, 31 March and 7 April 1933. William Noble Warbey (1903–80) was elected as a Labour MP in 1945. He represented the Luton constituency and later Broxtowe, then Ashfield until he retired in 1966. The NUWM was the National Unemployed Workers' Movement, founded by Wal Hannington in 1921. It was seen by the Labour Party, with some justification, as a Communist front and is now mainly remembered for its organization of the hunger marches. As we shall see in the next chapter, the question of what attitude the ILP should take towards it became inextricably linked to that of relations with the CPGB.
55. *New Leader*, 14 April 1933.
56. Ibid.

Chapter 15: Turbulent Waters

1. Paton to Aplin, 10 March 1933, ILP Collection.
2. Paton's letter dated 16 March 1933, ILP Collection.
3. Minutes of the Consultative Committee of the N.A.C. Held on Thursday March 30th in the House of Commons, London, 11.
4. Minutes of NAC meeting, 14–15 April 1933, 4.
5. *Report of the Annual Conference Held at Derby, April 1933*, 30.
6. NAC *Report, 1933*, 3.
7. Ibid., 17.
8. Ibid.
9. Fenner Brockway, "The Next Step: Towards Working-Class Unity," Chairman's Speech, I.L.P. Conference, Derby, 1933, 3–5.
10. Ibid., 16.
11. *Report of the Annual Conference, 1933*, 18.
12. Ibid., 19.
13. Ibid., 20.
14. Ibid., 34.
15. "Final Agenda: Resolutions to Be Submitted to the 41st Annual Conference, Derby, Easter, 15th, 16th, 17th and 18th April 1933," 26.
16. *Report of the Annual Conference, 1933*, 25.

17. C. K. Cullen, "Democrats and Democracy at Derby," *R.P.C. Monthly Bulletin*, May 1933, 3.
18. *Report of the Annual Conference, 1933*, 15, 31.
19. Ibid., 33, 31.
20. Ibid., 31.
21. Ibid.
22. "Final Agenda: Resolutions to Be Submitted to the 41st Annual Conference, Derby, Easter, 15th, 16th, 17th and 18th April, 1933," 25–26.
23. *Report of the Annual Conference, 1933*, 16, 28.
24. Ibid., 29.
25. *Constitution and Rules of the I.L.P., Together with a Statement on the Place of Parliamentary Activities in the Policy of the Party, as Adopted at the Derby Conference, April 1993*, 3.
26. Gidon Cohen, *The Failure of a Dream: The Independent Labour Party from Disaffiliation to World War II*, 12.
27. *New Leader*, 21 April 1933; *R.P.C. Monthly Bulletin*, May 1933, 1, 5.
28. *New Leader*, 5 May 1933.
29. *Report of the Annual Conference, 1933*, 15, 16, 24.
30. Minutes of Meeting of National Administrative Council Held in the York Hotel, Derby, on Tuesday, April 18th 1933, 1.
31. *New Leader*, 21 April 1933; *Report of the Annual Conference, 1933*, 36.
32. Minutes of NAC meeting, 14–15 April 1933, 3.
33. Cohen, *Failure of a Dream*, 88.
34. *Forward*, 15 April 1933.
35. Cohen, *Failure of a Dream*, 86–87.
36. NAC *Report, 1933*, 8.
37. *Report of the Annual Conference, 1933*, 4–5; *New Leader*, 21 April 1933.
38. *Report of the Annual Conference, 1933*, 6–13.
39. Ibid., 36, 37.
40. Ibid., 37.
41. *New Leader*, 21 April 1933.
42. Minutes of NAC meeting, 18 April 1933, 3.
43. *Forward*, 23 April 1933.
44. *New Leader*, 6 January 1933.
45. *New Leader*, 3 February 1933. Harry Pollitt (1890–1960) was elected general secretary of the CPGB in 1929 and, apart from a period at the beginning of World War II, continued in that position until 1956.
46. *New Leader*, 5 May 1933.
47. Ibid.
48. Minutes of NAC meeting, 13–14 May 1933, 16.
49. Ibid., 9–12.
50. *New Leader*, 19 May 1933.
51. *New Leader*, 2 June 1933.
52. *New Leader*, 16 June and 23 June 1933.
53. Minutes of NAC meeting, 24–25 June 1933, 7.
54. Cohen, *Failure of a Dream*, 47.
55. Minutes of NAC meeting, 24–25 June 1933, 8.
56. Ibid., 9, 10.

57. Ibid., 13, 14.
58. Ibid., 15, 16, 17. On Guy Aldred, see Mark Shipway, *Anti-Parliamentary Communism: The Movement for Workers' Councils in Britain, 1917–45*. Shipway quotes Aldred as explaining his recent (February 1933) resignation from the Anti-Parliamentary Communist Federation he had founded in 1921: it was "no longer necessary to pioneer Anti-Parliamentarism, because Anti-Parliamentarism has conquered" (130). No doubt his view seemed supported by the post-disaffiliation developments in the ILP.
59. Ibid., 18, 21.
60. *New Leader*, 30 June 1933.
61. Cohen, *Failure of a Dream*, 114.
62. Minutes of the Subcommittee on General Policy, 1 July and 2 July 1933, 1–2.
63. Ibid., 1–4.
64. "The Policy of the I.L.P.," report of the Subcommittee on General Policy to the NAC (marked in pen "Confidential"), 3.
65. John Paton, "The Policy of the I.L.P.: A Minority View," 1, 3; John Paton, "Party Policy," 1.
66. Fenner Brockway, "Party Policy," 1, 2, 4.
67. Ibid., 5, 6.
68. Minutes of the meeting of the Subcommittee on General Policy, 22–23 July 1933, 1.
69. Minutes of NAC meeting, 5–7 August 1933, 13, 14.
70. Ibid., 14, 17.
71. Ibid., 17, 19, 20, 21.
72. Ibid., 21, 22, 23.
73. *New Leader*, 11 August 1933.
74. James Maxton and Fenner Brockway, *A Clear Lead*, 13.

Chapter 16: Lancashire Revolts

1. Minutes of NAC meeting, 18 April 1933, 1. See also Gidon Cohen, "Special Note: The Independent Socialist Party," 233. As Cohen points out, the Power Fund (as it was generally called) "led to increasing demands on divisional finances to support the top-heavy party centre" (233).
2. Minutes of NAC meeting, 13–14 May 1933, 4.
3. *Labour's Northern Voice*, June and July 1933. The *Voice* began to carry advertisements for *The Adelphi*, a publication now edited by Rees but still closely associated with Murry, in July.
4. Gidon Cohen, "Special Note: The Independent Socialist Party," 232.
5. *Forward*, 22 July 1933.
6. Minutes of NAC meeting, 5–7 August 1933, 9–10.
7. *New Leader*, 25 August 1933; *The Adelphi*, August 1933, 318.
8. Minutes of NAC meeting, 23–24 September 1933, 15, 17–21. The *New Leader* reported on the NAC meeting on 26 September 1933.
9. *Labour's Northern Voice*, September 1933.
10. *The Adelphi*, September 1933, 391.
11. *Labour's Northern Voice*, October 1933.
12. *Labour's Northern Voice*, November 1933.

13. *Forward*, 11 November 1933.
14. *Controversy*, December 1933.
15. *New Leader*, 2 February 1934.
16. *Labour's Northern Voice*, February 1934; Gidon Cohen, *The Failure of a Dream: The Independent Labour Party from Disaffiliation to World War II*, 98–99.
17. *Labour's Northern Voice*, February 1934; Cohen, *Failure of a Dream*, 98–99.
18. Minutes of NAC meeting, 6–7 January 1934.
19. Minutes of NAC meeting, 10–11 February 1934, 7, 15.
20. *Labour's Northern Voice*, March 1934.
21. "Final Agenda: Resolutions for the 42nd Annual Conference, Cooperative Hall, York, March 31st to April 3rd 1934," 17–19.
22. NAC *Report, 1934*, 7.
23. *Decisions of the 42nd ILP Annual Conference, Together with the Statement of ILP Policy Endorsed at the Conference Held 31 March–3 April 1934 in York*, 4–5, 13.
24. *New Leader*, 6 April 1934.
25. Ibid.
26. *London R.P.C. Bulletin*, June 1934, 1.
27. *New Leader*, 6 April 1934.
28. Minutes of NAC meeting, 6–7 January 1934, 4.
29. Minutes of NAC meeting, 3 April 1934, 3.
30. Ibid.
31. *Labour's Northern Voice*, April 1934.
32. *New Leader*, 20 April 1934; Cohen, *Failure of a Dream*, 101. The Socialist League, which was affiliated to the Labour Party, already contained many former ILPers who had opposed disaffiliation in 1932. More will be said about its fortunes in chapter 21.
33. Minutes of Executive Committee meeting, 19 April 1934, 2.
34. Minutes of Inner Executive meeting, 26 April 1934 (a single page).
35. Cohen, *Failure of a Dream*, 101.
36. *Forward*, 5 May 1934.
37. *London R.P.C. Bulletin*, June 1934, 1.
38. *Controversy*, June 1934.
39. *Controversy*, July–August 1934, 1–3, 6.
40. *Labour's Northern Voice*, June 1934.
41. *Labour's Northern Voice*, July 1934.
42. *Labour's Northern Voice*, August 1934.
43. Minutes of Executive Committee meeting, 10 August 1934, 3; *New Leader*, 17 August 1934.
44. Minutes of NAC meeting, 16–17 November 1934, 7.
45. *Report of Meeting of Inner Executive with Representatives of the Communist Party*, 12 December 1934, 1.
46. Minutes of NAC meeting, 9–10 June 1934, 13.
47. *London R.P.C. Bulletin*, June 1934, 11.
48. *Report of Meeting of Inner Executive with Representatives of the Communist Party*, 12 December 1934, 2.
49. *New Leader*, 3 May 1935.
50. Robert E. Dowse, *Left in the Centre: The Independent Labour Party, 1893–1940*, 43.
51. "Constitution and Rules," in *Report of the Annual Conference Held at Leicester, April 1918*, 95.

52. *Report of the Annual Conference Held at Glasgow, April 1920*, 111.
53. NAC *Report, 1924*, 9.
54. Cohen, *Failure of a Dream*, 45.
55. Minutes of NAC meeting, 10–11 February 1934, 4.
56. *Decisions of the 42nd ILP Annual Conference*, 7, 10.
57. *Labour's Northern Voice*, May 1934.
58. *Labour's Northern Voice*, August 1934.
59. Cohen, *Failure of a Dream*, 101.
60. *Labour's Northern Voice*, August 1934.

Chapter 17: The Abyssinian Crisis and the Fate of Democratic Centralism

1. I use the name "Abyssinia," most commonly used at the time in Britain, although the use of "Ethiopia" was not unknown. Sylvia Pankhurst's anti-fascist newspaper, founded in response to the Italian invasion, was called the *New Times and Ethiopia News*, and *The Adelphi* also used Ethiopia (see *The Adelphi*, February 1936, 290). The ILP's *New Leader* generally used Abyssinia but did refer to the "Ethiopian Legation" in its issue of 22 February 1935. On Sylvia Pankhurst's involvement with Ethiopia, see Richard Pankhurst, "Sylvia and the *New Times and Ethiopia News*," in Ian Bullock and Richard Pankhurst, eds., *Sylvia Pankhurst: From Artist to Anti-Fascist*, 121–48.
2. *New Leader*, 22 February 1935.
3. *New Leader*, 8 March, 21 June, 12 July, and 19 July 1935.
4. *New Leader*, 23 August 1935.
5. *New Leader*, 6 September 1935.
6. In addition to *Abyssinia—Crisis for the Workers* and *Workers' Action Can Stop the War!* the London Division circulated other, similar leaflets, including *Abyssinia . . . and You* and *Abyssinia—Workers! Watch Your Step!!* All are now in the ILP Collection.
7. *New Leader*, 13 September 1935.
8. *Forward*, 31 August and 21 September 1935. See also Gidon Cohen, *The Failure of a Dream: The Independent Labour Party from Disaffiliation to World War II*, 171.
9. Minutes of Executive Committee meeting, 13 September 1935, 1.
10. *New Leader*, 20 September 1935.
11. Cohen, *Failure of a Dream*, 103–4.
12. *New Leader*, 4 October 1935. Describing James as "a Negro Socialist," the paper identified him as the chairman of the Finchley ILP branch.
13. *R.P.C. Bulletin*, October 1935, 11.
14. Minutes of NAC meeting, 9 October 1935, 2–3.
15. *New Leader*, 11 October 1935.
16. NAC *Report, 1936*, Appendix 2, "NAC Manifesto, October 1935," 15–16.
17. Jack Gaster, "Abyssinia—Where Does the I.L.P. Stand?" *Controversy*, October 1935, 17–19.
18. *Controversy*, October 1935, 16; *R.P.C. Bulletin*, October 1935, 1. Cohen quotes more from this passage in *Failure of a Dream*, 93.
19. *R.P.C. Bulletin*, October 1935, 1.
20. Ibid., 6, 2.

21. Ibid., 6, 3, 10.
22. Jack Gaster and Hilda Vernon, "The War Situation—And the League," *R.P.C. Bulletin*, October 1935, 7–10.
23. *R.P.C. Bulletin*, November 1935, 1.
24. This presumably refers to the "Communist Opposition," which was inspired by Bukharin rather than Trotsky.
25. Ibid.
26. Ibid., 1–5, 6.
27. Minutes of NAC meeting, 30 November–1 December, 1935. Gidon Cohen, who interviewed Gaster in 2000, writes that because of the position Gaster had taken on the issue, he was initially denied membership in the CPGB. He was only allowed to join after making an appeal to that party's general secretary, Harry Pollitt. He subsequently played a significant role in the CPGB for more than half a century. Cohen, *Failure of a Dream*, 94.
28. *New Leader*, 13, 20, and 27 December 1935.
29. *New Leader*, 10 January and 6 March 1936.
30. *New Leader*, 7 February 1936.
31. Minutes of NAC meeting, 15–16 February 1936, 17.
32. *New Leader*, 3 April 1936.
33. NAC *Report, 1936*, 2.
34. The ILP had played a major role in the IBRSU since the formation of the Bureau in 1931, and its secretariat had been moved to London in 1935 under the wing of the ILP. The International Bureau would remain the "London Bureau" until transferred to Paris in 1939. Cohen, *Failure of a Dream*, 166–68.
35. NAC *Report, 1936*, Appendix 9, "Resolutions of the International Bureau," 26–28.
36. *Official Report of the 44th Annual Conference Held on 11–14 April 1936 at Keighly*, 3.
37. *Report of the Annual Conference, 1936*, 5.
38. Minutes of NAC meeting, 14 April 1936, 3.
39. *New Leader*, 17 April 1936.
40. *Forward*, 18 April 1936.
41. Minutes of Executive Committee meeting, 23 May 1936, 1–2.
42. Cohen, *Failure of a Dream*, 174.
43. *New Leader*, 29 May 1936.
44. "Report of the Scrutineers," 30 June 1936, signed by Francis Johnson and John Aplin, 1.
45. Minutes of NAC meeting, 4–5 July 1936, 2, 3.
46. Ibid., 3, 4, 5.
47. NAC *Report, 1937*, Appendix 3, 21.
48. "Report of the Scrutineers," 2.
49. *New Leader*, 26 June 1936.
50. Cohen, *Failure of a Dream*, 175.
51. *United Policy Against War: Important N.A.C. Decision Following Plebiscite*, 1–2.
52. Cohen, *Failure of a Dream*, 176.
53. Minutes of NAC meetings, 1933 and 1934. For a description of the two cases, see Cohen, *Failure of a Dream*, 88–89.
54. *Controversy*, April 1935, 1.
55. *Report of the Annual Conference, 1936*, 4.
56. *Controversy* leaflet, ILP Collection.

57. NAC *Report, 1937*, 11.
58. "A Survey of the Party Position," marked "Confidential," signed by Fenner Brockway and dated 13 November 1937, 6.
59. NAC *Report, 1939*, 15.
60. Minutes of Executive Committee meeting, 23 May 1936, 2.
61. C. A. Smith, "Re-establishing Party Discipline," *Between Ourselves*, July 1939, 8, 9.
62. Ibid., 10.
63. Minutes of Inner Executive meeting, 25 March 1936, 1.
64. Cohen, *Failure of a Dream*, 109.
65. Minutes of NAC meeting, 23–24 April 1935, 3–4.
66. Minutes of NAC meeting, 2–3 August 1935, 8.
67. Minutes of NAC meeting, 10–12 August 1935, 5.
68. NAC *Report, 1936*, 13.
69. Minutes of NAC meeting, 30 November–1 December 1935, 6.

Chapter 18: Soviet Foreign Policy and the League of Nations

1. Bernard Crick, *George Orwell: A Life*, 255.
2. Fenner Brockway, *Socialism at the Cross Roads: Why the I.L.P. Left the Labour Party*, 8–9.
3. *Revolt*, 18 June 1932, 2.
4. *Daily Worker*, 18 July 1932.
5. *New Leader*, 24 March 1933.
6. *Controversy*, June 1934, 4.
7. Gidon Cohen, *The Failure of a Dream: The Independent Labour Party from Disaffiliation to World War II*, 87–91. As Cohen explains, the Communist-sponsored Affiliation Committee which included undercover members of the CPGB, who were not content with the reliability, from their point of view, of the RPC, 87.
8. For a detailed and convincing analysis of the development of the Webbs' view of the USSR over the period, see Kevin Morgan, *The Webbs and Soviet Communism*.
9. *New Leader*, 24 January and 31 January 1936.
10. For MacDonald and Snowden's initially relatively sympathetic view of the Bolsheviks, see Ian Bullock, *Romancing the Revolution: The Myth of Soviet Democracy and the British Left*, chaps. 3 and 4.
11. John Paton, *Left Turn! The Autobiography of John Paton*, 394.
12. Fenner Brockway, *Socialism over Sixty Years: The Life of Jowett of Bradford*, 310, 327.
13. *Labour Leader*, 7 March 1918; Bullock, *Romancing the Revolution*, 148–49.
14. Bullock, *Romancing the Revolution*, 205; Keith Laybourn, *Philip Snowden: A Biography, 1864–1937*, 86.
15. *New Leader*, 16 April 1926.
16. *New Leader*, 30 December 1927.
17. NAC *Report, 1924*, 33.
18. *Forward*, 25 October 1930; *New Leader*, 16 January 1931.
19. *Forward*, 5 January 1929.
20. *New Leader*, 27 September 1929.
21. *Controversy*, October 1935, 5.
22. *New Leader*, 10 January 1936.

23. *Labour's Northern Voice*, February, April, June through October, and December 1931 and March 1932; *Forward*, 16 January and 23 January 1932; *New Leader*, 12 February 1932.
24. *Annual Report and Resolutions to Be Submitted to the Annual Conference of the Independent Labour Party Welsh Division, 1931*, 7.
25. Fenner Brockway, *"A Socialist Plan for Unemployment": A Speech Against a Conservative Party Motion of No Confidence in the Labour Government, April 16, 1931*, 6.
26. *New Leader*, 6 May and 19 June 1932.
27. *Report of the Annual Conference Held at Derby, April 1933*, 37, 17; *Constitution and Rules of the I.L.P., Together with a Statement on the Place of Parliamentary Activities in the Policy of the Party, as Adopted at the 1933 Annual Conference at Derby*, 4.
28. Fenner Brockway and James Maxton, *A Clear Lead*, 13.
29. *"A Socialist Policy for Britain": Statement to Be Submitted by the National Administrative Council of the I.L.P. to the Annual Conference of the Party to Be Held at the Keir Hardie Hall, Derby, April 20th to 23rd 1935*, 3, 13, 5.
30. "New Russia Supplement No. 14," *New Leader*, 12 May 1933. The Four-Power Pact or (sometimes called the "Quadripartite Agreement," a term also applied to several other pacts) originated from a document drafted by Mussolini that sought to encourage closer cooperation among Britain, France, Germany, and Italy, in part by awarding them greater power within the League of Nations. After considerable revision, a somewhat tepid version of the pact was signed on 15 July 1933 by all four countries, but it was never fully ratified.
31. *New Leader*, 16 June and 23 June 1933.
32. *New Leader*, 30 June and 7 July 1933.
33. *New Leader*, 14 July and 21 July 1933.
34. *I.L.P. and Comintern with the 21 Points of the Communist International: Correspondence Between the Secretaries of the British I.L.P and the Executive Committee of the Communist International*, 3–7 (Kuusinen) and 8–11 (Brockway). Brockway noted in his memoir *Inside the Left* that Kuusinen had "become known to the whole world as the head of the ill-fated puppet government set up by Russia in Finland." Fenner Brockway, *Inside the Left: Thirty Years of Platform, Press, Prison, and Parliament*, 249.
35. *New Leader*, 4 May 1934. This issue also carried an article headlined "Russia Is Not Starving, Oft Repeated Lies of the Capitalist Press Answered by the Facts."
36. *New Leader*, 27 July and 21 September 1934.
37. *New Leader*, 30 November 1934.
38. Ibid.
39. Ibid. Graham's book had appeared earlier that year from the London publisher Victor Gollancz.
40. Minutes of Inner Executive meeting, 5 December 1934, 1, and 10 April 1935, 2; report of the Inner Executive to the NAC, April 1935, 2.
41. Minutes of Inner Executive meeting, 15 April 1935, 1.
42. Minutes of NAC meeting, 19 April 1935, 1.
43. Minutes of NAC meeting, 23–24 April 1935, 4.
44. *New Leader*, 5 January 1934.
45. *Controversy*, December 1933, 1.

46. Telegram from the Secretariat of the Communist International, 30 April 1933, sent from the Rundschau Press Agency, Zurich. ILP Collection.
47. Minutes of NAC meeting, 10–11 February 1934, 15–16; Cohen, *Failure of a Dream*, 87–89.
48. Minutes of NAC meeting, 30–31 March 1934, 7.
49. Paton's letter (now in the ILP Collection) was dated 6 March 1933 and was written on behalf of the ILP, the Independent Socialist Party (Holland), the Socialist Workers' Party (Germany), the Independent Socialist Workers' Party (Poland), the Party of Proletarian Unity (France), the Socialist Party (Italy), and the Labour Party (Norway).
50. Minutes of NAC meeting, 30–31 March 1934, 9–10.
51. *New Leader*, 22 February 1935.
52. *London R.P.C. Bulletin*, June 1934, 8.
53. Minutes of NAC meeting, 29–30 June 1935, 3.
54. Minutes of Inner Executive meeting, 19 July 1935, 1.
55. NAC *Report*, 1936, 9.
56. Minutes of Inner Executive meeting, 10 April 1935, 2.
57. Minutes of NAC meeting, 23–24 April 1935, 4.
58. *London R.P.C. Bulletin*, 31 July 1935, 3.
59. Ibid.
60. *R.P.C. Bulletin*, November 1935, 13.
61. Fenner Brockway, *Workers' Front*, 59.

Chapter 19: The ILP and the USSR

1. *New Leader*, 13 March 1936.
2. *New Leader*, 28 August 1936.
3. *New Leader*, 28 August and 4 September 1936.
4. In *Inside the Left: Thirty Years of Platform, Press, Prison, and Parliament*, Brockway tells us that, at the ILP summer school in 1937, he learned of Maurin's survival from his wife, Jeanne, who had just received a letter from him (290). Maurin was imprisoned by Franco for several years and went to the United States when he was released. Brockway's 1938 book, *Workers' Front*, is dedicated to Jeanne and Joaquin Maurín.
5. Gorkin's "undelivered speeches" were published by the ILP under the title *"We Conquer or Die": Spanish Workers Appeal to You*. The publication was described on the title page as "Two Speeches which Sir John Simon tried to Stop." Simon was the Home Secretary responsible for refusing Gorkin entry to Britain.
6. NAC *Report*, 1937, 3–4. On the Spanish Exhibition, see Gidon Cohen, *The Failure of a Dream: The Independent Labour Party from Disaffiliation to World War II*, 179. Brockway chaired the exhibition's organizing committee, which included veteran anarchist Emma Goldman as well as artist Roland Penrose, who, according to Brockway, "designed its layout beautifully," in addition to gathering materials. Fenner Brockway, *Towards Tomorrow: The Autobiography of Fenner Brockway*, 1977), 121. Penrose travelled to Spain with his first wife, Valentine Boué, the two of them both "sponsored by the Independent Labour Party and described as 'trustworthy Socialists' in the introductory letter" that the party provided them. Elizabeth Cowling, *Visiting Picasso: The Notebooks and Letters of Roland*

Penrose, 27. A friend and later biographer of Picasso, Penrose also organized a tour of Picasso's Guernica in 1938, in support of the Republican cause. One of the founders, in 1946, of London's Institute of Contemporary Arts, he married the celebrated photographer and war correspondent Lee Miller—the former associate of Man Ray—in 1947.

7. NAC *Report, 1937*, 4. A Catholic—although, he insisted, an opponent of "clerical domination from the pulpit" since the age of eighteen—McGovern held that "where the Church has remained on the side of the people they have been treated with respect and reverence," citing the Basque provinces in support of this view. *Why Bishops Back Franco: Report of Visit of Investigation to Spain*, 11.
8. NAC *Report, 1937*, 4. For a detailed and well-illustrated account of the ILP volunteers in the Spanish war, see Christopher Hall, *"In Spain with Orwell": George Orwell and the Independent Labour Party Volunteers in the Spanish Civil War, 1936–1939*. Bob Edwards (1906–90) chaired the ILP from 1943 to 1948, was elected general secretary of the Chemical Workers' Union, and was a Labour MP from 1955 to 1987, becoming, in 1983, the "father of the House," that is, the oldest MP in the House of Commons.
9. *New Leader*, 29 January 1937.
10. *New Leader*, 2 April 1937.
11. Ibid.
12. NAC *Report, 1937*, 4.
13. Letter from O. W. Kuusinen to Fenner Brockway, 20 February 1934, in *The I.L.P and Comintern with the 21 Points: Correspondence Between the Secretaries of the British ILP and the Executive Committee of the Communist International*, 4.
14. *New Leader*, 19 February 1937.
15. *New Leader*, 12 March 1937.
16. Bernard Crick, *George Orwell: A Life*, 317.
17. Paul Preston, *The Spanish Civil War: Reaction, Revolution, and Revenge*, 6.
18. Hugh Thomas, *The Spanish Civil War*, 20, 29; Ian Slater, *Orwell: The Road to Airstrip One*, 134.
19. Fenner Brockway, *Workers' Front*, 74.
20. Crick, *George Orwell*, 317.
21. Fenner Brockway, *The Truth About Barcelona*, 13.
22. See Cohen, *Failure of a Dream*, 102–9.
23. *New Leader*, 20 March 1936.
24. "Left Communists," or "council Communists," were active in the short-lived Comintern Sub-Bureau in Amsterdam. The leading members were Antonin Pannekoek and Herman Gorter. In Britain, this tendency flourished for a few years in Sylvia Pankhurst's Communist Party (British Section of the Fourth International). They were perceived to be a serious enough threat for Lenin to denounce them dismissively in *"Left Wing" Communism: An Infantile Disorder*. Pankhurst's later Communist Workers' Party was an affiliate of the original Fourth International, also known as the Communist Workers' International, which preceded the Trotskyist organization of the same name by roughly a decade and a half. Officially formed in 1922, it was made up of a number of small groups similar to Pankhurst's, of which the most important was a faction of the KAPD—the Communist Workers' Party of Germany. Over the course of the 1920s, it disintegrated and, by the start of the 1930s, was essentially inactive. On

"Left Communism" in Britain, see Ian Bullock, "Sylvia Pankhurst and the Russian Revolution: The Making of a 'Left-Wing' Communist," 121–48; and Bullock, *Romancing the Revolution: The Myth of Soviet Democracy and the British Left*, chaps. 9 and 11.
25. *Daily Worker*, 6 April 1937.
26. *New Leader*, 14 May 1937.
27. *New Leader*, 21 May 1937.
28. Brockway, *Truth About Barcelona*, 3, 7, 10.
29. Ibid., 11, 14–15. Brailsford's article had appeared in the *New Statesman and Nation*, 21 May 1937.
30. R. Palme Dutt, "Spain Organises for Victory," *Daily Worker*, 23 May 1937.
31. *Daily Worker*, 19 June 1937.
32. *New Leader*, 28 May and 4 June 1937; *Daily Worker*, 10 June 1937.
33. Thomas, *Spanish Civil War*, 581; *New Leader*, 18 June 1937.
34. Tom Buchanan, *The Impact of the Spanish Civil War on Britain*, 110. Buchanan devotes an entire chapter of his book to the circumstances of Smillie's death, basing his account mainly on the David Murray papers at the National Library of Scotland (acc. nos. 791415). He concludes, after considering the possibility that "intent" as well as negligence may have played a part, that "the full facts of Bob Smillie's death may never be established" (121). In *Failure of a Dream*, Cohen says that Smillie died as a result of the "extreme neglect of his Republican captors" (139).
35. Ibid., 116–20.
36. Ibid., 110.
37. Minutes of NAC meeting, 11–12 December 1937, 1, 3.
38. Ibid., 1.
39. NAC Report, 1938, 6; *New Leader*, 11 March 1938; Fenner Brockway, *Towards Tomorrow: The Autobiography of Fenner Brockway*, 125.
40. *New Leader*, 13 August 1937.
41. Thomas, *Spanish Civil War*, 579–81. The Soviet secret police operated under the NKVD (Narodnyi komissariat vnutrennikh del, or People's Commissariat for Internal Affairs), which was responsible for carrying out the Stalinist purges of 1936 to 1938. Organized in 1934, the NKVD incorporated the OGPU (Obyedinyonnoye gosudarstvennoye politicheskoye upravleniye, or Joint State Political Directorate), which, in 1922, had replaced the Cheka as the Soviet Union's secret police. In 1934, the OGPU was renamed the GUGB (Glavnoe upravlenie gosudarstvennoi bezopasnosti, or Main Directorate for State Security), which eventually evolved into the KGB, founded in 1954.
42. Brockway, *Truth About Barcelona*, 14; *New Leader*, 4 June 1937. The Left Book Club, founded just over a year before, had been advertised in the *Leader*, but now the ILP paper began to question the club's "political limits." It cited a Gollancz "editorial" sent out to convenors of Left Book Club discussion groups that urged them not to tolerate "Leftist" criticisms. *New Leader*, 11 June 1937. For a brief discussion of Sloan's book, see Bullock, *Romancing the Revolution*, 326–31.
43. *New Leader*, 11 June 1937.
44. *Daily Worker*, 14 June and 18 June 1937. The reference was to the farcical trial and subsequent execution of Marshal Tukhachevsky and a number of other senior officers of the Red Army.

45. *New Leader*, 18 June 1937.
46. *New Leader*, 25 June 1937.
47. *Daily Worker*, 13 July; *New Leader*, 16 July 1937.
48. *New Leader*, 17 November 1937.
49. *New Leader*, 24 December 1937.
50. *New Leader*, 14 January 1938. A review, in the same issue, of seven recently published books on the Soviet Union noted that "Stalin gets a majority here by the odd vote in seven." Whereas Paul Winterton's *Russia—with Open Eyes* and Hubert Lee's *Twenty Years After: Life in the USSR To-day* both offered "the orthodox Communist apologia for Soviet foreign policy, the 'Trotskyist' purge, the 'democratic' Constitution etc.," the "most valuable" of the seven was Eugene Lyons's *Assignment in Utopia*. Lyons wrote that, although he had gone to the USSR in 1928 as "an enthusiastic supporter of the Communist Party," he was now "thoroughly disillusioned." In his view, the system that had evolved there should be called "not Communism but 'Sovietism'"—a system "backed by armies and secret services."
51. *New Leader*, 25 February 1938.
52. *New Leader*, 4 March 1938.
53. *New Leader*, 11 March 1938; Brockway, *Inside the Left*, 260. The Communist Opposition, which comprised a number of small organizations in several countries, began as the "Right Opposition," who were supporters of Bukharin (as distinct from the "Left Opposition" followers of Trotsky) in 1929.
54. *New Leader*, 11 March 1938.
55. Ibid.; NAC Report, 1938, Appendix 3, 26–27.
56. *New Leader*, 18 March and 15 April 1938.
57. *New Leader*, 22 April 1938.
58. Brockway, *Workers' Front*, 25.
59. John McGovern, Terror in Spain, 5, 13, 15. Brockway said that the Communist-controlled secret police was "organised on the model of the Russian O.G.P.U." *Workers' Front*, 123. The acronym refers to the main Russian secret police organization between 1923 and 1934.
60. Fenner Brockway, *Pacifism and the Left Wing: Address to "After the Crisis" Weekend Conference of Holborn and St. Pancras Group of the Peace Pledge Union*, 15.
61. *New Leader*, 29 April and 6 May 1938.
62. Crick, *George Orwell*, 314–15, 317. See also Michael Shelden, *Orwell: The Authorised Biography* (London: Heinemann, 1991), 276. In fact, Orwell may not have been misled about the need for socialist credentials. Brockway described how a Spanish border official had rejected McNair's British passport on the grounds that it had been issued by "a Capitalist Government." After McNair produced a letter from the ILP, however, he was allowed to enter Spain. Brockway, *Workers' Front*, 91.
63. *New Leader*, 12 March 1937. In the second half of *The Road to Wigan Pier*, Orwell tackles the question of why socialism—which clearly represents a solution to the terrible conditions described in the first half of the book—holds such little appeal to most people.
64. Quoted in McArthur, *We Carry On*, 4. Brockway still referred to Orwell as "Mr. Eric Blair" in *Workers' Front* (1938), mentioning his service with the North West Frontier Police (111).

65. Crick, *George Orwell*, 348; Shelden, *Orwell*, 308.
66. *New Leader*, 13 August 1937. Jeanne Antonino was the wife of Joaquin Maurin.
67. Buchanan, *Impact of the Spanish Civil War*, 14.
68. *New Leader*, 24 September 1937.
69. Crick, *George Orwell*, 364–65; *New Leader*, 24 June 1938.
70. *New Leader*, 8 July 1938.
71. Shelden, *Orwell*, 328; Crick, *George Orwell*, 380.
72. *New Leader*, 2 September 1938. The report was signed "GOEM."
73. Brockway, *Workers' Front*, 224.
74. NAC *Report*, 1939, 3.
75. George Orwell, letter to Raymond Postgate, 21 October 1938, in *Orwell in Spain*, 310. One of the founding members of the CPGB, Raymond Postgate (1896–1971) split with the party only two years later, in 1922, over the Comintern's insistence that its constituents abide by Moscow's directives. A novelist, journalist, social historian, and founder of the *Good Food Guide*, Postgate remained committed to the socialist cause.
76. *Basic Resolutions for ILP Annual Conference, 16–19 April 1938, in Manchester*, 10.
77. *New Leader*, 10 July 1936.
78. *New Leader*, 8 May 1936.
79. *New Leader*, 27 November 1936.
80. A review of her novel *The Pure Flame* appeared a little later that year. *New Leader*, 6 March 1936. As well as novels and travel books, she also wrote seven volumes of autobiography, beginning with *Confessions and Impressions*, published in 1930, and ending with *Sunset over Dartmoor: A Final Chapter of Autobiography*, in 1977. Brockway says that Mannin was "a Maxton worshipper" who joined the ILP after it disaffiliated from Labour. He says that later, under the influence of her friendship with Emma Goldman, her views "came to approximate closely to the anarchist position." He also pays tribute to her for donating all her available capital to buying a ship to break the Bilbao blockade during the Spanish Civil War. When this failed, the money raised was used to finance a refuge for Basque children in Somerset. Brockway describes her as "heroically generous." Brockway, *Inside the Left*, 299, 320–22.
81. *New Leader*, 17 January 1936. Mannin's book critical of the USSR, published in 1936, was *South to Samarkand*.
82. *New Leader*, 31 January 1936.
83. *New Leader*, 14 February and 21 February 1936.
84. "Final Agenda of Resolutions and Amendments to Be Presented Before the 48th Annual Conference, 23–25 March 1940, at Nottingham," 28.
85. Brockway, *Inside the Left*, preface to 1947 edition.
86. *Between Ourselves*, October 1939, 10–12.

Chapter 20: Calls for Unity as War Approaches

1. *A Socialist Policy for Britain*, NAC statement for 1935 annual conference, 11.
2. The march, billed as an "Anti-War and Anti-Fascist Demonstration," was advertised in a leaflet issued by the St. Pancras branch, titled *Abyssinia! Workers' Action or World War?*

3. The names of the speakers were listed on the postcard-sized admission ticket, headed "Abyssinia—Workers' Action or World War?" which extended an invitation to "Bearer and Friend." See also *New Leader*, 11 October 1935.
4. *Election Manifesto of the Independent Labour Party: Against War! For Socialism!*
5. Gidon Cohen, *The Failure of a Dream: The Independent Labour Party from Disaffiliation to World War II*, 69–70. In chapter 4 of his book, Cohen provides a brief, but comprehensive, survey of the ILP's electoral activities, national and local, during the years following disaffiliation.
6. F. W. Jowett, *Parliamentary Election: To the Electors of the East Division of Bradford, 1935*, 2, 3, 4.
7. *R.P.C. Bulletin*, November 1935, 7, 9.
8. Cohen, *Failure of a Dream*, 72. In both cases, the ILP candidate came in second.
9. *New Leader*, 20 December 1935.
10. "Report of Meeting Between J. Maxton, A. F. Brockway, H. Pollitt and W. Gallacher held at the House of Commons, April 12, 1935," 1.
11. James Jupp, *The Radical Left in Britain*, 46.
12. NAC *Report, 1936*, 2.
13. *Get Round the Table!* The letter was dated 4 August 1936 and later appeared as an appendix in the NAC's report to the 1937 annual conference (23–24).
14. *New Leader*, 7 August 1936.
15. NAC *Report, 1937*, 6.
16. Minutes of NAC meeting, 4–5 July 1936, 2, 6.
17. *New Leader*, 10 March and 31 March 1933.
18. Brockway, *Inside the Left*, 270.
19. The speech of "La Pasionaria"—Isidora Dolores Ibárruri Gómez (1895–1989)—was broadcast on radio on 18 July 1936.
20. Robert Benewick, *The Fascist Movement in Britain*, 226.
21. *Daily Worker*, 5 October 1936; *New Leader*, 9 October 1936.
22. No doubt the figure cited by the ILP is a very generous estimate of the number who took part in the protest. That said, it is notoriously difficult to estimate the size of even an orderly demonstration taking place with police consent. How much more difficult it must have been in the Cable Street context.
23. *New Leader*, 9 October 1936.
24. *Daily Worker*, 5 October 1936.
25. *They Did Not Pass: 300,000 Workers Say No to Mosley*, 3, 4, 8.
26. *East London Advertiser*, 10 October 1936.
27. Benewick, *Fascist Movement in Britain*, 225, 226. For recent books on Cable Street, see Dave Renton's review in *Socialist History* 44, 91–94, of a number published in 2011.
28. Brockway, *Inside the Left*, 272. According to the *New Leader* report of 9 October 1936, before the fascist march was diverted by the police, Brockway phoned the Home Office from a call box and was later told by the Press Association that the decision to prevent Mosley's march taking its intended route had been made half an hour after his call. "I have always doubted whether my message had anything to do with the decision to call off the procession," Brockway concluded, probably accurately enough.

29. NAC Report, 1937, 6; minutes of NAC meeting, 7–8 November 1936, 6; minutes of Executive Committee meeting, 24 November 1936; Cohen, Failure of a Dream, 134.
30. New Leader, 1, 8, 22, and 29 January 1937.
31. Cohen, Failure of a Dream, 135.
32. Ben Pimlott, Labour and the Left in the 1930s, 95.
33. New Leader, 15 January 1937. More of this article is quoted in Cohen, Failure of a Dream, 134–35.
34. Labour's Northern Voice, February 1937; Forward, 2 January 1937.
35. New Leader, 12 February 1937.
36. Tribune, 1 January 1937.
37. Patrick Seyd, "Factionalism Within the Labour Party: The Socialist League, 1932–37," 220. The voting was 56 for, 38 against, and 23 abstentions.
38. Cohen, Failure of a Dream, 136.
39. New Leader, 2 April 1937; Tribune, 14 May and 21 May 1937.
40. NAC Report, 1938, 13. This was not too different from Forward's assessment, which appeared on 12 February 1938 and gave the following four reasons for the breakdown of the unity campaign: the pledge to refrain from criticism of the USSR; the Communists pushing for an alliance between Russia, France, and Britain while the ILP wanted a "pact with Working Class Governments"; tensions over Spain, with ILPers being denounced as fascists; and the Moscow trials.
41. Fenner Brockway, "A Survey of the Party Position," November 1937, paras. 2, 5, 6.
42. Ibid., paras. 8, 11, 12. The "minimum conditions" for ILP reaffiliation would appear again in early 1938 in Fenner Brockway's Workers' Front (217).
43. "Survey of Party Position," paras. 38, 39.
44. Minutes of NAC meeting, 11–12 December 1937; "Preliminary Agenda of Resolutions, Forty-Sixth Annual Conference, April 16th to 19th, 1938," 13; Socialist Policy for 1938 [Resolutions Adopted by the Annual Conference of the I.L.P., Manchester, April 16th–18th, 1938], 9.
45. Brockway, Workers' Front, 154–55, 238.
46. Simone de Beauvoir, The Prime of Life, 147.
47. Brockway, Inside the Left, 338–39.
48. New Leader, 5 February 1937.
49. New Leader, 15 October and 24 December 1937; 22 July, 29 July, 2 September, 9 September, 23 September, and 30 September 1938.
50. Cohen, Failure of a Dream, 191.
51. New Leader, 7 October 1938. More of McNair's report is quoted in Cohen, Failure of a Dream, 194. Maxton's speech was also published separately by the ILP: James Maxton, Maxton's Speech in Parliament.
52. Brockway, Inside the Left, 332–33; Cohen, Failure of a Dream, 191–94; John McNair, James Maxton: The Beloved Rebel, 277.
53. "Independent Labour Party: Final Agenda of Resolutions and Amendments, Forty-seventh Annual Conference, Roscoe Rooms, Scarborough, April 8th to 10th, 1939," 48; Joseph Southall, "To Members of the I.L.P.," 1 March 1939, 3. In support, Southall cited an article by H. G. Wells in the News Chronicle.
54. "Independent Labour Party: Final Agenda of Resolutions and Amendments" (1939), 48, 50.

55. *New Leader*, 7 April 1939; Brockway, *Inside the Left*, 334; Cohen, *Failure of a Dream*, 195.
56. Fenner Brockway, *Pacifism and the Left Wing: Address to "After the Crisis" Weekend Conference of Holborn and St. Pancras Group of the Peace Pledge Union*, 6–17.
57. Brockway, *Workers' Front*, 252.
58. Cohen, *Failure of a Dream*, 31.
59. Ibid., 210.
60. "Survey of the Party Position," 6–7. Brockway listed the following books as "in hand": C. A. Smith, *Power and the State*; George Orwell, *Barcelona Tragedy* (presumed to be an early version of *Homage to Catalonia* although no additional information is available); Ethel Mannin, *Women and the Revolution*; Victor Serge, *From Lenin to Stalin*; and his own *Workers' Front*. In the latter book, Brockway described the Left Book Club as the CPGB's "main instrument" for promoting the Popular Front policy. It was "a clever device to use a sympathetic and enterprising publisher for the purpose of influencing the large class of readers who are interested in 'Left' questions" (244).
61. *New Leader*, 15 July 1938; Minutes of NAC meeting, 30 July–1 August 1938, 5–6.
62. *New Leader*, 29 July, 5 August, and 2 September 1938.
63. Brockway, *Inside the Left*, 273.
64. NAC *Report, 1939*, 10.
65. NAC *Report, 1939*, Appendix, 25.
66. "Independent Labour Party: Final Agenda of Resolutions and Amendments" (1939), 36–44.
67. *New Leader*, 7 April and 14 April 1939.
68. *New Leader*, 14 April 1939. See also Cohen, *Failure of a Dream*, 158–60.
69. Cohen, *Failure of a Dream*, 160.
70. Minutes of Executive Committee meeting, 23 April 1939, 3.
71. *New Leader*, 14 July 1939.
72. *Between Ourselves*, July 1939, 2.
73. Ibid., 2, 3.
74. Minutes of NAC meeting, 5 August 1939, 1, 2, 3.
75. Ibid., 5, 6.
76. Ibid., 7.
77. *New Leader*, 11 August 1939.
78. *New Leader*, 25 August 1939.
79. NAC *Report, 1940*, 9.

Chapter 21: The Ex-ILP

1. Robert E. Dowse, *Left in the Centre: The Independent Labour Party, 1893–1940*, 96.
2. Ben Pimlott, *Labour and the Left in the 1930s*, 101.
3. *Forward*, 13 August 1932.
4. *New Clarion*, 27 August 1932. After the original *Clarion* closed in 1931, there was a short-lived attempt to revive it the following year. Brailsford contributed regularly during its short life.
5. *Forward*, 20 August 1932; *New Leader*, 19 August 1932.
6. *Forward*, 27 August 1932.

7. *Forward*, 19, 17, and 24 September and 19 November 1932; 14 January 1933.
8. *Forward*, 4 February and 18 March 1933.
9. *Forward*, 1 April 1933 and 30 March 1935.
10. James Jupp, *The Radical Left in Britain*, 54; *Forward*, 27 April 1935.
11. *Forward*, 21 January 1933.
12. *Forward*, 9 December 1933 and 24 February 1934.
13. *Forward*, 9 November 1935, 20 November 1937, and 12 February and 5 March 1938.
14. *Forward*, 21 May 1938.
15. *Forward*, 8 January and 12 February 1938.
16. *Forward*, 26 March 1938.
17. Pimlott, *Labour and the Left in the 1930s*, 101.
18. *Forward*, 31 March 1934 and 30 March 1935.
19. Gidon Cohen, "'Happy Hunting Ground of the Crank': The Independent Labour Party and Local Labour Parties in Glasgow and Norwich," 60.
20. *Forward*, 5 November 1938. Only the four largest cities in Scotland—Edinburgh, Glasgow, Dundee, and Aberdeen—have Lord provosts. Others have provosts whose function is similar to that of mayors in other parts of the UK. The Lord provosts combine this role with that of the largely ceremonial Lord lieutenants of the county.
21. *Forward*, 26 March 1938, 29 April 1939; Pimlott, *Labour and the Left in the 1930s*, 101.
22. Jupp, *Radical Left in Britain*, 28; Pimlott, *Labour and the Left in the 1930s*, 44. See also Michael Bor, *The Socialist League in the 1930s*.
23. Ernest Bevin and G. D. H Cole, *The Crisis: What It Is, How It Arose, What to Do*.
24. Michael Stewart, *Forms of Public Control*, 10.
25. Patrick Seyd, "Factionalism Within the Labour Party: The Socialist League, 1932–37," 210.
26. *New Clarion*, 13 August and 27 August 1932; *Forward*, 27 August 1932.
27. *New Leader*, 23 September 1932.
28. Pimlott, *Labour and the Left in the 1930s*, 46.
29. Jupp, *Radical Left in Britain*, 125; Seyd, "Factionalism Within the Labour Party," 207.
30. Pimlott, *Labour and the Left in the 1930s*, 49.
31. Charles Trevelyan, *The Challenge to Capitalism*, 3.
32. Seyd, "Factionalism Within the Labour Party," 207.
33. Pimlott, *Labour and the Left in the 1930s*, 48, quoting *Manchester Guardian*, 3 October 1932.
34. Seyd, "Factionalism Within the Labour Party," 207, 225nn9–10. See also Pimlott, *Labour and the Left in the 1930s*, 217n28.
35. Seyd, "Factionalism Within the Labour Party," 209.
36. Ibid.
37. Jupp, *Radical Left in Britain*, 42.
38. *Communist International*, 20 March 1935, quoted in Jupp, *Radical Left in Britain*, 74.
39. E. F. Wise, *Control of Finance and the Financiers, 1934*, 4.
40. *Socialist Leaguer*, 15 January; March–April; May 1935.
41. David Howell, "Traditions, Myths and Legacies: The ILP and the Labour Left," 220.
42. "Forward to Socialism," National Council document for decision at 1934 Socialist League conference, 10–11.

43. Pimlott, *Labour and the Left in the 1930s*, 53.
44. *Socialist Leaguer*, December 1934. See also Pimlott, Labour and the Left in the 1930s, 55.
45. *The Socialist: Journal of the Socialist League*, no. 4, n.d. [but probably early 1936].
46. Pimlott, *Labour and the Left in the 1930s*, 22; Jupp, *Radical Left in Britain*, 72.
47. Quoted in Seyd, "Factionalism Within the Labour Party," 222.
48. Pimlott, *Labour and the Left in the 1930s*, 49.
49. Seyd, "Factionalism Within the Labour Party," 221.
50. *Labour's Northern Voice*, July 1934.
51. *Labour's Northern Voice*, August 1934.
52. *Labour's Northern Voice*, September and October 1934.
53. *Labour's Northern Voice*, October 1934.
54. Gidon Cohen, "Special Note: The Independent Socialist Party," 234; *New Leader*, 7 September 1934.
55. *Labour's Northern Voice*, January 1935.
56. *Independent Socialist Party Manifesto*, 2.
57. Ibid., 2.
58. Ibid., 3.
59. *Behind Rearmament: Preparing for Fascism in Britain!* 6, 8.
60. Ibid., 8.
61. Cohen, "Special Note," 235–36. The advent of the Nottingham branch was reported in *Labour's Northern Voice*, January1935.
62. *Labour's Northern Voice*, September 1935; May 1936. Herbert Read (1893–1968) was an anarchist poet and art critic. He was a cofounder, with Roland Penrose, of the Institute of Contemporary Arts.
63. "Speech to the I.S.P. Convention" (draft), John Middleton Murry Papers, MS 2508.27, 1, 2.
64. Ibid., 3–4.
65. Ibid., 4, 6. There is a certain irony here. Although Murry opposed emphasizing ILP traditions, his call for unity echoed Robert Blatchford's Clarion campaigns for "socialist unity" in 1894, the year after the ILP's formation, when the notion of the "unattached" first saw the light of day for ILPers. Logie Barrow and Ian Bullock, *Democratic Ideas and the British Labour Movement, 1880–1914*, 83.
66. Cohen, "Special Note," 235–37.
67. Jennie Lee, *This Great Journey*, 45–46.
68. Kenneth O. Morgan, *Labour People: Leaders and Lieutenants, Hardie to Kinnock*, 40, 49.
69. Martin Gilbert, *Plough My Own Furrow: The Story of Lord Allen of Hurtwood as Told Through His Writings and Correspondence*, 204.
70. "Speech to the I.S.P. Convention" (draft), John Middleton Murry Papers, MS 2508.27, 3.
71. *New Leader*, 8 January 1932.
72. *New Leader*, 15 February and 22 February 1932.
73. *New Leader*, 29 January and 19 February 1932.
74. *Workers' Monthly*, February 1932.
75. *Workers' Monthly*, July 1932.
76. *New Leader*, 13 May 1932.
77. *New Leader*, 12 August 1932.

78. *News-Letter: National Labour Monthly*, 1 October 1932, 8–9.
79. Gilbert, *Plough My Own Furrow*, 205.
80. Arthur Marwick, *Clifford Allen: The Open Conspirator*, 130.
81. *The Next Five Years: An Essay in Political Agreement*, 312, 316.
82. Ibid., 3.
83. Ibid., 12.
84. Ibid., 17–18.
85. *Daily Herald*, 26 July 1935.
86. *Forward*, 8 September 1934; 22 May 1937.

Conclusion

1. Keith Laybourn, *Philip Snowden: A Biography, 1864–1937*, 86; Ian Bullock, *Romancing the Revolution: The Myth of Soviet Democracy and the British Left*, 202–5.
2. Peter James Thwaites, "The Independent Labour Party, 1938–50," 255.
3. Dennis Pilon, *Wrestling with Democracy: Voting Systems as Politics in the Twentieth-Century West*, 53.
4. *Report of the Annual Conference Held at York, April 1924*, 98–100.
5. Clifford Allen, *Socialism and the Next Labour Government: Presidential Address at the I.L.P. Conference*, 4.
6. John Beckett (1894–1964) edited the British Union of Fascists' *Action* and *Blackshirt*. He later broke with Mosley and founded the National Socialist League. He was interned during the Second World War and continued to play a role in the fascist movement in the postwar period.
7. Jennie Lee, *This Great Journey*, 167–68.
8. Tony Judt, *Thinking the Twentieth Century*, 191.
9. Friends of the Soviet Union, *The New Democracy: Stalin's Speech on the New Constitution*; Friends of the Soviet Union, *Spies, Wreckers, and Grafters: The Truth About the Moscow Trials*; W. P. Coates, *More Anti-Soviet Lies Nailed*. Coates and his wife, Zelda, were founder members of the CPGB.
10. Coates, *More Anti-Soviet Lies Nailed*, 7.
11. Charles Trevelyan, *Soviet Russia: A Description for British Workers*, 7, 25, 31, 29.
12. Eric Hobsbawm, *Interesting Times: A Twentieth-Century Life*, 201.
13. Kevin Morgan, *Bolshevism, Syndicalism and the General Strike: The Lost Internationalist World of A. A. Purcell*, 53.
14. Bullock, *Romancing the Revolution*, 233–36.
15. Thwaites, "Independent Labour Party, 1938–50," 34.
16. Franz Borkenau, *The Totalitarian Enemy*, 26.
17. David Howell, "Traditions, Myths and Legacies: The ILP and the Labour Left," 224.

Bibliography

Archives

British Library, London

ILP (Independent Labour Party) Collection, 1893–1978, British Library of Political and Economic Science, London School of Economics

James Maxton Papers, Glasgow Digital Library, Centre for Digital Library Research, University of Strathclyde

John Middleton Murry Papers, Special Collections, Centre for Research Collections, University of Edinburgh

Archive and Study Centre, People's History Museum, Manchester

Collections, Working Class Movement Library, Salford

Contemporary Newspapers and Journals

NOTE: When a paper had a recognized organizational affiliation this is indicated in parentheses. Other papers were independent publications.

The Adelphi
Bradford Daily Telegraph
Bradford Pioneer
The Clarion
Controversy (ILP)
Daily Herald
Daily Worker (CPGB)
East London Advertiser
Forward
Guild Socialist
The Internationalist (left-wing of the ILP)
Justice (BSP, SDF)
Labour Leader (later the *New Leader*) (ILP)
Labour Monthly
Labour's Northern Voice
London R.P.C. Bulletin
Manchester Guardian
National R.P.C. Monthly Bulletin
New Clarion
New Leader (formerly *Labour Leader*) (ILP)
News-Letter: National Labour Monthly
Revolt (later *Revolt: The London Workers' Paper*)

Bibliography

R.P.C. Bulletin
The Socialist (SLP)
Socialist Leaguer (later *The Socialist: Journal of the Socialist League*)
Socialist Review (ILP)
The Times
Town Crier: Birmingham's Labour Weekly
Tribune
Workers' Monthly (CPGB)

Contemporary Publications

Abyssinia . . . and You. ILP, London Division, n.d. [1935].
Abyssinia—Crisis Faces the Workers. ILP, London Division, September 1935.
Abyssinia! Workers' Action or World War? ILP, London Division, St. Pancras Branch, n.d. [1935].
Abyssinia—Workers! Watch Your Step!! ILP, London Division, n.d. [1935].
Allen, Clifford. *Britain's Political Future: A Plea for Liberty and Leadership*. London: Longmans, Green, 1934.
Allen, Clifford. *The I.L.P. and Revolution: Chairman's Speech to ILP Summer School, Easton Lodge, August 1925*. ILP, 1925.
———. *Putting Socialism into Practice*. ILP, 1924.
———. *Socialism and the Next Labour Government: Presidential Address at the I.L.P. Conference*. ILP, 1925.
Attlee, C. A. *Economic History—with Notes for Lecturers and Class Leaders*. I.L.P. Study Course No. 4. ILP Information Committee, 1923.
Behind Rearmament: Preparing for Fascism in Britain! Manchester: General Council of the Independent Socialist Party, n.d.
Belloc, Hilaire. *The Servile State*. London and Edinburgh: T. N. Foulis, 1912.
Bevin, Ernest, and G. D. H. Cole. *The Crisis: What It Is, How It Arose, What to Do*. London: New Statesman and Nation, 1931.
Boothby, Robert J. G. *I Fight to Live: Autobiography*. London: Gollancz, 1947.
Borkenau, Franz. *The Totalitarian Enemy*. London: Faber and Faber, 1940.
Brailsford, Henry Noel. *The "City" or the Nation? Reprinted from the New Leader*. ILP, 1931.
———. *Socialism for To-day*. London: ILP, 1925.
Brailsford, Henry Noel, John Atkinson Hobson, Arthur Creech Jones, and E. F. Wise. *The Living Wage: A Report Submitted to the National Administrative Council of the ILP*. ILP Publication Department, September 1926.
Brockway, Fenner. *Bermondsey Story: The Life of Alfred Salter*. London: Allen and Unwin, 1949.
———. *Inside the Left: Thirty Years of Platform, Press, Prison, and Parliament*. London: Allen and Unwin, 1947. First published 1942.
———. *"Make the Workers Free!" The Industrial Policy of the I.L.P.* ILP, 1926.

Bibliography

———. "The Next Step: Towards Working-Class Unity," Chairman's Speech, ILP Conference, Derby, 1933. London: ILP, 1933.

———. Pacifism and the Left Wing: Address to "After the Crisis" Weekend Conference of Holborn and St. Pancras Group of the Peace Pledge Union. Pacifist Publicity Unit, 1938.

———. Socialism at the Cross Roads: Why the I.L.P. Left the Labour Party. ILP, 1932.

———. Socialism over Sixty Years: The Life of Jowett of Bradford. London: Allen and Unwin, for the National Labour Press, 1946.

———. Socialism—with Speed: An Outline of the I.L.P. "Socialism in Our Time" Proposals. ILP, 1928.

———. "A Socialist Plan for Unemployment": A Speech Against a Conservative Party Motion of No Confidence in the Labour Government, April 16, 1931. ILP, 1931.

———. Towards Tomorrow: The Autobiography of Fenner Brockway. London: Hart-Davis, MacGibbon, 1977.

———. The Truth About Barcelona. ILP, 1937.

———. Workers' Front. London: Secker and Warburg, 1938.

Coates, W. P. More Anti-Soviet Lies Nailed. London: Anglo-Soviet Parliamentary Committee, 1933.

Cole, G. D. H. Guild Socialism Re-stated. London: Leonard Parsons, 1920.

———. Workers' Control in Industry. I.L.P. Pamphlet, New Series, No. 25. ILP, 1919.

The Communist International. I.L.P. Pamphlet, New Series, No. 37. ILP, 1920.

Cook, A. J., and James Maxton. Our Case for a Socialist Revival. London: Workers Publications, [1928].

Crooks, Will. "A Living Wage for All": An Appeal for a Weekly Minimum Wage of 30 Shillings—A Speech Given to the House of Commons, 26 April 1911. ILP, 1911.

Cullen, C. K. Memorandum on the Present Political and Economic Situation of the ILP. London: By the author, 1932.

Dalton, Hugh. Call Back Yesterday: Memoirs, 1887–1931. London: Muller, 1953.

de Beauvoir, Simone. The Prime of Life. Harmondsworth, UK: Penguin, 1960.

Democratic Control. I.L.P. Position Leaflet No. 2. London: National Labour Press, 1916.

Election Manifesto of the Independent Labour Party: Against War! For Socialism! ILP, 1935.

Elliott, Sydney R. Co-operation and Socialism. ILP, 1926.

Friends of the Soviet Union. The New Democracy: Stalin's Speech on the New Constitution. London: Lawrence and Wishart, for Friends of the Soviet Union, 1936.

Friends of the Soviet Union. Spies, Wreckers, and Grafters: The Truth About the Moscow Trials. London: Friends of the Soviet Union, n.d.

Get Round the Table! London: National Labour Press, 1936.

Henderson, Fred. Socialism of the I.L.P. I.L.P. Programme Pamphlet No.1. ILP, 1922.

Huntz, Jack. Spotlight on Spain. London: ILP, 1937.

The I.L.P. and the Labour Party: What Is the Difference? Bristol: ILP, 1919.

The I.L.P. and the Third International: Being the Questions Submitted by the I.L.P. Delegation to the Executive of the 3rd International and Its Reply, with an Introductory Statement by the National Council of the I.L.P. ILP, 1920.

Bibliography

ILP Industrial Policy Committee. *Trade Unions and Socialism: A Report to the I.L.P. Conference, 1926, on the Industrial Aspect of Socialism.* ILP, 1926.

The Independent Labour Party and Its Future Work. ILP, n.d. [1922].

Independent Socialist Party Manifesto. Manchester: General Council of the Independent Socialist Party, n.d.

Hobson, S. G. *National Guilds: An Inquiry into the Wage System and the Way Out.* Edited by A. R. Orage. London: G. Bell and Sons, 1914.

Johnson, Francis. *The Independent Labour Party and the International: A Memorandum for Members.* ILP, 1920.

Jowett, F. W. "*Down with the Parasites*": *Jowett's Chairman's Address to the Labour Party Conference at Edinburgh.* ILP, 1922.

———. *The I.L.P. Says No to the Present Standing Orders of the Labour Party.* ILP, 1932.

———. "Labour and Cabinet Rule," Reprinted from the "Bradford Pioneer," December 6th, 1929. ILP, 1929.

———. *Parliament or Palaver? Answers to Objections to Proposal for Reform of Parliament.* ILP, 1926.

———. *Parliamentary Election: To the Electors of the East Division of Bradford, 1935.* ILP, 1935.

———. "*Socialism in Our Time*": *Address of the Chairman to the ILP Annual Conference, Whitley Bay, April 1926.* ILP, 1926.

———. *What Is the Use of Parliament?* Pass On Pamphlets No. 11. London: Clarion Press, 1909.

Jowett, F. W., and H. B. Lees Smith. *The Reform of Parliament: Speeches by F. W. Jowett and H. B. Lees Smith at the ILP Conference.* ILP, 1925.

Kirkwood, David. *My Life of Revolt.* London: Harrap, 1935.

Kneeshaw, J. W. *Democracy "Done Brown."* I.L.P. Pamphlet, New Series, No. 36. ILP, 1920.

———. *The Hidden Hand in Politics.* I.L.P. Pamphlet, New Series, No.12. ILP, 1919.

Lee, Jennie. *This Great Journey.* New York: Farrar and Rinehart, 1942.

MacDonald, J. Ramsay. *The History of the I.L.P.* I.L.P. Study Course No. 1. ILP, 1921.

———. "The I.L.P. and the Labour Party." *Socialist Review*, April–June 1918, 119–95.

———. *Parliament and Revolution.* London: National Labour Press, 1919.

———. *Socialism After the War.* Manchester: National Labour Press, 1917.

———. *Socialism and Society.* The Socialist Library II. ILP, 1905.

———. *Socialism: Critical and Constructive.* London: Cassell and Company, 1921.

———. *The Socialist Movement.* London: Williams and Norgate, 1911.

———. *The Story of the I.L.P. and What It Stands For.* London: I.L.P Information Committee, 1924.

McAllister, Gilbert. *James Maxton: The Portrait of a Rebel.* London: John Murray, 1935.

McArthur, Dan. *We Carry On: Our Tribute to Bob Smillie.* ILP, 1937.

McGovern, John. *Terror in Spain.* ILP, 1938.

———. *Why Bishops Back Franco: Report of Visit of Investigation to Spain.* ILP, 1937.

McNair, John. *In Spain Now!* National Labour Press, 1936.

Maxton, James. *Maxton's Speech in Parliament.* ILP, 1938.

Bibliography

———. "Roads to Socialism": Chairman's Address to the I.L.P.Conference 1929. ILP, 1929.
———. Twenty Points for Socialism. ILP, 1925.
———. "Where the ILP Stands": Presidential Address of James Maxton to the ILP Conference, Together with a Declaration on the Relation of the ILP to the Labour Party. ILP, 1930.
Maxton, James, and Fenner Brockway. A Clear Lead. ILP, 1933.
Moscow's Reply to the I.L.P. Glasgow: Left Wing Group of the I.L.P., Kirkwood and Co., [1920].
Mosley, Oswald. Revolution by Reason: An Account of the Birmingham Proposals, Together with an Analysis of the Financial Policy of the Present Government Which Has Led to Their Great Attack upon Wages. ILP, 1925.
Murry, John Middleton. The Necessity of Communism. London: Jonathan Cape, 1932.
The Need for the I.L.P. ILP, 1920.
The Next Five Years: An Essay in Political Agreement. London: Macmillan, 1935.
Now for Socialism! The Call of the I.L.P. ILP, 1923.
Paton, John. Left Turn! The Autobiography of John Paton. London: Secker and Warburg, 1936.
Penty, Arthur J. The Restoration of the Gild System. London: Swan Sonnenschein and Co., 1906.
Reckitt, Maurice B., and C. E. Bechhofer. The Meaning of National Guilds. London: C. Palmer and Hayward, 1918.
Resist War! ILP, 1938.
Salter, Alfred. "A Living Wage for All": Dr Salter's Speech in the House of Commons on 7 March 1923. Bermondsey ILP, 1923.
Shinwell, Emanuel. Conflict Without Malice: An Autobiography. London: Odhams, 1953.
———. Nationalisation of the Mines: A Practical Policy. ILP, 1929.
Snowden, Philip. Socialism Made Plain. ILP, 1920.
Socialist Policy for 1938. ILP, 1938.
Stewart, Michael. Forms of Public Control. S.S.I.P. Study Guide No. 7. Society for Socialist Inquiry and Propaganda, 1932.
Strachey, John. Revolution by Reason: An Account of the Financial Proposals Submitted by Oswald Mosley at the Thirty-Third Independent Labour Party Conference, and Endorsed by the Birmingham Borough Labour Party and the I.L.P. Federation. London: Leonard Parsons, 1925.
Swanwick, H. M. Builders of Peace: Being Ten Years' History of the Union of Democratic Control. London: Swarthmore Press, 1924.
Symons, W. T. A Living Wage or a Living Income: An Attack upon the Living Wage and an Alternative Policy for the Independent Labour Party. London: Blackfriars Press, 1927.
They Did Not Pass: 300,000 Workers Say No to Mosley. ILP, 1936.
Trevelyan, Charles. The Challenge to Capitalism. London: Socialist League, 1933.
———. Soviet Russia: A Description for British Workers. London: Gollancz, 1935.
United Policy Against War: Important N.A.C. Decision Following Plebiscite. ILP, 1936.
Waugh, Evelyn. Vile Bodies. London: Chapman and Hall, 1930.

What the I.L.P. Stands For. ILP, 1935.

Wintringham, T. H. *Facing Both Ways: The I.L.P. and the Workers' Struggle.* London: Communist Party of Great Britain, 1929.

Wise, E. F. *Control of Finance and the Financiers.* London: Socialist League, 1934.

Workers' Action Can Stop the War! ILP, London Division, 1935.

Secondary Sources

Alberti, Johanna. *Eleanor Rathbone.* London: Sage Books, 1996.

Barrow, Logie, and Ian Bullock. *Democratic Ideas and the British Labour Movement, 1880–1914.* Cambridge: Cambridge University Press, 1996.

Benewick, Robert. *The Fascist Movement in Britain.* Rev. ed. London: Allen Lane, 1972.

Bennett, Gill. *"A Most Extraordinary and Mysterious Business": The Zinoviev Letter of 1924.* London: Foreign and Commonwealth Office, 1999.

Blaazer, David. "Guild Socialists After Guild Socialism: The Workers' Control Group and the House of Industry League." *Twentieth Century British History* 11, no. 2 (2000): 135–55.

Bor, Michael. *The Socialist League in the 1930s.* London: Athena Press, 2005.

Branson, Noreen. *Poplarism, 1919–25: George Lansbury and the Councillors' Revolt.* London: Lawrence and Wishart, 1980.

Brockway, Fenner. *Bermondsey Story: The Life of Alfred Salter.* London: Allen and Unwin, 1949.

———. *Socialism over Sixty Years: The Life of Jowett of Bradford.* London: Allen and Unwin, for the National Labour Press, 1946.

Brown, Gordon. *Maxton.* Edinburgh: Mainstream, 1986.

Buchanan, Tom. *The Impact of the Spanish Civil War on Britain.* Brighton: Sussex Academic Press, 2007.

Bullock, Ian. *Romancing the Revolution: The Myth of Soviet Democracy and the British Left.* Edmonton: Athabasca University Press, 2011.

———. "Sylvia Pankhurst and the Russian Revolution: The Making of a 'Left-Wing' Communist." In *Sylvia Pankhurst: From Artist to Anti-Fascist,* Ian Bullock and Richard Pankhurst, 121–48. London: Palgrave Macmillan, 1992.

Cohen, Gidon. *The Failure of a Dream: The Independent Labour Party from Disaffiliation to World War II.* London: I. B. Tauris, 2007.

———. "'Happy Hunting Ground of the Crank': The Independent Labour Party and Local Labour Parties in Glasgow and Norwich." In *Labour's Grass Roots: Essays on the Activities of Local Labour Parties and Members, 1919–45,* edited by Matthew Worley, 54–78. Aldershot, UK: Ashgate, 2005.

———. "Special Note: The Independent Socialist Party." In *Dictionary of Labour Biography,* vol. 11, edited by Keith Gildart, David Howell, and Neville Kirk, 231–38. Basingstoke, UK: Palgrave Macmillan, 2003.

Cowling, Elizabeth. *Visiting Picasso: The Notebooks and Letters of Roland Penrose.* London: Thames and Hudson, 2006.

Bibliography

Crick, Bernard. *George Orwell: A Life*. London: Penguin, 1982.

Cross, Colin. *Philip Snowden*. London: Barrie and Rockliff, 1966.

Dowse, Robert E. *Left in the Centre: The Independent Labour Party, 1893–1940*. London: Longmans, 1966.

———. "A Note on Ramsay MacDonald and Direct Action." *Political Studies* 9, no. 3 (1961): 306–8.

Foot, Michael. *Aneurin Bevan: A Biography*. Vol. 1, *1897–1945*. London: MacGibbon and Key, 1962.

Gilbert, Martin. *Plough My Own Furrow: The Story of Lord Allen of Hurtwood as Told Through His Writings and Correspondence*. London: Longmans, 1965.

Greenleaf, W. H. *The British Political Tradition*. Vol. 2 of *The Ideological Heritage*. London: Methuen, 1985.

Hall, Christopher. *"In Spain with Orwell": George Orwell and the Independent Labour Party Volunteers in the Spanish Civil War, 1936–1939*. Perth, Scotland: Tippermuir Books, 2013.

Hinton, James. *The First Shop Stewards' Movement*. London: Allen and Unwin, 1973.

Hobsbawm, Eric. *Interesting Times: A Twentieth-Century Life*. London: Abacus, 2002.

Howell, David. *A Lost Left: Three Studies in Socialism and Nationalism*. Manchester: Manchester University Press, 1986.

———. *MacDonald's Party: Labour Identities and Crisis, 1922–1931*. Oxford: Oxford University Press, 2002.

———. "Traditions, Myths and Legacies: The ILP and the Labour Left." In *The ILP on Clydeside, 1893–1932: From Foundation to Disintegration*, edited by Alan McKinlay and R. J. Morris, 204–32. Manchester: Manchester University Press, 1991.

Jenkins, Roy. *Mr. Attlee: An Interim Biography*. London: Heinemann, 1948.

Jones, Raymond A. *Arthur Ponsonby: The Politics of Life*. London: Christopher Helm, 1989.

Judt, Tony, with Timothy Snyder. *Thinking the Twentieth Century*. London: Vintage Books, 2012.

Jupp, James. *The Radical Left in Britain*. London: Frank Cass, 1982.

Kendall, Walter. *The Revolutionary Movement in Britain, 1900–21: The Origins of British Communism*. London: Weidenfeld and Nicolson, 1969.

Laybourn, Keith. "The Failure of Socialist Unity in Britain, c. 1893–1914." *Transactions of the Royal Historical Society*, 6th ser., 4 (1994): 153–75.

———. "The Independent Labour Party and the Second Labour Government, 1929–31: The Move Towards Revolutionary Change." In *The Second Labour Government: A Reappraisal*, edited by John Shepherd, Jonathan Davis, and Chris Wrigley, 100–116. Manchester: Manchester University Press, 2012.

———. *Philip Snowden: A Biography, 1864–1937*. Aldershot, UK: Temple Smith, 1988.

Leventhal, F. M. *The Last Dissenter: H. N. Brailsford and His World*. Oxford: Oxford University Press, 1985.

Marquand, David. *Ramsay MacDonald*. London: Jonathan Cape, 1977.

Bibliography

Marwick, Arthur. *Clifford Allen: The Open Conspirator*. Edinburgh: Oliver and Boyd, 1964.

McKenzie, R. T. *British Political Parties: The Distribution of Power Within the Conservative and Labour Parties*. 2nd ed. Aldershot, UK: Gregg Revivals, 1963. First published 1955.

McKinlay, Alan, and R. J. Morris, eds. *The ILP on Clydeside, 1893–1932: From Foundation to Disintegration*. Manchester: Manchester University Press, 1991.

McNair, John. *James Maxton: The Beloved Rebel*. London: Allen and Unwin, 1955.

Middlemas, Keith. *The Clydesiders: A Left Wing Struggle for Parliamentary Power*. London: Hutchinson, 1965.

Miliband, Ralph. *Parliamentary Socialism: A Study in the Politics of Labour*. London: Merlin Press, 1972. First published 1961.

Morgan, Austen. *J. Ramsay MacDonald*. Manchester: Manchester University Press, 1987.

Morgan, Kenneth O. *Labour People: Leaders and Lieutenants, Hardie to Kinnock*. Oxford: Oxford University Press, 1987.

Morgan, Kevin. *Bolshevism, Syndicalism, and the General Strike: The Lost Internationalist World of A. A. Purcell*. Vol. 3 of *Bolshevism and the British Left*. London: Lawrence and Wishart, 2013.

———. *Labour Legends and Russian Gold*. Vol. 1 of *Bolshevism and the British Left*. London: Lawrence and Wishart, 2006.

———. *The Webbs and Soviet Communism*. Vol. 2 of *Bolshevism and the British Left*. London: Lawrence and Wishart, 2006.

Newman, Michael. *John Strachey*. Manchester: Manchester University Press, 1989.

Orwell, George [Eric Blair]. *Orwell in Spain*. London: Penguin, 2001.

Peart-Binns, John S. *Maurice Reckitt: A Life*. London: Bowerdean, 1988.

Pelling, Henry. *A Short History of the Labour Party*. Basingstoke, UK: Macmillan, 1961.

Pilon, Dennis. *Wrestling with Democracy: Voting Systems as Politics in the Twentieth-Century West*. Toronto: University of Toronto Press, 2013.

Pimlott, Ben. *Hugh Dalton*. London: Jonathan Cape, 1985.

———. *Labour and the Left in the 1930s*. Cambridge: Cambridge University Press, 1977.

———, ed. *The Political Diary of Hugh Dalton, 1918–40, 1945–60*. London: Jonathan Cape, 1986.

Preston, Paul. *The Spanish Civil War: Reaction, Revolution, and Revenge*. 3rd ed. London: Harper Perennial, 2006.

Seyd, Patrick. "Factionalism Within the Labour Party: The Socialist League, 1932–37." In *Essays in Labour History, 1918–1939*, edited by Asa Briggs and John Saville, 204–31. London: Croom Helm, 1977.

Shelden, Michael. *Orwell: The Authorised Biography*. London: Heinemann, 1991.

Shepherd, John, and Keith Laybourn. *Britain's First Labour Government*. Basingstoke, UK: Palgrave Macmillan, 2006.

Shipway, Mark. *Anti-Parliamentary Communism: The Movement for Workers' Councils in Britain, 1917–45*. Basingstoke, UK: Macmillan, 1988.

Skidelsky, Robert. *The Economist as Saviour*. Vol. 2 of *John Maynard Keynes*. London: Macmillan, 1992.

———. *Oswald Mosley*. London: Macmillan, 1975.

———. *Politicians and the Slump: The Labour Government of 1929–1931*. Harmondsworth, UK: Penguin, 1970. First published 1967.

Slater, Ian. *Orwell: The Road to Airstrip One*. 2nd ed. Montréal and Kingston: McGill-Queen's University Press, 2003.

Stocks, Mary D. *Eleanor Rathbone: A Biography*. London: Gollancz, 1949.

Taylor, A. J. P. *English History, 1914–1945*. Harmondsworth, UK: Penguin, 1970. First published 1965.

Thomas, Hugh. *John Strachey*. London: Eyre Methuen, 1973.

———. *The Spanish Civil War*. Harmondsworth, UK: Penguin, 1965. First published 1961.

Thompson, Laurence. *The Enthusiasts: A Biography of John and Katharine Bruce Glasier*. London: Gollancz, 1971.

Thompson, Noel. *John Strachey: An Intellectual Biography*. Basingstoke, UK: Macmillan, 1993.

Thorpe, Andrew. *The British General Election of 1931*. Oxford: Oxford University Press, 1991.

———. *A History of the Labour Party*. 2nd ed. London: Palgrave, 2001.

Thwaites, Peter James. "The Independent Labour Party, 1938–50." PhD diss., London School of Economics, 1976.

Wedgwood, C. V. *The Last of the Radicals: Josiah Wedgwood, M.P.* London: Jonathan Cape, 1951.

White, Stephen. "Labour's Council of Action 1920." *Journal of Contemporary History* 9, no. 4 (1974): 99–122.

Winter, Barry. *The ILP Past and Present*. Leeds: Independent Labour Publications, 1996.

Worley, Matthew. "Class Against Class: The Communist Party of Great Britain in the Third Period, 1927–1932." PhD diss., University of Nottingham, 1998.

———. *Class Against Class: The Communist Party in Britain Between the Wars*. London: I. B. Tauris, 2002.

Worley, Matthew. *Labour Inside the Gate: A History of the British Labour Party Between the Wars*. London: I. B. Taurus, 2005.

———, ed. *Labour's Grass Roots: Essays on the Activities of Local Labour Parties and Members, 1919–45*. Aldershot, UK: Ashgate, 2005.

Index

Abbot, Tom, 242, 243, 246, 261, 322–23, 324, 326

Allen, Clifford, 142, 363n57: "Allen-Attlee" alternative, 64–66, 68–70; chairman of ILP, 95, 338, 361n79; on disaffiliated ILP, 329; elected ILP treasurer, 72; on first Labour government, 100; industrial democracy, 58; and ILP 1922 program, 66, 71, 114, 130; inspires *Living Wage*, 101–3, 113, 118; interpretation of parliamentary democracy, 95–96, 100–101, 161; and Maxton, 143–45; Moscow mission, 32–34, 57, 58, 68–70; National Labour in the House of Lords, 134, 139, 179–80, 184, 326–31; *Next Five Years*, 329–31; relationship with MacDonald, 95, 116, 180, 337, 375n17; resigns as ILP chairman, 118

Angell, Norman, 42, 329

Anomolies Bill, 175, 377n23

Aplin, John, 204, 217, 244, 252–53, 256–57, 362, 307–8, 310, 314

Attlee, Clement, 21, 62: "Allen-Attlee" alternative, 64–66, 68–70

battle of Cable Street, 300–302, 393n22, 393n28

Beckett, John, 64, 69, 74, 76, 191, 398n6; joins New Party and later BUF, 168, 172, 184; suspended as MP in 1930, 168, 374n41

Benewick, Robert, 300, 301

Bevan, Aneurin, 129, 172, 302

Bevin, Ernest, 99, 318, 319

Blatchford, Robert, 85, 103, 350n8, 397n65

Bondfield, Margaret, 71, 162, 175, 194, 359n20, 377n23

Bradford resolution, 16–17, 21, 166–67, 198

Brailsford, Henry Noel, 351n46: advocates price stability, 102–3, 106; advocates proportional representation, 21–22; on Allen, 327–28; attacked by Maxton, 201; *The "City" or the Nation?* 178; on Communists, 284; dispute with MacDonald, 116–18, 121, 122; editor of *New Leader*, 22, 23, 76–78, 95, 131, 141, 338; English Revolution of 1640s, 104, 365n36; expelled from ILP, 202; "gradualness," 104–5, 112, 133, 153; and Liberals, 121, 131–32, 137; *Living Wage* report, 103–7, 113–116, 118, 125–26, 130, 338, 347; opposes disaffiliation, 179–80, 183, 191, 193, 195–96; pleas for Labour Party unity, in 1931, 177, 181, 183, 188, 196; refuses to speak at ILP summer school in 1932, 200–201; resigns as editor, 131; Russian Revolution, 103, 267–68, 287; on "scenes" in Commons, 91; *Socialism for To-day*, 103–7; 111–12; Socialist League, 302, 320, 321, 335; supports "Allen-Attlee," 64; supports Jowett, 23, 24, 350n26; UDC, 42

Brockway, Archibald Fenner, 7–8: on Abyssinia, 251–52, 256; "anti-Soviet slanders," 271–72, 281; attacked by *Daily Worker*, 236; battle of Cable Street, 300, 393n28; Clifford Allen, 72–73, 81, 100; Clynes, 87; Cook-Maxton, 147; conversation with Arthur Henderson in Geneva, 192; debate on failure to nominate MacDonald as treasurer, 145; defends POUM, "not a Trotskyist party," 282; disaffiliation, 191–93, 201; editor of *New Leader*, 181, 226, 255; General Strike, 119–20; ILP chairman, 7, 190, 193, 195, 204, 205, 219, 220, 222, 236; *The I. L. P. in Crisis*, 178–79; ILP secretary, 232, 267,

409

275; Living Wage, 129; Member of Parliament, 161; Moscow trials, 279, 287, 288–89, 290, 293; No Conscription Fellowship, 42; pacifism, 290; political activities post-1945, 7–8, 346; praises Wedgwood and MacDonald, 88–89; rejoins Labour Party, 346; relations with the Communists, 230, 244–45, 265, 275–76; *Socialism with Speed*, 135; Soviet foreign policy and League of Nations, 272–74, 276–77, 294; Spain and the POUM, 282–84, 286–87, 290; supports Allan-Attlee alternative, 64; supports Jowett's constitutional reform proposals, 24; suspended from House of Commons, 167–68; *Workers' Front*, 282, 289, 305–6, 309, 317

Brown, Gordon, 91

Brown, W. J. (William John), 165–66, 172

Bruce Glasier, John, 43, 49, 244, 335, 355n12

Bruce Glasier, Katharine, 35, 36, 65, 73, 355n12

Buchanan, George, 148, 181, 185, 189, 191, 199, 298, 312

Buchanan, Tom, 285, 292, 390n34

Bundock, Clement J., 54, 73, 357n59

Buxton, Charles Roden, 42, 76, 159–60

Carter, Bertram C., 65, 73–74, 358n32

Clynes, John Robert, 44, 86–88, 162, 178, 336, 361n9

Cohen, Gidon, 4, 5, 8, 181, 191, 200, 214, 221, 223, 227, 228, 253, 258, 259, 262, 302, 308, 309, 318, 323, 326, 349n7, 382n1, 385n27, 386n7, 390n34, 393n5

Cole, G. D. H. (George Douglas Howard), 58: collapse of Building Guild and NGl, 79; founds SSIP with Margaret Cole, 318; and ILP 1922 program, 46, 69, 72, 78; resigns from Socialist League, 320. *See also* guild socialism and "functional" democracy

Comintern (Communist International): affiliation committee, 223, 260; "an instrument of the foreign policy of Soviet Russia," 286; biennial world congresses, 269; "class against class," 268, 372n70; Gaster's call for "sympathetic affiliation," 275; ILP branches invited to Comintern conference, 244; ILP hostility to Comintern, 254, 267, 275, 290; ILP offer cooperation, 274; "Left Wing of the ILP" campaign for affiliation, 5, 31–38, 51, 60; organizes international brigades, 280; popular front policy, 273, 310; relations with ILP after 1933, 271–72; replies to ILP queries, 1921, 353n31; sub-bureau in Amsterdam, 389n24

Communist International. *See* Comintern

Communist Party of Great Britain (CPGB): attempts at intervention in ILP, 205, 223, 244–45, 266; foundation, 3–4; hostility to ILP, 272, 279; ILP membership losses to, 37, 195, 203, 336, 354n51; policy "somersaults," 269; prospect of merger with, 34, 37, 38, 226, 237, 240, 263, 322; seeks Labour Party affiliation, 4, 273, 298, 300, 302

conferences, ILP: Birmingham (1930), 165, 168–70; Blackpool (1932), 189–91, 203, 208; Bradford (1893), 11; Bradford (1914), 18, 166–67; Bradford (1932), 200–202, 218, 343–44; Carlisle (1929), 136–37, 154, 155, 159–60, 170; Derby (1933), 214, 217, 218, 220–24, 228–30, 238, 270, 271, 272; Derby (1935), 274, 276, 297; Glasgow (1920), 20–21, 29, 31–32, 38, 46, 51, 53, 57, 191, 246; Glasgow (1937), 258–61, 280, 281, 283, 300; Gloucester (1925), 22, 80, 99–101, 103, 108, 125, 337–38; Huddersfield (1919), 20, 30; Keighley (1936), 249, 255–57, 260, 262–63, 299; Leeds (1917), 19; Leicester (1918), 27–28, 246; Leicester (1927), 144–45; London (1923), 21, 77–78; Manchester (1913), 16; Manchester (1938), 286, 289, 304, 305; Merthyr Tydfil (1912), 16; Nottingham

(1922), 63–70, 72, 76, 221; Nottingham (1940), 289, 314; Scarborough (1931), 170, 171; Scarborough (1939), 293, 308, 309, 311–14; Southport (1921), 29, 30, 36–38, 60, 62; Whitley Bay (1926), 71, 118–119, 125; York (1924), 94, 95, 143–44, 246, 268; York (1934), 214–15, 242–43, 246

Cook, A. J. (Arthur James), 181, 371n30: Cook-Maxton, 137, 145–56, 163, 339; General Strike, 120

CPGB. *See* Communist Party of Great Britain.

Creech Jones, A. (Arthur), 141, *Living Wage* report, 113–14, 347

Crick, Bernard, 265, 282, 291, 292

Cripps, Stafford, 260, 302–4, 320, 322

Cullen, Carl (Dr), 186, 189, 203, 204–5, 220–21, 226, 249, 251–54

Dalton, Hugh, 114, 122, 143, 322, 370n13

dictatorship of the proletariat, 21, 32, 33, 35, 47, 51, 52, 54, 60, 102, 151, 153, 186, 206, 286–87

Dollan, Patrick, 94, 97, 113, 117, 137, 146, 150, 153, 165; attacks Maxton, 163–64; attempts to refer back ILP program, 62, 72; critical of Allen, 102; criticizes Cook-Maxton, 148–50; expelled from ILP, 202; fails to refer back *Living Wage* report, 136–37; Lord Provost of Glasgow, 318; opposes disaffiliation, 186, 187, 189, 192–94, 198, 199, 200; "A Rebel against the Rebels," 170–71; Scottish Socialist Party, 315–18; third in 1929 ILP chairman election, 155

Dowse, Robert E., 4, 5, 8, 12, 28, 29, 48, 58, 68, 73, 76, 78, 80, 91, 95, 245–46, 315

Edwards, Bob, 389n8: Labour MP, 346; POUM militia, 291, 306; supports disaffiliation/opposes reaffiliation, 183, 313; supports "workers' sanctions," 257; suspended from ILP, 223

Fairchild, E. C., 35
Foot, Michael, 78, 172

Garton, C. G., 189–90, 237: ILP policy subcommittee, 228–31

Gaster, Jack, 275, 298: and Abyssinia, 240, 251–54; against Sandham, 241–42; censure motion *v*. Lancs Division, 237, 239; and CPGB, 266, 385n27; ILP policy subcommittee, 228–31; a leader of RPC, 186–87, 205, 221, 228; and London Division, 218, 224, 227, 236; and Russian foreign policy, 274; warns NAC about Communist League, 245

general elections: 1895, 11; 1922, 76, 79; 1923, 92, 98; 1924, 97; 1929, 155; 1931, 166, 180–81; 1935, 287–89

General Strike, 1926, 119–20

Gilbert, Martin, 143, 180, 327

Gorkin, Julián, 280, 282, 285, 388n5

Grayson, Victor, 43, 49, 89, 90

guild socialism and "functional" democracy: influence in ILP, 6, 49–50, 54–55, 58, 256n40, 357n59

Hardie, David, 316
Hardie, George, 171, 194–95, 316
Hardie, James Keir, 3, 12, 30, 43, 85, 86, 87, 146, 154, 155, 179, 189, 315, 316, 339

Henderson, Arthur, 361n4: on clash of Clydesiders and MacDonald, 86; defeat, 1931 election, 180; as Labour leader, 177–78; as member of Labour's "inner leadership," 92; on post-disaffiliation ILP, 192; and UDC, 411

Henderson, Fred, 71, 360n14
Hobsbawm, Eric, 343
Hobson, J. A. (John Atkinson): influence, 69, 103, 109, 110, 114, 117, 122, 366n57; *Living Wage*, 6–7, 113, 117, 121, 125, 127, 132, 141, 172, 347; *New Leader* articles, 102, 130; UDC, 42

Howell, David, 8, 29, 79–80, 87, 91–92, 130, 132, 142, 321, 345

411

Hughes, Emrys, 120, 137, 186, 191, 257, 268, 318, 346

Independent Labour Party (ILP): affiliation committee, 223, 260, 266, 274 386n7; Cable Street, 300–302; conflict over Labour Party standing orders, 5, 165–70, 174, 178–79, 182–95, 197–200, 208, 243, 311–13, 335; democratic centralism, 6, 245–47, 255–69, 261–63, 340; devolution, 7, 53, 55, 64; ethical socialism, 126, 127, 130, 209, 210, 211–12, 240, 243, 244, 344, 348, 367n8; Guild of Youth, 200, 211, 225, 280, 285, 311; House of Lords, abolition, 13, 15, 29, 50, 62, 152, 239, 324; identification with the POUM, 284, 286, 340; intellectuals, 6, 44, 77, 322, 325; International Bureau for Revolutionary Socialist Unity (IBRSU), 256, 275, 279, 281, 283, 286, 385n34; "Left Wing of the ILP," 5, 20, 31–32, 51, 60, 61, 223; membership decline, 4, 309; Vienna Union, 38

James, C. L. R. (Cyril Lionel Robert), 252, 255, 256, 282
Jewson, Dorothy, 149, 194, 336
Johnson, Francis, 35, 353n40
Jowett, F. W. (Frederick William): Bradford councillor, 14, 351n42; Bradford MP, 12–13, 351n42; chairman of ILP, 17, 118; contests 1935 election, 298; Cook-Maxton, 150; critic of foreign policy, 17–19; defence of representative government, 14, 20, 215, 226, 343; First Commissioner of Works in 1924 government, 13, 93, 97; *The I.L.P. Says "No,"* 197–98, 377n35; and Labour Party leadership, 86; opposes reaffiliation in 1939, 312–13; *Parliament or Palaver?* 22–24, 352n51; radical parliamentary reform, 6, 9, 13–16, 19–25, 161, 166–67, 168, 314, 335, 343, 347; refusal to wear court dress, 13, 94; on "scenes" in Commons, 89; UDC, 41; USSR, 267; *What Is the Use of Parliament?* 15, 402
Judt, Tony, 341
Jupp, James, 299, 319, 322

Keynes, John Maynard, 102, 106, 109, 121, 122, 127, 131, 171–72, 193
Kirkwood, David: attacks Brailsford's high salary, 78, 141; Clyde group supports MacDonald, 86–87; Clyde Workers' Committee, 353n22; Cook-Maxton, 148, 150–51, 154; dismissive of first Labour government, 98; Maxton's popularity, 142; moves pro-Bolshevik motion in 1920, 31; records of ILP candidates, 160; refuses to leave the Labour Party, 181, 185, 199

Labour Alliance, 3, 11, 30
Labour Party: attitudes to ILP, 81, 116–18, 137, 145, 154, 159, 163, 169, 171, 182–83, 192, 194–95, 310–11; bans cooperation with CPGB, 299; constitution of 1918, 3, 5, 27–30, 38–39; influence of ex–ILPers after 1945, 334, 346; refuses to endorse ILP candidates at 1931 election, 179
Labour Representation Committee (LRC), 3, 12, 14
Lane, Hilda, 194
Lansbury, George, 171, 174, 180, 183, 301, 311, 341–42
Laybourn, Keith, 97
Leach, William, 21, 42, 68, 69, 71, 163, 167, 351n42
Lee, Jennie, 219, 222, 298, 346, 376n54: advocates revolutionary policy, 227; on Clifford Allen, 326; and Communists, 226; supports disafffiliation/opposes reaffiliation, 188, 312; on USSR, 293, 341
Lees Smith, H. B. (Hastings Bernard), 22, 23
Left Communists, 214, 343, 389n24
"Left Wing of the ILP," 5, 20, 31–32, 51, 60, 61, 223

Index

Lenin and Leninism, 4, 196, 205, 208–9, 210, 219, 246, 262, 268, 282, 283, 284, 289, 348, 353n31, 389n24
Leventhal, F. M., 101, 103, 105–6, 122, 133, 350n26, 360n43
Living Wage Bill, 138–39
Longden, Fred, 69, 359n10
LRC. *See* Labour Representation Committee

MacDonald, James Ramsay: biological analogy, 45; constitutional conservatism, 45–46, 54, 89; on devolution, 53; editor of *Socialist Review*, 28, 41, 48, 55, 116, 143, 144; failure to nominate as Labour Party treasurer, 144–45; first government, 92–98; foreign policy, 97; and ILP, 41–56; and ILP 1922 program, 64; importance of ILP support, 39; Labour Party leadership, 4–5, 12, 86–89; National Government, 156, 174–180, 185, 190, 327, 328, 335; opposes abolition of cabinet system, 20; personal attacks on, 354n45; second government, 155, 159–75; and the UDC, 41; Woolwich by-election, 36; writings, 44–45
Maclean, John, 43, 54, 211, 355n9
Mannin, Ethel, 207, 291, 294, 379n16, 392n80–81
Marquand, David, 44, 50, 93, 94, 97, 99, 122, 125, 129, 130, 132–33
Marwick, Arthur, 13, 32, 58, 64, 78, 87, 134, 143
Marx and Marxists, 4, 53–54, 130, 148, 198, 204, 206–12, 217, 219, 221, 227, 284, 295, 320, 325, 345
Maurin, Joaquim, 280, 282, 388n4
Maxton, James: abstains on Education Bill, 191; Abyssinia, "rival dictators" and plebiscite support, 251–53, 258; Allen's defection, 328; attacks Brailsford, 20, 173–74, 229; chairman of ILP, 71, 141, 169, 222, 232; Cook-Maxton, 146–56, 339; cooperation with CPGB, 302–3,

317; critic of USSR, 288; Insurance Bill, 162–65; on Lenin, 205; Living Wage Bill, 138–39; Living Wage policy, 122, 125, 131, 132, 136; Munich agreement, 261, 307–8; "murderers" episode, 90–92, 362n18; popularity and support, 164–65, 198, 239, 258, 260, 338–39; re-elected MP, 289; second Labour government, 138–39, 162; on Spain, 286; supports disaffiliation, 185–86, 190, 192, 193, 195; threatens resignation, 256–57; on Trotsky and Stalin, 287
McAllister, Gilbert, 138, 142, 148
McGovern, John, 257, 262, 286: Abyssinia, 267–68; Clydeside MP, 181, 185, 191, 228; Communists as "good little lads," 269; and Lancashire "revolt," 242; Munich agreement, 307–8; *Terror in Spain*, 290; West of Scotland Disaffiliation Committee, 193; *Why the Bishops Back Franco*, 280, 389n7
McGregor, Don, 295
McKenzie, Robert, 27, 56, 167
McNair, John, 279, 280, 282, 284, 285, 291, 292, 303, 307, 308, 312, 391n62
Mellor, William, 146, 303, 318
Middlemas, Keith, 129
Miliband, Ralph, 27, 30, 67, 170
Morel, Edmund Dene, 42, 354n3
Morgan, Austin, 47
Morgan, Kenneth O., 327
Morgan, Kevin, 6, 8, 59, 343
Mosley, Oswald: and Birmingham proposals, 107–112; and Cable Street, 300–302; forms British Union of Fascists, 5, 172; forms New Party, 172; headed for Labour Party leadership, 172, 339; *Revolution by Reason*, 107–112
Murry, John Middleton: and ILP, 6, 206–12; and ISP, 323–26; opposes RPC and cooperation with CPGB, 208, 217, 224, 236, 240; resigns from ILP, 243; resigns from ISP, joins Labour Party, 326; *The Necessity of Communism*, 206, 208–9

413

Index

National Labour, 134, 179, 180, 327, 329, 335
Newbold, John Turner Walton, 34, 38, 184
Nin, Andrés, 282, 286
No Conscription Fellowship, 42, 73, 81
Norman, Clarence Henry, 20, 31, 46, 61

Orwell, George (Eric Blair), 6, 391n64: *Homage to Catalonia*, 280, 290, 291, 292, 395n60; joins/leaves ILP, 292; in Spain, 290–92, 391n62; *The Road to Wigan Pier*, 291, 392n63

Pallister, Minnie, 317: on building successful ILP branch, 66; in "Now for Socialism" campaign, 77; organizer for South Wales, 75; pamphlets, 358n41
Palme Dutt, Rajani, 153, 154, 223, 284, 372n64
Paton, John: on Allen, 80; alternative revolutionary policy, 212–13; and Communists, 205, 224, 235, 244, 267, 340; Cook-Maxton, 147–48; critic of Maxton, 142, 370n6; edits *New Leader*, 165, 168, 181; on Living Wage Commission, 113; on Living Wage program, 134; opposes Comintern affiliation, 37, 354n50; opposes RPC, 204, 217–18, 230; "permanent opposition" of ILP to second Labour government, 169; on recruits from Liberals, 42–43; resignation, 203, 217, 232, 267, 275; secretary of ILP, 80, 147; supports disaffiliation, 190, 193, 195
Pelling, Henry, 41
Penrose, Roland, 380, 387n62, 388n6
Pethick Lawrence, F. W. (Frederick William), 71, 102
Pilon, Dennis, 336
Pimlott, Ben, 180, 183, 302, 315, 319, 322, 351n43
Pollitt, Harry, 224, 225, 245, 291, 299, 300, 302, 303, 381n45
Ponsonby, Arthur, 3, 4, 18, 41, 76, 93, 350n30, 354n3, 363n41, 363n43

Preston, Paul, 282
proportional representation, 20, 21–22, 45, 49, 131–32, 196, 369n28

Radice, E. A., 319
Rathbone, Eleanor, 102, 114, 127, 300, 365n23, 367n8–9
Rees, Richard, 206, 228, 236

Sandham, Elijah, 174, 375n74: and ISP, 323–24, 326; and Lancashire revolt, 237–40, 261; opposes cooperation with CPGB, 226–27, 23; opposes RPC, 218, 225, 236; removed from list of parliamentary candidates, 241–42; resigns from ILP, 322; supports parliamentary politics, 215, 228, 235, 241; Unity Group, 236
Salter, Alfred (Dr), 51, 101, 182, 183–84, 267, 356n49, 364n19
Scottish Socialist Party, 7, 315–18
Scurr, John, 21, 59, 112, 149: Labour MP, 154, 358n12; resigns from ILP, 154
Seyd, Patrick, 319, 322
Shinwell, Emanuel, 64, 68, 70, 72, 92, 131–32, 149, 164, 361n7; on MacDonald, 44, 86, 96; as minister, 93, 97, 170–71; second in 1929 ILP chairman election, 155; supports Insurance Bill, 163
Skidlesky, Robert, 109, 110, 111, 112, 171
Skinner, J. (James) Allen, 137, 141, 167, 218, 325; opposes RPC, 205, 221, 225, 226, 228, 236–37; resigns as chair of London Division, 225
Slater, Ian, 282
Smillie, Bob, 280, 285–87, 291, 390n34
Smith, C. A. (Charles Andrew), 215, 218, 225, 227, 231: and Abyssinia, 257–58; attacks Stalin, 288; chairman of ILP, 173, 261, 312; edits *Controversy*, 258, 260; elected to NAC, 222; opposes reaffiliation, 312; "Re-establishing Party Discipline," 261–62
Snowden, Ethel, 42, 51–52, 267, 333, 356n49
Snowden, Philip: against the war, 13; chairs

Index

ILP, 2, 60, 62; clash with Katharine Bruce Glasier, 73, 354n44; election of MacDonald, 86; financial orthodoxy, 174; leading role in early ILP, 12, 31, 43; member of "inner leadership," 92; memoirs, 331; National Government, 185, 196; prominent in UDC, 13, 42; resigns as treasurer, 68, 72; resigns from ILP, 141, 149; reviews *Socialism for To-day*, 112, 122; *Socialism Made Plain*, 59; socialist resolution, 197, 377n33

Social-Democratic Federation (SDF), 14, 43, 48

Socialist League, 7, 242, 318–22, 335; unity campaign, 302–4, 310

Southall, Joseph, 99, 165, 185, 257, 308, 310, 364n3

soviet democracy, 13–14, 21, 32–33, 37, 61, 214, 283, 286–87, 343–44

Stephen, Campbell (Rev), 191, 205, 226–28, 231, 237, 239, 242: advocates disaffiliation, 195, 196; clash with Dollan, 171; and Cook-Maxton, 148; elected MP, 181, 298; elected to NAC, 222; secretary of ILP parliamentary group, 169

Stocks, Mary, 114, 367n7

Strachey, John, 3, 102, 365n49: breaks with Mosley, 179; *Revolution by Reason*, 107–111, 118; *Socialist Review* editor, 141, 151, 153; supports Communists, 183, 293; *The Theory and Practice of Socialism*, 293

Swanwick, Helena, 42, 327

Tawney, R. H. (Richard Henry), 69, 95, 141, 206

Taylor, A. J. P., 27, 93, 132

Third International. *See* Comintern

Thomas, Hugh, 107–8, 282, 285, 365n49

Thomas, J. H. (James "Jimmy" Henry), 92, 93, 171, 196

Thompson, Noel, 110, 172

Thorpe, Andrew, 129, 181

Thwaites, Peter, 8, 333–34

Trades Union Congress (TUC), 48, 92: and Cook, 148; and General Strike, 119–20; and Mond conference, 135, 151

Trevelyan, Charles, 342: Education Bill, 191; as founder of UDC, 18, 41; leaves Liberals for Labour and ILP, 4, 41, 76; resigns as Minister of Education, 173; Socialist League, 318, 319, 320; on USSR, 342

Trotsky and Trotskyists, 5, 196, 203, 245, 252, 261, 272, 275, 279, 281–86, 287, 293, 309, 317–18, 326, 334, 340

TUC. *See* Trades Union Congress

UDC. *See* Union of Democratic Control
Union of Democratic Control (UDC), 18, 41–42

Vernon, Hilda, 251, 253, 254

Wallhead, Richard: attitude to Bolsheviks, 32, 37; chairs ILP, 32, 34, 37, 67, 68, 77, 339; not elected to NAC in 1933, 222; ILP program, 64; Moscow mission, 32–33, 353n33; opposes cooperation with CPGB, 222–23; opposes Left Wing, 37; resigns from ILP, 203, 215, 222, 242; returns to Labour Party, 181, 339; survives 1931 election, 222

Warbey, William, 215, 219, 224, 286, 380n54

Walton Newbold, J. T. (John Turner): Communist MP, 184; and Left Wing, 34, 38; supports National Government, 184

Webb, Sidney and Beatrice, 93, 103, 266, 341, 342, 386n8

Wedgwood, Josiah, 76, 86, 89, 182, 362n13

Wheatley, John: Housing Act of 1924, 97, 147; and Maxton, 86, 90, 147–48, 164; opposes minority government, 161; refusal to wear court dress, 13, 94; on "scenes" in Commons, 91; suspended from Commons, 90

Wilkinson, Ellen, 115–16, 121, 131, 135

Williams, Percy, 227–29, 230, 231, 285
Winter, Barry, 8
Wise, E. F. (Edward Frank), 113, 347n4, 378n49: *Control of Finance and the Financiers*, 320; critic of Snowden's "financial orthodoxy," 174; *Living Wage* report, 103, 108, 113, 128, 135, 137, 141, 347; on Mosley, 173; opposes disaffiliation, 174, 177, 179, 184–85, 186, 189, 200, 202, 315, 335; Socialist League, 302, 319, 320
Worley, Matthew, 8, 29, 87, 129, 132